To: Grace Tompos

Dirty

October 9, 1997

Lisa— This is the book Mr. Kuda (author) gave me. Eventually, should it go to Library or should you keep it in your office?

Grace Tompos

The Kuder
Book of People
Who Like Their Work

First Edition

Compiled by

John A. Hornaday, Ph.D.
Motivation Research Corporation

Lucinda A. Gibson, M.A.
The Performance Alliance, Inc.

A word of thanks from the author of the Kuder inventories to our 1,460 participants

This volume has been made possible through the generosity of many people who have contributed their knowledge, thoughts, and experience in the interest of developing better ways of helping young people find enjoyable careers.

You have participated in the creation of a new and valuable guidance tool. I thank you for your kindness and generosity. This is the first publication of its kind that consists of job descriptions written by the people themselves. It could not have been done without your help and that of other kind people like you.

There are many publications about occupations, but this is the first that is composed of descriptions written by the workers themselves.

WELCOME TO THE CLUB! I hope you are as pleased as I am.

--Frederic Kuder

Motivation Press
Amherst, New Hampshire
1995

The Kuder Book of People Who Like Their Work

Suggestions, permission requests, and other inquiries can be addressed to the senior compiler of these data, John A. Hornaday, Daniel Webster College, Twenty University Drive, Nashua, New Hampshire 03063.

Published in 1995 in the United States of America by Motivation Press, 135-21 Amherst Street, Amherst, New Hampshire 03031.

Printed and bound in the United States of America by Maple-Vail Book Manufacturing Group

Library of Congress Cataloging-in-Publication Data

Library of Congress Catalog Card Number 95-094686

ISBN 0-9647625-0-1

To Linn
who brightens the world for everyone around her

...and to Fritz
whose inventories have been used in the
counseling of millions of young Americans

J.A.H. & L.A.G.

An Invitation to the Reader......

Close your eyes.

Choose at random any three pages in this book.

Open your eyes and read those pages.

You will almost surely find immediate information

of significance in your job search.

If you don't, try again. You'll be reading descriptions of jobs

that were written by the workers themselves. This is a

new and very valuable way to learn about an occupation.

The Kuder
Book of People
Who Like Their Work

ACKNOWLEDGMENTS

In a variety of ways, many helped in compiling the material in this book. Very valuable assistance was given us by Michelle Amundson, Leland Draper, Geraldine Klein, Paul LaBarre, Marion S. Lacker, Pamela Loper, and Lynn Schur. In addition, there were those who supplied good support for us: Maria Clarke, Karen Jordan, William Lacker, Mary Marks, and Lee Stinson.

A survey requiring computer analysis accompanied the questionnaire from which the job descriptions in this volume are drawn. For their help with that analytical work, we appreciate the contributions of Darin Krauss, George W. Waggoner, John Cole, Mary Lynn Edwards, and Brian Mobbs.

A number of students at Daniel Webster College contributed their professional help to us, some of them over a period of a year or more. Our appreciation to: Michelle Gear, Jean LoGiudice, Darlene Meely, Majbritt Neilsen, Erika Schmidt, and Jennifer Singleton. Significant help was received also from Adam Beckoff, Amy Burdett, Kimberly Eighmie, Dunja Hein, Theresa Marshall, Steve Nadeau, and Lora Ryan.

The Administration of Daniel Webster College was very helpful in lending strong support services to this project. To all of these and to the hundreds of respondents who completed our extensive questionnaire, we express our appreciation.

John A. Hornaday

Lucinda A. Gibson

July, 1995

INTRODUCTION

The career information in this book may be used by many groups: young people in grades 9 through 12 in public or private schools, college students at any level who are about to select a major course of study or who are considering various jobs, and adults of any age who may be considering a job change or who have been displaced and are seeking information about a new job for themselves. The collection of "interviews" in this book, all taken from open-ended questionnaires, will have value also for research persons interested in job characteristics as seen through the eyes and in the words of persons employed in various jobs. Thus, this volume is intended to allow the reader to "interview" employed persons, and there are hundreds of respondents in a very wide array of jobs from which the reader may choose.

The respondents' comments were guided by the open-ended questionnaire; that is, a series of brief questions was asked with ample space provided for a thoughtful, written response. Some persons in answering may have merely listed their points with partial sentences or a list of single words. For those cases, the rewrite staff expressed the thought as a complete sentence while fully retaining the idea. It is for this reason that the reader will find some similarities in the structure of paragraphs in this book. Of course, the structure of the occupational questionnaire itself led to a certain amount of homogeneity in the comments. Actually, there was very limited editing of the responses; most were used in the words of the respondents, without quotation marks, so as to reflect the various workers' own opinions and feelings. As mentioned in the cover letter that was sent to the respondents with the questionnaire, it is an opportunity to share their information with someone interested in knowing about the skills and attitudes that would contribute to success on the jobs in which the respondents have been both happy and successful. If they were not happy with the work or not successful in it, they were not used in this publication.

As you will discover in this book, learning about jobs can be fun. At the same time, it can be helpful if you want it to be. It may even help you identify and find a career. The book represents a vast array of ideas about jobs in the words of the workers themselves. Keep in mind, however, that no two people ever do the same thing, of course, and no two careers are ever exactly alike. In a real sense, as observed by Ghiselli (1969), [1] "There are as many jobs as there are people."

You can enjoy thinking about jobs and still be serious at the same time. In fact, that is probably the best way to go about planning your future. In that case, the first thing to do is go to the counseling center at your local school or university. In an introductory interview, they will probably tell you to take an interest inventory of which there are several. If you do not already know the occupations that interest you, such a

---

[1]Ghiselli, E. E. *The Validity of Occupational Aptitude Tests*. New York: Wiley, 1969.

survey will be a helpful first step. If you already know the job or occupations in which you are interested, you should turn through this book now and find those fields. Then you can read about those jobs in paragraphs written by persons who know them first hand!

For those who wish to take a survey of interests first, it will be helpful to know that Dr. Hornaday recently has developed a technique that allows a comparison of your interests with those of everyone in this book. When you learn from an interest survey which kinds of occupations you might find most interesting, this book will give you job descriptions, written by people employed in those jobs, and they will tell you the facts they think you should know about the job and their opinion of the personal characteristics needed for success.[2]

You may never find the perfect answer, but you should keep searching. This book represents only a start, not a comprehensive solution. The people in this book have been kind enough to share their thoughts and experiences with you, the reader. But they are not everybody. If you are serious in your quest for an interesting occupation, you should really explore further.

In considering the jobs described here, the reader should recognize that interest in the work is only one of the many factors determining success on the job. Interests and motivation are very important, but the skills to do the job are essential. Sometimes education or training is required. Abilities, aptitudes, personality, and experience can also be measured with the result that, if these areas are properly pursued, the work force in the United States can be more stable than in the past.

It is expected that this volume will help achieve that goal.

John A. Hornaday

Lucinda A. Gibson

---

[2] Methodological details are in a forthcoming book on the measurement of interests. Previous lumping of data from all the people in an occupation prevents developing an inventory that makes the desirable fine distinction now possible with the new technique we call person-match. In the past, differences between individual members of the same occupation have been ignored--possibly because no one thought these important but more probably because it was not practical to deal with these differences. Fortunately, Dr. Hornaday has worked out a way to compare your interests with those of other individuals rather than just with the average of a group, and it is now appropriate to deal with the theory involved. That will be published in detail in a book now in preparation by Kuder, Hornaday, and Gibson titled *The Measurement of Interests: A New Approach*. It will clarify the way in which refinements over the years have reduced the number of overlapping facets of vocational interests from about 90 to 17 very nearly independent areas while still covering the same domain as the larger number did. That new publication will build upon the theoretical structure originally published in *Activity Interests and Occupational Choice* by Frederic Kuder (1977).

ACADEMIC LANGUAGE THERAPIST

I was an art teacher and a professional artist. However, my career changed when I found that I had three dyslexic children. Getting them diagnosed was the easy part, but finding help for them was another story. I decided to be the one to provide the help. I then returned to school and earned a Bachelor of Science degree in Education and now work with other dyslexic children.

As an academic language therapist, I work with dyslexic children in a one-to-one situation and teach them to read, write, and spell. I see my students for one hour a day, five days a week. I go to their homes or they come to my office. Each lesson has eleven segments which deal with alphabet-dictionary skills, reading, handwriting, writing, spelling, listening skills, and verbal expression.

Patience and an understanding of the student's learning style are necessary in order to accomplish your goal of teaching these children. You are also required to have a strong knowledge of linguistics in order to perform this work.

I like this kind of work very much and the people I work with. The only thing I really dislike is marketing my services and finding the clients. I wish people would come for help sooner, before severe emotional damage has been done. It is so much simpler to prevent a low self-image than to repair one.

I am going to continue on this track for the next two years. At that time our youngest daughter will be driving, which will give me more flexibility in my schedule. I haven't definitely decided what to do after that. I may go back to school to get my certification in reading or psychology, or I may write and illustrate children's books for dyslexics.

ACCOUNTANT #1

As an accountant, I prepare data for payroll and run payroll through the computer for 200 employees. Preparing and reconciling all bank reconciliations for the three divisions of the large retail company I work for are also my responsibilities.

Having the ability to concentrate and a passion for accuracy are necessary skills.

I like to "work smart." By this I mean that I get satisfaction from my work by completing each task accurately in the shortest time possible.

After working in this occupation, my major complaint is that I do not receive much recognition or remuneration.

1

ACCOUNTANT #2

When I entered college, I was a pre-med major. I changed my mind and earned my bachelor of arts degree plus a master of arts degree, and have then pursued a career in accounting for more than 25 years!

I own an accounting business whose primary function is to prepare tax returns and maintain the books for the clients' businesses. On a typical work day, I either stay in the office working on client accounts and checking staff work, or I go to clients about their accounting and tax problems.

To perform well as an accountant, it is important to have excellent basic math skills, the ability to analyze, and be observant to details.

I particularly like my kind of work and am enjoying the opportunity it has provided me to own my own business. This has also allowed me to have a choice in whom I work with. Because of this, I like the people I work with. The most frustrating part of my occupation is working with government agencies. Other than that, I have found much job satisfaction from problem solving in my kind of work.

ACCOUNTANT #3

My career since earning my Bachelor of Arts in Accounting has been as a controller for a small corporation, a director of personnel for a private university, and now as an accountant for a local government agency. I work with 9 major programs funded in part by federal or state grants. The difference in costs is supplied by the county government. Among these 9 programs, there are 3 different fiscal years; therefore, I am either preparing a budget or preparing to prepare a budget. This work is done on a personal computer. In order to do this kind of work, it is essential to have basic fund accounting knowledge and a familiarity with operational requirements of programs, which the department provides.

It has been my experience, in working with a social service organization as opposed to a private business or my work at the university, that they do not give accountants the same kind of responsibilities. I have found the pay to be good and the actual work moderately interesting, but there is a lack of responsibility in this position which tends to make it boring. Basically, though, I still like accounting as an occupation.

ACCOUNTANT #4

As an accountant of twenty-six years, I prepare financial statements and tax returns for my clients, and I assist them with financial planning. My job entails talking with clients and meeting with clients regarding their accounting statements which I prepare for them.

To work as an accountant, you must complete a minimum of a Bachelor's degree in college, possess good math skills, have the ability to deal with and pay constant attention to details, and be experienced with computers.

I like my job and find that my helping small businesses with their accounting needs and financial planning allows my clients to do what they do best, run their business. I also like the fact that every project must balance at the end; my work is black and white. Being self-employed, I have total control over the growth of my business and the number of clients that I take on, so I have no one to blame but myself if my job causes me any dissatisfaction.

Before starting in this career, I worked as a bookkeeper on a part-time basis; I enjoyed that job so much that I decided to start a bookkeeping service. That endeavor proved to be very successful, so I decided to return to school to earn an accounting degree, making it possible to upgrade my service to a full scale business.

I plan to continue to work hard and expand my practice; if my business continues to grow, I may consider taking on a partner or selling a portion of the business to finance another endeavor.

ACCOUNTANT #5

I have always enjoyed working with figures. Since high school my interest in this area has always led me to occupations related to working with numbers. This past year I moved from the finance area to operations in a manufacturing company. My career started as a bank teller.

As an accountant, I work with budgets and perform other accounting functions including publishing department budgets, preparing weekly/monthly journals, reconciling accounts, and monitoring expenses. More specifically, I receive and review various reports generated by the system, reconcile ledger accounts, process capital asset requests, review department expenses and perform various administrative activities for my group such as assigning projects.

To perform this kind of work, you must have a background in accounting. A "customer first" attitude to everyone you interact with is also important. I have also found that this work requires the ability to work as a team player.

I like almost every aspect of my work. However, I would recommend the following changes in order to make the work more satisfying. There should be better documentation available so that those who deal with programs they haven't developed will better understand the functions. When transitioning work responsibilities, have people who develop a program become more involved in an active role, not just drop the work in someone's lap.

Job satisfaction for me is the ability to work independently, but have at hand the expertise needed. I like the fact that I am always learning something new and being given the opportunity to do so.

I have almost completed my studies in order to earn a Bachelor of Science in Business Management. I am hoping I can then assume a supervisory position.

ACCOUNTANT #6

I always have enjoyed math and working with figures as my work background will show. Prior to becoming an accountant, I have been a cashier, bank teller, and accounting clerk.

As an accountant, I balance the accounts on a monthly basis and all the financial reports at the end of the year. More specifically, I enter adjusting journal entries for the current month, do the cash flow analysis, prepare and submit reports to the Federal and state government, and continually balance all cash accounts.

You need to be a detail-oriented person to deal with figures. If you are not accurate, your reporting will be incorrect and reflect bad financial reports.

In spite of the job being tedious at times because the work is so repetitive, I like most other aspects of my job.

If given the opportunity to start over and prepare for any occupation, I would still choose accounting. I am satisfied with my work because I do it well.

My future career plans are to work for the I.R.S. at a later time.

ACCOUNTANT #7

An income tax accountant in a small CPA firm, I prepare personal federal income tax returns. After a fact-finding interview with the client by me or a CPA, I gather the information and prepare the return. I also do research work on current tax laws and possible future changes in the law.

The ability to work well alone with little supervision, after training, is essential in this field. Math and computer skills are equally important. Having a relationship with a client you interview only once a year is a challenge requiring strong people skills. My Bachelor of Science Degree is in Construction and Accounting, so education has been helpful.

I experience satisfaction when a client expresses satisfaction with my work. I don't dislike anything about my job and there's nothing I'd change about it. I spent 20 years in the U.S. Army and have been with this firm for 10 years. After I retired from military service, I was asked by my brother, who is a CPA, to join his business. My plans are to retire again soon and look back on a pleasant and successful career.

ACCOUNTANT #8

I got interested in the accounting field in a class in accounting while working on a Bachelor of Science degree. I went on to earn a Masters in accounting. Eventually, I'd like to open my own tax consulting firm.

Job satisfaction for me comes in helping others. I like saving the clients' money and I also enjoy the excitement of completing a difficult task. My coworkers make my job satisfying as does the fact that there are opportunities for advancement. If there were more client involvement, I'd like my work even more. It would be easier if there weren't really busy times and, then, quieter times. Much overtime is needed in the busy seasons. You have to be able to deal with the pressure of meeting deadlines when there is a great deal to do.

My days are spent doing a great deal of research relating to taxes. I prepare tax returns, spending lots of time on the computer. Preparing and working on spreadsheets are part of my job.

An accountant needs strong people skills in working with clients. You should be a good communicator and especially be able to work well under the stress of deadlines. Research and computer skills are needed. Finally, being self-motivated is very important. It is often solitary work.

ACCOUNTANT (CPA) #1

As a Certified Public Accountant of thirteen years, my duties are to prepare and review financial statements and income tax returns, to consult with clients by interviewing clients and answering their questions, to study new tax laws and accounting pronouncements, to supervise and train my staff, and to set schedules for my employees.

In addition to the certification to perform Public Accounting, you must have at least a Bachelor's degree. I completed a Master of Arts degree in Math Education. For success, you need an aptitude for figures and math calculations, strict adherence to accounting policies, accuracy, patience, good writing skills and good communication skills. You must also be honest and trustworthy to be successful in this field.

I enjoy the interface with clients and other accounting professionals or colleagues and the respect they hold in the public eye. I also find it a challenge to stay current on changes in tax laws and accounting procedures. My work would be much more rewarding, but not as challenging, if tax laws were simplified, there were fewer deadlines, and tax return due dates were spread throughout the year. I would also like my work more if I did not have to deal with difficult clients.

Prior to becoming a Certified Public Accountant, I held positions as a bookkeeper and as a high school math teacher. I left teaching to return to college to study accounting, I have always enjoyed it and had the desire to become an accounting professional. I took the CPA exam and found employment with the public accounting firm where I work now.

ACCOUNTANT (CPA) #2

The work of a Certified Public Accountant involves consultation with clients about their taxes, preparation of tax returns, researching tax issues, reading and studying new tax laws, and writing research papers.

In addition to a Bachelor of Science degree, the work of a Certified Public Accountant requires the ability to comprehend what one reads, the ability to write to be understood, patience, the ability to explain technical tax issues to laypersons, and persistence in seeking the best solution to problems.

I really enjoy my job; I like this kind of work very much because I find it mentally stimulating, especially when I am able to arrive at a conclusion that is satisfactory to both the client and myself. I also enjoy my professional contacts, and I like to communicate with other tax professionals.

In the many years I have been working in this field, my only complaint is that I would appreciate having less pressure to meet the set tax deadlines.

Before becoming a CPA, I worked as an auditor; I find my present work more challenging and I am glad that I chose this as my career.

ACCOUNTANT (CPA) #3

I work in the audit department of an international public accounting firm and interact with a variety of clients, usually meeting at their places of business. The typical day is from 8:30 to 5:30, with overtime as needed to complete the work. My job is to audit the financial statements of businesses to determine if there are ways we can help our clients. In addition to improving a client's situation, we provide a basis to report the information to third parties. We further furnish advice to a client on improving aspects of their business.

Critical to my work are analytical skills. I must evaluate information and develop ways to resolve problems which differ from situation to situation. An accounting degree with enough hours to qualify for the Certified Public Accountant exam are necessary qualifications for this job. Flexibility is important due to changing schedules and working conditions. In dealing with clients, people and communication skills are very important.

I chose accounting as a major and then learned there was an industry built around it. Until college, I never realized my profession existed. I was hired by my present employer right out of college.

With my degrees, a Bachelors in business accounting and a Masters in public accounting, one day I hope to own and operate the family business that I've grown up around and kept in contact with. Although I like the accounting work I've been doing for 4 years, the future for me lies outside public accounting and in the corporate world.

Gratification for me is seeing the work completed and the final report issued. I like getting to know new staff members and feeling appreciated when I teach them something. I really appreciate receiving feedback from supervisors on a job well done. I like the people where I work, the work that I do, and I like the fact there are opportunities for advancement. I don't like the politics of my large organization or its management. I would really like to see a reduction in bureaucracy and a decrease in the amount of administrative tasks that must be done.

ACCOUNTANT (CPA) #4

Because I like math and did not want to teach, my dad suggested I try accounting. I looked into the field, discovered I enjoyed it, earned a Bachelor of Science degree in accounting, and found a position with my present firm. Now, my aspirations are to become a partner/owner in this company.

I particularly enjoy the feeling of closure when a specific job is completed. Further, the group with and for whom I work are marvelous people; I appreciate the professional atmosphere here. While I really like the variety of clients we have, if we could eliminate the pressures of billing them along with the stress of deadlines, this would be a perfect job.

My work includes preparing financial statements and tax returns. It involves tax planning and advising businesses. Generally, I have three or four jobs going simultaneously: an end-of-the-year accounting to complete for a client along with its corresponding financial statement and tax return; a business evaluation; and a year-end tax projection to update.

Strong organizational skills are required in my work. You must be detail-oriented and be able to persevere. Being able to handle disruptions is also essential for I am constantly interrupted by client phone calls or by my boss. You need to have good business sense and be self-motivated. Finally, solid human relation skills are required.

ACCOUNTANT & CRAFT SHOP OWNER

While in college just after high school, with plans to earn a degree in accounting, I was sidetracked. I opened a shop to sell my own crafts. I love to paint and do most any craft. My college education then got interrupted. I returned to college 13 years later to complete my degree program in accounting, and after graduating, I opened up my own accounting business. Consequently, I now have 2 careers.

I work as an accountant 2 days a week providing financial advice, preparing reports, and recording transactions for a business and several individuals. My craft business is seasonal. Six months out of a year I paint and produce craft items which I sell.

Each of these careers requires different skills and attitudes. As an accountant, you must have a good mental attitude, and the skills to do repetitive work with numbers. Talent is required as a painter and craft person.

I find job satisfaction because I have a feeling of accomplishment. It is also the satisfaction of others for my work which spurs me on. Although I derive satisfaction from both careers, I think that I will pursue full time accounting work in the future.

ACCOUNTANT & OFFICE MANAGER

My job evolved into accounting work from an entry level position with a municipality. I found that accounting offered more career advancement opportunities than secretarial work. Prior to this I had worked as a flight attendant and airline operations and maintenance clerk.

As an accountant/office manager, my typical work activities include: preparing accounts payable documents; assisting in inventory reconciliations; assisting accounts receivable clerks as needed; maintaining checking accounts; analyzing general ledger accounts; preparing journal entries; preparing payroll documents; answering telephones; and assisting with customers.

The various skills and attitudes which I consider important in order to perform this kind work well are: calculator, typewriter and computer knowledge; accounting knowledge; customer and personnel relations; and willingness to put forth extra effort for the good of the company and customer satisfaction.

I like most aspects of my work including the organization and people I work for; the people I work with, and the kind of work I do. Job satisfaction for me is found from working for a company that has a good reputation in the community for fairness, honesty and service. I plan to continue with my current employer in my present position.

ACCOUNTANT, IRS

My career as an accountant started out immediately after graduating from college with a Masters of Science in Accounting degree. I got my first accounting job as a cost accountant for a manufacturing company from a college interview. I am now an IRS accountant. It is my job to audit tax returns. It is my responsibility to see that the taxpayers are complying with the tax laws of our government. To perform this kind of work you must have knowledge of accounting practices and procedures, auditing, and tax laws. It is important to have the ability to work well with people in order to do well at this job.

I am very satisfied with my career in accounting. I would choose this occupation again if given the chance to start over. I like the people and organization I work for, the kind of work, and opportunities I have had for advancement. I particularly like the variety involved in each audit, and observing business practices and people.

ACCOUNTING & SCHEDULING CLERK

Budgeting other people's money has always been of interest to me. That is probably why I like my job so well as the bookkeeper for a plumbing company. In order to prepare myself for this kind of work, I earned an Associate degree in Business Technology and Secretarial Science.

I could certainly use more time in a day to finish all the paperwork I am responsible for handling such as writing and planning the budget, updating monthly and annual accounts, summarizing account activity, writing financial reports, and preparing the weekly payroll.

To perform this kind of work well, it is important to have mathematical skills, speed, and knowledge of budget balancing. The most critical skill might be accuracy; therefore, when in doubt, double check and triple check.

I like almost every aspect of my job including the organization and people I work for, the people I work with, the opportunity for advancement, and the kind of work I do. My work is challenging and provides me with the opportunity to use the skills which I have learned.

ACCOUNTING CLERK #1

Although my educational background, which includes a Bachelor of Arts in psychology degree, does not correspond with my employment, I am fairly satisfied with my job in general accounting and am now planning to continue my education in business. I plan to earn a bachelor's degree in accounting and possibly to become a certified public accountant. As the general accounting clerk in a small office, I handle the various accounting functions for the company. My regular duties include: handling accounts payable, receivables, payroll once a week, journal entries, and phone calls with vendors and/or customers to discuss account problems.

I like the kind of work I do, and the people I work with. I find job satisfaction in the challenge of my work, in problem-solving, and in the socialization within the workplace.

ACCOUNTING CLERK #2

As an accounting clerk, I disburse money for travel expenses; audit and process expense reports; process, sort, and distribute payroll; perform data entry functions; and coordinate audits.

The skills required to perform my job are accuracy, attention to detail, knowledge of company policies, a courteous disposition, a helpful nature, good communication skills, an aptitude for basic accounting skills, and knowledge of debit and credit procedures for accounts.

I like my job, especially when a specific job I am working on balances, or when I collect money from employees who owe it to the company, because I know that I have done my job and taken care of my company's resources well. I like the company I work for and I enjoy the interaction I have with my co-workers and my boss.

Although I have not completed the undergraduate degree program in the field of accounting that I have started, I believe that upon completion of that degree program, I will have a broader range of choices for career advancement.

Previously, I have held jobs that involved working with numbers, such as a cashier and a bank teller.

My main goal is to take on more challenging phases of accounting and complete a Bachelor's degree in Accounting.

ACCOUNTING CLERK #3

I work as an accounting clerk in a company's travel department. Job responsibilities include the payment of airline and rental car bills on behalf of my company, the review and processing of credit card applications, and interaction with travel agencies and employees with regard to travel expenses. I have been employed in this position for five years at a company with which I enjoy working.

To succeed as an accounting clerk, you should possess good customer relations skills, an aptitude for figures, a positive attitude, and good phone skills.

I like this kind of work because, among other things, I like to see everything run smoothly. It is satisfying to save the company some money. I believe there is opportunity for advancement here.

I have worked in various positions after completing high school. These included jobs as a bank teller and teller supervisor before my present position in a big corporation. I prefer the corporate environment with a good benefits package and greater chances for advancement as I have at my present company.

In the future, I plan to get a degree in accounting and work toward my long-range career goal of becoming a financial analyst.

ACCOUNTING CLERK, NEWSPAPER

As an accounting clerk at a newspaper, I keep records of newspaper carriers in the computer and I pay the carriers. I update computer records with any changes or adjustments. Other duties are: preparing reports for various departments, inputting cash payments from state distributors, designing payment schedules for city carriers, and disbursing checks.

I was referred to this job by the unemployment compensation service. I spent 4 years in the Advertising Accounting Department; then I was promoted to a supervisory position in Circulation Accounting. I've been at my present job for 14 years, and like it fairly well, but I would like some changes in the working conditions and some of the people I work with. I like the varied and diverse special projects, most of the people I work with and for, and the organization itself. I wish there were an opportunity for advancement.

 The skills needed for my work are knowing the computer, being skilled in problem solving and being level-headed, efficient, and calm. I find satisfaction often in being asked questions and in seeking prompt answers. Also, I try to make a minimum number of mistakes.

I graduated from college with a B.A. in sociology and have also taken accounting courses.

My other occupations have been secretarial for both a rehabilitation center and an insurance company. I've also been a mental health worker. My aspirations are to take classes in computers or get another degree, perhaps in science/biology or in education.

ACCOUNTING SUPERVISOR #1

My career in accounting started by accident. I was originally hired as a secretary. I became bored and wanted to take on additional responsibilities. I was cross-trained with the cost accountant and enjoyed the work tremendously. The cost accountant finally left and I was promoted to that position. I have pursued the career because I enjoy the work and excel in the types of requirements needed.

As accounting supervisor it is my job to motivate and delegate to the staff, prepare financial reports, and perform various projects requiring research and analysis. My typical daily activities might include: completing 3 or 4 financially related spreadsheets; being interrupted about 25 times a day from staff to answer questions; spending at least an hour a day answering questions over the phone; gathering information for personnel; putting out various fires; working on ongoing research projects (i.e., cost savings plans, ways to motivate); and job performance reviews.

In order to perform this kind of work well, you need excellent organizational skills. You must be versatile--have the ability to switch from one project to another within minutes. A person who is analytical, logical, and can work with numbers has the right qualifications for accounting work. Additionally, you must have patience.

Aside from the pay scale, I am satisfied with my work. I like the kind of work I do and the organization and people for whom I work. I find job satisfaction when a project is complete--the finished spreadsheet or other end result- and knowing I did a good job. I also derive satisfaction from teaching staff how to perform their jobs or new jobs and then seeing them complete it with no problems.

I am presently working on a bachelor's degree with only 4 more classes to go. My career plan is to become the controller of a company.

ACCOUNTING SUPERVISOR #2

I was always good at math in school and had good teachers in this area. I also enjoyed an accounting course I took in high school, and it made such an impression on me that I finally chose that area for my career. After earning a bachelor's degree in accounting, I started working in the accounting field and am now accounting supervisor.

As an accounting supervisor, I supervise 2 accounting clerks and am responsible for maintaining and preparing the trial balance, general ledger, fixed assets and financial statements. I start work at 8:30 and spend about a half an hour reviewing the work for the day with the clerks. The rest of the morning is spent working on the computer doing the trial balance, general ledger, etc., taking care of accounting matters which are brought in with the daily mail, and reviewing billing for the day. During the afternoon, I review the accounts payable clerk's work (if needed), work on financial statements, and do bank reconciliations.

To perform this kind of work well, you need a very good understanding of accounting principles. A lot of the work is done on a computer and a PC, so a good working knowledge of computers and computer spreadsheets is very helpful.

I like the kind of work I do. I just wish there were more respect from upper management for our function. Accounting is usually viewed as a necessary evil in manufacturing firms like the one I work for. Management only tolerates us because they have to. I would like to see them show us more respect and listen to our suggestions more often.

In spite of these frustration with my occupation, I plan to stay in the field. I hope to some day have a Master's in Business Administration and work for a certified public accountant.

I enjoy seeing the completed monthly financial statements, knowing I am the one responsible for producing them. Having the respect of the clerks I supervise is also very important.

ACCOUNTING TECHNICIAN

The work of an accounting technician at a state agency involves writing up potential overpayments for unemployment insurance, placing calls to employers to verify wage information, preparing quarterly, computer-generated reports for employers, and weeding out the data that does not meet our criteria. I have worked as an accounting technician for five years and in that time I have found my greatest job satisfaction is derived from completing my work on time; receiving a one hundred percent review from my superiors; and getting help from my co-workers, working as a team.

I graduated from college with a Bachelor of Science degree in Business Administration with a concentration in Finance. My job also requires that you have a positive attitude, be accurate, know how to use a calculator, and have knowledge of computers.

Although I feel somewhat overwhelmed at times with constant pressure that comes from the expectation that my group maintain high productivity in as short a time as possible, I believe I have a good job with good benefits. I like the people I work with especially when we work as a team. I believe there are many opportunities for advancement, and in general I believe working for a state agency has proven to be a good career move for me. I previously held positions as a recreation leader, a secretary, and a sales manager; I believe these positions helped me develop the people skills needed in my present work.

My future plans include working toward a promotion to become the Senior Accounting Officer at the agency.

ACCOUNTS PAYABLE CLERK #1

I have always enjoyed working with numbers and researching problems, and therefore I find my accounting job very satisfying. As an accounts payable clerk, my major responsibilities are to pay invoices and reconcile accounts to the general ledger every month. In the process of paying invoices, I must match invoices with receivers, check prices, and research problems.

To perform this kind of work well, you need to be motivated, with the ability to research effectively. You also need patience because a lot of times the answer will not jump out at you.

I like most aspects of my work but sometimes it can be monotonous to look at figures all day. Having more variety in my work would be welcome. I do, however, find it very rewarding to balance my figures against the ledger and find I have accounted for everything.

I plan to stay in the accounting field, hopefully working my way up to a staff accountant's position.

ACCOUNTS PAYABLE CLERK #2

Since I have always enjoyed working with numbers, I find that I like working as an accounts payable clerk. I was able to move into this job after working for the company as an assembler and quality control inspector. I saw there was an opening in the accounting department, so I applied for the job and was hired. I have found that I like this kind of work so much that I am now working on a degree in management with a finance minor in order to obtain a position of accounts payable supervisor or staff accountant.

As an accounts payable clerk, I follow invoices through the complete accounts payable process. This process includes the filing of receipts, opening and matching the mail to receivers, filing vouchers, doing the check run, matching the checks to vouchers, and filing paid invoices.

To perform this kind of work well, you should like working with numbers, have the ability to do filing and be able to deal with stress. Also important is a good attitude and communication skills.

I like this kind of work and I have gained from the exposure this job has given me to accounting processes. I find satisfaction in being very busy and keeping my mind active doing fast, accurate work.

ACTUARY

As a partner and president of a small pension consulting administration firm, I apply mathematical principles to solve financial problems. I am an actuary who performs annual evaluations of pension plans to determine the cost to a business. My evaluations help companies ensure that their pension plans have enough cash available for employees when they retire. I don't foresee changing jobs unless business decreases to the point where we have to sell the company.

An actuary must have an extensive mathematical background. Problem-solving abilities are very important in this work.

With a Bachelor of Science degree in mathematics and a Master of Arts degree in educational research, I first was a math teacher. After investigating careers in mathematics, I found actuarial work interesting. I enjoy mathematics and love being able to apply it in my work to help others. My job would be more satisfying if government regulation of the pension industry were reduced.

ADMINISTRATIVE ASSISTANT #1

As an administrative assistant in a real estate office, I manage the office, not the people. I work for brokers, typing all agreements. An additional responsibility is ordering office supplies, which is usually done by phone. My activities on a typical day might be: answering the phones, preparing Purchase & Sales agreements, filing, notifying brokers of "dates" approaching, keeping track of deadlines, ordering supplies, and keeping the "up-desk" updated.

To perform this job well, good organizational skills are a must. I would also add typing and plenty of patience to the list of skills and attitudes which I consider important for this career. Prior to this job, I was a rental property manager, a bookkeeper, and administrative secretary to the president of a radio station. It has been my job experience that has qualified me for work. I do not have a college degree.

I like this work very much primarily because I just enjoy working with people and keeping materials in good order. I am satisfied too with the organization and people I work for.

My future career aspirations are to become an independent worker - to work for my own company/myself. However, I'm not sure "what."

ADMINISTRATIVE ASSISTANT #2

While in high school, I found that I had an aptitude for secretarial studies. Therefore, I went on in school in order to get training for this career by earning an Associate in Science in Secretarial Administration degree.

As an administrative assistant, I assist the executive director of an international non-profit organization. In order to perform the duties of this job, it is necessary to have skills in typing, keyboarding and composition. An open mind to new technologies (i.e. computers, fax machines), stress control techniques, and leadership skills are also important to have for this kind of work.

Aside from desiring more recognition and higher pay, I like my job. I particularly like the kind of work I do and the people with whom I work. I find job satisfaction when I write a composition that my boss is willing to put his signature on. It is also satisfying to produce an error-free document that looks professional. I take pride in meeting deadlines.

My future career plans are somewhat diverse. I would either like to continue doing office work and move up to a management position, or own my own retail boutique.

ADMINISTRATIVE ASSISTANT #3

I planned for my secretarial career by earning an associate degree in business. Now as an administrative assistant to a building contractor, I handle all aspects of office management. My typical daily activities include getting messages off the telephone recorder, opening and disbursing incoming mail, checking the schedules for the day, confirming meetings if necessary, processing various paperwork, and taking telephone calls.

In order to perform this kind of work, you should have computer and telephone skills. It is also important to be well organized and to have the ability to put your assigned tasks in priority. An upbeat, friendly attitude helps with clients.

I like this secretarial work, the people I work with, and the organization for which I work. I find job satisfaction in knowing that the whole "picture" is going well because of my input.

However, I do find that there is a lack of opportunity for advancement. I eventually plan to use some of my prior experience in clothing and cosmetics sales to open my own color analysis business.

ADMINISTRATIVE ASSISTANT #4

After many years of customer service work dealing with people and clients and medical billing as a medical billing clerk, I found a satisfying career job as an administrative assistant manager in a collection agency. As such, I assist the management and office staff in all areas of the operation, including the staff, computer and clients. This work consists of many phone calls from clients, management, co-workers and debtors. It is a constant flow of questions and suggestions in which an opinion is required. There is never ending paper work and mathematical evaluations. I am basically responsible for keeping the office on track and free of problems, plus keeping a staff of ten busy.

To perform well in this kind of position, the following skills and attitudes are important: get along with others, strong management skills, great personality, well organized, good memory, exceptional math and accounting skills and medical insurance knowledge.

I have found that I like almost every aspects of my work, including the people I work with, the opportunity for advancement, the kind of work I do, and the people and organization for whom I work. To see the company improve year to year and to be a part of that successful team is indeed satisfying. I also find job satisfaction when I get recognized for a job well done.

I am presently enrolled in college to better myself. I am considering going into patient account management in the hospital setting sometime in the future.

ADMINISTRATIVE ASSISTANT, INVESTMENT MANAGER

As an administrative assistant in an investment management firm, my typical duties include opening the mail, retrieving information from the computer, answering the phones, handling follow-ups on trades, preparing reports, making appointments, filling out forms, paying bills and ordering supplies.

To perform my type of work well you must show responsibility, follow through on the various duties, be detail-oriented, and have decision making abilities.

My job satisfaction comes from doing my work well. I would find my work to be more satisfying, however, it there were more variety, more challenge, and more opportunity to advance.

After receiving my BA, I became a teacher. I have also had secretarial experience.

I have future career aspirations of opening up my own business. This should provide me with the challenges I find lacking in my present job.

ADMINISTRATIVE COORDINATOR

I have utilized my work experience as a disbursement clerk and Canadian exchange clerk and my educational background, which includes an Associate degree in Business Management, to procure my present job as an administrative coordinator. Assisting co-workers in their tasks is a basic summary of my responsibilities as an administrative coordinator. During the course of a typical work day, my duties include typing letters for the associates of the company, inputting advertising material, sorting mail, posting the mail, copying, invoicing, answering questions, answering the phone, shipping the Federal Express mail, and answering more questions.

To perform this kind of work well, it is important to have typing skills, a positive attitude, and good communication skills. The key to performing my job successfully is to be aware of what everyone in the office is working on and to be available if they need assistance.

Although I like the kind of work I am now doing, I do feel somewhat stifled and would like to have more opportunity for advancement. I do find satisfaction in this position from helping people, helping clients, and having knowledge of everyone's job.

Because of my desire to find career advancement, I plan to earn a bachelor's degree. It is my career aspiration to become the Director of Human Relations.

ADMINISTRATIVE LAW JUDGE

As an administrative law judge, I make decisions involving disputed claims for Social Security benefits. I investigate shipping casualties and seaman misconduct and review medical and vocational reports to determine any degree of disability.

To be an administrative law judge, you need a law degree. I have a Bachelor of Law degree, an L.L.B. In this job you must be able to evaluate medical records and ascertain the truthfulness of a claimant. You must also be able to cross-examine medical and vocational expert witnesses.

Prior to my career as a judge, I was a Coast Guard Officer. Clearly, I found both of these occupations satisfying. A couple of minor jobs I held very early in life were selling women's shoes retail and serving on an airline ramp crew. I did not find those jobs to be nearly as attractive as administrative law.

I particularly enjoy making decisions which involve tremendous responsibility for another person's complete life style. Although I do not like the pressure to do more work, I enjoy the people involved, the prestige of my position, and the fact that I'll always have my title of "judge."

ADMINISTRATIVE SECRETARY #1

I didn't exactly choose my career. My liberal arts college degree had not really prepared me for work in a specific job, and since I enjoyed the medical field and secretarial work, I accepted a job as a part time receptionist/medical transcriber/secretary in a hospital. I have been working my way up the ladder to obtain my present position as an administrative assistant in the radiology department of the hospital.

I perform a variety of tasks for many people--8 radiologists, 3 managerial staff persons, and other department staff. The work includes word processing, statistical reports, writing meeting minutes, keeping appointment calendars, and supervising the transcriptionists. As a supervisor, I prepare work schedules, do performance reviews, and oversee the day-to-day activities of the transcriptionists.

My work as administrative assistant requires the following skills and attitudes: word processing; computer knowledge; ability to "keep cool" in a hectic workplace; and the ability to get along with the variety of co-workers, bosses, etc. Basically what I am saying is "people skills" are as important as "technical" type secretarial skills.

My only dislike about my job is that I am too busy! Otherwise, I like my work very much, and the people I work with. I particularly like the variety of tasks. I enjoy working in the health care field, being part of the behind-the-scenes team providing part of the overall hospital services. There is job satisfaction from doing a good job.

I have no changes planned other than seeing where my present job leads--in the 5 years I've been in the job, it has expanded and changed enough, with added responsibilities, so that I am still satisfied.

ADMINISTRATIVE SECRETARY #2

On a daily basis my job involves office management, typing on a word processor, answering the telephone, scheduling appointments, and anything else required to keep the office running smoothly -- such as budget preparation and reports of various kinds. I have done this for 7 years.

It takes patience and basic secretarial skills but no college degree. A big plus is the feeling of accomplishment each day, and the lack of stress since I can leave at end of day and go home without taking any problems with me. I have flexibility of time if I need it.

On the other hand, there is little room for advancement and I would rather be giving orders than taking them. For that reason, I hope to obtain a bachelor's degree in business and run a business with my husband. If that doesn't work out, I have aspirations to become a manager in a medium-sized business.

ADMINISTRATIVE SECRETARY #3

I work as an Administrative Secretary in the high tech industry.

I assist my boss with running our organization, and, in seven years, I have found this task to be anything but monotonous. Employing computer databases, I am constantly dropping one project to work on something else.

I earned an Associate degree in secretarial science, and I believe that allowed me to choose this field rather than wait to be chosen; other requirements for this position are a positive attitude, good people skills, flexibility, and time management skills.

The rewards are numerous. I have no one standing over me and watching to see if I do my work; I am able to work independently.

I like the people I work with, and I have a good boss and work for a good organization. There is not much opportunity for advancement, but I do enjoy this kind of work.

My goal is to get more involved in the administrative functions of this organization, perhaps even move into the sales support area of the company.

ADMINISTRATIVE SECRETARY #4

The job of Administrative Secretary involves secretarial duties -- answering phones, making travel arrangements, and running the copier machine; but also some administrative functions, such as proof reading documents and maintaining system files. In addition to these duties, my job requires the preparation of presentations with the aid of computer software packages. I create these presentations, given to me in rough draft form, using state of the art computer graphics.

The presentations require a pleasant manner and refined presentation skills; overall, the skills necessary to perform the functions of an administrative secretary are organization and computer literacy in addition to good office skills.

It is very rewarding to be trusted to handle presentations of such importance and it is particularly satisfying for me to make a rough draft look fantastic! I like the people I work with and this kind of work although I would prefer to handle more computer work and less secretarial work.

In the five years in this position, the only thing I really dislike is the politics of working for a large company.

After high school, I worked as a manager at a fast food restaurant, then on an assembly line. My interest in computers led me to take the temporary assignment that led to my current full time position.

I plan to pursue a career more in line with computer software development and testing, and will possibly further my education to become a software specialist.

ADMINISTRATOR

One of the advantages of this job is the variety of activities in any day or week. The wide diversity of jobs and new problems arising from time to time appeal to me. Interacting with clients, employees, government regulators, and others is very satisfying (usually), especially in dealing with employees. Personally, I like the politics that operate in any organization (or in most anyway). I like seeing things fall into place the way I want them, after much interacting with people to get them to go that way. Occasionally, I have been involved in a successful group which I find particularly satisfying. Of course, there is always a risk too, but that makes it more exciting.

If you are thinking of going into an organization to function in a leadership position, it is helpful (but not essential) to have a college degree--I have a BSBA--and to have confidence in your own abilities. You need to know when to speak up and when to be quiet.

My experience has been to work my way up in the organization over the years. Upon retirement, I will look back with satisfaction over the accomplishments in which I have had a part.

ADMINISTRATOR, CONSTRUCTION

My career has evolved from property management, to real estate development, to construction. I also worked as a police officer initially in my career life.

I work for an institution, planning space, designing and engineering expansion and capital improvements, and managing energy and construction of buildings. My typical daily/weekly activities include coordinating construction work, reviewing design drawings, planning future construction projects, reviewing billing applications from contractors, recording and tracking energy bills and usage, planning for energy saving programs and projects, designing space for minor construction and alterations, and planning and reviewing for capital renewal projects for the physical plant.

As well as my job experience, I also bring a strong educational background to this position. I have earned two bachelor's degrees and a master's. This background has equipped me with the business, engineering, and finance skills necessary for this kind of work. I also think it is important to have a positive attitude, the ability to handle pressure, and the personality necessary for coping with emergency situations.

Although I like most aspects of my work, I would like it better if the administration in my institution utilized long-range planning goals and objectives. I would like them to recognize that their physical plant is just as important as academic programs in terms of financial returns.

Despite these drawbacks, I like the kind of work I do. I find job satisfaction in projects completed as designed, fruition from drawings to actual use. My reward is when the work is appreciated and also in knowing that savings generated are shared.

My future career plans are to become the vice president for facilities planning or administration in a larger institution.

ADMINISTRATOR, DAY CARE

For the last six years I have worked as the administrator of a day care center with a regularly scheduled forty-five hour work week. Mostly, I do office work consisting of account and record keeping, handling finances, supervising the staff, and scheduling day care programs. I also get involved with conducting interviews, and interfacing with many different people such as parents, staff, salespeople, and of course the children.

I love children; I also possess a Bachelor of Science degree in Christian Education. In addition to this, in order to succeed in the day care business, you must have flexibility, confidence, creativity, a sense of calmness, diplomacy, good judgment, good communication skills, and the ability to make decisions.

I like my job, especially because I believe that my staff and I manage to have a tremendous effect on the future world leaders.

In my opinion, the general public is not aware enough of the importance of this work. Part of the certification process should include educating potential staff members in practical skills in relating to people and dealing with difficult situations.

I began my work in this field on a part-time basis while still in college; I enjoyed my work so much that I decided to pursue day care work as a full time career upon college graduation.

I have always worked in positions where I dealt directly with the public; I enjoy my interaction with people very much. I like the people I work with and this job also has the benefit of flexible hours.

I plan someday soon to open my own day care center and train my staff as I believe a day care staff should be trained. I believe that I have the experience and the abilities to succeed in such a venture.

ADMINISTRATOR, ELEMENTARY SCHOOL

A brief description of my work would be that I administer elementary school programs, supervise staff and programs, and do routine administrative tasks such as scheduling. More specifically, my regular duties include supervising pupil arrival, observing several classrooms. I must meet with staff members, review the budget, order supplies, prepare papers to be delivered to PTA meetings, and supervise dismissal.

To be an effective school administrator, it is important to have the ability to get along with people by having respect for self and others, and to have common sense and a knowledge in all areas of education.

This position has been satisfying work for 24 years for me mainly because of the joys of seeing success in others as a result in some part of my efforts. I like the people I work with, the opportunity for advancement, the kind of work, and the people and school district I work for.

Previously, I was a teacher for twelve years. I have earned a bachelor's degree and master's degree in education.

I got into teaching because while, in the army, I was placed in teaching roles. I liked it, and I subsequently went to college to train as a teacher.

ADMINISTRATOR, PUBLIC SCHOOL DISTRICT

As a central office administrator in a small public school district, I am responsible for the professional development of the educators in my area. A lot of my time is spent answering the needs of the teachers in the school district. I wear several hats in my job: grant writer, assessment coordinator, and program administrator. Ordering materials, working on program budgets, editing our monthly newspaper, and completing numerous forms for the State Department of Education are also part of my duties. In addition, I enjoy learning new methods of instruction, then sharing what I've learned with my teachers.

I have a Master's degree and I have worked as a bank teller prior to entering the educational field as a teacher and then guidance counselor. My job satisfaction comes in helping others, both teachers and students. I'd like my present position more if there were less paper work, but my plans are to continue on in this capacity. One day I'd like to be a superintendent in a small school district.

Very important to a school administrator is the willingness to learn and to change.

Strong writing skills are also necessary. You also need to enjoy working with people, be able to teach others, and be flexible.

ADMINISTRATOR, RELIGIOUS ORGANIZATION

As a parish pastor for 18 years before entering executive administration for our denomination, I've found the ability to work well with people essential to my work. As an Associate Executive, I learned that having a sense of humor, together with the ability to laugh at myself, is very useful.

In my position, I am the corporate secretary, treasurer, and business administrator. My education includes a Bachelor of Arts degree in social psychology, a Master's of Divinity degree from a seminary, and a Doctorate of Ministry. Working easily with figures and being well organized is necessary in my job. I must also be able to retrieve information quickly from the computer for I track clergy changes, keep a variety of records, and manage the budgets.

As secretary for several boards, I prepare minutes and reports on finances. In addition, I manage property sales and loans as well as sign official correspondence and legal documents. Acting as parliamentarian in interpreting our church constitution as well as policies and procedures is also my responsibility.

I particularly enjoy the diversity of my work. There are frequently new challenges to meet. I also appreciate my contact with people. Developing new skills to handle the various tasks is pleasant. I'd like to have more time to do all I'm supposed to do or I'd like full-time clerical help to handle some of the more tedious jobs. A better salary would also help. My plans are to continue what I'm doing, and, perhaps, to become an executive myself someday.

ADMINISTRATOR, TRAINING DEPARTMENT

In a corporate training department, I work as the administrator of training; developing the curriculum, coordinating seminars, presenting workshops, setting up the logistics for these seminars and workshops, and hiring consultants to conduct some of the more specialized workshops and seminars for which we have no expertise on our staff. I also travel extensively to training sites, handle organizational development, and speaker updates.

My educational credentials consist of an Associate degree, a Bachelor degree, a Master of Arts degree, and a Master of Education degree. In addition, the work of a training administrator requires excellent verbal and written communication skills, the ability to pay attention to details, experience in coordination of events, intelligence, a sense of humor, a pleasant personality, a professional appearance, skills in group dynamics, presentation skills, and negotiation skills.

In my present position for nine years, I have really enjoyed my job. It affords me a high degree of independence and self-direction; I also believe I am quite fortunate to work with a group of people that I like.

Some of the aspects of this job that I personally enjoy are the positive end results, organizational change, personnel staff growth, creativity, numerous rewards for my accomplishments, and the opportunity to network effectively.

Prior to my work as a training administrator, I worked as a social worker, a district director, a training specialist, an area administrator, the director of a personnel department, and a director of corporate policy and planning.

While continuing in my present employment, I plan to finish writing a book and numerous periodical articles, then continue with plans to start a private consulting company.

ADULT CAREER COUNSELOR

As an Adult Career Counselor/Career Information Specialist it is my job to help people find jobs. I work for a city in their library where I assist patrons in their job search. In order to do this, I establish and maintain job listings, order career materials, refer to community agencies, counsel the job hunters, assist with resumes, plan and lead workshops, seminars and job fairs.

To perform this kind of work well, it is important to have: an acceptance of and openness to people as individuals; the ability to establish rapport; organizational skills; initiative to ask questions; assertiveness in going after information, speakers, resources, etc.; excellent oral communication skills; knowledge of the community; and flexibility and willingness to go above and beyond duty. I returned to school at age 40 to receive my degree in sociology. I had just earned my degree and was working as a summer youth counselor when I found out about this new position which was being opened up by the city. I was looking for a "career level" position in the social service area. The job looked interesting, and I like the idea of working in a library. I also like to help people with minimal hassle. My career background includes jobs as: field interviewer and crew leader for the Census Bureau, field interviewer and coordinator for a market research firm, insurance inspector, assistant bookkeeper, sales clerk, and credit authorizer.

What I particularly like about my job is the fact that I am assisting people in their vital life work. I like networking in the community and heading workshops. I feel I could do my job more effectively, however, if I had an assistant to do routine paperwork, correspondence, answer phone, etc., and an area of the library more conducive to privacy and interaction between job hunters. What is satisfying about my work is the sense of helping people gain direction, hope and self-esteem. I also like being totally in control of my department. I plan to continue in this field and build up my skills through a masters degree.

ADVANCED APPLICATIONS ENGINEER

For eight years, I have been working as an advanced applications engineer for printed circuits. My job requires that I write processes and prove them out, order tools and materials necessary for each job, and perform research and development on new ideas and technology.

While serving in the U.S. Navy, I specialized as an interior communications electrician. In addition to the proper training, to succeed in a position such as mine, one should possess the qualities of attention to detail, the ability to communicate effectively, the ability to work with minimal supervision, the ability to perform tasks of an engineering nature, a positive attitude, the desire to help others, creativity, and open-mindedness.

I enjoy the interaction I have with my co-workers, I like my boss, and I believe in the company I work for. I can work at my own set pace, and I especially enjoy having the opportunity to work on a project and ship a quality product made by my own hands. I also enjoy knowing that I'm one of the best at what I do and that people can and do come to me for help and open discussions on how to do certain aspects of my job.

I plan to further my education and continue expanding my knowledge of printed circuits. Eventually, I would like to work my way into some sort of staff engineering position.

ADVERTISING AGENCY CREATIVE DIRECTOR & COPYWRITER

I found out about my career in advertising primarily through my wife's career. She was a junior fashion stylist at an agency when I was still in college earning a Bachelor of Science degree. I used to visit the agency often, and the copy and art people often asked me to look at rough work and "react" to or critique it. I discovered I had a good talent for analytical and creative responses, and most of all that I enjoyed it immensely. I have now been in the business for 29 years.

As the creative director and copywriter for an advertising agency, I create T.V. commercials and print advertisements, and supervise others. I also devise strategies and present the ads. My typical day or week might include some/all/most of these activities: conceive ideas for ads; write scripts for TV and radio; write text for print ads; supervise filming and still photography sessions; production work; presentations to internal and client groups; visit photo and client factory locations; supervise others who do above.

To perform this kind of work well, it is important to have imagination, writing skill, some diplomacy, "public speaking" ability, graphic judgment, high energy, and logical thinking.

Except for some of the people I work for, I like almost all aspects of my work. My concern is that some of the account executives for whom I work don't have the level of intelligence I think they should have-- particularly for their level of work. I do, however, like the organization and some of the other people for whom I work. I like the kind of work I do, the travel involved, working with film and print techniques, and learning about products and services. I have also found that this career has offered me the opportunity for advancement. I love seeing my work produced. The people I work with are mostly wonderful; bright, funny, creative. I find much satisfaction from learning about new places, products, processes, people.

ADVERTISING EXECUTIVE

I am retirement age, but I am still working at the company's request to help train others in this advertising business. I have been in advertising for many years because I enjoy the challenge this job offers.

In my position in the agency as advertising executive, I direct and create advertising, develop marketing programs for clients, supervise other account executives, and help manage the agency. On a regular basis, I contact clients, review current advertising promotions, check sales, and keep abreast of competition. I meet with creative people regarding work in progress or a need for a new campaign.

To perform well as an advertising executive, it is important to have a knowledge of marketing and public relations. You need a creative bent to come up with ideas. It is important to have a knowledge of writing and other communication skills. Advertising includes many different job needs. In my position, I must be able to communicate well with clients and convince them of my agency's capabilities.

The most significant problem I see in this occupation is occasional poor communication from the creative staff to the account staff and to the media production people as well. This job has offered me the opportunity for advancement. I have very much liked working with young, creative people. I find satisfaction from the results achieved through good creative campaigns, the opportunity to be part of that creative decision, the fast pace, and the work with optimistic people.

AEROSPACE ENGINEER, MANAGER

As an aerospace engineer I design and build aerospace systems and supervise others at this work. It is difficult to explain what I do on a typical day because of the variety of activities to be considered. I will broadly explain my job progress over the years that I was in the field of aerospace. In the early years I obtained, calculated and analyzed wind tunnel data to provide reports on aircraft performance. Later, I designed, built and operated aerospace facilities and now I manage and guide people in these areas.

I feel I have had better than average work experience. I have the ability to control (or try) my destiny. I enjoy the opportunities I have had for advancement.

The main satisfaction I get from this work is the gratification of accomplishment. Not to be overlooked is the satisfaction from the pay for this kind of work, but overall that is to a lesser extent than the intrinsic satisfactions.

AGRICULTURAL ECONOMIST

I have found my work interesting and varied in the United States and a number of foreign countries. In order to prepare myself for my various jobs in agriculture, I have an extensive educational background including a Bachelor of Science in Agriculture, a Masters of Science in Horticulture, and work on a Ph.D. in economics. Prior to my current position as agricultural economist, I worked as an agricultural technician doing research for a horticulturist and extension agent, as an agricultural farm credit supervisor for a federal agency, as a professor of agricultural economics in a state university, as an agricultural chief, and as a deputy and country mission director. I also spent many years working in China for the United Nations.

As an agricultural economist/marketing specialist, I work on developing products that lesser developed countries can produce, assist with the storage and packing of these products, and then assist in marketing.

In order to perform this kind of work, it is important to have an inquisitive mind, and knowledge about potential production; reliability of producers; facilities for harvesting, processing, storage and packaging; and marketing skills.

A major concern in this field of agriculture is to be able find the means for providing adequate financing at reasonable rates for both the producer, processor, and the market. When I am able to accomplish this, I have the satisfaction from assisting in planning, securing the production, and marketing of the quantity and quality of food products that enable people to eat better and have food available every day.

Because of my long experience and successes as an agricultural economist, I now have received requests to do consulting in 6 foreign countries. I have also been honored with 2 meritorious service awards and personal "thank yous" from heads of state. This is definitely a rewarding career.

AGRICULTURAL ENGINEER

In my role as an Agricultural Engineer, I specialize in the design of farm machinery. I accomplish these designs by first studying farming processes, obtaining samples of products and machinery currently on the market, and following up to be sure the machinery I design is working as it should once in use. The design process may include breaking a farming process down to basic tasks, assigning a priority to each task and developing a design to suit those needs. In addition, there is review of past performance of machinery of my own design for possible improvements, checking costs of proposed designs and design improvements, or meeting salespeople to learn from their interaction with customers.

In addition to formal education beyond high school, I earned a Bachelor of Science degree and was awarded an honorary Doctorate degree in the field of Management. You must possess the qualities of neatness and accuracy, be hospitable, and enjoy keeping busy. This is a very creative job and requires good creative instincts on the part of the designer.

I love my work and enjoy knowing that my work affords other businesses the opportunity to achieve higher profits. It gives me great pleasure to design products that are economical, attractive, and productive. I admit at times I have found great frustration in having to design machinery within a very limited budget although I pay very close attention to economy of design whenever possible. However, I believe you cannot cut corners on quality or place a dollar figure on quality.

This career was a logical choice for me. I was born and raised on a farm, and I have operated farm machinery since the age of ten.

I will continue with my designs until retirement and will most likely, at that time, share my experience with those who have not been as fortunate as I.

AIR CARGO AGENT

As an air cargo agent for a major airlines, I accept, sort, transfer, and release air freight. My day-to-day activities in carrying out this service work includes: answering phones, giving rates and schedules, accepting cargo for shipment, connecting cargo between flights, storing shipments, and releasing cargo to customers.

To perform this kind of work well, you must be able to do teamwork with fellow employees. It is also important to be able to follow policies, and to work well with the public. As far as physical requirements for this work, you must be strong and in good health.

In order to qualify for this job as air cargo agent, I received training at an airline career school. The school's placement service then assisted me in getting my first job which was with a commuter airline. After working for this small airline for a while, I was able to get a job with a major airline. I have now worked as an agent for 13 years. Prior to this, I was a representative on a cruise ship assisting passengers, a night auditor at a hotel, and a service station attendant.

I have liked working as an agent because of the variety of work available. I like the organization I work for and the people I work with. In fact, if I were given the chance to start over and could choose any career, I would again choose to be an air cargo agent. I find job satisfaction in happy customers. I also enjoy the great rates and discounts on my personal travels which is a benefit in this work.

AIRCRAFT WEAPONS TECHNICIAN

As a technician on the weapons release system of fighter aircraft, I am the troubleshooter. My day is roughly one-half at a bench in the shop tearing down and rebuilding mechanical items related to the weapons release system. The other half is spent finding problems in aircraft or testing equipment.

To perform this work I have had to develop electronics and mechanical skills.

These were not skills which I gained from my education by earning a Bachelor of Arts in education degree nor from my previous job experience in teaching, accounting, and finance. I gained these skills on the job.

I like what I do and have done for the last 12 years.. I find satisfaction from my work in that we develop an aircraft that maintains a high performance record.

AIRLINE CAPTAIN/U.S. NAVAL AVIATOR

I started in the aviation field while serving in the Navy. I have flown both as a naval aviator and as an airline captain. In the role of airline captain, I am in complete charge of a commercial aircraft, transporting people on both domestic and international flights. I prepare for the flight by checking the flight plan, fuel loading, and weather charts; I keep the aircraft maintenance log book and take-off performance chart.

It is very satisfying for me to take a multi-million dollar aircraft with a load of passengers and crew on a flight of ten plus hours from the west coast to Europe or Asia safely; I know all aboard are depending upon my competence as a pilot and I am always up to the challenge.

I love my job, and I have a great crew, but I would find greater rewards from this field if the Federal Aviation Administration (FAA) shortened the allowed flying time and on-duty time within a twenty-four hour period; the current allowance can make for an overwhelming schedule when pushed to the limits.

I have no opportunity to advance further in my field as I will soon be forced to retire, by law, at age sixty. I strongly disagree with the forced retirement restriction, especially since I am still in perfect physical condition, and, in my opinion, still up to the challenge for several more years.

AIRLINE FIRST OFFICER

As a First Officer for a Commuter Airline, I do more than just fly; I offer advice in emergency situations and handle all the paperwork that this position involves. After I check in and perform a preflight inspection of the aircraft, I check the weather reports and conditions for my travel route, and go over the flight plan with the Captain. When we return from our flight, I perform the post-flight check out.

This position requires flight skills, knowledge of aircraft, and a positive and professional attitude toward the Captain and passengers.

I enjoy performing the duties of a first officer and knowing that I am qualified to handle any emergency situations. Most of all, I love to fly - as a senior in high school, I went for a ride in a C-152 and decided a career in flying was for me.

A Bachelor's degree in Aviation Management/Accounting, combined with one and one-half years' experience as a Flight Instructor and a healthy respect for safety prepared me for my career. I take great pride in the positive reputation I have built while accumulating flight time and training others to fly.

My background and desire to succeed in aviation will no doubt lead me to a position as a Captain (of one of the larger aircraft, I hope) with one of the major airlines or to the position of Captain on one of the more advanced types of corporate aircraft for a private company.

AIRLINE PASSENGER SERVICE REPRESENTATIVE

My job is to make sure the arrival/departure procedure of aircraft is as smooth as possible for passengers at the international terminal of the airport. My specific daily work activities include meeting two 747 flights and making certain baggage reaches customs hall for passengers to pick up. I greet passengers and assist them through arrivals. Supervising the check-in of two flights, answering questions, coordinating the departure procedure, writing reports to improve service, and making schedules for staff are also my responsibilities.

To perform these duties well one should have language skills, typing skills, computer knowledge, an outgoing personality, and be able to work under pressure.

I have been satisfied working in this occupation for 15 years because each day is different and a challenge. I enjoy meeting people and being able to solve a problem and see an upset passenger leave happy.

I would be more satisfied if my working facilities were improved. There should be better control of airport facilities on which passengers must rely. Prejudice should be put aside when dealing with people from all over the world.

I have always dreamed of working for a foreign airline. I started working for them part time. Prior to my airline job, I worked for a travel agent. I am also working on raising three children.

In the future I plan to go to school to study what I also enjoy-- nutrition, history, and water color. I realize that a career isn't all there is in life.

AIRLINE PILOT #1

Although I graduated from college with a degree in electrical engineering, I found that my love of flying dictated my career. I got my flight training through the military, and am currently a second officer/flight engineer for a commercial airline.

I typically fly 4 days per week - usually two 2-day trips. I report to flight operations, then proceed to the aircraft and conduct a thorough preflight. We fly several short "legs" every day during which time it is my job to manage the aircraft systems and backup the pilots.

To be a pilot, it is , of course, necessary to have the technical knowledge and skills to operate an aircraft, the aircraft systems, and know all the procedures. Also, it is essential that you are able to work well with the rest of the crew.

I like my kind of work very much and the people I work with. However, I am somewhat concerned about job security.

It is my intention to remain in this career and move up in position to first officer/pilot or captain.

AIRLINE PILOT #2

For twelve years, I have flown as a pilot for a major airline. My route takes me all over the continental United States and at times to other overseas countries. I fly for a limited number of hours, then stay in a designated hotel, paid for by the airline. Usually after the entire crew checks into their rooms, we go out and visit the city and take in a restaurant.

I have a Bachelor of Science degree and twelve years of experience. In addition, you need good motor skills and a very determined attitude.

Although there is nowhere to go from here for career advancement, there are many benefits to being an airline pilot. I love flying and the opportunity to travel and see different places. At times, I see great irony in the fact that I like my job so much, I should be paying for the privilege; it does not seem like work to me.

I enjoy flying for a major airline. They treat their pilots very well, and I find a certain public prestige associated with my job. I also work with some very nice and dedicated people.

I knew when I took my first ride in an airplane that this is the work that I was born to do; while serving in the U.S. Marine Corps I was trained as a marine pilot and upon discharge from the service, I was hired by the airline for which I now fly.

My career ambition is to be a Captain on a jumbo jet.

AIRLINE PILOT #3

My job of twenty-four years involves conducting flight operations as an airline pilot in command of a large aircraft. Before the aircraft leaves the ground, there are many procedures that must be followed without exception. I check the flight plan on the computer, check the weather reports, meet with the other crew members, and preflight the aircraft. I am in control of the aircraft while in flight and I make all of the in-flight decisions. One trip may last from one to four days of a series of flights anywhere in North America, Europe, and the Orient.

In addition to an intensive training program, an airline pilot must have the following attributes: thoroughness, preciseness, preparedness, a stubborn desire to overcome seemingly endless training, education, academic testing, physical testing, and a thorough knowledge of the rules and regulations governing commercial flight.

I very much enjoy my work. The money is good and I have been working as an airline pilot for such a long time that I have seniority in choosing my schedule. I generally work ten to sixteen days per month. I derive great satisfaction from doing a difficult, but pleasurable, job. I like the airline that I work for and the people I work with. It had been a life-long goal of mine to become an airline pilot; I started flying in the Air Explorers as a young boy in scouting. Since then I have flown aircraft in private aviation, flight instruction, and charter flights. Other positions I have held over the years are as an electronics and computer technician, electronics field service technician, and computer production testing technician.

I have an Associate's degree in Electronics and I believe that experience with computers is essential to be a successful pilot. Everything on the pilot's console is now computerized.

Although a medical condition has currently grounded me, I plan to regain my medical certification shortly, and I will then return to flying. My career choice has given me many personal rewards and I hold high enthusiasm for the field of aviation.

AIRLINE PILOT #4

As captain of a B-747, I make 3 to 10 day flights, domestic and international. I like flying a trip without problems. Should problems occur, I enjoy finding good solutions.

While college degrees are not required to be a successful pilot, I have two: a Bachelor of Science in Civil Engineering and a Master of Science in Management.

There is nothing I dislike about my work. I enjoy the people and the work I do. Yet, being able to fly regularly with compatible crew members is my ideal situation. Very soon I will retire and plan to travel and golf.

Formerly, I served as an officer in the United States Army where I began flying. I loved it, and I've been an airline pilot for 28 years. Knowledge of aircraft systems, close attention to detail, and love of flying are all fundamental to a pilot. Equally important is the ability to work with your flight crew.

ANALYST, DEFENSE DEPARTMENT

For seven years, I have worked as a management analyst for the department of defense. I develop, enhance, and test a comprehensive disaster recovery program and perform miscellaneous administrative tasks. Consulting with associates concerning progress on the project in their respective areas, I also offer assistance to other analysts as requested. Because I constantly must respond to my boss's daily crises and I have to deal with the political climate in the nation's Capitol, there is considerable stress.

Although I see few opportunities for advancement, I do like my job; I feel fortunate to work with some very good people. I enjoy the sense of camaraderie that is present in this organization and the ability to snoop into all areas of the organization.

I have a Bachelor's degree in Business Management. The job requires patience and a slow fuse; you must also have the ability to compartmentalize, the willingness to stay with a project until its completion, diplomacy, and the ability to work through problems and arrive at workable solutions.

Prior to my present position, I held several different jobs; among these were accounting clerk for an aircraft builder, a system designer, and while in college I mowed a lot of lawns.

I plan to keep working with my current organization for as long as possible. There is a unique uncertainty to working as a federal employee; budget cuts and changing political climate may reduce the size of my department at any time. I try not to worry too much about the future of my job, as I believe that the privilege of working as a federal employee has paid in ways that cannot be measured by monetary compensation.

ANIMAL GROOMER

I have worked as a human services technician for 10 years and have owned my own animal grooming shop for the past 6 years; I like both jobs. I have also had a number of other jobs in various careers which I have liked to a degree such as truck driving, bookkeeping, and housekeeping. The one career which I went to school for (cosmetology) is the one which I did not like.

As an animal groomer my daily schedule includes checking the appointments for the day, setting up the grooming room, bathing dogs or cats, blow drying their hair, clipping and styling, making out reports and files for each animal, and doing the bookkeeping before closing the shop for the day.

As a human services technician I help where I am needed. This might include filling out reports, counseling with the handicapped patients or assisting them in getting around.

The skills needed to operate a grooming shop are good personal skills in dealing with the animal owners, good manual and finger dexterity, a love of animals, and kindness toward them, the ability to make good judgments, and bookkeeping and office skills.

The skills which are important for my human services work are good personal skills, the ability to work with the handicapped, the ability to make good judgments, and to set a good example.

It is satisfying for me to have my own grooming shop, because I am able to do most all the things I enjoy: be with animals, work alone or with one or two people, and bookkeeping. Improving the condition of the animals is rewarding.

Human services work is satisfying to me as well because I am helping people on an individual basis, and watching handicapped people learn to do things on their own.

APPRAISER, MERGER/ACQUISITIONS

With background experience as an Appraiser of Businesses, I now specialize in Mergers and Acquisitions. I prepare appraisals of businesses that are up for sale, or will soon be up for sale. I assist both buyers looking for an acquisition or merger opportunity and sellers looking to sell. I travel in the United States about 25% of the time. I conduct research, prepare appraisal reports and spend a great deal of time on the phone contacting buyers and sellers in an attempt to put together a business deal where all parties benefit.

In addition to a Bachelor's degree in Business, my job requires analytical skills and a desire to search for the truth out of what I am told.

I take pride in a job well done and try to maintain a high level of professional competence; I really enjoy my work.

Previous occupations were: accountant, chief financial officer of public and private firms, stockbroker, and internal auditor for a chain of department stores, auditor for electronic and aircraft firms, analyst for the Securities Exchange Commission, and budget and fiscal officer in the Air Force. All of that was before leaving the corporate environment to start my consulting firm. I believe my business firm provides a valuable service to smaller businesses in helping them solve financial and marketing problems.

I love my work and plan to keep at it until I am forced to retire.

APPRAISER, REAL ESTATE

After 32 years of supervisory work with a large chemical firm, I chose to go into business for myself as an independent contractor making residential real estate appraisals. I appraise houses for clients to determine their market value. I start by visiting the house, talking with the owner, and examining the house. I usually then visit 5 to 8 comparable houses in the nearby area to get more needed information. It is then mostly paperwork that needs to be done after that.

Rather than utilizing the knowledge I gained by earning a Bachelor of Science in Chemistry degree and my supervisory job experience, I have enjoyed gaining knowledge about appraising and using my common sense for this kind of work.

This has been a good change of pace for me because it allows me independent action as opposed to my rigid large corporation work. I like the people I work for and the people with whom I work. The variety in the work and having each day different is satisfying to me. If given the chance to start my career over, I would go into real estate appraisal initially.

ARBORIST

An arborist, or tree surgeon, services trees in many ways, such as pruning, fertilizing, examining for diseases or parasites, planting, and cabling of young or weak trees. Pruning involves removal of dead wood and trimming in the proper fashion to ensure continued healthy growth, as well as to protect the tree from injury; diagnostic skills are necessary to be able to determine what measures should be taken if a tree has problems with disease or insect infestation; planting a tree involves proper evaluation of location with respect to sunlight and room for a healthy root system; fertilization in the proper amount and combination is essential to every stage of a tree's growth; respect for and attention to proper safety procedures is always a consideration to a successful tree surgeon.

Although there is not much opportunity for advancement, there are numerous benefits to this job--especially the opportunity to work outdoors and the knowledge that the work done has the effect of enhancing the environment. This is extremely rewarding. Tree removal, when performed with skill, allows sunlight to reach barren areas and promote other plant growth; strategic placement of new trees produces oxygen and provides shade for enjoyment of leisure time, as well as adds esthetic beauty to the landscape.

After completing high school, I held various positions, one as a chimney sweep, in which I learned many safety techniques valuable to my present work.

As a tree surgeon for nine years, I enjoy my work so much that I would like to start my own business. Then I could select and purchase for myself the proper equipment necessary to perform at full peak.

ARCHITECT #1

An architect starts a new project by discussing with clients the needs that the client perceives he or she has, then developing sketches of the structural and aesthetic expression of these needs into building form, designing and preparing drawings to be formalized by our drafting staff, and developing job specifications. Once the project is in progress, the architect supervises construction and negotiates with contractors on bids. Working as an architect for thirty-five years, I believe a good education is an essential tool for success in this profession. I completed a Bachelor of Arts degree in Architecture. You must also possess the imagination to convey the concepts of the project into pictorial form and, later, into a physical form. A thorough understanding of materials, structures, and general building aesthetics are key qualities to a good architectural knowledge foundation.

To be happy in this type of work you must like people and have the desire to see them happy in the structures you create--consideration of creature comfort is a big part of the job. I am always pleased and very proud to see a building take form as if it were my child--I feel that I have given life to my creation; it is then that I know those who will occupy the structure have been well served.

As a child while travelling abroad with my parents, it was my privilege to see the great and beautiful structures of Europe; my parents also encouraged me to read about different architectural designs in books they provided for me. As a matter of fact, architecture was the first merit badge I earned as a twelve year old Boy Scout. As you can see, my interest in my career choice began many years ago.

I plan to work in this field as long as I am able and, upon retirement, I will keep active and probably be involved in some kind of people-oriented activities.

ARCHITECT #2

For fifteen years I have been working as an architect; there are many fascinating aspects of my work. I prepare architectural designs and generate construction drawings per customer specifications and engineering concepts for custom residences. There is a wide variety involved in the design phase of a project, such as sketches, organizing programs, drawing plans, and figuring out structure and details for the buildings I create. I spend a lot of time on the phone, answering questions from builders about plans or details; from clients about the design itself, the drawings involved, or details that cause them concern; and from consultants regarding their involvement in one of my projects. I am responsible for coordination of the efforts and concerns of agencies, engineers, consultants, and clients; I also have to deal with a lot of paperwork such as billing, agency application forms, and building permits.

I graduated from college with a Bachelor of Arts degree. While in school, I always enjoyed art and tried architecture--that was all it took since I have an aptitude for math and engineering. I have always been comfortable with reading maps and plans; it all made sense to me.

Besides a good education and a natural interest in architecture, you must be a highly organized individual. There are a lot of factors involved in design such as the site, the people, the structural requirements, and government building codes. All have to be considered. There are many factors in the finished product that must be considered in the planning stages and incorporated into the engineering drawings. You must also possess an aptitude for conceptual design work and strong communication skills as concepts must be clearly communicated to clients, engineers, contractors, and governing agencies involved.

I find it extremely satisfying to design a pleasing structure that meets the client's needs, then I have the pleasure of watching my ideas take shape as the structure is being built. The only aspect of my job that I do not enjoy is all of the paperwork, but I must admit I have the advantage of operating as a sole proprietor with no employees. As a sole proprietor I am able to avoid the paperwork that employees in large architectural firms must endure. I strive to spend my work day designing and drawing, but that does limit the amount of work I can take on as well as limit the amount of money I earn.

ARCHITECT #3

As an architect for 20 years, I meet with clients, determine building needs, design, review, redesign, and then produce construction documents. I have worked as a staff architect for approximately 10 years for a large urban firm and several smaller firms. For the past 10 years I have been a partner in 2 different firms. I have designed a wide variety of building types.

My day can include typically 3 or 4 hours at the drawing table, 1 or 2 hours on the computer preparing correspondence and working on business activities, and perhaps an hour for meeting with clients. I visit job sites, read technical research manuals, and meet with government agencies.

Some attributes needed in my job are self-motivation when working in smaller offices and effectiveness in teamwork with the engineers of each project. In the larger offices, specific task accomplishments are required. Problem-solving and communication skills are much needed. Drawing skills and knowledge of construction are obviously needed. I have a Masters Degree in Architecture, and, while the advanced degree is not essential, it is a plus. My uncle, who had interests similar to mine, was unable to get a college degree. He, therefore, became a builder.

Architecture is a profession of delayed gratification. Yet, I find great satisfaction in the challenge of working with clients and their notions of design and construction. I am pleased to be an integral part of the immense struggle to get a building built with some degree of building integrity, purpose, and beauty. I'd like to continue trying to design energy-conscious buildings and to push for fewer consumptive buildings.

ARCHITECT/DESIGNER

My career as an architect/interior designer evolved from my interests at an early age. I had much involvement in art while in grade school and high school, and I became aware of architecture as a good career choice for me while in high school. I earned a bachelor's degree in architecture and have now been working in the field for 12 years.

As an architect/interior designer, my major work activities include meeting with clients to review their projects, designing the building by progressing though the various design phases from preliminaries to working drawings, and reviewing projects with contractors.

To perform this kind of work well, it is important to have flexibility, talent in working with people and in design, and knowledge about building construction. I like the kind of work I do as an architect/interior designer, and I find satisfaction in seeing a project constructed and having a happy client. My career plan is to stay in this field and to become a partner in an architectural firm.

ARCHITECTURAL STUDENT

At present, I am studying to become an architect. I have been working actively toward this goal for five years now; most of that time has been spent, seven days a week, studying and drawing. I also got the opportunity to put those studies to use on a very special and practical project; I got the opportunity and privilege to design my parents' new house and to help build it. I cannot describe the satisfaction I derived from seeing the building I designed being built.

I became interested in this field by my talent in drawing and my aptitude for design. I believe that working as an architect will be very rewarding.

My previous work as a translator and a tour guide helped me develop the people skills necessary for my career choice.

My career aspiration is to work as an international architect and run my own architectural firm.

ARMY COLONEL & OFFICE MANAGER

I retired from the military as a colonel after 32 years of service and am now the manager of a tax office during the tax season. As office manager, I consult on tax matters and do tax forms for over 600 clients. The office is open January through April 15th each year. During this time, I set up the office, arrange work schedules for employees, and prepare tax forms for clients.

To perform this work it is necessary to take yearly classes in tax laws, forms, etc.

I am a college graduate having earned a Bachelors degree in Business Administration and a Masters in International Relations. My first occupation after graduation was as a personnel manager for a shoe manufacturer. I then joined the military as a regular army officer. After retiring from the military, I took a course in tax preparation and was recruited as the tax office manager.

I enjoy working with tax problems, and I find interesting the people and organization I work for. I particularly enjoy the yearly contact with clients. The major drawback is the low pay. However, I enjoy this work because I enjoy helping clients in the preparation of income taxes, and I feel good about effectively managing the work force.

ARMY NURSE PRACTITIONER

My career has been in the military, starting as an enlisted soldier, then working through college in order to get my commission as a registered nurse. All of my military assignments have been in the medical field, as a medic, a sea and air rescue medic, and now nurse practitioner/head nurse.

In my nursing position, my major responsibilities are for patient education and health maintenance plus managing a large internal medicine clinic. The amount of work required is somewhat overwhelming, and I sometimes think that I have to be a bit crazy to take all this on; however, I like the kind of work I do very much. It helps to be flexible in this position because of the diversity of work that is required during the course of the 10- to 12-hour work day. Some of the daily activities include head nurse duties, caring for patients, teaching medical students, tending to emergencies, teaching patient education classes, and military duties like physical fitness.

I could certainly use an assistant, but despite the long hours and heavy work schedule, I like the job because of the organization and people I work for, the people I work with, the opportunities I have for advancement, and the kind of work I do. I find self-satisfaction from my work and am always happy to have survived the day.

ARMY OFFICER #1

After graduating from college with a Bachelor of Science degree in horticulture, as well as a Bachelor of Science in civil engineering, I received my commission into the U.S. Army. I tried it, liked it, and made it a career.

Recognition for doing good work is particularly satisfying for me. Further, I appreciate the opportunities for career advancement, and my work itself. I also enjoy my fellow servicemen and my superior officers. My only recommendation, which would make my job more rewarding, would be to decentralize the entire organization.

My work week varies greatly depending on the current assignment. It mostly involves dealing with people and being able to function within established guidelines. I have to make a lot of decisions regarding the personnel who work under me as we train them to defend our country.

During my 22 years as an officer, I've found that strong organizational skills are very important. Creativity, a positive attitude, and intelligence are needed to be successful. You should also be self-confident and self-motivated.

ARMY OFFICER #2

After graduating from West Point with a Bachelor of Science degree, I was commissioned into the Army as a regular officer. There is absolutely nothing I would change about my career; I've enjoyed it very much.

The knowledge that I am actively providing a safe environment for the citizens of this country to live in is very rewarding to me. Also satisfying are Army life itself, my fellow servicemen, my superiors, and the opportunity for advancement. The only thing I would wish for is the chance to use my initiative and make decisions on my own more.

My particular job involves a great deal of planning. I am responsible for seeking out all resources available and supervising the Army's command and control systems.

An Army officer must be tough, morally and mentally. You should have a positive attitude as well as initiative. Finally, you must be courageous.

ARTIST/GALLERY OWNER

I always wanted to be artist. I worked hard to save enough money to study and then was an apprentice until I was skilled enough. I earned my Bachelor of Arts degree and taught elementary school for a while and then worked as a draftsman/secretary for an architect prior to going out on my own as an artist.

As an artist and gallery owner, I create works of art and sell them, as well as selling works by other artists. My gallery clients are mostly tourists. My typical day is spent greeting tourists, selling arts and crafts, and working on my own paintings and other crafts.

To be a successful gallery owner and artist, you must have the determination to produce, willingness to put in many hours, friendliness to strangers, and the ability to endure endless questions about your work . The biggest frustration with my job is dealing with artists and craftsmen who are less skillful than they think. I would also like to be able to get higher prices for my work.

Despite these drawbacks, I like my work as an artist very much, and most of the people I work with. I particularly like being my own boss. My job satisfaction comes from creating precisely what I want in a way that expresses what I see and what I feel about it. I'm doing MY thing, depending on myself to succeed.

ARTIST/PICTURE FRAMER

Framing seemed a natural outlet for someone like me, an art student in college. I began working in a retail art gallery doing picture framing and have now done this for 12 years. I earned my Bachelor of Arts in Fine Arts/Political Science. My real love is painting, however. Although I would like painting to be my full-time career, I have not found this to be financially possible yet.

I spend about 20 hours a week doing wholesale picture framing for a few art galleries. I own the business. Twenty to forty hours a week are spent painting. Doing framing work requires both technical/artistic skills and the knowledge of framing tools and devices.

Although I like framing, I do find it occasionally monotonous, although there is some opportunity for creative freedom. I find satisfaction with my painting from learning about myself through my work and successfully capturing that on canvas. My picture framing work is satisfying in knowing that my efforts pleased the person for whom I did the work.

My future career plans are to continue to paint and become a more successful artist both critically and financially, and my expectation is to be a better artist creatively.

ASBESTOS WORKER

I became an E.P.A. asbestos worker because I found it new and interesting, and I liked the fact that I am helping to clean up the environment and making it safe for others living in this world.

As an E.P.A. accredited asbestos worker, it is my job to remove the asbestos off walls, tubes, and pipes in all types of buildings including schools and refineries. I work seven days a week, twelve hours a day in this rough and serious job. Removing asbestos insulation and disposing of it is very risky and dangerous. In order to perform this kind of work, it is important to get the proper training and experience. You must also have the attitude of knowing you have to do the best you can to remove the environmental hazard.

I find job satisfaction from this work because, even though I know I am risking my life, I'm saving thousands of people, adults and children, from getting cancer diseases produced by asbestos. That is something that satisfies my heart.

I have had many types of jobs in the past including work on a ship, furniture factory worker, and maintenance work. Although there is considerable satisfaction from my present job, I am earning very low wages from this work and am looking for a better career opportunity. I am considering work in the electronics field, or, because I seem to like risky and dangerous work, I am considering pursuing work as an investigator, private detective, or undercover policeman.

ASSEMBLY LINE WORKER

As an assembly line worker for an automotive manufacturing plant, I perform many different tasks as part of my job. For sixteen years, I have worked with many different types of heavy power tools to assemble vehicles on an assembly line.

Due to the nature of this work (heavy manual labor), the skills needed to get the job done are the ability to learn a task quickly, to work fast once performance of the task is mastered, to work well with and get along with many different types of people, to perform a task accurately on an ongoing basis (as the job involves many repetitive tasks), and the necessary experience to work with the tools of the trade.

I enjoy my work for the most part; I especially enjoy the good feeling and sense of team spirit I share with my co-workers and the knowledge that I do my job well and that I do my job right the first time. I feel that I accomplish something important with my work--a quality product that the buyer will be happy with.

At times, I wish we could buy more modern tools to make the assembly line even more efficient, but I also know that would raise the price the consumer pays for the vehicle--it's a tradeoff.

I chose this line of work as I enjoy working with my hands and the sense that I am helping to improve the quality of American cars.

I would like to complete my college education some day. I believe that you can never learn too much. Then perhaps I could use my assembly line experience in a management position at this plant to improve the processes and the overall efficiency of the workers on this line.

ASSET MANAGEMENT

There is really nothing I dislike about my work as an asset manager. I oversee tenants on a farm as well as make investments in stocks and bonds. Selecting investments and determining any changes to be made describes my work.

You have to have knowledge of how to invest to do this work. After graduating from high school, I was employed by several financial institutions. I learned on the job about investing and gained much experience. The ability to work with people is also important. To supervise the farm tenants, you need to be an especially good manager of people.

I really enjoy my work. It is rewarding to manage assets and be able to select investments with reasonable success. I like my job so much that, if I had to start over, I'd choose it again. My plans are to continue with my investment successes and to bring others into the venture.

ASSISTANT BANK CASHIER

As an assistant cashier and head teller at a bank for a number of years, I've very much enjoyed the public and my coworkers. Working with math has always been fun and I find solving problems a challenge. Helping people is rewarding as well.

My work day includes opening the bank vault and distributing money to the tellers. I handle the general ledger as well as help with the night deposits and the mail. Waiting on customers, taking orders at the window, and solving in-house problems along with those of the customer are part of my job. I order currency, travelers cheques, and money orders, when necessary, and maintain the travelers cheques log. Attending bank-related seminars, training new tellers, and bringing to management's attention any problems or suggestions from tellers are my duties, too.

A high school graduate, I've worked in a grocery store, as a factory worker, and did tax preparation--all which I liked. I'd enjoy my current work more if this particular bank had more work space as well as storage room. We, and our customers, also need a less time-consuming program for opening new accounts and certificates of deposits. I do regret the lack of opportunity for career advancement here.

To succeed in my work, you need to really like people and have the ability to work well with the public. You must be able to smile and be pleasant under all circumstances. Enjoying math along with problem-solving are also necessary. Flexibility and accuracy are very important in banking.

ASSISTANT CONTROLLER

As an assistant to the controller, I am responsible for helping to prepare financial reports and analyzing the payroll distribution for the payroll clerk. I prepare payroll tax returns; answer phones, fielding and directing calls; handle the processing, reporting and follow up on Workman's Compensation claims. My day also includes performing secretarial work for the president and vice president.

Previously, I worked as an emergency medical technician, but in this job there's a wider range of skills and tasks which I find most satisfying. Each day as an assistant has been challenging--there's never any boredom. I find great job satisfaction in a job well done. Following through from beginning to end is very rewarding. I also like it when I'm one step ahead.

In my bookkeeping assignments, I find you need an aptitude with figures. Computer literacy as well as being able to work with all office equipment is also vital. Strong communication skills are most important and you must have the willingness to listen, to encourage, and always be open to new ideas. Being able to follow directions and learn has made my job easier.

A high school graduate, I chose the clerical/bookkeeping field in school. With college out of the question at the time, I wanted an occupation on which I could rely to earn a living. My only regret in my present job is that there is little opportunity for advancement.

ASSISTANT, INSURANCE AGENCY

Especially satisfying to me in my work as a part-time assistant to an insurance agent is the service I do for our clients. I appreciate the favorable feedback I get in subsequent contacts with them. The variety in my work also makes my job enjoyable. I particularly like completing a project when all the components involved come together.

Since graduating from high school, my work life has always been in secretarial positions. I left the field for a period of time to raise a family. When my children were in high school, I went back to work as a substitute secretary in our local public school. Later, I became a temporary secretary in this insurance agency while they looked for someone permanent. That was fifteen years ago, and I'm still here.

Skills required in my job are typing, word processing, communication, and computer skills. You must be able to write effective business letters, be attentive to details, and have a strong desire to help people. An "unflappable" attitude is also helpful as I often have to do several things at one time while being interrupted by the telephone or by my boss.

My job involves all phases of secretarial work: filing, transcribing dictation, composing and typing letters. I assist with insurance policies from submission of the application, through the underwriting process, and to the issuing of the policy. My responsibilities include keeping all information on policies updated in the computer files as well as in the home office. In customer service, I help our clients keep their policies up-to-date. My work also consists of managing the office, maintaining supplies, and handling payroll. I plan to work for several more years and then I will finally retire.

ASSISTANT MANAGER, FINANCE COMPANY

As the assistant manager of an office in a finance company, I handle loans, mortgages, and collections and attempt to develop new business. My work of four years has been mostly to collect on delinquent loan accounts, post payments to accounts, take loan applications and make recommendations for approval or denial, and close loans.

In addition to an Associate's degree in Business Management, to succeed in a position such as mine, you must also be organized, good with figures, sympathetic to customers' problems, patient, and have a friendly telephone manner.

I like the people I work with and this kind of work in general. I especially enjoy having the opportunity to help someone out of a financial bind or stick with them until they get back on their feet financially.

I started as a bank teller and continued working in a few banking departments. After receiving a degree in business management, I wanted to put my education to use and seized the opportunity to work for a finance company. With my previous experience in banking, I was pleased to be able to land a management position in my present company; I have found that working for a finance company holds more career opportunities and the pay level is on a higher scale than in the bank where I worked.

I am taking a new turn in the field of finance and learning about income tax preparation; perhaps the future will hold something in that line for me as well as expanding my knowledge in my current field. I believe that you must always be open to new opportunities.

ASSISTANT MANAGER, PRODUCTION

I work as the assistant production manager at a regional theater company; I have been working in this position for three years.

Basically, I tend to the details of three productions going on at the same time. The job varies daily with respect to the tasks to be accomplished. I track budgets, take care of housing and travel arrangements, attend meetings, draw up contracts, monitor performances, prepare the payroll, and perform daily trouble shooting to ensure all is well with my company.

Although there is a lack of opportunity for advancement with my company, I like my job, the people I work with, my boss, and the overall company. This job gives me the opportunity to meet some interesting people that I otherwise would not have the chance to meet. All my hard work is worth it for me when I see the final production on stage.

I have a Bachelor of Fine Arts degree. In addition, my job requires a sense of humor, keen observation skills, theatrical knowledge and experience, the ability to read people and be diplomatic, the ability to motivate and persuade people, and basic computer skills.

My past experience includes working as a wardrobe mistress and teaching guitar.

I would like to take on more responsibilities and become a full- fledged producer. I plan to return to college (graduate school) and earn an advanced theater degree.

ASSISTANT PRINCIPAL

Although I've been in education 23 years, I've been assistant principal at a vocational technical center for only 3 of those years. I've enjoyed these last years because my students appreciate a concerned, caring, and supportive administrator.

In my work I counsel students as well as encourage at-risk students to continue their training programs. I observe and evaluate staff and students. I am also responsible for discipline. Plus, there are also a great number of meetings to attend, 4 to 6 per week.

I really enjoy almost every aspect of my career: the institution, my immediate superior, the chance for professional growth, and my colleagues. It would be even better if our boss, once in a while, would give us encouragement and a little positive reinforcement. One day I, myself, would like to be the principal or the Director of our vocational center.

An assistant principal must have high self-esteem along with a positive attitude toward life. You should have the ability to work cooperatively as a team member and be able to make decisions and be willing to lead. The proper training and experience are very important, and some kind of college degree is important for this work. My own degree is a Master's of Arts in education. I've been a high school principal and a teacher, but this present job is the one I enjoy most.

ASSISTANT PRINCIPAL, K-8

I have been in school work most of my life. After graduating from college with a bachelor's degree, I spent 15 years teaching grades 6, 7, or 8, and 1 1/2 years teaching college level sociology. My former principal asked me to prepare to be his assistant principal. I expressed the desire to be a counselor and he convinced me I should complete an administrative graduate program, which I did. I then moved to my present location and am certified to be an administrator in the state in which I live.

As assistant principal, I am responsible for buses, lunch program, discipline duties, a sounding board for teachers, and a complaint center for everyone. More specifically, my daily and weekly activities include: checking on staff, buses, and students for immediate needs; writing daily notices; walking through each classroom; attending grade-level team meetings; visiting one classroom and writing a formal observation; pre- or post-conference with teachers for evaluation; writing parent letters; supervising lunch and break recesses; tending to and documenting all discipline problems; interviewing applicants for lunch crew, aides, and substitutes; and meeting with parents and the school board.

To perform well in this kind of job, it is important to have a knowledge of educational procedure and laws; a sense of humor; a mild, friendly, non-threatening temperament (people skills); office and time management skills; leadership skills; clear goals; and those subtle abilities necessary to generate enthusiasm for progress and new programs.

Every day is different in this kind of work; some days are better than others. At times I can get very frustrated dealing with angry, demanding, unreasonable parents; and I don't know how to change the situation. Other times, I am very satisfied with my role as assistant principal because of the fun with the kids, fun with the teachers, and the thrill from a project well done. I am also pleased with the pay and have a feeling of financial security.

I plan to stay in education, but probably not in administrative work. I would like to continue graduate studies in a doctoral program which would result in college-level teaching and supervising new teachers.

ASSISTANT PRINCIPAL, SECONDARY SCHOOL

My career began as an English teacher. I liked administrative duties and working on school-wide issues and projects. Classroom repetition became boring to me. In administration, I have found no 2 days are alike. Administration is not boring.

As Assistant Principal in a junior high/middle school, I assist the principal in making sure the school runs smoothly and the kids are getting an education. I spend a great deal of each day following up on discipline concerns that parents, teachers, and bus drivers report. I talk to kids, parents, and monitors all day. I try to make sure an environment exists where instruction can take place without interruption.

My educational background to prepare me for this career includes a bachelor of arts and master's in science, plus certification in school administration. To perform my work well, I think it is also important to have patience, common sense, efficiency, compassion, speaking/listening skills, and the ability to work with many diverse people.

The biggest frustration I am now facing is with the inefficiency of the school district in which I am now working. It seems that computers, copiers, and phones are often broken. Certain procedures make no sense. There are cumbersome ways to do things and no one cares.

Aside from these frustrations, I like my kind of work very much. I like playing a key role in a school building. There aren't 50 of me--only one. I like talking to kids and parents and teachers. I really BELIEVE what we're about is important. I'd like to keep moving up the ladder at a District--right now, to Assistant Superintendent for Instruction.

ASSISTANT PRODUCTION SUPERVISOR

A typical day for me, as an assistant production supervisor, includes checking with the previous shift to see what problems they had, looking over the schedule, and making sure everyone has come in for work. I give directions for each employee's work, determine each worker's need, and make certain each has what is needed to start up production.

My day consists of managing any necessary paperwork and computer work. I tour the work area, handling whatever problems arise. Talking with the workers helps keep open the lines of communication and keep the employees motivated.

My supervisor lets me run my area with little or no supervision. That is job satisfaction for me. What I would like is more power to hire and fire workers; but I do enjoy the people I work with, my bosses, the company, and the fact that there is the chance of furthering myself.

A supervisor needs very good leadership skills. You also have to be able to work well with people and organize things.

After graduating from high school, I was in maintenance. I liked that work, I liked the company a lot, and I decided I wanted to work for them. I had to start at the bottom. I moved into being an assembler, and I worked up from there to assistant supervisor. My plans are to be a maintenance technician and maybe, some day, an engineer.

ASSISTANT SCHOOL SUPERINTENDENT

There is no such thing as a typical day in my work as an educator serving as an assistant superintendent. That's why I love my career. For me, knowing my work makes a difference is the greatest satisfaction.

I have a Bachelor of Arts degree, a Master of Arts, and a Doctorate in education. While in college, I worked in merchandising as a means of earning extra funds. In a public school of 3,600 students, kindergarten through adult, I am responsible for the personnel, administration, and curriculum. I love my work; students basically remain the same throughout their school years--bright, curious, challenged, and often at risk.

My work requires a thorough knowledge base, including excellent communication skills. Versatility and flexibility are key characteristics for a person in my position. Further, one needs skills in leadership, in the ability to work with people, the belief that all people are basically good, and the conviction that young people are great.

It would be more satisfying if there were not only fewer meetings, but also more educational focus in those meetings which are required. More input from educators, as opposed to decisions being made by public officials, is needed. I also would like to see more educational projects implemented. My future plans are to retire--and then to start teaching again!

ASTROLOGICAL WRITER, PUBLISHER

My career as an astrologer is outside the mainstream of conventional fields of endeavor, and I am not in a high-paying field. Therefore, to become an astrologer, generally you must enjoy this subject and be highly motivated to pursue it, as I am.

My work in this field is as an astrological writer of biographical almanacs and I am the publisher of a newsletter. Basically, I correspond world-wide to collect birth data and exchange information, compile data, and carry out research.

In a typical work week I handle international correspondence by letter and phone, do data entry and updates on the computer, clip and file magazine and journal articles, and do library research of public figures. I also give lectures about a dozen times throughout the year.

To pursue this career, I want to re-emphasize that you must enjoy the field of astrology and probably tend to be idealistic and independent.

Self-employment requires self-motivation. Also important are computer processing skills and the ability to communicate and reach people. You must have enough intelligence to make astronomical calculations and handle multivariables of symbolic interpretations.

I totally enjoy my work and field and have for 30 years. I like being my own boss. I'm a data collector. I like the tedium of handling thousands of items of information, compiling, editing, recording; the manipulation of facts to present a journalistic finished product. I work at my own pace, time, and place, and at my own level of interest, i.e. independently. I'm interested in people, both public figures and private individuals--their motivations, goals, and handicaps.

There are several changes I would like to see in my field. The academic ignorance of astrology is even more appalling than the public image (i.e. sun-signs in the local paper). I would like to witness academic acceptance. There should be within the field a central voice, a national and world-wide exchange of information to a greater degree, and a clearing house (or organization) for research projects.

Prior to this career I was in restaurant management, a pilot, a model, a talent agent and a secretary. My future goals are to finish publishing my two books, and I plan to further develop my data-bank on an international level.

ATHLETICS DIRECTOR, COLLEGE

I seem to be most satisfied when working with young people, which is the primary reason I like my job as director of athletics at a college. My work background is somewhat diverse and yet tied together with a common thread in that it is people-oriented. Prior to my current position, I was a high school history teacher, a vice president for a major corporation in advertising and public relations, and a reading teacher for young people who had reading problems. My educational background includes a Bachelor of Arts in History/Education and a Masters of Art in Reading. I chose to get into athletics because athletics is always something I have been involved with.

As a college athletics director, I plan and direct on a daily basis the total operation of the athletic department. My day begins at 8:30 and ends at 6:30 or 7:00 p.m. During the course of the day, I plan all the athletic events, supervise the coaching staff, handle and administer the athletic budget, and work with students.

In order to perform this kind of work well, it is important to have good budgeting skills, be able to communicate well with people, and be able to listen.

I like almost every aspect of my job, but I wish that it was possible for my athletics department to offer more programs for students and provide more services.

My future career plans are to continue to work with young people but I intend to change subject matter again. My aspiration is to get a law degree and then teach history and political science on the college level.

ATTORNEY #1

Typically I'm at the office by 8:30 a.m. During the course of the day or week as a civil and criminal litigation lawyer, I might have various appointments with clients, have court appearances, research legal issues, prepare memoranda, complaints, interrogations, interview witnesses, engage in settlement negotiations, try cases to judges and/or juries.

An attorney should have an analytical mind, good writing and speaking abilities, be able to think quickly on your feet, and a knowledge of the law in the area in question. Always be open minded and open to compromise.

Helping others resolve legal conflicts without resorting to physical attacks gives me job satisfaction.

My job could be accomplished better if the court system were streamlined so that matters could be resolved in a quicker fashion.

I entered this profession through education and hard work.

ATTORNEY #2

As an attorney, I practice corporate, bankruptcy and environmental law. My 10-12 hour work days include: using all forms of communication, such as the telephone, letters and meetings, doing research, attending and participating in court hearings, and office management.

I chose this profession, first of all, because I liked the intellectual challenge of law school. Now that I am practicing, I am still enjoying the challenge. I also like the people I work with and the firm I work for. The variety of cases is stimulating. I find satisfaction from solving complicated problems or negotiations, helping people accomplish goals, and winning contested arguments.

My major dislike about my profession is the pressure and deadlines. I would like more time to devote to each matter. Another thing I would like to change would be to improve the professionalism of other lawyers.

To perform well as an attorney, it is important to have good communication and reading skills, the ability to speak and think on your feet, the will to want to know more about the facts and the law than the other side, and be able to make objective analyses.

My future career aspirations are to continue to improve as a lawyer, the constant challenge.

ATTORNEY #3

My career has taken me into a variety of fields and it wasn't until I was in my mid-thirties that I decided to go into law. After graduating from college with a Bachelor of Arts degree and before pursuing law, I was a journalist, Peace Corps volunteer, housewife and mother, and writer and editor. I earned my master's degree, after which I became a college English teacher. My father is a judge and I'd always thought about going into law on and off. I was involved in the anti-war movements and the Women's Movement in the 60's and 70's and thought that law was a good way to change things.

As an attorney in private practice, I handle negligence cases, family law, general litigation, municipal law, estates, etc. It is very difficult to describe a typical day or week in my profession. There is no routine schedule. I might see clients on various matters Monday, return telephone calls, do research; be in court Tuesday and Wednesday; have depositions in a negligence case Thursday; motions in court on Friday and some work in the office.

To perform your job well as an attorney, it is essential to be able to write well. Getting along with people and a willingness to work hard are also important attributes to have for this kind of work.

My biggest frustration with my occupation is that I never have enough time. Aside from that, I like this kind of work very much, and the people I work with. I am very satisfied with my decision to be an attorney, and have now been in practice for 15 years. I find job satisfaction in winning an important legal point; accomplishing a good result for a client; learning about clients' problems and needs and doing research; and constructing an argument.

In the future, I'd like to write more, but otherwise I like what I do and have no real plans to do anything different.

ATTORNEY #4

I attended law school at age 35. I was tired of having unchallenging and unrewarding jobs. I had dreamed of maybe becoming a lawyer since I was a child, and just decided I'd never be satisfied unless I at least tried to get into law school. So I took the entrance exam and was admitted to the school of my choice. I now have my J.D. Prior to this, I worked as a waitress, in telephone sales, and as a human resources clerk in an electronics firm. I have also been a Vista volunteer working as an outreach worker for legal services.

As an attorney in general practice, I work long hours making phone calls, appearing in court, doing research, writing motions, interviewing new clients, and counseling clients, in the process of planning and implementing lawsuits.

To perform this kind of work, you must be able and willing to work long and hard. This career also requires intelligence and a competitive nature. However, you must also know when it is more advantageous to be cooperative.

The one thing I wish I could change in my occupation would be to lower the cost of new legal material. Aside from that drawback, I have found that I am indeed enjoying this occupation and its challenges. I like the people I work with, and the opportunities I have for advancement. I find this career satisfying because I am helping people get something they want or need. I plan to continue my work as an attorney and become successful in my field.

ATTORNEY #5

For many years, I have worked as an attorney; my case load is usually two or more law suits at a time.

Working as an attorney requires superior communication skills, knowledge of the law in a classroom setting, passing the bar exam, and practical application of the theory learned in the classroom. I have two degrees in the field of law; you can never know all there is to know, or learn too much about law.

I like working in this field. My job gives me great intellectual stimulation, but more than that, I like winning.

I decided early in life that I wanted to become a lawyer. I have relatives that work as lawyers, and they were my inspiration.

Because I do not always enjoy dealing with clients, I may at some point get involved in legal research.

ATTORNEY #6

I have a Bachelor of Arts degree, a Law degree, and have been in law practice for a year. I like almost everything about being an attorney, especially the ability to help people. A sense of accomplishment along with having the ability to do well are part of my job satisfaction. I only wish there weren't so many long hours required.

I chose the legal field because my skills and abilities were best suited for the law. Ever since I was a youngster, I've wanted to be an attorney, so, if I could start over, I'd again elect law. My future is unsure. While I plan to stay in law, I don't know whether I'll find a career in politics, or own my own firm, or become a judge.

An attorney's day consists of any variety of projects. Included may be preparing a pleading or consulting with a client. Handling internal administrative matters also takes my time.

To be a successful lawyer, you must have strong reading skills along with the ability to comprehend what is read. Reliable memory skills with sound recall capability are a great asset. You must be able to work well under pressure and have the ability to work well with others. Research skills are especially important in this field.

ATTORNEY #7

Mental flexibility and dexterity, tenacity, and persuasiveness characterize the field of law. An attorney must be able to relate to people in a variety of situations. A "fight hard, don't quit" attitude is a must. I enjoyed my work in advertising, but being a trial lawyer has given me the opportunity to research, write and draft legal pleadings and documents. I have no future plans. The stress of the work, the lack of sufficient time for each client, and the conflicts in schedules created by clerks of the court have all made my job less satisfying than it could have been. My college major was Business Administration; my minor was English. My law degree followed. You might say that law is a family tradition; I'm a 3rd generation attorney and the 6th in the family. I've enjoyed the mental challenges, the people I've met, and the law profession. There is a great variety involved in my work. Especially notable has been the personal contact with my clients, with witnesses, and with adversaries and their attorneys. I am delighted when I have happy clients and I appreciate respect from skilled opponents.

ATTORNEY #8

I always knew I wanted to be a lawyer; I loved to argue positions, even those with which I disagreed. My family had a history of labor involvement and my school had a great labor program, so it was labor law for me.

A typical week in labor law for a union includes researching legal issues and new developments in the law; meeting clients; writing legal memorandum, motions, complaints and answers to complaints. A lawyer answers correspondence and telephone calls from clients and attorneys, responds to other attorneys' inquiries, and spends some time in court. Court intervals consist of motions, depositions, and sworn testimony.

Thoroughness, compassion, and trustworthiness are vital to a successful lawyer. Persuasive writing and speaking skills are required. Credibility is mandatory to a union lawyer. Being able to do research well is also very important. I have a Bachelor of Arts Degree, a PH. D., and a law degree.

I'm very gratified when I can help individuals solve a disaster in their lives. It's great to know you gave a regular gal or guy a second chance. I would like more contact with people and less desk work, but the desk work is a necessary part of the job. I work 30 hours at the desk for every one hour in the courtroom.

ATTORNEY, GENERAL PRACTICE

Interestingly enough, the major influence in my life was my mother, especially in the way she encouraged me during my childhood and adolescence.

Becoming a lawyer just seemed to be the natural career choice for me. As long as I can remember, I have wanted to be a lawyer, and from early childhood I was told I would make a good lawyer. My career life, however, has not all been in this field. I was a Russian linguist, an intelligence analyst in the Air Force, and an operator of a service station and hot dog stand.

As an attorney in general practice, I arrive at the office at 6:30 a.m. and leave at 5:00 p.m., 5 days a week. My typical daily/weekly activities include reading the mail, reviewing my schedule, discussing plans for the day with the paralegal, meeting client appointments preparing legal documents, receiving phone calls, and attending court hearings and trials.

In order to perform this kind of work well, I consider the following characteristics and skills to be important: honesty, dependability, professional skills, and concern for individuals and society. A desire to work against an incompetent judicial system is also necessary.

Being an attorney has offered me a sense of participation in life as it is. I have found satisfaction from interacting with all types of clients and employees. I have also been rewarded by the trust others place in me. Satisfaction has also come from having the ability to respond to people's needs.

ATTORNEY, PATENT LAW

I am very satisfied that I made a change many years ago from engineering to law. Originally, I earned my Bachelor of Science in Mechanical Engineering degree and had jobs as a test engineer, design engineer and draftsman. When a recession hit the air and space industry in which I was working, I took a job as an examiner in the U.S. Patent Office. I then decided to pursue this career further and attended law school at night to earn my J.D..

As an attorney specializing in patent law, I prepare and prosecute patent applications, and prepare and negotiate technology license agreements. My typical 10-hour work day includes reading incoming mail, proofing the previous day's work before mailing it that day, reviewing inventors disclosure from a client to determine what may be patentable after comparing the disclosure against what has been identified by a patent search, discussing the invention with the inventor, formulating the claims to be pursued, preparing the invention description for the patent application, and reviewing comments from the patent examiner and other cases, etc.

To perform well in this career, it is important to have a knowledge and understanding of patent law, contract law and general engineering principals, and the ability to communicate well with engineers, business people, government bureaucrats and other lawyers.

I very much like this kind of work. I receive satisfaction from seeing new technology utilized successfully.

ATTORNEY, U.S. NAVY

After earning a Bachelor of Arts degree in political science, I decided to attend law school since I didn't feel my undergraduate field was marketable. I'd been interested in the Navy since high school, so I got my law degree and am an attorney for the U.S. Navy.

For 5 years, I've advised command on disciplinary and legal issues. Giving counsel to individuals regarding legal problems is also my job. Much of my time is spent in meetings, sorting through mail, and preparing responses to correspondence.

Besides the required training in law and a legal degree, one needs good political skills to be a lawyer for the Navy.

If I should leave the Navy, I plan to go back to school and specialize in tax or environmental law. I'd like to get away from what I see as inefficiency and a waste of time in meetings and concentrate on getting a job done.

ATTORNEY, VICE PRESIDENT--INSURANCE COMPANY

I am an attorney with the position of Vice President of Claims for a casualty insurance company. I daily wade through a large amount of mail, involving complaints, requests for appointments to sell services, equipment and supplies used by the department, industry publications and reports, etc. I review various reports of claim activity and have consultations with others on unusual claims. Reviewing audit reports of the quality of claim activity by office, area or region are part of my regular work. Committee meetings with staff personnel and representatives from other company divisions plus reports to the President also are part of my responsibility.

To perform well in my occupation one should have initiative, planning and organizing skills, decisiveness, control, leadership and organizational sensitivity and awareness.

I find my work satisfying when I see the development of people and the efficient operation of the department because of my efforts.

It is my opinion that an attorney's work could be more satisfying if there were less interference by uninformed governmental agencies.

I started my job when I returned from military duty during the Korean War. Prior to that I had a private law practice.

Upon retirement I plan to do volunteer work with the elderly, such as Medicare counseling and income tax assistance.

AUDITOR

I audit company records to support procurement actions with the government and to assure regulation compliance. My numerous administrative tasks as an auditor for the government usually involve setting up and organizing assignments so that the audits can be performed and a conclusion can be arrived at, whether it be a proposal, claim, contract, etc.

The most important skill necessary to perform my type of work is a detailed knowledge of accounting rules and regulations plus government procurement regulations. You must know audit techniques necessary to arrive at conclusions.

I have enjoyed auditing work for 15 years. My job satisfaction is from personal contacts with people I meet during audits and with whom I work. If I had a chance to start over I would choose this same kind of work. However, I would like to see the elimination of a number of job related rules and regulations that I find inhibiting or confining, such as strict adherence to and excessively heavy evaluation based on factors related to assignment budgets.

To prepare myself for this accounting work, I earned a BA in Science and an MA in Business Administration. I have been in the US Navy and worked as a supply clerk. Prior to my current job with the government, I was an accountant for a manufacturing company.

I plan to continue in this profession because I like it and I can build financial security for myself and my family.

AUDITOR, FEDERAL OFFICES

As a federal auditor, I examine the financial statements of federal offices. I verify the accuracy of these statements and affirm the efficiency and the economy of the office's operation. A typical day consists of planning for an audit, or doing the audit, or reporting the results of the audit.

In planning for the audit, we learn about why the office was established. We study how it is structured to carry out its mission. In the audit phase, we examine the office's system of internal controls. We review its program accomplishments, the efficiency of its operations, and its accuracy of reporting its results. Comments on any weaknesses found come in the report stage when we cite problems or causes of problems and make recommendations for corrective actions.

I'd choose my career as a federal auditor again. For 15 years, I have enjoyed the independence that comes with the job and having my recommendations respected. Knowing that they are accepted and that they result in a significant improvement in the efficiency of operations is really important to me.

A background in accounting and in business administration is helpful to an auditor. I have my Bachelor of Science degree. You should have analytical skills as well as enjoy research. Being able to summarize data would be very useful as well.

AUDITOR, INSURANCE AGENCY

Part of an internal audit team for a large insurance agency, I'm also the licensing and sales coordinator. As a member of the audit team, I'm responsible for quality control and policies for errors and omissions coverage. Further, my work involves securing and renewing agents' and brokers' licenses in my state and in 49 other states. I prepare internal sales reports on a weekly basis, as well as provide preliminary tax and corporate reports. My job includes tracking continuing education requirements for the various licenses and, in general, monitoring the numerous requirements for these licenses.

Proper training is essential to this work. I currently hold several designations in the insurance field. My tax accounting background and my current credentials help in preparing tax and other reports required for nonresident state licensing.

Strong people skills are needed to get the information required for the many sales reports. Adeptness on the computer and with word processing is necessary in the production of reports. Being well versed in all areas of the insurance field is essential. Additionally, close attention to detail, being organized, and being accurate are vital.

In my job, I especially enjoy working with people. It's satisfying to answer questions, keep track of license needs, and make sure tasks are done well and in a timely manner. I'm proud of our company and its progress. I like being part of a large, but friendly, family-oriented agency. My job would be perfect if there were more knowledgeable people in our internal departments of insurance, and in insurance companies elsewhere.

My plans are to continue training in my field to be ready for any advancement opportunities. I'd like to further my computer skills as well as identify a better computer system to produce reports more efficiently as well as to reduce tracking time.

AUTHOR & PUBLISHER

My publishing company is small; therefore, I wear many hats as an author and publisher. As an author, I write mathematics books, as well as supplemental math materials, for schools. My work as a publisher requires that I spend time preparing advertising and promotional matter. Some part of the day is also spent dealing with administrative business: opening the mail, responding to government requests, preparing bids, ordering supplies, and supervising accounting operations as well as company staff.

Previously a classroom teacher and a supervisor of curriculum, I now enjoy having the freedom to "do my own thing." My teaching experience provides the ideas and the background for my present work. I've written many mathematics textbooks for a major publisher and, now, it is rewarding to be creating unique products for my own company. The feeling of satisfaction from starting and managing a successful business is remarkable.

I'd choose this profession again except that I'd wear fewer hats. I'd like to devote more time to developing my educational products. All the government paperwork involved in collecting and paying taxes as well as preparing government reports is a bother. With both a Bachelor degree, a Master of Science degree and a high interest in publishing, I don't believe I'll ever retire, but plan to continue writing and developing my business.

My profession requires strong writing skills. You need to develop useful math materials and have a "feeling" for the teacher and the student in the classroom. My work also demands patience because much time is needed to produce a product. To run the business, good service is required in order to aggressively compete.

AUTOMOBILE MECHANIC

Being an auto mechanic was a natural career for me because I have always had an interest in cars. I started by doing the repairs on my own car because I couldn't afford to have someone do it for me. Even my hobbies, like racing rallies, are centered around cars. My background includes 3 years of college and work as a photographer for a newspaper, plus construction work.

I work for an automobile dealer where I diagnose and repair cars. I also install radios, air conditioners, and other optional equipment on new cars, and perform preventative maintenance operations.

In order to perform this kind of work well, it is important to have good mechanical skills. As an automobile mechanic, you must be able to determine what a problem is from clues, and then perform the repair. Basically, you must understand why something works.

I enjoy the job, but I would like to have better communications between customer and mechanic, worker and management, etc. I have also found that there is a lack of opportunity for advancement. Therefore, I plan to finish college in order to put myself into a better position for advancement. I hope this will lead to a management position in the car dealership, or some sort of industrial safety job. Despite the drawbacks of the job, I have remained with this kind of work because I find satisfaction in fixing broken things.

AUTOMOBILE SERVICE TECHNICIAN

There are constant challenges in my job as an automotive service technician. I enjoyed my earlier jobs as a photographer, a welder, and a graphic artist, but I like the continual changes and the fact that there is minimal supervision in my present job.

As an automotive service technician, I listen to customers' complaints, diagnose the causes of the problems, sell the maintenance or repair work to the customer, and then make the repairs. Good listening skills, confidence, and integrity are all very important in my work. The job requires exceptional mechanical skills along with the ability to see spatial relationships. Abilities to read and write well, and to get along with people are also necessary.

I'd like more respect for the level of skill required to do my job and better pay.

I got into this line of work because I took a job as a lube technician with the company. Then in 1969 I studied mechanics. I'd like one day to have my own independent automotive service shop.

AUTOMOTIVE ENGINEER

My technical specialty as an automotive engineer is with engine combustion. I study engine operation, fuel economy and emissions. This involves studying reports and literature relevant to a problem. The next step is to prepare test plans, run the test and analyze the results. Writing and presenting reports on the conclusions drawn from the tests are other stages in my work process. I also frequently consult with other departments.

To perform well in this career, a background in science, technology, math and statistics is necessary. It is also important to have good writing and speaking skills and to work well with others.

I have been working as an engineer for 20 years after receiving my bachelors of science degree in engineering and like the work very much. I derive satisfaction from solving problems and understanding how things work. I like the people I work with, and the people I work for. However, I do not like the organization I work for. It is too big which creates a lot of bureaucracy. I would prefer more personal responsibility. I plan to continue in this field and aspire to be a technical leader.

AVIATION DEPARTMENT MANAGER & CORPORATE PILOT

All my jobs have been aviation related. I have always been interested in aviation, so I decided to learn how to fly. From there, I continued to pursue flying to obtain the knowledge and requirements to pilot the type of aircraft I currently fly. Before being offered my current job as Aviation Department Manager and Chief Pilot for a corporation, I was a flight instructor, aircraft salesman, co-pilot, and I ran my own aviation related business. My educational background includes a Bachelor of Science degree.

My work responsibilities are to manage the corporate aircraft travel needs for the corporation, plus pilot the aircraft. I fly to various places in the U.S. and occasionally Europe.

There really isn't anything I dislike about my career. I like the kind of work I do, the opportunities I have had for advancement, the people and organization I work for, and the people I work with. I find satisfaction from my work because I enjoy flying and managing people.

The skills and attitudes which I consider important for performing this job well are a dedication to perfection, desire to travel, and interest in machines and how they work.

I plan to continue in my current job. If, however, the possibility arose, I would like to manage an international flight department.

BAKER/BAKERY MANAGER

Cooking has always been one of my favorite things to do, so when an opening came up in a bakery, I was happy to fill the position. I started out by waiting on customers and bagging bread and rolls. My training came on the job by previous bakers. In addition to the on-the-job training, my educational background, which includes an Associate degree in Business Management, has prepared me for this work. I have worked previously as a dental receptionist, mail clerk with a greeting card company, and in food preparation at a fast food restaurant, but I have found this work more satisfying to me.

As the bakery manager/baker, I arrive for work at 2:30 a.m. I must make sure all the equipment is working and the ovens, proof boxes, and fry-o-lator are turned on. I start making donuts, fill the proof boxes, and start making products that were set up the day before. Baking different products throughout the day, setting up products for the next day's production, and recording all products baked and any stales from the previous day are all my daily responsibilities.

To perform this kind of work well, you must have training in baking and food preparation. You must be committed to early hours. Punctuality and low absenteeism are important. It is also essential as a manager/baker that you take pride in your work and have the ability to adjust in different situations.

I like most aspects about my work; however, I have found that working in a supermarket bakery can sometimes be difficult because the management does not always allow enough time to produce all that is needed. Despite this frustration, I am satisfied particularly when seeing the nice looking products being bought and knowing that I made it.

BANK AUDITOR, INTERNAL

While I have a Bachelor of Arts degree in theology, I also have a Bachelor of Science in business administration and have found a satisfying career as an internal bank auditor. My plans for the future are to continue in my bank auditing work of the past 8 years. Perhaps one day I'll be the manager of a bank department.

A bank auditor should have strong verbal and written skills and be able to solve problems easily as well as possess good analytical skills. Knowledge of accounting principles, along with banking regulations and procedures, is essential, of course. Familiarity with general business procedures is useful also.

In my work, I examine bank policies and procedures as well as accounting controls for accuracy. I accomplish this through interviews with employees and through personal review of bank business. On occasion, when errors are detected, we redo work and make certain information is reliable. Then, I prepare and submit a report on the effectiveness and efficiency of our bank's systems and controls.

I'd like the salaries to be more competitive with other industries. It would also be more efficient if we could automate our work as much as possible to eliminate the routine grunt work. But it is personally rewarding to me to be able to find solutions to problems we've identified and to correct these problems. I enjoy, on an ongoing basis, acquiring thorough knowledge of banking principles. My fellow bankers, management, and the fact that there are opportunities for advancement, are all fulfilling to me.

BANK LOAN OFFICER

It is important that a banker have analytical skills and strong written and oral communication skills. A friendly personality to help with selling bank products is great to have. A banker must also have perseverance and problem-solving skills.

I've worked in insurance sales, as a retail store manager, and as a factory manager. With a Bachelor of Arts Degree in economics, I entered banking 21 years ago. In my work in the indirect automobile loan division, I review loan applications for individuals and dealerships. I am a credit manager as well and that work requires me to write reviews and make presentations to the credit committee. I must make sales calls, analyze financial statements, and write policies and procedures.

Helping others gives me a great sense of job satisfaction. I'd enjoy my work more if some of the "red tape" could be reduced. Work flow would be more efficient if we'd do away with the formal written presentations and if other employees would be responsive to inquiries.

The way I got into banking was by answering an ad in the newspaper. I've worked my way up in the business and my plans are to continue in this line of work. I want to add more business to the bank.

BANK LOAN RECORDS CLERK

I have had numerous occupations during my career, but after finding out about careers in banking through a temporary assignment, I now plan to stay in this industry. Previous jobs have been as a cashier, accounting clerk, bakery manager, restaurant manager, and waitress.

As the records clerk, I receive and audit new real estate loans. My typical daily activities include receiving new loan files, making sure all information is correct, auditing new loans to make sure all the documents are in the file and correct, and entering necessary information into the computer. Since I am also in charge of my area, I make sure all my charges are working and I answer their questions. Despite the fact that this can be tedious and the tasks are often repetitive, it is critical that the work be done with accuracy and attention be paid to details.

I have found that I like this kind of work and find job satisfaction in getting my work done accurately and in a timely manner. As I mentioned earlier, I plan to stay in banking and take courses in order to qualify myself for other positions within the banking industry.

BANK OPERATIONS DIVISION MANAGER

As Bank Operations Division Manager, I direct the operation of the bank services division which includes hiring, firing, budgeting, purchasing, and monitoring services. This involves problem solving, report/statistical preparation and review, and employee counseling.

I earned a bachelor's degree in business administration and have been working at elevating my position in the business world by working at different positions. Prior to my current job, I have been a bank teller, head teller, returns unit manager, and management consultant. I plan to continue my business climb in hopes of achieving senior management status. I like the kind of work I am doing as a bank operations manager. I find job satisfaction in providing quality customer service. It is also satisfying for me to make the job easier for other employees through equipment purchases and procedure enhancements.

BANKER #1

I am in my present position because, while serving as a bank director, I was asked if I was interested in becoming the Chief Executive Officer. My prior professions as a C.P.A. (Certified Public Accountant), attorney, and industrialist, along with the educational background which I have had in order to pursue these other careers, probably contributed to the C.E.O. position being offered to me. I guess you can conclude from this that I like many phases of business, and like to be in decision- making positions.

As a C.E.O. of a bank, my responsibilities include the management of meetings, reviewing reports and financial reports, community volunteer work, and planning. The proper handling of these responsibilities requires analytical, human resource, and financial skills.

My biggest frustration with my work has been because of all the regulatory constraints imposed upon banks by the Government. Aside from this frustration, I like my kind of work very much. I also like the organization I work for, and people with whom I work. I find job satisfaction from helping others, and helping the community. Performance is my responsibility and I derive personal satisfaction from carrying out this responsibility.

BANKER #2

Twenty-four years ago after leaving the Air Force, my first job was in banking. I earned a Masters of Business Education degree, having earned a Bachelor of Science before I entered the Air Force, and today I am Chief Operating Officer with all operating units of a bank reporting to me. While the degrees are not absolutely necessary, they are a help.

My work includes a variety of meetings to make decisions regarding the bank, its products, its services, and its employees. Determining the most efficient way to perform tasks is also a purpose of these meetings. Satisfaction for me is giving exemplary service to customers of the bank and charging a fair price for these services.

Being a competent banker requires very strong verbal skills. One needs to be able to write reports and correspondence as well as be able to present the bank in a favorable light to the public. A knowledge of finance and good people skills are equally important. Some day I'd like to be the Chief Executive Officer of the bank or of a financial company.

BANKER, PRIVATE LOANS BROKER

As a private banker and loan broker for twenty-three years, my job is to arrange financing for various projects. I take information from clients about their credit needs and arrange financing from various sources.

This position requires a good education, the ability to analyze financial statements, the ability to analyze what people mean versus what they say, the ability to say no diplomatically without damaging the future financial relationship with the customer.

I love everything about my job, but I especially enjoy making deals!

It is a pleasure for me to assist people to obtain the funds they need and to complete a loan transaction. The only discouraging aspect of this job is that people are not always completely truthful with me and that always is revealed sometime before the transaction is closed, usually during background or credit checks.

Previously, I worked in industrial sales and tax accounting. After completing a college degree, I plan to stay with this field and expand into international financing.

BANK TELLER #1

I like my job as a bank teller because it allows me to have the people contact which is the part of the job I enjoy most. In fact, I get the most job satisfaction from turning an angry customer with a problem into a happy, satisfied customer. I also like the people I work with and the people for whom I work.

My responsibilities as a bank teller are to cash checks, take deposits, balance accounts and solve customer banking problems. Although there are no highly technical skills required to handle these duties, it is important to have good basic math skills and to be accurate. It is also essential that you like dealing with people.

My educational background includes an associates degree. Prior to this job, I worked as a secretary.

Although I like the kind of work I am now doing, I think I would choose the career of court stenographer if given the opportunity to start over and prepare for any kind of work.

BANK TELLER #2

I've been a bank teller for three years, and I find this work very pleasant, and I hope to continue working in banking. Two years from now I would like to work in banking customer service. I would enlarge the customer service area and perhaps teach seminars about savings accounts and IRA funds.

It is satisfying to me to offer a service which is helpful to people. I enjoy greeting people and going the extra mile. In my work I post bank transactions and fulfill services offered by the bank to its customers. I open the mail and the night deposits. Serving individual depositors and commercial customers with small and large amounts of money and balancing all the money orders are some of my duties. I also balance the automatic teller machine reports. I assist in customer service by selling products and services and I explain our accounts to customers.

In banking you need good, basic arithmetic skills, good eye contact, a smile, willingness to serve people, and ability to identify needs. You need a pleasant attitude and the ability to be a team worker.

To get this job, I answered an ad in the local paper. After my interview and the job offer, I accepted because I thought I would like the work, and that has turned out to be true. The pay and the location are good. The environment at the bank, the people I work for and with, and the organization are pleasant, but the lack of opportunity for advancement is discouraging. My lack of a college education will slow my progress significantly, but it does not preclude success in the field. I'd also like more training, especially in areas that could benefit the customer. I'd like the bank to offer incentive plans for savings programs to help and encourage people to save.

BANK TELLER #3

I grew up wanting to be a movie star or a wife and mother. I always knew if I couldn't have both, homemaker was the more important. Before marriage, I earned a Bachelor of Science in Elementary Education, and worked as the production director of a magazine. I have now been a homemaker for 40 years and a part-time bank teller for the past 15 years. Since I consider my career as a homemaker to be of prime importance, I will describe this occupation as I see it.

Every moment is full from a baby's first cry until the last teenager arrives safely home from a date. It's a constant challenge to find more efficient ways to get it all done and keep everyone happy. To handle these responsibilities well and effectively, the following attributes are important: a consistent philosophy, a knowledge of psychology, a sense of humor, a respect for justice, and an ability to do three things at once.

Although I am satisfied with most aspects of my work as a homemaker, I would have had someone else do the windows, floors and yard work for me if money was no object. What I particularly like about being a homemaker is the freedom of my own schedule and being in charge. Having a part time job provides the change of pace I need. I have found satisfaction from my homemaking career from the two well-adjusted children I have raised who are now parents themselves. It is rewarding to watch my interesting grandchildren discover all over again the wonders of life and living.

Another sidepath that I have taken in my life has been that of a writer. I've written two novels which I would like to get into shape for publication but I'm not as ambitious as I should be and rejection tears me apart so I'll probably never submit them. (They're good, though.)

BARTENDER #1

For a number of years, I have been working as a bartender. Essentially, I make drinks and serve them to the public. My day begins, before the customers arrive, by preparing the bar workstation for the day's business. Opening the bar involves getting all my juices and mixes ready, cutting up fresh fruit for garnishes, checking my stock to be sure I will not run out of something during my shift, and making sure that the last bartender working at my station left everything clean and where it should be. When the customers start arriving, I mix drinks, take food orders, and make my customers feel comfortable by talking with them and generally being friendly and sociable.

Training to become a bartender is available through vocational schools; you must have some knowledge of standard drink recipes, especially the proportions, and training in handling people in a situation where they have been consuming alcohol. Tending bar requires good math skills, good judgment skills, the ability to think quickly; the ability to get along with people, and some psychology helps, as a bartender is called on to be a part-time shrink.

Although bartending is a job with limited opportunities for advancement, it can be a lot of fun; I enjoy making people smile. I really like my job and I enjoy the people I meet; I am a person who really likes people.

I previously worked as a secretary, a bookkeeper, and most recently as an administrative assistant. After a layoff at my company, I decided, on the spur of the moment, that I would try bartending as an in-between job; but I enjoyed the work and the people so much that I'm still doing it!

With my training and experience in the restaurant business, I eventually plan to become the owner/operator of my own bar and restaurant.

BARTENDER #2

I've been a bartender for five years and, although I don't like the people, their lack of motivation and professionalism, nor the organization I work for, I do enjoy the people I work with and serve. I like the social interaction with people and the casual party-type atmosphere. I particularly like being in control of the bar.

Currently, I am attending college, but I've been a receptionist, a cocktail server, and a video store clerk. In my present work, you need to be able to attract customers as well as deal with difficult customers. I have to be able to stop serving customers when necessary and to dismiss people when required.

Usually, a day consists of checking stock, setting up the bar, preparing drinks for the customers and food servers, and visiting with our clients. I keep the bar clean, ready, and well-stocked. It is a relaxing, pleasant job and I like it. Eventually, however, I hope to earn a degree in veterinary medicine.

BIOCHEMICAL ENGINEER

I've been a research engineer and a credit collector, but I enjoy the tremendous amount of freedom in my current job as a biochemical engineer. For 10 years, I've helped support the movement of technology from the laboratory into the business environment. I enjoy meeting new and interesting people across a wide range of business communities. I like traveling throughout the United States and Europe, identifying and evaluating new technologies. It is never boring, repetitive, or tedious.

My work consists of visiting university and corporate labs to identify commercially promising technologies and evaluate the commercial merit of funding proposals from technical and business perspectives. I meet with diverse groups involved in education, science, corporate, financial, and government communities who want regional economic development. I also recruit new companies to the state.

I got into this field because I grew tired of being a research engineer. I was heavily involved in bringing technology out of the laboratory into commercial practice. Acting as the agent between the universities and traditional industries, I helped start a regional economic development organization. My organization is a private, non-profit company which receives 90 percent of its funding from the state legislature. As a result, and this is part of what I dislike about my work, we are very aware of political correctness. We tolerate inefficiency and are somewhat bloated staffwise. If one quarter of our staff could be streamlined, salaries could then be improved.

This job requires technical and scientific competency along with good interpersonal skills and an outgoing personality. One needs a solid sense of self and a great deal of presence. Strong negotiating skills, the ability to make decisions, and being able to operate in a straightforward manner are important. Foreign language skills, a well-developed business sense as well as awareness of the global market are all vital. I have a Bachelors in biochemistry and a Masters in chemical engineering. For the future, I'd like to develop a new position in the same field.

BIOLOGICAL RESEARCH ASSISTANT

I found that my bachelor's degree in biology led me into this career as an alternative to medical school which, was my initial intention. I still have the desire to become an M.D.. However, at the current time I am satisfied with my job as a biological research assistant. Additional background information about myself is that my bachelor's degree included a double major in art history and biology, and I also liked my work as a word processor/secretary which I did prior to my research job.

As a biological research assistant, my work includes setting up experiments, carrying out experiments, collecting and analyzing data, and doing literature searches for changes in experiment protocol.

To perform this kind of work well, it is important to have a basic science background, pay careful attention to detail, have logical and analytical thinking , and have patience.

I like the organization and people for whom I work. However, I do not like the solitary aspect of this kind of work. I would prefer to have more contact with people. Aside from this, I find satisfaction from my work because I feel that somehow my work will improve life or help preserve it in some way.

BIOMEDICAL ENGINEER/TECHNICIAN

I got my initial training for my career as a technician while in the U.S. Air Force. I feel fortunate to have gotten training which helped me in my career development for my civilian future. After the military, I worked as a computer technician for 2 years. The experience and training in both hardware and software has been very beneficial to my biomedical career as PC's are a necessity for record-keeping, and computer hardware is becoming an integral part of modern medical instrumentation.

As a biomedical engineer/technician, my major responsibilities are to inspect, repair and calibrate medical equipment, and to train equipment users on the proper and safe use of equipment. I repair equipment on an "as needed" basis and inspect equipment on a quarterly or a semi-annual basis depending on the equipment category. When I perform inspections, I am checking for electrical safety, calibration, wear and tear, and general condition. My in-service training on new equipment focuses on safety and function.

The qualities and skills which I consider to be most important for this kind of work are: good mechanical skills; electronics training; following logical thought processes; relating well to a large number of people (only a few at a time).

I like almost all aspects of my work except for the lack of opportunity for advancement. In order to overcome this drawback for myself, I plan to pursue a bachelor's degree in computer science. I should then have the skills to write software, which I would plan to do to make extra money (possibly in the biomedical area, but on my own time). I like having a steady career in a stable field. It also offers me continuous challenge as technology advances and because of the large variety of equipment on which I work. I have found that people are always friendly; they think I'm doing them a favor fixing their equipment, even if I'm "just doing my job."

BIOMEDICAL INSTRUMENTATION TECHNICIAN

I design, repair, and fabricate experimental electrical instrumentation. As a biomedical instrumentation technologist, I find success in creating useful products, and successful it is very evident to all. Previously a fast food owner and an insurance salesman, I enjoyed the work, but I've most liked the constant variety in this present work for the 14 years that I've been in it.

Knowledge of math, an inquisitive mind, and being logical and curious about cause and effect are all needed in my occupation. I got into the work as a hobby which became a profession. I'd like more personal control over decisions and policy. I'd also like more opportunities for advancement, and eventually I plan to move on into management to achieve those ends. Nevertheless, this work is enjoyable and satisfying.

BISHOP/FRIAR

I had previous occupations as a salesperson, a school teacher, writer, and critic and have now been called to serve the church as a bishop/friar.

My daily schedule includes prayer, work preparation, study and pastoral visitation.

To perform well as a bishop and friar it is important to have sympathy, patience, listening skills, sensitivity, and perseverance. It also involved years of educational preparation.

After many years in this career, I can still say that I like the work very much; however, I am somewhat dissatisfied with my particular church because I feel they should be more resistant to excessive liberalism.

It has been my reward to have the joy of helping others and of bringing people to the Lord.

BOOKKEEPER #1

In high school I was encouraged by a counselor to enroll in an accounting class. I enjoyed it and was successful, so I decided to go to college to get an associate degree in accounting.

For the past five years I have done bookkeeping for a production company. I match packing slips and purchase orders to vendor invoices, bill all customers for outgoing products, handle payroll, do bank reconciliations, and reconcile intercompany balances.

You have to have an enjoyment of math and an understanding of double entry bookkeeping to perform well. After three years on the job I became Senior Bookkeeper in this sole proprietorship company that I work for.

I like knowing that the president of the company directly benefits from the work I do in billing, accounts payable, analyzing accounts, and period-end closings. My work provides checks and balances on the status of the company.

I have held jobs in banking and as a retail clerk, but bookkeeping is more satisfying to me.

I plan to take my CPA exam eventually and own my own accounting business since my present occupation provides little room for advancement.

BOOKKEEPER #2

Because of the knowledge and skills I learned while earning my Bachelor of Arts in Business Administration, I was able to set up a bookkeeping service at home. This also allowed me to stay at home and care for my children. I started after my first child was born with one client, as part-time work, and the work has now grown into a full 40 hour per week job.

As a full charge bookkeeper, I do all the accounting work (including financial statements) for a very large church and several charitable organizations. My hours are flexible enough for me to be able to handle my home obligations as wife and mother of 3 also.

In order to perform this kind of work, you must have a basic knowledge of accounting and be able to type fairly well (computer and typewriter skills are essential). I believe it is important to have good communications skills also, because I have to interact on a face-to-face basis with people from every walk of life.

I enjoy being able to meet deadlines satisfactorily. But most of all, I enjoy knowing that, indirectly, I am providing a service for those in need, however slight the need is. I must add, though, that it is not easy to keep a home for my family and keep up with my children's activities. I would like to work less hours, but I find that I must work full time in order to earn the money necessary to put our children through college.

BOOKKEEPER #3

Working as a bookkeeper specializing in the area of accounts payable for the past five years, I handle the vouchers for bills to pay, enter those voucher bills into the computer, update the cash book with the balance of cash available, credit the proper accounts for bills paid, handle filing of invoices, process checks, and mail those checks out to their destinations.

While in high school, I took business courses and enjoyed them. After graduation I worked in several other positions, in a fast food restaurant kitchen for two hours--I hated it, in an office as a secretary which I thought was all right, in a restaurant as a waitress which I liked, and in a bank as a teller which I also liked.

In addition to training in the basics of bookkeeping, you must have good typing skills, solid math skills, and a knowledge of invoices.

Working with figures is very enjoyable for me, so I like this kind of work. I like my job very much and the company I work for. I enjoy typing, paying bills, and keeping the accounts balanced.

Unsure of what is ahead, I would like to travel and meet some new people. I enjoy my work in bookkeeping and perhaps I can find a job that combines my interests as well as my skills. I believe the best way I can achieve a balance between skills and my interests is to return to school and earn an undergraduate degree.

BOOKKEEPER #4

After graduating from high school, I worked as a receptionist and in sales, but have now found more job satisfaction from my work as a bookkeeper.

My typical responsibilities include handling the accounts payable, accounts receivable, and the general ledger. During a typical day I may be processing payroll, paying bills, or sending out invoices.

In order to handle this kind of work and to perform it well, it is necessary to have a knowledge of accounting procedures and have a positive attitude.

I like this kind of work and find satisfaction in making everything balance. I plan to continue pursuing my accounting career and am currently enrolled in college evening classes in order to earn a degree in this field.

BOOKKEEPER #5

A bookkeeper, I am responsible for everything that has to do with accounts receivable, payroll, as well as invoicing and collections on current and past-due accounts. I receive and post deposits, maintain time sheets and balance sheets, and purchase office supplies. Along with preparing end-of-the-month reports, I also handle some accounts payable. In addition, I explain benefits to new employees and act as go-between with employees and management.

At different times, I worked as a secretary, a sales coordinator, and a credit investigator. Having always liked working with figures, I went back to school to get my Associates degree in accounting and marketing. I chose this career, and would choose it again, because this is what I like to do. There's always a variety of tasks to do; I never get bored. I like being busy.

I like the company I work for and the work is rewarding, but I have some difficulty with a few of the people and the fact that there is little opportunity for career advancement. Enjoyment for me is getting everything done on schedule as well as reconciling figures on end-of-the- month reports. Doing a good job with collections is satisfying. I'd like the work flow to run more smoothly and for there to be more inter-departmental cooperation.

My work requires good office skills. Most important are computer skills, accounting ability, competence with the calculator, and good typing skills. A pleasant personality along with the ability to work well with people is essential. It is necessary to be forceful, yet gracious, when doing the collections. An advanced education in accounting and marketing would be helpful. One day I'd like to go back to school and get my Bachelor of Science degree in accounting.

BOOKKEEPER/ACCOUNTANT

I came into my career in accounting kind of by accident. I took an accounting course and found out I loved it. I also found I was good at it. It is satisfying work for me because in accounting things must balance, so there must be an answer.

My background includes a bachelor's degree in business management and accounting and previous job experience as a secretary, waitress, and teacher of preschool children. Now that I have found my niche in accounting, I plan to continue in this field with a goal of becoming a certified public accountant. I will then have more opportunity for advancement.

As a bookkeeper/accountant, I keep the books for a small company. This work includes posting accounts receivable/accounts payable, answering accounts payable calls, calling accounts receivable, and processing payroll. I have found it helpful to have all the accounting courses I can manage to take in order to perform my work well.

BOOKKEEPER/HARDWARE STORE OWNER

I took bookkeeping in secretarial school and accounting in college. Consequently when I became 1/2 owner of a retail hardware store, the natural area for me to manage was bookkeeping.

I am responsible for the daily bank deposits, accounts payable, payroll, and staff management. My daily duties include: making bank deposits; checking accuracy of credit card charges and cash sales; posting invoices to be paid to the computer. Weekly duties include: paying all bills including payroll and taxes; preparing, printing, and analyzing financial statements.

To handle this kind of work well, the following skills and attitudes are important:

good attention to detail; the ability to work alone; general understanding of taxes, computers and accounting procedures.

Aside from disliking my responsibility for training new employees, I like my job. There is fairly quick job gratification--every day some- thing is completed. You can work for a right answer--2 + 2 is always 4 if put in the right places. In addition, I like being my own boss, which gives me a lot of freedom.

My future plans include expanding my expertise in accounting. I want to learn how to make the computer do what I need it to do.

I am my own boss already, so promotion is not an issue.

BOOKSELLER

I am now into my third career. I enjoyed my 15 years of teaching, but got burned out from that kind of work. Then, as a real estate salesperson, I loved finding affordable homes for first time buyers, but was frowned on by the company for not concentrating on high priced homes. A friend suggested I try bookselling at a state-of-the-art bookstore. I passed their stiff book test and, happily, was hired and trained.

My work in this large bookstore with 75,000 titles includes manning the information desk, operating the cash register, managing a section of books, inputting computer data, and taking turns cleaning. I manage the garden, ecology, animals, literary critics, poetry, drama, and foreign books section. The weekly schedule is staggered. Sometimes I work from 9 a.m. to 6 p.m., and other times from 12 noon to 9 p.m. Monday and Tuesday are my weekends.

To perform well as a bookseller, it is important to have a knowledge of and love of books and reading; familiarity with tools necessary to find books; patience and courtesy with customers who expect you to produce books after being given very little information.

Despite some frustrations I have with the management of the bookstore and the lack of opportunity for advancement, I like this occupation.

I like the democratic environment in which I work. Everyone does everything so it's not boring. I also like the profit-sharing plan at this bookstore. I find job satisfaction being around all the books and working with people who are highly literate, funny, helpful, socially conscious, and idealistic.

BRANCH BANK MANAGER

I started at the bottom rung and worked my way up to bank manager. Doing this has meant working hard, having the skills to work with the public and bank personnel, having a methodical, accurate approach to work, and acceptance of a highly responsible position.

As a bank manager, I must arrive on time to open the bank. My typical duties include: opening the vaults; supervising 5 tellers and solving their problems; meeting with savings bank life insurance, mortgage loans, and personal loan customers; responsibility for all employees; responsibility for money transactions; building and training of new personnel; and balancing out at the end of the day and having to find any discrepancy.

I like almost every aspect of my work, except that I do not feel the salary is commensurate with the responsibility. I like the kind of work I do, the organization and people I work for, the opportunities for advancement, and the people with whom I work. I find job satisfaction in pleasing the public and running a "tight ship." There are also rewards of being stable, dependable, and honest.

BUILDER, REAL ESTATE MANAGER

After getting my Bachelor of Science in finance and real estate, I began a career in construction. I build houses as well as manage and maintain apartment rentals. Also, I develop land I own for subdivisions and apartment sites.

Of course, knowledge of construction is needed to do this work. Good math skills are also required in the drawing of plans. Basic knowledge of civil engineering is helpful. You also need to be competent in accounting and finance. Good people skills help keep employees happy, loyal, and performing well. It's also useful to be able to think ahead to anticipate problems and to be prepared.

Knowing that our houses are well built, that they are good buys for the purchasers, and that the buyers are getting their money's worth is very satisfying to me. In the apartments we manage, I very much enjoy our long-time renters. I also like the people I work with, that I am my own boss, and that there are opportunities for advancement. If our computers could be upgraded and if we could get more skilled office staff, I'd be completely happy.

My work in construction includes being on site when the workers begin work. I order and pick up building materials as well as schedule work with subcontractors. Planning ahead for future needs and jobs is also part of my work. When not on a building job, I show apartments which are for rent. I also manage the repair materials supply and I maintain the rental units. Finally, it is my responsibility to review cost and income figures.

BUILDER, SINGLE FAMILY HOMES

I have been in the carpenter business for 30 years. My work includes supervising of home building trades, arranging financing, and performing of finished carpentry.

On a typical day my job will be either to arrange the flow of men and materials to a construction site or supervise various construction trades. I also meet with home buyers to determine colors, choices, etc., pay and approve invoices for sub-contractors and suppliers, and meet with real estate agents.

To be able to perform my job with perfection, it is important to have personal organizational skills and good relations with various types of people ranging from bankers, customers, lawyers, tradesmen, and construction laborers. You also need the ability to make quick decisions and stand by them or change them if they prove to be incorrect.

After having been in this business for 30 years, my greatest satisfactions have proved to be the physical evidence of my work. There are structures that will still be in place 50-100 years from now.

I would be more satisfied if I could find more responsible subcontractors or be able to instill in these people the same pride in workmanship that I feel myself, and the sense of urgency that the building business seems to require to be successful and profitable.

I started in my line of work by working for a building corporation. Prior to that I was a bookkeeper for 15 years and also an assistant manager of a branch bank.

BUILDING CONTRACTOR/FARMER

My work as a building contractor and an alfalfa farmer is controlled a great deal by the weather. Both are outside jobs, so my income is at risk. But I enjoy the great feeling of accomplishment I get in both jobs.

After getting my high school diploma, I studied and earned a two-year Associate's degree. Higher education is not required for the work I do, but you should have training and experience. After these 15 years, I've found you also need to be able to keep your mind working all the time.

I was a ski area mechanic for a while, but I enjoy my work building houses. Raising hay as a farmer is also a rewarding business. My long-range plans are to work less and enjoy life more. Nevertheless, if I had to start over, I'd choose what I'm doing now.

BUILDING MAINTENANCE

For seven years I have been working in building maintenance. Basically, I repair broken building parts, such as windows, overhead doors, light bulbs, starters, alternators, or assemble new office partitions, or repair and install heaters. These are some of the kinds of jobs that come up.

My work requires mechanical aptitude, the ability to work with tools, and some common knowledge of maintenance.

Although there are no opportunities for advancement in my present work, I do like my job, and I feel that I learn something new almost every day.

After my high school graduation, I held several jobs, including in an electrical supply house, in a cleaning service, and in a grocery store.

I plan to continue to work in maintenance. I would like to get a job in a large corporation where I would have a greater variety of work assignments and develop greater versatility in skills.

BUSINESS CONSULTANT

To be a good business consultant, you need to be able to think analytically, independently, and be creative. Strong interpersonal skills are required as well. Managerial talent along with a positive attitude and persistence are very important. A consultant combines these skills when developing his or her own leads.

The day normally starts with phone calls. Some of my time is spent writing proposals or researching and writing reports. I attend meetings with company officers and also attend various luncheons, presentations, and networking sessions. My future goal is to open my own consulting practice and be successful with it beyond just making a living.

I started my career in consulting right after college graduation. After my assignment in general management and experience in an import/export operation, I earned a Masters in business administration and returned to consulting. Helping a client solve problems and improve productivity satisfies me most. When recommendations are adopted and implemented, I'm pleased.

I'd like to be able to concentrate on work-related areas of greater interest to me. If I could be more selective in assignments, I'd be happier. I do like the freedom of being my own boss in this line of work.

BUSINESS CONSULTANT/ADJUNCT PROFESSOR

I work for myself as a business consultant. I have been doing this kind of work for many years in several different industries including banking, industrial, federal, high tech, and woodworking. As well as my consulting work, I am an adjunct professor in marketing, computers, and business management. My educational background includes two master's degrees and I am currently working on a Ph.D.

As a consultant, I guide companies in their business needs to help them reach their goals. I meet with clients to explore their needs and then, after research, I come back to them with results or solutions.

Good "people" skills are important for my kind of work. It is also essential to have strong technical knowledge and analytical ability.

Although the consulting work involves long hours and an unpredictable cash flow, I like almost every other aspect of my occupation. I find job satisfaction from a job well done (when things work correctly). It is also gratifying to know that I have made a positive difference for a company.

My career goal is to promote myself more in order to get more steady work and allow me to hire others to do the work. I then envision myself as "a money machine."

BUSINESS DEVELOPMENT MANAGER

I always wanted to be an "engineer" from a very young age, although I didn't really know what it was all about until college. I have now found that "business development" as related to engineering, rather than "pure engineering," better suits my abilities and interests. After earning a Bachelor of Science in Mechanical Engineering, I tried out a strictly engineering job, but made the transition to the business side after several years.

As a manager of business development for an electrical power generation company, I seek new project opportunities for the company. A typical week for me would include 2 days of travel making business development contacts, and 3 days in the office writing reports, reading literature, and making phone calls.

I can't think of any major dislike I have about my job. My plan is to stay in this career and even in the electrical power generation industry, and work my way up to executive management.

I like the feeling that in a small way in this job I am making the earth a better place for all of us to live.

BUSINESS EDUCATION INSTRUCTOR/SWIMMING COACH

Although I consider my career as a high school business education instructor/swim coach to be lacking in opportunity for advancement, it's not a problem for me. I love working with high school students and their environment. I started college with a finance and insurance business major, but decided that continued work in this field would not be satisfying for me. Business education looked interesting, there were not many people taking these types of courses, and grades in general were tough for me but business ed was easier for me. Little did I know that it would lead me to thoroughly enjoying my work. I have been a swim coach during summers and year round. I left teaching for two years to work with swimmers on a year-round basis as a marketing director and age group swim coach. In addition, I coordinated all fund-raising for a USS swim club.

I teach juniors and seniors Business Law and Business English, and coach the guys and girls swim teams. I teach five classes of 30-35 students a day: 4 in Business Management & Law, and 1 of Business English. In the afternoons and certain mornings, I coach high school swim teams. I have to allow time for lesson plan development. My day starts at 7:30 a.m. and ends at 5:30 p.m. There are some days, however, that I have swim practice starting at 5:00 a.m., and then there is a weekly swim meet that starts at 6:15 p.m., ending around 9:00 p.m.

To perform all these functions well, I find it is important to have organizational skills and stay on top of my swim practice/lesson plan development; to go home with my desk cleared! As a high school teacher/instructor, you should have a basic understanding of what working with high school students is all about. I try to remember from my own experience and draw on my students--know that learning never ends, and that you can learn from your students as well as their learning from you.

I would like to see a higher wage scale for teachers, perhaps commission-based on the number of students that enroll in my classes, or on the success of our swim program.

My job satisfaction comes from the interest my students take in the law and English I teach, and the success and work ethic my swimmers and divers develop. I am rewarded by my relationship with my students and athletes as well as with their parents.

BUSINESS PROFESSOR

After retiring as a Lt. Col in the U.S. Army, I needed to find a guaranteed income and lots of time to pursue my own interest. I found that a career as a business professor would fit these qualifications. Additionally, I felt qualified for this profession because of my experience while in the military and my educational background. I served in the infantry, as a helicopter pilot, and a foreign affairs officer (Army attaché, U.S. Embassy in Jakarta). I have earned two master's degrees and a Doctorate in Business Administration.

As a business professor, I teach and do research in entrepreneurship, strategic management, and business pedagogy (the art or profession of teaching business). A typical working day includes: teaching, course development, and research work.

To qualify and perform well in my profession, it is important to be intelligent, a self-starter, and have good writing and speaking abilities.

The frustration that I have found with this career is that I am generally disappointed in the capabilities and dedication of those in academe as compared to professional officers I encountered during my Army career. However, I like this kind of work very much and would make the same choice again if given the opportunity to start again. I find satisfaction in making things work. Teaching is gratifying because I enjoy challenging students. Creating new programs, and challenging old assumptions and ideas of peers are also factors contributing to my job satisfaction.

My plan for the immediate future is to attend Fulbright scholar leadership classes at an international university.

BUYER

For the past four years I have not had a work day that could be classified as typical. I work as a buyer, and my job is to buy raw materials as well as finished products at a cost savings for my company. I get involved in solving problems, handling crises that arise daily, placing orders, and attending meetings with associates and outside vendors.

Although I have not yet finished my college degree program, I believe the classes I have already taken have helped me greatly. In addition to a good educational background, my job requires people skills, an open mind, negotiation skills, the ability to cope effectively (as one must take the good days with the bad), and good communication skills. In this line of work, you should always remember to treat others as you would like to be treated. I have observed that those who have failed in this position did not treat their fellow workers fairly; at no time should you belittle another.

Until I finish my degree program, I see very limited advancement opportunities; even so, I do like the company I work for and this kind of work. I feel fortunate to be working for a boss that I like and with people that I also like. Satisfaction comes from the times that my boss has praised me for a job well done or expressed thanks for my efforts; I really believe that my efforts help the production line to run in a smoother fashion with fewer problems.

Previously, I worked as a clerk/typist for an insurance company, as a data entry operator, and as an accounts payable clerk.

I intend to finish my undergraduate degree program and earn a promotion to senior buyer. I have not made plans beyond that yet, but with a good college education, I believe there are many opportunities both within my present company and in the overall industry.

BUYER, AIRCRAFT ENGINE PARTS

A senior buyer for an aircraft engine manufacturer, I find my work is very challenging and rewarding. I am responsible for large amounts of money; it is my responsibility to seek the best product for the lowest total cost. Interesting and never boring, my job is to purchase various electronics, exotic and common metals, robotics and many other materials for the engines.

Job satisfaction for me is being able to contribute to the production of a safe, reliable, and economical jet engine. I don't always get along with senior management because I think they use short-term fixes of symptoms instead of long-term treatment of conditions. Other than that, I really enjoy my colleagues, the company, my work, and the opportunities for advancement.

After earning a Bachelor of Science degree in psychology and serving as a U.S. Army officer, I began my present buyer's job. Yes, I like the job, and I'd choose this work again. My plans are to continue on this current track while concentrating on becoming a procurement specialist.

Math is one of the skills needed in my line of work. You should be of at least average intelligence with the ability to work well with people. A good personality is needed in the constant contact with vendors and coworkers. If you have all these things and an interest in the product, you should be a successful buyer who is well satisfied with the occupation.

BUYER, BRIDAL FASHIONS

For 20 years, I have been a bridal consultant with a broad range of services. I used my Bachelor of Arts degree in home economics creatively and have enjoyed my career.

Twice a year I go to New York City to buy samples of outfits for the bride or the bridal attendants. I write special orders for garments or I sell the gowns I buy. For some occasions, I consult with the family helping to prepare for the event. Guidance on the proper wedding etiquette is part of my service if the customer is interested. Depending on what the customer wants, I have spent an hour up to 30 hours planning invitations, flowers, music or caterers, or just providing the wedding clothing.

It's a great deal of joy for me when I am able to plan a really beautiful wedding. I have enjoyed my customers and my work very much. If I could begin again, I'd certainly choose my career in bridal consulting.

My work requires a great deal of hours on the job. I'd have liked working fewer hours and I'd have liked some of my customers to be more pleasant, even under the pressure of a wedding. My greatest worry has been always getting orders back on time. There is a stress factor.

A bridal consultant should like being and working with people. In this field you must have a sense of style and fashion. Being able to work under pressure with a positive attitude is critical.

BUYER, CATALOG SALES

My strong retail store management background in all phases of operations and department merchandising led to my job as catalog control buying specialist. Even my 4 years of active military duty and work as a dental lab technician provided me with training in getting along with people that have proved valuable as a buyer.

As a catalog control buying specialist, I project sales quantities for the length of time the catalog is active, and make many purchases of merchandise so as not to be left with overstocks. I work in a semiprivate office for a very large corporation with millions of dollars in buying power. I use numerous computer programs to provide me with available daily updated information regarding trends, historical records, future projections, etc. A vast array of special and specific information is necessary for the decision-making in buying merchandise.

To perform well as a buyer, you should have the ability to make reasonable decisions. A good sense of figuring (math) in your head is important. Sure, we all use calculators, but knowing side-rule ratios, etc., can be most beneficial. You should know marketing profit formulas. A pleasant attitude will generate a great deal of help (i.e. short cuts) from your working associates.

If I could change anything about my occupation, it would be to receive more financial rewards for outstanding work. I believe for new items that just arrive with no past history, if successfully presented and vast profits realized, that the team of people that took the risks should be financially rewarded with some small percent of that item's profit.

I like being in a job that rewards careful and intelligent planning. Sometimes the plans are made months in advance of the actual results. When you see all developments going smoothly, according to the way they were projected, and you see results accepted and generating profit for the company--that is a very satisfying part of this work.

BUYER, COMPUTER RESELLER

My current position as a purchaser/buyer for a computer reseller began as an accounts payable position. I was given a little bit of the purchasing function to relieve pressure off a co-worker. I performed very well and was eventually given all the purchasing responsibilities at my company. This kind of work seems to suit me because I feel I have always had a high aptitude in dealing with figures and people.

As a buyer for a computer aided design value-added reseller, I am responsible for generating and processing purchase orders for orders in progress and maintaining proper inventory levels. A typical day involves cutting purchase orders for new sales, following up on purchase orders in progress, insuring all parts for a particular sale arrive on schedule, acquiring the best possible cost on items, and arranging for the return and replacement of defective/damaged equipment. In doing this work, I interface with sales and the accounting departments. It is also essential to maintain rapport with vendors and search out new sources or alternative items to meet an order's delivery.

To perform this kind of work well requires the ability to work well under pressure, to be adaptable, to possess a measured amount of congeniality, to be firm and aggressive, and to make quick, well informed decisions.

The power of controlling what is used for an order and where items will be purchased gives me the most satisfaction. Also, seeing a completed order being delivered with all components required gives me a real feeling of accomplishment.

In response to my ideas for any changes in my occupation to make it more satisfying, I would like to be less involved in handling credit issues with the vendors I deal with as this creates a conflict of interest.

My future plans are to complete my college degree work and get more into management of people, while remaining in the purchasing field.

CAPITAL ASSETS CONTROLLER

I tried out many jobs before settling into this position as capital assets controller, and I have found that I like this kind of work. Prior to this I worked as an apprentice electrician, waiter, restaurant manager, cook, factory machine operator, sales clerk, construction laborer, and cashier.

As a capital asset controller, I move equipment, take inventory, update records, and compile various data about the equipment. More specifically, I collect unused, idle equipment, check its financial status and decide what the company wants to do with it according to their policies. I answer questions from people looking for used equipment and try to keep accurate records. Sometimes I help people with special equipment needs.

I consider the following skills and attitudes to be important in performing this kind of work well: a good sense of organization; attention to details especially with numbers; ability to communicate well; self-motivation; conscientiousness, discipline; the ability to cope with many different types of people; and the desire to be helpful.

I like the kind of work I do and the people with whom I work. I do not particularly like the person I work for and also the fact that there is a lack of opportunity for advancement. Despite the drawbacks, I find benefits to this job like working in a clean, safe environment, and getting many things I need free. I find job satisfaction from meeting the needs of people who can't afford to buy new equipment and from their gratitude when I help them out.

CAPTAIN, STATE POLICE

The only thing wrong with my job as a Captain for the State Police is that frequently I have to put in some long hours. Otherwise, my work is ideal. The people I work with, the organization, my supervisors, and the job itself are all gratifying. Plus, being able to actually "fix" some of the problems I perceive in society is extremely rewarding to me.

My job with the state marine patrol involves mostly office work, which I like. I do legal research and write preliminary documents. Getting new regulations into public awareness, answering complaints or requests for interrogatories (formal inquiries) are some of my duties. I assist officers in drafting an affidavit or an application for a search warrant. My responsibilities are also to sort mail, return phone calls, draft letters, and prepare drafts of new regulations or laws.

Interestingly, I originally was a paint contractor who won a bid to paint the state police station. The more I thought about it and the more I saw, the more an officer's job appealed to me. So I earned a Bachelor of Science degree and soon will receive my J.D., the law degree. I've been in police work for 16 years; I anticipate a promotion when I complete law school. I plan to stay until retirement (at an early age) and practice law.

One of the important skills needed in my work is being able to read well and comprehend what you've read. Proficiency in writing is also necessary. You need a strong vocabulary as well.

CAPTAIN, U.S. NAVY

There is nothing I dislike about my work as a Captain in the U.S. Navy. I like the people, the Navy itself, and the fact there is room for advancement. Fulfillment for me in my work is accomplishing a specific goal or task and knowing I am serving my country.

I'm glad I chose this work; if I had it to do all over, I'd again choose a career in the Navy. With a Bachelor of Science and a Masters in electrical engineering, my career goal is to reach a senior executive management level position in the private sector after retirement.

To be a good officer, one should be motivated as well as goal-oriented. Confidence and dedication along with a high sense of integrity are required. An officer should have strong communication, good listening, and excellent analytical skills. A high energy level helps as does determination and reliability.

There is not a so-called typical day, except in the sense that each day is planned so any goal or task at hand is accomplished. During the day, adjustments to the plan are made as required to perform the tasks.

CARDIOLOGIST/RESEARCHER

For seven years, I have been working as a cardiologist and as a researcher. I diagnose and treat people with heart disease, perform evaluations of patients in the hospital, change medications, order and perform diagnostic tests, follow up on patients that I have treated to ensure that their health remains stable or improves and that they stay on the assigned medical regimen. I am also involved in research, evaluating the effects of beta blockers on patients with valvular heart disease.

In addition to a Doctorate degree in Medicine, you must be able to listen, understand, interpret what people mean out of what they say, and also gather and interpret all pertinent data relevant to medical diagnosis from the patient's history, physical condition, and diagnostic tests performed.

I enjoy my work very much; I find it especially rewarding when patients show their appreciation for my skill and efforts. The intellectual stimulation of my work keeps me excited and involved in the research aspects of my work. I believe it also goes without saying that I enjoy the earnings level and status that goes with being a doctor.

I previously worked as a research scientist in the field of physiology; that experience has proved invaluable in my current work. It was the job security among other factors that led me to practice medicine instead of devoting my life to research.

CAREER COUNSELOR

A career counselor assists individuals and groups in the career decision making process--from self assessment, vocational testing, and career exploration, to choosing appropriate training programs. As a part of the assistance I provide, I teach job search skills.

To succeed as a career counselor, you must have the ability to work well with the public and possess a certain degree of empathy as well as counseling skills--I have a Master of Arts degree in Counseling. You also need knowledge of career information resources, and knowledge of the career counseling field.

Personally, I derive great satisfaction watching those I have helped follow through, complete their action plans, and attain their goals; I would like to have the time to follow through with those I have counseled. I am in the position now that I do not know what is going on with their careers unless the person reports back to me or, in some other way, stays in touch with me.

Originally, I intended to choose teaching as my career, and I served at a community college in a related internship while in graduate school. I enjoyed the experience and that led me to investigate and pursue a career in career counseling. I have worked in this field for fourteen years now and I expect to consider an expansion of my present work into the field of rehabilitation sometime in the future.

CARPENTER #1

Carpentry has been my job for 30 years. It hardly needs an explanation because everybody knows what a carpenter does. My own specialty is installing acoustical tile ceilings but I handle other standard carpentry jobs too. Like most carpenters, I make house calls -- go from job to job and do the work that the owner wants. You meet interesting people that way and that is one of the rewards in this work. The major satisfaction is in producing a high-quality finished product and in making a good living salary-wise.

You need to have a good attitude, be able to get along with all kinds of people, and of course be good in using your hands. You have to be able to visualize the final appearance, make accurate measurements, and move toward the goal without errors. Experience does that for you.

Sometimes I work as an independent but most of the time I work on the crew of one or another developer or contractor. There are periods when no work is immediately available in this area, and that is a disadvantage of getting into this kind of work. I have always been interested in construction and have been a carpenter since I was 20. When I am financially able, I'll retire although some carpenters keep on working into their 70's.

CARPENTER #2

I've enjoyed my work as a carpenter for many years. There's nothing I'd have changed; I like the customers and coworkers, carpentry itself, my supervisors, and the company. Besides the fact that there has been opportunity for advancement, I like producing something which is both usable and attractive.

As supervisor for a home builder in a construction company, I am in charge of the whole operation. I manage the workers as well as the schedules. I also sign the company checks.

After graduating from high school, I worked as a welder and in auto service. But, if I had my choice, I'd be a carpenter all over again.

As for the skills required, the trade doesn't require the same abilities as it did when I first learned it. The times are different and the machinery is different.

CARPENTER #3

I wanted to build houses ever since I watched one being built when I was a child. After graduating from high school, I first was an apprentice. Then I quit the union and got a job with a contractor who taught me all about construction. Now I'm a residential carpenter.

There are two basic parts of construction: first, frame the house, which means build the primary structure, then, second, trim the house or hang interior doors, cabinets, window trim, etc. Generally, a large company does both, or someone can specialize in just one of the operations. I do all aspects of the construction job since I build new customer homes. I also remodel and add to existing houses.

Seeing what was accomplished at the end of each day's work is highly rewarding to me. It encourages me to try to get more done each day. I like the contented physical weariness at the end of the day knowing I have worked hard to earn my living. I'd like to be able to find faster, better, and more economical ways to perform each feature of the building process. Besides my work, I also enjoy my coworkers and bosses. I plan to continue as a carpenter until I retire someday; then, I'll do odd jobs for others as long as I can.

You have to have a general knowledge of woodworking tools (hammer and power saw, for example) to be a carpenter. Depending on how much of the building process your company does, you may have to be familiar with cement and roofing tools as well. You can learn a lot on the job with the tools, but you need some natural ability to excel. A willingness to work hard physically eight hours each day is required. You can't have a fear of heights either. An open mind and the willingness to learn help make a well-rounded carpenter.

CARPENTER/CABINET MAKER

My carpentry work for a fine arts museum includes setting up displays for incoming shows, general building maintenance, and building and repairing office workstations. Each day can be boring or exciting, the latter being the more frequent.

To perform well, it is important to like your job. Having the ability to get along and work with different people without overly compromising yourself is vital. In carpentry, a very high concern for safety for yourself and others, concern for those you work with, in and out of work all contributes to doing a job well.

I find satisfaction when my employer and recipients of my work say to the effect: "Thank you; good job." Ultimately you know best how well you did.

After 20 years as the "jack of all trades" with a theater company, I took a temporary job at the museum, to fill in for a vacationing "swing" man. I have now been with the museum for many years, and I expect to stay in this job since I do enjoy it. Between my teens and early 30's I had too many jobs to enumerate, but they have all given me experience and these experiences have later come in handy.

CARPENTER/FOREMAN, UNION

I became a carpenter mainly because I was always good with my hands, and I liked working outside. After getting into the occupation, I found that I liked working on big buildings, so I joined the union. The union has helped me to earn good wages and benefits.

As a foreman, I supervise the interior finish mill work. My typical day's work includes: laying out the work to be done, assigning jobs to the carpenters, and making sure the work done is of good quality and done according to specifications.

My suggestion for skills and attitudes which are important to perform well as a carpenter are: working well with your hands, knowing how to use all power tools pertaining to your job, and being conscientious to be able to see the job through from finish to the end.

I earned an Associate in Architectural Engineering degree to prepare myself for this career. Prior to becoming a carpenter, I was a steel foundry worker, in the Navy, and a telephone equipment installer.

I like almost every aspect of my work, the people and organization I work for, people I work with, and the kind of work. Job satisfaction, for me, is found in the finished product--a real nice finish job. Teaching the trade to young carpenters is also rewarding.

CARPENTER, UNION

While in high school, I attended a vocational technical school for carpentry, because I figured that if I didn't make the Army a lifetime job, I would have something to fall back on. I did go into the Army and was a combat engineer, but decided not to become a "lifer."

As a union carpenter, I build wall partitions on construction projects. This involves constructing the metal stud framing and hanging drywall. To do this work, it is necessary to have math skills, and the ability to read blueprints. The right attitude to work hard and a strong back are also important for this occupation.

I find job satisfaction from my carpentry work because I start with nothing and, with my hands, I create something. Although I like this kind of work, I dislike the distance I have to travel to the various jobsites and the lack of opportunity for advancement. Therefore, I am now going to college to earn a degree in the technical aspect of this field. I am working toward an associate degree in architectural engineering technology. This will enable me to stay in the construction industry.

CASEWORKER

I have spent my career life in service professions, initially as a second grade teacher and now as a case worker for a state department of income maintenance. My educational background includes a Bachelor of Science and Master of Arts degrees.

As a caseworker, I am the eligibility technician. It is my responsibility to determine the eligibility of cases--if they are initially eligible or if they can remain eligible. More specifically, I make determinations of eligibility for AFDC, food stamps, T-19, convalescent cases and state supplement. To accomplish this, I check forms and conduct interviews.

To perform this kind of work, it is important to have patience and to be able to deal with the young and the old.

One of my biggest frustrations with my work is the amount of time that is wasted because of downtime on the computer. I also find that working for the government can be very unrewarding at times. However, I like my work because I am being of service to others, and my pay check is higher than when I was a teacher.

CASHIER, RETAIL STORE

I work as a cashier at an Hawaiian food store. In my job, I wait on customers as well as stock shelves with food items. I am also responsible for keeping the merchandise organized on the shelves.

The only thing I'd change about my work is the attitude of some of the customers. Otherwise, I enjoy the people I work for and with, the shop, and being a cashier. What I like most is the opportunity to meet new people. Even though I never graduated from high school, there are still opportunities for advancement.

I've found being able to get along with people very important in my work. Being a cashier requires strong math skills as well.

I got this job because a friend offered me the position. I've been here for four years, and I'd accept this job again because I like the work.

CASHIER/STOCKPERSON

I work part-time as a cashier/stockperson in an import store. I operate the cash register, ring up merchandise, take cash from customers, give them their change, stock merchandise, straighten up the store, and help customers with merchandise selection decisions. I do not hesitate to give a customer my opinion of the merchandise because I want them to be happy with their selection.

This kind of work requires math skills for duties as a cashier, good communication skills, a positive attitude, a cheerful personality, and an outgoing disposition.

I like my job; it feels good to help people decide on a purchase and assure them they made a wise decision. This is a job that is to you what you make of it.

I previously worked as a math tutor and as a clown.

When I finish my college education, I plan to become a teacher. I like working with people; I am studying to be an interpreter for the deaf and a teacher of elementary school age children.

CASINO EMPLOYEE, SLOT MACHINES

As a slot machine floorman I supervise the cashiers and change people, assist customers, and repair the slot machines.

It is important to have good customer relations, patience, and a pleasant personality for this job. Some math skills are also necessary to perform this job well.

I have been satisfied with this job for 10 years because of good pay/tips, the comfortable working conditions, and the opportunity I have had to meet all different types of people.

I graduated from high school and did not attend college. I became a casino worker because there was nothing else available at the time. In the future, I am hoping for a promotion with even better pay.

CATALOG EDITOR

I got into my present occupation as a catalog editor because I have always been interested in and enjoyed the English language, though it can be difficult at times. I started in this career after graduating from high school and have been satisfied with this kind of work for the past 10 years.

Because the technical catalog is published quarterly, the work week can be extremely busy or extremely slow. I can work as many as 70 hours or as little as 25. Therefore, it is necessary to be able to keep a flexible work schedule in order to perform this kind of work. You must also be articulate with the English language and be able to work well with many types of personalities to succeed in this field.

I find my job satisfaction each quarter when the catalog is published. It is nice to see what I have done with the "raw" technical data--making it simple so that customers can understand it and use it to order equipment.

Although I like almost all aspects of my work, it would be less frustrating if there were a process whereby all contributors submitted data on time and in which one person would be a reliable source. There is a need to streamline the operation.

I would like my career to progress into advertising where I could handle things such as making decisions as to what source to use and planning the strategy. I am now enrolled in college courses to help me advance in my career.

CATHOLIC PRIEST

I became a priest because I was aware that I had the skills and interests to meet a real need in our society for spiritual leadership. I started my career in journalism as a newspaper editor after earning my Bachelor of Arts degree. I then realized that I was better suited for parish life. I have now been a priest for 31 years and like this kind of work very much.

As a Catholic priest, I pastor a parish of 500 families. This is extremely demanding work, particularly with the size of my church, and my biggest concern is the danger of burnout. There are just not enough priests to do the job needed. What is needed is people with a creative spirit, an optimistic attitude, and care for people.

I like this vocation because it has given me the opportunity to be creative. Job satisfaction comes when I reach people with good sermons and when I can provide personal care. My reward is seeing people helped, encouraged, and comforted.

CATTLE RANCHER

In my work as a cattle rancher, I feed, brand, doctor, and move cattle. Job satisfaction comes for me when I have a good head of cattle and good crops of hay. The hours are long and hard, but this is necessary to stay out of financial trouble.

Although I've enjoyed my work for many years, I dislike the small income associated with it. It's hard to keep up with expenses. I expect to continue cattle ranching in the future and then retire when I have to.

In the past, I was a banker and I enjoyed it, but I prefer cattle ranching. If I had it to do all over again, even with the financial problems, I'd choose the same work. My entry into this business came when I married a cattle rancher's daughter. It's been hard trying to keep ahead.

You should have a high school diploma if you want to do this kind of work, but you do not need a college degree nor do I have one.

A cattle rancher must rise early in the morning. The cattle are checked, as are the irrigation and the hay. Sometimes you have to repair equipment. One of the main qualities you need to do this work is patience. You have to have mechanical ability, and you should like working with animals.

CEO, INDUSTRIAL TRAINING COMPANY

After receiving my GED, I earned a Bachelor of Science Degree in biology, a Bachelor of Science in history, and a Masters in educational administration. I've been a biologist, a college administrator, and a Superintendent of Schools. For the last two years, I've been Chief Executive Officer of the company I began.

The company, which I hope to franchise, offers training in the business industry. My aspirations are to build this company to national status. When it is successful nationwide, I'd like to turn the position over to someone else, and then create a publishing company.

I like everything about my work, especially the opportunity for advancement. Creating a national company from zero with a limited budget is thrilling. Bringing a new concept into reality with cutting edge performance is very gratifying to me. If I had to begin again, I'd make the same decisions and do just what I've done.

My work involves planning, organizing, and implementing the company's product training materials. I stay very busy getting the company ready to go nationwide. To do this work, you must possess great leadership skills and have a "good comfort level in your own skin." Strong people and management skills are essential. Very important is having long range vision.

CEO, MECHANICAL CONTRACTING COMPANY

I guess you could say that it was first luck, and then by hard work, that I have made it up the ladder to the position of Chief Executive Officer of a mechanical contracting company. I was hired 30 years ago as an apprentice into this field, and have gone from there. I do not even have a mechanical engineering degree or a college degree at all.

As the executive officer, I handle the financial and technical management of the firm. This involves financial decision making, management decision making, customer contact and meetings, and project management.

The key ingredient to obtaining my kind of management position is experience. You also need technical education, whether on the job or through schooling. Besides these requirements, you must also be willing to subjugate all other interests.

In response to the question about the changes I would like in my occupation, I would kind of like to go back in time a bit. I would like to return to the market opportunities of 1965-1975 and to see a return of the work ethic of the 50's. I also dream of more leisure time and being free from corporate financial worries.

Despite the frustrations I face in my work, I very much like the kind of work I do, and the people with whom I work. I find satisfaction from my position and resulting success, including financial success with the added percs. I take pride in my accomplishments and my reputation.

My ultimate career goal is to retire comfortably!!!

CEO, REAL ESTATE COMPANY

The beauty of the position as chairman of the board of my own moderately large and fast-growing real estate company is that each day is different.

To perform this job well, you should have knowledge and expertise in theory "Y" management techniques. That is highly democratic and involves employees deeply in the decision-making process, especially when the matter being considered affects them or their department. You need to use the participative approach for most small companies. You also will need huge energy, the ability to see through problems to solutions, creativity, and concern for the needs of others.

My job satisfaction comes from helping people achieve their dreams. As much as I like being self employed, I would like to find some way to make my job more secure.

After coming in second in a race for the U.S. Congress, I began university administration and prepared to enter the real estate field. After significant successes, I formed a real estate company with a partner. Prior to this, I had been a teacher and farmer at the same time, a laborer, a part-time tour guide, and vice president of marketing at an aviation firm.

In the future, I plan to build the real estate company, sell it, and travel.

CERAMIC ENGINEER

Since obtaining my B.S. in ceramics years ago, I've worked as a ceramic engineer doing a variety of tasks related to ceramics. Mixing ceramic compositions, forming ceramic shapes, and then drying and firing the shapes are some of the steps followed. Next comes the testing and the evaluation. New ceramic compositions and forming methods are developed. I then write reports of the results of my work.

You need an education in ceramic engineering to do this work. At least 5 years of experience is necessary. A person must have the desire to create, to originate, and then to revise.

Everything about my work has been enjoyable: the people, the work, the location. I am glad to see my developments manufactured and sold. I like the fact that there is opportunity for advancement.

Of the jobs I had before becoming a ceramic engineer, the ones I liked best were dishwasher and short order cook. I got into my present job through acquaintance with other ceramic engineers.

CERAMIC TECHNICIAN

As a ceramic technician, I load and unload high temperature furnaces and run forming machines. In this position for four and one-half years, I derive satisfaction from seeing the finished product shipped on time.

After finishing high school and before working as a ceramic technician, I worked as an electrical harness assembler, an assistant auto mechanic, and a cook and driver.

I like this kind of work and the people I work with.

In the future, I plan to get a degree in ceramic engineering.

CERTIFIED PUBLIC ACCOUNTANT #1

I guess I have always liked working with numbers and money. I chose this career field in accounting while I was in high school taking an accounting class. I also had a strong interest in math and enjoyed my job as a cashier. I earned my Bachelor of Science in Accounting degree. It has been because of my education and work experience in the accounting field that I was able to pass the C.P.A. (Certified Public Accounting) exam.

As a certified public accountant, I prepare and analyze financial statements for several corporations. As well as using my mathematical skills, I find that writing and oral communication skills are important in order to perform this work well.

Although I like this kind of work, I am finding there is a lack of opportunity for advancement. Therefore, I plan to go back to school to earn my Masters in Business Administration in order to have the qualifications necessary to get a job as a controller or treasurer of a company.

I really feel that accounting is the right career choice for me and I would not change professions even if given a chance to start over. I find job satisfaction in the completion of my work in a timely manner.

CERTIFIED PUBLIC ACCOUNTANT #2

I'm very pleased with my career as a Certified Public Accountant. Previously I was Chief Financial Officer for a manufacturing firm, but if I could start over, I'd choose my CPA work.

Client appreciation is very rewarding to me, but I also get a great deal of satisfaction just from service to my clients and from the variety in the work. Respect and understanding are valuable to me as well.

Financial accounting along with tax planning and reporting describe my work.

There are meetings to schedule and technical work to do related to our efforts. I review the work my subordinates do in this area. I also market our services and I'm involved in the administrative and planning aspects of our accounting firm.

A CPA needs to be responsive and responsible. Honesty, integrity, and sincerity are essential characteristics to have. You need strong accounting skills as well as good communication skills. Being understanding and service-oriented is important to an accountant. You also need creative logic. Training is important as well; I have a Bachelor of Science degree.

I'd like to be free of routine activities so I can have the freedom of creativity and development of the business. My future goals are to see the firm's horizons expand to offer a variety of services: litigation, business acquisitions, mergers, and sales. I'd also like to teach and publish articles.

CHARGEBACK ASSOCIATE

I consider my work to be a "job," not a career. I never had the ambition for a career. I just want a job I can leave behind at the end of the work day. I would honestly love to be well enough off to spend my days working out, gardening, reading, being a homemaker (baking, especially), and doing things with my daughters.

This job started out as part-time, temporary Christmas work in the catalog department and I ended up as chargeback associate when the company could not find any voluntary replacements for my predecessor. Actually, I have found that I like this job fairly well.

As a chargeback associate in a department store, I handle disposition of defective merchandise, shipping errors, etc. To do this, I check references on different suppliers to see how to handle the problem merchandise and follow through. I enter information into the computer, and package and ship out merchandise where called for. I also put in some time in our catalog department binning orders from incoming shipments and scanning packaging returns.

Reading and writing are absolutely essential for this kind of work. You must be able to follow directions, and to figure out how to handle one problem for which you do not have specific directions, by relating it to other similar ones. A positive attitude is always helpful.

I particularly like the people with whom I work. I find job satisfaction in completing what is needed on each problem and getting my area emptied out--not having things sitting around waiting for authorization from suppliers.

CHEF/CATERER

I have found great satisfaction and success from my career in the food service industry. I only wish the attitudes that so many people have toward the food service industry and its workers could be changed. Many believe it's a "last option" type career with no future or advancement. Not true!

I got my start by answering an ad for a part-time restaurant position while I was in high school, and I was anxious to earn extra money. Ever since then I have never had a job unrelated to food service. Now, I am a full time chef and I have my own catering service as well.

As a full time chef and part-time caterer, I do much the same kind of duties, and my daily and weekly schedules are all dependent on client demand. Some are more hectic, some less, but I can almost always count on more than a 12 hour day. If I were to describe a somewhat typical schedule it would be as follows, starting at 5:30 a.m.: Monday and Wednesday I'm doing bookwork and banking for 2 1/2 hours a day, inventory and ordering for 1 hour daily, meeting with clients and finalizing menus and details for their functions for 3 hours a day, meeting with new clients can take 1 1/2 hours daily, and I allow 1 1/2 hours for preparing function sheets for the week. Tuesday and Thursday are spent finalizing detail, accepting deliveries, and shopping for odds and ends; Fridays and Saturdays are spent cooking and executing functions; Sundays are my day off.

Of course, you need a strong background in culinary knowledge and the skills related to that background. Adaptability is a major part of that, as well as organizational and managerial skills. A cooperative attitude is of major importance, not to mention team work.

The major drawback to this kind of work is that there is never a set schedule and the hours are long. The food service industry in any aspect is extremely challenging--presenting less than your best is never acceptable. I'm most satisfied when I know that I've met that challenge in accepting the trust my clients have put in me to ensure a delightful and successful evening for their guests and for themselves.

CHEMICAL ENGINEER #1

I earned my bachelor's degree in chemical engineering and got a job immediately in the profession. I work for a major international oil company. After the first year or two, however, my job assignments tended to become more and more oriented toward economic studies and into business planning and coordination as well as devising solutions to business problems. Although I am not doing the work I was educated for, my degree qualified me to start with this company.

The work has been satisfying, and this career has offered me opportunity for advancement. I enjoy the people I work with and the company I work for. I find satisfaction from this work when I experience accomplishment of objectives.

To perform well in business, it is necessary to have intelligence, perseverance, a positive attitude, ability to understand and get along with other people, willingness to work hard, and the ability to achieve goals.

I plan to retire eventually and concentrate on writing.

CHEMICAL ENGINEER #2

I was encouraged to study engineering in high school because I excelled in math and science. I selected chemical engineering because there was, and still is, a high demand for people in this occupation in the state of Maine where I live.

As a chemical engineer in a paper mill, I coordinate construction projects, design industrial instrumentation, and develop capital plans. My typical job activities include: attending department meetings; meeting with construction personnel to coordinate shut-down work; answering phone messages; reading mail; skimming technical journals; developing scope of work for new products; reviewing detailed drawings from outside consultants; reviewing construction progress at job site; and conducting safety audits.

As well as a degree in chemical engineering, I think the following attributes are important: organizational and time management skills, the ability to grasp technical details, and the ability to work with people of diverse groups.

I have experienced some frustrations with my occupation because of the frantic environment in which I work and the long hours. It has been difficult as a women in this demanding work to manage both my family and my career. However, I like this kind of work very much, and find job satisfaction in seeing something that I designed or developed actually built and working.

My future career aspirations are to either run my own consulting engineering firm, or to manage major capital investments for my present company.

CHEMICAL ENGINEER #3

A typical day for me as a chemical engineer includes determining boiler performance, sizing auxiliary equipment, and writing studies and reports. I analyze a boiler or part of a boiler to detect any problems and monitor any changes. My work is documented by my written calculations, reports, or memos. I spend a few hours each day dealing with the mail, paperwork, and filing. It is very gratifying to me to be able to determine what the problems are and find solutions.

A chemical engineer must be able to work accurately and quickly. Being able to work well in a group or by oneself is very important. A person should have an engineering degree as well as computer skills. Technical writing and presentation skills are essential, and you must not be afraid to ask for help.

I like everything about my work except that, at the company I work for, I am not able to work "hands on" in the field. I would like to work 50% of my time out of the office and 50% within.

I entered this field because I liked chemistry and math in high school. I decided to major in college in chemical engineering. My career plans are to perhaps change to work in an environmental field. I'd like to earn a Masters Degree in Science in environmental engineering.

CHEMICAL ENGINEER #4

To be a chemical engineer, basic skills in chemical engineering are required. These skills are particularly necessary for the technical phase of a program. As head of an engineering team, I've found it good to have the ability to motivate people, along with enough leadership to guide the team members.

It's the responsibility of the project engineer to maintain the schedule and manage the budget for any projects we undertake. At each phase of the venture, he oversees the progress in holding to schedules and to budget.

While in college, I enjoyed chemistry and earned a degree in chemical engineering. I have spent many years in my career, finding the most enjoyment in seeing a project finally completed and operating. My coworkers, the company, and the engineering work itself are all very rewarding to me. About the only negative is the great deal of travel involved in my work.

CHEMICAL ENGINEERING CONSULTANT

I first built up my knowledge of chemical engineering by working my way up educationally to earning a Ph.D. I then looked for employers with engineering problems and applied for a position as a consultant.

There has been no typical day in my chemical engineering consultant work of 30+ years. Engineering problems are endless in variety. However, problem solving methods follow a pattern: 1) defining the problem, 2) collecting information on alternative problem solutions, and 3) making recommendations.

As well as the technical knowledge required for a career in chemical engineering, you should have a curiosity about what takes place in chemical processing operations. My advice for people planning to enter this occupation is to first spend a lot of time acquiring broader problem solving skills.

There is really nothing I dislike about my occupation. I like the organizations and people I work for, the people I work with, the opportunity for advancement in this career, and the kind of work. I find job satisfaction in successfully meeting the challenges involved in solving chemical processing problems.

CHEMICAL PLANT SUPERVISOR

I am currently working as a chemical plant supervisor and have done so for 11 years. I am also attending college and am hoping that my degree will enable me to have more opportunities for advancement.

I work out of an office at the chemical plant, supervising the production people and being responsible for the equipment. It is one of my primary duties to see that my people produce the required number of units. In order to carry out these duties, I think it is important to have good communication skills, and to be able to perform well despite the stress and pressure of the work.

Prior to this occupation, I was a welder, pipefitter, and high pressure water cleaning operator. I now plan to stay with the chemical plant and advance in my position there.

I like the kind of work I am now doing, the organization and people I work for, and the people I work with. I find job satisfaction from making the unit run well. Satisfaction is harmony among the troops!

CHEMICAL TECHNICIAN

I do not have any logical explanation as to how I started working in the chemical industry, but I am glad that I found my job as a chemical technician. It has given me direction for my career. My plans now are to earn the college degree necessary to become an environmental or chemical engineer. My job experience so far in related jobs has been in pollution control operations, as an environmental technician, and in waste water treatment.

In my current job as a chemical technician, my tasks involve the purification and blending of chemicals. The pre-weighing of the chemicals in order to get the right blend is a critical part of this operation. This kind of work demands accuracy and attention to safety measures. Because there are no particular skills required or learned at this stage of work in the chemical industry, there is also not much opportunity for advancement. Therefore I have found it necessary to pursue academic training to build my knowledge and skills in order to advance myself.

CHEMIST--INSTRUMENT ENGINEER

My job title is chemist; in reality, I am an instrument engineer. I maintain the company-wide instrument calibration and correlation program. Semi-annually, I travel to outlying plants to ensure proper equipment operation and conformance to company procedure and policy. I calibrate certain pieces of equipment and run a statistical correlation to a historical population.

For my job, you need analytical reasoning ability, mechanical aptitude, mathematical skills, and knowledge of statistics. Problem- solving skills in the scientific realm and organizational skills are also needed. Attitudinally, you need to be tenacious, be attentive to detail, and be diplomatic. I particularly like correcting correlation problems between multiple pieces of scientific equipment. I like keeping equipment in reliable operating condition and having a reputation for being good at doing that.

Earlier in my career development, I was a computer programmer/analyst and a quality assurance technician. I particularly enjoyed the latter job. I attended college and earned two Associate degrees, one in data processing and the other in electronics.

I like my work very much, particularly the people and the pleasant surroundings. It is my expectation to remain with this company indefinitely. I'd like one day to work my way up to becoming an analytical services department manager.

CHIEF ENGINEER, OIL TANKER

I entered this occupation after I completed studies at the U.S. Merchant Marine Academy. Choosing marine engineering as an occupation was natural for me because I like the sea and working on a ship going to various ports. I also like 5+ months a year vacation.

As the chief engineer on an ocean-going oil tanker, my daily and weekly duties include: checking all machinery aboard the ship; making decisions on repair to equipment; scheduling repairs to vessel; accounting for all water and fuel used; and inputting description of repairs in the computer.

A good mechanical and math background, and the ability to work long hours are important to perform this job well.

I find satisfaction from making decisions concerning the operation of the vessel. Teaching new people how to operate an engine room is also a part of the job I find satisfying.

What I would like changed is to have more hands on repairs and less repairs with the computer.

CHIEF UNION STEWARD

Eighteen years ago, while working as a U.S. customs inspector, I was asked to help my union, the National Treasury Employees Union, by becoming the Chief Steward. Prior to these careers, I earned my Bachelor of Arts degree and taught school.

It is now my responsibility as the Chief Steward to prepare and present employee complaints and handle negotiations. My daily activities to accomplish these goals are: making appointments; meeting with employees; analyzing and researching questions of law and regulations in the process of preparing and presenting complaints; and writing briefs. I consider the basic skills of reading and writing to be the most important skills necessary to perform this job well.

I like this kind of work very much. However, I do become frustrated because of the incompetence I observe within our government. If I could initiate any changes in my occupation, it would be to eliminate all the idiocy which exists throughout the federal government.

The bottom line to why I like my job is that I find job satisfaction in winning.

CHURCH MINISTER/MISSIONARY

I have worked as a church minister and missionary for twenty-eight years. My primary duties are counseling and visitations, generally working with people; administering the church; praying; studying; and preparing sermons.

I completed a Bachelor of Arts degree in theology while working as a clothing salesperson and customer service supervisor.

The most important skills a good minister must possess are a positive attitude and a people-oriented nature, as well as the desire to serve God in a church environment.

There is great fulfillment in being called by God to be a minister and being an integral part of people's lives.

There are personal sacrifices to this job, but they are far outweighed by the rewards and blessings I receive.

I really love being a minister; I know it is what I was born to do with my life.

I will stay in my position for as long as I can. I do not look forward to retirement as do many people with other fields of endeavor, which they find less satisfying than I find this calling.

CHURCH SECRETARY #1

I very much enjoyed one of my previous jobs as a secretary to the managing editor of a Christian magazine and I love working now as a church secretary. Working with words and in word processing on the computer gives me great job satisfaction.

Interruptions and not having privacy when I need to concentrate are my only complaints in this job. As one of several secretaries for a large church, I have no typical day. My responsibilities include helping the other secretaries with their word processing duties, assisting in proof-reading the printed materials, and maintaining the database records for our church mailing list. Occasionally, I relieve the receptionist, serve as back-up for the telephone, or take dictation. My work is with a variety of ministries, my favorite being the area of music.

I was offered this job because of my excellent typing skills. I accepted it because I wanted a change from being secretary to a registrar. As a pastor's wife, I was already oriented to the life of a church. I may choose to remain where I am while furthering my education in music. My degree is a Bachelor of Science, but I'd like to be able to participate more in the ministry of music.

Strong verbal and written language skills are needed to be an efficient secretary. Word processing and computer skills are essential as well. The ability to work well with people is also very important. While I am actually shy, I do like people and they sense this, which helps me in my work.

CHURCH SECRETARY #2

As a church secretary, I've found the need to be very familiar with the computer and its functions. You should understand as well as be able to efficiently use office equipment. Strong communication skills are also necessary. Very important is the ability to listen well.

In my work in the church office, I prepare the weekly church bulletins and the newsletter. Opening and answering the mail and preparing the pastor's calendar are also my responsibilities. I handle telephone calls and set appointments for the staff. Finally, I listen to whoever needs me.

For 7 years, I've enjoyed being able to meet and talk with interesting people. I've developed good listening skills from working with these people. The church and the secretarial work I do are very rewarding to me. I also like the flexible hours. My only complaint is that I work primarily by myself, so, on occasion, it gets lonely.

A high school graduate, before coming to the parish as a church secretary I worked as a police emergency radio dispatcher and a police department clerk, but I really enjoy my work as church secretary.

CITY MANAGER

I love what I am doing because I get to help people solve problems in my field of expertise. My career started after my military tour of duty in which I served as a Squadron Commander of a base hospital. I read about the work of city managers in a newspaper article, investigated further, got my wife's approval, signed up for 4 years of college and never looked back. I earned a Bachelor of Arts in Public Management.

As Municipal Administrator (City Manager), my problems are varied and always an interesting challenge. Dealing with irate people who want immediate solutions to unsolvable problems is the norm. However, no two days are the same and occasionally you do solve a knotty problem and the community is a better place because you did. The gratification then is fantastic. While this does not happen every day, it occurs often enough to keep you striving.

To perform this kind of work well, you should be a good listener, be polite, attentive, and interrupt only to get a better picture of the problem. Always explain what you can do to solve or ameliorate the situation and what you can't do. Attempt to direct them to a source that can help if you can't. When they leave, wish them well and tell them when they can expect the solution. Be sure to deliver. NEVER promise what you cannot deliver.

Although I love my work, I often get frustrated with mayors and council members. I would certainly like to see better trained mayors and council members.

Job satisfaction is knowing that the community and its people have benefited from your work. You left it better than it was and you NEVER VIOLATED the ethics of your profession. With this sort of effort you sleep well nights and arise each day to go forth and do good.

My future aspirations are to live long, to do a few worthwhile things, to enjoy my children and grandchildren, and to leave many friends as I report to the Main Gate.

CIVIL ENGINEER #1

In my civil engineering job, I supervise a small group of engineers and technicians working on primarily water resources projects doing preliminary engineering studies. As a supervisory engineer, I spend a great deal of my time in planning, scheduling and budgeting. I do a considerable amount of coaching and review of projects as plans are developed by my subordinates. We are challenged every day with unprogrammed work that is assigned to us. This requires some creative scheduling and development of priorities as we have a limited staff.

The skills and attitudes which are important to performing my kind of work well are: organizational and time management skills, communication skills (verbal and written), the ability to think and reason through problems using minimum data and making reasonable assumptions based on experience, training and education, the ability to separate things that are important from things that are not, and flexibility and open mindedness.

I decided that I wanted to be an engineer when I was in high school. I liked math and science and felt it would be a good career. I earned my Bachelor of Science in Civil Engineering degree and have now worked in this field for a number of years. I do like my kind of work very much because of the people I work with, the organization I work for, and the variety of work and challenging problems to solve. My major frustration, however, is the uncertainty of the programs I work on which are controlled by politics. Sometimes bureaucratic procedures and political pressures keep us from doing our best work. Our funding comes primarily from the U.S. Congress. I am also concerned about erosion of my health benefits and retirement plan, and to a lesser extent on the lack of pay comparability due to budget cutting efforts and other priorities and demands on federal funds.

There is great satisfaction in developing a conceptual plan for a project and then following it through the design and construction process to a finished product. My current project, involved with fish passage improvements to help rebuild salmon and steelhead runs, is rewarding.

CIVIL ENGINEER #2

I worked for many years as a public employee after graduating from college with a Bachelor of Science in Civil Engineering degree. For the past several years, I have been working in the private sector as mass transit and highway consultant, and have found this work to be most rewarding. As such, I supervise the design and construction of highways and mass transit systems. There are few typical work days. There is a variety of activities including meeting with engineers, planners, and politicians to present design concepts, schedules, etc. It is definitely because of my years of experience in this field that I have the expertise to consult in the field. As well as the knowledge and experience necessary for this work, it is also important to have the ability to communicate technical competence.

Although I like my civil engineering work, the one area I most dislike is working under conditions where you suspect graft. Aside from that, I like the opportunity for public service. I would again choose civil engineering even if given the chance to start again and train for any kind of work. I find satisfaction in creating a worthwhile facility.

CIVIL ENGINEER #3

After being a housewife and then spending some enjoyable time in mining engineering, I moved into civil engineering. In my work, I visit all construction sites, inspect the work done, and arrange for any required testing. I must negotiate change orders and prepare progress payments to contractors. Approving materials submittals, preparing Local Improvement Districts, and anything else my office requires makes up my day.

I graduated from high school and my career plans are to complete my last semester of college work for my degree in mining engineering. I'd like to go into public works administration.

A person who wants to get into engineering needs college course work in an engineering discipline. You must also have an even temperament, and good public relations skills help a great deal.

There's really nothing I would change about my job, except maybe some of the people I work for and with. Satisfactorily completing a project within the contract time and under budget makes me feel great.

CIVIL ENGINEER #4

From childhood, I always wanted to be a civil engineer. So, I earned a Bachelor of Science degree in civil engineering and an associate's degree in technical design and drafting.

My job is to design the structural parts of state highway bridges. I review their structural design and plans, then write the necessary special provisions. I then estimate the bid costs. It's also my responsibility to handle all the calls from contractors and/or estimators who have questions about a bridge's plans.

The skills most important in my work are mathematical. You also need the ability to communicate and to write well.

I really like everything about my job: the people, management, the company, and the work itself. There are also opportunities to advance. Monitoring a project from its conception to its completion gives me a great deal of satisfaction. My plans are to stay in this field and look for ways to improve myself.

CIVIL ENGINEER #5

After graduating from high school, I intended to prepare for a teaching career and to coach. I went to college as long as I could, but I had to take a job eventually on a bridge construction gang, where I learned a great deal on the job.

Since I am involved in the design and construction of bridges, I am called a civil engineer. I am also the administrative crew. I like my job so much that if I could start over now, I'd choose it again.

Communication skills are very important in my work and being able to work with people. You also have to be extremely competent and be able to work as part of a team. I find humility to be an asset.

Particularly rewarding is knowing you've done a job well. The relationships with both superiors and subordinates alike are very satisfying. I wish some of the bureaucracy could be reduced. I also do not like the amount of political influence there is in bridge construction work. But generally, I enjoy the job I have, the company I work for, and the fact that there have been good opportunities for advancement.

CIVIL ENGINEER #6

With a Bachelor of Science degree in civil engineering, I started out in my career as a civil engineer 17 years ago. Other than finding little opportunity for advancement, I've enjoyed my work and would choose it again.

It was a childhood dream of mine to go into construction. As a civil engineer, I'm also involved in design supervision. My typical day or week, in fact, includes both construction and design supervision.

In my work, I very much enjoy working with people. It is rewarding to be able to find solutions to problems. I also like the people I work with and I like the company I work for.

To be a civil engineer you must have strong computer skills. Also important is the ability to work well with people.

CIVIL ENGINEER #7

For thirty years I have been employed as a civil engineer; my work has involved several aspects of engineering and management. The areas I have been involved in to the greatest extent are planning, design, construction, budgeting, and general management of projects and technical personnel. I designed a water treatment plant and a sewage treatment system; I was also responsible for supervising the construction of both projects.

In addition to a good college education, technical training, and practical experience, you must enjoy conceptual design work and drafting for the preliminary phases of a project, possess an interest in the area of civil engineering, possess knowledge of materials to be used, and have good working math skills.

I like my work very much; I especially find my job rewarding when a project is brought to successful completion.

I became interested in working as a civil engineer by working with my father; he is a civil engineer and he taught me a great deal about construction materials as well as the importance of this kind of work. I have always had a keen interest in math and enjoy working with numbers, so this was a logical career choice for me.

Before working as a civil engineer, I held jobs as a timber cruiser, which I enjoyed also, and a party chief for the U.S. Forest Service.

I plan to remain working in my chosen field for as long as possible.

CLAIMS REPRESENTATIVE

As a claims representative, I accept disability and retirement claims. These claims are then processed for payment or they are denied. For 25 years I have enjoyed helping people.

I would like more time to spend with applicants in interviews. The pressure to always accomplish more takes some of the satisfaction from my job. I am looking forward to retirement.

After graduating from high school, I got into claims by working my way up within the company from my position as a secretary. For my job, a person must work with and enjoy the public. One needs to be caring and considerate. Additionally, computer skills are essential and working well with fellow employees makes this job easier.

Prior to joining this company I worked briefly as a bank teller.

CLERGYMAN

A clergyman for quite a few years, I've found nothing I dislike about my work. If I were to start over, I'd elect the ministry again.

A clergyman must have strong speaking skills. Teaching ability is needed as well. You also should have a love for people. I think wanting to be of service is important in the ministry.

My work is most satisfying to me. Helping people find meaning and guidance for their lives has been fulfilling. I enjoy being involved with the church and the people I work with.

Mornings are spent in the church office with administrative work and with study. Some afternoons I visit church members in hospitals or in their homes. I also work on sermons or prepare for classes. Then there are sometimes meetings to attend in the evenings or there'll be rehearsals for church functions.

I had a Bachelors degree in music and enjoyed building and maintaining pipe organs before I was called to the ministry. I then earned a Bachelor of Divinity at a seminary and began my years of service in the church.

CLERK TYPIST

I work in the classification department of a state prison. My job is to calculate and update sentences of inmates and answer questions from within the prison and from external agencies or people.

Good mathematical skills are important in this work. You must also have the ability to comprehend laws pertaining to the calculating of sentences. A college degree is not necessary for this job.

Working within the department of corrections is very interesting in that no inmate is exactly like another-each one has a different personality background, and criminal activities vary vastly.

What I dislike about my job is the overcrowded working area and the lack of opportunity for advancement.

I chose this work because I found it interesting. I applied for the job when an opening became available. Previous job experience has included legal secretary, bank teller, real estate/insurance office worker, salesperson and customer service representative. I plan to continue to build up and use the skills and knowledge I have obtained to further advance my career in the same type or similar work as I am presently working.

CLINICAL NURSE SPECIALIST

I have always wanted to be a nurse or teacher, and I think I have been able to combine both professions into one with my current and previous positions. I am a clinical nurse specialist working with clients with multiple sclerosis in an out-patient setting. It is my job to examine patients, talk with them, educate both the patient and the family, and recommend treatment through their physician. My regular activities include obtaining the history of my clients/patients, performing a physical exam on new patients, answering questions about MS, rechecking patients who return for follow-up visits, making recommendations with the physicians, and returning phone calls from patients with questions/concerns.

To perform this kind of nursing work, and to do it well, requires good neurological assessment skills, good communication skills, and patience.

My occupation as a nurse is very satisfying. However, there are aspects of my current job which are frustrating--the disease MS is chronic and patients have frustrations in health/illness. Working with 3-4 physicians is also difficult for me to deal with at times.

I have basically always been in nursing. At one point I taught staff development for nurses. I have also been a head nurse and had administrative responsibilities. What led me into my present position was working on a neurological floor where I started learning and liking neurology. Eventually, I specialized. My future career plans are uncertain. I may possibly pursue more education, maybe a Ph.D. or another Masters. Staying in out-patient nursing or moving to an administrative position is another option I am considering.

I find satisfaction from nursing because it is social; you meet new people daily. I also like the position I am now in because it offers considerable autonomy.

CLINICAL PSYCHOLOGIST

I changed in mid-life from a prior profession as doctor of optometry when I increasingly realized that, even though optometry was enjoyable, my unique talent and urge lay in the field of understanding people and responding to their needs.

As a clinical psychologist, I help people achieve higher levels of self appreciation and better solve life problems. I accomplish this through counseling sessions, i.e., psychotherapy to individual adults, couples, children, families, about the dysfunction in their lives. These dysfunctions could be anger, unhappiness, poor coping skills, dysfunctional relationships, inability to achieve desired goals, etc.,

To perform psychotherapy well, it is important to have a high intellect that is prepared to understand and accept what one hears and senses, without judgment. Because of in-depth training in under- standing communication, covert meanings and the dynamics of relationships, the therapist is able to assist people in making the desired changes.

I have been enjoying this profession for 20 years primarily because of my own tremendous sense of satisfaction that my clinical skills and strategies are working. My reward is also the feedback from clients who tell me their lives are changed for the better.

CLINICAL RESEARCH COORDINATOR

As a research pharmacist, I am working for a pharmaceutical company as their Clinical Research Coordinator. I have always been interested in research. While working on my graduate degree in pharmacy, I accepted a research fellowship sponsored jointly by a university/corporation which led to my permanent position with the corporation.

It is my responsibility to coordinate trials where patients receive study drugs in preparation for new drug applications to the Federal Food and Drug Administration. My regular activities include: obtaining status updates from investigators and subordinates, organizing and managing data, assigning tasks or jobs, and reporting weekly to the clinical leader.

To perform well as a clinical research coordinator, it is important to have the following skills and attitudes: a science and medicine background, understanding of research principles, organization, patience, and the ability to work well with a team.

I have always liked working in the pharmaceutical field, and have held previous positions as a hospital pharmacist and nuclear pharmacist. I plan to continue in this field and work toward a corporate management position as clinical leader/manager of a team of scientists and associates.

I find job satisfaction when I come to the end of a 4-year project. It is also rewarding when we find that the drug which we have tested will be marketed successfully when approved.

CLINICAL SOCIAL WORKER, STAFF DIRECTOR

For the past 16 years I have been both director of staff development in a psychiatric hospital and a clinical social worker. I like my career as a clinical social worker and do not particularly like the staff development job; therefore, I will only discuss the former job.

Five evenings per week I conduct individual and couple psychotherapy in a part-time private clinical practice.

To be qualified to perform this work I earned a Master's degree in Social Work. As well as education, the important attitudes and skills which a clinical social worker should have are a non-judgmental attitude, openness, empathy, and a clear theoretical approach balanced with warmth and caring.

I decided to become a clinical social worker as a result of my own growth and change going through therapy as an undergraduate.

In the future I plan to expand my private practice, because of the satisfaction I get from watching the growth and change in my clients as they work through their problems.

COLLEGE ADMINISTRATOR

As a college administrator, I try to help people interested in improving the educational process at the university where I work. I am currently involved in the set-up of a new operation to provide support for services to users of personal computers. I observe, listen, gather information, interact with the users, attend meetings, come up with ideas, put those ideas into written proposals, and then forward those proposals to the necessary parties for consideration.

My educational background includes a Bachelor of Science degree in Science and Math Education, a Master of Science degree in Education, and six years in audio-visual education. In addition, my position requires an understanding of human behavior, motivational skills, critical thinking skills, problem solving skills, the ability to be objective, the ability to work efficiently, the ability to accomplish the most with the least, the ability to place self-satisfaction over ego gratification, and a genuine like of people.

I like my job very much, and in the twenty-six years I have been involved in this kind of work, my only complaint is the lack of commitment to the mission of the university that arises when financial crises occur. But, overall, I like the people I work with, and working in a university is very rewarding. I am happy that the work gives me the opportunity to make a contribution to the improvement of the educational process, help people grow, and derive self-satisfaction from my work; I feel that my job provides me opportunities for on-going learning.

Although I have held several other jobs over the years, the only other jobs that I enjoyed were within the educational system, in the field of teaching.

I plan to continue to make as much contribution to improving the educational process as I possibly can. Years from now, I will probably spend my time writing and producing video cassette programs as an outlet for my creativity and desire to share my experiences in the pursuit of excellence in the field of education.

COLLEGE STUDENT

I am not in any occupation yet; I am a college student trying to earn a B.A. in Business. I now have an Associate Degree in Business Administration. I have been in this job for 15 years and I plan to apply this in an occupation when I have completed my degree. With luck, I will also obtain a bachelor's degree, and then, perhaps, a Master's degree.

My activities will not be described in connection with an occupation but in connection with being a college student. The "work" involves taking notes, studying, writing papers, research, and other activities of the student at the college level. I believe that my majoring in Public Relations with another major in Communications will be of value to me in public relations work within an established organization.

The characteristics that are important in being a student are optimism, perseverance, adjustability, reading, and sharp writing skills. I find satisfaction from getting a paper or exam back with an A. Sometimes just getting the work, that had seemed so overwhelming, finally finished, can be extremely rewarding.

COLLEGE STUDENT/HOMEMAKER

I am a college student and a homemaker; basically I study and run a household. My days are long and my schedule requires careful planning.

My success balancing both endeavors requires extreme concentration, organizational skills, the ability to comprehend course material, study, written and oral communication skills, and budgeting techniques for whatever money I have available to me.

For all my efforts, I gain peace of mind. I previously worked in real estate sales; the draw to that profession was essentially money. It was only superficially satisfying; I do not believe that money is all that you should work for as it limits and inhibits natural talents and abilities.

Before spending fifteen years of my life in real estate sales, I held several jobs including meter maid, secretary, office manager in a dentist's office, waitress, and several sales positions. None of these positions fulfilled my need to grow into the person I know I can be.

After completing the Bachelor of Arts degree program in progress, I plan to join the Peace Corps and give my time to children living in Africa to teach them the English language.

After the Peace Corps, I hope to return to graduate school to earn a Master's degree and then put my education and teaching experience to work teaching children in this country.

COLLEGE VICE CHANCELLOR

I enjoy every aspect of my work as Vice Chancellor in a community college system. My work can best be described as serving the needs of a systems office staff of 100 individuals and the college personnel in 23 colleges. By monitoring the human resource functions of the systems office, I find it particularly rewarding to be an agent of change. I like providing guidance and assistance to college personnel.

I found this position through a competitive search process. The announcement of the opening appeared in the Chronicle of Higher Education and I responded a little over two years ago. After receiving my Masters of Divinity, I had served as a Director of Minority Student Affairs and as a Dean of Student Affairs. One day I hope to become Executive Vice Chancellor of a community college system or, perhaps, a Human Resource Director for a private corporation.

My position requires a great deal of patience. Also important are a good sense of judgment and independent thinking, in accord with the structure of the organization. Two days are never the same. Flexibility is important for there are always new challenges, new correspondence, new problems, and new possibilities.

COMMERCIAL AIRLINE PILOT

I have always wanted to fly since childhood and much to my satisfaction my career has been that of a commercial airline pilot for more than 20 years. My educational background includes a Bachelor of Science degree from the Naval Academy. After serving in the Navy for a number of years, I was able to get my civilian job largely due to my Naval aviation training and experience.

As a pilot of a commercial, turbine powered, passenger aircraft, I generally make three-day trips. My flights originate from my base city, from which I fly two to five legs with a 10-18 hour layover. The second day is the same, and the third day the crew and I return to our home base. I am then off for two to three days.

Aviation and motor skills are essential as a pilot. As well as these skills, the correct mental attitude is very important. A pilot should have an even disposition, not inclined to be excitable or easily angered, and able to handle stress.

Except for the lack of a set schedule, I like every aspect of my work. I like the people I work with, the people and organization I work for, the opportunity for advancement, and the kind of work I do. I would not change careers even if given the opportunity to start over and prepare for any kind of work.

I find job satisfaction because of my pleasure in flying, for serving people, and seeing different places. My future career plans are to continue flying.

COMMERCIAL ARTIST, FREELANCE

I have been a free-lance commercial artist for thirty-five years. I chose this as a career because I have always loved to draw and, if given the choice again, I would still choose this career. I graduated from college with a bachelor of fine arts degree in order to prepare myself for this career as an illustrator.

My typical work day is spent illustrating in various mediums. My illustrations are mainly for advertising and are sometimes black and white, sometimes four colors.

To perform this job well you must have the ability to draw and have a good sense of color and design.

I receive satisfaction from my work by doing what I love to do, knowing that I have completed a job, and knowing that I have done my best.

The thing that I would most like to change about my career is the pressure of deadlines. I would definitely like to be given more time to work on each job.

COMMERCIAL BANK JUNIOR LOAN OFFICER

My Bachelor of Science in Economics degree led me into this career as a commercial banker/junior loan officer. I was recruited from college, and chose it because I was offered a year of training in a bank credit program, up-front. My summer job work as a secretary, pension benefit analyst, and financial analyst also made my qualifications better for this training program.

Although I like my work, I have found the corporate culture to be somewhat annoying to deal with. In working for a large corporation, you are constantly faced with many people trying to get ahead, and I have observed that a focus set too far ahead leads you to downplay the importance of your present duties.

My basic responsibilities are to analyze the credit worthiness of a customer, to structure financing by working with large corporate clients in obtaining financing for their activities, and go through the steps to secure their loans using research and analysis techniques. I also help promote and sell the bank's products and services, and I assist internal credit personnel in working with customers.

The qualities essential to success as a commercial banker are flexibility, the ability to work independently, the inclination to be detail-oriented, knowledge of financial issues, and experience with credit issues.

I find my work rewarding; it is interesting to me. One has the opportunity to learn a great deal, and the work itself is very relevant to what goes on in the public markets.

I intend to start a new venture in the near future; I would like to run my own business, allowing me to work with a smaller, more specialized group. I believe my education, past experience, and people skills will ensure success in my future endeavors.

COMMERCIAL DESIGNER INSTRUCTOR

While I was working as a commercial artist/designer for a toy company, I was asked to teach part-time at night at a community college. I took the night job and continued at the toy company for a year until I was hired as a full-time instructor. Prior to teaching commercial art and advertising design and working for the toy company, I was a public school science teacher, and an artist/designer for an electronics manufacturer. My educational background includes a Bachelor of Fine Arts, and a Masters in Education degrees.

As an instructor at the college, I teach a variety of drawing, design, and computer graphic classes. My typical day includes: preparing for classes, teaching; returning materials used; meeting office hours; attending meetings; grading papers; and preparing for the next day. I often work on artwork at home in the evening.

In order to perform this kind of work well, it is important to have the ability to: organize material, speak, and demonstrate art media and techniques.

Although I like most aspects of my work, I dislike the paperwork and forms required by the state departments. I would also like to have up-to-date equipment without having to go through such a hassle to get it. Aside from that, I like the kind of work I do. I like the organization and people I work for and the people with whom I work. My flexible schedule, when I am not in class, is also a definite plus to college teaching. I find satisfaction from working with students on a personal level, and working with fellow faculty members. It is also satisfying to know that students who complete the program get good jobs.

COMMERCIAL FISHERMAN

Other than knowing how to catch fish, a commercial fisherman in Alaska must know boat operation, navigation, boat maintenance, book- keeping, and radio operations. There is no typical day. Some fishing days last 24 hours, others can last 15 days without stopping. The scenery is great; human population is sparse.

The elements I don't like about my work are being away from home, government restrictions, and the constant hassle and misrepresentations by the environmentalists, as well as the canneries we sell to. And the price of fish is not equitable. Our overhead is destroying us as is the unfair foreign competition.

I've been in my present work for 14 years. Added to those years are 6 years of fishing through my college years. I was with Douglas Aircraft and then I was a merchant seaman during World War II. I studied theology (though no degrees were given then) and served as a pastor for 28 years. I've worked for Metropolitan Life, operated a burglar alarm business, and, right out of college, I sold vacuum cleaners.

I love the independence of owning my own fishing business. There's a high degree of excitement and challenge in this business and there is always something new to learn.

COMMERCIAL PROPERTY OVERSEER

As a national real estate property portfolio manager, I oversee the commercial property management offices of a national insurance company. I had enjoyed my previous work in leasing and sales marketing personnel, but I particularly enjoyed the opportunities to problem solve in my real estate work. I liked creating new management techniques and developing subordinate workers for promotion.

I would have liked greater recognition in the business community. Few seem to be aware of the professional qualifications required in my job.

Strong oral and written communications skills are valuable in this managerial position. In addition, you need to have a positive mental attitude, flexibility, and persistence. You must approach problems with a view to solving them, not being intimidated by them. Real estate management requires a team approach so if you are a loner, you should not be a manager. Encourage initiatives in your employees and my advice is to hire people who are smarter than you. One must maintain professional attitudes and results along with the continual desire to learn if you are to be successful in this arena.

A college degree is not essential for this work if you are a good manager.

My usual day consists of analyzing and approving leases, contracts, and environmental statements. I review disability contracts and legal actions for national commercial properties. I advise national mortgage/equity/appraisal groups on commercial property management and leasing questions.

COMMODITIES TRADER

I wanted a performance-oriented career where I could apply my math skills. I started out in institutional sales after graduating from college, but was not satisfied. I then took a lot of interviews and finally found a company that wanted to hire me as a commodities trader. I have found this work to be very satisfying for a number of reasons: being able to find new ways to make money; dealing with important, multi- million dollar deals; seeing the application of what I learned in school (especially math and finance); fun people to work with; ideas are communicated by talking--reports and memos aren't required.

My basic job as a commodities trader is to look for new ways to arbitrage markets. I negotiate trade swaps, and options on natural gas, gasoline, heating oil, and crude oil. My typical activities are: evaluating deals other trading companies want to do, evaluating deals for clients, looking for new trading strategies, meeting with clients, reading/writing contracts, and calling brokers.

In order to perform well as a trader, the following skills and attitudes are important: self starter; sharp mentality; mathematical quickness; desire to do well; maturity; quick thinking; common sense; a sense of priority; self confidence; aggressiveness; ability to work well with people; and ability to keep it all in perspective.

As with anything, there are some drawbacks, and at the present I would like the market to move more. My other point of frustration is how long it takes to put a deal together. Aside from that, I like the kind of work I do and the opportunity I have for advancement. The casual atmosphere and money are additional pluses to my career.

My future career plan is to run a bigger trading position.

COMMUNICATIONS TECHNICIAN

As a radar technician in the US Air Force, I volunteered to retrain into the technical control field. I then spent 8 years in this field before retiring from the USAF. Based on this training, I was able to find the job I now have as communications electronic technician. This, in turn, has expanded my experience into field service work.

My work schedule varies depending on whether I am assigned to the field or the control center. My day could consist of working in a communications control center handling incoming trouble calls on terminals ranging from PC's (personnel computers) to multi-port telex terminals. It could be calls on high speed data circuits requiring testing of local international transmission media. On the other hand, I could be assigned field work for the week and be installing new circuits or terminals or called on to test, reprogram, or repair existing terminals and circuits.

A positive attitude and ability to deal with various types of people is absolutely essential to perform the job well. Electronics schools ranging from basic electronics through data transmission testing is also necessary. I also recommend schooling in various terminals and PC's along with their peripherals.

Although I am not completely satisfied with the people and organization I work for, I do like the people I work with and the kind of work I do. I particularly like meeting new people in my field work and solving their problems. I find job satisfaction from a relieved look on my customers' faces when they realize they are able to resume using their communications again, along with the thanks usually accompanied by a smile.

COMPENSATION ADMINISTRATOR

My work as a compensation administrator in the area of human resources involves the processing and reviewing of salary changes for my company. It involves the processing of newly-hired employees, employees that have been terminated, requisitions to hire additional employees, and employee promotions and performance appraisals including merit raises. I also spend time writing and updating job descriptions; participating in salary surveys by gathering, researching, and communicating information to outside sources; researching and compiling statistics; offering advice and assisting with matters pertaining to salary and performance appraisals; maintaining and updating personnel files; and writing custom computer reports.

In addition to a college degree, my job requires the ability to think quickly, problem solving abilities, good interpersonal and listening skills, good written and verbal communication skills, good math skills, computer literacy, and a positive and dynamic mental attitude.

I find my work very interesting; it allows me to see most of the changes occurring throughout the organization. I enjoy dealing with many different people through my position, becoming familiar with who they really are. I also enjoy dealing with personnel laws and applying these laws in challenging and dynamic ways. I strive to keep current. I enjoy the fast-paced work environment and I enjoy the feeling that I have accomplished a goal that will benefit others. Essentially, I like that I work as an integral part of a service organization.

Currently, I am completing a Bachelor of Science degree in Business Management; I look forward to completion of that program as I believe this degree will help me in human resource management, specifically in the area of compensation.

I may consider branching out to be involved in more general types of human resources. That would require that I receive additional training and experience in other areas of human resources such as benefits, employment, training, and employee development.

COMPUTER ANALYST

A computer analyst needs a great deal of patience. Being able to translate users' feelings and needs into technical performance are required. Equally needed is the ability to listen well. Also important are an understanding of people and being able to diffuse tense situations.

I work with personal computer users, teaching them how to use the software they need. Trouble-shooting computer problems to determine hardware or software errors is also part of my work. Then, I refer the defined problems to others for repair. It's my job to determine user requirements in order to develop new programs or to change existing ones appropriately.

Getting a task done right and having satisfied clients pleases me. The people I work with and the job itself are very rewarding as well. However, I'm having trouble with my supervisors and with the company. I wish there were more opportunities for advancement. Working more in the business administration arena appeals to me as a good lateral move.

Although I'd earned an undergraduate degree in history and later a Masters in Business Administration and a Masters in Education, I got into this work during a period of unemployment. I passed a battery of tests and went through extensive interviews. Then, I was placed in a training program to learn specific computer programming languages and systems. Eventually, I'd like to get a Ph.D. in information systems.

COMPUTER ANALYST & PROGRAMMER

Specifically, my programming in the last two years has been in the area of EDI (electronic data interchange) although I have been in the occupation of programming for nine years.

In this job I have several functions. One is to keep in touch with customers/vendors we are getting "set up" on EDI or who are in production so that we can iron out any problems. In those calls, we determine the best way to meet the needs of our customers/vendors with our business systems and vice versa. It is necessary to think beyond the immediate situation. I might ask: What solution holds the greatest opportunity to answer the problem for the most customers/vendors OR is most flexible and easy to change? The job also requires that I work with middle managers in our own company to determine how we will integrate customer data into our systems. Finally, I test and analyze the test data to see that the agreed-upon methods are working properly.

Clearly, to be effective in this kind of work, you need the ability to see the long-term, "best" solution and you should then have a commitment to work toward that best solution. You will need to present abstract concepts to business managers in concrete terms; that is, take the customer/vendor's EDI specifications and describe how they will appear in our business systems. All of this requires abstract intelligence and attention to detail. Obviously, you must have a background of training in programming. In my case, I took a Bachelor of Science degree in Agricultural Education and included many courses dealing with computers.

The rewards for all this are good feelings when you remove repetitive data entry functions so that you have a highly effective program. It is important for me to know that

I am helping to build a foundation that will serve our company for years to come. The satisfactions far outweigh the occasional frustrations caused by inaccessibility of people who need to make decisions about how they want the data presented.

Other occupations I have had (less satisfying to me) were campus minister, factory worker, heavy equipment operator, and construction foreman. My plans are to continue in programming indefinitely.

COMPUTER CONSULTANT #1

As a computer consultant, I help clients assess new technology and its applicability to and impact on their organization and problems. I regularly attend meetings with clients about work, plan how to market our capabilities and how to build a group, figure out how to use a new computer tool, review proposals for other groups (as a critic), talk to peers about work-related issues, and keep up with contacts outside of the company.

To perform well as a consultant it is important to have creativity, imagination, inability to leave an unsolved problem, people-handling skills, and the ability to tolerate ambiguity (at least initially).

I have been in this kind of work for 30 years and been satisfied mainly because I like solving problems and selling solutions. This occupation has always been fun, but organizational politics, alas, have not always been fun. If I could change anything about my profession, I would like to see more demand and reward for excellence.

I earned a bachelor of arts degree in Spanish. I was recruited out of college and was required to learn programming; consulting just kind of chose me after that. Previous work experience involved teaching and writing.

My future career aspirations include writing, consulting, and teaching as an independent professional.

COMPUTER CONSULTANT #2

My goal, as a freelance computer programmer and consultant, is to create a corporation which electronically links the public domain to all universities. I would use interactive multimedia to eliminate the barriers of distance, costs, and time-constraints that tend to prevent many people from attending universities.

Before entering this field, I served a while in the U.S. Army. My degree is a Bachelor of Science in Electrical Engineering. My work requires a tremendous amount of reading for marketing purposes. In my reading I look for niche markets which I can enter. Once a market is recognized, I interact with market principals to identify problems and solutions.

Reading is the primary skill needed for my job. Highly effective oral and written communication skills are vital. Having an extensive knowledge of computer networks along with programming skills are essential. In addition to all of this, one must possess business savvy, patience, and a willingness to take risks.

I dislike the amount of time and effort it takes to "close" a sale. Other than that, I pretty much like everything about my work: the people, the work itself, and the freedom of self-employment--"being my own boss." I am gratified simply knowing that my efforts have improved another company's productivity.

COMPUTER CONSULTANT & PROGRAMMER

For 16 years, I've worked as a consultant and programmer in the computer industry. Over half of my time is spent consulting, discovering the objectives and the requirements of my clients. There is a great deal of interaction with others, giving and receiving technical information, exchanging ideas on new technology, analyzing problems as well as developing solutions.

In general, I help people with computers and software. I enjoy building software systems and seeing them function. I like watching my clients' satisfaction as they use these systems. There is great satisfaction in exploring a problem, or opportunity, and then, drawing pieces into a solution that works for the client.

I got into this work through dumb luck and hard work. Corporate politics changed the department where I first worked as a financial analyst, and, although I have a Bachelor of Science in business, I found that I must move to computers. The computer systems people gave me training and let me work as hard as I wanted to learn my new trade. I very much enjoy my work now, but my earlier experience in computers would have been less frustrating if there had been less bureaucracy. I am now an independent consultant with my goal being to build a successful practice on my own.

To be an effective software consultant, you must be a good listener and active learner. Because of the changes in technology, you are constantly thrown into new and unfamiliar situations. The fastest way, and often the only way, to get information is by listening to and learning from others. Being able to define problems and then solve them is very significant in this work. Very importantly, you need to keep an eye on the client's objectives, and to remain tactful in dealing with the client. Strong communication skills are vital. It is also important to be able to convey information in a clear, straightforward, nonjudgmental manner. Further, you need to read, write, and speak clearly to be successful in this work.

COMPUTER CONSULTANT/TEACHER

Self-employed, I work as a computer consultant and software instructor. I teach others how to use certain software packages such as LOTUS and various word processing packages. My work requires that I travel to see my clients and offer assistance with their problems, or teach them how to use different software, and that I send out literature about my business to prospective clients in an advertising effort that will hopefully bring in new customers.

I have an Associate degree in Computer Science. In addition, my job requires an understanding of the different software currently on the market; knowledge of computers in general; a patient attitude, especially with beginners; and the ability to communicate clearly.

I like this kind of work. Being self-employed, I have the flexibility to be available to my family; I like making my own hours and keeping my own schedule.

I was drawn to this type of work because I wanted to combine my past experience in business with my computer skills; I previously worked as a secretary in an office environment.

I am also involved in a separate venture through which I sell medical software; I plan to expand the market area that I service through that venture.

COMPUTER ENGINEER #1

For thirteen years I have been employed as a computer engineer. For the most part, my work has involved the design and writing of computer software programs. There is a great deal of planning and organization that goes into my work. Daily I review my previous day's work and that of my colleagues before planning the tasks I expect to accomplish each day. I write and test the computer programs that become the software packages that my company utilizes and sells.

While serving in the U.S. Air Force, I was trained in computer engineering; in addition to the proper training, one must be self reliant, self disciplined, organized, and have the ability to adapt to constant changes in plans.

I really like my job. I work for a great boss and a good company, and I believe there are many opportunities for advancement from my present position. I like the people I work with and the fact that I have the opportunity to work with computers. I find special satisfaction in the completion of a project and I am especially pleased when I have the opportunity to see a product perform as it should in a real customer environment.

I plan to continue in this field and with this company. I would like to become a project leader and a researcher for larger, more technically advanced projects in software development.

COMPUTER ENGINEER #2

My job is my hobby. I have been pursuing my career as a computer engineer for the past 23 years and, if given the chance to start over, I would still choose the same occupation.

My job is to design custom computer systems to customer specifications. The progression of my duties goes from reviewing the specifications, to researching components, designing the system, writing the design documents, training manufacturing, and then supporting installations.

To perform this kind of work, you must have the knowledge of computer science and electrical engineering. It is also very important to have the ability to work with others in order to perform well.

I particularly like the kind of work I do although I have found a lack of opportunity for advancement without going into management. However, I enjoy my current level because I find satisfaction from seeing my designs solve customers' problems and perform useful work.

My career plans for the future are to continue to keep my education up to date as I am now doing by attending night school classes in order to continue in my career as a computer engineer.

COMPUTER HARDWARE MAINTENANCE ENGINEER

I chose this field of work because of my personal interest in the electrical engineering field. My career in technology started after earning an associate degree in electrical engineering technology. My first job in the field was as a field service radar technician. Then, after attending a company school, I worked as a computer field service technician. I was then sent to another internal company school, plus I took outside college classes, before going before the engineering review board.

Now as a computer hardware maintenance engineer, I offer high level support to customer services on telecommunication equipment. My typical daily activities include: returning phone calls from voice mail; reading electronic mail and replying if needed; checking for any new customer problems from customer service centers; checking with design engineering about resolutions of old problems; setting up test configuration to work on current problems.

To perform this kind of work well, you should have the following skills and attitudes: technical knowledge of computers, computer networks, and data communication; and the ability to work well as a buffer between groups with divergent interests. I find satisfaction from this problem/solution type work where the problems and solutions are usually well defined. The work lends itself, for the most part, to a strictly logical approach.

COMPUTER MANUFACTURING TECHNICIAN

I have been in the computer business for 7 years. For the past three my job has been to provide technical information to the manufacturing people of mini and super computers. Before that I was a printed circuit board and systems integration technician in the same field.

I like very much all aspects of the job and organization I work for. I have several years of college and plan to obtain a bachelor's degree eventually. I went into this job for financial reasons but plan to stay with it in spite of, or perhaps because of, the independence I have and atmosphere of crisis as we rush around "putting out fires," so to speak, i.e. problem-solving as I go along.

Liking the independence and lack of routine would be important characteristics in this work. You set your own goals, depending on what is needed, and try to come up with solutions by being versatile and creative.

COMPUTER OPERATOR #1

I was an aide at the high school when the decision was made to computerize student records. Three other aides and I were given the information which was to be entered, and we were shown the basics on operating the computer. This was my first exposure to computer operations. After several months, I was given the computer operator's job because of my efficiency and accuracy. Prior to my work as an aide, I was a secretary.

As the school's computer operator, I enter all data, grades, schedules, attendance records, and discipline reports on 1200 students. In order to perform these functions, I deal with all of the school's personnel, including the 85 teachers and 1200 students. This requires patience and a pleasant attitude. Along with this, I think a sense of humor is a must in dealing with the high school level.

I have liked this kind of work; the people and school district I work for; and the people I work with. It is satisfying work because I enjoy the students and teachers. I have also benefited by gaining computer knowledge and skills. I plan to stay with computers in the future.

COMPUTER OPERATOR #2

I'm proud to be involved in the kind of work I am doing. I dropped out of school when I was a senior. I did, however, attend business school for data entry which helped open up this opportunity for me. I chose data entry because I've always liked to type. I became a computer operator because I was in the right place at the right time. Our computer operator was fired at a moment's notice, and I was asked to take his position. I learned how to operate the computer over the telephone, with the help of our part-time programmer.

As computer and data entry operator, it is now my responsibility to run reports and key all the data that's entered into the computer at an appraisal company. My day at work starts at 6:30 a.m. I key the information and update the computer system. I also do research on sales of residential and commercial properties. If reports are required to be printed and readied for distribution, I run the reports and get then ready. My regular job ends at 3:30 p.m., and then I have a few hours off before starting work at a video store at night.

To perform this kind of work, you must be able to change programs in the computer when needed. Also, you have to be a very fast and accurate data entry operator. I have a lot of responsibilities and it tends to be a very stressful job.

I stay very busy in my line of work, and I try to be the best at what I do. I'm proud to be making the kind of salary I do--considering that I dropped out of school. I've learned an awful lot being employed at this company.

I would like to go out to our on-line customers' offices and learn how to hook them up to our system. I could also use a data entry assistant.

I plan to remain in this career because I am really happy with it. I would like to retire early, however, so I can do volunteer work for children or the elderly. Volunteer work has always been a dream of mine for as long as I can remember. I would just like to be in a position to help others that are in need.

COMPUTER OPERATOR #3

I was a janitor at my present company when I saw the position open for operator trainee and decided to apply. I always had an interest in computers but no experience. I got the position, and in 2 1/2 years I rose 4 seniority levels and am now training operators myself.

As a computer operator, I assist computer users with hardware, software or general problems, do some programming and editing, account for computer materials, and maintain the computer facility. If there happens to be problems with any particular computer, I try to fix it; if I can't, a service call is placed. I may have to repair a minor program error, or set up an account for a user on a given machine. When hardware needs to be moved, I do that also.

In order to perform this kind of work well, I recommend good common sense and judgment, a good understanding of formats and certain methods to deal with problems, an applied understanding of how computers work, and the ability to work with others.

I like almost every aspect of my work.

It is satisfying work for me, and in fact I find it exciting, because I seem to be able to deal with almost any problem that comes up. I also am asked my opinions and for help, even from senior staff. It is also satisfying to be in a good learning environment.

I am currently attending college and am enrolled in the computer science degree program with future plans to continue in the computer field.

COMPUTER OPERATOR #4

I began at this company as a college coop student, took a full time position upon leaving college, and changed jobs within the company as my needs and aspirations changed. I was trained on the job and acquired more computer skills with each position held.

My major responsibility as a computer operator is to run backup programs. My typical work day starts with a brief meeting with my supervisor to review events of the day and advise on any problems or peculiarities. I then proceed to the routine jobs of preparing log sheets, mounting tapes, and running backup programs. Troubleshooting and hardware/software problems seem to be a daily occurrence also. I do a minimum of clerical work.

An aptitude for computers, organizational/logical skills, and patience are what I consider key requirements for performing this kind of work well.

As a mother, I am content with the job I presently have as it is tailored to my needs and skills--second shift/part time. As my responsibilities at home change or diminish, I would like to take on a more challenging position in the computer field; one with more diversity. Meanwhile, my main satisfaction comes from solving problems, by programming and checking hardware--the "hands on" aspects.

COMPUTER OPERATOR #5

My 30-year stint as a computer operator almost matches the development of those machines as we know them today. As they have grown so have I grown with them. My current job is operating and maintaining a large mainframe computer. I deal with terminals, printers, copiers, and cartridge drives designed to facilitate maximum productivity in a busy environment.

Basic to being able to do this job is a knowledge of computer functions, several of the languages they use, and the fundamental keyboard. You should be able to think and work independently of others, yet you must be able to work with others when there are group assignments to be done. In addition, a college degree, while not essential, is very helpful in the job. I have a Bachelor of Arts degree.

It is a challenge--which I enjoy meeting--to complete work in the most efficient way possible. If some changes could be made in the work schedule, we could utilize the equipment better. I wish I had more opportunity for advancement in this job; then I could put some of my ideas to work!

Although my education is not in the computer area, I became interested in this field by reading magazine articles concerning future job markets. It has turned out to be a good choice for me.

My secondary interest is archeology, and some day I will have time to pursue knowledge in that field.

COMPUTER OPERATOR, CADD

I began my career in manual drafting after earning an Associate's Degree in Industrial Product Design. Computers began to be used for drafting and I received on-the-job training. Each time I changed jobs, I learned to use different computer hardware and software, as well as switching to doing graphics and/or design of different types of products.

Currently, I make specialized maps and graphs of geologic data using a computer. This is done by referring to sketches, verbal information, and other documents. I use a graphic/drawing program on a P.C. to create the figures for the reports my company writes. My drawings are specialized types of maps. I also use a spreadsheet/database program to tabulate geologic data and then make graphs to illustrate trends. I work at the computer 75% or more of the time.

In addition to the computer skills which are obviously required to perform this work, you must also pay attention to detail, have a manual drafting background, be somewhat of a perfectionist, have an understanding of maps and graphics, and have math skills.

I like the kind of work I am doing very much. However, I would be more satisfied with improved working conditions such as better lighting and ergonomic furniture and equipment, and more advanced and appropriate graphics software. Despite these drawbacks, I find job satisfaction in several ways: I am doing something creative, I am NOT doing military product design, and I am using a computer.

I am planning to get a Bachelor of Science Degree in Computer Science in order to be more flexible in career choices as the economy fluctuates. I would like to work at an environmentally and socially conscious company and be paid well. I plan to continue to work with computers whether programming them or using them to create graphics and designs.

COMPUTER OPERATOR, COLOR GRAPHICS

For twenty-six years I have worked as a Graphics Illustrator on a computer. Working for an Arts department at a large company, I do graphic illustrations on a computer terminal; I design color slides, prepare the artwork for color brochures, and do color presentations.

Besides having a natural ability in art and computer skills, one must be accurate and precise when working with the computer.

I feel fortunate to be working for what I believe is an excellent company. I really enjoy my job and the type of work I do.

I was previously employed in retail sales, and that was interesting work, but I prefer to work in a more creative environment.

I plan to stay in this field and learn more about the computer system I work on.

COMPUTER PROGRAMMER #1

As a computer programmer, I write, maintain, and develop computer programs to solve business needs. My typical daily and/or weekly activities include: writing and changing computer programs to solve business problems and provide information; discussing problems with customers and answering questions; attending meetings to define problems and needs; and reporting to management.

To perform well as a computer programmer, it is important to have logic skills, an understanding of others, and the ability and desire to pay attention to details.

After graduating from college with a Bachelor of Arts in speech, I took a test in order to qualify for the position. I was initially attracted to the job because of the high pay. After working in this career now for 26 years, I can still say I like the salary, but I can also say I like the kind of work, and the social interaction in my workplace. The drawback to this kind of work is the high pressure to meet deadlines which I consider to be irrelevant sometimes. I do, however, find satisfaction in helping solve problems.

COMPUTER PROGRAMMER #2

I got into my occupation as a computer programmer through hard work and an understanding of and interest in computers. When I was in high school, I leaned toward electrical engineering or computer science. I chose to work with computers because it was more interesting to me and I felt I could do more in this field. In order to qualify for this kind of work, I earned a bachelor's degree.

As a computer programmer/analyst, I am a team leader in building customer credit card processing systems. My regular daily activities include meetings, development of program applications, preparing technical specifications, handing out work to others, and answering questions.

To perform this kind of work well, it is important to have imagination, a good outlook toward oneself, and the skills and understanding to work with others (personalities).

One aspect that I dislike about this work in not having enough time for everything and always working under the stress of deadlines. Despite these frustrations, I like the kind of work I do.

It is satisfying to see something I have developed work as planned and work efficiently.

My career aspiration is to advance to an upper level management position or to own my own company.

COMPUTER PROGRAMMER #3

The career which I had planned for myself, as an accountant, took an unplanned turn after I earned my Masters degree in Business Administration and was going through a 1 1/2 year internship as a bank branch manager trainee. I was recruited by a credit union software support company to help train clients to use the computer. Since then, this job has evolved into a programming job.

As a computer programmer, I train users, and design and write programs used by credit unions. I spend 2 to 3 hours answering questions and training users. The remaining time is divided between planning, writing, and testing programs.

The most important attitude for this kind of work is tolerance for people who are NOT computer literate, because so much of my job involves customer contact. The predominant skills are to be detail-oriented, persistent, and well organized.

Aside from feeling that there is a lack of opportunity for advancement in my current position, I like the kind of work very much. I also like the people I work for. The main satisfactions are immediate feedback--programs either work or don't work. My job involves considerable customer contact which is fun and breaks up any monotony.

My future career plans are to have my own computer consulting business or to manage a company for someone else.

COMPUTER PROGRAMMER #4

Working as a programmer for three years, I assist users in working with application tools, write programs, and run and maintain production jobs. I work with software programs and the documentation of those programs.

I have completed a Bachelor of Science degree in Business. In addition to a college degree, my job requires logical thought processes, organization, skills in time management, people skills, typing or keyboarding skills, and extensive knowledge of computers--programming languages, hardware, and networking.

I really like my work as a programmer; I like the people I work with, my boss, and the company I work for. I get a sense of accomplishment from performing a job from start to finish, and combining my computer skills with my people skills to get results from the computer system.

I started out as a financial analyst for business systems, then became a business systems analyst, and ended up as a programmer analyst. I am happy with my present position. The only difference I would make if I had it to do over is that I would have pursued a degree in computer science instead of business.

I am taking programming and computer courses at the undergraduate level; I plan to become a Management Information Systems (MIS) Manager within the next five years.

COMPUTER PROGRAMMER #5

As a programmer for eight years, I create a series of programs to accomplish a specific goal and work toward a set deadline. Most of my work is problem solving, but I also write new software; I either write new code or move existing code between DOS and UNIX hardware platforms.

In addition to a good education (I have an Associate's degree and a Bachelor's degree), one must be able to sit in one place and be willing to be stimulated intellectually by tracing problems.

Although there is no opportunity for advancement within this organization, I like my job.

This kind of work is enjoyable because I have the opportunity to keep the product running and I enjoy working independently. The only complaint I have is that I wish I had more time to learn new approaches to problems.

I really like computers and at times my work seems like play; I have always been interested in computers. I have also had the opportunity to work as a manager of a department, a commercial photographer, a lab technician, and a cab driver.

I plan to continue taking courses offered through in-house training and advance to manage more network software development in this company.

COMPUTER PROGRAMMER #6

Over a period of seven years I have worked my way up through the ranks of the company I work for, and for the last four years, I have enjoyed my position as programmer. I analyze existing programs, correcting programming bugs when I find them, and create new programs for our inventory control system; I also help users with their programming problems.

The skills required for success as a programmer are: logic; stubbornness--you need to be able to outwit the computer when program errors occur; people skills, as you need to be a good listener; resourcefulness; and an innovative mind. You must constantly come up with new ideas to solve the new problems that arise daily. I also have previous data entry experience and my people skills were developed in a previous position as an assistant manager.

My greatest job satisfaction comes from correcting a problem on an existing program that someone else could not fix or completing a program that others could not complete.

I would like to get involved in more challenging work, perhaps work on a more complicated computer system than the one I presently deal with. I enjoy being part of a team, but I would prefer to work on a higher level, maybe running a project of my own within a department of my present employer.

Long-term goals include acquiring more education. I presently have earned an Associate degree in Computer Systems; I know that a Bachelor's or Master's degree would help me qualify for an engineering or teaching position.

COMPUTER PROGRAMMER #7

I chose my career as a computer programmer/business systems analyst in answer to my search for a stable, interesting, challenging occupation with a future. I based my decision on exposure to computer programming in high school, almost ten years prior. I am satisfied with my decision.

As a computer programmer/business systems analyst, my job is to analyze business computing requirements and then to deliver the solutions. This involves interacting with business managers and their representatives to determine their computing needs and define/analyze the problems. Then, to meet their needs, I modify existing software to solve problems or design and develop new software. An additional part of my job requires transferring analysis knowledge to my peers and support juniors.

To perform these duties well, it is important to have the following skills and attitudes: tact, professionalism, good written and verbal skills, excellent analytical skills and technical skills to support the computing environment.

I like the work I do primarily because of the opportunity for advancement, the kind of work I do, and the people with whom I work. I have found satisfaction from the variety of my responsibilities, in the delivery of solutions and in the development of solutions. I think that as long as the work environment is one that promotes professional development and technical advancement, this work will remain satisfying.

My future career plans are to remain in this career and to continue to grow technically into a consulting role.

COMPUTER PROGRAMMER #8

An interest in computers and solving problems led me to pursue a degree in computer science. I worked for many years as a field engineer repairing computer mainframes and peripherals before making a job change to computer programmer.

As a computer programmer, my responsibility is to correct problems found in existing software and make required changes to the code defined in approved software change proposals. In order to perform this kind of work, you need typing skills and a knowledge of the programming language and the supporting software packages. In addition to these technical skills, it is important to have good logistic and organizational skills and a capacity for detail work.

I like almost every aspect of my work.

I find job satisfaction in knowing that the software works and is being used.

COMPUTER PROGRAMMER #9

I've been involved in computer programming with a large company for the past 10 years. I enjoy everything about my work except the fact that there seems to be little chance for advancement. I started as a computer operator and moved into programming when the opportunity arose.

Being able to deal with frustration has been valuable to me in my work. The ability to think logically and to work with difficult supervisors are important in this work.

Good interpersonal skills make it easier to interview people to determine their computer needs or problems. Sometimes I have to maintain high production level under pressure. That is difficult but it can be done.

A normal day for me includes prioritizing a task list for the day's work. I interview users about project needs, and then I load and test programs on our computer. I enjoy seeing the completed program perform well, resulting in people being able to do a job easier and faster. My work would be more satisfying if we could reduce the backlog of projects and educate users on how hard making their changes can be.

I worked into this position without having a college degree, having had only courses in computer operations. At first, I was assistant manager of a restaurant, then a truck driver. Later, I became an office clerk, and, after completing some computer training, a computer operator. I've worked up to programmer, but I still have ambitions to move on to the position of Director of the Management of Information Systems department.

COMPUTER PROGRAMMER/ANALYST #1

While working as a bank proof operator, I found I was fascinated by the machines (computers) I was working with. I went to a community college during off hours (days or nights, depending on the job) learning computer languages. One thing led to another, and I finally got a job as an entry level computer programmer at the community college I was attending. The migration to programmer/analyst, and systems analyst, was through normal promotions.

As a computer programmer/analyst, I analyze computer-related problems and design solutions, and I write computer programs. I would describe my work as a daily hassle of unending surprises. The system problems are well known for the most part. Fixing them requires some mean feats of technical "pretzel making"! On a week-to-week basis, my job involves analyzing problems, coming up with creative (sometimes very creative) solutions, coding the programs and testing them, and getting the programs into production as fast as possible so the users can get back on line and do their jobs.

To perform this kind of work well, the important skills and attitudes are patience, ability to listen to others, analytical ability to break down a composite problem into its component parts and cross-reference to other problems of a similar nature, ability to understand machine logic intuitively, computer programming skills, a positive attitude, and then more patience.

In the main, I am satisfied with this kind of work very much.

The only drawback is that I feel there is a lack of opportunity for advancement. This technical world advances so rapidly, it is hard to always keep up. Aside from these frustrations, I like my work and find satisfaction from getting the job done right.

My career aspiration is to become my own boss some day by opening a consulting business.

COMPUTER PROGRAMMER/ANALYST #2

As a computer programmer/analyst of three years, I am involved to a great extent in computer programming, customer support, trouble shooting, and training customers about the uses of the computer system and its software capabilities. I revise computer programs to be more useful for the customers; I write custom programs for our customers and write the manuals that go along with those programs; I trouble shoot problems with customers over the telephone; and I occasionally train new customers in use of the programs.

In addition to a Bachelor of Science degree in Computer Science, which I have, to succeed as a computer programmer/analyst you must be well organized, have an aptitude in math, and possess the ability to be very patient in situations when things don't work out the way you expect.

Although there are not many opportunities for career advancement in my present position, I really like my job; I look at my programs with almost an artistic view. I like my programs to be easy to use and nice to look at; when I accomplish that goal, I'm satisfied. I also get personal satisfaction when I get positive feedback from a customer. I really like this kind of work; I feel fortunate to work with a great group of people and I have a good boss.

While in high school I made the decision to become a computer programmer, which led me to choose to major in Computer Science in college; I was hired by my present company directly from college, so I have not held any other jobs.

While I am uncertain about my future plans, I know that whatever I do, I will be working with computers.

COMPUTER PROGRAMMER/ANALYST #3

I have held jobs in a variety of fields during the course of my career life, some of which I liked and others I disliked. I have earned a Bachelor of Arts in Art and have enjoyed being an art instructor. Other jobs which I liked were as a preschool teacher, monument designer, and assistant store manager. My job as a dental assistant did not appeal to me. Ten years ago when I was unable to get a teaching position, I accidentally got into a retraining program and acquired the skills necessary for computer programming. I have found this to be a career which I like very much.

As a computer programmer/analyst, my job includes the following responsibilities: analyzing solutions to business problems, designing computer systems, coding computer systems, interacting with users and coworkers, and reacting to computer problems.

In order to do computer programming and analysis, you must be logical and organized, have good communication skills, and have good writing and technical skills.

The reason I like this kind of work is that I find job satisfaction from finding successful solutions to business problems and improving existing business procedures.

I do not have plans to leave my current job in the near future, but I have thought that eventually I might make another job change which would combine two of the jobs, computer work and teaching, which I like, and seek employment as a computer teacher to children.

COMPUTER PROGRAMMING MANAGER

I supervise developers of business software. The bulk of the day is usually meetings with staff, clients, vendors and/or management. The remaining time is spent reading or writing correspondence.

My educational background is not in computer science but rather I have a BA in Political Science and an MBA in Management. I do, however, have 17 years of experience in data processing.

The skills and attitudes which I find are important for performing this job well are: analytical skills for identifying and resolving business issues, to be logical, structured, and organized to handle details required to design, code, and test programs, and good communication and interpersonal skills.

I derive satisfaction from my work by successfully implementing systems that meet business needs. I could do without the long hours and deadline stresses.

I fell into this job after college. I worked for the company in the general business office while in college and found the job in the process. I plan to continue with this company and build up additional/increased responsibilities in the department's management.

COMPUTER PROGRAMMING TEACHER

As a computer programming teacher at a vo-tech center, my day begins at 5:15 a.m.. I usually review computer-related material while having coffee or doing exercises. My office hours are from 7:15 until 2:45. Students are with me from 8:30 until 2:00 with a 30 minute lunch. I never take breaks; I am standing most of the day, debugging at the computer or helping students write programs. I also do some lecturing and paperwork after hours.

The following skills and attitudes are important in order to perform well in this teaching profession: a degree in business education or computer education; continued education to update; a love for students; sacrifice of time and personal needs; willingness to perform record-keeping tasks that are not related to teaching.

Aside from my dislike for the paperwork involved in teaching, I like about every other aspect: the people I work with, the opportunity for advancement, the kind of work, and the people and organization I work for. I particularly enjoy the student-teacher relationship. My job satisfaction comes from providing students with training that gives them an opportunity to change or advance their position in life, advancing myself through continual studies and practice, and association with fellow educators.

COMPUTER REPAIRMAN

After earning a Bachelor of Science degree in management, I served in the military before I moved into the field of electronics as a computer repairman. Even though there is little chance for advancement, I enjoy my work for it's never boring.

Each day is different. On any day, I never know what I might work on. In repairing computers, the job is always a challenge. Although I enjoy the work, I would prefer fewer hours be required at night plus shorter work hours overall.

Working with customers who have problems with their computers describes the work I do. I often conduct preventative maintenance work on the systems as well.

My job requires competence in the fields of electronics and mechanics. It is also important to be able to work with distressed customers in all types of circumstances and be able to calm their concerns; therefore, good people skills are essential.

COMPUTER SCIENTIST

I have earned a Bachelor of Science in Computer Science in order to pursue my career as a computer scientist. As such, I manage relational database software. More specifically, I manage the operations of a relational database and help users of the database with problems they may encounter while using it or an associated product. In order to perform this kind of work well, analytical problem solving skills are quite important.

I became interested in computer work through my father who has a similar career. Now after working in this field myself for a while, I have found that I like it very much. If, however, given the chance to change anything about my occupation to make it more satisfying, I would increase the amount of time given to answering users' questions and decrease the amount of time spent on written reports. What I do find satisfying is helping users of the product with problems they encounter.

COMPUTER SERVICE REPRESENTATIVE

As a secretary at a major computer company, I felt undervalued and transferred to the customer service area when the opportunity came to me. This job is challenging and never boring. For the past 4 years each day has been different in that I speak with or meet people from all over the world and am always learning new things.

I work with customers, sales reps, account managers and other groups on issues such as special discounts, software and licensing matters and customer contracts and orders. I also send out letters, mostly on legal matters of taxes, software contracts, etc.

Good communication skills and product knowledge are essential. Typing, word processing/computer skills, and a math aptitude are also important.

I would prefer that things were organized differently so that more work would get done in the same amount of time. If I were in charge I would eliminate those employees who don't perform their job efficiently.

The variety of the work is its main appeal to me. The company I work for is outstanding also.

I am working to obtain a college degree and would like to become an Account Manager or do demonstrations of computer products in the field eventually.

COMPUTER SOFTWARE DEVELOPER

My work as a software developer for six years has entailed writing computer software and instruction manuals, developing new software computer programs, fixing computer software "bugs," providing customer hardware and software support to system users, project planning, and computer engineering.

I completed an Associate in Science degree and previously worked as a grocery manager. In addition to a college degree, my job requires good communication skills, imagination, creativity, organization, confidence, a willingness to help people, and experience in computer programming.

Although there is not much opportunity for advancement within my present position and upper management is at times not very flexible, I do really like my job; I like the people I work with, this kind of work, my boss, and overall the company I work for. I find that my job gives me a good sense of accomplishment.

I plan to continue in evening college courses and further my studies; I have always been interested in Aeronautical Engineering and I may apply my computer skills in a position in that field. In any event, I plan to always work with computers and people over the span of my career.

COMPUTER SOFTWARE ENGINEER

My job as a software engineer is such that I always have multiple projects in progress; basically I fix problems in software and design new computer software programs. If there is a problem of a piece of software malfunctioning, then I have to find a solution in a very timely manner. Small software problems arise on a daily basis and these can get to be very time-consuming; such problems can delay the completion of some of my long-term projects that are scheduled to take several months of work.

In addition to a Bachelor's degree in Computer Science, the work of a software engineer requires curiosity, persistence, patience, and the ability to break large problems into smaller, more manageable pieces.

In the seven years I have been working as a software engineer, I have found that my greatest satisfactions are derived from balancing multiple projects at one time, having competent co-workers to share technical problems with, management recognition for a job well done, the knowledge that I am a skilled problem solver, and possessing the ability to design and build new projects. There is nothing that I dislike about my job; I work with some really great engineers, there are many opportunities for advancement within my corporate organization, I have a boss that I like, and I believe in the company I work for.

Since any previous positions I have held were in unrelated fields, I know that I have finally made a career choice that is right for me.

As I am an individual who enjoys learning, I plan to widen my area of knowledge in the field of software engineering, specifically, and in the field of computers, in general.

COMPUTER SOFTWARE SUPPORT

As a computer software support person, I help people learn to use the software they buy and don't know how to operate. In that sense, I'm a trainer as well. After I leave a customer's office, I'm on the phone a lot with them, answering questions about the individual problems with the software.

I like my support work very much. The teaching is very rewarding to me; I like my customers and the people I work for and with. It would be even better if there were more access to software packages.

To do this work, you need strong communication skills since in teaching and helping people with their computer problems it is crucial to be a good "explainer." You need a lot of patience as well. Finally, a positive attitude is essential. I graduated from high school, but my future plans are to continue my schooling to keep up with the changing technology.

COMPUTER SPECIALIST

On a daily and/or weekly basis I collect and analyze statistics, check the status of our communication network, detect problems, look for solutions, and indicate implementation.

A systems engineer needs to be knowledgeable about computer communications hardware and software and computer protocols. A good attitude and control when interacting with people is an important attribute for the job.

The job is satisfying to me because I solve problems and am always learning. However, it would be even more satisfying if it were less routine and a little more challenge to creativity.

I started as an Industrial Engineer and later became an Electronics Engineer. Finally I did programming and have loved my work since then.

I plan to continue working in this career until I am old enough to retire at an advanced age.

COMPUTER SUPPORT SPECIALIST

My work background is diverse including cook, musician, disc jockey, teacher and writer. I was then accidentally led into computer work after I found that I liked computers. I had also come to the realization that I would starve in the music field. My work in the computer field has included positions as programmer, analyst, data processing manager and competitive consultant.

Now as a data communications support specialist, my job is to interconnect three types of networks. I travel to customer sites, install hardware and software, and teach the customers about their new product. While in the office, I answer telephone inquires concerning support of these products.

In this type of work, I have found it necessary to be able to have people moan and complain to me without having it affect me. As well as having this ability, software, hardware and data communications skills are essential. In addition, you must know many network topologies.

I would like to be able to force customers to learn about their purchases. Aside from the minor frustrations I have because of customer's attitudes, I like the kind of work I do and most of the people I work with. There is real job satisfaction for me in getting customer's systems up and running for the first time. I plan to continue with my work in the computer field with aspirations of becoming a consultant.

COMPUTER SYSTEMS ANALYST #1

As a computer systems analyst, I conduct interviews with users of computer systems, translate user requirements into system inputs and outputs, design screen and report layouts, and put requirements into written report format.

I have two college degrees, a Bachelor of Science in Economics and a Master of Business Administration in Systems Analysis; I also have seven years of experience. In addition to a good educational background, one also needs patience and understanding with all levels of employees in business, written communication skills, including the ability to describe business processes in written form, and programming or technical experience.

I specialize in translating business requirements into a final computer system and I enjoy the fact that I have an excellent reputation in my specialty.

I like my co-workers, the users that I interface with on a regular basis, and this kind of work; I believe there is no limit to opportunities for advancement in the computer field. Easier and faster programming techniques and less written documentation requirements would be a plus.

I previously worked as a word processor consultant, an office manager, and in customer service; all helped me to develop the essential people skills and computer skills needed in my present position.

I plan to work at becoming a System Development Manager for an international company in the future.

COMPUTER SYSTEMS ANALYST #2

I have been in my present work as a computer systems analyst for eight years. My work includes designing, specifying, and creating computer programs for a retail sales company. Typically, I test software systems, investigate users' requirements, and problem solve.

I like my work, but, as a college graduate with a B.S. degree in mathematics, I dislike the lack of advancement opportunity here. Yet, even if I could begin again, I'd choose this occupation.

Some of the satisfactions I've found in my work are giving other managers the tools and information which help them with their work, and I enjoy solving particularly difficult problems. I also enjoy designing computer systems which are complex and reliable. It would be helpful to me if others were aware of what a computer can and cannot do.

Other jobs I've had are retail salesman at a small airport (selling fuel, oil, services, and aircraft rental) and fire fighter for the forestry service. I'm 29 years of age, and my future plans are to own my own business in the computer software field.

The following abilities have been helpful in my work: problem- solving skills, logical thought processes, good communication skills with non-technical people, attention to detail, and ability to keep long-range goals in sight while working on small details.

COMPUTER SYSTEMS CONSULTANT

After graduating with a Bachelor of Science degree in business administration 5 years ago, I tried selling as a career. I didn't like prospecting for clients or closing the sale, but I was good with people and I like explaining new products. My job now as systems consultant for a payroll service is perfect for me.

My work schedule varies from day to day. I meet with prospective clients to analyze their payroll systems to determine their needs. After presenting the results of the analysis, I demonstrate our computer payroll software. I also help organize client seminars where I demonstrate our product.

Self-confidence is a must in this work. You also need a positive attitude at all times. Knowledge of the product is, of course, a requirement. You need to be able to speak in front of large groups in presenting to an audience in our seminars.

I like just about everything about my work, the people I work for, and the company. Being considered "the expert" by a client is great. It is also very satisfying to wind up a complicated deal. Being involved with a complex sale is exciting to me.

I'd like, though, to be more than a support person. Having more control and being busier would please me as well. One day I'd like to develop and implement computer-generated 401k financial plans (for retirement purposes) to companies throughout the country. This would not include sales, but it would have the direct contact with human resources departments and with the employees that I especially enjoy.

COMPUTER SYSTEMS MANAGER #1

As a computer systems manager, I am the first line manager of a team of computer programmers who generate and maintain a payroll processing software application for a bank offering business services. I organize and supervise a staff of twelve programmers: assign tasks, clarify expectations, assist the programmers to reach their intended goals, or make decisions with regard to progress and project expectations. Supervising my staff involves tracking and reporting the progress of my staff with assigned tasks and related items, such as attendance, training, salary administration, and career counseling. I also meet with business partners to identify needs and determine solutions.

Work of this kind requires a good education. I completed a Bachelor of Arts degree as well as a Master of Arts degree. It also requires good communication skills--verbal, listening, and written; problem solving skills; the ability to make decisions; organization; an openness to sincerely consider the opinions of others; genuine concern for the welfare of one's staff; flexibility; and dedication.

I enjoy my job and this kind of work, the staff with which I currently work and the people I deal with on a daily basis as well as opportunities that exist for advancement both on business and personal levels.

I have been engaged in this type of work for the last nine years; prior to working as a manager, I was employed as a junior high and high school teacher.

I plan to continue working in my present job for some time on projects in progress that will require several years to complete. I may return to the classroom to learn more about computers; it is a rapidly growing and fascinating field.

COMPUTER SYSTEMS MANAGER #2

As a Computer Systems Manager, I oversee and manage the employees of my computer laboratory, perform troubleshooting and problem solving in the laboratory and develop new procedures for system users. I also manage the academic computer system with my experience and technical knowledge of the operation and enhancement of computer systems.

This position can be frustrating at times as you have to communicate technical information accurately to those not technically learned; this requires the ability to work well with others and superior communication skills. Of course, you must be highly skilled in use of the computer.

After two years with this company, I do not see much opportunity for advancement, but I do like the people I work with. I have a sense of pride when the computer systems run well and when things run smoothly. I do not believe that this position offers much technical challenge; it involves more employee management.

With my Bachelor's of Science degree, I believe my educational background would be better utilized in computer research, especially in the area of artificial intelligence; that is where my future lies.

COMPUTER SYSTEMS MANAGER #3

Before becoming a computer-aided design (CAD) systems manager, I was a computer network administrator where I programmed for engineering purposes. Now I get even more satisfaction from using the computer to make drawings and designs that engineers used to have to do by hand.

My first degree was an Associate's Degree in computer-integrated manufacturing. Then, I earned a Bachelor of Science in computer systems. Someday I plan to be vice president of engineering at this company.

My coworkers, the company, and the designing work I do all give me a lot of job satisfaction. The only thing I'd change is to reduce the high level of stress. There's a lot of pressure to make absolutely certain a computer network functions correctly.

In my work, I search for new technologies in computer-aided design. I also maintain already existing computer networks. My job is to develop ways to blend product design and the manufacturing of the product.

My job requires expertise with the computer as well as strong communication skills. Knowledge of mechanical design along with engineering skills are also needed.

COMPUTER TECHNICIAN #1

I find satisfaction from my work as a computer technician because it allows me to accomplish what others say cannot be done. It is my job to set up, configure and repair all types of computers and associated devices. I am also responsible for shipping of computer equipment and supporting software development.

In order to perform this kind of work well, you should have a good disposition with people. Problem solving ability is also necessary for handling this job well. Taking the initiative with duties will also help you succeed.

Prior to this job, I worked as an electrician and maintenance mechanic. I plan to stay in the technical field that I am now in because I like this kind of work and aspire to become a systems manager of a large corporation.

COMPUTER TECHNICIAN #2

My love of mathematics and desire for a challenge were the reasons I chose this field. I was hired as a contractor by a large and well known computer company doing quality control work. This exposure to the company product, in addition to my previous electronics training, enabled me to obtain an electro-mechanical test technician position within the same company. I later progressed to an electro-mechanical technician I, to an electro-mechanical technician II, to my current position as an electrical engineering technician III.

In this position, I stage computer systems and peripherals to perform development testing and analysis. My typical daily activities include interfacing with engineers to design, specify, install, analyze, and develop computer system solutions, software and hardware components. This includes doing experimentation and data gathering to generate test reports.

In order to perform this kind of work well, the following factors are important: communication--the ability to work with others (team work); writing skills (the ability to write memos and test reports); excellent logic/code/digital debug skills; the ability to work independently and with minimal directions; typing skills (computers are a way of life now); and not being afraid to try to learn something new.

I like most aspects of my work but I would be more satisfied if the stress level could be reduced. The tight schedule to complete a project is due, in a large part, to the intense competition between companies to produce "new and faster" products. What I do find satisfying is being able to work with state-of-the-art hardware and software components. I like working with others to develop solutions to help customers manage their companies more efficiently. It is rewarding being a part of a project that is a total success. My plans for the future are threefold: to obtain my degree in engineering science (should have done this sooner); to progress to the level of senior hardware or software engineer; and to take part in many training programs that are specific to the types of products with which I work.

COMPUTER TRAINING SPECIALIST

A typical day includes scheduling and preparing equipment/systems for four-hour student lab sessions. During the labs, I explain how to operate systems and answer questions. Additional duties include repairing the equipment, ordering parts, consulting vendors, evaluating students and scheduling work for subordinates.

Technical and interpersonal skills are necessary for my job. In order to relate to my students I constantly remind myself what it was like to be an entry level employee with limited experience.

The job is satisfying when I am recognized for my technical skills. Perception of student weaknesses, working with students to improve and overcome their limited experience and emotional trauma when entering the labor force also cause me to feel good about doing this job.

Increasing manpower and funding to complete and improve training and educational systems would be desirable changes in this occupation. Some engineers seem to expect a computer to do everything for them, and I wish they were not so naive. However, I like this job very much and I expect to continue in this work until I retire a decade or so from now.

COMPUTER USER SUPPORT TRAINER

I found that being a secretary is a good way to "look around" at different jobs in an organization if you're unsure what you want to do. I "evolved" into user support. About 10 years ago, I took my first computer course (word processing) and found I "got along" with the computer. I was tired of secretarial work so I took all the courses I could find (most on my own time and money). I started doing user support in my spare time and, when a position was created, I was hired full-time. Since I already understood the office operation, it was not hard to learn the computer related operations.

My general responsibilities as a computer user support is in training and minor repairs. My typical activities in order to carry out these functions are: doing some routine reports/administrative work; researching/reading up on new products or new and better ways to do things; making recommendations on buying new hardware/software or redistribution of what we have; doing training sessions; handling a lot of telephone work; diagnosing problems and giving advice/instruction. Then there are all the calls and visits from people demanding that I immediately react to their problem.

The ability to make good use of available time is important, and the ability to communicate clearly is essential. I also consider the ability to read and understand technical manuals, and then to pass on this information in simpler terms, is a requirement for this kind of work. Patience is essential; if you try to teach someone and lose patience, they often will quit trying.

What I dislike about my job is that there is no money to buy needed equipment. (I work for the Federal Government). I would also be more satisfied if fellow employees were to accept computers for the amazing helpers that they are - but recognize that they're not a panacea. I especially like training/demonstrating new equipment and software. I find satisfaction in seeing someone master a new technique--learning new things myself. I like the feeling that I contribute to making the office's work smoother and easier. It also helps, too, that the people I work with appreciate my help and don't hesitate to say so.

CONCERT MUSICIAN, PIPE ORGAN

I had recognized keyboard abilities at an early age and always wanted to be a concert organist. In order to pursue this as a career, I earned a Master of Arts in Music degree.

As a concert organist/choral director, I perform concerts on pipe organs and direct church choirs and music ensembles. Part of my work is coordinating 15 music groups at the church, private teaching, practicing, and planning. As a concert musician, I would, of course, prefer to have the time for more practice and performances, rather than spending so much time with administration work. However, it just isn't economically feasible for me to give up the lessons and choir and ensemble directing.

To pursue my kind of career in music, it is essential to have keyboard ability. Experience in knowing "what will please" the congregation is also necessary. You must be able to take a lot of unexpected, often harsh criticism.

I like the work I do because of the people and organizations I work for, and the people with whom I work. I am finding satisfaction from my career because the response from the public, in general, is very good. I get a lot of positive support, and programs continue to grow. My career goal is to survive and be "relevant" in my old age.

CONCRETE CONTRACTOR

My typical day starts at 7:00 A.M. when I go out to see the jobs and the men. I make sure they are doing the right job and help make decisions if they have problems. A client always likes to see the boss on the job.

Be honest with a client. It never pays to lie. Be patient with people. The bottom line is you are dealing with their money.

I find job satisfaction from doing the job right, being the best around, and getting paid for it.

This occupation would be more satisfying if people who do not bring anything good to the construction industry could be eliminated. Free loaders should get out! Unions should be supervised by the federal government.

CONSTRUCTION ENGINEER

I studied construction methods in a technical high school and have worked my way up to construction engineer over the years I have been in the industry.

As the construction engineer on the job site, I first did the layout on the ground relevant to control points to be followed by construction workers for the project. As they work, I supervise the accuracy and quality of their work. I also regulate and guide their adherence to the project's time schedule.

To perform well as a construction engineer, it is important to have good math skills, to know how to use surveying instruments, have knowledge of construction principles and characteristics of materials, have patience, and the ability to work with different personalities.

If I could initiate any changes in this occupation, it would be to find ways of communicating easier with superiors. I think that there needs to be a better forum for exchange of ideas and constructive criticism from the field workers.

I like almost every aspect of my work - the kind of work, the people and organization I work for, the people I work with, and the opportunities for advancement. I feel a sense of accomplishment when the project is finished on time and under budget.

CONSTRUCTION LABORER

A high school graduate, I'm a construction worker. I've been a quality control inspector as well as a laborer in the construction field. My work involves rigging and construction of steel structures and equipment on job sites. I also do some of the grinding, drilling, sanding, and cleaning of all sorts of mechanical parts: motors, generators, gears, and shafts.

I got into this job through a friend while working as a mechanic's helper in home construction. Previously, I worked as a dishwasher and a gas attendant.

To be a construction worker, you must be physically capable, but you don't have to be a "Hulk Hogan." Good math skills are also helpful. You must be alcohol and drug free to be alert and aware of all activity on the job site at all times. Dependability along with the willingness to work overtime are important. The ability to help others and work well with other people is required. Also, a good attitude "goes a long way." You must be conscious of safety as well.

I enjoy almost everything about my work because, overall, it is rewarding to know I help build things that are useful and functional. I could do more and earn more if I had training in other various fields, such as welding, electrical work, or plumbing. My job would be more satisfying if everybody had a positive, caring attitude about their work.

My occupational goals are to continue in my present field, furthering my career as an assistant to a millwright group. I want to become a certified millwright, a worker who installs or repairs the machinery in a mill. Perhaps I'll pick up some skills in other related jobs as well.

CONSTRUCTION MANAGEMENT CONSULTANT

I work as a management consultant specializing in the construction industry. I offer advice to construction contractors who have problems and businesses that deal with engineering or construction contractors. In the three years I have worked as a consultant, I found the essential qualifications for success are: a thorough knowledge of the construction industry; the ability to identify problems, the ability to develop solutions to these problems, and the skills to persuade my clients to accept the solutions I develop. You also need the ability to work with a wide variety of people with a great diversity of temperaments and personalities.

Prior to employment as a consultant, I held various positions in the construction industry. During this time I earned a Bachelor of Science degree in Architectural Engineering and a Master's degree in Business Administration. I was drawn to this line of work in an attempt to follow in my father's footsteps--I never considered any other type of work. I have no regrets about my choice of career fields; my present work is extremely satisfying--I enjoy developing successful resolutions to construction problems or helping to avoid problems in the first place.

My work is interesting; construction is a field in which you do not get stuck in a career rut--there is no such thing as a typical day.

I intend to work in my chosen field for as long as possible; my career goal is to someday assist a client to successfully resolve a multi-million dollar construction problem.

CONSTRUCTION MANAGER/VICE PRESIDENT

I took a part-time job with a civil engineering company while I was going through a career change. I had been a high school teacher and was trying to get into the medical field. The part-time job turned into an exciting full-time career.

As the vice president of a construction management company, my goal is to build buildings on time and on budget. More specifically, my work activities include organizing the construction projects, putting them out to bid, selecting bidders, writing contracts, scheduling projects, monitoring construction, resolving problems, maintaining financial records, pursuing other work, and consulting.

Organizational skills are very important in construction management. Another key ability is problem solving with a rational mind. Persuading people to work with you to get the job done properly is also essential.

I am very satisfied with my career change, and except for clients who don't pay in full, I like all aspects of my work. I like the organization I work for, the people I work with, and the good earning potential. Job satisfaction for me is seeing a project come to fruition. I love the challenge of getting it done on time and budget.

I presently am an associate with a small firm. I have a five year plan with the owner to buy the company so he can retire. When I am the majority owner, I want to enlarge it and get into bigger construction projects.

CONSTRUCTION PROJECT ENGINEER

The work of a project engineer in the field of construction is varied and interesting; for the past three years, my duties have included supervising the overall construction project from planning, through design to the actual construction of the structure. I organize and check on my staff's work assignments; respond to mail correspondence and answer phone calls; perform on-site inspection of construction work; make design and construction changes involving calculations, new specifications, and cost estimates; and organize and plan future work projects.

In addition to a Bachelor of Science degree in Engineering, my job requires good communication skills, a strong knowledge of engineering principles, and a talent for decision making.

Among the many benefits of working as a professional in my position: the opportunity to be in charge, work outdoors, and see progress taking place before my eyes, as I am involved in all phases of the construction and design processes. I particularly like the people I work with and this kind of work, although I would like it more if I had more authority and less paperwork.

I plan to continue working in this field and perhaps move up into upper management or a consultant's role in this same field.

CONSTRUCTION PROJECT MANAGER #1

My summer employment in construction projects while in college has led me into my career as construction project manager. I have now been employed in this capacity for 10 years, after graduating with a Bachelor of Arts in Economics.

As a construction project manager, I manage people and resources to build homes and streets. I meet with other department personnel and customers to find out what needs to be produced and what resources are available to construct the project. It is then my responsibility to work up a schedule and manage the project so the desired results are achieved.

In order to perform this kind of work well, it is important to have organizational skills, confidence, mental toughness, drive, aggressiveness, intelligence, and persistence. When this is done, you will be able to have the satisfaction in accomplishing "concrete" results!

I like the kind of work I do, the organization and people I work for, the people I work with, and the opportunity I have for advancement in this career. It is my career goal to advance my position and eventually to be in charge of a construction company. It is indeed satisfying work for me in seeing the completed product of my efforts being utilized by a family or the public.

CONSTRUCTION PROJECT MANAGER #2

I was born into a family with a history of work in the construction industry, and I am gladly following in their shoes. . My father and grandfather are both general contractors. I have held various jobs in the construction field from laborer through project manager.

As the project manager, I am the owner's representative charged with overseeing the construction of company-owned facilities. My regular work activities include answering phone questions, processing pay requests, resolving problems, and traveling to the job site to inspect the projects in progress.

To perform this kind of work well, you must have a good working knowledge of building construction and an assertive/positive attitude.

I like almost every aspect of my job as project manager.

It is satisfying to see a physical item, the planning for which I have been a part, constructed at the end of a project. I like the fact that there is a finite time frame for a project, and then I can go on to another. I also enjoy the certain amount of power and the responsibility of this work. In fact, I would like to be able to take more responsibility. I plan to advance through the ranks of the company with which I am currently employed to become part of middle and upper level management.

CONSULTANT

As a consultant who offers advisory services in increasing excellence and applied statistics, I help organizations improve the performance of their operations and the quality of their products or services. Solving difficult problems as well as helping others improve gives me great joy.

Marketing my services takes up a great deal of my time. I also develop the training materials I use in my seminars. In general, I consult with managers or engineers, depending on the organization, on their group's organizational performance or the quality of their products or their services. Then, after analyzing the company's procedures and their need, I train their people in statistical or quality management and improvement.

I enjoy my consulting work, which I've been doing for 19 years. If there were less travel involved and not so much need for marketing of my services, I'd be happier. My plans are to remain in consulting and to continue to develop my practice.

To be a successful training consultant, you have to have strong teaching skills. You must be able to write clearly and concisely. Analytical skills, along with being able to sell your services, are very important. Being able to advise, rather than manage, people is also necessary. You must want to help others. Finally, a good education is required; I have a Bachelors and a Masters degree in physics and a Masters in Business Administration (MBA).

CONSULTANT, BUSINESS

I became a consultant by a series of events not of my own creation or planning. Prior to this work, I earned my Masters in Business Administration and worked as an intelligence officer for more than 20 years.

As an consultant, I extend assistance to the C.E.O.'s (chief executive officers) of several corporations. There is never a dull moment in this work, no typical day. My schedule is always different because the situations are always changing depending on my current clients and the problems I am working out for them.

To perform well as a consultant, it is important to have common sense, positive thinking, and general and current knowledge of the world and political situations.

Despite the major drawback to this career, the fact that it is not very secure, I have liked doing this kind of work and have managed to make a good living at it for the past 10 years. I find satisfaction in the respect I receive from my clients.

CONSULTANT, BUSINESS START-UPS

I was a stockbroker with a degree in finance before becoming a business consultant. I now spend time with clients, listening, analyzing the client's situation, and recommending action, general or specific. The rest of my time is spent creating opportunities and following through. I identify companies or individuals who are doing similar things, ask them about strategy, and propose alliances or mergers. In my work, I determine the opportunities and create a written plan. I implement the plan while adjusting it to market conditions.

Primarily, I enjoy the challenge, the opportunities for me, and the recognition I receive. I find personal fulfillment in making unique contributions to business success. I value the recognition, the appreciation, and the monetary rewards. It is great when creativity turns into tangible progress.

While a stockbroker between the ages of 23-30, I most admired those who owned their own businesses. So I bought a business and resigned the same year from brokerage to run the business full time. After making it successful, I sold it. Following the sale of my second business, I became a consultant.

I'd like more time for personal things: my wife, my family, travel, visiting museums. I want to do some charity work and help where I am needed. I want to continue to build my 3 year old startup business in online information for the health care industry. Then I'd like to semi-retire at age 55.

Fundamental to success in this work is knowing the business, the marketplace, and the effect of one on the other. Knowledge of finance, accounting, marketing and psychology are essential. Being innately creative is an asset. Computer skills and familiarity with database manipulation are a must.

CONSULTANT, CHEMICAL BUSINESS

As an industrial consultant, I am involved with businesses dealing with chemicals. I provide advisory services to groups striving to improve their processes. Selling my services to prospective clients is also part of my work.

I got into this work after retiring from a position actively managing chemical operations. In the past 3 years in my current position, I've found I enjoy the people I work with, my clients, and consulting itself. It is rewarding to see my clients improve their operations with my help. It would be even better if I had more business.

An effective consultant needs solid technical knowledge. You have to have good selling skills as well. Strong teaching skills are essential to this work and adequate training and education is important. My degree is a Bachelor of Science in chemistry.

CONSULTANT, COMPUTER OPERATIONS

My career path has changed from drafting to computers because drafting was moved to CAD systems. Prior to my current position as UNIX Operating System Consultant (Specialist), I worked in drafting, mechanical design, P.C. layout, and software programming. I found I had good common sense when it came to computers. I taught myself how to program and then wrote programs to extract information from hardware designs (CAD) and drawings (parts list, wire list, etc.). From there I moved into software programming.

As an operating system consultant, I answer questions which do not have simple answers, questions which sometimes take much research. More specifically, I help line employees who call with problems they cannot solve, research and try solutions, and then return the call with a solution. My job also involves researching new products, both hardware and software, giving reports on new products, purchasing hardware and software, and reading trade magazines.

In order to perform well in this kind of work, it is important to have math skills, be able to solve puzzles, work with people, have an open mind, and have patience. I also think you must be a pioneer exploring new ideas.

I have liked almost every aspect of my occupation which I have been now doing for 18 years, particularly because I am on the leading edge of technology. My only major frustration is that I am too busy and under much stress which leads to inefficiency. I could use more people to help with the work load. I now continue in this field, however, because I find satisfaction in discovering solutions to the problems and from learning new hardware and software.

I am still keeping my mind open to new career opportunities because I know there is a whole world of possibilities. Sometimes I feel like I haven't yet decided what I want to be when I grow up.

CONSULTANT, FAMILY PLANNING

I am now an international management consultant doing comprehensive organizational and management reviews in family planning associations in third world countries. My job is to carry out overall family planning program evaluations in these countries which include development and management analysis and in depth discussions with the boards and management. This obviously means extensive international travel is involved in carrying out the responsibilities of this position.

The key to success in this career is outstanding communication skills and a flair for searching. Years of executive experience and experience in international business negotiations have been a valuable asset to me.

I earned my master's in business administration and held the position of chief executive officer of third world country subsidiaries of a Swiss multi-national chemical/pharmaceutical corporation prior to accepting this position. I chose this because I want to be directly connected with development efforts of the third world now and even into my retirement.

I am very satisfied with my choice of careers and receive satisfaction from being actively involved in developing projects. If I could initiate any changes in this field, it would be to give more hands-on support to the associations to implement a more efficient and result-oriented management system. After 12 years in this job and many more in my previous CEO position, both of which involved international travel, I am somewhat weary of traveling. However, I am personally committed to my involvement in these projects and do not plan any changes in my career in the future.

CONSULTANT, O.S.H.A.

For 19 years, I've worked as an occupational safety and health consultant for a major corporation. A registered nurse, I provide expertise on safety and health issues. In my work, I analyze principles from the Occupational Safety and Health Act (OSHA) and the Canadian Safety and Health Standards. I answer employee questions as well as develop corporate operating guidelines and compliance directives. Conducting inspections, identifying issues, developing recommended action plans, and writing reports on findings occupy a great deal of my time. Doing administrative activities and statistical reports complete a description of my work.

I don't feel there is much opportunity for advancement; I'd like there to be a promotional ladder that would provide career opportunities without having to leave the field. But, I do like my co-workers, the work I do, the managers, and the corporation. It is rewarding to feel that what I do contributes to the safety and well-being of all employees. This is evidenced by a decrease in work-related injuries and illnesses. There's a pride in being viewed as a technical expert.

I've applied my nursing skills as a public health nurse and within a hospital environment before moving into the corporate world. I would like to remain in my field and have greater responsibilities for managing safety and health at the corporate level.

For my job, you need a medical degree, technical understanding of the processes and the equipment as well as the applicable regulations. Both verbal and written communication skills are very important. You also need organizational skills to be part of a self-directed team.

CONSUMER ADVOCATE

I was a secretary with a bachelor's degree in sociology looking for advancement. An opening came up for a consumer advocate, and I took it. As a consumer advocate, I work as a mediator between a utility customer and the utility company for better pay arrangements. When I walk into my office on Monday, 5-6 phone lines are usually ringing. I answer the phone, screen the calls, and go with the complaint. People yell, cry, and curse at you, trying to get you to relieve a problem they have with their utility company. Turn on/turn off.

In order to handle this kind of work, I consider the knowledge gained through earning my degree in sociology to be very important. It is also necessary to be able to get along with people who are emotionally upset. A caring attitude, and a need to seek answers to questions is another job requirement.

If I could change something based on my occupational experience, I would change the rules that dictate regulations of the utility company and how they treat their customers. It is because of my feelings on this issue that I am finding satisfaction from my job because it offers me the opportunity of being proficient with the rules and regulations, in order to help the citizens of my state with their utility service.

Eventually, as I get burned out from this kind of work, I would like to get a Masters in Business Administration, and use this knowledge to run my own retail business.

CONTINUING EDUCATION COORDINATOR

I started my career as a kindergarten teacher but, while also working as an adult education instructor part time, I found out I enjoyed working with adults more. So, I took the job opportunity as continuing education coordinator when it became available. A typical day might include any of the following; interview/hire/train new instructors, supervision of adult continuing ed classes, ordering supplies/materials, budget planning/forecast, and meet with area agencies/businesses/community leaders to discuss/plan adult continuing education needs.

The skills and attitudes which are important to perform this job well are; knowledge of community needs/ resources, ability to forecast/plan (foresight), a positive attitude, and desire to "make a difference" in the lives of others.

When I made the career change from elementary to adult education, I returned to school to add to my bachelor of science degree in education, and I eventually earned a master's degree in adult education.

What I find somewhat unsatisfactory in my occupation is the lack of stimulating resources. Other than that I am very satisfied with my work. Seeing positive results from my work and happy "customers" (students) is rewarding.

CONTRACTOR, DEPARTMENT OF ENERGY

My years of experience in medical technology and as a safety officer, plus my education, have been major factors in securing this job as a contractor for the Department of Energy, employed by a privately-owned laboratory. I am very satisfied with this work for many reasons. I like the people and organization for which I work, the opportunity for advancement, and the kind of work I do. I enjoy the opportunity for domestic travel involved and the opportunity for "making things work."

Prior to this job, I was a diagnostic medical bacteriologist for a state health department, a medical technologist for a hospital, and I have worked in laboratories and private clinics/labs. I have a Bachelor of Arts in Bacteriology and a degree in medical technology.

As a Dept. of Energy contractor, I manage technical tasks done by the contract lab. I write policy and review and edit technical writing. I am the coordinator/liaison for technical tasks performed by the laboratory for the Environmental, Safety and Health Office of the U.S. Dept. of Energy.

To perform well at my job, it is important to have a medical background which you need to be able to apply to occupational safety and industrial hygiene.

The frustrating part of my job is working with employees who have a lack of motivation. Also, I would like to have less bureaucracy involved in my work. Then I would feel I could make things happen more expeditiously. Aside from these frustrations, I like my job very much and get satisfaction in working toward a safe and healthy working environment.

CONTROLLER

As a controller for ten years, I am responsible for all accounting and finance in the company. My work day starts at 6:30 a.m., usually by sorting my mail and going through and returning my calls from the previous business day, reviewing production reports from the day before, and signing materials purchase orders. I meet with my employees to check on their progress and update them on current issues. In the early afternoon, I usually meet with sales and marketing groups to keep myself current with new products and promotions. Later, I catch up on my written communications to vendors and customers. I enjoy my job, especially when we have accomplished a profitable month, when I see a new product sell, or the success of a new promotion.

Combined with a Master's degree in Business Administration, negotiation skills, people skills, and analytical skills are essential to success as a controller of a large company; you must also be disciplined to sit down and prepare the enormous amount of paperwork involved.

Prior to employment as a controller, I held positions as accounting manager, financial analyst, teacher, and sports official.

Future aspirations include teaching college full time in the day division at a four-year institution.

CONTROLLER (CPA)

At my company, the responsibility of a Controller is basically to oversee the Accounting Department and ensure its smooth operation. I review reports from regional offices, determine the work load for my subordinates as well as reviewing this same work upon completion, and determine the cash needs for our department.

The job of a controller requires a minimum education of a Bachelor's degree and the usage of theoretical accounting skills to gain practical accounting experience.

I have thirty-five years of experience as a Certified Public Accountant and a Bachelor of Science degree in Business Administration with a concentration in Accounting.

I really like my work and I am very glad I chose this as my career field. As a controller, I really enjoy being in charge of all financial concerns of my company and I know that I am good at it - I derive great satisfaction from doing a good job. I have no regrets about my career choice.

I believe that the credentials of a Certified Public Accountant will open doors in any business; you have the choice of a career in a corporate environment, as an independent businessperson in charge of her/his own company, or a combination of both worlds--as I chose.

I am a very active person and though I am nearing the age of retirement, I envision continuing in this profession, perhaps volunteering to help out those with businesses just starting out. I enjoy sharing my wealth of knowledge with those who may benefit from my work experiences.

CONTROLLER, COMPUTER COMPANY

I consider it pure coincidence that I am in my present occupation. On several occasions during the past 13 years people have recognized my general ability to accomplish things quickly and accurately. (I work hard and this is visible to lots of people.) Upon recognizing this ability, mangers have offered me career opportunities that have led me through various finance jobs to the one I have today. My educational background includes a Masters in Business Administration.

As controller for a computer company, my responsibilities include budgeting, forecasting, planning, analysis, business controls reporting, and influencing business decisions. Much of my work day is spent in meetings with middle to senior management to review and discuss various investment opportunities. Other meeting topics include: budgets, forecasts, resource requirements and strategies to manage the operation/business. I spend 25% of my time reading and responding to mail. I meet with my subordinates to discuss their responsibilities and offer guidance where appropriate.

I consider the following skills and attitudes important in order to perform this kind of work well: analytical skills; influencing skills; a very open attitude to other viewpoints; negotiating skills; and the ability to articulate the same vision to different audiences. You need to be able to identify cost savings opportunities and intuitively size the opportunity before bringing it to management's attention.

I have one basic suggestion when asked what I would do to change my occupation and that is to eliminate those fellow workers who have negative attitudes, and/or are very adverse to change. My favorite saying is, "Lead, follow, or get out of the way!"

I particularly like the entrepreneurial spirit of my kind of work. No one tells me how to do my job. They give me very high-level general directions and goals and then expect me to deliver an end result. Also in my job there are more opportunities to add value than I will ever be able to take advantage of. I would like to continue in Finance, increasing the span of control over larger and more diverse business groups.

COOK

I cook meals for customers in a small restaurant. My day starts very early with preparation several hours before the restaurant opens.

After graduating from high school, I enrolled in some culinary courses at a food service school. I always enjoyed cooking and I like meeting people. I have worked as a cook for six years now.

To succeed as a cook you must be preparing food for 7-8 hours daily, which includes being on your feet all day; you must enjoy cooking, have good people skills even with those customers that are disrespectful, and maintain a professional attitude.

I enjoy working with the general public and I also find that my job has a low stress level associated with it which is a plus.

I have worked at other positions where I also dealt with the public (carpenter, department store clerk), but I like this job the best.

I plan to open up my own restaurant in the near future, but as the owner I will still do most of the food preparation.

COORDINATOR, PUBLIC RADIO

I work as a coordinator for a public radio station. It is my responsibility to ensure that all work shifts are covered, which means that I need to anticipate the possibilities of volunteers being unable to attend assigned shifts, and I have to be constantly prepared to find replacements, often times without much notice. I am also responsible for recruiting volunteers from the community, training these volunteers, keeping the training manual current, and evaluating the volunteers to be sure they are working out in a way that fills our needs. I also prepare the station's newsletter, conduct a staff meeting once a week, and handle some of the on-the-air announcements.

I completed college studies with a Bachelor of Arts degree in communications. My job requires flexibility, creativity, the willingness to learn from others, self-motivation, the ability to work with minimal supervision, and certain persuasive skills to get and keep the shifts filled.

I enjoy working with the volunteers and this kind of work in general. I enjoy working for a public radio station since it is something I really believe in. The creativity involved in designing the training sessions, the opportunity to make my own decisions, and having the opportunity to get involved in on-air announcing are pluses in this work.

After working with a college radio station for several years, my present position seemed a logical and enjoyable next step on my career ladder.

I plan to continue my work in public radio at a more in-depth level, in the area of development. I believe that will help me achieve my long-term goal of becoming station manager. Perhaps after that, I will move on to public television.

COORDINATOR, TELEMARKETING

For some time now, I've been working as a telemarketing coordinator, organizing and overseeing on-going and future telephone marketing programs. I prepare the paper work which provides the product information for our telephone people to use when they contact the public.

In my work, I interact with marketing personnel in the company and with outside telephone shops to coordinate our selling programs. Compiling and analyzing financial reports on the results of our marketing programs is part of my job. I'm involved with a great deal of problem solving and with researching.

I enjoy almost all aspects of my job: my colleagues, the work itself, and my supervisors. I'm pleased when my efforts have made a telemarketing program run smoothly. I don't like the fact that my position in the company is not stable though. I'd also enjoy my job more if I had less "grunge" work to do.

My job requires strong computer skills for designing and maintaining spreadsheets and for word processing. You should have good communication skills, both written and verbal. Solid interpersonal skills are needed in addition to the above characteristics.

After earning an Associates degree in college, I worked as a secretary, an office manager, and a bank teller. I came to my present position by being transferred from another department within the company.

CORPORATE LAWYER

As a corporate lawyer, I am the Vice President and General Counsel for an insurance company: their chief legal officer. This involves many hours on the telephone in order to solve problems with insurance claims dealing with medical claims, accidents, theft, etc.

While in law school, I started working for this insurance company as a research assistant. My major field of law study was in taxation. However, I was unable to find a job using this specialty. It was therefore fortunate that the insurance company offered me this job as their corporate lawyer.

I find job satisfaction from performing a job well. However, I personally do not like my boss and am therefore working toward the day that I can open up my own firm and be my own boss.

COSMETOLOGIST #1

I became a cosmetologist, because it is something I have wanted to do for years, and I am very satisfied with this career.

My basic duties are cutting hair, doing permanent waves, coloring hair and styling hair. A typical day's schedule is: cut hair, shampoo hair, perm hair, wait for someone to call to make an appointment, wait some more, and then get so busy there is no time to eat or to sit down.

Beauty school training is mandatory for this profession to learn the basic hair styling skills. Aside from this training, I think it is very important to have the attitude that you are the best, but you are not perfect.

My major frustration with my work is with clients who are not able to make themselves clear on what style or color they want. Despite this problem, I like my work and would choose it again if given the opportunity to start over. I like the people I work for and the people I work with. I find job satisfaction in knowing I have helped someone look their best. It is also satisfying to have immediate results from your work. I plan to continue in this career and to be the best I can be.

COSMETOLOGIST #2

Cosmetology has been my career for more than 30 years. I didn't really plan to go into this field, but it was what I found available when I started looking for a job after graduating from high school. Actually, it seemed sort of glamorous, and maybe at times it is, but it is mostly hard work.

As a cosmetologist, I sell services and cosmetics. My work is done in the normal sales job routine of contacting prospective customers, setting up appointments, making sales calls to new and current customers, and processing the paperwork. Despite the fact that the activities might be routine, you must maintain your enthusiasm in your work and for the products and services you are selling. Experience is also another key ingredient in successful selling.

I like almost every aspect of my work, except for government red tape that I must work through because I am in business for myself. I can even say that I like it so well that, given a chance to change careers, I would stay with cosmetology. I find satisfaction in making people feel better about themselves. It is also satisfying to be making a living from my work financially.

COST ACCOUNTANT #1

My job is somewhat broader than that of the usual cost accountant in that I also function to some extent as a financial analyst. In this broadened function, I create reports reflecting costs of sales, prepare budgets, write monthly reports to management, report inventories and reconcile inventory reports, make variance analyses, and other similar jobs.

To anyone entering this occupation, I would warn you that good communication is essential. Obviously, you must be skilled and accurate in dealing with numbers, but interpersonal skills are important too. Occasionally it is necessary to question various management procedures and this must be done effectively and with a certain sensitivity. Basic to all of this is the needed ability to reason--to think through numerical problems logically.

The requirements are rigorous, but there is much satisfaction in knowing that the work I do is accurate and that it is used by management in making key decisions. It would perhaps be even more satisfying to me if there were greater demand for the financial analysis instead of straight accounting and if I were more involved in the decision-making that the managers do. Perhaps becoming Chief Financial Officer of a company would be my aim, but to reach that I will have to get a Master's degree. I am continuing work toward my Bachelor's degree and may eventually get the needed graduate education. I would prefer work in a high tech industry over the low tech company I have worked for over the past seven years.

COST ACCOUNTANT #2

My responsibilities as a cost accountant have been to keep accounts for all equipment being built, pay on invoice accounts, and supervise accounting procedures used by junior accountants in my department.

Although there is not much of an opportunity for advancement within the organization, I do like my job and this kind of work in general. I especially like my boss and the people I work with.

In addition to a good education, my job requires good math skills, accounting experience, close attention to detail, and extensive knowledge of accounting and billing procedures.

I find the most job satisfaction comes from putting each dollar where it should be - I know that I am helping our group with financial decisions.

As an accountant generally works alone, I would like my job better if I had more interaction with other people.

I plan to complete a program of studies on the college level to earn an undergraduate business degree; that combined with previous experience of secondary marketing manager in banking, legal secretary, and real estate broker, in addition to experience in my current position, I believe will be a valuable assets I could offer a major corporate organization. I would like to train individuals to use accounting software and get involved in the design of a marketing and accounting software system.

COST ESTIMATOR

I do cost and price estimating in the aerospace business. As such, I work on proposal estimate work to be done. I estimate labor and material costs and proper rates to establish a cost and a price. On a typical day I will read incoming mail and route to employees, review cost estimating proposals, analyze proposed costs and meet with representatives of functions-engineering, manufacturing quality assurance, material, contracts, and accounting ongoing business and proposals.

To perform this kind of work well it is necessary to have analytical skills, be bright and intelligent, have a cheerful attitude, and have good writing and speaking skills. I did not find it necessary to earn a college degree. I did go for two years. However, through my work I became a certified professional estimator (CPE) and a certified cost analyst (CCA). I have also had extensive work experience of being employed as an accountant, in all levels of supervision, as a cost analyst, salesman, speaker, writer, computer systems analyst and more. I authored a textbook on cost estimating.

I liked almost all the kinds of the work I have done because I gained satisfaction from finding the solutions to the problems which I met daily and periodically.

If I could make changes in cost analysis and estimating, it would be to try to eliminate as much overtime as possible and still do a creditable and a very good job. I sought a challenging occupation in an aero-space firm and investigated the skills and education and experience needed and went after the job.

COST ESTIMATOR, DEFENSE CONSTRUCTION

If given the opportunity to start over again and prepare for any kind of work, I would choose to progress through my career path in the same way as I have done. I started by getting training while serving in the military. Upon leaving the service, I worked as a machinist for 10 years. My experience in the machine shop and ability to read blueprints gave me an edge in securing the job I now have as a cost estimator within the same company.

As a cost estimator for defense contracts, I accumulate data from multiple departments and organize it to fit the needs of the project on which the company is bidding. In reviewing a "request for price" from the government on a complex piece of hardware, I must break down the complete unit into various assemblies using the blueprint drawings. Developing a plan as to who needs to estimate what, including any special requirements, is the next step. Once all other departments have given prices for their components, I then retrieve the data and formulate the answer, giving the government a price for the total.

I consider organization, communication, blueprint reading, and a knowledge of all departments' functions to be the key requirements for being able to perform well at this kind of work.

I like almost every aspect of my work, except that there is a lack of opportunity for advancement.

I particularly like the freedom I have in a small office. It is satisfying to have the freedom to receive general instructions and guidelines and then to be able to organize this information on my own.

COUNSELOR & EDUCATOR

I have been a counselor and educator at the graduate school level for 16 years. Previously, I taught psychology and counseled students in a junior college.

My colleagues, my students, the institutions, and my career are all very satisfying to me. I love watching students develop. It is a pleasure to me to help students solve problems. There are always things in any situation you'd like to change, such as physical equipment, space, time, more help, but I have very much enjoyed my work in education.

My work involves much preparation for classes, teaching classes in counseling and psychology, and I also counsel students with their personal, class, or professional problems.

An educator and counselor needs a strong background in psychology and in counseling techniques. My degree was a Bachelor of Science in math education. I taught 6th grade for a while, earned a Masters in educational psychology, and later got my Doctorate in education. One should be intelligent and have the ability to relate well to people.

COUNSELOR, COLLEGE LEVEL

After retiring from the U.S. Air Force with the rank of colonel, I returned to college and earned a Master of Science degree in behavioral science. I was then employed at a community college's career and guidance center.

My responsibility is to advise and guide students in their college curriculum choices and in their plans for their future. Besides assisting students in degree planning, my work includes academic as well as personal counseling. Work in the evenings is sometimes required.

College counseling demands adequate training. I also found trying to lead by example helped me. Always representing my organization with unquestioned loyalty was important to me. The willingness to update your professional abilities in order to cope with the changes in life style and technology is required. As the military says, "Be the best you can be."

An escape from poverty caused me to enter the Armed Forces. The G.I. Bill, after

I retired, helped me earn the credentials to become a counselor, which I enjoy. I particularly like knowing I help shape my students and their success. Living in the college community I see and hear about the people I have helped.

COUNSELOR, ELEMENTARY SCHOOL

I taught grades 3-6 for 13 years before earning my Master's of Education degree in counseling. As an elementary school counselor for the last 7 years, I counsel young students, individually and in groups.

Helping kids solve problems is very satisfying to me. I enjoy my fellow educators, the administration, the school, and the counseling itself. Not having enough answers to the many problems I deal with is frustrating. I like kids, but I don't have much patience with poor parenting.

My job involves working with lots of abused children in a high-need school. Seven out of 10 of our kids get free lunch; 150 get free breakfast. My responsibility is to counsel the students who need me, helping them find solutions to their problems.

An effective counselor has strong communication skills and is able to listen well. You have to have good self-control as well as be able to manage your anger. A good counselor is a caring, compassionate person.

COUNSELOR, HIGH SCHOOL GUIDANCE #1

As a high school guidance counselor, I advise students on programs of study, course selections, and personal problems that affect their studies and academic progress. I assist students in choosing possible careers and colleges to prepare them for those careers, refer students in need of outside help to agencies that may be able to help with those personal problems, and hold conferences with parents of the students in my care.

I have a Master's degree in counseling and psychology. A career in this field requires patience, compassion, attentive listening skills, training in psychology, and good organizational skills.

I like this kind of work and I derive particular pleasure from seeing former students years later and having them tell me that I made a difference in their lives. The only way my job could be more enjoyable for me is if I could eliminate or delegate the clerical duties associated with my job to someone else.

Although I also have experience as a teacher, I would like to become a principal, vice principal, or school psychologist at some time in the future.

COUNSELOR, HIGH SCHOOL GUIDANCE #2

As a high school guidance counselor, I find a typical day depends on the time of year. During the term there are students to advise as well as meetings with parents, students and staff. My work involves assisting students in planning their high school program, helping them with problems, and guiding them in their plans after high school. Later in the school year, we devote time to recommending appropriate colleges to our students and discussing curricula and work opportunities that might be available to students with financial needs.

It is very satisfying to see a student experience success. Knowing I had some part in making that accomplishment happen, even if the student doesn't realize I did, feels really good. I enjoy everything about my career; I hate the fact that I'll eventually have to retire.

While I earned a Bachelor of Arts degree in general science, my Master of Arts in guidance has been very valuable to me. Besides having the appropriate training, a guidance counselor needs the ability to listen intelligently. You must be able to see a problem from many points of view: the student's, the parents', the teacher's, and the principal's. A counselor must be knowledgeable about all possible options which are available for students. Further, being creative in coming up with inventive solutions to problems is important if you are to give your students the best possible service.

COUNSELOR, PRIVATE PRACTICE

My career has progressed into counseling from my work as a recreational therapist, leading groups in an in-patient hospital. I went back to school and earned a Masters in Educational Guidance/ Counseling, and was encouraged by social workers to go into private practice.

As a counselor in private practice, I counsel and guide others who are in some need of objectivity. During the day and early evening, I hold 50 minute sessions with individuals, couples, or families. I also lead 2 hour group sessions. Besides conducting my work through counseling sessions, I also keep in contact with my clients by phone.

There are 4 major skills necessary to perform this kind of work well: people skills (personable, like people); counseling skills (listening, empathy); problem solving skills; and negotiating skills.

Although I feel there is a lack of opportunity for advancement in what I am presently doing as a counselor, I do like this kind of work, and plan to stay in the field. I find satisfaction from my work by helping people take charge of their lives--feeling, acting, and thinking more clearly, more positively, and more effectively.

My future career plans are to do more education-oriented classes, and less one-on-one counseling.

COUNSELOR, SENIOR SERVICES

As an information and referral counselor to senior citizens for thirteen and one-half years, I work for an agency on aging, offering advice and guidance to the elderly and their families in my area. At times I may help my clients over the phone, answering questions and offering helpful information about our services; at other times I travel to senior centers to see my clients. I also develop informational fact sheets to mail or give out at the centers, or at speeches, special events, and mall booths.

In addition to a good education, my work requires a caring, knowledgeable attitude toward my clients, knowledge of resources and services available to assist them, a sense of humor, and the ability to show and assure people that you sincerely care about and for them and deserve their confidence in return.

I like the people I work with and this type of work. I believe my work is worthwhile. My greatest pleasure is derived from the friendships developed with the senior citizens and their families; the elderly people I deal with display such warm affection and gratitude; I know from their actions and words that I am giving them the assistance and understanding they need and appreciate.

Prior to my current employment, I worked in a business referral organization for a long time; I believe the move to my present position was the best move I ever made.

I plan to remain in this field, working at this agency as long as my health and ability will allow. I also have a strong interest in volunteering my time to nursing homes, children's education, or environmental programs.

COUNTY DIRECTOR, AMERICAN CANCER SOCIETY

I've been the Executive Director of the American Cancer Society for the past 12 years. Before this job and after earning a Bachelor of Arts undergraduate degree, I was a teacher for 19 years, a career I enjoyed very much. I came to this work after responding to a classified ad; the position perfectly fit my qualifications.

An Executive Director has to have strong management and communication skills. A very positive attitude is also helpful. You should have the ability to get along well with people and keep them motivated for top performance.

My days are spent in both educational and patient services. But, most of my time is used in fund-raising efforts. It is my job to implement programs through the efforts of my staff and the volunteers.

I love helping people and I have the pleasure of working with choice volunteers. The variety in the work and the opportunities for creativity also give me satisfaction. Even the fund-raising is fun, but it is extremely demanding. There's also excessive pressure and time demands to meet our goals.

My plans are to retire some day. I look forward, then, to working in part-time sales.

COUNTY ENVIRONMENTAL SUPERVISOR

As a county environmental health supervisor, I "sell" our health programs as well as our decisions and plans related to these programs. I also enforce health standards, and

I conduct inspections of food and restaurants, water and wells, swimming pools, mobile home parks, and sewage systems. All the qualities of a good salesperson are required to do this work as is proficiency with the computer. Although my college degree is a Bachelor of Arts, I have gained specialized knowledge in sewage, water, landfills, housing, and occupational health.

I got into this work after retiring from 22 years in the U.S. Air Force. I entered this field because I thought it would be interesting work, and it is. I like my current job; however, it has been frustrating in some ways. The public doesn't grasp our role in protecting environmental health. I think this is because the government is unwilling to spend enough time or money to educate the public.

My job includes attending planning commission meetings, Board of Supervisor meetings, and public hearings to justify our positions, when needed, to these groups who are still learning about protection of the environment. I must recommend to the Planning Commission all land use projects. I also report to a Board of Supervisors and at public hearings regarding the proper disposition of both sewage and water. My usual day includes meetings with staff to organize the day's events. I hold staff inspections as well. Much of my time is spent writing, reviewing, and organizing reports and recommendations from the staff. On field visits, my staff and I solve problems related to special environmental issues.

In my work, I particularly enjoy dealing with people. There are all sorts of individuals, developers, engineers, and professional people to whom to "sell" our product--environmental health.

COUNTY EXTENSION DIRECTOR

My work as county extension director requires me to be responsible for planning and implementing county programs that are beneficial to farmers in this area. I supervise professional as well as support staff, and I manage the budget. Some of my job requirements are writing informative newspaper articles, answering questions about agriculture, and approving expenditures that my employees may need to make. I make visits to farms, attend meetings, and read both popular periodicals and research journals about the most recent developments in agriculture.

I have always been interested in farming--as a child I was a 4-H member and as an adult I have served as an extension specialist for a 4-H Club. That development is very satisfying in itself.

I like being admired and recognized as a leader, and I get great satisfaction from helping people. My work would be even more enjoyable if there were fewer federal report requirements. I have been Chief Operating Officer for a fishing supply company and I have served as Vice President of a poultry research company. My communication skills and my knowledge of agriculture have been of much benefit to me. I hold several degrees: Bachelor of Science, Masters of Education, and a Ph.D. Some day I would like to be Secretary of Agriculture for this state.

COURIER

Although I have a degree in accounting, I am a courier because it pays very well. I've been doing this for 4 years and I would pick this job again over accounting.

We couriers are considered self-employed, a fact I like. I appreciate the company I work for and my boss even though I'm really my own boss. Some day, perhaps within the next 5 years, I'd like to buy my own courier company.

My work consists of picking up and delivering packages. I drive throughout the state doing this.

To be a courier, you have to know your geography well. Being able to read maps properly is necessary, too. Since you deal with so many people, you should have good interpersonal skills.

COURT RECORDER/INTERPRETER

I have been employed as a court recorder and interpreter for three years. I work in a courtroom on family cases; I operate a tape recorder; I keep trial logs of the voices on the recordings; and I interpret when necessary, from English to Spanish and vice versa.

Skills and characteristics required for my job are attention to detail, organization, fluency in Spanish and English, a professional attitude, the ability to interpret honestly and keep confidentiality, and the desire to treat everyone with respect.

There is not much opportunity for advancement with this position, but I enjoy having the opportunity to help people; I perform a critical service interpreting for those who cannot speak or understand the English language.

I was hired into this position after completing high school; this position requires that you achieve a high passing score on the civil service exam.

This is very interesting work; I would like to improve my skills as an interpreter and work in other areas as a freelance interpreter.

CPA

I've been a certified public accountant for many years. I most enjoy creating new improved procedures which strengthen the client firms. If there were less government interference, fewer federal regulations, and less involvement with lawyers, I'd enjoy my work even more. I look forward to retirement one day and becoming a consultant in the computer field, or perhaps I will go into writing.

Advising businesses and individuals on financial management, taxes, and economics is part of my work. Further, my work consists of meeting with clients and discussing their problems. I study their financial programs, review with the client, and write out recommendations for improvement.

As a young person, I liked management and business. I could handle numbers well, and I liked precision and getting things right. To be an accountant, especially a CPA, a college degree is needed; when I was in college I worked toward a Bachelor of Business Administration degree with concentration on accounting. That allowed me to be in contact with many businesses.

A successful accountant has common sense, good judgment, and an open mind. Knowledge of business procedures, the tax laws, and awareness of the current economic situation are necessary as well.

CREDIT MANAGER #1

For the past seven years, I have worked as a credit manager. I maintain direct accounts; make collection calls; prepare sales, commission, and shipping reports; perform research; keep accurate financial records; answer direct questions; approve warranty payments and transportation costs; help with the switchboard and assign work for our receptionist; meet with retail customers; review and change credit terms; handle deposit reconciliations; analyze financial data; apply cash to accounts; type; file; and enter data into the computer.

In addition to a good education, you must have good math skills and common sense; a positive, cheerful, and friendly attitude toward people; a great deal of self confidence; and dedication to the work as well as belief in the fruits of one's labors.

Although there are not many opportunities for advancement with my present company, I like my job; I particularly enjoy researching a problem, finding a solution, then implementing that solution.

Prior work experience for me includes such positions as nurse's aide, receptionist, sales secretary, waitress, inventory controller and purchasing agent.

My future plans include furthering my college education in accounting and financial management.

CREDIT MANAGER #2

My work as a credit manager for nineteen years has been to develop credit systems, report accounts receivable results, and train credit representatives. I develop and enhance automated accounts receivable systems to meet users' business requirements and set and monitor schedules for work to be implemented. I analyze and report accounts receivable results to sales account managers, I train others in the use of the accounts receivable system and other organizational skills, and I act as the senior consultant for the credit organization.

In addition to a good education, my job requires interpersonal skills, good oral and written communication skills, attention to detail, and an understanding of the complete business model.

Although I do not always agree with the company policies and procedures, I like my job. I enjoy the people I work with and I like the fact that my job allows me to help others understand how to obtain information that will help them in their decision-making processes.

I plan to continue to work as a consultant in this field and I will try to remain aware of other opportunities that exist in the areas of credit and finance within this company.

CREDIT MANAGER #3

For four years, my job has been to handle accounts receivable, controlling accounts, and dealing with orders; I work as a credit manager.

I have an undergraduate degree in business. In addition, my work requires an aptitude in math and good communication skills--both verbal and written.

I really like my job; I enjoy keeping accounts current and keeping sales flowing.

Previously, I worked in accounts payable, billing, sales, and secretarial functions in an office environment.

I believe that I have reached this point within my career because of my own advancement tactics.

Although I am uncertain in which direction my career will go next, I believe that I will either return to college for an advanced degree or start my own consultant business, or both.

CREDIT REPRESENTATIVE

I have now found a career which I like as a credit representative. Prior to this occupation, I was dissatisfied with my work in telephone sales and as a factory worker.

As a credit rep., I make collection calls, analyze business reports, and work with financial statements. As orders are received, I obtain financial statements on the companies placing the orders and analyze their credit records. Based on the analysis, I release the order, set up a new account and/or reject the order.

In order to handle these kinds of responsibilities, it is important to have good communication skills and to have good judgment.

This job appeals to me because I find satisfaction in making a successful judgment call and in seeing a problem through. I like the people I work for and find there is opportunity for advancement for me.

CROSS-CULTURAL CONSULTANT

As a self employed cross-cultural consultant, I teach business people and educators about the essential cultural differences between Japan and America and how this affects behavior. I studied cultural anthropology which led me to an interest in modern cultural comparisons. Why I specifically chose Japan is still unclear to me, although the current political/economic situation makes Japan-America relations of primary world concern. Perhaps the sheer degree of difference attracted me. I then lived in Japan for a couple of years and decided/realized that cross-cultural relations is the field in which I want to spend my life.

I have been unofficially involved in this type of work for 6 years after graduating from college with a Bachelor of Arts in Cultural Anthropology. It has now been 2 years since I started my own business, and I am still in the process of determining exactly what form this business should take: nonprofit, partnership, public company, sole proprietor, etc. I work on a subcontract basis. The administrative work involved in running this business is my least favorite part.

The strengths and skills necessary for this type of work are understanding of cultural differences, the ability to articulate and teach well, tolerance, drive to learn, general business skills, willingness to pioneer a very new field, organization, risk-taking, perseverance, record keeping, planning, and public speaking abilities.

It is a very exciting and promising new field. I enjoy teaching, research, postulating new ideas and approaches to problems. I have a passion for this kind of work and derive much satisfaction from the sense of improving the world situation. I am personally fascinated with cross-cultural comparisons and the immediate need for such.

Prior to this career, I had a wide variety of other jobs: human services work, research, teaching, secretarial, waitress, sales, labor, and driving. I now plan to remain in my profession as a cross- cultural consultant by myself, with a partner, or in the academic field. It may include advanced degrees and certainly a return to Japan.

CULTIVATION SPECIALIST

For many years I've worked for a company which grows sugar cane. When I first started, I was the lowest man on the company promotion scale. I am now the cultivation supervisor, the top position in the department. I oversee the activities of 9 department supervisors and 129 workers in the growing of sugar cane.

My day starts at 5:00 a.m. when I check the night shift log. Then I arrange with the repair shop to make any needed repairs in preparation for the next 2 shifts. It is up to me to give the section supervisors plans so they can handle their shifts.

I like everything about my job: my coworkers, the company, the bosses. I also appreciate the recognition for a job well done, but I'd like more training available for potential supervisors. The fact that there is opportunity for advancement is great.

Very important to a successful supervisor is knowing your job well. Being able to get along with people at all levels is necessary, too. My motto is "Be firm, be fair" and I praise workers publicly while giving criticism privately. It is also important to be patient and to be humble in dealing with people.

CUSTODIAN, PUBLIC SCHOOL

As the substitute custodian for a public school system, I enjoy doing a job well and seeing a room well-cleaned. I'm pleased when I get many compliments from teachers that I do a better job than the regular custodian. I also like working around the children and the fact that they recognize me outside of school.

The working hours in my job may vary from day to day. I might work from 5:00 a.m. to noon, or from 10:30 a.m. to 9:00 p.m., from 7:00 a.m. to 3:30 p.m., or from 3:00 p.m. to 11:00 p.m. Usually, I begin the day by setting up the tables for lunch and then cleaning them. Some days I work in elementary schools, other days in high schools. I clean bathrooms, halls, individual classrooms, lockers, cafeterias, and gyms.

Although I enjoy my work, I'd like one day to find a career in accounting or bookkeeping since I have an Associate degree in business administration and accounting. In the past, I worked in carpentry, as a truck driver, and in farming and hog inspection. I got into my present work through family connections and a situation that developed which called for a substitute custodian in the school system.

You need to be efficient with work schedules to do this job. Some mechanical knowledge to make minor repairs is also needed. Being productive and proficient with cleaning equipment is necessary. An attitude that calls for the best possible work to be done in a short time is important. You must get along with the school administration, supervisors, and teachers. In addition, I make it a point to be respectful of children and to teach them to have regard for others as well as for school property.

CUSTOMER SERVICE, GROCERY CHAIN

As a service specialist for a retail supermarket chain, I am involved in resolving customer service problems for the twenty-eight stores in my service area. I visit each store at least once every two to three weeks, handling bad checks, cash shortages, front-end expenses, bookkeeping methods, and overall store operations.

In addition to a good education, my job requires knowledge of the operation and accounting system of a large supermarket chain, well developed interpersonal skills, good communication skills, and management skills.

I love my job! I believe that I am fortunate to work for a good company and I like the people I work with; this kind of work is very interesting and I have the opportunity to meet some very nice people. I take great pride in showing positive results in stores that previously had problems. In the time since I took over this position, our stores have shown a noticeable reduction in costs. I also appreciate that I have good open communications with my front-end managers; that makes it such a pleasure to do my job.

Previously, I was involved in retail food store management, but I felt that I wanted to explore other avenues with my company; I was surprised to find that I was offered this job soon after I expressed the desire to change the direction of my work.

I plan to stay in this position for at least the next three or four years, taking classes to improve my management skills and perhaps taking on more responsibility within this company.

CUSTOMER SERVICE MANAGER

I evolved through my career (with the same group of management) by hard work, loyalty, and continued education. I started as a computer technician after earning an Associate in Electrical Engineering degree. From the technician job, I was promoted to group leader, then supervisor of systems testing, then manager of the test department, and now quality assurance/customer service manager.

In this position, I manage a staff that assists our customers with their questions about computer design and drawing software, and they ensure quality software for our customers. My typical activities in handling this work are: a weekly staff meeting with my people; answering numerous calls a day from our sales force on questions to help sell our products; providing support for our sales force; writing performance appraisals, and delegating work assignments.

In this kind of service-oriented work, it is important to have flexibility, an easy going personality, self motivation, and an easy temperament. You must be able to take criticisms from irate customers.

I like this kind of work and feel that there is opportunity for advancement. I am, however, getting somewhat impatient to get the next promotion and have my authority increased. The job satisfaction I find in this work is in helping sales support close a big sale, and in solving a difficult customer question and having them satisfied in turn.

CUSTOMER SERVICE REPRESENTATIVE #1

By combining my job experience and my education, I plan to move myself into a marketing position. I am currently attending college to earn an associates degree in marketing. I then plan to go on for a Bachelor's degree in Business. As a customer service representative in a sales environment, I am also moving toward my goal in marketing. Prior to this job, I was employed as a bank teller, and floral designer.

As a customer service representative, my primary tasks involve processing orders, expediting items with purchasing on shipping dates, answering phone calls from customers and sales executives, typing, filing, updating order activity reports and maintaining open order reports. To do this kind of work, it is important to have typing skills, computer knowledge, good reading skills and the ability to sort priorities. I find that I must be able to handle multiple tasks at once and always use my time efficiently. In order to have the ability to help others, which is the primary goal of the customer service rep., you must maintain a positive and professional attitude.

I like almost every aspect of my work including the opportunity for advancement, the people I work with, the kind of work I do, the organization and most of the people

I work for. My only frustrations are with one of my bosses and the lack of complete guidelines and procedures in regard to warranties. I like the fact that I have the busiest region to cover. This also gives me a sense of job security.

CUSTOMER SERVICE REPRESENTATIVE #2

During the past five years I have been the primary contact between the company and the customer, to represent the organization to its clients and to handle special problems on service agreements. More specifically, this job involves, mainly, informing distributors of proper business procedures and practices. In addition, I must write reports for management that track daily revenues for services so that we can keep up-to-date records of orders for services. I work up all exception orders, maintain a report of backlog and other work issues. When applicable, I issue commissions on orders.

All of those functions require someone in this job to have good communication skills, good telephone skills, and to be a team player in relation to other employees in the organization. You must be able to handle changes in the rules, to act as a "trouble-shooter" when various problems arise, and to manage your time effectively.

This work offers rewards and satisfactions. It is a good feeling to be able to solve problems from start to finish and to know you have made a difference in a customer issue. I appreciate the fact that people rely on me and that I can handle matters satisfactorily. I would like it even better if I had total control over this job, and perhaps someday I will realize my ambition to become a manager of a business department that deals with external customers.

Other jobs I have had, including cashier in a grocery store, school bus driver, and data entry clerk were far less satisfying although the data entry work was pleasant enough. My own major interest was working with customers and working in a professional atmosphere. I have worked my way up to this position and I enjoy it, but at age 40 there is little chance for advancement in the present job. By taking night courses, I may become able to move into a managerial position.

CUSTOMER SERVICE REPRESENTATIVE, TAXES

I am a Customer Service Representative for the United States Treasury Department. In my work, I assist people with their federal tax problems. Preparing federal tax returns for individuals and businesses and providing tax information is my primary work. For the past twelve years, I've answered questions for taxpayers and explained letters or notices they have received.

My greatest pleasure is being able to resolve a taxpayer's problem, or answer an inquiry to their satisfaction and to their relief. I would like more independence in making decisions which affect the taxpayer. My job would also be more satisfying if there were opportunities for advancement. Right now, my career goal is to become a Certified Public

Accountant.

I'd earned a Bachelor of Arts degree in education and was a secondary school teacher before moving to this field. After completing the Civil Service Exam, I applied for my position which was advertised through the newspaper.

To do this work, you need proficiency in communications--especially verbal skills. A great deal of patience is needed as well. I've also found being able to feel empathetic to be very helpful. Finally, competence to do the job well is required.

DAIRY FARMER

My father was a dairy farmer. I worked for him part-time while attending school. After earning my Bachelor of Arts degree with a chemistry major, I worked at other jobs for 8 years. These jobs included: teaching at the high school level, wood cutting, and maple sugaring. I then returned to my father's farm and purchased the business.

I manage all aspects of a dairy farm grossing $400,000 per year on total assets of $1,000,000. This includes supervising 2 full time and 2 part-time employees, tracking performance of 250 dairy animals, doing some daily chore work, and much of the crop work and repair work. My work days are 10-12 hours/day, 6-7 days/week, and sometimes there are years between vacations. 2-4 hours/day are spent doing management and office work, planning, reporting, bill paying, and accounting. For 2-4 hours/day I do routine daily chore work like milking, feeding, and cleaning. 6-10 hours/day are spent on repair and maintenance, crop work, and problem solving.

To perform well as a farmer, you should have the ability to plan ahead and set priorities, disciplined work habits, keen observation for detecting problems early, and the knowledge for correcting those problems. Also important is physical and mental stamina.

Although I like farming very much, I would be more satisfied with a lighter work load and the opportunity for more regular contact with other people. I also feel there is a lack of opportunity for advancement as a dairy farmer. On the other hand, I plan to stay in farming because I am satisfied that I am successfully operating a complex small business. I love working with animals and crop production--seeing things grow. I also enjoy the seasonal nature of the job.

My plans for the future are to manage this business better-- improving profit and labor efficiency. I would like to develop a nationally recognized herd of registered Jersey cattle and to participate more in farm organizations.

DAIRY FARMER, CATTLE BREEDER

I have always had a love of cattle and while going to school I read publications about all breeds that were available. My folks were crop farmers where the income was seasonal with many ups and downs. It was the steady income of dairy farming that kept us going.

My work as a dairy farmer and breeder of registered cattle varies with the seasons. Summer is mostly farm work, preparing for winter which is a time for study of different cattle families and their traits.

To perform well as a farmer and breeder you must have be willing to work hard and have a love of animals. In breeding registered cattle, I have found a study of the history and origin of the breed and their inherited traits most interesting and helpful in planning a breeding program.

My only dissatisfaction with my career is not being able to keep up with all the new methods. I am satisfied, however, that I have been able to do this kind of work and have it pay its own way. I have been able to pursue many areas of interest like making records of production, showing cattle in competition with other top breeders, and sales. I have seen my cattle blood lines go to Canada, England, Channel Islands, Africa, and Australia. I keep reading and tracing back breed traits that go back to the ancient polled cattle and the heavy producing cattle of Epirus.

DATA COMMUNICATIONS SPECIALIST

I like the challenge of finding things (problems) and fixing them. Maybe I should have been a detective, but instead I chose a career in computer technology. I attended computer programming school, started as a computer operator, went to programming, and then systems analysis. I was a project leader (Supervisor of Programmers and Analysts), but I didn't like it. I had been involved on and off with data communications during this entire period and found it very interesting. I was a "maintenance" programmer/analyst involved in "fixing" programs, tracking down problems. When the opportunity came up to do full time work in data communications, I took it.

As a data communications specialist, I install and maintain data communications lines and devices within my company. It is my responsibility to determine why a particular communication data line is not functioning and to correct it. I also coordinate the routing and installation of cables for a new line. Another part of my job is discussing improvement to current applications and planning future installations with department supervisors and manager.

To perform this kind of work well, it is important to have good analytical ability to track down problems. I guess my main motivation is challenge; I won't let a problem get the better of me. If it breaks, it can be fixed.

I like almost every aspect of my job; especially the diversity of my work. It is satisfying to me to know that I am doing the best job possible to keep data communications functioning. Our organization depends very heavily on the capabilities of data communications. Another satisfying aspect of this job is the variety that is built into it.

My future career plans are to keep abreast of current data communications technology. We are now getting into fiber optics at my company which is very interesting to me. I would also like to get into more voice communications, telephone and the like.

DATA ENTRY CLERK #1

I like my work very much as a data entry person and have been doing it for 18 years. I like not only this kind of work but also the people I work with and the organization and people for whom I work.

My work is done on a PC (personal computer) on which I keypunch data as a primary responsibility.

To do this job well it is important to have speed and accuracy on the computer. You do not need a college education for this occupation.

The main satisfaction that I find from my data entry work is doing well, which goes hand in hand with liking the job. There is nothing about it that I find dissatisfying. If I could start over and could prepare for any kind of work, I would still choose this career.

I was given this job by Job Services and have continued with it for 18 years and plan to stay with it.

DATA ENTRY CLERK #2

Currently, I am the registrar at a community college where I've been for a year and a half. Following retirement from the United States Air Force (Intelligence), I spent 11 years in the clerical department of a major railroad. Now, since I never went to college myself, I enjoy the interaction with students and faculty along with my evening job as building administrator for the college.

I appreciate the feedback I receive from both instructors and students when I have been helpful to them. It is also rewarding when I've advised students to elect classes which turn out to be just what they wanted or needed. Yet, I'd like it if I could perform my administrative duties full time.

Typically, I go to work at 11:00 a.m. where I register students, enter information on the computer, and accept payments for the college until 5:00. At that time, I put on another hat and begin my work as the building administrator until 8:00 p.m.

I found this work through an acquaintance who asked me to help out by doing data entry during peak registration periods at the college. Another employee's illness created the vacancy for the administrator's position. My plans are to continue working for the college for another 10 years, then retire and devote more time, with my wife, to our hobby of raising Morgan show horses.

My work requires the ability to communicate well with people. Instructors often present a dilemma to you and expect an immediate solution. Therefore, problem-solving skills and the capability of making quick decisions are needed.

DATA ENTRY TERMINAL OPERATOR

In my work as a senior data entry terminal operator of four years, my job is to check that all systems and remote network links are up and running, handle problems with the system and all remote locations, print off my daily work, and handle user problems.

My work requires a high school education, extensive knowledge of computers, the ability to learn quickly and handle a busy work load with varied tasks, a polite disposition, an outgoing personality, and the ability to work well with people.

Although there is no opportunity for career advancement in this organization unless I return to school, I like this kind of work, especially my co-workers and the range of knowledge that I gain.

I plan to learn as much as I can about computers and their uses. I would like to further my education on an undergraduate level and be able to someday use my knowledge to help others.

DATA INPUT TYPIST

I made a career change into data input in order to have a less stressful and less physically exhausting job. Prior to this I had waited on tables for many years and also worked as a nurse's aide. I went to a computer school in order to learn the skills for this work.

As a data input typist, I type information, batch work, verify other's work, and train new employees. At the end of the day after cleaning the machine, I can go home and relax and not be stressed out. This also allows me to have the energy I need in order to pursue my other interests: volunteer work as a reader for the blind and as a volunteer in a rehab class.

Not only do I like the work because of the low stress level, but I like the organization and the kind of work I do. This work requires typing skills and the ability to get along with others. I also find it necessary to be able to accept criticism. I enjoy the challenge of doing the job well--performing well and having few errors in my work.

My plans for the future include taking a writing course in order to learn how to write children's stories.

DATA PROCESSING ENGINEER

Both my educational background and work experience are somewhat unrelated to my present career. I earned an associate degree in court reporting. My career background includes work as an administrative assistant, and a Peace Corps Volunteer teacher. After taking a career training/evaluation, I started working as a data processing systems engineer. I have now been in this occupation for 13 years.

As a data processing systems engineer, I see to it that several manufacturing applications, programs, and systems in a large car assembly plant run correctly. I have the job as trouble shooter and systems enhancer. I also am responsible for customer support.

To perform this kind of work well, it is important to have computer training, curiosity, willingness to accept a challenge, and good communication skills.

The major dislike about my job is the fact that I am involved in a 24 hour operation. I only have control for 8 hours, and yet I must troubleshot for many things which happen when I am not on duty. Aside from this, I like this kind of work very much.

My job satisfaction comes from satisfied customers and from systems that run without error.

DATA PROCESSING MANAGER

I was going to become an accountant. I changed my mind after being exposed to the computer while doing my lab work. Once I saw and got a hands-on feel for the computer, I knew that was what I wanted to do. In the data processing field, I have held positions in programming, operations (running the computer) and analysis (defining and writing the technical specifications).

Now as a data processing project manager, I help to define and arrange the creation of computer systems to meet business needs of the company. My typical activities include attending scheduled meetings with users to define requirements to solve business problems, reviewing with subordinates the technical solutions to meet business needs, reviewing results of technical work, preparing status reports, doing administrative progress of subordinates, and interviewing prospective candidates for open positions.

Today, a 4 year computer degree is necessary to be sure you have the knowledge of the computer environment. However, other skills are needed: interviewing, to be able to get accurate information from people who are asking for a new system; understanding the business flow of a process to be able to define the real business needs; writing so that documentation can be prepared and communicated to different levels of the organization; negotiating; and analysis.

If I could make a change related to my occupation, I would like to change the method of compensation. Annual compensation is standard. However, in this field, the feeling of satisfaction and boost in morale could be better sustained if this were done as the product is completed, or stages of the product are completed. This would make the reward more in line with the activity.

I like almost every aspect of this kind of work except that it gets frustrating at times because technical advances happen so fast that I cannot keep up with them. I have been enjoying the challenges of this field of data processing for 22+ years. The biggest satisfaction is seeing a "creation" come to life when one takes an idea and turns it into a tangible product. Also, I find satisfaction in designing an efficient state-of-the-art technical solution for a business need.

DEAN & PROFESSOR, COLLEGE OF HEALTH PROFESSIONS

Very simply, I like my job because of the power. I have the power as the dean of a college of health professions to try new things with a limited tolerance of failure. I have the power of helping students succeed. With this power, I have started 5 majors plus 2 master's programs for 1500 students in the health field. I have had the satisfaction of building a major and seeing the first class graduate four years later.

I work in a private office with a personal secretary from approximately 9 a.m. to 5 p.m. During the course of the week, I hold formal and informal meetings with the 5 department chairpersons, plus attend a formal meeting with all other university deans, the president of the college and academic dean. These meetings usually involve decision making and/or solving problems. I have the general responsibility of budgets, students, hiring and firing, ordering, and leadership. For the programs which I started, I secured the 50 faculty members, set up the support system, and handled curricula development and accreditation.

Because I started the college of health professions from nothing and built it into the 5 bachelor health major degrees plus 2 master's programs, the main skills needed were innovation, perseverance, knowledge of the health field and of curricula, organization, and the ability to work with every type of person.

My career started with night shift work in a war plant testing superchargers. This was "man's work" and paid well. I later worked as a nurse where I preferred the administrative aspect of the job. I also preferred the administration part of my teaching career. My educational background includes a bachelor's, master's, and doctorate degree, plus I am a Registered Nurse. Because I was academically prepared, I was chosen for this position as dean.

My plans for the future are to retire from my current position eventually and to continue to work by exploring new avenues (i.e., real estate, travel and tourism, and the computer field).

DECISION SUPPORT SPECIALIST, HOSPITAL

As a decision support specialist at a hospital, I do case mix reporting on a quarterly basis, and coordinate the installation of the financial/budgeting software package.

To perform my type of work well you need excellent computer skills, the ability to work independently, as well as with others, and common sense.

I like my job and the main satisfaction I find from my work is doing a job to the best of my ability and achieving personal goals. What I dislike is that in my present position I do not have the opportunity I would like for advancement. I would like more responsibility.

To prepare myself for this career I earned a B.S. in Statistics/Operations Research and an M.S. in Industrial Engineering Management Science. Before pursuing this career

I was a legal secretary. After that, I began work in technical support for health care decision making, and I found association with the health care service to be very satisfying. I do not want to work in a manufacturing environment.

In the future, I plan to gain analytical experience in the areas of case mix reporting, budgeting, and other decision support responsibilities.

DENTIST #1

To be a dentist, you need strong hand and eye coordination. Sensitivity to people is also very important. You should enjoy learning, have a curiosity about science, and have good business sense. Having an artistic ability along with being very tenacious have been helpful to me.

As a Doctor of Dental Surgery, I've been in family dentistry for 14 years. I've also been a swim coach and a lab technician, but I love my work in dentistry and the people here.

I decided on dentistry after doing research into different occupations in high school. Dentistry looked like a good combination of art, science, and business. My work requires that I balance time and motion into an efficient routine of handling problems of varying intensity. I solve these varied problems using my science training and my artistic skills.

Although it's great being self-employed, I dislike the required administrative paperwork. I'd enjoy my work even more if there were less government intervention. Still, I like working at my own pace and I love challenging work. In the future, I will continue learning new aspects of dentistry, the materials involved, and new techniques.

DENTIST #2

My father, who was a dentist, encouraged me to enter the field. After earning a Bachelor of Science degree and a Master's degree in dentistry, I've spent 22 years in the field. I'd like to retire around the age of 59 and begin studying physics, if I'm still mentally able.

As a dentist, I provide restorative care to my patients' teeth. It is rewarding to help make patients aware of the need for oral health and caring for their teeth and gums. I don't feel there's much opportunity for advancement, but I do enjoy the people I work with and the work itself. It would be ideal for me if I were able to increase my income without increasing stress.

My day starts at 8:00 a.m. when I begin examining or treating approximately 25 patients each day. I spend about an hour on paper work in the office. Arriving home around 7:00 p.m., I have more paper work to complete.

Strong interpersonal skills are essential for a dentist to have. Helping relieve patient anxiety is very important. Good vision as well as having excellent hand coordination is essential.

DEPARTMENT OFFICER & FUNDRAISER

I like the variety and diversity in my work as development officer and fundraiser for a large non-profit group. Developing programs, writing proposals, and researching government and corporate funding sources for these programs are part of my job description. Encouraging current and potential patrons is one of my duties. I work much of the time on the telephone, but I also visit sites of programs.

My previous work as a journalist and as an administrator for a publisher was enjoyable, yet I get a great deal of satisfaction raising monies to help the needy and to help the organization I work for. It would be even more satisfying if office procedures could, or would, be updated in this 106-year-old organization. I dislike the bureaucratic behavior of some of the people and regret the lack of advancement opportunities.

My work requires flexibility, research ability, oral and written communication skills (in fact, I was a journalist for five years before taking this job), and adeptness at working with people. Devotion to details, meeting deadlines, telephone talent, and follow-through skills are equally essential. I also keep up with where "money" is generally through the business section of the newspaper. You must be devoted to the group or the cause and, especially, be able to communicate effectively. If someone says "No," do not take it personally.

Future plans are to continue as grant proposal writer in a freelance capacity. I'd like to try to develop a screenplay and I have one "in the works."

DEPARTMENT STORE SALES MANAGER

As the sales manager of a cosmetics department, I manage the sales associates, monitoring their work habits, productivity, and performance; coordinate and supervise floor moves; perform the necessary data entry and computer work--on and off the system; monitor floor maintenance and stock control; and conduct meetings with peers and subordinates.

In addition to a Bachelor of Arts degree in Business Administration, my job requires flexibility, cooperation, devotion to customer service, physical endurance for the long hours on my feet, tolerance for problems, analytical skills, and the ability to welcome change.

I enjoy my job. It gives me a sense of accomplishment, respect, and I am always busy; my job is never boring. The only aspects of my job that I would like to eliminate are the long hours and the need to work on weekends.

While still in college, I held several positions in an office environment and in retail sales; these positions helped me develop good interpersonal skills.

Although I plan to work in my current position for some time, my next career goal is to work toward becoming my company's Group Sales Manager. After I accomplish that, I plan to return to college and then move on to become the Director of Sales.

DEPUTY CLERK, U.S. COURT

I found my present occupation as a deputy U.S. Court clerk by accident. I was desperate for a decent job, after waiting tables at a restaurant and clerking in a jewelry store--and having only a high school diploma--when a relative told me about work available with the Clerk's office. After I got the job, I determined which position there carried the most responsibility, autonomy, and compensation. I educated myself for the position, and, when it became available, I was hired.

There are some aspects of my job which I don't enjoy, but, overall, I like what I do. One of the nicest compliments someone can pay me is to say, "You make this look so easy." I get the most satisfaction from a job well done; when the Court runs smoothly, I've done my work well. I have no immediate or near future plans to change jobs.

My duties require that I schedule hearings, call court into session, keep a record of rulings, and act as liaison with attorneys. I see that the Judge is aware of the next day's court calendar, that the day's hearings are posted, and attorneys who have not submitted orders are notified. I go through the pleadings, determine which need hearings, and decide which to submit to the Judge and which to put aside. My responsibilities also include rescheduling any matters needing more time and drafting short orders, when necessary.

Computer skills are very important in my work. Strong organizational skills to order your time well, the capability of focusing and to refocus if interrupted, and the ability to communicate effectively are vital to this job. You must be able to deal with stress and to act professionally with professionals.

DEPUTY PROBATION OFFICER

I became a Deputy Probation Officer after retiring from a career in the Navy. In my work as a probation officer, I investigate people who have been referred for probation. I then write reports recommending, or discouraging, their probation and evaluating their suitability for supervised freedom.

As a naval officer, I worked with and liked people. I chafed a bit at the strict structure of the Navy. When I left the Navy, I continued to interact with people in probation work. Previously, I'd also been a Naval ROTC instructor at my college, where I'd earned my Bachelor of Science degree in Naval Science.

I really like the people I am in contact with in probation work. My desire is to help them as well as protect society. It's a good feeling to know you have done a little something for the benefit of mankind.

DERMATOLOGIST

A dermatological physician for 25 years, I treat patients with skin problems. My weekly patient load is 40-50 individuals. I enjoy solving their skin-related problems. It is very satisfying work and I'd choose this profession again.

Although I like my work very much, I'd prefer that there not be so many government regulations. I'd also like more control over my time.

You need extensive training to be a physician. My education is a Bachelor of Arts degree and an M.D. In addition, a dermatologist needs to have surgical skills.

DESIGN/DEVELOPMENT ENGINEER

I always had an interest in mechanical things. I enjoy the challenge of fixing something broken or simply analyzing the way something works. My previous job experience includes work as an auto mechanic, an electrician, and a machinist.

In my current job as a design/development engineer, I design various types of electro-mechanical switches for radio and microwave communication--satellite links, computer data, radar, etc. My design work encompasses a large variety of tasks. A typical day may consist of writing engineering change requests for enhancements to existing products, to manufacturing problem solving, to new product concepts for customers, to initiating long term programs for new product development.

Design/development engineering requires a good mechanical aptitude, good communication skills, and mathematics skills. A broad range of thinking (there is more than one way of doing something) is important in this kind of work. Most important for succeeding in this career is COMMON SENSE.

I like this kind of work very much but would be even more satisfied if given more opportunity to be in touch with other related functions. I think more product enhancements would be realized with more communication between various department working with the same product. Despite the problems, I have enjoyed many successes in my 13 years as a design/ development engineer. It is indeed satisfying to design a product from scratch and have it satisfy the customers' needs.

DIRECTOR, ALUMNI RELATIONS

After serving on University Alumni Committees and as President of an Alumni Association and former faculty professor, I was recruited by the University President to become Director of Alumni Relations.

For the past 14 years the job has satisfied my social service instincts in helping people, the University, and the larger community. My education included a Bachelor of Science and a Master's degree in Social Work and my work experience has been as a social worker, police officer, and professor.

On a daily basis I supervise a staff of 7 professional and 12 support staff, planning and executing programs that serve both alumni and the University. We utilize a computer database for mailings and relate to alumni one-on-one by phone and by letter.

To be successful in this career, you must have verbal and writing skills, the ability to budget time, money, family, and personal emotional resources. Liking people and liking to work long and hard is important. It is more than a 9-5 job. The work is satisfying to a large degree and I would only wish to have even greater involvement of volunteers in the life of the University.

DIRECTOR & CEO, ALCOHOLISM TREATMENT CENTER

The ability to communicate clearly and concisely is essential in my work as Executive Director of a Drug and Alcoholism treatment facility. You must have leadership skills to direct, motivate, and inspire others to achieve goals. Excellent skills in understanding behavior, both group and individual, are necessary.

I have a Bachelor of Arts Degree in sociology and a Master of Arts in psychology. My duties as Executive Director of this special hospital include directing the activities of a diverse group of professionals consisting of doctors, nurses, and counselors. I coordinate and supervise all aspects of the hospital's activities.

It's been very gratifying for me to watch the blending of diverse professionals as they treat addicted patients and then to see the patients reach sobriety and good health. Unfortunately, I don't see much opportunity for my personal advancement. I also dislike all the problems with the insurance companies.

I've been involved in this work for 16 years. Previously, I was a Lieutenant Colonel in the U.S. Marine Corps. I became interested in this field based on my personal experiences and received the appropriate education and training while an officer in the service. I also directed a treatment program for the Marine Corps.

DIRECTOR, AREA AGENCY ON AGING

As the Director of an area agency for the aging for four years, I plan for and administer funds which come to the agency for the purpose of helping older adults, and I delegate to and supervise the staff of the agency so that we can achieve our objectives. My position requires that I spend one or two days per month out of town attending regional meetings; I manage the agency's budget, meet with staff, file reports, and spend a lot of time talking on the phone. Sometimes I close my office door and just think, but not often!

My education includes a Bachelor of Arts degree in Sociology and some graduate work in progress. My job also requires, above all else, sensitive communication skills, organization skills, the ability to plan, and patience. Also needed are skills in the areas of budgeting and networking, and a pleasant disposition.

I love my job; it is satisfying for me to see my visions and plans come to life. Personally, I like change and challenges and my job has both components. I like working with the seniors and my wonderful and dedicated staff. The only real problems I face on an on-going basis are issues dealing with salary and funding for our programs. We always need more money for services.

I have been working in the field of gerontology for ten years; as a homemaker and supervisor, as the owner of an in-home service business, and as an administrator of a small (3 country) rural agency serving 8000 older adults. Before that, I taught emotionally-disturbed pre-schoolers and kindergarten.

I plan to finish my graduate studies and work on my writing skills-- right now I write a newspaper column on aging issues; I would love to see my column syndicated.

DIRECTOR, COPYING CENTER

As director of a duplicating and copying center at a college, I plan and direct the daily activities of 14 student employees. I coordinate the flow of work by overseeing equipment and supervising workers. I attend committee meetings, counsel students, and deal with sales or repair people.

While I enjoyed my earlier work as a receptionist and as a private secretary, the last several years in this present field have been very rewarding. Helping others accomplish their work and seeing customers happy with the completed product pleases me. I like helping student employees learn the expectations and demands of a work environment. Having them return after graduation and say they learned as much from me as from the classroom is very rewarding. When I retire, I plan to work on my hobby--genealogy.

There are many skills needed to be successful at a college copy center: office management, mechanical ability, clerical skill, computer knowledge, organizational capability, and customer service capability. Knowledge of safety laws, copyright laws, budgeting, and accounting is necessary. Oral and written communication skills as well as the desire to serve others are also essential. You must be able to identify, measure, and meet duplicating and copying needs of a college and must know how to compile and maintain a departmental budget. There is a need also to interview, select, train, schedule, and evaluate other employees.

You need to be tolerant of the occasional selfish and ungrateful customer and of the sometimes unpleasant personalities of those you may serve.

My future career plans are to be involved in youth ministry either at a regional or national level, or to be director of a church related camp.

DIRECTOR, EMPLOYEE RELATIONS

I earned my Bachelor of Science and then my Masters in Science in Economics, and was then recruited from college by the company I have now worked for 35 years. I have always held employee relations positions. My first position offered variety and I also knew the company was large but diversified enough so I could eventually work in many businesses within the same company over my career. Prior to my current position, I was

Director of International Personnel.

I am now Director of Employee Relations with responsibilities for hiring, firing, selling businesses, setting compensation plans, benefits containment, labor relations, and business planning. I handle the complete range of employee relations issues both domestically and overseas. I rise at 5, arrive at work at 7:30 a.m., and leave at 6:30 p.m., making a 5 1/2 day week. The 4 hour commute is definitely the thing I most dislike about my job.

A strong educational background in business and economics is one of the first requirements for this kind of work. To this, I would add common sense, trust, and integrity.

These many years of work in employee relations work have given me the satisfaction of a job well done. I am looking forward to eliminating my 4 hour commute by retiring and relaxing.

DIRECTOR, EMPLOYMENT TRAINING

As an Employment Training Director, I supervise and plan our center's activities. I update the staff on program changes, write proposals, plan the budget, assign work areas to staff members, monitor staff on paper and in the field, coordinate all training, tend to all written correspondence and prepare reports, evaluate the staff, provide leadership for staff meetings, and prepare public presentations about the work of the center.

In addition to a high school education, this position requires good communication skills for written correspondence and oral presentations, interpersonal skills and public relations experience, knowledge of statistical analysis, state and federal regulations pertaining to the work of the center, leadership abilities, a caring nature, a sense of humor, and current knowledge of the employment and labor markets.

I like my work; I enjoy working with all types of people and helping many of them set employment goals and realize those goals; it is also very rewarding to watch my staff grow and reach their individual potential.

I gained valuable experience through my work as a Head Start teacher, an Employment counselor, a Sales Manager, Nurse's Assistant, and various office work positions.

My career goals are to grow personally as a supervisor and develop a team spirit with my staff, to assist the agency in its mission of helping poor people become more self-sufficient and prepare themselves for careers to make their dreams come true.

DIRECTOR, ENGINEERING RESEARCH

I have spent my entire career life in engineering research, starting with my tour of duty in the U.S. Army. As Director of Engineering Research at a major university, my brief job description would be that I process requests for grants, check on deadlines, evaluate projects, and assign funds if more are needed. Some of my typical daily activities might include: visiting research in progress; meeting with a professor interested in getting a research grant; meeting with representatives from other schools in preparation for a joint effort for a grant; attending and/or conducting a meeting of department heads in a college. Sometimes, I make several day visits to D.C. to check on the status of requests at the National Science Foundation.

To perform this kind of work well, you should have the ability to listen, a positive attitude in order to encourage people, general knowledge in the fields of engineering in which the research grants are being requested, and the personal drive to do everything possible to motivate young staff members to get into research.

In order to prepare myself for my career in engineering research, I earned several degrees. I have a Bachelor of Science in Civil Engineering, a Masters of Science in Geology, a professional degree in civil engineering, and a doctorate.

I have made this my life work because I like having the freedom of action and decision making. I like being a part of new discoveries. Getting the job done properly is a source of great satisfaction to me.

DIRECTOR, FINANCE, U.S. POSTAL SERVICE

As the U.S. Postal Systems Director of Finance, I am responsible for the budget, accounting, data processing, and the supply functions for the 200 post offices in my area. In my 12 years in this position, I've enjoyed knowing when I've done a good job and receiving the praise of others. Formerly, I was a part-time real estate salesman and an income tax preparer, but I like the responsibilities of my job with the postal service. Seeing my subordinates, including the people I have trained, earn promotions is very rewarding.

I do not approve of the organization's lack of appreciation for dedicated employees. There is also, in my opinion, an excessive amount of paperwork.

When my mother died after my freshman year in college, I went to work for the post office to earn and save money to return to college. However, I married, had a family, and never returned to school on a full-time basis. I've taken several management courses, though.

For my work, solid skills in human relations, tact and diplomacy, along with a sense of fairness, are very much needed. You must be capable of interpreting instructions and of meeting deadlines. The ability to control your temper when others lose theirs is very important. Accounting skills together with proficiency in using calculators and computers are necessary.

In my job, I attend top management meetings and hold organizational meetings with my own personnel. I visit associate post offices and I analyze reports. I counsel employees, recommend merit awards when deserved, and, as a member of the promotion board, I also am responsible for long-range planning.

DIRECTOR, FORGING SALES

As Director of Forging Sales, I am the head of sales for a $60 million company with a specialty in custom steel products. While I enjoyed other occupations I have had, specifically being a musician in a rock band and a piano salesman for a while, I'm glad I went on to earn a Bachelor of Science degree in metallurgical engineering. I also got my Master's degree in business administration.

I enjoyed being a metallurgical engineer working with metals, extracting them from their ores, refining them, and preparing them for use. As director of sales and marketing efforts for this steel company, these last 10 years have also been very rewarding.

I really enjoy the challenge of selling. The daily contests of making the sale and managing the people who sell in difficult market situations are very gratifying. The potential for additional opportunities for advancement interests me as well.

In my job, I assess new sales proposals or inquiries with my sales force. I also review our sales figures. Meeting in the office or traveling to meet customers is part of my work. It is up to me to follow up on the status of large projects or important proposals. I also interact with top management as well as with operations managers.

A sales director needs strong communication skills, both written and oral. You should work well with people, be innovative and resourceful, and be self-confident. A winning attitude, never accepting defeat or second best, is a must. Solid negotiating skills are useful as well. You must be willing to work hard and you should have the talent for analytical thinking. Problem-solving skills are essential in this work, but the financial rewards of sales careers can be great.

DIRECTOR, GOVERNMENT FIELD OFFICE

My official title is Director of U.S. Government Regional Office for the Nuclear Regulatory Council, which evolved from the Atomic Energy Commission several years ago. In this position for twenty-five years, I prepared for it with a Bachelor of Science in Mechanical Engineering, training received in my position as a Reserve Officer in the U.S. Navy, and experience gained through working as an engineer involved in the construction of power plants. My job involves managing a regional sales office, made up of professional inspectors and an administrative staff, to assure the accomplishment of our assigned programs on schedule.

In this position, you have to be human--admitting mistakes and trusting your people; you must know your staff individually, their competencies and shortcomings; and you must delegate responsibilities and let the staff know that they can perform their tasks to their individual ability without undue influence.

My greatest rewards have come from the friendship and respect of my colleagues and the personal feeling of accomplishment my position affords.

This was a natural career choice for me as I had always been associated with technical or engineering programs. I enjoy my work very much and take great pride in a successful career that I believe has been managed very well.

I am soon approaching the age of retirement and intend to get involved in volunteer work.

DIRECTOR, HOME CARE SERVICES

I worked for a year as a free agent for my organization. During that time, I helped them get their home care program off the ground. I wanted to find out if I could be a manager so I accepted the position of Director of Home Care Services.

My work varies from IV infusions and wound care to staff education, program development, and research. I am also responsible for marketing, advertising, sales, and administration.

I've most enjoyed the clinical field work with direct patient contact. The socializing and exchange of marketing is an aspect I find enjoyable as well as program design and development. If there were clearer lines of authority from the higher ranks to my position, my work would be easier. Power struggles are currently the problem. I'd also like to be able to do my work with clients and have fewer administrative duties. Since I've been a nurse for 18 years and a Home Care Director for the last year, I'm particularly glad there are opportunities for advancement in this field.

Having strong motivational skills is very important in my work. You must be able to organize, plan and prioritize tasks, and must be able to delegate. Trust is also a significant attribute in this work. Having a sense of humor is essential.

My usual Monday includes administrative catch-up and planning for the week's activities. Tuesday and Thursday will find me out doing clinical field work and marketing the program. Wednesdays and Fridays are occupied in staff and program development, research, and follow-up with problems that need attention. I often alternate Tuesday and Thursday activities with those of Wednesday and Friday.

My future plans are to complete the year in this directorship and use this experience as a launching pad to do some short-term travel assignments in the field. I have a nursing degree from a junior college, but I'd like to return to school to earn my Bachelors and Masters degrees.

DIRECTOR, HOSPITAL SPECIAL STUDIES

I run cardiology, neurology and vascular studies on patients in the hospital. Doing daily paperwork is also one of my major duties.

To perform well in this technical field you should have patience, years of training and be able to work with the super educated as well as the uneducated.

I have been satisfied working in this occupation for 34 years because of the good people I work with. I have however been dissatisfied because there have not been many chances for advancement.

My training for this technology work started in the Air Force and has continued into civilian life.

DIRECTOR, HUMAN RESOURCES #1

It was my desire after military service and upon graduation from college 3 years later, to get into my present occupation in human resource work. I had read about selling, motivation, and persuasion while in the military, and found it fascinating. In the Navy, I was a weather observer & tracker, and prior to that an insurance salesman. My college degree is a Bachelor of Science in Business.

As Director of Human Resources, I support a manufacturing operation in all employee relations opportunities and problems. This involves recruiting, compensation/benefit management, employee relations, training, and safety. My regular activities include: interviewing employment candidates; listening to and resolving employee complaints; writing letters, bulletin board notices, and job positions; conducting benefit and safety meetings; and handling all paperwork concerning hiring, transferring or terminating an employee.

The following skills and attitudes are important for performing human resource work well: verbal/written communication, listening/responding with empathy, maintaining/enhancing self-esteem, asking employees help in resolving problems, a strong desire for detail and to help other people, leadership in trying better ways to improve morale/productivity, selling skills, follow-up, and objectivity.

If I could initiate any changes in my occupation, it would be for more computerization of details that require storage and tracking. I would also like to see a higher pay scale for this kind of work. In spite of these drawbacks, I have liked doing this kind of work for 25 years. I like the organization I work for and the people I work with. It is satisfying when employees feel good about working with our organization.

I plan to continue to advance in human resources management. I also want to write books or articles on what has worked for me. My other career goal is to teach college students human resource principles and practicalities.

DIRECTOR, HUMAN RESOURCES #2

My current position as Director of Human Resources has evolved from my educational background and previous work experience. I earned a Bachelor of Science in Business Administration degree. Prior to the job I now have, I was an insurance administrator & hiring manager, loan officer and personnel director of a bank, owner/manager of an asphalt paving company, and administrator of my local Chamber of Commerce. While I was administering programs for the Chamber of Commerce, one of the board members thought my talents could help his company and he offered me a job. Since this job in private business paid more than the public (non-profit) organization

I was working for, I accepted the offer.

I am responsible for benefits, employment and community relations. As Director of Human Resources, I manage personnel who administer our benefit programs, and the personnel who administer employment, EEO/AAP. Working with numerous community organizations by representing my company's interests is another major duty. A typical day's activities might include: reviewing job openings; discussing employee problems; discussing employee benefit problems; attending a luncheon for a community organization; reviewing employment statistics; reviewing major medical claims; and answering numerous phone calls on policy interpretation.

To perform this kind of work well, it is important to be: a good listener, patient, a good communicator (verbal and written), confident, understanding, and a good counselor.

Although I am basically very satisfied with my job, I do get frustrated at times with what I consider to be antiquated thinking. If given the opportunity to make changes in my occupation, I would attempt to eliminate politics. I would also like to create more teamwork.

I am satisfied with the environment in which I work, and my benefits and salary. Helping other people, administering policy and procedures fairly, working with all types of people and organizing is satisfying to me. I plan to make a contribution each and every day.

DIRECTOR, HUMAN RESOURCES #3

Directing a staff of four and performing my own duties requires heavy personal interaction--in person and on the phone. I typically work up and evaluate various programs (relating to salary, incentives, benefits) as to their usefulness to our firm. Strong management skills, good industry knowledge, and technical knowledge are needed. A college degree is usually required; mine was in Business Administration.

I like working with people directly in recruiting them and later counseling them about career options. Also, it is satisfying to develop compensation programs or corporate policy statements, for example, that turn out to be valuable to the smooth functioning of the bank and its employees.

Previously, I had been a collector/repossessor, office manager, and personnel supervisor for a finance company. My present job is a very good one. In the future I would like to teach some human resource subjects at a bank training program (such as at the American Institute of Banking) or at a community college.

DIRECTOR, INFORMATION TECHNOLOGY

I am the Director and Chief Information Officer for a major Fortune 100 pharmaceutical company. For the past 5 years, I've developed and implemented the information technology strategies for this company.

Job satisfaction for me is being able to mentor employees. Giving them a chance to make mistakes by taking risks and allowing them to grow from that experience is very rewarding. I dislike the lack of a sense of urgency on the part of management, but I do like the people I work with and my job, which is exciting.

I meet with vice presidents to learn the directions of strategic business issues. Then, I work with the business units to determine their requirements. My job is to make presentations on these business strategies to the Board or to the company's Chief Executive Officer. It's also my responsibility to review the budget and the expenditures. I also attend vendor presentations on the latest technological changes.

To do my job, you need to be as courteous to fellow employees as you are to buying customers. Having motivational skills to guide employees toward a common objective and the ability to encourage new ideas is very important. Being able to persuade others is a critical skill as well. Experience and education are also necessary; I have a Bachelor of Science degree and a Masters in Business Administration.

DIRECTOR, MARKET RESEARCH

Providing senior management with factual, valid data for decision making describes my work as director of market research. I assemble data and make reports as well as collect information pertinent to the company by reading and talking with other persons employed here. Managing data on the personal computer is also part of my work.

I find accuracy, attention to detail, perseverance. and flexibility to be valuable skills in my work. The abilities to prioritize and to handle multiple assignments at one time are also essential. Although I very much enjoy my work, the people here, and the organization, I don't like that there is a limit on income potential and little opportunity for advancement.

I enjoy organizing data, solving problems, building a useful body of knowledge, and having virtual freedom to do my job without supervision. Further, I like achieving excellent job performance.

Earlier, I worked as an operations analyst and as a marketing financial analyst. I answered a classified ad for an operations analyst and later was promoted to this job. In the future, I hope to become a product manager or perhaps own my own business.

DIRECTOR, MERCHANDISING

My whole career has been food in some form, but in all different aspects. One job has always led to the next: from magazine food writer, to food and beverage restaurants/catering, to food public relations and advertising, to food commodity promotion. Now as the Director of Merchandising for a fresh fruit commodity promotion board, it is my job to develop retail promotion programs to increase the sales of a particular fresh fruit in the grocery stores. In preparation for work in the business community, I earned a Bachelor of Science degree and a graduate certificate in business.

My responsibilities as Director of Merchandising can be divided into 3 major segments. One-half of my job involves program development/ evaluation which includes contact with advertising agencies, artists, writers, and printers, and making reports, conducting surveys, and analyzing data. One-quarter of my work involves contact with the out-of- town staff of 5 and their training. The remaining quarter of my time is spent contacting retailers, public relations work, and selling ideas.

To perform this kind of work well, it is important to have written and spoken communication skills, supervisory skills for overseeing staff and outside groups, self motivation, and creativity. You should be a self-starter.

I like my job as merchandising director in many of its aspects.

I particularly like the high level of independence which I have with this job. I find satisfaction from my work when the audience accepts the points I present, and then my program works. I also find satisfaction in getting the most out of a budget and from board approval.

I plan to continue my career in marketing, but I hope to move to another location where I have access to a more stimulating environment than the one I am in now.

DIRECTOR, OPERATIONS

I have worked up through the ranks to obtain the position I am now in and am satisfied with that job. I studied business administration management, and became an industrial engineer for four years before moving into a management position in materials. My management skills continued to grow through positions in purchasing management, distribution center management, and manufacturing directorship.

As Director of Operations, I manage people to successfully provide our customers the services and equipment they have purchased. It is my responsibility to oversee activities and manage the personnel involved in engineering, materials management, field operations (installing equipment for our customers in worldwide locations), contracts, and facilities. My job also involves community activities and responsibilities i.e.: Chamber of Commerce, YMCA, Planning Commission, and several other agencies.

To perform this kind of work well, you must enjoy working with people and have good management skills. You must be willing to accept responsibility and make decisions in many areas. A positive attitude toward work and the people you work with and work for is essential. It is also necessary to focus on customer satisfaction and cost control.

My occupation is totally satisfying, but lack of time to adequately address some issues, at times, can be a bit frustrating. I like almost every aspect of my work, particularly the freedom to manage my organization. Building a successful organization through my employees, is what gives me job satisfaction. It is also rewarding to work with younger managers and see them develop their skills and become strong contributors to the organization.

I plan to continue to grow in my present position with emphasis on developing younger managers within my organization.

DIRECTOR, PUBLIC LIBRARY

I had enjoyed working in libraries in college and after. I was volunteering there when a position became available and I was willing to take a cut in salary to accept the job. Prior to my career as a librarian, I was taught on the job to be a carpenter, and later I became self employed. Also, I have been a teacher in both public and private schools. My background also includes earning a Bachelor of Arts in Philosophy degree and a Master of Arts in Liberal Studies degree.

As director for a public library, I organize and maintain two public libraries, handle collection development, and manage the budget, volunteers, programs, art exhibitions, etc. Mornings are spent selecting materials, ordering materials, processing materials, developing programs, and budget management. Afternoons are spent helping patrons find what they need.

The skills and attitudes which I think are important to perform well in my career are: patience, discipline, a somewhat compulsive nature, a desire to help people, a tolerance for different opinions and information needs, and a curious open mind willing to share.

Except for wanting more flexible working hours and a little more money, I am very satisfied with my library work. I receive satisfaction from providing people with their information needs from filing a divorce to recreational reading. I feel I am building a community resource that will grow in value over time. I'm putting more into a life than I take away from it.

In the future, I plan to complete a Masters in Library Science degree. It is my career aspiration to become a librarian on a research ship or research station and to be part of a librarian exchange with someone from New Zealand.

DIRECTOR, PUBLIC RELATIONS

It is my job as director of development and public relations to communicate to people what our ministry is. I help raise funds to support our work and I preach on Sundays as well. My work is so enjoyable to me that if I could start over, I'd choose this profession again.

I contact potential contributors by telephone along with visiting people by appointment. Three days each week are spent in the office meeting with contributors. I also make fund-raising presentations to organizations. Creative program development is part of my work as well. I also supervise 6 employees and have weekly meetings with each. Two days each week are spent doing administrative work in my office.

My work is very fulfilling to me. I enjoy relating to people and creating situations which bring out the best in others. There are opportunities for advancement as well as opportunities to meet new friends as I build support for a worthy charitable organization. Being able to develop and follow through on creative ideas is very satisfying. I'd have more time to do all of this work if I could delegate more of my administrative duties to other people.

In my years as a minister, the last ten as development director, I've found a strong emphasis on relationships important. You need to be able to maintain a positive attitude and you need to be a creative person. Good communication skills along with proficiency in the administrative areas are also essential.

DIRECTOR, PURCHASING

My work at the hospital started as part of a work-study program while I was attending college, and it has since become my career. My position as Director of Purchasing has evolved through experience and job advancement.

My responsibilities include managing a department, purchasing, inventory control, chairing committees, researching new products, and solving problems. More specifically, I manage the purchasing function, inventory, and the print and mail center. Typical activities include negotiating contracts, chairing the product and equipment standard committee, implementing new policies and procedures, and interacting with sales representatives and other staff.

To perform this kind of work well, you should have high negotiating skills, a philosophy of teamwork, the capability of analyzing problems, and creative problem-solving skills.

I like this kind of work very much. I also like the organization and people I work for, and the people with whom I work. I find job satisfaction in problem solving, and contributing to a fine organization.

My future career plans are to work in materials management and administration.

DIRECTOR, YOUTH MINISTRY #1

A youth minister's schedule is not usually the same from day-to-day or week-to-week. My duties depend on what activity we have planned. Depending on the activity it might mean I am running errands, researching, doing artwork, typing, or gathering items together.

The most important attitude for my work is to be able to understand, accept and love teenagers as they are, where they are, and what they're becoming.

My work is satisfying because I am giving something for the teens to believe in, and I am keeping them from the dangers of the streets.

I like the people and organization I work for and of course the teenagers I work with, but I would like more pay and more chance for advancement.

I wanted to give youth my full attention because I know what help a positive role model was for me. The position was also open in my church parish. Prior to this occupation, I was a hairstylist and a beauty college instructor.

One day I would like to be a Diocese Director of Youth Ministry.

DIRECTOR, YOUTH MINISTRY #2

I first thought of a career in youth ministry while in high school. I earned a Bachelor of Arts in Religion/Biblical Studies, and after being in a couple of low-paying jobs like assistant manager at a retail store and radio air personality, I decided to work at a youth camp. I enjoyed that so much, I looked and found this position as director of youth ministry in a church.

In this position, I program events and classes with youth from ages 10 through 18. My regular activities include writing articles concerning activities for the weekly bulletin, newsletter, and special mailings; contacting people (youth and adults) about upcoming programs; calling individual youths to see how they are; attending committee meetings, and assisting with various office staff functions.

In order to perform this kind of work well, it is important to be a good listener, to have organizational skills, and to have writing and typing skills.

Although I like the kind of work I am doing very much, there are several drawbacks to this kind of position. Because I am working for a congregation, everybody thinks they are your immediate supervisor. I also feel there is a lack of opportunity for advancement in this position. Aside from these problems, I find this work to be very satisfying. I like the organization I work for and the people with whom I work. Job satisfaction for me is when youth turn to me for help and advice.

DISK JOCKEY

I had a Bachelor of Arts degree in political science, certification to teach high school social studies, and couldn't get a job. So I started my own business, a disk jockey company. I handle all the entertainment logistics, including the disk jockey's job, for a scheduled function.

My work time is the weekends. It is a very hectic pace spent setting up for a day event, conducting the show, undoing everything and transporting to an evening performance. Then, the whole exercise is repeated.

It sounds like it's the same thing over and over, but it's not. I'm paid to dress up, have dinner, see people looking their best, and play music as a disk jockey. The money is great and you meet different people at every function. Presently, I am the most well known DJ in the area with 4 employees working for me.

What I don't like about my work is the poor treatment from banquet hall managers. They've probably had bad experiences with DJ's in the past, but I'd like them to just treat me like a human being. I also dislike the backstabbing behavior of competitors.

In my work, you should be very flexible, have a positive attitude, and a friendly disposition. Good people skills and motivational skills are very important. You should be a great problem-solver. Certainly, you need to understand and know how to manage music for events.

I still want to teach in high school and I would take a major pay cut in order to do it. My overall goal is to be a teacher during the week and a DJ on weekends!

DISTRICT MANAGER, NEWSPAPER ROUTES

As district manager for a newspaper, I supervise the motor route for the delivery of the newspapers. My responsibilities include hiring and supervising all route drivers, following up on serious complaints about the delivery of the papers, and aiding drivers with any questions or problems.

For this job, it is important to be able to have good communication skills to deal with customers, managerial skills to supervise the drivers, and acceptance of directions and demands from superiors.

After graduating from high school, I worked my way up from accounting clerk, then some sales and customer service work, to area manager for a newspaper, to regional distribution manager and now district manager.

I get job satisfaction from this work when I see a job well done with a minimum of errors.

DISTRICT SERVICE MANAGER

Excellent skills in working with people are a requirement for the job of district service manager. Being demanding yet understanding is a balance that you should try to achieve. You have to be tolerant because that will contribute to your success, but, underneath that, you must keep people moving in the right direction.

I oversee area managers in the operation of centers that repair appliances in shops and in customers' homes. Frequent car travel and regular meetings with local managers are necessary to be sure that company programs and policies are set into motion and are followed. I also conduct extensive training programs for managers. All these responsibilities will be part of your job description.

It has been helpful to me that I have a Master of Business Administration degree, but that is not essential. It is important to have an understanding of business, and getting a Bachelor of Business Administration degree is very valuable toward that end.

I enjoy seeing my managers grow, develop, and succeed. I also enjoy competing with the other district managers. I would be happier in this job if I had more freedom to make decisions; recently I have become more an administrator than a manager.

Although I like my work overall, I am about to accept the job of district manager for a competing company. I hope to achieve the position Vice President of Product Services there within the next five years.

DIVISION MERCHANDISE MANAGER

I was attracted by the glamour of retailing while interviewing in various fields after graduating from college with a Master's in Business Administration. Over the past 16 years, I have worked my way up to divisional merchandise manager for a large department store. As such, I lead merchandising operations and content decisions, supervise buyers, plan advertising, and develop plans and budgets. Typical daily activities include: planning advertising, attending meetings; holding meetings; analyzing selling information; and communicating to stores.

To perform this kind of work well, it is important to have management and leadership skills, analytical skills, fashion sensitivity, good forecasting and planning skills, people skills, and the desire to work long hours.

I like this kind of work. However, I could do without all the paperwork and red tape. I would also prefer to have less meetings held. Despite these frustrations, my satisfaction with this career comes from developing people and in achieving sales and profit plans.

DRILLING FLUIDS TECHNICIAN

I had worked as a carpenter and utility pole inspector and earned a Bachelor of Science in Biology prior to answering a newspaper ad offering training to become an oil field "mud engineer." I attended training school with pay for two months in Houston during the winter months. I returned to North Dakota and felt obligated to work for a period of time to even things up. Conditions were very good until the oil bust in 1983-1984. In spite of this, I have stayed with this career for the past 8 years. Although the job is fairly insecure, it has better pay and benefits by a 50% margin over virtually any other job I could do well. I plan to stick with the job for at least 10 more years if possible.

My job as oil field "mud engineer"/drilling fluids technician is a 7 day a week job with no holidays. I analyze and make recommendations of drilling fluids. I get up early enough to drive 40-130 miles to a drilling rig and make a chemical and physical property analysis of drilling "mud," fill out a report, and make treatment recommendations for the day, all before 7 a.m. in most cases. I am on call 24 hours a day.

To handle this kind of work, you must have patience and perseverance in dealing with people ranging from high school dropout roughnecks to petroleum engineers.

Despite the early morning hours and long drives, I like my occupation. I like the kind of work I do and the independence of working alone. I find job satisfaction from the variety of conditions and the problems to solve.

EARTHQUAKE SEISMOLOGIST

As an undergraduate student earning a Bachelor of Science degree, I changed from civil engineering to geophysics, the physics of the earth, or the science which treats the processes which modify the earth. In graduate school getting a Masters, I became interested in seismology (the science of earthquakes and their remarkable occurrence) through research work. I got some experience in the military, did my Ph.D. dissertation on seismology, and I'm now a seismologist.

A seismologist does research on the hazards of earthquakes, their occurrence, and the prediction of earthquakes. A lot of my time has been spent in the development of hypotheses or theories, the analysis of data, and the generation of appropriately-related computer programs. There are many discussions with colleagues, presentations at scientific meetings of results we've obtained, and preparation of manuscripts for publication in scientific journals. I often assess papers submitted by others as well as prepare and review proposals.

The scientific challenge, excitement, and exploration in my work are exciting to me. I am particularly rewarded with the sense of accomplishment and I enjoy the creativity in this science. One day I'd like to make an unparalleled scientific breakthrough in earthquake prediction and reoccurrence research; if I do, perhaps I can be a Nobel Prize recipient.

I'm not particularly pleased with the organization for which I work and the fact that there is little opportunity for advancement, but I love the work itself and my colleagues. I'd also like more job security, better salary, and improved benefits. We need more funding for state-of-the-art equipment, for research assistants, and for travel to scientific meetings.

The ability to recognize patterns, be persistent, and have scientific insight are all very important to a seismologist. You need to be competent using the computer as well as have strong communication skills, both oral and written. Finally, you must be very thorough, careful and objective.

ECONOMIST

My career in economics began after earning a Bachelor of Science degree in Economics and Finance with a job as a financial manager and then a government economist. I now am in business for myself as a private economist. As such, I forecast economic trends and forecast specific company sales/orders/revenues. This work involves analyzing economic data, studying trends, generating forecasts, writing reports, administrative work and presenting projects to the clients.

In order to perform this kind of work well, it is important to be able to conceptualize abstract pieces of information into a coherent tapestry. A good memory, respect for people and willingness to learn are also important. In addition, I have found that, as a private economist, I must have the ability to recover from being wrong and the ability to continuously learn.

I find job satisfaction from my work because people appreciate the work I do. They respect me and the firm. Another benefit in this work is the travel which brings me into contact with new and interesting people. The financial rewards can be good but the hours are exceptionally long and much time is spent away from home.

My goal is to become more profitable at what I do, thereby providing me with the opportunity to maintain my standard of living while working fewer hours. Retirement at age 55!

EDITORIAL CONSULTANT

Editorial consulting is interesting work because you deal with varied subject matters. It is also convenient for me because I work at home, except for occasional trips into the office for consultation with the editor. My hours are flexible; usually I work 3-4 hours in the morning and another 3 hours in the afternoon or evening. I have a rather extensive research library at home, acquired over the years, so I rarely leave home to use public libraries. In my work I check for grammatical and spelling mistakes; sentence structure; accuracy of factual information, etc.

To perform editing work well you must first have a sharp eye for detail; ability to concentrate; a good working knowledge of grammar, spelling, and punctuation; an interest in many aspects of life; tact in dealing with an author's needs when you revise or delete material in his manuscript; and an ability to work alone, unsupervised and self-disciplined.

I taught high school English, and during my own high school and college years worked part time in both public and college libraries. I took time off from teaching to be at home raising a family. During that time period, I heard of a press that needed a copy reader (one who reads galley sheets aloud, indicating all punctuation, paragraphing, etc. while another person follows along, correcting any errors in another copy of the galley proof). I began copy reading and gradually worked up to editing within a short time. The chance to work at home, with flexible hours, enables me to be with my family and work too.

The pay scale is low, but it is satisfying to have the mental stimulation, and every book provides to me new knowledge and insights.

EDITOR, PROGRAMMING PUBLICATION

I was hired by a major business machine manufacturing company just out of college and have spent many years satisfactorily employed by them in various capacities. I have just hung in there, so to speak.

Now, as the editor of programming publications, it is my responsibility to direct the technical writings through to their completion as publications. Editing involves taking the first draft of a manual, editing it for style, grammar, etc., leaving "holes" for illustrations, and overseeing the printing of the publication by the computer. There is no such thing as a "typical day"--whatever happens, you handle it.

I consider the following skills and attitudes to be important in performing this job well: flexibility, diplomacy, stubbornness to meet company guidelines where necessary, good English, good communication, good sense, and a feeling for audience needs.

I like the excitement and change in my work. Each job is more or less your baby. You nurse it and do whatever is needed to get the job done ON TIME.

EDITOR, WRITTEN PROPOSALS

Working in the area of proposal activity, I am a production editor. My job is to work closely with authors and other contributors to the writing of a proposal to ensure their needs are being met. I attend status meetings and make sure that all members of our effort are aware of schedule constraints and problem areas. I find workable solutions to these problems whenever possible. I initiate the process required to convert manuscript material into a deliverable document; then I proofread, edit and annotate changes on the draft copy for the art and text, making sure that there is strict adherence to the set formats. It is my job to keep the proposal on schedule and keep all members of the proposal team up to date on new inputs and draft changes.

My work requires a mastery of proper grammatical usage of the English language, especially knowledge of proper punctuation and spelling; the ability to cover a great deal of material in a short period of time; a positive attitude; strong interpersonal skills; and physical stamina as one is often called on to work long hours under extreme pressure.

I really like my job and the kind of work that I do. I especially enjoy seeing the final product come off the press fully assembled as I know that we are delivering quality work to our customers. I feel fortunate to work with people that I like, and there is a lot of talent within the organization I work for. I can see many opportunities for advancement if I decide to revise my job at some future time.

It would make my work so much easier if there were more computers and computer software services available for desktop publishing. Previous experience with word processor has given me the opportunity to see the advantages of using a computer to get the job done.

Since I have only a high school education, I intend to enroll in some undergraduate classes to prepare for the position of proposal specialist which I believe is the next step in my career development.

EDUCATIONAL ADMINISTRATOR #1

When still a young child, I decided on a career in education, but I entered the adult education phase by accident when someone asked me to substitute in a night class.

I am pleased when I see someone benefit from the programs I direct as an Educational Administrator. I enjoy the direct contact with the students, teachers, and community. My job would be more pleasant if the local school district and the state government would put more financial resources into adult education.

In my work, I administer and direct programs for at-risk students. My duties as an Educational Administrator are to supervise instructors and volunteer tutors, interview students, and review and revise curriculum. I also write numerous reports and answer lots of questions. I must review budgets and attend committee meetings as well.

Before moving into the educational field, I worked as a lifeguard, a tax preparer, and an author. My education is in mathematics and German. My plans are to complete a doctoral program and gain more responsibility as a program administrator.

I've found in my work that organizational skills, a sense of team work, and the ability to prioritize are necessary. Good communication skills and a strong work ethic are required. Good rapport with co-workers and subordinates greatly helps. Most of all, you need a great deal of patience.

EDUCATIONAL ADMINISTRATOR #2

My list of duties as an educational administrator/site principal include playground duty, plant management, crisis intervention, counseling, befriending, teaching, calling child abuse etc., meeting morning, noon and night, talking on the phone, ordering, planning, disciplining, answering mail, and reading by the midnight oil.

To perform my job you should have people skills, flexibility, and problem-solving skills.

This is my profession because I get satisfaction from helping children and making a positive contribution to society.

I would like to have counseling and community resources on site to help children so we can concentrate on traditional "education," not survival education.

I got into my present position after years of teaching children. I assumed leadership positions and obtained my administrative credentials and M.A. degree. Also in my background are many years as a wife and mother and as a service representative for the telephone company.

My future career aspirations include curriculum development, human resources work, and counseling.

EDUCATIONAL CONSULTANT #1

I am an educational consultant specializing in early intervention. I develop, implement and disseminate information about services for young children with disabilities and their families. I travel around the country doing public speaking and providing technical assistance to local and state educational and health agencies. I also teach graduate level courses, and work with individual families who have children with disabilities.

In order to have the skills and abilities to provide this service, I have an extensive educational background and am continually doing research on child disabilities. As a senior undergraduate honors student in psychology, I did an internship with children who were emotionally disturbed. This aroused my interest in developing methods and techniques for early intervention. I continued my studies and earned a Ph.D. in developmental psychology and have now been working in this field for 22 years.

As well as the extensive education necessary for this work, the following skills are important for performing this kind of work well: writing, public speaking, teaching, and communication/interaction skills.

There really isn't anything I dislike about my career. It is satisfying knowing I've helped to make a difference for children with disabilities and their families. I also find satisfaction from teaching effectively and watching students think.

I plan to continue my work to make an impact on the development of high quality services for children and families across the United States.

EDUCATIONAL CONSULTANT #2

Ever since I can remember, I've always wanted to be a teacher. I spent some delightful time in the classroom before becoming an educational consultant. My job now is to assist the school district where necessary.

My plans are to work in the school district as long as I'm able and as long as I'm needed. I love helping students and teachers. Finding solutions to problems which arise is very rewarding to me. I enjoy the schools, the people, the administration, and the students. If I could start over, I'd choose this work again.

One complaint is that there are no opportunities for advancement. Also, I'd like to have more help and more time to do my work. I'd like to be able to attend more seminars and workshops to update and improve classroom activities.

My work week is interesting. My contact is with the school district office. I find out what school is having difficulty and where I need to visit. I assist school personnel with problems they've identified. These problems may be related to a teacher, to a student, or to the curriculum.

If you are going to go into educational consultation as a career, you need to be able to work well with staff members and with students. It takes years of experience and training. Higher education is also necessary; my degrees are a Bachelor of Arts and a Masters of Arts. You also should be able to analyze a problem and find solutions. A desire to help others is important, too.

EDUCATIONAL MEDIA SPECIALIST

I worked as a volunteer in my children's school library. The media specialist there was instrumental in encouraging me to go to college and take courses in library science. My husband, who is also a teacher, gave me 100% support and encouragement to go back to school. I was anxious due to the fact that I was married, with three children, and I had never had a college course in my life! The people in my life, my husband, my children, even my neighbors, gave me the encouragement to pursue my career.

As an educational media specialist, daily I supervise a before school program called "Early Bird." Students come in to read or use computers. I have four or five scheduled classes during the day. During these times, I instruct students in the use of the library, cover research skills and assist students on individual projects. Usually every other week I have storytelling sessions, reader's theatre, or poetry readings. During non-scheduled times, I prepare budgets for all print and non-print materials as well as all audio-visual equipment. I am responsible for the selection, acquisition, and inventory of all media for the school. I am responsible for developing a new reading incentive program each September to encourage children to read more library books.

A media specialist must be well organized, highly motivated, and like to do a variety of jobs. Secretarial skills are highly beneficial(typing, use of machines, computer knowledge).

To work with children is the whole essence of the job. To see a child's eyes light up when you find just the right book for them or watch their faces when they're listening to a story is truly rewarding. When you succeed in showing the children easier ways to locate information and you get a genuine "Thank You," it makes your day.

I would like to expand my knowledge in telecommunications as well as journalism. I am presently taking night courses in educational computing. Possibly in the future, I would like to pursue a position as director of library services for a school district.

EDUCATOR

As an educator for thirty-three years, I work mostly in coaching and administration, making for some very long days--at times my day is fifteen hours long.

My education includes a Bachelor's and a Master's degree; for those considering this career field, I believe the qualities required for success are intelligence, good communication skills, open-mindedness, an open-door policy, a thick skin, a sense of humor, and social commitment.

I like my work; I find that my greatest satisfactions come from the work and fellowship of my educated colleagues, working with young people, the job security, and being engaged in a worthwhile profession.

I served in the U.S. Navy and chose education as my career after my tour of duty was over. I completed my college education on the G.I. bill.

I have also worked as a farmer, a real estate salesperson, and a volunteer for the

United Way.

In the future, I plan to remain active in civic, church, and volunteering activities as sidelines. I will continue my work as an educator as long as possible.

EDUCATOR & ADMINISTRATOR

An educator and administrator in the field of early childhood education, my career began after several years as a teacher. I always believed, as an adult, that I was attempting to solve personal problems which began at a much earlier age. My involvement with this early childhood education program is an attempt to help others avoid such problems and issues later in their lives.

My work includes providing parent education to families as well as supervising, observing, and training educators of parents. My duties involve writing curriculum along with program planning and design. Much of my time is taken in staff meetings as well.

Job satisfaction for me comes with helping people. I particularly enjoy working on new and better ways to do things. While I'm not crazy about the organization I've worked in for eight years, I do love the people.

You need flexibility to do this work well. Knowledge of child development is, of course, necessary. Also important in education is having insight into the feelings, needs, and skills of others. My training includes a Bachelor of Science degree along with a Masters degree in education, early childhood education, and liberal arts. My career plans are to continue my work in this field.

EDUCATOR & ATHLETIC DIRECTOR

As a youth, I wanted to teach and to coach. Now I am working in my eleventh year as an Athletic Director at the high school and junior high level. I've been in the field of education for 34 years and have a Masters degree. I enjoyed previous jobs as a teacher and as a coach and if I could start over, I'd choose education again.

Helping make the tasks easier for others, especially coaches, gives me job satisfaction. My job would be much easier if there were enough money to provide additional programs for our students.

An athletic director needs to have common sense and know how to be firm while maintaining a positive attitude. You should also enjoy working with adults and with students.

My work day usually includes handling phone calls, checking with head coaches, and checking bus schedules. There are letters and reports to be written. You also need to order equipment and check on equipment previously ordered. Another duty is to meet with other administrators and present your budget and other needs forcefully.

EDUCATOR, HEAD OF FOREIGN LANGUAGE DEPARTMENT

I was introduced to several languages in seventh grade and had a passion for them thereafter. Consequently, I have spent the last 33 years teaching foreign languages, and am now also department head.

As the head of the foreign language department in a high school, I prepare the programs, units and projects, and supervise the foreign language teachers. I also have my own teaching schedule to plan and organize.

To perform well as a foreign language teacher, you must have a thorough knowledge of the language. I would like to see more foreign university studying by teachers in preparation for this career. It is also necessary to know the best methods of teaching. I recommend using the conversational approach. A teacher needs an attitude of interest, concern and optimism.

I particularly like having the opportunity to speak to people in their language. I like the school district I work for and the kind of work I do. I find job satisfaction in working with young people, noting their progress and success.

My plans for retirement include traveling so I can use my knowledge of foreign languages for enjoyment.

EDUCATOR, LIBRARIAN, & ATHLETIC DIRECTOR

Since I am employed by a small school, I hold a combination of jobs as one must in an organization of this kind. The fact that I have been in it for 23 years indicates that I like it, and that is correct for the most part. I certainly do not plan to make a change now or in the future because that would result in a cut-back in salary. Of my jobs as teacher, librarian, and athletic director, however, I like the work in sports best and, if given a full opportunity to have whatever I wanted without loss of pay, I would be a full time athletic director or even assistant director.

My daily activities vary, and I have to decide whatever is most pressing at a given time. One day may be spent cataloguing library books and materials; another may be calling, contracting, and mailing information to officials in any one of several sports; and some days are spent working on student eligibility lists and rosters for state records. It is essential to place jobs in priority in this work. In addition, you must be organized and flexible.

Must of the adults and students with whom I work are great, and there is satisfaction for me in helping to run the various areas on my responsibility. However, I am spread very thin, and I would be happiest as a full time coach.

My jobs are a strange combination, but both reward me. I like things to be orderly and structured, and both functions provide for those needs. Also, I work on the side a bit as an official at college-level games, and that gives me a sense of personal accomplishment in that I can reach this level in sports.

In spite of my wish to be in sports all the time, my present job(s) are interesting, and I will stay with them through my career.

EDUCATOR, PSYCHIATRIC CASES

I have always been involved in some facet of education except for a one-year position as an executive secretary of a private tennis corporation. I initially trained as a teacher, and worked in a public school setting. I became recognized as a specialist, and thus held supervisory, curriculum specialist positions as coordinator of a preschool program for the handicapped, and supervisor of learning disabilities programs. I was recruited for my current position as education specialist in an inpatient psychiatric facility. My educational background includes two master's degrees.

My work as the educational specialist involves performing diagnostic assessments and treatments for educating children while they are patients in a psychiatric hospital. This includes supervising and implementing instructional programs; doing liaison work with receiving schools; interpreting diagnostic information to parents and professionals; providing parent training; participation on a multi-disciplinary treatment team.

To perform this specialized teaching well, it is important to have organization, initiative, the ability to work with other professionals on the treatment team, motivation to complete work independently, and flexibility.

Although I like the kind of work I do very much, there are several drawbacks in this career. I would like to see better interdisciplinary relationships with less bureaucracy, more flexibility in daily/weekly schedules, less clerical and paperwork responsibilities, and higher salaries. I do like the people I work with, and find the work to be interesting and dynamic. Therefore, I intend to stay in this field of medical/psychiatric specialized education and aspire to become a principal/administrator of a hospital school.

EEG TECHNICIAN

My career background is extremely diverse. I have been a chicken farmer, a factory worker, a credit manager, and now an EEG technician. I always liked lab work and was growing an ulcer in credit work. I found out about this lab technician job and applied and was accepted into a training program. I have now done this for 26 years and like it very much.

As an EEG technician, I perform brainwave studies on people. These are people who have brain damage or suspected brain damage, possibly from epilepsy, space occupying lesions or trauma, I usually do 3 or 4 studies per day. Each is different.

To perform this work well it is important to get along with clients, have a good memory, know the anatomy of the nervous system, have knowledge of electronics and pharmacology and have mechanical dexterity.

The major drawback to this career for me has been the lack of opportunity for advancement. However, I very much like this work and receive personal satisfaction from helping someone. I like it because EEG is one of the few noninvasive techniques for learning what is happening in the brain.

ELECTRIC COMPANY DISPATCHER & HORSE BREEDER

I have two occupations, one as an emergency dispatcher for 6600 hours/year for the local electrical company and the other as a breeder and trainer of Arabian horses. I particularly like my job as a breeder but my dispatch work is done primarily for money and convenience. I do my dispatch work from my house via the telephone and radio transmitter. I answer calls on power outages and call crews out to the various areas to restore the power. I work from 4:30 pm to 8:00 am daily and then from 4:30 on Friday, through the weekend until 8:00 am Monday. This adds up to 74 hours/week at a very low rate per hour.

It is important to try to be courteous to sometimes very rude and offensive people who are experiencing power loss. You must answer questions and keep a log of calls and outages. It is important to have a knowledge of the areas that the system is in. Skills in operating the radio system and switchboard are necessary.

I found out about the job through my husband who works for the electric company. Since I must be at home a lot with the horses, I know the area well, my husband could train me on the system, and no one else wanted this job, I got it.

I hope to devote more time in the future to the care of and showing of the horses.

ELECTRIC UTILITY SYSTEM PROTECTION TECHNICIAN

There is no typical day in my line of work, every job is different. Basically I maintain or install and then test electric utility protection systems as a relay technician.

It is mandatory to have a high regard for safety. You must have proper understanding of the instability of electricity and have the ability to work with small tools and test equipment.

I have found satisfaction from working at this job for 25 years because I like the results of my work, proper operation of equipment under operating conditions. What is particularly frustrating in this type of job is the "getting ahead" as a primary goal instead of understanding supervision. I would also like to eliminate "bottom line" thinking as the number one aim.

I chose this profession and worked my way up. I have also had experience as an apprentice machinist and a draftsman. I have not earned a college degree.

ELECTRICAL CONTRACTOR

Because of my abilities and interest in electricity while in high school, I was awarded a scholarship to a technical college. For nine years I was a coal miner and always involved with electricity before becoming self-employed as an electrical contractor.

My jobs include installing, troubleshooting, and maintaining electrical systems. I also do some design work. Typically, I go to the shop in the morning around 8 a.m. to check messages. I usually have my work schedule preplanned for the day. Unless something of greater urgency comes up, I go with my original plan. I work at a job until I get it done or until around 6:30 p.m.

My kind of work requires a fair amount of mathematics. I also need to be able to get along with people fairly well. Knowledge and respect for electricity and what it can do are critical elements for this occupation as an electrician.

I like this kind of work very much. I enjoy designing circuits, installing them and making them work. The more complicated the circuit the better!

I plan to continue my work as a electrical contractor in order to become the best contractor in the area.

ELECTRICAL DESIGNER

The only formal education I have had toward my career as an electrical designer has been the drafting courses I had in high school. I have gained the electrical knowledge on my own. I have now been employed as a designer for 25 years. Prior to that, I worked as a short order cook, and owned and operated my own hardware store.

As an electrical designer, I design lighting and power for commercial, industrial and residential buildings. This includes designing the lighting arrangements for all the rooms in a building, plus the powering of the entire building from the utility company source. The fire alarm systems and emergency lighting systems are also elements in the design. It is critical that everything in the design conforms to the latest codes applicable.

The skills and attitudes which I feel are important in this job are confidence in your knowledge of drafting design procedures, codes, and electrical construction techniques; intelligence; and willingness to do the best that you can.

Except for feeling that I am not recognized enough for my contributions to the company, I like my work very much and plan to stay in this line of work. I find job satisfaction in knowing that I have done the best job with the background and experience that I have to offer.

ELECTRICAL ENGINEER #1

Electrical engineering has been my profession for 20 years. It chose me from the start and I have stayed with this field. I am now doing consulting work, primarily RF design-communications, radar precision measurements. The work involves designing of electrical circuits or systems for various clients and solving their circuit or systems problems.

To qualify for this profession you should have analytical ability and a very thorough understanding of science and mathematics. You also must have an advanced degree in electrical engineering. I have received my Ph.D.

My greatest satisfaction comes from applying the laws of nature to a working system and watching that system do exactly what it was designed to do. What has been the least satisfying aspect of my work is that I don't feel the business people have the respect they should for engineers/scientists.

My future career aspirations are to continue consulting/ teaching/writing.

ELECTRICAL ENGINEER #2

As an electrical engineer, I plan large telecommunications systems. I gather information on problems to be solved and then an approach to solutions by myself. I then attend meetings where we discuss/refine solutions.

I entered this profession because I followed my math and science aptitude which was demonstrated while I was in high school and college. After receiving my bachelors degree, I continued on in school and earned my Masters of Science.

The skills and attitudes which I consider important to have to perform well as an electrical engineer are: mathematical aptitude, logical thinking, and expository writing and speaking.

I like the kind of work I do, However, I would like to see greater technical control of corporate solution, and less political decision making. I do receive satisfaction from my work because, for me, the sense of accomplishment is seeing something I planned being implemented.

ELECTRICAL ENGINEER #3

I was interested in electrical devices as a child and liked mathematics in school, so I studied electrical engineering in college. I was an insurance agent in my father's office for five years after graduating with a Bachelor of Science in Electrical Engineering degree. But I found out I was an engineer, not a salesman. I also found that an electrical background can be applied to many other fields: mechanical, chemical and even medical. This has led me into jobs as a biomedical engineer, a semiconductor product evaluator, and an electronic circuit designer, all prior to my current work as an electromagnetic emissions testing engineer (EME).

As an EME test engineer, after setting up and getting the machine running, I measure the radio frequency signals emitted from the machine using special radio receivers and antennas. If the signal levels exceed government limits, I work with the design engineer to find ways of reducing the levels of electromagnetic emissions. When the test is finished, I plot the results and write up a report.

To perform this kind of work well, it is important to: pay careful attention to details, cooperate with fellow workers, look for ways to make things better, and be honest.

I like my work. However, I am dissatisfied with my pay scale and feel somewhat trapped because of the lack of opportunity for advancement. I take pride in my work, though, and have the satisfaction of knowing that the machines I test and pass will not cause electromagnetic emission problems when they go into production and are placed in service.

My future plans include working on an experiment to convert mass totally into energy. I have hopes of helping to solve our energy problem, because in effect it will be like having a battery capable of delivering several kilowatts of power for years without wearing out or having to be recharged.

ELECTRICAL ENGINEER #4

My career has spanned several years and several different positions, all of which were in the field of electrical engineering and management of a sort. A college graduate, my degree is a Bachelor of Science in Electrical Engineering. The job titles I have held over the years are electrical engineer, regional engineer and field service district engineer, engineering and service manager, design supervisor for power circuit breakers, editor and publisher of an international newsletter, and editor of technical transactions.

In addition to an engineering degree, I urge anyone entering the field of engineering to continue their education, both in and out of the classroom, and always be open to new experiences. That is, after all, how we learn. Make it a goal to learn as much as possible over the entirety of one's career; participate in educational and professional societies when the opportunity arises, or seek out these societies and make the opportunity happen; and train to understand psychological problems before accepting a management position--it gives you a better understanding of people.

My career in electrical engineering has been very rewarding. I continued my education throughout my career as I believe all should do. I have been fortunate to be able always to work in a creative atmosphere without limits, as contrasted with a production environment. I grew up on a farm and knew at the age of ten that I was going to pursue a career in electrical engineering. I spent most of my leisure time playing with dry batteries used in farm clocks and flashlights. I was born with a natural curiosity for how things work. That is a requirement, I believe, for a successful engineering student. Early in my career I was a member of a six-person team which developed the first 440 volt, 400 cycle, alternating circuit power system for aircraft and this became the standard for all aircraft, large and small.

I am interested in the growth and development of engineering education, the search for new sources of electrical power, and a greater acceptance of nuclear power. I will continue to pursue these interests.

ELECTRICAL ENGINEER #5

For the past twelve years, I have worked as an electrical engineer. Most of my time is spent in front of a computer, designing circuits, preparing wiring diagrams, and generating spreadsheets to determine costs. The remainder of my time is spent supervising others.

I completed only a certificate program in electronics while still enrolled in high school and from there I have built my career, taking training whenever available to me, and through in-house training and seminars. In addition to ongoing training, my job requires a very close attention to details and good people skills.

I like this kind of work. I enjoy an above-average salary level and I gain a sense of accomplishment when my project goes well. I also enjoy making what I believe are good business decisions.

Without a college degree, I would probably encounter great difficulty in finding a job similar to this one at any other company, or, if I did, I would not make the same amount of money as I now enjoy. I have given a great deal of thought to opening up and operating my own business, perhaps as an engineering consultant at some time in the near future.

ELECTRICAL ENGINEER #6

Since I always enjoyed math and physics, electrical engineering seemed to be an excellent mix of both. This has turned out to be a good career choice for me, a career which I have now been pursuing for 18 years in the United States Air Force. My educational background includes a Bachelor of Science degree in Math, and a Masters and Ph.D. in Electrical Engineering. Prior to my current position I was an avionics (aviation electronics) technician responsible for the repair of the autopilot and instrument systems on the FB-111A.

In my current position as an electrical engineer, I work on applied electromagnetics research in radar and communications. This involves performing research and development on the scattering of radar energy from targets. A typical day consists of attending various meetings regarding ongoing projects and status. Once the meetings are done and correspondence completed, engineering and analytical solutions to particular problems are worked on (research). Basically, you could think of research as a very long word problem where there is no answer in the back of the book.

You need very keen analytical skills and a very strong mathematical and scientific background (particularly physics) to do this kind of work. Additionally, you need to be able to communicate effectively both orally (speeches/presentations) and written (articles and reports).

My only major frustration is that there are always many distractions such as administrative trivia and many different simultaneous demands on my time. Despite this, I do find satisfaction from my work in seeing a problem through from the first statement to the final solution. Sometimes I have the knowledge that is necessary to solve a problem that no one else has been able to solve.

My future career plans are to continue my career as an electrical engineer after retirement from the USAF.

ELECTRICAL ENGINEERING TECHNICIAN #1

As an Electrical Engineer Technician for four years, my job involves many different responsibilities. I file paperwork, build prototypes, translate directions to manufacturers, document materials lists, attend meetings, document assembly directions, seek out and obtain agency approval, deal with customer relations, keep track of special projects to which I am assigned, and answer technical questions or offer solutions to technical problems.

I have an Associate's degree of Applied Science; I find the skills most important to my job are being a team player, being mechanically inclined, troubleshooting, debugging, knowledge of electrical circuits, time management, and the ability to get along with others. I am constantly learning on this job.

I like everything about my job.

It is a relatively low pressure job, but it has its challenges and being challenged daily motivates me to do a good job. I chose this career because I like this kind of work; I believe the electronics/computer field is challenging and very interesting.

I plan to further my college education and earn a Bachelor of Science degree. I believe that will increase my abilities and technical level of knowledge while opening opportunities for further advancement in my field.

ELECTRICAL ENGINEERING TECHNICIAN #2

I particularly like the challenges from new technology I encounter in my job as an engineering technician working on high technology circuit boards. My main responsibilities in this position include working with research and development, process development, and troubleshooting. More specifically, my typical activities are to receive and review new circuit board design, run through process and debug, make recommendations for changes on future production runs, and compile a technical report on findings.

In order to perform this kind of work well, the following skills are important: overall knowledge of production process of circuit boards, innovation, and communication skills to relate to engineering and management.

I have now worked in this capacity for 12 years. Prior to this, I worked as a sheet metal fabricator, a truck driver, auto mechanic, and fast order cook. I do not have a formal education for this kind of work, and I have now found that there seems to be a lack of opportunity for advancement for me until I further my education. Therefore, I intend to get my college degree in order to work my way into engineering or circuit design.

I am very satisfied with this type of work with high technology circuit boards not only because of the challenge, but also because of the organization and people I work for and with whom I work. I find a sense of accomplishment in my work through successful implementation into the production environment and successful completion of first time builds.

ELECTRICAL ESTIMATOR & FIELD SUPERVISOR

My work in the electrical contracting industry started the summer I finished high school when I was offered a job with my friend's father's company. I attended college for 2 years, and then went back to work in the electrical contracting company with the position of electrical estimator and field supervisor because I found that I liked working in this industry.

My job is to prepare labor and material estimates to build a certain project and then to supervise projects under construction. With eleven projects going at one time, most time is spent getting materials to the proper project. Answering questions of the foreman and general contractor are part of my supervisory responsibilities as is job coordination. I am also usually involved in preparing one or two new bids for future projects during the course of the week.

To perform this kind of work well, it is important to know the job that the foreman and workers are attempting to perform. It is also critical to be able to work well with these people without making them feel that you are superior to them.

I like almost every aspect of my work including the organization and people I work for, the opportunity for advancement, and the kind of work I do. I am now satisfied mentally, physically, and financially. When I am able to, however, I plan to finish college with an electrical engineering degree in order to further my knowledge and create more opportunities for advancement.

Job satisfaction for me is when the power is turned on at a large office complex or any of my projects and the lights come on; you know then that something tremendous has been accomplished.

ELECTRICAL TEST TECHNICIAN

I started at a very entry level position as janitor/security guard for a company in the personal computer industry, and I have worked up to the position of electrical test technician. As such, I basically make life easier for the test operators by working out problems for difficult jobs. More specifically, I resolve any technical electrical difficulties concerning work performed in the area of my responsibility, personally handle any difficult first-run jobs, and document solutions to these problems.

To do this kind of work, you must have the ability to sort through a problem--figure it out. It is essential to work well with superiors and those who report to you. Additionally, it is important to have the ability to communicate ideas well and to write clear, precise instructions for jobs.

I like this kind of work, and the people with whom I work. I especially like the problem-solving aspect of the job and the gratitude/praise I get from those with whom I work and from my superiors when completing difficult jobs. The drawback to this job is the lack of opportunity for advancement. In order to overcome this obstacle, I plan to complete my college degree so that I can move into a position that is more challenging technically.

ELECTRICIAN

As an electrician, I usually work outside doing medium to heavy work for an electrical contractor on commercial jobs. This tends to be dirty and often hazardous work, which I find interesting and challenging. All the jobs are different, which makes it essential to be able to read blueprints. My typical work day is from 8 a.m. to 3:30 p.m.

To perform this kind of work well, it is important to have the following skills and attitudes: be careful; give your work thought; and have math skills, knowledge of electrical blueprint reading, and a positive attitude.

The biggest drawback for me to being an electrician is that I work outside, even during the very cold winters in my part of the country. Aside from this, I have always liked working with my hands and my mind, so this job suits me well. Prior to becoming an electrician, I did carpentry work, welding, operated heavy equipment, and auto body work. After 30 years as an electrician I still like this trade very much.

I find satisfaction in working with different people all the time-- mostly very interesting people.

Although I will be retiring soon, I plan to do many of the same things I've done all my life--working with my hands and mind--but in a warm climate.

ELECTRICIAN & INSTRUMENT TECHNICIAN

For 30 years I've worked as an electrician performing electrical maintenance, and trouble shooting equipment, including repair and replacement, in a large chemical plant. For the past two years I've been an instrument technician, which involves instrument maintenance. I prefer doing electrical work rather than work involving a combination of electrical and instrument maintenance. I keep records as well as update blueprints.

Sometimes I do work out in the field for the drafting and engineering departments.

My ability to work with tools and my hand dexterity are useful to me in my work. Proficiency in math, science, and mechanics are also needed. An exploring and analytical mind is valuable in this work too. There are three cautions: you should respect danger, should not be fearful, and should not be color blind. Because the system of wiring can be interpreted only by a high level of competence in matching colors, this last caution is more important than it might sound.

This is a good job for an employee with no college degree, and since I do not have one, I'm glad to be in this line of work.

If I could start over again, I'd choose this same occupation. The pay and benefits are good. I like the kind of work that I do and the people I work with, but I do not like the stress and the risk involved.

In the past I was a pipefitter, and I've been a carpenter. I've served in the U.S. Army and as a merchant seaman. I look forward to a retirement of fishing and travel.

ELECTRONICS ENGINEER #1

I have been an electronic engineer for many years. I like the job I have, the kind of work I do and the people I work with. If I could start over in a career, I would again choose electronic engineering. I never considered another profession.

I do systems engineering for avionics. It is my job to manage the people working on the system to ensure that the program is proceeding per plan.

To perform well at my work it is important to have good management skills and abilities plus technical knowledge in electronics.

The main satisfaction I derive from my work is being part of the design of a successful project. It would be nice, though, if I got more recognition for the work I do. I would also be more satisfied if there were less paper work.

To prepare myself for this career I earned a bachelor and masters of science degree in electronics engineering.

ELECTRONICS ENGINEER #2

As an electronics engineer working with embedded systems for three years, I design as well as monitor the design of small, very fast computers and computer software for missile systems. My job requires that I read over technical proposals and articles and provide a report assessing their applicability to various on-going projects; evaluate contractor progress on these projects through various mechanisms and try to anticipate any upcoming problems; and travel at least once a month to contractor or government facilities to be briefed on technical progress of these projects.

I graduated with a Bachelor of Science in Electrical Engineering. This is essential to work in the field of engineering. But to be successful, you must also have the ability to develop a working knowledge of different areas quickly and must be able to work comfortably with all sorts of people. Previously, I worked as an outside Plant Engineer where I designed cable runs for the telephone company; I was referred to my present position by a friend.

I chose this field because I have always been fascinated by computers.

I like my job; it gives me the opportunity to work with computers and software that are considered state-of-the-art in this field. My work also gives me the feeling that I am constantly increasing my knowledge in this area of expertise. The only thing I don't like and would change, given the chance, is the amount of time spent in contract evaluation. I would increase the amount of time spent in actual Research and Development.

I plan to further my education and finish the Master's degree program in which I am currently enrolled. After that is completed, I plan to go on to study at a Doctorate level of education and then work more directly in Research and Development.

ELECTRONICS ENGINEER #3

As an electronic/electrical engineer, I attend meetings, plan projects, get involved in the office computer activities, converse with customers and colleagues over the phone, and deal one-on-one with other personnel in my department.

I have a Bachelor of Science degree in Electrical Engineering. In addition, to succeed as an electronic/electrical engineer, you must be open to suggestions from various departments and groups, possess good communication skills, and be willing to continuously upgrade your technical skills.

I like this kind of work, the people I work with, my boss, and the organization I work for; I believe there are many opportunities for career advancement in my present position. I find my greatest job satisfaction comes from the interaction with other people in my department and my professional colleagues.

I previously worked as a real estate salesperson; I believe that position helped me develop interpersonal skills that benefit me in this position.

I will most likely continue to attend engineering classes throughout my professional career and perhaps pursue a graduate degree; I may even get more involved in project management.

ELECTRONICS ENGINEER #4

There is very little I dislike in my job as an electronics engineer working in radar systems engineering. I like my coworkers, my supervisors, the company, and the work itself. Most importantly, there are opportunities for promotion here. I'd prefer there to be more autonomy or independence. A major research library nearby for additional information would be helpful as well. This work pays well and I experience great satisfaction in solving users' (clients') problems.

An electronics engineer must have solid skills in math. You also need to have good analytical skills. Very important is a "can do" attitude. You must have the appropriate education as well. After earning an Associates degree in science, I obtained a Bachelor of Science degree in electrical engineering and a Master of Science degree in the same field. I've always wanted to work in science and electronics. Some day I'd like to run my own operation. With those college degrees, I tried teaching but I found that, for me, the applied area was more interesting.

With a variety of technical problems to address, there is no typical day. However, each day requires technical reading and writing as well as analyzing problems. There is also a great deal of interaction with other engineers inside and outside the office. It's a very pleasant job.

ELECTRONICS ENGINEER, MANAGER

As an electronics engineer and engineering manager, I design electronics and software packages and oversee other engineers and technicians who are working on my technical projects. The electronics designs I create are for system hardware; the software I design is to make the hardware work in an efficient manner.

In addition to an undergraduate degree in the field of engineering, my job requires that I never say "quit," continually follow my quest for knowledge, and think creatively.

Although I never have enough time to get everything done that I would like, I like my job. I enjoy creating things that didn't exist before. I like the people I work with and I believe there are many opportunities for career advancement in this type of work. I take a great deal of pride in seeing my creations work because I know that they provide the world with something useful.

In this line of work for seven years, I held several other positions prior to my present job. I worked as an engineering technician and as an engineer. I received extensive training during my years of service in the U.S. Air Force.

I plan to continue to work in my present position for several more years and then I may open a consultant service; it would be nice to be my own boss for a change.

ELECTRONICS MANUFACTURING TECHNICIAN

I am in the preliminary stage of my career life, and I am continually trying to work my way up the ladder through job experience and a formal education. I am employed as an electronics manufacturing technician/group leader while attending classes in order to earn a Bachelor of Science in Business Management degree.

As an electronics manufacturing technician/group leader, I evaluate the manufacturing procedures of microwave components for commercial and military industries, and I supervise the personnel who perform the procedures. A typical work week in this field would entail writing up production performance evaluations and analyzing the efficiency of the current procedures, overseeing production, and training the production staff.

You must be able to work well with others in order to perform this kind of work well. Applying intelligent reasoning when confronted with production problems concerning deadlines, personnel problems, or manufacturing difficulties is also an essential part of this job.

I have found job satisfaction from this work in being able to solve problems independently and in gaining respect from the people around me. I also like the educational value of this hands-on experience in this supervisory capacity. The fact that my employer is paying for my college tuition is also a positive aspect of my job.

After earning my bachelor's degree in business management, I hope to apply credits toward an aviation management/flight operations degree.

ELECTRONICS PRODUCT ENGINEER

Starting from the advice of a friend who often spoke of his job satisfaction, I began as a manufacturing technician of printed circuits. This job entailed working hand-in-hand with the engineering department in order to work out any problems with a job before it was released to the manufacturing floor. This, in turn, led to my current position as product engineer designing printed circuits.

Basically, my job as product engineer is to design and write procedures for the manufacture of printed circuits. The first step is to review the specifications from the potential customers. I then interact with manufacturing in order to produce the finished product.

Verbal skills are very important in order to communicate the procedures well. The ability to read and understand customer prints and translate them to a format that is readable by a person on the manufacturing floor is essential. Also important is a positive, upbeat attitude.

I enjoy seeing a product shipped in a timely manner to keep customer satisfaction. However, I receive the greatest satisfaction in being able to see something that just a few weeks before was just a picture and specification emerge as a finished product and to know I had a role in making it possible.

Although I enjoy most aspects of my work, at times the pressure to meet a customer's delivery requirements is extremely intense. I would like to be involved in improving some of our internal methods.

I plan to further my education in order to advance myself both personally and professionally. I would like to become more involved in the manufacturing processes of my job in order to better understand the requirements of the people who must work from the documentation I provide for them.

ELECTRONICS REPAIR TECHNICIAN

I have tried my hand at many other occupations before I found that I liked this kind of work. I have been an assembler in an automobile factory, a deckhand on a Great Lakes ore boat, a semitrailer truck driver, a delivery driver, and order desk clerk. I have always liked electronics, and after taking courses at my local community college, I answered an ad in the paper for an entry level position with a local company. I have now been employed with them for 10 years.

As an electronics repair technician on computers, photocopiers, and typewriters, I diagnose and repair this equipment. On a typical day, I go to the customer's place of business to diagnose and then repair the malfunctioning office equipment. I average 6 calls a day with 50 to 70 miles of driving.

On the one hand, an electronics repair technician needs the knowledge of electronic principles, mechanical knowledge, and diagnostic skills. On the other hand, interpersonal business relations with customers are important.

Although I am not particularly satisfied with the company I work for, primarily because I am required to promote and sell their supplies while making the repairs, I still like this kind of work. In fact, I plan to continue my studies in the field of electronics and hope to have a future career in robotics.

ELECTRONICS SPECIALIST

I searched out my job in electronics because I mostly wanted to work for the Defense Department. Prior to this, I returned to school several times to earn three separate associate degrees in liberal arts, accounting and business management. My job background includes work as secretary, electronics assembly and foster parent.

As an electronics specialist, I delegate work to others, update paperwork and ensure others are following their work processes. I work an 8 to 10 hour work day. My typical day includes: delegating all work to employees within my group, working hard to complete schedules; maintaining accurate records of work produced; and training employees for new tasks.

You must be a team player and have the ability to communicate freely with others to perform this kind of work well. Open mindedness and brainstorming is helpful in order to see what other employees can think of to make a job interesting and easier. Open communication is the key. In fact, I wish I could get other areas of the company to communicate more and work together as a team and not for personal goals.

I like almost every aspect of my job including the organization and people I work for, the people with whom I work, the opportunity for advancement, and the kind of work I do. I am glad I got into this field and plan to continue in it, working at moving up into middle management someday. I will also continue working on my bachelor's degree.

I find satisfaction from the feeling of being recognized by management and my co-workers. It is also satisfying knowing that my charges are working hard and producing accurate results and having the opportunity to explore and use creative thinking.

ELECTRONICS TECHNICIAN #1

I originally went to electronics school in the Air Force. I liked the field so well that I have been in it for 30 years. After leaving the Air Force, I joined a large company and continued my education. I have now worked for several companies in private industry as a test engineer in semiconductor fabrication and semiconductor equipment engineering.

Now, as an electronic technician I develop, install, and support host communications in semiconductor fabrication. My typical day includes checking my electronic mail, scheduling meetings, discussing application details with programmer, meeting with the customer (process engineer) to get the requirements on new applications, going out to manufacturing floor to test with programmer, making vendor calls to answer questions on specifications, and writing up progress reports.

To perform this kind of work well, it is important to have communication skills, computer skills, and a fundamentally sound technical background.

The one area of frustration which I face with my work is time pressure to get the job done. I wish there were less pressure and more time to do the job right. Aside from that I like the kind of work I do very much. I would even choose the electronics field again if given the opportunity to start over and prepare for any kind of work. I derive job satisfaction from putting together a good application that works well and does what the customer wants.

ELECTRONICS TECHNICIAN #2

As an electronic technician for twelve years, I test and evaluate power supplies with the use of loads, voltmeters, and oscilloscopes. I also repair power supplies that have had problems or that have been turned in to be reconditioned.

I have an Associate's degree in Industrial Electronics. In addition to some education, this job requires practical knowledge in electronics and a great deal of patience.

Although there are not many opportunities for advancement within this organization, I like this kind of work and the people that I work with. I enjoy that my job constantly puts me to the test and challenges me on a daily basis; every project is different.

The only fault that I find in working with the group that I work with is that some are reluctant to share their knowledge and information for the benefit of the entire group.

Previously, I worked in a warehouse as a stock clerk and as a painter; I also worked with electronics while serving with the U.S. Air Force.

I plan to continue in my educational pursuits and hope to become a computer programmer.

ELECTRONICS TECHNICIAN #3

My work as an electronic technician in a research and development lab has so much variety I never get bored. It also requires a lot of thinking, which I find satisfying.

I entered the field of electronics after receiving training through a publicly-funded program which enabled me to earn an Associates in Applied Technology degree in electrical engineering. Prior to my current position, I have worked in personal computer rework and repair, electro-mechanical assembly, and personal computer board inspection and wiring.

As an electronic engineering technician, I work with the electrical and mechanical engineers to design and develop prototype equipment, PC boards, test boxes, etc. This includes drawing layouts, building wiring, testing, troubleshooting and repairing these items.

The following skills and attitudes are important to perform this kind of work well: willingness to learn, work well with others, good communication skills, a good knowledge of electronics, some mechanical ability, soldering skills, experience with various lab equipment, and ability to wire and read schematics.

Although I like almost every aspect of my work, I would like to have the opportunity to learn more about the individual projects on which I work. I do plan to continue my formal education in order to become an electrical design engineer in the field of robotics.

The projects that I work on are usually pretty challenging, so when I complete a project, it gives me a good sense of accomplishment. I like to see something that I created operating--exactly the way it was supposed to work.

ELECTRONICS TECHNICIAN #4

For several years I have worked as an Electronics Technician for the military. My day usually starts off with testing circuit cards and, if they do not work properly, I spend the rest of the day trying to figure out why they do not operate as they should.

I enjoy this kind of work as I am an individual who likes to be right, and I know I am right when I have found the problem and can fix it. I enjoy finding an answer for myself without someone giving it to me or having to tell me that I am right.

I have an Associate in Science degree with a major in Computer Electronics. My job requires a lot of determination and technical knowledge of electronics.

For this career choice, my inspiration is my father; he also did this kind of work. I have been interested in following in his footsteps ever since I was a little boy. I like this kind of work very much and find my work fascinating and challenging. I work for a great boss and I like working for the military, even though I do not see much opportunity for advancement. It is good to have inspiration to perform this job--that gets me through the days when it seems I do not get paid enough for the skill level required.

I plan to pursue a Bachelor's degree, or beyond, related to computers and electronics and I believe my next career step will be to a programming position.

ELECTRONICS TECHNICIAN #5

A high school graduate, I've always been interested in electronics. After driving a truck for a while and trying my hand at farming, I went to trade school and became an electronic technician.

I've found patience to be very valuable in my years in this field. A person must be dedicated to be successful in this business. A long attention span is also helpful.

My job involves assembling electronic mechanisms. I trouble shoot and, if that doesn't work, I repair broken devices. Job satisfaction for me comes when the device works properly when it is assembled. Some of the work is too routine; I'd like it to be more challenging.

Career goals for me are to stay in the field and continue studying. I want to keep up with new technology.

ELECTRONICS TECHNICIAN, U.S. NAVY

I chose my occupation in high school. I always liked stereos and other electronic equipment and had a desire to know how they really worked. I learned my skills through the United States Navy and by attending night school. A good electronic's job is hard to come by these days, but through hard work and adequate education, it can be obtained.

I work as an electronic technician for a federal agency on communication equipment. My job is to maintain and repair this kind of equipment when it malfunctions and restore it to its normal working condition. A typical day will consist of completing daily routine checks on various equipment to ensure their proper working condition. Throughout the day, we ensure all spare parts are properly stocked and that there is adequate quantity. Then we work on repairs.

Math skills are very important in this field. In order to perform this kind of work well, you also should have the ability to calculate and evaluate things quickly in your head and to determine what is and is not relevant to the situation. Patience, the ability to work along side others as well as alone, and good communication skills are other necessary attributes for this kind of work.

Although I received training in the Navy, I want to continue my education and obtain a four year degree in computer science in order to advance myself professionally. Presently I am finishing up an Associates in Electronic Technology degree.

When equipment malfunctions and I am called upon to repair and restore that equipment, it is very rewarding when the job is complete. Many times I am alone and the only person with the skills and knowledge at the particular time who can repair it. It is very gratifying to see that others depend on my skills and that I can help them.

ELEMENTARY PRINCIPAL, K-4

Although my occupation is stressful, I very much enjoy my work, the people I work with, and the institution. I've spent 22 years in education, first as a teacher of 2nd and 3rd grades, and now (and for the past 11 years) as an elementary school principal.

A typical day for me might involve two special education meetings, three discipline problems, and a teacher conference. I handle many calls and write reports.

One needs tact, diplomacy, creativity, and warmth to be a principal. Other qualities are concern, honesty, and empathy along with technical skills, e.g., finance, instruction, law, and school policies. Of course, a college education is also necessary.

I come from a family of teachers; I've always been involved with children through church, swimming, and camp. I enjoy watching students achieve and grow. My future plans are to remain in education and perhaps one day get into counseling in psychology, teaching at the university level, or being involved in personnel work.

ELEMENTARY SCHOOL AIDE

I have a two-year teaching degree and am an elementary school general aide. An assistant to teachers and students, I have varied responsibilities. I type, copy, laminate, and correct papers. Other duties are to supervise the playground and the lunchroom. I also dispense any necessary medications daily.

Because I had small children and did not feel I had the time nor the resources to go back to college, I chose to be an aide. I also wanted to stay in education. Some day, I'll retire and substitute teach on occasion.

I love helping children learn either directly or through preparing their learning materials. I wish there were opportunities for career growth and I'd like to see reasonable means of discipline restored in the public schools. But my work, the students, and my colleagues give me great pleasure. If I could start over, I'd choose my job again.

My work requires strong social skills. You need to be able to get along with people, be patient, and be flexible. You need to have a general knowledge of elementary subjects as well. A lot of self-confidence and the ability to make decisions are important, too.

ELEMENTARY SCHOOL TEACHER

Being with and working with children is very rewarding to me as an elementary school teacher. Children are wonderful people with whom to deal and to teach!

In teaching, it is satisfying to me when I can gain the students' respect. My hope is that my efforts will bring good results and provide the skills the youngsters need. Working with my fellow teachers also brings me joy. If there were better communication between the administration and the classroom teachers, I would be happier. There is also not enough time for adequate daily class preparation.

My family sent me to a teachers' college after I graduated from high school. I earned a Bachelor of Science degree and did graduate work toward a Masters degree in education. Then I went into teaching 1st grade.

My days in education are spent in preparation for classes, in reading, and in teachers' meetings. I teach language arts, math, science, and social studies. There are scheduled times for the children's physical education, art, music, and library work. At the end of the day, I plan work for the next day and correct the students' papers from that school day.

A good teacher needs a natural understanding and insight into child development. You need to understand child psychology and appreciate individual differences in children. You should be able to recognize their weaknesses and learning difficulties and focus on helping. The ability to avoid "favorites" and to view children objectively is also important.

ELEMENTARY TEACHER, 5TH GRADE

A typical day for me, as an elementary school teacher, consists of 9-10 hours in the classroom. My hours are spent preparing lesson plans, correcting papers, and conducting classes. My subject load is quite varied; I teach science, social studies, math, English, spelling, health, and the computer. Every day there are adjustments made in the scheduling and in my teaching techniques. Each day I learn as much about my profession as my students learn from their subjects.

My education includes a Bachelor of Science degree in vocational agriculture and elementary education. After graduating from college, I began as a substitute teacher for a year. I've also worked as an operations manager and as a military policeman, but I especially like working with children. The students are a joy; the paperwork is a pain. I'd also like there to be more time allowed for classroom work. One day I want to become a school administrator.

Teaching elementary school requires a positive attitude in working with the students. It also demands a great deal of patience. You must have the ability to make rapid adjustment if a lesson plan is not working. You must be a keen observer, watch the students, and observe their reactions to what is being done.

EMPLOYEE RELATIONS SUPERVISOR

I've been a supervisor of an employee relations department for 3 years and there's nothing I dislike about my job.

Personal contact with people is what I most enjoy about my job. Helping employees resolve issues in this important part of their lives is very satisfying to me. Never having the same type of day twice makes my work quite interesting. I have a tremendous variety of responsibilities and activity with all kinds of people.

My job is to establish and maintain harmony in the workplace. I conduct company and union meetings to discuss issues of interest to both employees and management. Working with hourly employees, first-line supervisors, and all levels of management is challenging. We address and correct issues and problems affecting the employees and the operation of a manufacturing plant employing 500 workers. It is my job to ensure plant safety and prompt medical treatment for injured employees. Managing the selection process of new hires is also my responsibility. I'm in charge, too, of seeing that all governmental Affirmative Action regulations are obeyed. Finally, through arbitration, I respond to union grievances. If only there were more time in the day!

In my work, you need strong written and verbal communication skills to deal with people ranging from the president to hourly workers. You should be a highly organized and self-directed person. A positive attitude, as well as valuing human beings of all classes, is very important. You must be willing to be significantly involved in making positive changes in the workplace. The ability to motivate and to persevere toward compromise is critical to resolving work issues.

My plans are to sharpen my technical talents and develop company-wide management skills to take on further management responsibilities. I'd like one day to be the Director or Vice President of Employee Relations.

EMPLOYMENT OFFICE COORDINATOR

I had previously been an accounting clerk and bookkeeper but, for personal reasons, I was working doing temporary jobs through an employment agency when I was assigned to this job. I found the work challenging and interesting and now have done it full-time for 3 years.

I answer phones, talk with people who have inquiries on job openings, type reports, analyze reports, and do data entry.

One of the most critical requirements for success is people skills of friendliness and a willingness to help even under the stressful situation of people facing unemployment. It's very satisfying to be able to assist others.

Since this work has little opportunity for advancement, I may eventually try to go back to the finance area with an eye to becoming a financial analyst some day.

ENGINEER #1

As a mechanical engineer, I have used my knowledge and skills to design, develop and test refrigeration equipment. I provide engineering input and support for planning and implementing programs to create and maintain products for the marketplace. On a daily basis this requires analysis, reporting, planning, consulting, instructing and investigating activities. As far as the skills and attitudes which are required to perform well at this kind of work, you should have the technical skills, be a team player, and have leadership capability.

I like my kind of work as an engineer but would prefer to work for a company with an engineering organization that has less susceptibility to the current influences of the marketplace. I guess one of the reasons why I continue to stay with the refrigeration company is because I like the people I work with and feel that I am making a personal contribution to the achievement of the company's goals.

ENGINEER #2

If I had the opportunity to start over, I'd choose engineering again. I like everything about my job, including my coworkers, my work, and the company. I'd like more money now, but I do have the chance, professionally, to move up in this field. I particularly enjoy the sense of accomplishment I have in my work.

With a Bachelor of Science degree in industrial engineering and a Master of Arts in business administration and management, I served in the U.S. Army for two years. After referrals from friends who worked at this company, I interviewed and was hired 16 years ago. My career goal is to earn more money by becoming an expert in my field.

My job deals with developing a schedule with a logical time frame to plan all the work associated with building a refinery or a chemical plant. I also estimate, forecast, and control all the costs associated with a specific project. Watching for changes in the projected costs and seeking ways to save money are part of my job as well. I am also responsible for the procurement of all materials--from beginning to end--which are used in the construction of the plants.

An engineer needs to be able to work well with other people, so you need strong communication skills. The ability to make good decisions, to think, and to evaluate are all needed. A competent engineer also has good common sense. Being able to get a job done in the time allotted, along with the willingness to accept responsibility, is important in this field. Of course, you need a solid engineering background.

ENGINEER, FIBER OPTICS

There is very little I don't like about my career as a product development engineer for a fiber optic cable company. Fewer meetings and less bureaucracy is all I can think of. I really like developing new products, the fun I have, and being respected for my leadership skills. The people, the company, my supervisors, and the opportunity for advancement make this work very satisfying.

In my job, I develop new fiber optic cables. I supervise other engineers as well as manage other development projects. My day consists of attending meetings and planning or performing an experiment. Analyzing data is also part of my job.

I got into this work because I enjoyed math and I felt that engineering would be a marketable career. While working as a loss control rep for an insurance company, I earned a Bachelor of Science degree in mechanical engineering. One day I'd like to get into engineering management.

Analytical skills are very important to an engineer. You should have strong interpersonal skills and be a leader. Certainly, technical background and experience are necessary. Finally, solid planning ability is needed.

ENGINEER, MECHANICAL & INDUSTRIAL

I like everything about my work as a mechanical and industrial engineer. I've been doing this work for many years and haven't found anything to complain about. Some time ago I got my Bachelor of Science degree in industrial engineering and have never been sorry.

What I like most about my work, and most engineers will tell you this, is seeing a project completed. I also like my coworkers, the company I work for, and my boss (since I own 90% of the company!) The fact that there's opportunity for advancement is great as well.

In this business, we design equipment and processing systems. We also purchase any needed equipment. Conferring with other engineers is part of this work as well.

An engineer needs to be adequately trained. You should have insight and experience with a wide variety of processes. I got into this field because I followed a natural inclination for building things. One day I'll pass this business on to the employees.

ENGINEER, MILITARY ELECTRONICS

I'm an applications engineer for military electronics. Traveling by air to selected military bases, I consult with materials procurement officers, at the Colonel or Lt. Colonel grade, regarding their needs and available solutions to their problems.

In my work, I prepare audio/visual aids to assist in my presentations to customers. Demonstrating or testing electronic equipment and answering questions are also part of my job. Then, I convey the specific needs and interests of the customers to design engineers and follow up on the successful delivery of the products.

I'd had several technical and engineering jobs before I became an applications engineer. I had also earned an Associates degree in industrial electronics. During my years with this company, my qualifications were recognized by superiors, and the job and responsibilities have grown.

To do this job, a background in electronic engineering is needed. Also very important are marketing skills plus the ability to express yourself on your feet. You must have sensitivity to the audience's degree of interest, and respond accordingly. Effective "people skills" are necessary in order to have a good rapport with hardware design personnel. You must also be able to write proposals, carry out all financial and contractual obligations, and "lead the way" in all of the above.

Job satisfaction has been having satisfied customers and providing a vital service for national defense. I enjoy meeting with the high caliber military personnel and cultivating their respect and friendship. More defense appropriations to provide critical hardware to the military would make my job more satisfying. I would prefer less travel as well.

My plans are to stay in this job until retirement and then to use my computer as an aid in handling my investments.

ENGINEER, NUCLEAR UTILITY

With my strong interest in science, chemistry, and engineering, I decided to become a chemical engineer. I earned a Bachelor's degree in chemical engineering and joined a major nuclear utility. My plans are to strive toward an engineering management position eventually.

Each day I assist nuclear plants with any problems involving chemical engineering. There is some travel--2 to 3 days per week--to oversee 4 nuclear plants.

Although I don't see much opportunity for advancement in this job, I do enjoy the independence in setting priorities. If I could start over, I'd choose the chemical engineering field again. Not being stuck behind a desk and being able to travel is important to me. I also enjoy the people I work with. I would like more time to pursue professional organizational activities.

Very important to a chemical engineer are communication skills. You must also be highly organized. Certainly, having the training and technical knowledge is crucial.

ENGINEER, QUALITY CONTROL

In my job as a quality control engineer, I enjoy my small peer group, seeing the results of my effort, which is improvement in the quality of our product, and using my previous experience. I also enjoy passing along my knowledge of methods for testing materials. I've been in this profession for many years and I'd like to stay right here.

I like the combination of "office" and "hands on" work. But, because of the organization I work for, I sometimes find myself unable to function effectively. I'd like to see less bureaucracy and less paperwork.

Writing, reviewing, evaluating and approving work procedures are paramount in my work. Preparing and presenting training courses is also part of my job. I attend meetings and training courses; I evaluate and interpret the results of quality control inspections. Much of my work is reading of technical literature, attending seminars, writing reports, and communication with coworkers.

To be an effective quality control engineer, you need a good education (e.g., have a Bachelor of Science in Physics), the ability to learn "on the job," and writing skill. You should understand the "half art/half science" character of this profession.

ENGINEERING AIDE

My work as an engineering aide is to aid the engineers in the design and development of new products. I am involved in testing new products to see if they perform as designed; if the products don't perform as they should, new configurations must be tried.

In addition to the proper training, to work as an engineering aide you must possess a good imagination, a willingness to try new things, and patience.

In the six years I have worked as an engineering aide, I have found my greatest job satisfaction is derived from the success of one of my ideas. When one of my ideas makes it through the system and then makes money for the company, I know that I have chosen the work that will bring me the greatest rewards. This kind of work holds many challenges for me, and I believe there are many opportunities for me to advance in my career. I also work for a great boss, and that is an important factor.

I plan to return to school eventually in order to become an engineer in either the field of mechanical engineering or electrical engineering.

ENGINEERING DESIGNER

There is not a thing I dislike about my career which I have been engaged in for 30 years. My skills as a machinist were sparked when my dad got a small lathe for his home shop when I was 16. Although my family had a strong educational background (my father was the head of the electrical engineering dept. at a major university) I dropped out of college, one quarter shy of a degree in mechanical engineering. However, I have enjoyed job satisfaction all along and for a non-college graduate I am getting good annual reviews and having an above-average salary. For 12 years I had my own tool and die shop. For the last 18 years I have had the position of engineer designer at a medical and biochemical research equipment company. As well as my design duties, I also supervise 6 other designers. This involves hiring and firing, annual reviews, recommendations for pay increases, and overseeing their projects. As a designer, I carry out my own design projects from inception to release to the manufacturing department, a process which may take 6 to 24 months.

I arrive at work 10-15 minutes early every day. I check with all others working on my project (drafting, purchasing, prototype technicians, machine shop etc.). Returning all phone calls promised for the day, coffee breaks, talking with people regarding information to me or them, seeing my boss to report status of my project and my men's, are all part of my typical work day. I must be prepared for any inter-departmental meetings, get some design drawings done and get drafting started on them. I might work

1-2 hours overtime if necessary, but if it is too often, I talk it over with my boss.

To perform well at this job, you must know drafting and blueprint reading and machine shop practice at the tool and die level. It is important to be able to handle people and have them want to do their best for you. You should give verbal credit when someone does well, and get advice from the most qualified source you can find. Finally, be innovative. Having all people in the engineering dept. wanting to work on my projects has been satisfying. Also rewarding has been having the project engineers fighting to get me to run their projects. Receiving awards and being granted 13 patents has also made this career satisfying.

ENGINEERING GEOLOGIST

In my work of four years as an Engineering Geologist, I study the native stabilities of building sites in areas with high probability of earthquakes. I visit construction sites and "log drill" holes in the ground before a foundation is laid; these holes are designed to determine the nature of the subsurface materials.

I have a Bachelor of Science degree and a Doctorate degree in the field of Geology; I have experience as a Geologist dealing with precious metals, uranium, and petroleum.

In addition to a good education, other needs are: a background in geology, familiarity with drill rigs, familiarity with the techniques of logging, and a pleasant attitude toward one's surroundings as well as a positive attitude toward ordinary working people.

I enjoy my work because my job allows me to visit many unfamiliar places, provides me a good rate of pay, and I experience the practical application of geology while filling needs with civil engineering applications.

At times, I would prefer my work to be more technically demanding with a smaller percentage of my time spent on professional or administrative tasks, especially paperwork.

I plan to develop a higher personal expertise in engineering geology and in the field of environmental applications of geology.

Engineering Geology is a fascinating and challenging field, I recommend it highly to those with an interest in geology within an engineering discipline.

ENGINEERING INSTRUCTOR

Because I am a Christian, I prayed for guidance about a career. Teaching is what I felt God wanted me to do. In order to prepare myself for this profession, I first earned a bachelor's degree in mechanical engineering and worked as an engineer before going to graduate school so I could teach.

As an engineering instructor and division chair, I teach engineering, math, and physics, and perform duties such as scheduling, budget, curriculum development and faculty evaluations. The largest portion of my time is spent preparing lectures and laboratories, teaching classes and laboratories, and meeting with students who need extra help. Also, depending on the time of year, I work on curriculum development, instructor evaluations, course scheduling, budget planning, hiring of part time faculty, and giving on and off campus presentations.

In order to perform this kind of work well, math and reading skills are very important, as well as verbal and written communication skills. Also, it is important to be patient yet persistent and to be willing to keep learning and trying new things.

The only part of my job that I don't like is having to evaluate students and other faculty. However, this is an unavoidable part of my job. What I particularly like is getting to know the students, never being bored, and the stimulation of being able to learn new things. The most satisfying part of the work is my having a positive influence on someone else's life.

ENGINEERING MANAGER #1

As an engineering manager, I design large complex computer programs, lead a group of people to build the new design, and interact with other people/groups. More specifically, on a day-to-day basis, I work with other groups/managers to establish priorities, review progress of the group, work with group members to resolve problems, build portions of the system, and contribute to design of systems.

As a manager, it is important to have people skills and technical knowledge for the engineering part of the work. It is working successfully with both the people and the technology that makes this job satisfying to me.

I was studying to be a chemist when I entered the Air Force. Since the USAF had no need for chemists but rather a need for people with computers skills and I had worked with computers and liked them, I put two and two together. I continued in school to earn my Masters of Science in Engineering degree. I was an officer in the Air Force doing largely the same work I do now in industry. I plan to continue in this field and aspire to become a more senior technical contributor.

ENGINEERING MANAGER #2

For 10 years I've directed a maintenance department and worked on environmental projects, have done engineering as required, have overseen the work of those employed in my field, and, as a safety director, my tasks include those which keep the plant safe. I've found education, dedication, and satisfaction in doing a good job are needed in my field.

If I were to begin again, I'd choose the same job I have now because I like my work. I'd like it more if the pay were better and there were opportunities for advancement.

My main satisfaction from my work is doing a good job. Previously, I've been a factory worker, a maintenance man at a golf course, and I have earned my Masters in Business Education. My career aspiration is to continue to increase the quality of the work I perform.

ENGINEERING MANAGER #3

As an engineering manager, I supervise senior engineers and scientists in the development of advanced information systems. My work includes technical, scientific, and managerial coaching and counseling of my people.

I particularly enjoy watching others grow as we achieve mutual objectives. My colleagues and my work itself are very rewarding to me. What I don't like are the excessive administrative requirements of management; if our heavy workload were reduced, I'd like my job more. I want, in the future, to acquire major pieces of business by writing competitive federal procurement proposals.

An engineering manager needs broad and highly technical engineering skills. You need a strong background in mathematics and in computer science. A good sense of humor helps as does the attitude of a highly proactive, positive person. Appropriate training is also necessary; I have a Bachelor's degree in electrical engineering, a Master's of Science degree, and a Doctorate in engineering science.

ENGINEERING PHYSICIST

With my degree in physics, and a master's in electro-optics, I felt there were various scientific fields to choose from. In hard economic times, you must choose what is available and/or offered. Thus, I found a job designing laser and electro-optic systems and managing programs for government contracts.

This kind of work entails desk-work design, and then implementing the design in a laboratory. In addition, this research and development work requires analyzing data, writing reports, and program management. In order to perform this kind of work well, it is important to have a good math and science background with reading and writing skills. In addition to the skills, enthusiasm and perseverance are necessary attributes for accomplishing the work required of an engineering physicist.

I have no particular dislikes about my work except that I would like more opportunity to attend national conferences and to publish technical papers. I like the kind of work I do, the organization and people I work for, the opportunity for advancement, and the people with whom I work. My work is non-stressful and clean. I find job satisfaction from developing hardware (or systems) that perform specific tasks.

I do aspire to a research and development management job in the future, for more professional growth opportunities.

ENTREPRENEUR

I started my own business primarily because I wanted the freedom which this allows me to have. I chose the chimney sweep business because it had a fairly low start-up price and could be done part-time in the beginning. Prior to this and after graduating from high school, I have worked as a production test technician, a prototype technician, carpenter/builder, and a machinist mate in the Navy.

As an entrepreneur, I have not only started and now operate a chimney sweep business, but I am also now starting a filtered water cooler business. A typical week would consist of picking up materials to complete 5 jobs for the next week, promoting the business, doing the accounting, returning customer calls, and helping my employees do the jobs that need to be done.

An absolutely positive attitude is very essential in operating your own business, as well as a large variety of skills. Some days I have to be a carpenter/sheetmetal worker/chimney sweep and then become an accountant at the end of the day.

I find satisfaction in my work mostly from the freedom of determining my own destiny. I like having the ability to make as much or as little money as I want depending on how hard I want to work. The only major drawbacks for me are doing the filing and paperwork and controlling the cash flow.

My future career plans are to build more successful companies.

ENVIRONMENTAL ATTORNEY

I sought out a challenging career, away from politics and journalism, after my experience on the legislative staff of a press secretary. Therefore, I chose to go into practice as an environmental attorney.

In this legal specialty, I advise clients on compliance with environmental laws. My typical daily activities include researching issues, responding to client phone calls, drafting letters and memoranda, meeting with senior and junior attorneys, and reading periodicals on recent developments in the field.

To perform this kind of work well, it is important to have research and writing skills as well as personal skills. Diplomacy--the ability to convey self-confidence, the ability to inspire confidence--is critical for this profession.

I like almost every aspect of my work as an environmental attorney except the demanding schedule. This career involves long hours in stressful situations--client pressure and the adversarial nature of some parts of practice. What I do like about my work is the organization and people I work for, the people I work with, the opportunity for advancement and the intellectual challenge. I also find it very satisfying to be involved with and to deal with lots of people.

My future career plans are to do more of the same kind of work.

ENVIRONMENTAL ENGINEER CONSULTANT

I very much enjoy my work as an independent environmental engineer. If I could start over, I'd choose my present work without change. My employees include engineers, scientists, and consultants who offer assistance with problems with air, waste water, and waste. We work out plans of approach, estimate the cost to assess needs and pursue solutions. We evaluate alternative solutions to air pollution, waste water, and solid/hazardous wastes. Our company makes recommendations and at times implements technical, regulatory, and management solutions. We always evaluate our results.

After 26 years in the business, I've found that open mindedness, creativity, and objectivity are essential. Problem solving, as well as the ability to identify with the clients' dreams and hopes, are valuable tools. Professionalism accompanied by good naturedness and humor contribute to success. Solid morals, and a strong work ethic are also essential.

I enjoy my clients, but I particularly dislike collecting fees owed by slow paying clients. I like daily intellectual challenge, finding solutions to client problems, and then their satisfaction with the results. In the future I plan to bring on younger partners, expanding to cities in the Midwest. I'll act as consultant to these satellite companies.

My degrees are a B.A. and a Masters of Business Administration. Other jobs I've had and enjoyed are civil engineering, city planning, and economic research. I've also acquired stores and have been an administrator. As a 16 year old, I worked as a surveyor's helper. In the Army Corps of Engineers I served as a planning and construction officer. These skills translated into civilian life where I moved into civil engineering and eventually into environmental engineering.

ENVIRONMENTAL GEOTECHNICAL DRILLER

I am very happy in my job as an environmental geotechnical driller, which basically means that I am involved in and drill, install, and monitor wells. I acquire geotechnical samples to help in the designing of building foundations.

Striving to do more than is expected gives me pleasure in my work. I'd be happier if we had better machinery, more training, and higher pay.

After answering an advertisement in the newspaper for what I thought was for an oil field driller, I got into this work. I like the kind of work I do and my fellow workers. Unfortunately, there is little chance of advancement. One day I would like to become involved in alternative energy (e.g., solar and geothermal) heating and cooling.

To do this job well, you must be mechanically minded, like to work hard, not mind getting dirty, and be able to pay close attention to detail. A college degree is not required, but you should have a high school diploma.

I've been in this work 4 years and I'll probably stay in this or a related field because the pay is good and I like this kind of work. I've also worked as an offset pressman, an auto mechanic, a carpenter, a salesman, a house painter, and, just before becoming a driller, I was on an oil field factory production line.

ENVIRONMENTAL PLANNER

A brief description of my work is that I create environmental documents. To accomplish this I must first meet and make field checks with specialists, engineers, resource agency staff people and local government personnel. Somewhere along the line I actually begin to develop the environmental document. I also attend sporadic public hearings and meetings.

To be a good environmental planner, it is important to have interpersonal skills. Although you must have an understanding in various resources disciplines, it is not necessary to have actual professional competence in the various resources. Competence in environmental analysis/planning and an understanding of various environmental laws is mandatory, however.

This career has been satisfying to me for 11 years because I like getting a project through with environmental integrity and getting the best compromise worked out between engineering and politics. In my opinion, I would find it easier to arrive at compromises if engineers had more in-depth awareness of environmental constraints/laws.

I kind of got into this profession by default. I couldn't handle the math to be an astronomer or a meteorologist, and so I changed my major to geography/geology. Prior to my current job I was a land use planner and budget-policy analyst. I am now working on my master's degree in this field with aspirations of getting a Ph.D. so I can teach.

ENVIRONMENTAL SPECIALIST (EPA)

I am an environmental specialist in the area of waste water for the Environmental Protection Agency (EPA). My job is to conduct a site evaluation and specify what size and type of sewage treatment system is required. To enforce regulations, I then write to the property owners informing them of the requirements.

In my work, I review plans for sludge disposal and sewer line systems which are in place, as well as those proposed for development. Further, I inspect the operation of sewage treatment facilities and industrial treatment plants, and I attend public meetings where waste water will be a topic of discussion. Writing permits and evaluating task completion schedules are also part of my job. Currently, we are developing a computer program which will write permits automatically.

To do this job, you need to be a dependable individual. Patience and the ability to be flexible are also necessary. Even though I earned a Bachelor of Arts degree in

English and history, I've received specialized training for my job.

I enjoyed my previous jobs as social worker and as a teacher, but this work over 15 years has been very satisfying. I like the fact that every day is different and that there is so much variety. It is rewarding to serve people along with helping eliminate pollution. What I don't like is the bureaucracy of the system and some of the supervisors.

EPIDEMIOLOGY RESEARCH ASSISTANT

My work in the field of epidemiology as a research assistant involves many tasks. I use a computer to examine health-related data and run statistical programs on that data, develop data collection forms and instructions, analyze the data, report the results of my analysis to those in need of this information through meetings and correspondence, perform quality control and data entry to the computer, count items, keep track of events and people, match data across sources, and perform necessary administrative tasks.

I work for a family-run organization and so there are not many opportunities for advancement in my current position. But I do enjoy this kind of work and the people I work with.

I have completed a Bachelor of Arts degree in International Studies and have two years experience as an administrative assistant for a "quasi-public," health-oriented firm, which I also liked. In addition to experience and education, to work as a research assistant you must possess good problem solving skills and enjoy making pieces of a puzzle fit together. Working in the field of research also requires good computer skills, a willingness to discover, and persistence in tracking details--a personal quality that is essential to this kind of work.

I accepted this position because I have always had an interest in public health and a desire to do quiet, behind-the-scenes activities.

In another year I plan to return to college to earn a Master's degree in either Business Administration or Management Information Systems and, after that is complete, I expect to get into marketing research for a health-oriented industry.

EPISCOPAL PRIEST #1

My current position as an Episcopal priest is as the administrator in a diocese. As such I am responsible for filling vacant parishes and pastoral care of the clergy in the diocese. To perform these duties I meet with clergy and search committees, visit parishes in the dioceses and edit a newsletter. These do not take place in a 9-5 schedule.

To perform well as a priest with my type of administrative responsibilities it is important to have patience, be able to manage conflict, have the art of listening well, and then articulate what is being said. Skill at public speaking is also necessary.

I have not had another career, only odd jobs while in college such as sales clerking, ambulance driving, and as a church organist/choirmaster. I knew when I entered college that I wanted to study to become a priest. I first earned a bachelor of arts degree and then a master's in divinity. I was a parish priest for 22 years before the Bishop found I had the qualities he felt he needed for his chief assistant, and I moved to this position.

I like this work very much, but I would like to be able to study more carefully with allotted times for that.

I plan to stay where I am or possibly become a bishop because I find great satisfaction in the results of my work and in the relationships with many people.

EPISCOPAL PRIEST #2

For twenty-seven years, I have been the rector of a small congregation of the Episcopal Church. As an Episcopal Priest, I prepare sermons, preach the gospel, teach Christianity, provide pastoral counseling for my congregation, read, sort mail, visit those of my congregation who are ill, and attend meetings with my congregation and on behalf of my congregation.

I have completed graduate studies to earn a Master of Divinity degree. My work also requires listening skills, communication skills, faith, a willingness to risk, a willingness to depend on others, and a genuine love of all people.

Although at times I take on too many responsibilities, I really love my work and the gratification of the eternal significance of my efforts, which I derive from my work. I am truly blessed with a wonderful congregation in a lovely church setting; the respect and appreciation I get from my congregation makes all my sacrifices worthwhile. I enjoy the freedom to design my job--there are no limits, except time and money; I always am somehow able to find time to read and study, which I believe makes me a better priest to my parish.

The goal of my work at present is to help my congregation become more helpful to the community and more receptive to new people as potential members of our congregation.

EVALUATION SPECIALIST

I consider my job as an evaluation specialist to be the answer to a dream of mine of working for a highly-respected electronics company in the electronics engineering department. My electronics background from a vocational school helped me secure this position as an evaluation specialist.

My work involves analyzing cross-sections of a variety of electronic components. For example, I might take a microsection of an integrated I.C. chip, cut it, and evaluate it. This would include the plated holes through the P.C. board. Also I determine the extent of dye penetration in order to find very small cracks in a weld joint that might disintegrate under vibration conditions. There are many jobs similar to this that I do. It amounts to cutting and destroying a good piece of hardware in order to analyze its construction. If there is failure, analysis of the cause is needed.

In order to perform this kind of work, a combination of skills and techniques is required, particularly in the field of electronics. One of the most important keys for succeeding in this work is having a positive approach to the job and doing it with much concentration and attention to safety.

I find satisfaction in my work from the "thank you" I receive from the engineers. It pleases me to be working with others in much higher career positions and for them to accept my reasons and opinions. Making judgment calls and having the engineers use them is indeed satisfying.

My future career plans are to continue to increase my knowledge and skills in order to move into higher positions within the company such as a technician (group leader). My ultimate goal is to become a mechanical engineer.

EVALUATOR OF SURVEYS

This job involves a statistical analysis of evaluations of professors by students in evening classes at a university, either manually or by computer, from course evaluation forms completed by the students. I analyze the findings and prepare a report of the results.

In my twenty-one years in this position, I have found nothing I really dislike about my job. I enjoy this kind of work and I especially enjoy the faculty I work with. My job also affords me a high degree of independence, which is important to me.

I have both a Bachelor's and a Master's degree. You have to have the ability to conduct research and have knowledge of research methodology, to understand statistical results and interpret the meaning of the statistical results, and be able to prepare reports.

I have a strong interest in the areas of teaching and research; I previously held such positions as budget analyst, management analyst, management consultant, and merchandise wholesaler.

I have no plans to do any other type of work for the next several years; I am settled and happy with my position.

EXECUTIVE ASSISTANT

If I could start over, I would certainly choose my work as an executive assistant again. After graduating from high school, I was in retail sales and bookkeeping. I've also enjoyed being an executive secretary, helping give a good image of our company and of my boss.

My job requires the ability to make full and complete arrangements for large groups of manufacturing reps, from all over the country, who are visiting our factory. You also need a very cooperative attitude, particularly in dealing with vendors.

If anything, I would like more opportunity for advancement in my job and it would be nice if I had more chances to make my own decisions in specific areas.

Still, it is particularly satisfying to me when I successfully draw together all the details of some project or event. In my work, I organize all details for our sales meetings and perform all the secretarial office duties. These duties include opening and distributing the mail, making travel arrangements for the sales managers, and maintaining customer service. I take shorthand and type as well.

EXECUTIVE ASSISTANT IN RADIOLOGY PRACTICE

I work for 40 physicians in a large radiology practice handling various administrative tasks and purchasing. It is my responsibility to train and supervise the front desk secretaries. Preparation and distribution of agenda packages for Board and Committee meetings are included in my duties. I attend board meetings and take the minutes. I also assist the general manager with administrative projects, assist with building management duties, and plan business functions and corporate parties. Inventory control, and purchasing forms and stationery, are another part of my job.

To perform well at this type of work it is important to have initiative, a positive attitude, sense of responsibility, resiliency in dealing with various personalities, and problem-solving skills. Computer skills on word processing and Lotus Spreadsheet are also needed.

The main satisfaction I find from my work is the professional respect I get from managers and co-workers. Having the physicians express confidence in my ability is rewarding. I get personal satisfaction especially when accomplishing certain challenging projects.

I like almost everything about my job, the people, the type of work, and the organization. If I had more help, I would delegate some of the more routine tasks, and I could then work on more challenging projects. Originally, I was a legal secretary looking for a more responsible position. I would like eventually to become an office manager or a management assistant. I found this position listed in the newspaper under "administrative assistant." After the first year, the General Manager changed my title to executive assistant because of greater responsibilities.

I have an Associate's degree in business management. Prior to this position and my job as a legal secretary I was also a purchasing assistant, executive secretary to a bank president, a government secretary and an answering service switchboard operator. I hope to be promoted to a management position with the radiology practice. It is a good organization, and I would like to stay here.

EXECUTIVE RECRUITER

As an executive recruiter (headhunter) in the computer industry, I enjoy the ability to be my own boss and having the work scheduling flexibility which I need.

Because I am a single parent, I needed a well paying job, without travel so that I could work from my home if I needed to do so. With 12 years of experience in computer and real estate sales, I decided that the recruiting business fit the criteria and was an extension of my previous experience. I earned a Bachelor of Arts in Education and a Masters of Science in Education . Before my current career I was also an elementary, junior high and community college teacher.

A typical work day for me is: 50% on the phone calling clients, client companies, applicants, or cold-calling new applicants, 10% meeting new clients of established or new client companies, 10% meeting new applicants--interviewing them for technical skills and personality, and 20% administrative duties.

To perform well as an executive recruiter, it is important to have: Desire to make a deal--close the business. Ability to take rejection--not take it personally. Ability to talk with and meet new people in an effective way. Ability to follow through, taking the initiative to make things happen. Being well organized, smart, and timely.

One thing I think I should mention is that I work on 100% commission. I only earn money by placing clients. I would like it if I had better administrative help to make me more productive.

In spite of the drawbacks, I like the kind of work very much and enjoy the people I work with, and the flexibility. I receive satisfaction from closing a deal, and earning good money. It is rewarding when I find good people for jobs and find good jobs for people.

EXECUTIVE, SALES

My career focus has been in business management, and since earning a Bachelor of Science in Economics/Physics degree, I have held positions as Vice President of Sales and Marketing, President and Chief Executive Officer, and Director of Marketing.

Now as a company executive, I manage sales and marketing people. My typical activities include: directing the activities of the sales people; updating marketing plans; and participating in acquisition activities.

My key for success in business is enthusiasm, analytical skills, and maintaining a focus on key tasks.

Although I like the kind of work I do very much, I am somewhat frustrated with the lack of aggressiveness within the company. Aside from this aspect of the company, I like the organization and people I work for, the people with whom I work, and the opportunity for advancement. I find job satisfaction from my work because of the achievement of goals, development of people, and the opportunity I have to provide encouragement and motivation.

My future career plans are to continue to climb the ladder in business management and become president of the company.

EXECUTIVE SECRETARY #1

My job changes from day to day as an executive secretary. That is probably why I have liked this as my career for so many years. On a regular basis, I handle correspondence, appointments, the telephone, travel arrangements, act as an administrative assistant, plus an unknown quantity of things as they occur.

At times, I say that I would like there to be more stability as to how daily things progress so as to avoid things like the "last minute" response to get "things" out. However, I have to admit that I get enjoyment from this hectic, stressful, ever-changing job as an executive secretary.

To perform well at this job, it is important to stay cool and calm, have quick responses, and be alert, conscientious, dedicated and loyal.

I chose this as a career while I was in high school and took the high school business courses that would prepare me for secretarial work. The rest of my training has been mostly on-the-job.

EXECUTIVE SECRETARY #2

Through promotions and additional training I have worked myself up to the position of executive secretary for a state agency. As such, I do general secretarial duties, computer word processing, and research. More specifically, my duties include: receptionist work, answering the phone, typing, evaluating and researching state programs, conducting telephone surveys, communicating with staff, and making appointments.

In order to perform these duties well, it is important to have typing skills, to know word processing and how to efficiently use a calculator, have good telephone manners, be able to communicate with all kinds of people, and have an outgoing personality.

I like almost every aspect of my work.

On the other hand, I feel there is a lack of opportunity for advancement. I do plan to continue working for the agency, and through more training I hope I can get other promotions. I find this work satisfying because I like working with people, using the computer and doing research. I have also found that the traveling that is involved in my job adds another satisfying aspect to my work.

EXECUTIVE SECRETARY #3

I have enjoyed several different jobs during the course of my career. I was educated to be a high school teacher by earning a Bachelor of Arts in liberal arts (English, drama, speech), but out of the various jobs I have had, I have not taught high school. Prior to my current position as executive secretary to a college president, I worked as a library assistant in a children's library, a secretary to an elementary school principal, a section manager of a large university library, and a secretary to an academic dean.

As the executive secretary (or administrative assistant) to a college president, my duties are primarily secretarial. My typical responsibilities include opening and sorting the daily mail, making and serving coffee, composing correspondence, recording telephone messages, organizing, storing and retrieving information (filing plus), hosting office visitors, keeping the appointment calendar, editing and printing written material, relating to irate parents and students, and answering questions from all constituents.

In order to do this kind of work well, it is important to have judgment and sensitivity to all varieties of people, to maintain a positive attitude, and to be loyal to the supervisor and the institution. The ability to spell, to organize, and a knowledge of grammar are also essential skills for my work. I have found it necessary to have good health, stamina, and energy because my work schedule often goes beyond the normal work week hours. Above all the other requirements, however, is the willingness to contribute beyond what is expected. That is the key element.

If I could change any aspect of my work it would be to keep my work hours within the "normal" work week, and I would enjoy greater acknowledgement for the quality of my work. Despite these frustrations, I like almost all other aspects of my work and find job satisfaction from the belief that I contribute to the growth and progress of the institution and to the success of my boss, the president. My job is to help the president succeed. Her success is also mine. I enjoy the feeling that I am liked by the people to whom I relate.

EXECUTIVE SECRETARY #4

I've been an executive secretary for 11 years and I very much enjoy my work. I like the great feeling of accomplishment in working with people to accomplish intricate and difficult tasks. Being able to help people with their problems is great. I appreciate my boss and others making me feel that I am a vital part of the success of our scientific organization. I also like the pay.

Previously, I taught music in elementary school since I had a minor in music in my Bachelor of Science degree. My majors, however, were English and science, which turned out to be valuable in disciplining my thinking. Now, I handle the phones, take dictation, and arrange travel, meetings, and meals for those in the division who have these requirements. I write some of the correspondence for my boss, who supervises over 200 employees in our division. I maintain confidential personnel files, purchase orders for scientific books for our library, and research data for speeches he has to make at national scientific meetings.

To do the work of an executive secretary, you need to have excellent secretarial skills and good telephone manners. Being able to cope with pressure and deadlines is paramount. You must be self-assured and have self-confidence because you have to deal with a very wide variety of people such as laboratory technicians, vice presidents, scientists, clerks, college deans, government officials, and others. I cannot stress too much that good technical skills are necessary; the best jobs go to people with a lot of background knowledge on many subjects. Even my four years of Latin came in handy at times!

I have literally moved up through the ranks. I started in the company as a clerk typist, but my knowledge and background in English and science helped me move to secretarial positions with higher-level bonuses. It would suit my career plans if my present boss were to move up to be Vice President--and take me with him as his executive secretary!

EXECUTIVE SECRETARY #5

I am a missionary serving as an executive secretary at a college. Employee appreciation is an important part of job satisfaction. One of the greatest satisfactions with my work comes from the respect and consideration paid me by my boss. All I really need is more office space. My career goal is to work wherever I'm needed at the college.

My work involves organizing various events for the college. It's my job to attend administrative board meetings and record the minutes of the meetings. I serve, too, as Institutional Research Officer for accreditation. I also write and type much of the college's correspondence. Scheduling appointments and answering phones are my responsibility as well.

To perform my work well, requires respect for authority. You should also be a very hard-working person. I got into this occupation because my husband and I are appointed missionaries and were willing to work where needed. I've also been a preschool teacher and director. I have a Bachelor of Arts in English.

EXECUTIVE VICE PRESIDENT

I have worked my way up to this executive position and have ambition to go further. At the present time I manage 300 people in a distribution business. The day-to-day duties involved in this management position are meeting with people to define goals and objectives, sorting through alternatives, conducting follow-ups on performances, and maintaining an overview in the balance of the organization. In short, I worry about what is happening!

To perform well in this position it is important to have the following skills and abilities: listening, questioning, reasoning, challenging, cheerleading and honesty.

I find satisfaction in my work from the achievement of objectives, getting things done and getting others to get it done. I take pride and pleasure from seeing a subordinate do a great job.

What I find dissatisfying about my job is that I do not have enough influence over the balance of the organization. That is why I would like to eventually run a complete business, to be the boss. I hope to prove that people will do the job if properly led.

My previous business experience after receiving my MBA degree has been as the certified public accountant and partner in a Big 8 Firm, the Chief Executive officer of a small retail chain, and an investment banker. When the opportunity presented itself for my current position, I jumped, because it enabled me to satisfy one of my long time objectives.

EXECUTIVE VICE PRESIDENT, TRUCKING COMPANY

I was born into the trucking business and I too have found that this kind of work is satisfying to me. I have held other jobs like scuba diver instructor and real estate assessor, but have returned to the benefits of working in a family business.

As the executive vice president of the trucking company, it is my responsibility to buy, repair and rebuild the equipment. My work day is from 8 a.m. to 7 p.m. 6 days a week, and includes shopping for and buying parts and equipment, repairing equipment and diagnosing and correcting problems. In order to work well and endure this long work schedule, it is important to have patience, common sense and be physically fit.

I like most aspects of being part of a family business and can see one of the benefits being that we are working for a common goal. I find job satisfaction when I see all the pieces of the business working well. However, the downside of my work is that I have difficulty finding other willing, cooperative, honest employees.

I plan to stay with the trucking business and help it grow. My goal is to have the business grow enough to support more staff in order for me to get more free time and more money.

EXPEDITER, MANUFACTURER & SHIPPING

Six years ago I started a job as a machinist in a machine shop and then transferred to the shipping department. Pretty quickly I become head of shipping and then worked my way up to being manufacturing/shipping expediter.

Although I would prefer having closer relationships with customers, I am pretty well satisfied with this position that involves daily supervision of shipping and receiving.

I make up schedules for jobs that are due, correspond with management, expedite all open orders and reply to customers' inquiries.

You should be a high school graduate for this job. As far as personal traits are concerned, you should be well organized, able to work quite independently, and get along well with other people. In addition, you should have considerable knowledge of the company's product.

I would like to have more control of "due dates" on orders, but I think I would take this job again if I could start over in any kind of work.

EXPLORATION GEOLOGIST

As an exploration geologist for sixteen years, I use geology and geophysics to discover new reserves of oil and natural gas. Gathering geologic and geophysical data to develop prospects, I analyze the economy of the prospect and make recommendations to management. Once I receive approval, I arrange to drill the wildcat well, evaluate the well results, and then make further recommendations on the prospect.

I have three degrees in geology and geophysics; the highest level of education I have achieved is on the doctorate level of studies. In addition, in order to achieve success in this field, you must have a strong technical background in geology and geophysics, the ability to reason in an analytical fashion, and the ability to think in a logical manner; you must enjoy problem solving.

Although there are not many opportunities for career advancement from my present position, I really enjoy my work, especially the search for prospects and the evaluation process. I like the people I work with, my boss, and the company I work for. The only disadvantage of this type of work is that you move often in this line of work; it is the nature of the business; someday I would like to settle in one town that I like.

I plan to get involved more in research; I would like to design a rank exploration program that is successful.

EXPORT BROKER

An export broker deals in international sales, sourcing goods for sale on the international market and inquiring about international trade requirements.

I have both a Bachelor of Arts and a Master of Arts degree. You need to have knowledge of cultural traits, international trade contacts, a positive mental attitude, and considerable patience.

Although export restrictions can be a real hindrance, I enjoy this kind of work and the people I deal with; there is the opportunity for considerable monetary rewards.

My previous career of twenty years was in manpower management for the United States Air Force, after which I spent several years in college administration as a counselor and dean of students. I enjoyed the latter a great deal, but became interested in becoming an export broker through a contact in another country who requested information from me concerning the pricing and availability of goods in this country.

I am enjoying my present work and have not considered moving on to any other projects except perhaps to return to school to learn more about international trade.

EXPORT/IMPORT EXECUTIVE

For the last six years, my work as an export/import executive has involved the responsibilities of an international transportation executive, salesperson, and lecturer, to provide export forwarding and import brokerage services. I work as a consultant offering advice and contacts to those desiring to sell their merchandise on the international market, as a salesperson on commission handling forwarding and brokerage services, and as a lecturer for a flat fee at companies attempting to break into the international market. Usually, I visit various exporters and importers to help them solve problems and offer advice related to transportation documentation and customs clearance, but I occasionally conduct full day seminars at client companies.

I have a Bachelor of Science degree in Marine Transportation; in addition to a good educational background, my work requires good communication skills, analytical skills, the ability to listen, and the desire to perform research activities for the international and domestic markets.

I really like my work. It offers enough of a daily challenge and I know that the people I assist gain in professional levels--I give them a better understanding of the way to conduct business on the international level. I enjoy utilizing skills that I have developed over my entire career in the export and import business; my prior experience includes working as a merchant seaman, working in the export/import department in a manufacturing company, and being self-employed as an export forwarder.

I plan to remain involved in the international trade market. Perhaps I will return to school to complete graduate studies in the area of international marketing.

FACTORY ASSEMBLER

As a factory assembler, I take pride in a finished product with my name on it that will be shipped all around the world. It is my responsibility to troubleshoot, repair, and customize electronic amusement and gaming equipment. In a day, I build 2 to 12 machines, depending on type of machine and complexity. Other routine activities include: consulting with 8 other departments at various times about their problems, repairing up to 30 various machines, instructing others, inspecting incoming and outgoing parts, and making other decisions.

To do this type of work well, it is important to have good hand/eye coordination, the ability to take orders and perform them to the letter- within bounds of common sense, a good memory, the ability to work well with others, initiative, and tolerance.

I consider myself to be a multi-faceted person and have held jobs in virtually all kinds of work including: plumbing, carpentry, electrician, mechanic, rancher, farmer, truck driver, police, security, store manager, yardman, laborer, and mason. When I was working as a store manager, a friend of a friend noticed my abilities, such as they are, and talked me into going to work for his company as an assembler.

I like this kind of work and get annoyed by other people's neglect, ignorance and lack of respect or pride for their work performed. I take satisfaction from my assembly work because I can assemble from scratch a properly functioning intricate machine and electronic equipment.

I plan to continue working for myself and my family for the betterment of the human condition and peace of mind.

FACTORY REPAIR MECHANIC

I'm the trouble shooter on the second shift in a manufacturing plant. It's my job to respond to operator/supervisor problems with machines and repair them.

Because the operators or supervisors are sometimes irate because they are having difficulty getting their job done due to machine problems, it is important to have people skills. In addition to mechanical skills, I must be able to communicate well and have the ability to keep an open mind.

I get the same satisfaction you get when finishing a large jigsaw puzzle. I find satisfaction from changing peoples faces from unhappy(to say the least) to happy(or at least relieved).

FACTORY WORKER & ORDER ENTRY CLERK

I have recently moved myself up the career ladder from a factory worker to an order entry clerk. With this promotion has come various duties including placing and entering orders, being a part time receptionist, working on the computer, answering the telephone, and filing. In addition to rechecking my own work, I am also responsible for checking the work of other employees.

This work requires some secretarial and computer skills. I also consider optimism, communication and people skills to be important for performing this job well. By this I mean getting along with everyone and speaking to others so that they know and understand what you are saying to them.

I like my job particularly because of the people I work with. I find job satisfaction from receiving a call or letter from a customer thanking me for something I have done for them. It is gratifying to know that I am doing a good job. Finding an alternative way to do projects faster and better is also satisfying.

FARMER #1

I have been a farmer for years and before that I was a machinist and I am not going to tell you how old I am. As a farmer I till and prepare the land for raising crops and then harvest the crops. In the spring of the year, I do field preparation, planting, spraying for insects, and cultivating. In the fall of the year, I do combining of soybeans, corn, operating the corn dryer and trucking to the market.

To be a farmer you need mechanical skills for operating machinery, and an understanding of chemicals and marketing. It is important also that you have the ability to repair your own equipment.

I enjoy being a farmer because I can be outdoors. I get satisfaction from seeing crops emerge from the soil, seeing the harvest of my efforts. However, I don't like receiving prices for crops set by the government and Board of Trade. I would like to be able to set my own price on the products I produce.

I became a farmer primarily because my family was always on the farm. If I hadn't become a farmer too, I think I might have chosen a career as a dentist.

FARMER #2

I am doing what I have always wanted to do. I was given the opportunity to become a farmer through by father who was also a farmer. I went out on my own some years ago after earning my Bachelors in Business Administration, and would not change careers even if given the chance to start over.

My work varies with the season. I can generally summarize what I do by saying that I use Sundays for planning and organizing, such as planning the sequence of planting fields. My Monday through Friday work includes: buying inputs, checking the adjustment of equipment, directing which fields and what inputs to use, and repairing breakdowns.

To do well as a farmer, it is important to have patience, to be observant and give attention to detail, to be good at decision making, and to have organizational skills.

The major problem with my career as a farmer is coping with the weather and the insecurity due to uncontrollable conditions like the weather. However, I very much like being my own boss. This gives me the opportunity to do my work as I think it should be done. I also find this job satisfying because it has allowed me to have time for my family and to have fun when I want.

FARMER #3

Except for my time in the Army Air Corps which I liked, I have been a farmer all my life. You could say that my career chose me since the farm has been in my family for four generations. I like this kind of work and would choose to be a farmer even if I were given other career choices.

On my farm, I raise grain. There is a endless variety of duties to perform every day. The work also changes from day to day, week to week, and season to season. The skills and attitudes I have found to be most important for performing well at my work have been: mechanical, math, knowledge of bookkeeping and law, and patience.

The most frustrating aspect about being a farmer is the tremendous amount of work that needs to be done. However, I like this kind of work, the people I work with, and the opportunity I have for advancement. These years have been satisfying because I have enjoyed the comfort of success from doing a good job. Also, this career has rewarded me with friendships.

FARMER #4

I have worked as a farmer for quite a few years; in that time I have raised many small grain crops over the years on a dry-land farm. My days start early in the morning with a lot of the same physical chores to be accomplished each day, depending upon the season.

To do the work of a farmer, you have to be a jack-of-all-trades, and have the ability to do messy work in an environment of some unpleasant smells and a lot of dust.

Although the hours are long and there is small monetary return , \I enjoy my work; I am my own boss and the work is seasonal. I take a lot of pride in raising a crop and seeing it grow, mature, and ripen so it can be harvested.

I was born and raised on a farm; I always wanted to become a farmer, like my father; I was given that opportunity when he retired.

I plan to remain in farming for as long as I possibly can; then I, too, will pass it on to my son, if that is what he wants to do with his life.

FARMER #5

Farming hasn't a typical day. My work hours are sunup to sundown when I work. There are approximately 5 to 6 months that I hardly work at all. The tasks are also very different throughout the year, which makes it fun and rewarding.

As a farmer with a high school education who owns and manages a small spread, I have to be optimistic, competent, and self-motivated. I have to be willing to recognize when I've made a mistake and cut my losses. A farmer must have mathematical and mechanical skills, be part lawyer, and have a strong dose of common sense.

I grew up on my dad's farm and inherited my grandfather's homestead at age 10. I gradually was given control of the operation. I would like to see the government get out of controlling the farmers' prices and income. Farming should be allowed to be free market based.

Job satisfaction for me is the joy of working outdoors and having control over my life. Being my own man does not mean I have to like repairing broken machinery. My future plans are to expand the acreage of my farm to be able to increase cash crops. This would provide an income more capable of supporting a family of four.

FARMER & RANCHER #1

Self-employed and loving it, I've been a farmer and rancher for years. I buy and run cattle in Texas, New Mexico, and Mexico. Growing up on a farm, I found I liked cattle ranching better than farming. But actually the two go together well.

I like just about everything about my work except, maybe, government interference. There are possibilities for advancement and the people around are nice. I enjoy what I'm doing and being my own boss. My plans are to keep on doing what I'm doing the rest of my life.

To be a cattle rancher you need to really like the work. You stay busy with farming all summer and part of the winter. Cattle keep you busy all year long, sometimes for 12 to 14 hours a day. Having a good attitude is really critical. A lot of common sense is pretty important, too.

FARMER & RANCHER #2

As a farmer and a cattle rancher, I work the land striving for optimal seed beds and planting conditions, tend to my seasonal crops, breed cows, assist in calving and other veterinary needs, tend to the grazing herd, plan the planting and breeding schedules, and keep track of my weekly and monthly budgets.

I have a Bachelor's degree and in addition, to work as I do, you need a mechanical aptitude, veterinary skills, the ability to work well with others, the willingness to work alone at times, some experience in planning and budgeting strategies, good organizational skills, and self motivation.

I like the people I work with and, in general, this kind of work; I especially enjoy being self-employed, so it goes without saying that I like my boss. I enjoy tending to the crops and watching the calves grow, especially the ones that were difficult to deliver, and the opportunity to learn this business.

Because I do not like working with chemicals, I would prefer to farm organically and grow more fruits and vegetables; then I would feel really good about opening my own shop and selling my own produce.

I plan to increase my cow herd, experiment with raising other animals, and learn more about the veterinary needs of farm animals; for this I plan to return to the classroom.

FARMER & RANCHER #3

As a farmer/rancher, I have little money, no voice in government, and no access to Broadway. I do have a sow who will farrow later tonight, dirt under my fingernails, and such deep peace. My grandfather came to Oklahoma in a covered wagon and homesteaded our farm in 1898. My father farmed after him. Since I am a woman and an only child, farming seemed unlikely. However, after college (B.A. in English), I spent a summer just thinking about my future--city or country? The farm next door was for sale, so I decided to go for it. I farmed with my dad until he died 2 years ago, and now my mom, myself and my 7 year old son are farming alone with the help of a hired man.

We raise cattle, hogs, sheep, chickens, wheat, cotton and hay. Each day is different and rewarding. I work with animals--feed them, doctor them, deliver babies, fix fences, and provide daily and seasonal care. Each morning, all animals are fed and watered. The rest of the day is spent outdoors doing animal-related chores. Our hired hand does field work with tractor and plow or hay baler or whatever is seasonal. The weather dictates a lot of our planning. There are no weekends off, no 9 to 5 working hours. We deliver pigs at 3 a.m. and still have to do feeding at 8 a.m.

There is no such thing as a "dumb" farmer. Growing up on a farm is the best preparation. However, you need to be able to do everything somewhat well. A good farmer knows welding, carpentry, electrical wiring, mechanics, vet. medicine, bookkeeping, fencing, horticulture, and everything knowable about each breed of each animal in the herd.

The worst thing about farming is the prices we receive for our crops. Right now 2 bushels of wheat are the same price as one box of cereal.

Mainly, we stay with farming because there are very few family farms left and it is a privilege and a challenge to hang on. Secondly, we are surrounded by gentle animal and bird noises (no traffic or people), we breathe fresh air, we eat our own nonchemical food, and there is nothing else as neat as a day-old soft piggy or lamb or calf or cat. My child grows up with this lifestyle, so free and so untouched by large city problems. My future is still on the farm whether I can continue to own it or rent it. I will send my son to college and give him his own choice.

FAST FOOD ATTENDANT

While I am a student in nursing school, I'm energetically earning my tuition working as an attendant at a fast food restaurant. In my job, I serve food and friendliness in an effort to help people as I try to "make their day."

My typical week is quite hectic. The restaurant work requires 40 plus hours each week. Job satisfaction for me means getting to meet so many different types of people. It always makes me happy when I can satisfy a customer. I enjoy my work, except the pay is very low. I'd like to see the perception of the fast food worker changed. Many of us are just trying to get by in life and pay for our school tuition.

For a while I was a day care teacher, and loved it. If I could have concentrated on interacting with the children, instead of worrying about the political stuff, I would have stayed in the field. My goal has always been, and will continue to be, to help people make their lives better and to live life as best I can.

To do this job well, you must be very "people-oriented" and be very patient. You need the ability to shed the grief a customer may give you and be ready to pleasantly help the next person. This is important, no matter what you do in life!

FEDERAL AUDITOR

I have served fifteen years as a federal auditor in internal operations. A typical week involves development of audit plans and programs after extensive research, followed by the implementation of such plans and programs. I enjoy traveling and meeting people, the advancement opportunities, and the kind of work I do. There is relatively little supervision and I like that but would be more satisfied if there were even fewer levels of supervision. From time to time, I am able to improve the quality of office operations, and I enjoy doing that.

A good background in accounting and business are needed in this field. The ability to write well is also necessary. You have to be able to test program efficiency and the economy and effectiveness of operations.

With the desire to provide a public service, I majored in accounting and business administration leading to a Bachelor's degree in college. I enjoyed my earlier work as Veterans' Administration Claims Examiner and I have also served as an I.R.S. Agent. Eventually, I plan to retire and enjoy my time with family and friends.

FEDERAL CLERICAL EMPLOYEE

My job as a federal employee in Social Security is as a Post Entitlement Examiner. A high school graduate, I've spent 35 years in public service.

My duties are to stop and start benefits, or to adjust benefits as required. My department refers appropriate cases to the claims authorization people for their determination, then we process the cases according to their instructions. It is part of my job to prepare letters when beneficiaries are involved. On occasion, it is necessary to contact the district office for additional information before processing a case. In general, the main purpose of our office is to keep benefits going out to beneficiaries.

It is a good feeling when a difficult case is completed. I enjoy the satisfaction of doing exact work and the awareness of performing a real service to the public. I appreciate the close cooperation of coworkers required to accomplish this task.

My career would be more satisfying if there were a more realistic production quota, i.e., one designed with the average case in mind. I am always looking for improved ways of doing a better job in line with procedures. If the people in leadership were more qualified as managers and more in touch with the reality of the work, things would be better.

To do my job, you need to have a thorough knowledge of the procedures manual. This means remembering instructions well so as not to waste time looking up answers. Being able to concentrate and think quickly is important. General math skills and good writing are necessary. Concern for the beneficiaries, appreciating their need for benefits, and correctly computing benefits are essential.

A high school graduate, this has been my single career. I now look forward to retirement when I will do volunteer work for our church in assisting the homebound.

FEED MILL MANAGER

I became a feed mill manager by buying the business. I chose it because it was located where I wanted to live. I have had many jobs while going to school, and since graduating with a Bachelor of Science in Physics, I have been an electrochemical engineer in the aerospace industry and a stress analyst in the nuclear reactor industry.

On a typical work day I review the day's work schedule with the mill foreman; buy ingredients; arrange for trucks to ship feed; input information into the computer; print and analyze reports; pay bills; make bids on custom feeds, wait on customers if the retail sales force gets behind; review with mill foreman what has been accomplished; and schedule the next day's work.

To succeed in this business, you must have patience, the ability to do many things at the same time, acceptance of interruptions, engineering skills to design and maintain the mill equipment, accounting skills to direct the flow of business, management skills to keep work force working together, along with sales ability and telephone communication skills.

I like the variety of tasks involved in being a feed mill manager; however, I could do without so many interruptions. I would like to find more time to develop innovative ideas. I find satisfaction from the pleasant people I work with, and the challenging problems I get to solve.

My future career plans are to continue helping the feed business grow and expand into new and innovative areas.

FICTION WRITER

I am a writer of fiction, short stories and novels, and I babysit to support myself. Typically, I wake up at 5:00 am and write for two hours, break until 8:30 when I write for two hours until 10:30, babysit for three hours, write for two hours from 1:30-3:30, babysit for four hours, read from 7:30-10:30, and go to bed. On Wednesdays I meet with a writer's group.

Self-discipline, unswerving belief in yourself, your ability and your artistic quest and tenacity are important skills and attitudes needed to perform well in this type of occupation. Also, you should be well read in a number of fields and fluent in at least one foreign language. Any activity which broadens understanding of life is an asset.

As a writer, I have autonomy--freedom of expression. I can bring myself and my convictions without censorship or compromise into my daily life. I can avoid the tiring politics of working with others.

I've always loved literature and the subjects it dealt with and I've always loved writing. After trying journalism and finding no satisfaction there in terms of creative expression, I decided to move into fictional writing. Previously, I have been a journalist and a teacher.

I would like to establish myself as a writer over the next 3 years. Then, I'd like to do some graduate work in literature so that I can lecture at the University level. I would like to be paid for work in progress so that I could concentrate wholly on my work rather than have to do odd jobs to take care of the survival issues.

FIELD REPRESENTATIVE, FEDERAL GOVERNMENT

For 13 years, I have enjoyed the varied duties and sites in my work as field representative for the federal government. Two days a week I travel to contact stations in three county seats, reviewing senior citizen services. I generally have at least one or two public presentations each week. I also go to hospitals and nursing homes to assist with claims. Other duties are preparing articles for news media and speaking on radio or TV.

In my job, I enjoy working with and meeting individuals from all walks of life. The pay could be better, but the benefits for federal employees are good. Also, the work is highly varied in duties, people, and job sites, so it is not boring. You meet many individuals from all walks of life. I will enjoy my retirement, my active involvement in children's services, and teaching literacy volunteers.

The skills needed in my work include the ability to speak well in public. You need to have "meet and deal" qualifications. Good people skills are also necessary. Stressful situations for my clients, such as death of a loved one, dealing with a disability, or problems in retirement are common occurrences, so you need the ability to make people feel at ease, even when they are having a difficult time in their lives.

Since I was unable to attend college when I was younger, this is a particularly good job for a person with only a high school education.

FIELD SERVICE ENGINEER #1

Basically, I watch or oversee people working on or testing the electro-mechanical systems which my company has made. I must ensure the equipment is properly installed and tested so that it will serve the customers well. Reading and correcting technical manuals on equipment and making suggestions to the designers on how to improve specific items, systems and procedures are part of my regular duties.

To perform this job well, you must have knowledge of equipment, systems, procedures, good mechanical skills and ability to pass knowledge to tradesmen without "ruffling feathers." The ability to not be belligerent when it would be very easy is important. To perform well you should have the ability to solve minor problems without getting "lots of people" involved. Of utmost importance, however, is the ability to get the job done!

Job satisfaction has come from solving problems that stump others, saving time and reducing unnecessary work.

This is dirty work. I would be nice to work in cleaner conditions. It would create a more pleasant environment.

After receiving my BS in mechanical engineering, I started working for a large company and kind of fell into this job. I chose this field for the compensation.

FIELD SERVICE ENGINEER #2

As a field service engineer, I have been involved in repairing computer software and hardware for seven years, . Essentially, I diagnose problems with computer equipment and determine if it is a software or a hardware problem; then I fix the problem. I keep a customers log of calls made requesting repairs on their systems, I respond to these service requests, and I diagnose the problem. The most common problems I encounter are part failure or software that is set up improperly. Once repairs are complete, I call in to log my time with my boss. I also get involved in the installation of new options for computer systems and installation of the computer system itself.

In addition to an undergraduate degree in Computer Science, my job requires a thorough understanding of electronics and computer software, and the ability to interact with customers.

I like my job and the company I work for. I enjoy my work when a problem is solved; I gives me a certain amount of self-satisfaction. But I find the greatest job satisfaction comes from customers showing their appreciation and gratitude for solutions to their problems.

Although there is some variety in my work, I believe there would be more challenge for me if I ware able to work on a bigger variety of products and systems.

After working with hardware for such a long time and only getting involved in minimal software support, I plan to get into the software field full-time, not as a programmer, but as a system manager or a system analyst.

FIELD SERVICE ENGINEER #3

I am glad that I was able to get into field service work, even if it was somewhat through the back door. I started as a maintenance man in a semiconductor plant where I met the people in the field that led me to this career.

As a field service engineer, I maintain software/hardware for manufacturing computer chips. My typical daily duties include reviewing a customer's data to control process problems or repairing the piece of equipment my firm sells. This kind of work requires very good math, technical reasoning, and interpersonal skills.

I like the kind of work I do; however, there is a lack of opportunity for advancement. In order to overcome this problem, I plan to continue my education, although I might also change direction and move into medical electronics. At the present time I have earned an Associate's degree in electronics engineering.

I am satisfied in this job when an assignment is completed and a customer makes a profit based on my input. There is also satisfaction in working with little or no supervision.

FIELD SERVICE ENGINEER #4

I did not know what I wanted to do when I left high school. A friend of mine recommended computer repair and a school for training in this field. I took the entrance exam for the school, passed, and more or less decided on the flip of a coin to enroll. I am now very pleased that I did because after now working in this field for nine years, I have found this to be a good job choice for me.

As a field service engineer, I fix computer hardware and software. I work on scheduled problems but am often interrupted with emergency calls (down systems). I often teach users how to use the system and fix minor problems themselves. Ninety-five percent of my work is now installing and fixing software.

In order to perform well at this kind of work, it is important to have the ability to deal with all types of people, have public speaking skills, organizational skills, to like a good challenge, be creative, and enjoy fixing things.

I find satisfaction from fixing something that was broken. Watching a multi-million dollar computer system come to "life" after taking it apart and putting it back together or after fixing a software problem is rewarding. I also enjoy working with and teaching others. There is always a new challenge in this line of work.

Although I like my work very much, I would be more satisfied with less administrative work and more time to work on software problems, plus with less corporate politics.

I am now in night school and plan to proceed with that. I hope to become a systems analyst and continue working with customers, not spending too much time in an office behind a desk.

FIELD SERVICE TECHNICIAN

My job as a process control technician consists of maintenance, replacement, and monitoring of equipment. I work with electrical gear and components, and with calibrations, temperatures, pressures, and levels. Toxic gas and the handling of chlorine are also involved.

I enjoyed my earlier job as a park ranger, but my work as a process control technician is exciting. I like everything about my occupation. Running a crew of 10-15 men on a $250,000 electrical instrumentation job is very challenging to me. Job satisfaction comes when I am successfully struggling with a difficult task that very few others could accomplish. I really like getting an entire process back on line without undue down time. Although I do not have the benefit of a college education, you do not really need that for this job. I did get basic electronics and trouble-shooting techniques in the U.S. Air Force, which I joined immediately after high school.

A couple of examples will help explain this job. A plant engineer calls our shop--says he can't get his compressor started. His is a paint factory and 150 people are standing around because so much of the plant works with compressed air. The shop pages me and, depending on the job I'm on, I'm on my way. Control called once saying that their filling machine was not working correctly. On arrival I determine that the drive is the problem--further follow-up--the drive is German and the machine was made in Italy. After several calls I've located the only replacement drive in this country. I have it shipped UPS and install it the next day.

Qualities you must have are perseverance, problem-solving skills, and the ability to trouble shoot. You must be able to read and follow prints as well as schematics. Communication skills are needed to be able to talk to engineers, foremen, plant managers, and operators so that they will understand the problem and procedure and so that we can understand their needs and fulfill them quickly and efficiently. You must be able to stand back and take in the larger picture.

More and more these days I am directing the work of others, a responsibility I like a great deal. I expect to continue in that direction.

FILM TECHNICIAN

I work for an instructional film service which ships and receives 750-1000 films per day to and from schools in just one county of Pennsylvania. As a film technician, it is my job to inspect and repair damaged film, order footage for repairing film, and make decisions if the film is to be repaired or replaced. In order to do this, I run the damaged films through a viewing computerized inspection machine which records the damage on cards. The cards are given to a communication specialist who orders new films or footage. I then replace the footage when it is received by the film company and keep records of all transactions.

To do this work, you must be able to spot film defects in sound and quality. If you do not keep the films in good condition and keep them updated, you cannot keep the interest of the viewing children.

I did not have any previous training for this job and am happy I was hired for this work after answering a newspaper ad over 13 years ago. I have graduated from high school and worked previously as a file clerk, billing clerk and salesperson.

I do not have any dislikes about my work except that I would like to have my own room to work in where I would not be disturbed by outside noises and distractions.

It is a very rewarding position knowing that I am a part of providing a very valuable learning tool for our youth. There is so much available to young people today in education. If they take advantage of all that is there in film and video, it would be easy to educate all kids.

FINANCIAL AID OFFICER, COLLEGE

Before becoming a financial aid officer and data systems manager, I was a college recruiter for a corporation. While I enjoyed that work, I like being closer to students, helping them learn responsibility, and watching them succeed. I also have the satisfaction of managing computer programs and getting them to run right when people need them.

The bad news is that on a daily basis the pace is very hectic and stressful. There's little time for myself. Plus I'm always dealing with rules which are constantly changing. Additionally, there's not always the needed cooperation from others.

The good news is my work is very rewarding in the sense that I am helping to contribute positively to a student's future. I assist in distributing financial aid to college students. I also maintain the financial aid computer data base.

If you are going to do this job and do it well, you need patience and understanding. Being a decision maker and standing by your decisions are also important. In my work with determining student needs and in using the computer, I find good detective skills are useful. In addition, you should be a cooperative team player.

My college degree is a Bachelor of Arts in psychology. I also have a Master of Science degree in applied psychology with emphasis on human resources. One day I'd like to be a counseling or clinical psychologist. Being the director of a human resources department for a business also interests me.

FINANCIAL ANALYST #1

I am pleased to have worked up from a data entry operator for a stock company, to secretary for a computer company, then secretary for the finance group and now financial analyst.

In this position as financial analyst for a sales group in a computer company, it is my responsibility to analyze and report spending against revenue. This involves tracking capital equipment, reporting actuals and graphing results, and attending meetings regarding project spending.

To perform this kind of work well, the following skills and attitudes are important: accounting, the love of numbers, organization, problem- solving, and flexibility to tackle "fire-drills."

I like almost every aspect of my work including the people I work for, the kind of work I do and the people and organization I work for. I would like it even better if there were travel involved and more opportunity for advancement. Therefore, I plan to earn a college degree in accounting with aspirations of moving into a finance group in an international organization.

My job satisfaction is found in the completion of projects on time, finding ways for the group to cut spending, and helping people find financial solutions in a particular project.

FINANCIAL ANALYST #2

After serving in the US Air Force as an air traffic controller (a job which I liked), I started my civilian career at a low level position of packager of computer systems and parts. The advantage of working for the company was that they paid for college courses. Consequently I started going to school, and I became interested in finance. I began looking for job positions in that area within the company. I was able to get into an entry level accounting position as an inventory controller from which I advanced to my current position as financial analyst.

As a financial analyst in the freight administration department, my main responsibility is to assist internal clients in the reconciliations of their freight accounts. This is done by creating reports, looking at microfilm, and speaking with vendors, carriers, and others in my group. I also have responsibility for two balance sheet accounts which I must reconcile at month's end.

To perform well at this kind of work requires the ability to prioritize work load, the ability to adjust to changes in technology and the work environment, good communication skills, and good analytical skills.

Everyday there are new challenges. Helping others when they need it gives me a great deal of satisfaction. It is also gratifying to know that I have done the best I could possibly do. I also find job satisfaction from having the ability to bend when the job dictates and push back when it's necessary - being in control of what I am working on, rather than it controlling me.

My future career plans are to continue to grow within the department I am in. With a solid education and work experience, I hope to move into a supervisory position, and from there, into a management position.

FINANCIAL ANALYST #3

After 3 1/2 years of college, further study and certification, I am a chartered financial analyst. I evaluate financial instruments, such as equities (cash value) and fixed income annuities (money received on a regular basis), for investments. Making recommendations to clients and managing their portfolios describes my work.

For 25 to 30 hours each week, I research financial activity, read and work with the computer in financial database inquiry. Additionally, I do technical analysis and make contact with the home company. I spend 8-10 hours in contact with my clients as well as reviewing their portfolio. The rest of the time, 10 to 20 hours, I'm doing office work, writing correspondence, and generally managing the office.

There's never a dull moment in this work. It's always challenging. I like the fact that there are opportunities for advancement. The people, the job, and the organization are all great, but I truly dislike all the paperwork. If the government-mandated reports could be reduced, it would help a lot.

To be a financial analyst, you have to be a disciplined person who can consistently apply solid investment principles. You need teaching skills to help the client adjust their investment methods and learn from their mistakes. An inquisitive nature is important to be able to seek out information, ask clients penetrating questions, and review a variety of investment possibilities.

One day, I'd like to manage just my own finances and, perhaps, those of a few select clients. I'd also like to spend some time teaching financial principles and I am interested in integrating those with the ethics as found in the Bible.

FINANCIAL PLANNER & ENTREPRENEUR

In the field of financial planning, securities sales, and entrepreneurial ventures for twenty-six years, I have spent a great deal of time on the phone. When I am not on the phone, I spend my time reading to keep up with money and financial markets, and attending meetings.

This kind of work, which I like very much, requires math skills, listening skills, communication skills, and a dynamic personality.

Although my income fluctuates in accordance with the investments I make, and the money I persuade other people to spend, I like my job very much. I enjoy the income level I have managed to attain, the accumulation of wealth I have now achieved, and the friendships I have made over the years.

I have also been involved in the field of life insurance sales, but that was not challenging enough for me.

I plan to continue in my present field. I like working with money matters, and I will continue to stay involved in entrepreneurial ventures for as long as I am still breathing.

FINANCIAL SERVICES MANAGER

In my work as a financial services manager for 20 years, I approve loans for individuals and for corporations. Making these kinds of decisions is important because sometimes considerable amounts of money are involved. I also solicit new business from current customers and I follow up on business leads. Supervising employees as well as collecting on real estate accounts are also part of my job requirements.

To be a successful financial services manager, you must have very good people skills. Being a competent salesperson is important as well. Capability in judging which applications are sound is a basic need.

Job satisfaction for me is helping people with budgeting their money and solving financial problems for customers. I'd like my work better if there were less strain involved, but in dealing with large amounts of other peoples' money, that strain cannot be avoided. Eventually, I'd like to move into area supervision with my present employer.

Although I like the job quite well, I do not plan to continue in it after I am 65 and can retire comfortably.

FIRE CHIEF

I have been employed as a fire fighter for over twenty years. I am now working as the Fire Chief of a 140 member fire department, and have held this position for two years. In a nutshell, I handle the daily operation of the fire department and plan for the future needs of the department by supervising the training of fire fighters, writing and issuing orders, answering phone calls and departmental correspondence, preparing the budget, issuing rules and disciplining those who break the rules, and handling the transfer of personnel from one station to another to keep station coverage consistent.

In addition to a good college education and training in the field of fire fighting, you have to be fair, be able to motivate others, be patient, possess a great deal of physical energy, have a good sense of foresight, and possess a thick skin. The general nature and accountability aspects of this work can be ruthless at times.

I find working as a fire chief very rewarding, especially because I had to work my way up to this position by passing difficult examinations and progressing through a series of promotions--lieutenant to captain to deputy fire chief and then finally to fire chief. Rewards also come in my attempts to make the department more professional, the interaction with my crew, and helping them with their problems if possible. I take pride in my crew and in the knowledge that I am a good fire chief. The aspects of my position that are at times difficult are negotiating with the union, attending meetings, and the occasions when I must engage in public speaking; too often, budget constraints also make it difficult to operate efficiently and a lack of funds threatens lay-offs and station closings. The hiring process, under the constraints and regulations of Civil Service, also can be a source of great frustration.

When I entered the field of fire fighting, it was considered to be a very secure field of employment. That has changed drastically over the years, and the job no longer offers the security it once did.

I plan to continue in my present position for as long as I possibly can. It took me several years to achieve this success; I plan to enjoy it.

FIRE FIGHTER

I have found my work as a fire fighter to be intrinsically rewarding and have no dislikes about this career. I started at a young age as a volunteer and then went into the Air Force as a fire fighter. After my tour of duty, I began my fire fighting work in a civilian fire department. I have also worked as a machinist, carpenter, and in sales, but have been most satisfied as a fire fighter.

My work schedule consists of 2 (10 hours) days, 2 (14 hours) nights, and 4 days off. At work I do cleaning (same as in a house) in the morning. When emergency calls come in, I go to render aid. A typical fire call involves a lot of physical work, plus potentially crawling in dark, hot, smoke-filled rooms, breathing smoke, getting wet and then cold (winter), or sweating profusely (summer). Medical calls are anything from minor to death.

In order to perform this kind of work well, you need good common sense, intelligence, a mechanical background. Plus, as you move up the management ladder, leadership skills are necessary. Most importantly, you MUST be dependable and trusting . . . your life may depend on it. You must have a positive attitude and be willing if need be to sacrifice yourself to save someone else. The main and biggest satisfaction for me is helping someone.

My future career plans are to be promoted and, during my off time, to start a business.

FISHERY RESEARCH SCIENTIST

Although there isn't much opportunity for advancement, I like the kind of work I do as a fishery research scientist. In my work I determine fish populations in lakes and streams by catching them (temporarily) in nets; I measure and tag fish, sample available plankton, and carry out hatchery studies. I also write scientific reports for publication in journals.

I've found my ability to supervise personnel, to analyze data to determine the value of my research, and to write well are important to perform my work well. Knowledge of mathematics and chemistry as well as competence in the use of the computer are all essential in this job. It's also important to enjoy the outdoors, rain or shine.

Earlier, I was a Finance Department officer in the Army, and I have been a construction worker as well as a photographer.

Even though I've found no advancement opportunities, I've enjoyed my work for many years. Being outside and working with other professionals in my field have given me great pleasure. Job satisfaction also has come to me from seeing my writings published.

Future plans are to write a book about my interesting adventures. For me, I couldn't think of any occupation more satisfying than the one I selected.

FLIGHT ATTENDANT #1

I do international flying so my work days are long (12-20 hours) and I'm away from base usually 4-6 days. I have worked up to a supervisory capacity so I oversee the other flight-crew members.

The skills and abilities which I think are most important to perform this job well are patience, understanding and flexibility.

I like this kind of work because I enjoy meeting many different people, traveling worldwide, and making foreign friends. I would like my job better if I could work for new management. I am personally dissatisfied with the organization and people I work for, and the lack of opportunity for advancement.

I chose this career after being previously employed as an insurance adjuster and financial analyst. I wanted to travel and see the world. By doing this job, I get to do this and get paid for it. Eventually, however, I plan to utilize my Bachelor of Science degree in Business Management and be self-employed.

FLIGHT ATTENDANT #2

My career includes 10 years of flying as a flight attendant and 10 years of working in an airline office. Airline work for me has meant good working conditions, time off, good pay, and a chance to work with the public.

As a flight attendant, your main function is to serve passengers. On a typical day of flying, the first order of business is to be punctual-- you can never be late. Once on the job, you organize the galley, and prepare the cabins for the passengers. Receiving the passengers on board in a friendly, outgoing manner and maintaining that manner at all times is important. This work can often involve long, long days.

To perform these duties well, the following skills and attitudes are important: flexibility, punctuality, teamwork, friendliness, organization, good general appearance, and helpfulness to others--"caring."

The major drawback to this work is the long hours; the time differences tend to be really hard on the body. However, I have had other jobs outside the airlines including work as a legal secretary, model, general bookkeeper, and office manager, and I think that I have preferred my job as flight attendant the most. I like this kind of work primarily because I like people. I find it satisfying to serve and please the public, especially people in need such as the elderly and children.

FLIGHT ATTENDANT #3

As a flight attendant, I am responsible first, in case of an accident, for ensuring the safe exit of passengers from the airplane. Secondarily, I act as a hostess, serving meals and beverages.

Before my flight, I arrive at the airport an hour early. Using the computer, I pull up information on the day's flights. In addition to serving as a hostess, I organize supplies on the plane to promote efficient service. It's my job to visit with the passengers, as time permits, answer questions, and reassure them when they are concerned. I change planes on an average of 3 times a day and my on-duty time daily is approximately 8-10 hours.

I enjoy the travel benefits and discounts in my work as well as the good pay.

Working for a reliable company with retirement benefits and health insurance is grand, so I plan to stay with the company. Finally, I like the fact that I have had excellent training, but I don't have to tolerate a lot of direct supervision.

Though I don't like the unpredictable schedule each month, I do enjoy all the great time off. I'd like more holidays off as well. The stereotype the public has of the flight attendant annoys me a bit. Actually, there's great competition for our jobs. One of the deciding selection factors with personnel is having a college degree. With a Bachelor of Arts degree in commercial French with a minor in Spanish, I love having the opportunity to visit and explore other cultures and cities. I'd like to see more European destinations offered out of my base.

A flight attendant should have a pleasant attitude, be patient and courteous, and want to work with the public. You must be punctual as well as organized. A 5-6 week training class given by the employer is also required. Finally, you must have the ability to keep calm in stressful situations.

FLIGHT TEST ENGINEER

For 17 years I've worked as a flight test engineer. In my work, I prepare and document flight plans and schedules. There are meetings to attend, test ranges to schedule, systems to be tracked. I conduct flight tests of aircraft as well as participate as a primary crew member on test flights.

A flight test engineer needs knowledge of a variety of aircraft, common sense, and excellent communication skills. Abilities to understand what you can't see, to conceive and accept new concepts, and to focus using your knowledge of the aircraft are essential. Math and writing skills are very important. Also, I've found you have to learn to be very diplomatic and not require that your own ego needs be met.

My degrees are a Bachelor of Science in Mechanical Engineering and a Master of Science in the same field. I got into aircraft work directly out of college. I became a test flight engineer by being in the right spot at the right time.

I enjoy flying and the uniqueness of being a flight test engineer. I like the recognition, acknowledgement, and the reputation. Overall, the job is very satisfying. However, the opportunity for advancement is limited because the community is very small. I must either wait for my chance or move into another field. My plans are to stay in the aircraft realm and move up into management.

During my earlier days I held various short-term jobs including service station attendant, farm laborer, fast food cook and worked in construction briefly.

FLORIST

A florist sells plants and flowers, and designs and creates floral arrangements. There are many steps involved that make the business of a florist a very rewarding field.

After planning my daily floral purchases, I make my selections from the fresh flowers and plants at the market, buy them, and transport them back to my store, where I arrange and price the items in preparation for my customers. I may arrange them in baskets, in a vase, or in a number of ornamental ways for the different seasons.

Although I have a degree in Library Science and was formerly a librarian, the skills necessary for the work of a florist can be learned at a trade school, or through a period of apprenticeship. Needed are artistic skills, a good eye for color, knowledge of the care and selection of healthy flowers and plants, bookkeeping skills, and the desire to help people--basic people skills.

I really enjoy my work; it gives me a wonderful opportunity to be independent and provides a great outlet for my creative talents. In the eight years I have worked as a florist, I find the greatest satisfaction from working with flowers and taking care of my customers. I have been fortunate to meet some very nice people through my work. I was drawn to work in this field because of my love for flowers and people, and I enjoy it so much it hardly seems to be work.

I plan to keep making my flower arrangements and selling plants. I have found a job that I really enjoy--except for the business aspects of my work.

FOOD BROKER

In my work as a food broker, I have been involved in sales promotions in both the retail and wholesale food markets. In the retail market, I indirectly control the market by controlling the shelf position to stimulate interest in the promotion of the food lines I display and advertise, and by introducing new and expanded lines of my food products. In the wholesale market, I directly control the market by my attempts to control the supply, by introducing new and expanded lines of my food products.

My family has been involved in the grocery business for as long as I can remember. After completing high school, I managed a small retail food store.

Besides a desire to succeed in this field and some experience in the food industry, you must have, above all, good communication skills, knowledge of the food lines, the ability to schedule promotion dates and plan the supply of perishable food products, and knowledge of product shelf placement.

I enjoy my work, especially the customer respect I receive and customer appreciation for the services I render. I feel I am fortunate to work for a person that I like.

I plan to continue to live comfortably on the financial fruits of my labor for several more years, and perhaps return to school to expand my business knowledge.

FOREIGN SERVICE OFFICER, STATE DEPARTMENT

As a foreign service officer for the U.S. Dept. of State, I have represented the United States in embassies overseas, been a delegate to the United Nations, the

Organization of American States and more. My work entails interviewing foreign diplomats, preparing speeches and developing reports on political and economical situations as they occur. I must understand the people in the countries where I serve, and learn their languages, customs, needs, etc.

To perform well as a foreign service officer it is important to have political awareness, linguistic capability, analytic and writing skills, conversational capabilities, and a genuine interest in other people.

I have been satisfied with this work for 32 years because it has provided me the opportunity to travel. In retirement I plan to be involved with community activism in social welfare, drug and substance abuse, and homelessness.

Some satisfactions that I find from this job are that I know more about foreign cultures and I better understand the workings of our government; its similarities and differences from other countries and cultures. In reference to changes in my occupation, I would recommend that only seasoned, experienced diplomats be considered for ambassadorial or ministerial positions. Also I recommend that officers receive more language and area training.

Before entering the office of foreign service I experienced a diverse career background as a newspaper editor, a musician, trombone and french horn, a social worker and in the infantry as both an enlisted man and officer. I got into the foreign service after taking an examination and also after my overseas military duty.

FOREMAN, FACTORY

I ended up in my present occupation as a floor leader in a factory because it is what was available after I graduated from high school. I have found from doing this work that I like working with machines and leading people. I enjoy showing or teaching people how to do things. I like the challenge. Prior to this job I worked as a truck driver, but didn't like it at all. I have also taught myself carpentry skills, and built a house. Carpentry is something else which I might like to do.

I am a floor leader in a factory overseeing machine operators working on vertical mills, lathes, drill presses, screw machines, and other programmable machines. I set the daily work flow for each operator, check parts regularly for quality, and fill in when employees are not at work. My work day starts at 7 a.m., and my first task is to schedule work for all areas of production. During the course of the day, I am involved in the following activities: helping, answering, or giving directions in how to carry out production; checking parts for quality; helping fill in to make sure work gets done; informing next leader where we are and what needs to be accomplished. I leave work at 5 p.m.

In order to perform this kind of work well, it is important to have a positive attitude, patience, and knowledge of technical machines and blueprint reading.

Although I like the kind of work I do, I do have some frustration related to this occupation. I am bothered by the amount of scrap made and loss of production because of it. I would like to see an improvement in workers' approaches to their jobs, and to get people more involved. On the other hand, I like the people I work for and the people I work with. I find job satisfaction in knowing that I did the best that I could with what tools were given to me. I also find satisfaction from working with, helping, and teaching others about their job.

FORESTER

As a kid growing up, I worked with my hands, out-of-doors, doing farming and ranch work. A career as a wildlife forester was the natural field open for me. There is no opportunity for advancement, but I like my work a lot and would choose the field again if I could start over.

In my work as a staff forester, I am responsible for planning the budget and for the programs already in place. I am also in charge of the range, wildlife, and fire programs. My duties include coordinating program areas, and acting as a mentor to the younger staff members.

It is my function to act as a resource specialist for all levels of planning, including project planning and design. I serve as the technical expert and spend a lot of time reviewing others' work.

I really enjoy my work implementing programs to improve environmental conditions. It is a pleasure to be a mentor to others and help in the development of new resource professionals. I'd like my work more if there were less governmental intervention, but my plans are to finish my career with the government. Then I'd like to become a range manager for some big farm or ranch operation.

To be a forester, you need the proper training; my degree is a Bachelor of Science in forestry. Since forestry and related resource management leads to very little immediate response, except for fire management, you should be a very patient person. Usually the results from decisions made and work done will not be evident for many years.

FUND RAISER #1

As a development consultant to a public television station, I underwrite corporate contributions and get heavily involved in the station's fundraising campaigns. I write scripts for use on the air and revise tapes when needed, write fact sheets for telemarketing operators' use in responding to donor calls, give suggestions to station management for upcoming special events, review upcoming station news- letters, and have influence even in such decisions as the station's new logo design.

I earned a Bachelor of Arts degree, a Master of Arts degree, and some teaching credentials before pursuing this position. This kind of work requires an open mind, a willingness to share ideas and work as part of a team to improve the overall project, and a willingness to accept constructive change. In my belief, change keeps us alert and inventive.

I enjoy the vast variety my work provides; although the ultimate direction remains the same, each day or week provides a new challenge. I also enjoy that my work benefits the community and at the same time allows me to utilize my talents and abilities; this work has a high degree of creativity associated with it.

Public television operates on a lean budget and like any service organization, it is difficult to raise funds for anything other than the primary service--we must run rich and be poor, but that is also the challenge that keeps us going.

Previously, I had positions as a teacher, a federal program director, and a YMCA director; I have always been drawn to working with people.

I plan to continue to work at this job. I truly appreciate the opportunity to be selective while exercising my creative talents.

FUND RAISER #2

As a fund raiser for the last ten years, I plan, direct, and execute the fund raising activities for a large hospital. My duties are to direct and prepare mass mailings, write grant proposals, direct special events, handle phone calls, conduct committee meetings, attend board meetings, and manage the general activities of the fund raising office to accomplish the hospital's goals.

In addition to a Bachelor of Science degree, my job requires writing skills, interpersonal skills, a positive and optimistic outlook, an extroverted temperament, good organizational skills, and the ability to follow through on projects.

I really like my job, the people I work with, this hospital organization, and this kind of work in general; I believe that I am making an important contribution to good causes with long-term benefits to society.

Although there is sometimes a negative connotation associated with fund raising, I enjoy contacting people to enlist their funds and help.

Prior to working as a fund raiser, I was employed as a salesperson, a linguist, a member of the Peace Corps, a bill collector, and in the field of public relations. I use many of the skills learned in those positions in my present work.

I plan to stay right where I am and make this endeavor as big a success as I possibly can.

FUNERAL DIRECTOR

In the funeral business, every day is different; the clientele and the services both vary. As a funeral director, you meet with families, discuss their needs, and coordinate all aspects of the funeral. Quite often people come in to make arrangements in advance. Each body you embalm brings different and sometimes very complex circumstances.

In embalming you must treat each individual with the same respect and dignity you would if he or she were a member of your own family or a friend. It is gratifying to me to make people look their best after embalming, especially in accident cases. It is important that the deceased be remembered as looking as natural as possible. The last image of the deceased that the family sees is a mental image they will carry with them for a long time.

I'd like my profession more if I weren't on call 24 hours a day and if I had some time away from work. I'd like my profession better if there were fewer unfeeling, disrespectful members in it. I'd like all funeral homes to operate under the same Federal Trade Commission regulations--the overcharging by some funeral homes needs to cease.

I entered this profession as an apprentice in a newly opened funeral home in town. My training was in Funeral Management and Embalming Sciences. Some day I hope to own my own funeral home.

One must have a very compassionate and comforting nature when dealing with families. You have to be able to read the personality of the family itself to help them through the difficult time they are having. A person must resist becoming hardened toward death, for each family deserves your full attention and compassion.

GAS TURBINE ENGINEER

I decided on a career in mechanical engineering at the age of 8. I earned a Bachelor of Science in Mechanical Engineering, and then went on to earn my Masters in Business Administration while working part-time and paying for school through the G.I. bill. During the course of my career life, I have worked as a machinist, computer wireman, and survey crew member.

Now, as a gas turbine engineer, I design and test gas turbine engines. It is my responsibility to plan, organize, and conduct tests on gas turbine engines. My test plans and final report of my findings must be written up. This kind of work involves skills in writing, mechanical ability, and the ability to work well with people.

I like my occupation because of the kind of work I do and the people with whom I work. However, I am not particularly satisfied with my pay scale and the deadline pressures. Despite these drawbacks, I find it to be satisfying work because there is measurable job progress. It is rewarding to be part of technological advances and to find creative solutions to old problems.

I plan to continue with my career as a mechanical engineer working toward raising my position to a higher management level.

GENERAL ACCOUNTANT

As a general accountant, I prepare monthly closings, profit and loss\ statements, and balance sheets. I work with cost cards to process weekly cost of manufacturing reports and maintain inventory balances; perform credit, purchasing, and accounts payable functions; calculate and publish various financial reports on a weekly and monthly basis; and provide information to the manufacturing group on their performance.

To perform this job well, you must be versatile and organized, must have a thorough understanding of accounting principles, and should possess the ability to work with the pressure that time constraints produce.

I have worked as a general accountant for ten years. Previous positions include inventory control clerk, secretary, order entry and billing clerk, and customer service representative.

My educational background includes an Associate's degree.

I enjoy my job, especially providing manufacturing with performance evaluations and recommendations for process improvements.

My long-term goals include self-employment in the next ten years.

GENERAL CONTRACTOR #1

A general contractor builds schools, stores, and other commercial buildings. I contract work for the company by working up an estimate for the job we are seeking, submitting the bid with all the security bonds and paperwork in order, and then winning the bid, usually by having the lowest cost. My estimates must be accurate in order for the company to make money and be able to construct the building according to the specifications. This kind of work involves many phone calls, experience from other jobs, writing letters, and technical knowledge in the various construction trades.

To perform well as a general contractor it is important to have common sense, a working knowledge of construction, and the ability to judge a situation and make decisions.

I like my job very much and have been in the business for 20 years after receiving my bachelor of science degree in industrial management. I always wanted to be in construction. The opportunity came up to work for a large construction company after college and I started there. I then figured I could run my own company and went out on my own 16 years ago.

The main satisfaction I get from my work is seeing a project built. I also like the people I work with. I would be more satisfied if the subcontractors we work with were a little smarter and more professional.

My career plans for the future are to see the company grow and have a more secure base.

GENERAL CONTRACTOR #2

A general contractor operates machinery to construct buildings for customers; I have been working as a general contractor for seven years. Any contract job starts with a bid or an estimate of the cost of getting the job done. I prepare an estimate and, upon receipt of the job, I put a great deal of effort into purchasing the materials needed to complete the job, making sure that there is also enough labor available for hire (subcontractors). I then proceed with the job, obtaining blueprints from the client and constructing the project to the customer's satisfaction.

In addition to a good education and some experience in construction, my job requires good communication skills, both verbal and written. There is a great deal of paperwork associated with this type of work, and I am constantly explaining my construction decisions to the customer. A healthy respect for the competition in this industry keeps me on my toes. Creativity to come up with solutions that satisfy the customer and allow me the highest possible profit margin is important.

I like my job; I love being my own boss! The construction business has been very rewarding, especially when my customers make comments praising my work at times that I am not expecting them. I also find the construction industry very challenging; I take a great deal of pride in my work.

I have experience in several areas that help a great deal: plumbing, welding, electrical repair and installations, and finished carpentry. I have a strong aptitude and interest in mechanical things; I always want to know how things work and how they go together.

I enjoy working for myself and I plan to continue for as long as I can; I plan to go back to school to learn more about drafting; then I could also add that service to my business.

GENERAL MANAGER, PACKING DISTRIBUTION COMPANY

I have worked my way up the ladder primarily through hard work and job experience. After graduating from high school, I have been a factory worker, a salesman, and photographer. I started out with the packaging distribution company as a salesman, and have worked up through the organization to my present position as the general manager.

As the general manager, my duties include: reviewing customer contacts; reviewing products for sales; reviewing operation--sales, accounting, delivery, purchasing, etc.; creating sales forecasts and plans; and interviewing new candidates for hire.

I feel it is important to have enthusiasm, people skills, product knowledge, drive, and ambition to perform well at my kind of work. I like my work because I am satisfying customer needs. I like the organization I work for and the people I work with. What I do not like is working with non-ambitious people.

Job satisfaction for me is found in developing people in the company, recognizing the success of the organization and solving problems. It is my plan to continue with the company in order to develop a new and innovative organization which would help to make us a dominant supplier to the marketplace. I will then develop my replacement looking toward my own retirement.

GENERAL MANAGER, TELEPHONE COMPANY

After earning a Bachelor of Arts degree, I worked as a bank manager. Because of the recommendation of a family member who loved his work at the telephone company, I applied for work there. I have now spent 30+ years with the telephone company and I have also enjoyed working for them.

As the general manager, I manage a large work force, a large revenue and expense budget, and deliver service. My typical activities include making field visits to sites, listening/asking, budgeting, and planning.

The keys to success in this field of work are communication skills, integrity, interest, innovation, people handling skills, and financial knowledge.

I like every aspect of my work. If given the opportunity to start over and choose any occupation, I would again choose this kind of work. I find job satisfaction in good results--in service, in productivity, and financially. I also derive satisfaction from being told, "Good job!"

GENETIC & DNA RESEARCH GROUP LEADER

I work as a group leader for a builder of instruments for genetic and DNA research. I oversee our building 60 - 80 instruments per quarter and I am also responsible for the necessary paperwork, the ordering of materials, and, when needed, training new employees or experienced employees in new techniques and procedures.

To do this kind of work, you need assembly skills, technical knowledge, and a lot of patience.

In the two years of working as a group leader, I find satisfaction in knowing that the instruments we build help the various medical schools and laboratories develop new techniques and possible cures for various diseases.

I was hired in this position through a temporary assignment that became permanent a few months after I started. I have worked in various positions prior to this as a solderer, a machine operator, a sales clerk, and a deli clerk.

I like my job and the people I work with, although layoffs have left us short-handed in the group.

I hope to further my education and get an Associate's degree in business management.

GEOLOGIST, OIL & GAS OPERATOR

As a geologist and oil and gas operator, I search for places to drill for oil and gas and operate the oil and gas wells. This involves doing subsurface geology, looking for potential places. I must make the decisions regarding the day-to-day operations of the wells.

You must have the ability to mentally visualize the configuration of subsurface shapes from a limited amount of data. This takes patience but also a high degree of geological knowledge.

To prepare my self for this kind of work I earned my bachelor of science and master's degree in geology. I also received training and experience through my father, who was in the oil business.

This is satisfying work for me because I enjoy developing an idea, selling it, and seeing it tested. I would be more satisfied in my work if there were a decrease in the amount of government regulation. I would like to be able to raise the price of the product.

I have been in this business for many years and plan to continue what I have been doing.

GEOLOGIST, PETROLEUM CONSULTANT

When I was 11 or 12 years old, I wanted and decided to become either an archeologist or a geologist. In high school I decided upon geology since I felt that it would allow me more intellectual independence and would be more rewarding both from the point of view of a family life and monetarily.

I have earned both a B.A. and M.A. degree. While in college, my summer jobs included working in a factory, on a freighter on the Great Lakes, and as a dispatcher in a concrete yard. During WWII I was a pilot in the Army Air Force. Prior to becoming an independent petroleum geologist, I was a geologist and district and staff geologist for a refining company.

Fortunately, being independent I may work as long and as much as I wish to. Even though I am now 67 years of age I plan to work until I am at least 80 and hopefully be involved in the discovery and development of several more oil and gas fields.

Basically, my work involves working up prospects for drilling, supervising drilling and well evaluation, doing independent geological studies of oil and gas fields and evaluations of properties. My more specific daily or weekly tasks are working on maps, preparing reports, making recommendations, dictating letters, selling ideas to clients and investors, working out trades, acquiring information and leases, sitting on committees, and evaluating drilling wells.

The skills and attitudes necessary to perform well in my career are the ability to think in more than one dimension, preferably a Master's Degree in Geology, the ability to communicate both verbally and in writing, a curiosity to learn to think as nature "thought" and to always remember that nature is logical, to learn not to dwell on but to learn from your mistakes. In my profession this means "dry holes." You must be an optimist and as Polonius said to Laertes "unto thine ownself be true."

The main satisfaction I find from my work is the euphoric feeling of occasionally being right! I have liked being a geologist for 39 years and have no intentions of changing.

GEOPHYSICISTS & MINING CONSULTANT

I have always been interested in geology, in physics, and in prospecting. My career has included work as an underground miner, in Naval underwater demolition, as a mining engineer, and as a prospector. I have earned a Bachelor of Science in Mine Engineering. My work as a geophysicists started while I was working for a copper company. After returning to the company from military leave, I was asked to take over a new geophysical program that was being initiated. I am now using my experience in this field working as a geophysicists consultant specializing in mining exploration.

In my consulting work, I use a combination of geophysical and geological techniques to search for base and precious metal deposits. My work week might include the study of the geology, airborne magnetics, and gravity of a region (say 15 x 15km) for a client. As part of the study, the available publications and drilling knowledge would be reviewed. Computer modeling of known and suggested geologic conditions to compare with magnetics and gravity results is usually attempted. This sounds straightforward, but it involves much fumbling and rejection of ideas. It usually takes longer than a week.

To perform this kind of work well, patience and doggedness are most helpful. An open mind helps keep up with technological advances as well as with rapidly changing concepts of the earth's history. I like this kind of work very much and find it to be stimulating and intellectually challenging. I find job satisfaction in partially answering complex questions that arise in these studies; there are never complete answers. The joy of looking for something hidden and unknown is also satisfying.

My only regret with my career is that I wish I had the Ph.D. in geophysics that I once had the opportunity to earn. I would then pursue research in earth science. Instead of looking behind though, I look ahead to finishing the design of a metal detector that has multiple uses: gold and silver nugget discovery, buried military ordinance, buried waste and garbage sites, etc. I also plan to write several papers on the use of geophysics in defining volcanogenic and intrusive systems. Spending some time looking for deposits of precious opals is also in my future plans.

GIFT STORE OWNER

As a retail gift store owner for 35 years, I have a continuous variety of chores to perform every day. Generally my day involves placing orders, unpacking goods, setting up displays, paying bills, waiting on customers, and packing and shipping.

To be successful in this kind of business you need to enjoy (or at least tolerate) most all types of people and want to please them. A certain artistic bent is helpful.

This was satisfying work for me, because of the relatively short hours, from 10 to 5. I enjoyed travelling around the U.S. and other countries to gift markets for buying. There is also satisfaction from being my own boss.

A problem which retailers face is the high rent and space limitations.

I learned the retail business from my father who was in the furniture business. I did not think I would follow in his footsteps, but I guess merchandising rubbed off on me.

GOVERNMENT CONTRACTS ANALYST

As government contracts analyst, I negotiate bids for the company's product line utilized by the Dept. of Energy, Dept. of Defense, and their prime contractors. The various job activities which I am involved in on a daily or weekly basis are: answering customer calls related to proposals for quotations; coordinating order placement (when bid is awarded to us as the supplier) and production schedules to meet delivery dates; reviewing a proposal's terms and conditions, material specification and additional federal regulations--taking exception to those parts not agreed upon by my company when drafting bid; reviewing purchase orders for total agreement before acknowledging acceptance of order.

To perform well at this job, it is important to have data management skills. Concise verbal and written communication skills are also mandatory in a world of heavy jargon, acronyms and legal verbiage.

I got into my present occupation through a network of associates. I was approached to interview for an open position (company does not advertise openings). It was a position that had challenges and growth potential. The people of the new organization presented themselves on a very professional level, but were also very personable. Prior to this, I held secretarial positions for the banking and the chemical industry. I also worked several years as secretary to several doctors of chemistry and chemical engineers. I was promoted to a technical level in a chemistry research and development laboratory, wherein I acquired my regulatory responsibilities related to federal and state regulations impacting our chemical products for compliance to these regulations. This also included interacting with customers, agencies and industry representatives.

I like my job as government contracts analyst very much. I also like the autonomy in my workplace. My future career plans are to expand my position to incorporate marketing and advertising functions, as well as to maintain the growing government business. I find job satisfaction in coordinating a team to effect an efficient, accurate supply of quality products to an exceedingly high tech industry for the benefit of our country's security and future standing of excellence in the world.

GOVERNMENT OFFICER, EEOC

Since I am a minority, I have had great interest in the education of minorities and their future opportunities. Through my involvement with human rights issues at the local and state level, I was encouraged by minority leaders to apply for this job as Equal Employment Opportunity Officer.

It is my job to implement and monitor the Affirmative Action Plan, investigate complaints, and participate in community involvement. My typical duties include: reviewing hiring procedures; providing information to directors, managers, etc.; recruiting minorities for new positions; attending community meetings dealing with minority issues; and handling complaints.

To perform this kind of work well, it is important to be able to communicate well, be able to be impartial, be a positive person, be able to think and analyze facts, details, etc. and be able to make clear decisions, be organized, and have a vision.

Although I like my work, I do face some frustrations because I do not have the control over top management that I need in order to implement some of my plans. I am also dissatisfied to some extent by the lack of opportunity for advancement with my job.

I have brought a diverse work background with me to this job which I feel is beneficial. I have been a bilingual tutor instructor, a telephone operator for the Federal government, a bar waitress, a housekeeper , and a court translator. My educational background includes an associate degree.

Despite the frustrations I have encountered with this position, I am basically satisfied and like the kind of work I do, and the organization I work for. I find job satisfaction when my decisions and plans turn out well even though I may have had a lot of problems. I feel a sense of reward when I can show positive growth. It is also satisfying when other employees respect me and see me as a professional.

It is my future career aspiration to become an elected official in state government.

GRAPHIC ARTIST, FREELANCE

The kind of work I do as a graphic artist primarily consists of designing brochures and ad fliers and preparing them for printing. As a freelancer, I set my own schedule each day but primarily I meet with clients, work on designing their projects, and deal with printers.

To do well in this field you must have creativity. Dealing well with people and organizational skills are particularly important as a freelancer in this business.

I find that the main satisfaction from the job comes from seeing a finished product. I find working for myself has additional advantages. In prior work I felt I did not have the opportunity for advancement and I did not like the people I was working for, so I have eliminated these two objections.

My aim is to develop my artistic skills. To prepare myself for this career I earned a BA in Art and a BA in Communications. Prior to freelancing I taught art, worked as a library aide, and did sales work.

GRAPHIC COMPUTER ARTIST/OPERATOR

This career chose me! I was good at drawing and decided to make money at what I did best. I worked for 5 years as an illustrator which is a very related field. Other unrelated jobs in my background have been as soldier, in wood working, and in wood cutting.

As a graphic computer artist/operator, I prepare industrial graphics such as charts, graphs, and work slides. My hours are erratic and my work is self paced unless it's a rush job. It seems my work is either boring or hectic, never in between. Yet, it is satisfying. Beside the technical computer skills which are necessary for this job, it is also important to have flexibility in accepting varying work loads, creativity and innovation.

Despite the lack of opportunity for advancement in my present position and lack of new challenges, I like the kind of work. I also like the people for whom I work and the people I work with. It is satisfying because of the good pay, the absence of physical labor, and the good overall working atmosphere.

I plan to start my own business and would hope to integrate more creativity into standard or usual work specifics. I also think it is important to up-grade equipment regularly, and I systematically do that and would like to be able to influence others to do the same. Not entirely unrelated to computer art is music, and as one of my long-range future goals, I would like to make the transition to a musical career. That may be merely a hope and dream, however.

GRAPHIC DESIGNER #1

The duties of a graphic designer are varied and interesting; I have worked at this job for three and one-half years. A graphic designer discusses incoming project specifications with company division representatives; coordinates the art job with the typesetting, proofreading, and photography departments; prepares the art from concept stage to the stage where it is ready for press; performs the actual design of the art; and acts as the keyline coordinator for slide show presentations of corporate and promotional literature.

The requirements for this type of work are good visual aesthetics, good organizational skills, good hand and craft skills, the ability to work independently, and education beyond high school. I earned a Bachelor of Fine Arts degree in Graphic Design and previously worked as a free-lance designer for a book publisher.

I enjoy my job and I take pride in watching a job go from a thumbnail sketch to a printed piece of literature. Art has held high interest for me for a long time--since grade school; I took extracurricular art classes while in college to prepare for a job in art since the college program in which I was enrolled required an internship at a local business. After that temporary internship, I found my present position.

I would like to find a position in which I deal with more creative, conceptual, and larger budgeted projects. Eventually I envision myself working as an art director.

GRAPHIC DESIGNER #2

I followed "my bliss" and became an industrial illustrator. I always had an interest in art, developed my natural artistic abilities and have been able to pursue a career as an artist.

As an industrial illustrator, I perform the many tasks required to prepare artwork for reproduction for many concerns and individuals. The artwork I provide must be reproducible in black and white or color and must fit the job order requirements. To perform this kind of work and do it well, it is important to have a thorough knowledge of a variety of art forms and the ability to apply them. You must want to do your work well!

The drawback to this career for me has been the lack of opportunity for advancement and consequently a low pay scale. I have gotten the impression that employers sometime consider artwork "kid stuff," and therefore do not pay fairly for the services in accordance with the skills required. Despite these frustrations, I like my work very much and would not switch to another career even if given the opportunity to start over.

My background includes 4 years of art school after high school although it was not a degree program. My duty as photographer while serving in the Navy also helped to broaden my experience in art forms.

I find job satisfaction when what I have done works. It is also rewarding to see how well my artwork looks in proof.

GREYHOUND DOG FARMER

My wife and I got tired of living in the city, plus we both also had a love for dogs and greyhound racing. So, after working as a meat cutter, auto mechanic, auto center manager, and owner/manager of 2 auto paint supply stores, we bought land in the country and changed careers to greyhound dog farming.

As such, I raise, feed, and train 300 racing Greyhound dogs. This is a 7 day a week job from daylight to dark. To have the stamina and dedication to do this work all day and night, you must have a very good attitude toward these animals. You must also be alert to their individual needs in order to care for them properly.

What keeps me going is seeing the Greyhounds race. I do like this kind of work, and the people as well as the dogs I work with. I will keep on working at this in hopes of getting more of my dogs into the racetrack.

GUIDANCE COUNSELOR, HIGH SCHOOL #1

Being a high school guidance counselor requires a great deal of patience. You should have strong listening skills and a sense of genuine concern for people.

Mine is not a field unfamiliar to students. I schedule appointments with them to talk about career choices as well as what courses are appropriate to take. Occasionally, students bring their personal problems to me.

I really enjoy helping young people. It would be easier if there were fewer interruptions; otherwise, I like everything about my work. So, my plans are to stay in my present position.

My degrees are a Bachelor of Science, a Master of Arts, and a Doctorate in education. My first position was as a teacher. Then I moved up to assistant principal and to principal. I found I liked helping youngsters so much, I decided to become a counselor.

GUIDANCE COUNSELOR, HIGH SCHOOL #2

A high school counselor, I also was a business education teacher for many years. My degrees are a Bachelor of Science in education and a Master of Science in education. My plans are to stay in some area of counseling, perhaps eventually marriage counseling or career guidance. I belong to many organizations related to my profession and keep my skills sharp by attending workshops and seminars.

My work as a counselor is to help students in high school understand themselves so they may be more successful in their relationships and in the world of work. Part of my work involves conferences with parents, students, and teachers. There is a great deal of planning in my work: for testing, classroom activities, and scheduling various activities. What I dislike most (what I consider unnecessary) is the paperwork. The only other job I have had was working in my parents' country store as a small child. When I was on break from college, and afterwards, when I'd go home for a visit, I'd work there.

In counseling, I've found great satisfaction in helping students flourish. Seeing them choose occupations related to their interests and aptitudes has been very rewarding. A good counselor has a strong desire to help others become all they can be. Solid counseling skills and the ability to plan are necessary. Additional job satisfaction has come to me from observing students and parents (or other adults) living happily. This includes, of course, happiness in their chosen professions or occupations.

HAIRDRESSER

I liked my jobs as a secretary and customer service representative; however, I wanted to change and to find work that allowed me to work part time and take care of my baby and husband. I decided that I would like hairdressing, so I attended a local cosmetologist school in order to prepare for this career.

As a hairdresser, I style and perm hair plus some cosmetic work. Greeting my clients and deciding what they want done, then doing it as well as possible and going on to the next person is the basic routine in this kind of work.

Patience and good communication with clients are important for performing this work well. However, I consider the key to excellent performance as a hairdresser is TO CARE about what you do.

I like many aspects about this kind of work and particularly the opportunity which this career has for owning my own business. I find job satisfaction from changing clients' appearance so they feel good about themselves. It is very rewarding when a client leaves the salon in a good mood because of the new look I have created.

HAIRDRESSER & BARBER

I've been a hairdresser and barber for 20 years and I love the work. I own my shop and enjoy the smiles on my customers' faces when they like my work. Giving my customers my best, and knowing they will be back, is very rewarding.

A high school graduate, I worked as a bookkeeper for a while and then in sales. My husband was in the hair business and needed more assistance, so I joined him in the shop to help out. I am a full service stylist now.

The typical day begins at 8:30 a.m. From then until 6:00 p.m. I check our appointments to be sure we have everything we need for them. Our clientele is varied; we take care of people from all walks of life who come into the shop. I also make coffee and I maintain the supplies.

Training is very important in the hair business. You need to stay current, so you need to continue to go to classes as often as possible. There's a lot of competition in this business. Neatness is a good quality to have; you should keep yourself and your work area tidy. Being professional and not talking too much to your coworkers while with a client is also important.

HAIR STYLIST

I went into cosmetology as a temporary means of making a living after graduating from high school. I thought I would see what I really wanted to go into before I went to college, but I have liked hairstyling so much I have wanted to stay in this line of work. I have now been doing this for 15 years.

My typical duties include cutting, setting, perming, coloring, frosting, and blow-drying hair. I also manicure nails. It is possible to service 8 to 10 people on a good day. If I don't have 8-10 clients per day, it is hard to make enough money because I work on a commission basis.

The skills and attitudes which I consider important for a hairstylist are: being good with hair, being very personable, looking neat, attractive, and well done (finished in your appearance), being up, positive, and creative with people.

I like working as a hairstylist because I like having the chance to be creative and to meet lots of people. I have job satisfaction when people are happy with what I've done.

Especially pleasing is when someone loves something that was totally my idea, but I never push my opinion. I suggest in a positive way.

HANDYMAN; FORMERLY NAVY MAN

There is no typical day in the odd jobs business. I do things when people ask.

My skills as a machinist, mechanic, electrician, electronics technician and in carpentry have all been useful. Most important is an acquired understanding of basic mechanical and electronic principles. One must be able to look at an apparatus and know how it works.

I am satisfied when I successfully repair something at a reasonable profit. I would like to set up a better repair parts source library. Finding parts takes the most time in this line of work.

I did not get into this business by choice. I retired from the navy with many skills. People knew I could fix anything, so I decided to do this as a part-time business.

Other previous occupations have been as a newspaper delivery boy, student, machinist, deep sea diver, U.S.N. master chief, U.S.N. master diver, V.W. repairman, T.V. repairman, coin dealer, Lionel train dealer, well driller, sky diving jumpmaster, and more.

HEALTH AIDE, PUBLIC ELEMENTARY SCHOOL

As a health aide at an elementary school for the past six years, I provide basic first aid for ill or injured students: keep immunization records, check immunization records on new students, call or write letters to parents regarding immunization needs, and give necessary medications to students as prescribed by a physician.

It is important to know the health laws regarding immunizations and all school policies. It helps to be able to type and communicate with worried or irate parents. It's very important to have a positive attitude and to be cheerful because ill or injured children are usually very frightened. To do this work, you must like children.

I feel good about my job when I am able to wipe away a child's tears and get a smile.

I worked for the school as an instructional aide and when an opening came up for health aide, I tested and was hired into this position. I chose this because I have always been interested in the health field, I love children, and since my own children were school age, working for the school allowed time to be home with them. I'm off on the same days and time that they are.

Although there is not much opportunity for advancement I enjoy my work. Previously, I was an administrative secretary in a prison, which was interesting but not satisfying. I have also been an instructional aide at a Junior High School--also no satisfaction.

I have returned to school, and am now working toward my Bachelor's degree in nursing and would like to continue working in the school system as a nurse. I would also like to work part time in a hospital on the obstetrics floor.

HEALTH CARE ADMINISTRATOR

I administer and operate a nursing home. About 85% of my time as administrator is spent dealing and meeting with individuals on all levels of the organization, as well as outside organizations. I must make sure daily regulatory requirements on a state, federal and local level are met. Meetings are held to report and review the fiscal operation of the home, for problem solving and for delegations of appropriate tasks to accomplish routine and new work requirements.

To perform this job well it is important to have the ability to be flexible, be a sound decision maker, produce change, meet challenges, provide for expert support when needed on issues or problems that require outside organizational assistance. Never think that you are able to achieve operational effectiveness by yourself--team work is essential. You should have the ability to think and decide on a large perspective of the total operation.

I am satisfied with my profession because it does not become routine, but provides a daily challenge of meeting the operational needs in a complex delivery system. It fine tunes your ability to see problems and issues clearly and act on these matters.

I would like to involve myself more actively in testifying before Congress and other governing bodies regarding issues, concerns, and problems associated with the delivery of care and LTC (Long Term Care).

It has been a life long ambition of mine to achieve an administrative level of work. To prepare for this I have earned the BA in Social Work and a Master's in Health Service Administration. Previously, the institution in which I work appointed me to be Director of Social Services, Administrative Assistant, and Assistant Administrator. The higher officials of the organization requested and appointed me for my current position. I plan to continue in the field of LT care on an administrative level.

HEALTH EDUCATOR

I chose a career as a health educator because I enjoy the subject area and am convinced of its importance. Therefore I get satisfaction from sharing it. I have also always enjoyed working with youth as evidenced by my previous experience as camp counselor and playground director.

I teach students in grades 6 through 12 about developing a healthy lifestyle. I meet with 5 classes of students each day to discuss the various health-related topics. I have found that a pleasant attitude is important. Good communication and organization skills are also necessary. I also consider it very important to bring personal experiences and insight into the classroom.

The only thing I dislike about my teaching job is the schoolday schedule. I think that school should start later than 7:30 because I have found that students are not thinking and functioning well that early. Aside from that, I like this kind of work very much and have for the past 18 years.

My future career plans are to continue to acquire as much knowledge in my field as possible by attending workshops and then sharing with my students.

HEALTH EDUCATOR & ATHLETIC TRAINER

My career has taken a natural course in that I earned a Bachelor of Science degree in Health Education with additional courses in athletic training and am now working as a health educator and athletic trainer. These are separate jobs. I teach 10th grade health and am an athletic trainer for a small college.

As a health educator, I teach 5 health classes a day. I then spend one to three hours in training sessions at a college. The primary requirement for handling these jobs is a knowledge of the subject matter and an interest and ability to handle teenagers.

I have found that I like almost every aspect of my work including the people I work with, the opportunity for advancement, the people and organization I work for, and the kind of work I do. There is one major drawback, however, and that is the low salary. Despite this, I am satisfied with my work because I find satisfaction dealing with teenagers.

My future career plans are to return to school to earn a Masters in Physical Therapy and to work in that field.

HEALTH INSURANCE SALESMAN

The general routine in my work as a health insurance salesman is to prospect for customers, drive to meet with various customers, give my presentation, and close on the business. You need strong people skills in sales work. High self-esteem is essential.

I particularly like the fact that there are advancement opportunities and I'm pleased with the work itself. Gratification in my work comes for me in meeting new folks and in helping people.

My job would be more satisfying if the insurance products and services were changed to meet the current needs of the customers. I also dislike all the travel and the high mileage each year. My future plans are to develop an employee leasing service to go with an insurance business.

After finishing high school and before getting into the insurance field, I enjoyed my work in office management, which was a requirement of the company before I could pursue insurance sales.

HEALTH LABORATORY ADMINISTRATOR

My administrative work at the laboratory is basically to oversee the review of lab surveys and program results of laboratory testing. The work must be done precisely and accurately so it is necessary to be attentive to pertinent details and have scientific knowledge.

I find satisfaction from program results which are achieved from efficient and accurate laboratory testing. My job could be more satisfying without all the government bureaucracy details work. I could also use more help.

I started my career after college as a laboratory technician and worked up to my administrative position.

HEAVY EQUIPMENT OPERATOR #1

After graduating from high school, I worked on highway construction, as an underground miner, a truck driver, surveyor, logger, factory worker, and in farming. I took the job as a heavy equipment operator in an open pit phosphate mine because of the money. I have now found that I actually like this kind of work and have therefore kept at it for 15 years. I like the organization I work for , the people I work with, and the opportunity I have for advancement. What I don't like is the shift work--changing shifts every 2 weeks.

My machine work can vary from day to day. I don't know until I report to work for the day what area I will get dispatched to and what work will be designated for me to do. I operate various heavy machines for reclaiming, ore separation, haulage, etc.

Safety awareness is the most critical aspect of this work. You must also stay alert so you don't waste ore or get it dirty. You must remember production. Finally, I think it is important to be aware of the cost of the machine you are running and to treat it with respect. I run a $750,000+ machine.

I find job satisfaction from the respect I receive from my co-workers. I plan to stay where I am and to possibly become a foreman.

HEAVY EQUIPMENT OPERATOR #2

I work as a union operating engineer specializing in large cranes. My position is also called a heavy equipment operator; my biggest responsibility is to go to a job site and safely and efficiently operate a large piece of equipment. In the fifteen years I have been doing this, I have helped in the construction of buildings, bridges, and nuclear reactors.

I have a Bachelor of Science degree in Business Administration and I feel that my college education has helped me understand the business side of my work.

My work requires safe, smooth operation of the equipment as there is always the possibility that someone will get hurt; the most important quality for success in my work is sufficient experience to give an individual confidence in his/her ability.

My work is rewarding; these rewards come in the form of a pat on the back for a job well done and a big paycheck.

In the future I plan to put my business education to use in starting my own business.

HOMEMAKER #1

I'm on my own time. I have no set hours. I have no one telling me what to do and how to do it. Of course, I do have a lot to do to take care of my family's needs. I take care of the house. I do the cleaning and the washing of clothes. I am a chauffeur for two teenagers, the bookkeeper, seamstress, etc,!

To perform well as a homemaker it is important to be a good organizer. You need many skills like cooking and sewing. Utmost, you need lots of patience and love.

A monetary award would be nice! I would like to have a weekly paycheck that was my own.

I guess it's obvious how I got the job, I married into it! Before homemaking, I clerked in a retail catalog store and was a steel mill worker.

In the future I will possibly work part time somewhere but never full time. I feel homemaking is fulfilling and if I had a full time job my home and family would suffer!

HOMEMAKER #2

My day varies between summer and the school year. In summer, we basically get up and dressed, have breakfast, do chores and then HAVE FUN. It is kids, kids all day. I enjoy it but appreciate school days. On school days I help get the family up and on their way by 8:30 a.m. I spend the day as I see fit--lots of variety. At 4:00 I listen to people as they come home from work and school and start to prepare dinner. There is often a rush to evening activities.

My job requires a variety of skills such as cooking, caring for the sick, cleaning, also organizational skills are important. I try to have a professional attitude about my work. I am not "just a homemaker." To do the job well takes all the love, creativity, strength, intelligence, on and on, a person may have; it is a career!

Seeing my children grow, do well in school and be happy, secure people gives me great satisfaction. I enjoy the teamwork between my husband and myself to accomplish goals and provide a steady home for our children. I also like the freedom to be in charge of my schedule.

I wouldn't change things in my occupation. However, I would love to take a break from all outside activities long enough to get my home totally organized. There is also a lack of uninterrupted time to be by myself.

Previous to becoming a homemaker, I worked for a printer which I enjoyed. Also

I assisted a tailor at a men's store making alterations. I have had no major careers and therefore did not have to make a traumatic choice between career and home/family. Instead of my choosing a career, it chose me, and I have enjoyed it for the past 12 years.

I may return to college and get a job to pay for my children's education. I attended for 2 years previously. I would prefer to stay "unemployed" and to use my time for volunteer and church work. Most importantly, I want to be available to my family especially as my small children enter their teen years.

HOMEMAKER #3

The role of a housewife for me has been extremely rewarding and filled with variety. I do the daily chores of preparing 3 meals daily, cleaning, and laundry. However, I have the freedom of choice as to the time when I want to do something and the chore which I choose to do. It has been my choice to spend much of my time on volunteer activities such as the library, a charity craft shop, a health care unit, Sunday school, and Camp Fire Girls.

The most important attitude to have is a willingness to accept the role of the homemaker. Being a housewife takes many skills. I have had the time and the rewards of personally caring for my ailing husband.

I have been able to have a variety of social-work positions over the years. I have been an assistant camp director, a housemother in a study home for delinquent boys, a supervisor of delinquent girls working in my home when the children were small, and director of an international house for foreign visitors.

My reward has been that I have a happy home.

HOMEMAKER #4

I love my work as a homemaker. I keep very busy with a steady flow of work all day and the time passes quickly. I consider my major responsibilities to be cleaning, cooking, and advising.

In order for perform well as a homemaker, I think it is important to keep smiling, and to work fast, but most importantly, to work accurately with no mistakes.

I think a homemaker's job would be more satisfying if the people for whom she worked were to say please and thank you and offer encouragement by noticing when the work is done well and telling you that it is good.

I graduated from high school and did cashier work for a grocery store and department store prior to becoming a homemaker and mother of two.

I do not have any major dislikes about my job as homemaker. I find satisfaction from a job well done, and from people who enjoy working near or with me.

HOMEMAKER #5

I like being a homemaker because I like being my own boss. I have had this as an occupation for 20 years because I believe it is the place for me to be while I have children to raise.

My daily and weekly duties as a homemaker are: taking care of a home including cleaning, shopping for supplies, doing interior decoration, etc., taking care of children, doing laundry, making arrangements for doctor's, etc. and social engagements, cooking, doing volunteer work in politics, gardening, keeping records for a family consulting business, keeping cars running, repaired and full of gas, arranging for home maintenance, and keeping in touch with children, family, and friends who are away.

I consider communication skills to be most important as a homemaker. You must also be flexible and care about others.

My educational background includes earning a Bachelor of Science in Math degree and a Masters in Statistics. Prior to having children, I worked for a large research and development firm as a computer programmer and statistician.

I like most everything about being a homemaker except I wish I had a less hectic schedule and more time to myself. I would choose to do this again if I had the chance to start over. I receive satisfaction from watching my children mature, having a reasonably well-organized household, and being able to determine my own schedule.

When my children are grown, I may teach math in a high school.

HOMEMAKER #6

I consider my current occupation as homemaker to be a chosen career path when I married. It is my personal/moral need to nurture children at home. Prior to becoming a homemaker, I was an Army officer and registered dietitian /food service director for a small pediatric hospital. My educational background includes earning my Bachelor of Science degree and Master of Science degree in Systems Management. I am married to a Navy officer.

A typical day for me includes doing laundry, cooking meals, playing with my children, going for walks, and diaper changes throughout the day. To perform my homemaking responsibilities well, I think it is important to have patience, organization, devotion, a sense of humor, and love.

The reward for my work has been the knowledge that I have helped make a safe and happy home. I have had the joy of watching the progress of my children grow and develop.

In the future, I plan to write a small book of inspirational thoughts for other military wives.

HOMEMAKER #7

I worked as a teacher, weather observer, and librarian for a number of years, and now that I have married a man who makes a decent living to support both of us comfortably, I am a homemaker. My educational background includes a Bachelor of Arts, a Master of Arts in English Literature, and a Master of Arts in Library Science.

As well as having the cooking and cleaning skills required of a homemaker, I feel that it is important to have the ability to enjoy a pressure-free life for yourself and your family. My daily schedule is set up to do that and includes: taking care of my cat, doing personal exercises, reading the newspaper, watching T.V. news programs, doing necessary outside and inside chores, preparing food, and reading.

I am very satisfied with my role in life and am pleased to get up in the morning.

HOMEMAKER #8

My life changed dramatically when I got married and had a child. Prior to being a homemaker, I was an account executive with a major investment firm in San Francisco, sold and rented real estate in London, England, worked as a waitress in a ski area, worked in a needlepoint shop in Toronto, Canada, and taught needlepoint in a women's prison in Canada.

Although I find my duties as a homemaker to be tedious and would like to have help with some of these mundane chores, I love my family and my home and feel I am doing the right thing at this time in my life.

My morning activities include: getting my son off to school, putting out the horses, cleaning up the barn, doing laundry, going to aerobics, and sometimes meeting a friend for lunch. Afternoons are usually spent doing errands, paying bills, riding horses if time allows, and meeting my son at the bus. In the evening, I plan and cook dinner, read to my son and get him to bed, and watch T.V. or read.

I have found satisfaction from being a homemaker for the last 10 years in raising my son and enjoying his company. It is satisfying for me to have a nice comfortable home with lots of animals around to keep it all interesting. My future aspirations are to continue to be happy and healthy.

HOMEMAKER #9

I quit working because I had always intended to raise my own children. I feel that others, no matter how competent, cannot care as much as a parent would.

Prior to motherhood, I was an advertising executive, bank officer (where I also taught adults finance), and a psychologist (I did some therapy). To qualify for these positions, I have earned two master's degrees. Ultimately, I'll go back to "work," however, it is now my choice to stay home while my children are young. I may even consider a career in law or medicine when I return to the work force.

As a homemaker, I awaken early and start the day by walking my daughter to school. My other routine daily activities include: cleaning, cooking, shopping, doing errands, making phone calls, organizing school functions, and other social activities for us all, answering mail, paying bills, and supervising home renovations, yard work, and many visiting children.

Organization is absolutely crucial as a homemaker. You have to be able to think ahead and plan without making too fixed a schedule, since it inevitably gets disrupted. Interpersonal/parenting skills are next. A "Zen" attitude helps a lot, or the tasks can be tedious.

It would be nice to have a little more time that isn't spoken for--a few more hours in the day, so to speak. This is by far the most exhausting job I've had--and I commuted to NYC and put in 10 hour days while I was "working." However, homemaking is in a separate world from the marketplace, and I sometimes feel out of touch with a big part of the adult world.

In spite of this, I like the flexibility/creativity I have as a homemaker. My satisfaction comes from knowing that while my children are young, no one could care more or take better care of them. I find satisfaction in knowing I'm giving them a foundation of confidence and knowledge which will last a lifetime.

I'm in the process of training to work with the Volunteer Ambulance Unit in town one day a week. I've also discovered that I like and am good at home design. Leading a therapy group for parents is also in my future plans. I like to follow a lot of leads, and then decide what's next.

HOMEMAKER #10

I was a professional women for 15 years before taking a maternity leave, intending to return to work. But after the birth of my first child, I decided I didn't want to pass up the experience of raising my children. I had fulfilled several of my career goals, and thought that I would prefer to devote my time to my family full-time. My life before children included earning a Bachelor of Science in Education plus some graduate courses, and working as a high school art teacher, an advertising production assistant, a layout artist, and an art director.

A description of a typical day or week for me as a homemaker is: getting 2 children and myself ready to start our day, feeding, cleaning, organizing my household responsibilities, sharing fun time with my children, keeping in touch with my women friends, participating in our local family center, and overseeing the building of our new home.

I have found the following attributes to be important for performing well as a homemaker: creative problem solving, patience, persistence, consistency, and knowing where to find support when necessary.

There are some frustrations and drawbacks to my work as a homemaker, which

I think are important to bring out. First, sometimes some of the tasks are routine and monotonous. Second, there is never enough time to oneself. Third, in my attempt to present a united front regarding discipline of our children, I have found it difficult to find ways to communicate my concerns with my spouse. We both are very interested, concerned and involved with the raising of our children but I worry that there is not consistency in how we raise them so they will learn the essential values, resulting in responsible productive behavior. Being a parent is about the most major responsibility you can have.

I like my occupation as a homemaker, and find watching the growth and development of my children is very rewarding. I find satisfaction in fostering their growth and potential.

When my children are school age, I plan to work in an art related profession. I also plan to be involved in the local school board, and volunteer in various community activities.

HOMEMAKER #11

I have been in my occupation as a homemaker for 16 years and consider it to be made up of many occupations including bookkeeper, chauffeur, teacher aide, laundress, cook, maid, and gardener. I chose to be home to care for my children. I see too many children with problems either in school or with the law when both parents work.

As well as the cooking, cleaning, laundry, getting to doctor and dentist appointments, paying bills, doing banking, buying clothes, and taking the children to school, etc., I include volunteer work in the school classrooms and library as a part of my homemaker duties. In order to handle these diverse responsibilities, I think it is important to have skills in cooking, hygiene, accounting, driving, and a patient attitude.

One of the reasons I like my occupation as a homemaker is that it includes many different types of jobs. I find satisfaction seeing my family healthy, secure, happy and knowing I've always been able to help my children grow.

I am considering going to college to earn a degree in library science after my husband finishes college.

HOMEMAKER #12

I have chosen to stay home to raise my three children. I feel that it is my responsibility as a wife and mother to do the cooking, cleaning, and household management. This includes the routine duties of bathing the children, playing or watching T.V. with the kids, and driving them around for various activities. Although these may sound like tedious and mundane tasks, they must be done with an understanding, caring and loving attitude in order to achieve the proper result--well-adjusted, happy children.

Prior to becoming a wife and mother, and after graduating from high school, I worked as a secretary/bookkeeper and a waitress. Since I have had my children when I am young, I plan to go back into the work force when they are raised. I would like to do juvenile welfare work or police work of some kind.

I find satisfaction in my work particularly when I hear "I love you, Mommy," or see the smiles on their faces.

HOMEMAKER #13

Four years ago, as I am the mother of two children, I chose to become a homemaker. My daily tasks include cooking for my family of four, house cleaning, running errands, and supervising the activities of my two children. This requires the ability to organize one's time and prioritize tasks, good listening skills, patience, and the motivation to do this job out of love for family.

It is satisfying for me to watch my children grow, knowing they need me, and returning the love I give to them.

If I could change anything, I would increase the number of hours in a day so I could get more rest.

I worked outside the home for seven years as a geologist, I have a Bachelor of Arts degree in geology, and I have worked also as a banker before making the decision to work at home full time. This decision would not have been possible without the patience of a very supportive spouse and I would not go back to either of those jobs; my present work is too important to me.

In the future, when my children are attending school all day, I plan to teach grade school science.

HOMEMAKER #14

As a homemaker, every task I perform is an act of love. Even though I have a Bachelor of Science degree and have taught school in the past, I love keeping a home and caring for a family.

My spouse was very supportive of my decision to make my family my career--it gave me the opportunity to explore the person I really am and grow to be the best I can be.

My career choice has given me the opportunity to explore volunteering; I have worked with crippled children to assist in their physical therapy and rehabilitation.

Though I completed a Bachelor's degree and have not worked outside my home, I believe education is never wasted; there is no wage that can give one a return equal to personal enrichment.

I will continue to perform volunteer work--I plan to give some of my time to an art museum sometime in the near future.

HOMEMAKER #15

As a homemaker of eighteen years, I perform the regular housekeeping tasks; I also am involved in volunteer community projects. During a normal week, I cook, clean, and garden at my home daily; deliver meals to shut-ins twice per week; visit nursing homes once per week; and play cards with shut-ins as often as I can, usually twice per week.

My job, which I love, requires the same skills as those required to be a good and successful employee at a business outside the home-- communication, a love of people, and dedication.

The people I administer to, I believe, help me more than I help them; I always receive more blessings than I give. The rewards of my volunteering are infinite, but there are not enough people giving of their time; I believe this is unfortunate for all concerned.

Past employment for me has held satisfaction, but nowhere near the rewards of the work I now do; although I never had a job I disliked. I had always worked with people in an office environment, but in my opinion, this is the best job I have ever held and I plan to continue as long as I possibly can.

HOMEMAKER #16

I have now chosen to be home with the children because it is most conducive for supporting my husband's career. Prior to being a full time homemaker, my background included jobs in somewhat diverse fields. I operated my own boarding kennel. I was employed for a long time as an academic assistant at a state university. I have also worked as a corporate executive secretary, a factory worker, and waitress. I suppose you could say I've been a "professional assistant." Most of my efforts have been of a supporting nature.

I describe my job as a homemaker as involving a great deal of cleaning and straightening up, plus caring for the children. I spend about 2 hours a day behind the wheel running errands and taking the children to school and other activities. I prepare meals and tend to all the house and yard maintenance. I also have lots of time to myself for reading or recreation.

I have found that organizational skills are essential to running a household. A carpe diem (seize the day) attitude combined with a be-here- now philosophy is also helpful as a homemaker.

I like my job as a homemaker very much. I find it satisfying to be spending my time caring for my family. Besides, I find that a big advantage is that I get to be home when I have leisure time.

HOMEMAKER #17

I am a homemaker because I find satisfaction in being at home with my children. I consider my basic responsibilities to be taking care of the children and my husband and keeping the house clean. My days are somewhat routine and typically include getting my husband off to work, the school age children to school, exercising, caring for the pre-schoolers, cooking meals, picking up the house, and getting the children bedded.

I have found that providing this care and performing these duties takes a variety of skills and attitudes including organization, patience, quick thinking, diplomacy, first aid, and nutrition.

Prior to becoming a wife and mother, I worked in banking and also in accounts receivable at a college. I have earned some college credits, but have not completed the requirements for a degree. I plan to continue to stay at home with my children guiding them to be mature, loving adults. I then plan to go back and finish college and work outside the home.

HOMEMAKER #18

I am a full time homemaker because I married a man who had the same views on homemaking as I have. We made sure he had an occupation that would enable our family to live on one income so I could quit work and stay at home with the children.

My responsibilities as a homemaker with two small children are to keep the house and lawn clean and tidy, and to care for the physical, spiritual and emotional needs of the family members. Some of the activities which are involved in carrying out these duties are ironing, preparing meals, exercising, cleaning, shopping, library visits, visits with friends, yard work, playing with the children, reading, sewing, and making cookies.

To perform this kind of work well, the following skills and attitudes are important: budgeting, cooking, sewing, patience, creativity, imagination, enthusiasm, consistency, optimism, compassion, knowledge of first aid, and a broad base of other knowledge.

Although I like being a homemaker, I do find household chores like ironing, washing dishes, and cleaning bathrooms to be monotonous work. I have also found that I miss receiving a paycheck for the work that I do. Despite these drawbacks, I certainly like the majority of my work because of the people I am working for and working with, my family. I particularly like having the freedom to make my own schedule. I find job satisfaction from being able to develop interests and talents, being with my children, knowing the things I teach my children and the example that I set for them will transcend time (be passed down through generations), and knowing my children feel secure because I am there for them.

I plan to remain being a homemaker until the children are raised. Then, I am considering a career as a nutritionist.

HOMEMAKER #19

I have always viewed the role of a wife and mother to have the greatest responsibilities a person could have. It is a responsibility for other lives whose lives affect others. It is the opportunity to shape "goodness" into our world.

As a homemaker, I plan and execute all the areas of a house and family. There are no typical days or week, but every day involves some tasks or chores related to housekeeping: bill paying, planning meals and preparing them, planning for birthdays and holidays, planning children's transportation, planning and shopping for clothing and household needs, plus whatever volunteer work one does. But, usually every minute is busy.

To perform this kind of work well, it is important to have a positive attitude that includes the confidence that what you are doing is important and makes a difference in the lives of people, planning skills, creative thinking, patience, endurance, the willingness to do for others, the ability to teach children in many ways, and a caring, helping, giving spirit. Some engineering skills and being a self-starter are additional assets.

Like many homemakers, I don't like scrubbing bathrooms and grocery shopping, but I do like the challenging and creative opportunities plus the great flexibility and freedom.

My work is always changing and yet some things about it never change. Some days I'd rather be doing something else--but wouldn't we all from time to time. Homemaking offers the freedom to choose from many volunteer or personal interest areas. It is always challenging. Throughout my homemaking years I have found challenges as a volunteer in my church as a teacher, Sunday school leader, moderator, committee chairman, choir member, and regular weekly visitor to nursing homes and to the elderly in the community. I find satisfaction in my work in creating an atmosphere where others can grow and develop. I am an enabler, a teacher, a mentor, and a "servant person." Being and doing for others is its own great satisfaction, but being the teacher of values for children is an awesome responsibility because it affects the future.

HOMEMAKER #20

I've always wanted to be a mother and wife, not part time, but full time. Although I have considered other professions, nothing is as appealing or stimulating.

My responsibilities as a homemaker are to keep house, care for the goats and chickens which supplement our income, help with building our house, and landscaping around our new house. My typical day starts with seeing my family off to school and work. The mornings are spent cleaning the house, and in the afternoon I take care of the goats and chickens. That may include building projects. I set aside time to refinish furniture, do landscaping, and gardening. When the children get home, we talk about their day and I help with homework. When my husband gets home, we discuss our day and make decisions. Dinner is next, and then family activities (games, TV, movies).

In order to perform this kind of work as a homemaker well, the following skills are important: all around handyman, communications, business, nutrition (family and livestock), child rearing, and psychology. A love for people and common sense are also necessary. My attitude toward my work as a homemaker is to do the best I can to benefit my family and myself.

I like the kind of work I do and the people with whom I work. I find satisfaction from the family unity and love we have. There is also satisfaction for me in a clean house and property, and healthy livestock.

In the future, I want to expand my livestock and acreage. I also want to run my husband's part-time hot tub business out of my home. Other future plans include selling my paintings and making quilts to sell. Through all of this, I want to support my family so they can achieve their goals.

HOMEMAKER #21

I have been in the "job" of homemaker all my married life, and that has been many years because I married young. In some ways homemaking is a job more challenging than other work. Anyone who decides to go into this kind of occupation would do the normal activities of a housekeeper--make beds, wash dishes, laundry, and other household chores. It does not require special skills, except perhaps in cooking, and the rest is doing what comes naturally!

As in professional occupations, there are many satisfactions, but in this job by far the major satisfaction derives from seeing the development of a happy and healthy family--a husband and, in my case, four sons. Since I am of a generation different from the persons who might be using this service, my attitude may be judged to be old-fashioned, but I would do the same thing again if I were presented with the opportunity of reliving my life.

I wish I had more time to do all the things I want to get done, but I expect that would be true of many other jobs as well. One of the reasons I need more time is because, in earlier days particularly, I did untold hours of volunteer work.

I enjoy very much the opportunities I have had to read, and being a homemaker does allow time for that. I read a great deal, exercise, watch my health, and continue to enjoy life.

HOMEMAKER #22

I decided to leave my secretarial job so I could stay home and raise my children. I have found this to be satisfying, watching the kids grow and learn new things.

My daily responsibilities are the typical home chores of a homemaker with young children like fixing meals, changing diapers, bathing and playing with the children, grocery shopping and running errands. In my opinion, the most important factor to perform well as a homemaker with children is to have patience.

Although I am glad I have chosen to stay home with my children at this time, I do plan to work part-time when they are in school.

HOMEMAKER #23

I have chosen to stay at home to raise my son. Prior to becoming a wife and mother, I served in the U.S. Navy for 7 years as a radioman.

I do not restrict myself to a set schedule, but rather I do what I want, when I want to do it. I must, however, accomplish the basic duties of a homemaker such as cleaning, cooking, and caring for my husband and child. I have volunteered some time every week to read stories at my son's kindergarten. I also find time to meet with friends and their children.

I have found that as a homemaker it is important to be flexible, have a sense of humor, and to be patient. Because I have been able to develop these traits, I find that I like my occupation. However, I wish homemakers got more thanks for doing what they do. Job satisfaction for me is smiles from my family.

I eventually plan to find a part-time job outside the home until my son leaves home, and then a full-time job for "life after kids."

HOMEMAKER & STUDENT #1

In a nutshell, I take care of 4 children, 3 cats, 2 large dogs, volunteer at my children's school, and attend college. I am doing what I always wanted: to have a large family, and have the children when I am young. In this way I feel we can grow together, and I'll still have time for my career choices and my husband.

My day starts early and includes feeding my animals, making lunches, waking up the family, making breakfast, getting kids dressed, hair combed, and homework in backpacks, driving kids to school, cleaning house, doing laundry, picking up the kindergartner, running errands, making lunch, finishing up housework, picking up other kids from school, fixing snacks, starting dinner, cleaning up dishes, helping kids with homework, giving kids baths and tucking them in bed, and feeding the animals. On some evenings, I go to school and do homework in between cleaning.

Prior to becoming a housewife, I worked 2 jobs while attending high school, one as a late night D. J., and the other was salesclerking at a department store. After high school, I worked as a grocery checker. I am studying elementary education and plan to teach kindergarten. My future aspirations also includes getting a master's degree in special education, and then my doctorate in psychology or administration.

To perform well as a housewife, the number one skill to have is patience. You must be able to sacrifice time and your personal needs for the sake of others. It is also necessary to be able to make money stretch.

I find my occupation as a housewife to be satisfying because I am rewarded by having children and a husband who are proud of me. I feel needed and know that I can't be instantly replaced. The best part is being there to watch my children grow and develop and know that I was a big part of the development. I do wish I could change the attitude of others about the role of a housewife: that they could be recognized for all they do and not taken for granted.

HOMEMAKER & STUDENT #2

For the past year I have been working as a homemaker and a student; I am in the process of raising my twin babies and working toward a degree in the field of Law. I perform the basic household duties required of any homemaker--cleaning the house, picking up after the twins, attending to their individual needs, keeping the household budget, and preparing meals; but in addition, I am attending Law School. My schedule requires that I do most of my studying during the twins' nap time in the afternoon.

My daily tasks require physical energy, organization, concentration, patience, and the constant reminder that I am doing all this out of love for my family.

The rewards are numerous: hugs, kisses, giggles, first steps, first words, books to read, and a wonderful sense that all that I do is so important. It is so wonderful to be home with my babies, watching them grow and change every day; I wouldn't choose any other career right now.

I have previously worked outside my home as a photographer, mini-lab trainer and manager, waitress, bookkeeper, computer operator, factory worker, and salesclerk.

I am going to finish Law School on a part-time basis until the children are enrolled in kindergarten, at which time I plan to take on a full-time college schedule of classes. I am also getting my twin babies into performing in movies and television commercials.

HOMEMAKER & TEACHER

I felt that being a full-time mother to my children was far more important than working full-time at a career and attempting to raise children at the same time. Both my husband and I felt the same way on this issue. Consequently we have had to make life-style choices based on this decision, i.e.: the size of home we could afford and the activities we could participate in.

After tending to housekeeping chores like dishwashing, laundry, and picking-up, I begin my chosen task for the day--sewing, working on church committee work, reading or whatever. In the evening, there is dinner to cook, and the children's homework and sports to oversee.

The skills which I consider important for a homemaker are: organization of time, creative solutions to problems, and making do with limited financial resources. The most important attitude for me is forbearance--the kids will grow up and move out. I'll get a job eventually in which I can be intellectually challenged. Humor is also necessary for me because this job can be dead boring with the repetition of tasks.

Being a homemaker does not generate income. If I could find a way to be paid for working at home, I would pursue it. I have done crafts and dressmaking to earn some money but have found them to be too labor intensive with little return for the time spent.

I was an elementary teacher prior to becoming a full-time housewife. I like not having to please 145 students, three administrators and countless parents. I have time at home to do what I like, when I like to do it.

My career plan for the future is to find a job which will be intellectually challenging and give me the opportunity to utilize my educational background. I have earned a B.S. in Elementary Education and a B.S. in Biology while staying at home as a homemaker.

HOMEMAKER, STUDENT, & OFFICE CLERK

Although I have held jobs outside my home (I am currently employed as an office clerk in a college office on a twenty-hour-per-week schedule and attend college computer classes twelve hours per week), I consider myself primarily a homemaker. I spend about twenty hours per week on household duties--cooking meals for my family, cleaning the house, doing the laundry, paying the bills, taking care of correspondence, and shopping for my family; I also take time to study computer skills for the classes I am taking and work at my office position where I primarily perform filing, typing, record keeping and word processing. I have never held a job that I enjoy as much as being a wife, mother, and homemaker.

A schedule such as the one I maintain requires organizational skills, good self esteem, the ability to do many tasks simultaneously, the motivation to be able to work for the satisfaction derived from performing some tasks purely for the benefit of others, and the ability to perform a job well without feedback.

I like working part-time in an office because I enjoy being among people--answering telephone inquiries about course offerings. The feeling of competence I get from doing a good job is very rewarding. I enjoy the feeling of being "in control" when my home is clean and in an orderly state.

I made several choices along the way and I wonder where I would be, careerwise, had I made other decisions. I have a Bachelor of Arts degree which has never been utilized to its full extent with respect to a job; I have never held a position for longer than three years, as my spouse's field of employment requires that we relocate often. I often wonder what I might have achieved if I had been able to build a career in one place; but, admittedly, I have enjoyed living in many different and interesting places.

I plan to use my computer skills and office experience to work at temporary office employment positions and then move closer to my goal of becoming a free-lance technical writer, writing at home.

HORSESHOER & BLACKSMITH

My father was a trainer/driver of harness horses. I helped shoe horses and served six years of apprenticeship with other horse shoers in order to qualify myself for this career. It has now been my primary job for 30 years. Along the way, I did calf roping as a part-time rodeo cowboy and was also a lumberjack.

As a horse shoer/blacksmith, also called farrier, my day starts at 7:00 a.m.. I shoe harness horses on an hourly appointment basis Monday through Friday, year around.

The art of shoeing is a skill on its own! As far as the attitude which is important in this trade, it is the attitude of caring and doing the best you can do.

In response to any changes which I would like to see in this occupation, all I can say is that this trade hasn't changed much in over 2000 years and I don't see any in the future.

I have stayed a horse shoer for so long primarily because I find satisfaction in doing a good job and receiving the appreciation from my clients.

My future career plans are to just work at my trade as long as I am able.

HORSE TRAINER/BREEDER

As a horse trainer/breeder, I attend to the health and safety of the horses in my care. My basic chores include training horses to be ridden and to be driven, and, when necessary, making preparations to breed a particular mare. In the summer, I also raise a crop of hay.

To engage in this type of work you should possess flexibility, patience, and lots of physical energy; an affinity toward outdoor work; an appreciation of horses; and respect for safety.

I enjoy working outdoors and expressing my love for horses, which in my opinion, is in the blood; the visible results are very rewarding.

Working with many different horses has given me the sense that each possesses unique and interesting personality traits and attitudes.

After three years in this position, I would like to be self-employed because then I would have greater autonomy regarding the way in which the horses are trained. I believe I could accomplish this by obtaining a degree in business or accounting and establishing a career that would afford me the means by which I could keep a number of horses to train in my own way.

HOSPITAL, DISCHARGE ANALYST

After sending my youngest child off to school, I attended college and earned my Bachelor of Arts in Anthropology degree. I then searched out a research-type job in a medical/university type setting. What I found was my job as a discharge analyst in a university hospital.

It is my job to analyze hospital discharges using an international coding system. I apply the codes to diagnoses and procedures for a data base, billing, resource utilization, etc. My typical daily activities include going to assigned in-patient units to pick up discharge charts from the previous day; reading the entire record; assigning codes from ICD-9-CM to diagnoses and procedures; entering codes in the computer; and, if a research request is pending, additional forms must be filled out. To do this work, I must know various assignment rules and regulations for Medicare patients. My work must be accurate!

In order to perform this work, you need a knowledge of disease processes, treatments, medical terminology, rules and regulations, and the coding system. A person in this position should be inquisitive and intelligent.

My only real complaint about my work is the lack of opportunity for advancement and the lack of feedback on how the hospital utilizes the data base which I create. I am satisfied with this work because I find it thought provoking. I enjoy doing this solo work and setting my own pace (within limits).I have found research work both at this job and as a data manager for chemotherapy research in a cancer clinic to be appropriate and satisfying for me.

HOSPITAL PLANNER

In my current position as a hospital planner, it is my responsibility to do the strategic planning, operational and business plans, grants, data requests, and special studies for the hospital. My work day is very varied. I do a good deal of reading and data compilation for a wide variety of projects, plus assisting departments with document preparation.

This job requires a person who is a self-starter, has writing skills, can do a quick study on varied subjects, and is good at explaining in an understandable way what others want to do.

I earned my health administration graduate degree. My first position in this profession was doing public health planning under a federal contract. When the funds dried up for the government contracting agency, I moved to my position at the private hospital.

I plan to continue in health administration and to someday head a health system planning/marketing effort.

This career gives me personal satisfaction by offering me the opportunity to deal with a wide variety of topics at a high level. This affords me an opportunity to show my abilities, and that gives me a reward in my work.

HOTEL MANAGER

I have spent all my career life since school in jobs related to the hotel business. I attended 2 years of hotel management school in Europe and then started as a cook/waiter and worked my way up and through the various levels in this profession. Previous positions have been as credit manager, beverage manager, front office manager, controller, assistant manager, and general manager.

At this stage in my career as hotel manager, I am responsible for operational and financial aspects of a hotel, including restaurants, bars, and meeting/banquet facilities. The typical activities involved in this position are: financial observation of revenues and costs; involvement in sales and marketing; public relations; observation of daily business and relating findings to respective department heads; setting goals for operational departments; new ideas; and preparation of budgets.

The following skills are important in order to perform this kind of work: good human relations in dealing with guests and employees; ability to motivate; good accounting knowledge; knowledge of basics of each department (front office, sales, service, food, etc.)

I like almost every aspect of my hotel management work.

I particularly like the frequent moves I have made and the option to live anywhere and still work in this occupation. It is very satisfying to work in an established organization and yet be highly independent.

My career plans are to get assignments for bigger hotels.

HOTEL SECURITY COORDINATOR

I am the office coordinator/security investigator for a luxury class hotel. As such, I assist the security director with departmental correspondence, write incident and accident reports, and conduct interviews, interrogations, and locker searches. I am responsible for back-of-the-house ingress and egress by hotel service personnel. More specifically, my regular duties include: checking the identity of all persons entering the building; checking packages going out; receiving and filing time cards; answering the phone and dispatching other officers to incidents, accidents, and requests by hotel associates for assistance; engraving name tags; typing correspondence; documenting all activities in logs and on summary sheets; issuing equipment and keys to hotel associates; monitoring 5 alarm systems and 4 TV monitors showing areas covered by 6 cameras; and administering first aid and CPR.

To perform this kind of work well, it is important to have a positive attitude, alertness, easy communication with lots of people from different social and academic backgrounds, diplomacy, attention to details, ability to compose thoughts and write them, the ability to place information in a chronological order, filing and typing skills, the ability to receive information of a confidential nature and not reveal it unless necessary to document activities in a report or to solve a case, and first aid and CPR training.

Prior to this job, I had been a secretary/girl Friday, a substitute elementary school teacher, and an office administrator and teacher assistant at a vocational/technical school. It was while I was working at the voc/tech school which trains security personnel that I was offered my current position.

I like this kind of work although I find some difficulty being accepted as competent in the security field because I am a woman. I particularly like the daily contact and communication with people from all walks of life, the management, hourly employees, and guests/clients. I find job satisfaction in assisting people who need help. I think I have the best of two occupations, clerical and investigatory, with the best benefits of both--a day-time schedule, most weekends off, people contact, mobility, etc. In the future, I would like to complete my degree and to either become a licensed private investigator, a U.S. Marshall, or lawyer.

HOUSE RENTAL BUSINESS OWNER

The business started when my husband and I decided to purchase a home to rent to help build up a retirement fund. We used the equity we had built up in our own home to buy this first rental , and we have now built up the business to 7 rentals. We also have a farm on which we raise beef. Since my husband is employed full-time outside the home, the rental business is managed by me. It is my responsibility to handle the bookkeeping, interviews for rentals, collecting the rent, and to stay on top of repairs. In order to do this kind of work, it is important to be a good mediator, stay on top of problems, and to be honest and fair.

I like this work because of the independence I have with it and the opportunity of meeting the public. What I don't like is when I have to turn someone down for a rental.

I feel I have done well with this business and plan to continue in it. I plan to take some business courses which I hope will help us expand.

HUMAN RESOURCES, BANKING

I've worked in human resources in a bank for many years. It's a grand job where I enjoy the respect of the bank employees who express appreciation when I'm able to help them. I also like it when senior management pays attention to problems I bring to their attention. Knowing that I have a positive impact on the way people are treated at work is very rewarding to me.

A human resource manager must be a good communicator with emphasis on writing and listening. You should maintain a positive attitude, especially when dealing with management. Very good analytical skills in uncovering and solving problems are very important. You must also understand the laws related to obeying state rules regarding work conditions, and be able to interpret these laws. Teaching skills are necessary since you often have to make presentations to groups.

In my work, I handle any employee relations matters involving salaries, job transfers, promotions, and complaints or concerns. I make sure all departments conform to employment laws. Making certain that managers and supervisors are trained in the bank's human resource policies is part of my job as well. I also answer technical questions about human resource matters and prepare progress reports for senior managers. Finally, intervening when management and employees have problems is my responsibility.

In my work I particularly enjoy the projects that give me authority. I also like the high visibility in my job. My supervisors, the bank, and my work itself make my job satisfying. Unfortunately, salary raises are limited. I also wish there were more than just one person doing the human resources work.

My plans are to move into a corporate position in human resources. Maybe I'll expand my education beyond my Bachelor of Science degree in business administration and earn credentials in counseling, perhaps to work in labor relations.

HUMAN RESOURCES COMMUNICATIONS ASSISTANT

Projects are presented to me from various departments--Employee Relations, Affirmative Action, Benefits, etc. I might write scripts, coordinate and produce videos or design posters for such employee programs as promoting US Savings Bonds purchase through payroll deductions.

Previously, I was doing mainly paperwork and record-keeping in the Bids and Proposals Department of a computer company. After two years of work I did not enjoy at all, I transferred to the Communication Division.

There are many intrinsic rewards to this job which I have held for three years now. I enjoy the opportunities I have to be creative. Writing scripts, making up brochures, and designing posters are more like fun than work to me. I am paid very well and have very little tedious paperwork to do.

I have to meet with different departments to complete projects so that communications skills and people management as well as good decision making skills are necessary. Computer software (graphics) skills are important in designing posters and brochure materials. When I coordinate large seminars with teams of people, it takes good organizational ability and management skills.

My career aspirations are eventually to become a manager in the communications field in either the graphics division, media division, or corporate communications.

HUMAN RESOURCES OFFICER

I've been a human resources officer in a bank for 10 years. My duties are to interview applicants and to train employees after they join the bank. I must also help them to deal with their problems. I am responsible for supervising some of them.

Job satisfaction for me is in the training, which I enjoy very much. I also like matching a particular person with an appropriate position. I like problem-solving too. If there were more contact and interaction with people, my job would be even more pleasurable. Although I enjoy my work in human resources, I think one day I'd like to become a mortgage lender in the bank.

A person working in human resources must have initiative and leadership. You need the proper training; my degree is a Bachelor of Science in psychology and business. You should have competent communication skills and be able to work well with people. Good organizational skills are also important. In addition, you must be willing to do the "crummy" jobs as well as the fun ones.

My job requires that I work on many projects and deal with many issues at the same time. I also assist managers in solving problems with employees.

HUMAN RESOURCES MANAGER #1

I started as a secretary. I expressed an interest in setting up a personnel department because the company did not have one. I was then given a promotion to personnel assistant, personnel administrator and finally human resources manager. Prior to working for this company and moving up the ladder with them, I earned my Bachelor of Science and Master of Arts in Business Education degrees, and taught for several years.

My routine duties in managing the human resources department include: phone calls and meetings with various members of management regarding problem employees, employee requisitions; interviewing and screening applicants and referring them to department heads; meeting with employees about problems or helping with benefit information; supervising two full time and one part-time clerk who handle payroll, all benefits, workers' compensation claims, new employee enrollment; and all record keeping and personnel procedures.

To perform well as a human resource manager, it is important to be a good manager of time and to enjoy working with people and people problems. It is also necessary to have an educational background which includes a degree in human resources or a related area.

The only real frustration I am now facing with my job is the pay scale, and because I think there is a lack of opportunity for advancement at this point, I feel somewhat trapped. However, with additional education and experience, I hope to be able to move into a human resources job in the manufacturing industry or at our company headquarters.

HUMAN RESOURCES MANAGER #2

If I had to start over, I'd choose my current career as human resources manager. I love helping people succeed. Working in staff development and supporting employees as well as management is important to me. Knowing I've "earned my way" each day is very rewarding too.

I have a Bachelor of Science in history and enjoyed past work as a project manager and technical trainer. For the past several years, I've worked with staff and management. In the data processing division and the administrative subsidiaries of a large insurance company, I help form and implement company policy. My job is to advise employees and administration and to help things run smoothly.

While I enjoy the ability to have an impact and make a difference, I don't like the long hours. Unreasonable expectations are discouraging to me as well. I'd like to see fair evaluations of the staff and fairness in the expectations of management. Still, my plans are to continue in my field and make the staff and the company itself members of my personal winning team.

A manager of human resources needs strong communication skills. You should be composed and unemotional, with a desire to make all situations better. Being able to handle many circumstances at the same time is necessary. You also must be very attentive to details.

HYDROGEOLOGIST

I am a hydrogeologist now, but I previously worked at several other jobs: surveyor in national forests, janitor, gardener, and crop harvester. After I graduated with honors with a Bachelor of Science degree in physics, I was a geophysicists in the oil industry. Then I earned a Master of Science degree in hydrogeology and entered my present field.

I evaluate the source, movement, and occurrence of ground water. In my work, a typical work cycle is 3 years. I get a project, perform it, and evaluate the results. Twenty-five percent of my time is spent in the field and 75% in the office. Currently, I use highly technical electronic instruments to evaluate water loss through evapotranspiration (or what takes place when water evaporates) in desert environments. It requires making models with the computer, working with statistics, and being able to visualize concepts. I also have to interpret my findings.

Job satisfaction for me is being able to provide information which helps people and communities make educated decisions related to the use of the earth's resources. In order to best use these resources, while minimizing the risk of property and personal loss, the public needs this information. I really enjoy my work as well as the people I work with. Some day I'll retire and continue my hobbies, which include the ham radio and cross country skiing.

What I don't like in my job is all the red tape and the need to find funding to do a project. I work for a federal agency which must locate 50/50 matching funds from the private sector in order to finance an undertaking. Federal laws often times are in conflict with our doing a good job within the time frame and within budget.

ICE SKATING PROFESSIONAL

Ice skating, as a profession, chose me. I skated as a child and have just continued. I have not had another occupation that I liked and if I were given the chance to start over, I would again choose skating. I am now teaching, but in prior years I have been in the Ice Capades, and then shows in Las Vegas, Hollywood, and other places.

I teach about 2 or 3 hours now that I am semi-retired, but I used to teach a lot more. I teach ice skating to adults and children, competitors and recreational skaters.

To be a good ice skating instructor, you must have patience, give constant encouragement, have a knowledge of the sport and of the muscles, bones and nerves in the body. Good communication skills are necessary so you can explain one maneuver 20 different ways so anyone can understand it.

I find satisfaction from my work when my students gain in their ability and are happy with themselves because they understand they have advanced in a very difficult physical sport. I hope to live long enough to teach at least another 40 years!

IMPORT COORDINATOR

I have tried out various jobs since graduating from high school including work as a customer service representative, receptionist, and data entry operator, but I was not satisfied. I then started working for a growing manufacturing company and through the process of being transferred to several departments including manufacturing, scheduling and merchandising, I gained the experience necessary to be chosen to help start up a new segment of the company's business in the import division.

As the import product coordinator, I have the responsibility for purchasing shoes from various overseas vendors. This involves expediting production, negotiating delivery, and creating reports to the sales department and customer service regarding delivery.

This kind of work requires good communication and organizational skills. You also need to be able to do long range planning and have a good memory to perform this job well.

Part of the reason I like my job as import product coordinator is that it allows me to work independently which I find satisfying. However, I am always striving to accept new challenges and after 3 years in this position I am getting anxious to move up and/or out.

My plans for the future include receiving a business degree and starting my own business.

IMPORTER & RESELLER, CHEMICALS & PLASTICS

My previous international experience with a large corporation and my educational background provided me with qualifications necessary for my present position as importer/reseller of chemicals and plastics. I earned a Bachelor of Science in Mechanical Engineering degree. Previous jobs include: sailor/Naval officer, engineering manager, director of manufacturing, planning director, and energy conservation manager.

On a daily basis, I make telephone contact with product manufacturers. I weekly contact contract haulers and banks. Monthly, I make telephone contact with financial advisers and customs service.

The skills and attitudes which I consider important to perform this job well are: language capabilities, ability to establish trust in others, knowledge of business management, accounting procedures, and knowledge of product advantages.

I like this kind of work very much; however, the lack of total commitment of others is sometimes discouraging. What satisfies me most about my work is that my success is completely dependent on my efforts.

INTERIOR DESIGNER, IN-HOUSE

I find great satisfaction in helping people function more efficiently, and in improving their interior environment. That is why I have enjoyed working as an interior designer for the last 10 years. However, I am now in the process of adjusting my career in order to accommodate my multiple sclerosis handicap. I plan to learn C.A.D. (computer aided design) since my drafting skills have deteriorated and this should enable me to stay in the profession.

I majored in interior design, and fashion buying and merchandising in college. I have worked for an office furniture store, home furnishings store, and most recently for a university as their in-house interior designer. In this capacity, my design projects ranged from offices for department heads, to classrooms, to auditoriums. I did furniture layouts, bid documents, color schemes, and material specifications. I worked closely with the in-house architects, engineers, and craftsmen/tradesmen. Projects took several months to over a year to complete.

To perform this kind of work well, it is important to have the following skills and abilities: drafting, working with color and space, knowledge of good aesthetic qualities, working well with a variety of people, good communication skills to give directions verbally and in drawings, good listening skills, and ability to be a good teamworker. It is also a state requirement to have a license to practice interior design.

INCOME TAX PREPARER #1

My work as an income tax preparer requires math skills and precision. A calm manner is very important in dealing with the stress of the job. Treating clients and colleagues courteously is part of the job.

A high school graduate, I took a course to train me for my work. Some day I would like to go to college and get my Bachelor of Arts degree. I'd like to get a job with more chance for advancement. Since the tax season is so short, I'd like work that lasts longer than 5 months a year.

I really liked being a computer operator once, but, now, I enjoy dealing with the great variety of people who come in for help with their taxes. The people I work with, but not the person I work for, and the type of work I do give me pleasure.

A typical day for me is to open the office and wait for people to come in for their appointments. I must interview people to get accurate information in order to correctly prepare the tax forms. "Walk ins" have to be worked in among the appointments.

INCOME TAX PREPARER #2

Because I like working with numbers and being around people, I joined this company as an income tax preparer. Actually, I asked the person preparing my tax forms what I had to do to get into the field, and I did what she told me.

I still attend tax classes every year. You have to know the tax laws and how to fill out all the many tax forms (there's a form for everything). Tax preparers have to be able to keep their cool when working with difficult clients. Smiling and being pleasant is very important in this work.

After graduating from high school, I tried a number of occupations including waitress, factory worker, cashier and secretary. I've been a tax preparer for 4 years. If I could start over again, I'd choose this line of work because I enjoy it so much. My work day generally consists of doing returns and filing them, answering the phone, and answering questions concerning taxes. I check other preparers' returns as well. Listening to clients' anger while trying to give them the best benefits is a difficult part of my work. I also write letters on behalf of clients for the Internal Revenue Service.

Knowing that I've done the best job I can do for clients and having them ask for me the next year is very satisfying to me. Helping the client to the best advantage pleases me. I'm also pretty much my own boss. Staying away from computers would make my job more satisfying. I'd like to keep preparing taxes; it's what I do best. But, my most important job is being a mom, a grandmother, and being friends with all of my clients.

INDUSTRIAL ENGINEER #1

As a department manager for quite a few years, I manage the industrial engineering department in a metal stamping plant by establishing the best methods of doing my department's work and by establishing and maintaining our plant's work standards. I walk through the plant and check all production lines that are running for problems, offering suggestions and providing help; I also attend production meetings and handle the engineering assignments.

To work as a department manager, you need to complete a Bachelor's degree in an engineering discipline and I strongly recommend the completion of a Master of

Business Administration degree, as I did. In addition one you need to be a good listener, to be interested in helping other people to get their problems solved, to have good analytical skills, and to work well with people.

Although there are not many opportunities for advancement at my level, I really like my work. I enjoy the people in my department and I like the company I work for. The aspect of my work that I enjoy most is helping people to improve their work performance; that makes me feel that I am a factor in the plant's overall improvement in productivity.

Previously employed as a production manager for an ice cream company and as an industrial engineer for a steel company, I brought a great deal of experience to my position.

I plan to continue working at my present job, helping as much as I can to keep my company's operation profitable.

INDUSTRIAL ENGINEER #2

As a co-op student, I'm working in my field of industrial engineering while completing my college education. Stress-related issues in manufacturing and in facility design are my focus. In addition, I design and analyze process flows and material handling.

For this kind of work, people skills and a modest attitude are needed in dealing with managers and operators. I must collect information without making anyone feel inferior or "in the dark." Good analytical skills along with proficiency in math are also necessary. Facility with the computer is essential. An open mind to accept new ideas and to possibly admit that an idea may not be the best is an essential quality.

A usual day is difficult to describe because jobs will vary depending on the problems that may exist. Typically, I meet with management to discuss certain new or old issues once or twice a week. At least one hour a day I'm out on the manufacturing floor talking with operators and collecting data. The rest of the day I spend analyzing data and effects. I use these results to formulate and analyze designs, which are almost always done via computer.

Job satisfaction mainly comes from the feeling of achievement when I complete a project and get to see in operation what I designed on paper. I like everything about my work except I'd prefer working without having to get approval for everything. I'd like to have less managerial "red tape" required for a project.

For the future, I'd like to stay in industrial engineering for about 10 years with some travel and, possibly, work in Germany. I'm currently obtaining professional qualifications in German. Afterwards, I'd like to get my Masters in business management and work a few years in management. Eventually, I'd like to start my own manufacturing company.

INDUSTRIAL HYGIENIST #1

I became an industrial hygienist after reading an article in the Wall Street Journal on the U.S. Dept. of Labor's training program. I researched the profession and found it to be in line with my education. I have a Bachelor of Science in Biochemistry and Master of Science in Molecular Biology. I have not had any other jobs except for miscellaneous jobs while going to school and have found this to be very satisfying work for the last 12 years.

I am involved in the identification, evaluation and control of occupational health hazards (chemical, physical (noise and radiation), biological and ergonomic). My typical work activities include: inspecting work and work locations to identify, evaluate and control occupational health hazards; discussing working conditions and operations with employees and management; using sampling collection devices and instrumentation to determine levels of employee exposure to chemicals, noise and radiation; identifying engineering and work practice controls for limiting employee exposures; and training employees and management in workplace hazards, controls, and personal protective equipment.

To perform well as an industrial hygienist, it is important to have: curiosity about how things work; chemistry, physics, math, and biology knowledge; the ability to communicate orally and in writing with employees with a wide range of educational backgrounds; enjoyment in "detective" work.

As an industrial hygienist, I have become aware of the importance of a healthful work environment, and I only wish there were greater societal understanding and acceptance of the need to provide this environment.

I like almost every aspect of my work and find that the variety of different problems to solve keeps away boredom. I have the enjoyment of seeing my work have a visible/positive effect on the health and welfare of the people I work for and with. I plan to continue in this profession with expansion of my knowledge of hazardous waste/spill clean up. I want to manage an industrial hygiene/environmental program and do consulting.

INDUSTRIAL HYGIENIST #2

Safety and industrial hygiene were a small part of a job I had as a project engineer. I enjoyed this work and left this job to do safety and industrial hygiene full time. I am self-employed as an industrial hygienist. Prior to this, I earned a bachelor's degree in chemical engineering, and also worked as a production engineer and research technician.

My major function as an industrial hygienist is to identify and evaluate health hazards in the workplace. My work varies from day to day, week to week, and month to month, because I am a consultant. I may be on a construction site supervising a crew monitoring gases from the landfill upon which the construction is being done. I may be on an asbestos abatement project monitoring the air. Another day I may be training asbestos workers. It is the variety of the work that is one of the most satisfying aspects of this occupation for me.

You should first have an interest in science to consider this kind of work. Then, after gaining the technical knowledge and skills, it is also important to have a somewhat analytical mind.

My career plans for the future are to stay with this field and my consulting business and to possibly hire other industrial hygienists to expand my company.

INFECTION CONTROL PRACTITIONER

Previously, I have worked as a teacher and a waitress, but I really enjoy the independence I have now as an Infection Control Practitioner. I like working with so many professionals and the job itself, which I have now done for eight years. My work would be more satisfying if there were more recognition from my superiors in the form of pay and praise for my accomplishments.

In my work, I am an advocate for patients and employees to ensure they are free of infectious disease exposure. Reviewing patients' lab results from their charts and determining if "hospital acquired" infection has occurred are my responsibilities. I examine the rate of infections as well. Teaching hospital staff about infectious diseases is also a part of my job. I'm a member of the Safety and Infection Control Committee for Occupational Health.

To be a practitioner, you must be proficient in epidemiology (medical science treatment of epidemics) surveillance. My background includes a Bachelor of Science degree, training as a medical technologist, and experience with infectious diseases and their control. Good communication as well as management skills are essential. In addition, you must be a competent public speaker.

I plan one day to retire and open my own small business.

INFORMATION SYSTEMS ANALYST

When I finished my tour in the Marine Corps, I found the experience I had gained in the service was appropriate for my present job as systems analyst and engineer. I used my training in operational telecommunications and system acquisition.

In my work, I analyze the communication systems to define problems as well as find their solutions. I'm in charge of ensuring that our client, the U.S. Marine Corps, remains constantly in communication with all the other Services. Reviewing the composition of messages and the method of information transmission is my responsibility.

For my job, you need to be very attentive to detail. You need the proper training along with being familiar with all the requirements of the work. A positive attitude when doing often humdrum, tedious tasks is critical. Some advanced education may be needed for this job, but not necessarily the Bachelor of Arts degree in business management that I have.

Job satisfaction for me is knowing I am doing something important. Besides my work, I enjoy my colleagues, the organization I work for, and the people I work for. I also like the fact that there are many opportunities for advancement.

My plans are to get my Masters degree in information systems management. I would like to install and manage an extensive internal and external telecommunications computer system, an expanding field.

INFORMATION SYSTEMS CONSULTANT #1

For the last five years, I have worked as an Information Systems Consultant for business applications. I perform business analyses with recommendations on process improvements and system development to improve productivity, search for opportunities for automation, develop documents and proposals to reflect the analyses, and attend/participate in numerous meetings.

A good education, a technical background with strong analytical skills, and the quality of being a good listener are required to work in this field.

I previously worked as an Applications Programmer/Analyst, which I found to be a more technical position. I chose the position of consultant because I wanted to work where I could contribute more as an individual.

I find the greatest satisfactions of this kind of work come from learning new things; the type of people I work with; and the opportunity to make a difference for the companies I work with, as I provide system direction for business partners and help develop productivity improvements. At times I would prefer to have more clout implementing some of my proposals, but that is not in the role of the consultant.

My future plans are to update my technical skills and work my way back into a Programmer/Analyst role. My transition into a consultant position has led me to work more with people than with machines, and since I enjoy the more technical aspects of working with computers, the position I seek will involve more work with computers than people.

INFORMATION SYSTEMS CONSULTANT #2

I am an information systems consultant, which means that I design and implement large scale computer systems. My job requires substantial analytical skills and the ability to work independently, without much guidance and feedback. Strong listening skills are valuable in my work.

There is no typical day in my work. My duties vary from week to week and from project to project. I have been in the field for 5 years and I am uncertain of my future plans.

It is helpful to me to have a Bachelor of Science degree in Industrial Management and another Bachelor of Science degree in Economics. Of course, computer training is absolutely essential.

I particularly like the people with whom I work, the work itself, and the fact that there are opportunities for career advancement. My job would be more pleasant if the politics were removed from the workplace. I don't like the pressure to sell a solution that may answer only short-term needs.

INNKEEPER

Twenty-two years of people contact occupations seem to have naturally led to a position where I could (eventually) run my own business using all my previous skills. The opportunity presented itself when my corporation offered a furlough package in lieu of a major household move due to the relocation of corporate headquarters. Bed and breakfast inns had been an interest of mine prior to this furlough offer. I also wanted to get off the corporate fast track.

My years in the corporate track have been as a secretary, flight attendant, flight service manager, corporate staff analyst, flight attendant supervisor, manager of inflight sales and hostess. I have not graduated from college.

As a Bed and Breakfast Innkeeper, my job responsibilities are contingent on the number of guests at the inn. Breakfast, lunch and dinner are available and breakfast comes with all room rentals. My daily schedule is as follows: 7-9 a.m. serve breakfast, 9-11a.m. refurbish/clean rooms and laundry, 11:30-1:30p.m. serve lunch (as appropriate), 6-9 p.m. serve dinner. Outside lawn and grounds maintenance is ongoing daily. Preparation and clean-up of meals must always be done as well. The inn is open 7 days a week.

As an innkeeper, people skills are critical--the ability to carry on a conversation that is not subjective; bring out the guest's interests and genuinely reflect a desire to please them. A high energy level will ensure that the inn is run efficiently. Never should a guest get the feeling they are imposing on you or that their requests or needs are a hindrance to your operation: the guest IS the operation.

Presently, the inn needs some cosmetic repair and there is a problem between me and my partners as to the extent of the work that should be done. Despite this frustration, I really like this kind of work. New ideas, attitudes and opinions are the spice of life. The guests who come to the inn bring their individuality and experiences that I truly enjoy sharing. The natural beauty surrounding the inn is a source of pleasure.

INSTRUCTOR, AIRCRAFT OPERATION

A rundown of my educational background and job experiences is probably the best way to understand how I have arrived at my present career as F-111 contract instructor and part-time teacher of history and political science. I have worked as a salesperson at a nursery, traffic cop, and US Air Force officer--F-111 weapon systems officer and pilot. I have a Bachelor of Arts in Botany and a Master of Science in International Relations degrees.

As an F-111 contract instructor and teacher, each day starts and ends at a different time. This varies from 0630 to 1400 starting and 1530 to 2230 ending, but most days are only 9 hours long. I may teach class for up to 8 hours, but usually less. Alternatively, I may instruct 2 flight simulator periods (these last 3 to 3 1/2 hours each). At other times when not scheduled to do anything specific, I work on lesson plans, new visual aids, monitor other instructors, study for the next day, or read.

A teacher/instructor should have the ability to tailor instruction to students' backgrounds and understanding. It is also important to have stamina for those long days of lecture; patience; ability to anticipate when students will have difficulty; credibility; and proven expertise.

I would welcome more regular hours with less evening work so I can teach part-time at a local junior college.. A maximum of 4 hours of lecture on any given day would also be desirable. However, I like the kind of work I am doing and the people I work with.

Future career aspirations include working on a Ph.D. and teaching college, or owning a garden store and still teaching part-time. In reality, I will probably continue in my present job and advance to management so I can move to a city where I can work on my Ph.D.

INSTRUCTOR, COMPUTER OPERATION

As an instructor of twenty years, I teach software operating systems and computer hardware maintenance to field engineers. This sometimes involves learning and preparing new material for upcoming lessons.

You must be able to communicate with and convey information to students with various skill levels. I also have earned an Associate of Science degree in addition to previous experience in my field.

I find the greatest rewards come from having a student come up to me at the end of a course and both tell me and show me what he/she has gained through the course.

I like teaching very much, although I would like to see more attention paid to ensuring that all students enrolled in one of my courses meet the prerequisites. I believe, because of the complex nature of the material taught, this would make the classes more enjoyable for everyone.

I am retired from a twenty-year career in the Navy, during which I spent six years as an instructor.

When I retire from teaching I plan to do a lot of fishing!

INSTRUCTOR, HIGH SCHOOL BAND

As a band instructor at the high school level, I rehearse several bands: concert, marching, and jazz. In addition to directing these bands, I also perform with high school instrumental groups, usually with a performance of some kind every other week.

I truly enjoy watching the students in my bands improve and learn to play their instruments expressively. Observing students grow and mature is part of the satisfaction of my job. I really like my work in music.

My work would be even more rewarding if there were less emphasis on, and less support for, sports in the school. I'd like more freedom to control the overall music program. We could also benefit from a more capable music staff.

A good band director should love music and be competent in the field. Being a caring person who loves kids is also very important. Strong organizational skills are necessary as well. Training is also critical. I earned a Bachelors in Music Education and a Masters degree in Music Performance.

I've never been, or wanted to be, anything but a music instructor. I'd like one day to direct college level musical groups. More composing and arranging music are also in my plans.

INSTRUMENTAL MUSIC TEACHER

As the instrumental music teacher for grades 5-12, I teach group band lessons for all these grades, and conduct elementary, junior high and high school bands. Every day I conduct junior high and high school band rehearsals. I travel between 5 elementary schools and teach group lessons to 5th and 6th grade students. I have a work load of about 350 students in grades 5-12.Despite the work load involved in teaching such a large number of students, I like my kind of work very much. I enjoy making music and discovered while in college that I am a good teacher. These are obviously the basic requirements for an instrumental music teacher. As well as enjoying music, however, it is also necessary to be able to play all band instruments. In handling so many students, organizational skills are needed. I have found flexibility to be another key factor in performing this job well. You must also like working with a diverse group of people.

My job satisfaction comes from getting students to make music. I love working with kids.

Despite my love of music and enjoyment of kids, when I get burned out from this kind of work, I may work in the business which my parents operate, modern packaging service.

INSURANCE ADJUSTER

After graduating from high school, I was working as a receptionist for an insurance company and found insurance adjusting work interesting. I began studying and taking courses and subsequently received my adjuster's license. I was gradually given more difficult assignments and eventually became manager of two of our branch offices.

As an adjuster, I appraise damage to autos, houses, boats, etc., investigate accidents, do interviews, give liability recommendations, review policy coverage, and recommend settlement figures. In a typical day, I may appraise damage to 2 or 3 vehicles, look at 1 or 2 homeowners' losses, have several discussions with repair shops and building contractors regarding ongoing work, dictate 10-15 reports to various insurance companies, and take a couple of statements from people involved in accidents.

Communication skills are very important since this job deals primarily with people who have suffered a loss and may be upset or irrational. Mathematical skills are important in preparing repair estimates. A straightforward, non-judgmental attitude is important when conducting liability investigations.

If given the opportunity to change something in this occupation to make it more satisfying, it would be to educate more people on what insurance policies are designed to cover or protect. Many conflicts come from people having false expectations of what coverage they are buying when they purchase an insurance policy.

Despite these frustrations, I like my job very much.

In doing this kind of work, I feel I help people recover from losses whether it be an automobile accident or house fire, etc. I also get satisfaction from knowing we help make sure a fair price is being paid for repairs, etc. The insurance company isn't getting ripped off and the person doing repairs is being paid for proper repairs.

INSURANCE AGENCY OWNER/BROKER

I got into my career in the insurance field by following in my husband's steps and I am glad I did. I like this kind of work very much. Prior to his death, I worked as the bookkeeper. Now I am a broker/owner.

There is no typical day when you are an independent insurance agent representing various companies. It is who calls or walks through the door that determines your activities. You take care of your customers' needs first. There are 7 agents/brokers in this office. We sell all types of insurance: automobile, fire, homeowners, commercial casualty, health, and life.

To be an insurance agent you first need a basic education and then special training in the insurance field. You are a service organization, so you are required to deal with people and people problems. Service is really the only thing you can offer--there are a lot of insurance agents. Also, since the insurance business is strongly regulated, the insurance laws govern what we do. This is sometimes difficult to deal with.

I find job satisfaction in the satisfied "insureds." I also am rewarded for my work by having built up respect in the field and respect in the community.

INSURANCE AGENT #1

I am an insurance agent and have been in this career for 40 years, ever since I graduated from college with a B.S. and found this to be the highest paying job available. I consider this career to have the opportunity for unlimited income.

On a typical work day, I start at 8 a.m. making calls. I have lunch with a prospect if possible. From 1-3 p.m. I do service work in the field. Office work usually consumes 3 more hours in the afternoon. After supper, I make calls on the phone.

To perform well as an insurance agent, I think it is important to be able to read and understand contracts and law, and have mathematical accuracy skills. You must like and enjoy meeting new people and listening to their problems and concerns.

I am always interested in finding the most competitive product with the greatest company backing it up. I can then have the satisfaction of concluding a good sale and making a new friend.

INSURANCE AGENT #2

Meeting new people and helping people with their problems is the part of my job as insurance agent that I most like. Basically, I sell insurance products, and then service the accounts after the sale. More specifically, my daily activities include: preparing quotes, meeting with prospective clients, making presentations, closing the sales, and then helping my customers with claims.

In order to perform this kind of work well, the following skills and attitudes are important: liking people, patience, ability to communicate well with others, accuracy, and good memory.

Although I like the kind of work I do, I feel that there is a lack of opportunity for advancement until I own my own agency, which is part of my career plan.

INSURANCE CLAIMS EXAMINER

I work as a claims examiner for a health and casualty insurance company. My duties for twenty years have been to review incoming claims, work with field claims adjusters, check incoming correspondences, set up new claims, assign claim handling to adjusters, and authorize the checks or insurance drafts for claims payments.

In addition to a Bachelor's degree, you have to know insurance terminology and have the ability to identify coverages and limitations in policies, meet with and gain the customer's trust, recognize the importance of good will in business, write clean and concise letters, and handle stress.

I find gratification in satisfying policyholders and claimants and meeting the needs of doctors, lawyers, repair experts, and pleased executives; I believe I receive sufficient recognition for my efforts.

I enjoy insurance work and the company I work for; I like my co-workers and the people I meet in connection with my work.

I have always engaged in work that required interaction with people. Among previous positions I have held are high school teacher and public opinion researcher.

I plan to keep working and learning all that I can about the insurance business.

INSURANCE CLAIMS MANAGER

Before becoming an automobile claims manager, I served in the U.S. Marine Corps. When I retired as a lieutenant colonel, I got my Bachelor of Arts degree and entered the insurance field where I have spent many happy years.

Helping people with their car problems and rendering good service is very satisfying to me. I also enjoy the customers, the sales, and the insurance company. The fact that there are opportunities for advancement pleases me as well. My job involves managing the field supervisors as they evaluate automobile insurance claims. They assess damages and file reports. I also oversee the work of the company headquarters supervisors. To be a claims manager, you should have broad knowledge of the automobile claims field and the ability to motivate adjusters and supervisors. Patience and tact are necessary when dealing with customers who've made claims and who have complaints. Strong interpersonal skills along with good administrative skills are important as well.

INSURANCE SALESMAN

I own and manage a life insurance agency, specializing in employee benefits. I prepare and sell group insurance, health and life, pension plans, and executive deferred compensation. My typical day-to-day schedule may include the following tasks: answering phone calls, handling mail, setting appointments with new clients, developing new programs, attending community service or educational luncheons, preparing new programs after extensive studies, and working with health legislation.

Mine is a service job. I have to care and want to make the best health care programs available. I need people with mathematical, legal, and diplomatic skills as well as people that know insurance programs and laws.

Employers finally learn that it is their obligation to provide benefits for their employees rather than fight government mandates.

The one thing I would like to change in my occupation is to get more women in agency management.

I was doing actuarial work in a home office of an insurance company when I saw that opportunities were in sales. When no one wanted a "female" in their agency, I opened my own company.

I attended college and studied liberal arts and mathematics but did not get my degree. I consider politics to be my avocation. My future aspirations include lecturing in Germany (country of my birth) to women about the opportunities in sales. There are no women in life insurance sales in Germany and the US sales force is now only 25% women.

INSURANCE UNDERWRITER & SALES

An insurance underwriter and salesperson for automotive, fire, life, and health insurance writes and sells insurance policies; I work for a major insurance company. I answer questions for people regarding their insurance policies and payment problems; I also assist co-workers in my office with their questions. Another part of my job is taking claim reports and selling insurance to prospective policy holders.

In addition to a good education, to work in insurance you must be service minded toward customers, have good organizational skills, and generally be a "people" person.

I have found that answering people's questions so they feel more informed brings me the most satisfaction; I also like it when a client is thankful for the work that I do on their behalf. I enjoy meeting new people and helping them solve their insurance problems.

I really like my job, the people I work with, and the insurance company I work for. I find the insurance business to be very interesting and I like this kind of work. The only change I could make to enjoy my job more is to have more flexibility in my work environment. I would prefer not to be confined to a desk most of the time.

As the company I work for requires an undergraduate degree in order to advance to the position of an agent, I plan to return to college and finish an undergraduate degree program. I would like to become a licensed insurance agent for this company.

INTELLIGENCE OFFICER (CIA)

As an intelligence officer for twenty-five years, I write reports, meet with many different types of people, and relate information to them as necessary, regardless of their station.

I earned a Bachelor of Arts degree and completed three years of military service before joining the ranks of the Central Intelligence Agency. This type of work requires strong interpersonal skills, a good command of the English language, strong mental faculties in communication of ideas, a good memory, listening skills, and the ability to express oneself succinctly when summarizing topics in verbal or written form of communication.

My work is very interesting and I love every minute of it. I have met some very colorful and fascinating people in the course of my work; I have enjoyed this interaction with many different types of people. My work also allows a certain degree of anonymity, which I like. Over the years I have come to realize that the sense of urgency, that has been ever present in my work, may not have always been needed; it makes this line of work very stressful.

While still in college, I interviewed privately for the job and accepted the position offered because it sounded fascinating and presented the opportunity to start on a really challenging career. I have no regrets about that decision.

There are not many opportunities for career advancement beyond this level of employment, and I am not interested in starting a new career after all these years. So when I decide to move on, I will most likely retire and spend most of my time traveling for the pleasure of it. When I am not traveling, I suppose I will grow flowers and then take the time to stop and smell them, as the saying goes--it will be a welcome change from the perpetual stress I have encountered in my nevertheless interesting professional life.

INTERIOR DESIGNER #1

I started out as a house painter, and kept increasing my creative skills by going to school and from work experience, so that now I am a decorative painting specialist and interior designer. I am part owner of the business which sells decorative painting services to designers. I figure out how each finish should be done and oversee the projects at various stages. More specifically my daily and/or weekly schedule includes meeting with clients and artists to review current projects, figuring out formulas for new finishes to match with clients' fabrics, etc., interviewing new artists, and showing our portfolio to new designers.

The most important skill to perform this type of work well is creativity. Yet, you must have the desire to please, be committed to excellence, and have a love of beauty. You must have the ability and desire to listen to others. In order to manage the business well you need organizational skills, discipline, assertiveness, and aggressiveness.

There are many ways I find satisfaction from my work. People admire my work. I make money at it. I make things beautiful. I provide work for other artists. I work for famous people. I work with and for many talented people and I meet a lot of interesting people.

Eventually, I would like to do more of the complete interior design of each space rather than just the decorative painted finishes.

As I mentioned previously, I was a house painter and felt the need to be more creative. I discovered and practiced decorative painting from a book, and I went to college to earn my associate degree in interior design. While in college I developed a client following among instructors who taught in the interior design program. Word-of-mouth increased business, which led to my forming a partnership and later incorporating with another artist.

My future goals include a thriving interior design business with a staff of 8 people and continued growth in the decorative paint business.

INTERIOR DESIGNER #2

My father was in the furniture business. This exposure to the decorating business probably accounts for my interest in this career. I went to college and earned my Bachelor of Arts degree. I then became a sportswear buyer and later switched careers to become a travel agent. Eventually I found that interior design was really the right career for me, and I have been designing for 30 years.

To perform well as a designer, it is important to have an ability to "create," an ability to deal with people, good taste, lots of patience and imagination, and good business abilities.

I receive satisfaction from the final result of my work. I like the freedom this work affords me--not being tied down to certain hours. I have also been monetarily rewarded--the earning potential is great.

Although I like interior design very much, I do have future aspirations of going into investments and trading.

INTERNATIONAL SALES & MARKETING MANAGER

As a Manager of International Sales and Marketing for an intravenous infusion pump manufacturer, I plan both short-term and long-term strategy in the international marketplace for intravenous medical devices. I place many phone calls to direct operations at client companies and to give information to dealers. I am constantly looking for new technologies and applications by reading medical journals and reports. I work closely with our Research and Development team on new product development to ensure that our products meet international market and business regulatory requirements.

To be successful in this occupation, you must have a solid educational background (including possibly Bachelor of Science and Master of Business Administration degrees as I have), like people, and be able to communicate with people who have different perspectives from oneself. You should possess certain business skills and knowledge of engineering with respect to product enhancements.

I enjoy knowing that my position gives me the opportunity to travel extensively all over the world. The only drawback I have encountered in working with international corporations is that Friday is not a good day to conduct business because many countries observe different customs and traditions. There is also the time difference; some countries are already into Saturday while we are still, timewise, in Friday. I believe that a four-day work week of four ten-hour days would increase the week's accomplishments.

I was promoted within my company several times, most importantly from Financial Analyst to Product Manager, before reaching my goal of working in International Sales and Marketing. I believe the key factor in obtaining this much sought-after position was my educational background.

I plan to become the Vice President of the international effort at my company within the next ten years. Beyond that, I will always be involved in public service.

INVENTORY & BILLING DEPARTMENT MANAGER

In my position as a Manager of Retail Inventory and Billing at a carpeting store, I manage people to get the customers' bills out in a timely manner and get their orders placed and processed. It is essential for me to check that deadlines are being met, to check on personnel, and to solve problems as they arise.

In addition to well-developed management and organizational skills, my job requires job product knowledge and good communication skills.

Although there is not much opportunity for advancement with my present company, I like the people I work with, the people I work for, and the whole organization in general. It is difficult at times to keep morale at a high level as this business is greatly affected by ups and downs in the economy.

After completing an Associate's degree in a secretarial discipline and a certificate in Fashion Design, I started with this company as a data entry clerk and was given several promotions over a period of nine years until I reached my present position. Coming up through the ranks as I did, I see areas of the company that could be organized differently to help other departments and the whole company run in a smoother fashion.

I enjoy having the ability to accomplish the company's tasks and meet deadlines, especially since I see that this is accomplished by the employees working together as a team.

I also enjoy retail sales and would someday like to work as a general manager in a retail store or perhaps open my own business in this area.

INVENTORY CONTROLLER

As a production inventory controller, I check and maintain inventory, figure out inventory problems, generate routing information, and adjust routings and bills of materials for stock. I also control raw materials inventory and prepare raw stock.

To work as an inventory controller, you should have an appreciation of the need for accuracy, knowledge of computer systems, knowledge of inventory and routing systems, patience, and the ability to work with people.

I enjoy the responsibility given me and the variety of my work as I am almost always busy and moving. However, I sometimes wish I had been given more authority to go with that responsibility. Inventory control can also be challenging and frustrating, too. As inventory interacts with many other production groups, you deal with many different people to get the job done. This can interrupt the work flow if the person you need is busy and you must wait until that person is available.

I previously worked in machine set-up. There is not much opportunity for advancement within my present organization, but I would like to work in middle management should the opportunity arise.

INVENTORY COST ACCOUNTANT

For three years I have been the Cost Accountant dealing with inventory in a manufacturing environment. Previously I had been a bank teller, head bank teller, and analyst in general accounting.

A typical day includes an early morning analysis of inventory activity using a daily report, developed by speaking with the data entry clerks and program specialists. I also review rejected transactions that were not accepted on the inventory report. After I reconcile inventory accounts on the general ledger, I discuss the inventory balances with the manager. I coordinate yearly inventories as well.

Good arithmetic skills and logical thinking are required, but not a college degree necessarily. You must also be very organized and detail oriented.

I rather enjoy the pressure of keeping computer records of material movement in an up-to-date manner and meeting the challenge of completing all journal entries for the month end close in just a day or two.

The only negatives in this work are that priorities change rapidly and there are constant job interruptions. You must be able to keep focused in spite of changing orders and interruptions because the work requires considerable accuracy. There is satisfaction in being able to accomplish that goal.

INVESTMENT BANKER

As an Investment Banker and former Chief Executive Officer for six different companies, I arrange for mergers and acquisitions between corporate buyers and sellers of companies and financial institutions. Arranging mergers and acquisitions requires a great deal of careful negotiations, setting up meetings, and handling business over the phone. I really enjoy knowing I have the ingenuity required for successful closings. Success as an investment banker also demands that you possess imagination; experience in negotiation, finances, operational company disciplines, and strategic planning; and the ability to delegate responsibilities. It gives me so much pleasure to be able to close a tough deal that everyone else gave up on or to build a company and watch the managers and employees grow.

My background includes a Bachelor of Science in Applied Engineering and positions as manager, corporate staff, and engineer.

I will remain on this career path as long as possible, perhaps in the direction of more consulting and less deals, or I will teach others the keys to success in this fascinating field.

INVESTOR

I definitely have a different life style from most people. I consider myself to have gotten the "luck of the draw." I am an investor and have luxury of spending most of my time outside with nature. My day starts by getting the kids off to school and then going off in my boat to check duck boxes, erect housing for animals, plant trees, and troop through the woods and streams doing my volunteer wildlife management work. I do spend some time keeping up with the financial market so that once every couple months I can manipulate my investments.

In order to live this kind of life, I consider myself to have skills in math, English, science, observation, and dealing with people. I graduated from college with a bachelor's degree in business and economics. I have previously done restaurant work, woodworking, and accounting.

I find satisfaction in what I have done for 11 years because I am helping wildlife and doing a job well. I aspire to earn more money, however, so I could eventually start my own business in the nature or recycling field.

IRONWORKER & GENERAL MECHANIC

There are several reasons why I wound up as an ironworker and general mechanic. I decided that by doing this work I could use my training which I received in the Army Corps of Engineers. Also, it paid the most and I was interested in mechanics. I am a journeyman bridgeman and ornamental ironworker.

My work starts at the foundation of the bridge, building, or dam. After the engineers layout the project, as a member of a team of ironworkers, we put in the steel reinforcing rods, anchor bolts, raise the steel and enclose the structure with steel or aluminum. The next steps involve installing windows, skylights, and doors and sashes; finally doing metal finishing trim; welding; etc.

It is important to like your work and not be afraid of new methods and materials if it's feasible. You should have a good mechanical aptitude and knowledge of blueprints. Having good common sense about the abilities and safety of your fellow worker is another critical aspect of this work.

Although I find many aspects of this work to be satisfying, the worst part of my work has been with companies who have not been safety-oriented. The construction industry is one of the most hazardous industries and safety should be of utmost importance. I do like this kind of work and find satisfaction in seeing a job completed well, on time, and, most important, with no injuries and no fatalities because someone was careless or wanted to try a shortcut.

If given the opportunity to change anything about this occupation, it would be to offer profit-sharing to workers who can be depended on and are loyal to the company, instead of raising wages.

I am now learning gunsmithing in order to provide myself with a marketable skill for retirement.

JEWELRY DESIGNER & ARTIST

While interviewing for "real"jobs, I found amusement and relaxation in working with my clay. Years before, I had sold some of my "creations" in high school. After the encouragement of a professional artist, I gave up the job search and began research into marketing my jewelry on a larger scale. My background also includes earning a bachelors degree in French and psychology. After college, I worked in several offices in a variety of capacities e.g. administrator and personnel.

Now that I am a self-employed jewelry artist, I try each week to create at least one new design as well as re-creating variations on my established designs. I also fill any orders I have, and often I have a show which I must prepare for and attend. This involves creating items for sale, organizing the sale items and collecting my sales tools. I also spend a couple of hours a week on bookkeeping. Additional time is invested toward improving my reputation and increasing my clientele.

Creative, artistic, organizational, and marketing skills are all important tools to me as an entrepreneur and artist.

I feel it is up to me to make my work enjoyable and productive. Creating an original work is very gratifying and, when I sell a piece, I enjoy the immediate monetary encouragement. It is wonderful to control my own day and to make my own decisions.

JOB PLACEMENT SERVICE COUNSELOR

A civil servant in the department of employment, I assist veterans with job searches and refer them to openings or to other supportive services. I arrive at work at 0800, put up the flag, and check both conventional and computer mail. I contact employers to discuss status and referrals. An important part of my job is assisting veterans with their job search or, if I cannot help, referring them to other supportive services. I attend staff meetings and give presentations to other employees on specific programs.

There is nothing about my work I dislike. I can make a difference in people's lives, help them feel better about themselves, direct them to the services they need, and assist them in finding employment. I wish to stay in this very job, in this office, working with these people until I retire. I would move my residence to be closer to this office rather than the other way around.

To be successful in this field you must be service-oriented. You must sincerely enjoy helping people. Being fully informed about the work requirements and being computer literate are important. Good verbal communication skills and the ability to listen are also needed.

I have had other jobs and they were all right, but none was as interesting to me as my present job. Other occupations were soldier, teacher, and director of human resources.

JOURNALIST, FARMER, & TEACHER

My occupational experiences are broad, have all been a significant part of my life, and I have liked them all. However, my career as a teacher has been my steadiest employment. I taught 2 to 10 year olds for 25 years and then have also taught for a number of years at the college level.

I thought it was great writing for a newspaper. However, as I watched my boys grow to hate school and, knowing how much I loved it, I was compelled to get into teaching. I was particularly interested in taking the regimentation out of learning to make it more exciting.

The skills and attitudes which I consider important to have as a teacher are: understanding of children and how they learn, a love for children, a good background of knowledge, and a clear clean discipline-- lightly dispensed.

If it were not for the red tape involved in the teaching profession, I would have no complaints. I love working with children of all ages. I find satisfaction in watching the development of a love for learning and its excitement.

JUDGE #1

As a Judge, I preside over misdemeanor criminal cases, smaller civil cases, and juvenile cases. I develop and refine procedures for the operation of the local court, and I handle some administrative matters as well.

Job satisfaction comes with feeling that my temperament, personality, and abilities are well-matched for my work. I entered this field because of my natural sense of justice and I really enjoy it. I earned a Bachelor of Science degree, served as an attorney, and I've now been a Judge for 17 years. My work would be more satisfying if I had greater freedom and flexibility in devising solutions for cases.

The ability to cope with stress and exhibit a great deal of patience are requirements in my field. Academic ability along with attention to detail are also important.

JUDGE #2

I've found my work as a judge sometimes mentally stimulating, sometimes boring. The working conditions are fine, but I don't necessarily like the irregular work hours. The pay is good, and I also enjoy my association with very intelligent people.

A typical day includes reviewing files for scheduled court proceedings and conferring with attorneys about any anticipated problems. I hold court between 9:00 a.m. and 5:00 p.m. with an hour and a half lunch recess. Between court sessions, I'll study legal briefs, research the law, and dictate decisions on matters I've already heard. I'll also dictate correspondence and work on administrative issues, i.e., personnel problems and the budget. Drafting court documents and briefs are part of my activities as well.

After being in the military service, I decided the law sounded like an interesting career. My college degree is a Bachelor of Science and I also earned a law degree. I've served as a lawyer and now a judge for a many years and I'd do it again. I have no future plans outside of law, other than eventual retirement.

Working in the field of law requires patience and good judgment. Certainly, you have to know the law and you have to be self-motivated. Being able to make decisions on issues and having an understanding nature are also necessary.

JUDGE, SUPERIOR COURT

In my work as a State Supreme Court Judge, I read briefs, hear legal arguments, and listen to evidence. I write decisions, and I control the courtroom. I've been a judge for 10 years; if I could begin all over again, I'd choose the same profession. I find pleasure in finding solutions to issues, but I'd like an occasional opportunity to practice law.

To be effective as a judge, one needs good English skills and analytical ability. Further, knowledge of the law along with an open mind are needed.

I enjoyed my previous work as an insurance adjustor, as a musician, and as a lawyer. I came to the bench through election. I chose to run because I liked the community and felt I could make a contribution that would be of service to society. I plan to retire as a judge and practice law as an avocation.

KINDERGARTEN TEACHER

I changed my major at least 4 times in college. In the end, I decided on elementary education because teaching meshes well with being a mom. Perhaps heredity was also a factor since my mom and my grandparents were also teachers.

As a kindergarten teacher, I teach children beginning school skills. Basically, my job involves planning lessons and teaching 2 groups of 20, 5-year-old students. I also meet with their parents, as necessary.

Being a good elementary teacher takes a positive attitude, organizational skills, a knowledge of the abilities of the children at the age you are teaching, and a knowledge of the needs of children.

Although I like this kind of work, and the people with whom I work, I dislike the sparse budget on which we operate, and dealing with angry parents. I also would prefer 15 children, rather than 20, in a class so each child could get the time and attention he/she needs. Despite the drawbacks, I find satisfaction from my work in seeing children grow in their academic abilities.

If I were to change careers, I would still center my work around children and maybe find a job involving publishing of children's books.

LABOR RELATIONS CONSULTANT

Now that I am somewhat near the end of my career and have acquired 30 years of experience in working for a labor union, the committee for whom I now work chose me as their labor relations consultant. My educational background includes two masters degrees, one in philosophy and the other in public management. My career background includes positions as a data processing director, college instructor, and contract department head.

As Labor Relations consultant, I direct a committee which helps companies and unions establish problem-solving committees. I am using my experience to teach companies and unions how to work together in problem-solving and to improve quality, working conditions, and job security. To do this, it is important to have leadership skills, verbal and written communication skills, negotiation and mediation experience, and a large degree of patience.

Except for the financial reporting and accounting aspects of my work, I like this kind of work very much. I also like the people I work with. I find job satisfaction from making a difference in the enhancement of the local labor climate.

LABORATORY OPTICIAN

I fell into my occupation. After graduating from high school, I had been working as a waitress, bartender, domestic, retail sales clerk, and cashier, but none of these jobs were satisfying to me. Through the recommendation of a friend, I started working for an optical lab at a very minimum wage and went through their journey person training program. Fifteen years later, I am still with this lab as a lab optician and have plans to continue my training in the field of optometry. I am presently enrolled in a college undergraduate program in preparation for optometric college. My plans are to be in practice as an optometrist in 10 years.

A lab optician has a skilled trade of manufacturing prescription eyewear. I work in the finish department of the lab and am responsible for making sure the prescription is correct per the doctor's prescription, and the lenses are properly fitted into the selected frame.

To perform this kind of work well, I have found that is important to have common sense, intelligence, math skills, hand coordination, and the ability to do teamwork.

My biggest frustration with my work is the lack of understanding between the different people involved in optometry. I would like the doctors and their dispensing staff to be more knowledgeable about lab work processes, and for lab technicians to know what is involved in the retailing and dispensing side of optics.

Aside from this frustration, I like the kind of work I do.

This work gives me the satisfaction that someone will be wearing a good, quality pair of eyeglasses. I also find satisfaction because I do my job well.

LANDSCAPE DESIGNER

Because of my dissatisfaction with my work in mechanical and electrical design, I took a self assessment and career development class. From this I found my values and skills led me to landscape architecture, occupational therapy or the engineering field. I chose landscape architecture. I broke into the operations and nursery aspect of this field because of finances and the need to have the knowledge of plant materials and landscape operations. I am continuing with my formal education in the evenings to earn a bachelors degree. I have already earned an associate degree and have a landscape certificate.

As a landscape designer, my responsibilities include: client contact, property evaluation, drawing landscape plans, and consulting with customers in the garden center. More specifically, my typical daily activities may include evaluating the site of potential clients who have requested a landscape plan; drawing a base plan; meeting with estimators; calculating cost of plant materials and square foot for seeding/sodding; calculating top soil requirement for other earth product needs; some client company relations; garden center work--customer consulting; personnel scheduling; ordering stock; and plant sales.

To perform this kind of work well, it is important to have the following attributes: a plant material knowledge; drafting skills; art background; math background; communications skills; a positive attitude; insect/disease control knowledge; knowledge of the history and trends in architecture; and effective speaking and listening skills. I have found that I have also needed to have the ability to do research for answers not readily available.

I like the field of landscape architecture and am getting anxious to have my own firm. I plan to wait until I have completed my educational and experience requirements, however. It is rewarding to work with clients to achieve an environmentally pleasant and safe outdoor living space which is aesthetically pleasing to the client, or resolving any problems clients may have with their existing landscape.

LAW CLERK

I've a Bachelor of Arts degree and a Masters in public administration, but I'm back in school as a 3rd year law student. Prior to returning to college, I was a secretary and then an admissions clerk in a hospital. Now I work as a law clerk as well as attend classes.

My work consists of doing a lot of legal research. I also prepare drafts of pleadings, which are plaintiff's cause or defendant's justification. Part of my job is to summarize the current status of the law in specific legal cases.

What I like most about my job as a law clerk is being able to use my intelligence. I am constantly learning new areas of the law, which is very helpful in my law studies. My work is very fulfilling and I enjoy the people I work with. I also see good opportunities for advancement, a fact I appreciate. My plans are to finish my law studies, get my J.D. law degree, and practice law.

In my job, you must be very detail-oriented and focused in order to pay close attention to the fine points in legal opinions. You should have solid analytical skills, making you able to examine carefully the legal issues. Having strong powers of concentration is also essential.

LAW ENFORCEMENT & CHEMICAL OPERATIONS

I work in the field of chemical operations and law enforcement. I respond to accidents involving hazardous materials and enforce the policies and regulations with respect to the laws governing these substances and materials. My work is very confidential in nature and requires a wide range of experience and education. I have completed college studies and have earned two degrees, in the fields of Architecture and Law Enforcement.

In addition to educational requirements, experience, and an understanding of the need for confidentiality, you have to possess quick reflexes, intelligence, a willingness to sacrifice yourself to help others, a willingness to work alone, current knowledge of world and national events, and an interest in political issues.

I derive great satisfaction from knowing I have helped other people. I enjoy my work for the most part; the drawbacks are the need to work long hours, be on call twenty-four hours a day, and not have much leisure time for family or friends.

I entered this career field after my discharge from the U.S. Army; during the time of my Army enlistment, I worked as an architectural technologist.

I plan to continue applying my knowledge and experience toward a career in the international applications of my work.

LAW ENFORCEMENT OFFICER, FEDERAL

Everything about my work as an investigator for federal law enforcement is satisfying to me. I enjoy helping the community and only the frustration created by bureaucracy at times prevents me from succeeding. The variety and the diversity of the work always keeps things interesting.

In my 17 years in law enforcement, I've found no day is typical. Depending on my assignment, I might conduct interviews, analyze evidence, or make arrests. Executing search warrants, conducting surveillance or testifying in court are also some of my responsibilities. In general, I investigate violations of federal law and assist in putting criminals in jail.

Along with a Bachelor of Science degree in criminal justice, self-motivation is vital to my work. The ability to work with minimal direction and supervision is essential. You must also have the desire to help people.

Before entering the federal arena, I worked in local law enforcement. I applied to several federal agencies at that time because federal law enforcement jobs offered better pay, greater benefits, and more interesting work. My plans are to continue in my present career.

LAW PROFESSOR & DIRECTOR OF LAW LIBRARY

I entered my career by accident. While in law school, I worked in a law library and found that I liked the organizational aspects and service-orientation of this career. After completing law school and earning my J.D., I enrolled in a specialized program for law librarians and earned a Masters degree in Law Librarianship. Prior to studying law, I worked as an admissions counselor for a college.

As director of a law library and professor of law, I manage the library operations with a $1.7 million budget and staff of 32. I also teach law librarianship courses. More specifically, this includes preparing and teaching one 3 hour class; handling budget, personnel, policy matters for the law library; drafting letters, memos, and reports; and making decisions.

To perform well in this career, it is important to have flexibility, a sense of humor, sound knowledge of legal materials and library operations, good verbal and written communication skills, organizational skills, and service orientation. You must want to help people.

There really is nothing I dislike about my work.

I have been satisfied in and intrigued by this career for 15 years because I find it intellectually challenging, and the duties are varied, never boring. I like teaching and working with good people.

LAW PROFESSOR & WRITER

After years of practical experience as a lawyer, I sought out this position as law professor. This seemed to make the most sense for me as a book writer who needs a salary. Prior to this, I also worked as a journalist, naval officer, and newsletter editor.

As a law professor, I teach one or two classes a week. Additional teaching activities include: meeting with fellow committee members for 2 to 4 hours per week; writing memos; preparing for classes; overseeing a group of 30 adjunct professors on a weekly basis; reading books, newspapers; skimming magazine articles; and talking to colleagues.

In order to handle the responsibilities of a law professor along with a career as a writer, I recommend that you have an open mind, the ability to do 9 things at once, and curiosity.

I like what I am doing. I would be even more satisfied if I had better students, more hours in a day, less administrative work, better software, and a filing clerk.

My main satisfactions come from the intellectual aspects of my work and from the personal freedom this job provides.

My career aspiration is to publish a book.

LAWYER #1

One of the benefits of my profession as a lawyer in a private practice is that I don't have to retire even after practicing for 48 years. My career life started as a claim adjuster for an insurance company. It was from watching lawyers while working as a claim adjuster that I got the initiative to study law myself.

As a lawyer in general practice my normal activities include interviewing clients, preparing documents, going to court to represent my clients, and negotiating contracts. As well as the legal knowledge necessary for this kind of work, I have found that it is very important to understand people, and have the ability to present a clear speech.

Aside from the hassle of collecting unpaid fees, I like most aspects of my work, particularly the people I work with, and the kind of work I do. The main satisfaction I find from my work is a job well done.

LAWYER #2

I have been a lawyer for forty-three years. I study law, prepare cases, write briefs, talk to clients, and attend hearings.

I have several degrees in law, the highest being Juris Doctor. In addition to education, you must have a wealth of legal knowledge, good writing and communication skills, knowledge of the local courts, and the ability to concentrate.

I enjoy this kind of work and I like my job very much. I derive great satisfaction from successfully completing a case and resolving a problem for a client.

My background includes such positions as a business owner and a law firm associate.

I plan to practice law for as long as I possibly can; I would also like to prepare a natural resource program for the town where my law firm is located.

LAWYER #3

I've been a lawyer for many years and there's never been a typical day for me. One day I may be in court defending a criminal case. Other days I spend in my office doing research or meeting with clients or prospective clients. In general, I try law suit cases and advise clients about their rights.

While I went to law school to prepare for a career in the diplomatic field, I've found practicing law and the work itself satisfying. I also enjoy the people I work with. What I dislike are the deadbeats who refuse to pay their fees. I'd like my business to be more profitable.

An attorney needs the ability to communicate with various types of people from different economic levels. You should be able to detach yourself emotionally from the client. I have found in my practice the need to understand basic science. The appropriate training is required as well: I have a Bachelor of Arts degree and an L.L.B. law degree.

LECTURER, MANAGEMENT SEMINARS

An instructor and lecturer for 16 years, I conduct supervisory and management seminars throughout the state for our company. There is no such thing as an average day in my work. Some days I plan and prepare lectures or presentations. I'll also organize and coordinate conferences. Other days I fly to the instruction sites and teach all day.

My background is varied. I've worked in architecture, urban planning, and landscape design. My degrees are a Bachelor of Science and a Master's in public health administration. Then came this managerial and supervisory training opportunity.

With my strong communication skills, I am able to speak and write well. You also need the ability to encourage and support people. I've found that respecting people, along with being empathetic to their situations, is important. Patience and optimism are also good qualities to have.

Recognizing progress in my students and in myself gives me great satisfaction. I love the interaction of active minds. In the classroom, being the "captain of my ship" makes me feel great. I also find building friendships very important to me. If bureaucratic stifling of creativity could be reduced, my job would be outstanding.

LEGAL ASSISTANT

I started my career as a teacher of adult education and business subjects. This required earning a Bachelor of Science and Master of Science in Teaching. I was also the office manager in a church before starting my career as a legal assistant 13 years ago.

As a legal assistant, I help in all aspects of managing a litigation legal practice for one lawyer. I work from 8:30 to 5:00 handling the following job responsibilities: opening mail, coordinating calendars, transcribing dictation, proofreading documents, drafting routine correspondence and documents, making appointments, billing clients, and timekeeping.

To perform well in this kind of work, it is important to have the following skills and abilities: typing, oral and written communication, accounting, ability to get along with people, willingness to learn new things such as computers, and understanding legal concepts.

I like this kind of work and the person I work for. I find job satisfaction in creating documents, dealing with people in all aspects of life, managing work load, coordinating projects, and meeting deadlines. However, because of my desire to continue my education and to have more opportunities for advancement, I plan to go to law school. I am also considering the possibility of returning to teaching.

LEGAL SECRETARY

As a legal secretary, I handle scheduling of appointments and meetings for 15 attorneys, and I type notices and letters on the word processor.

In this career, you must be precise, attentive to details and accurate. Dedication, good memory, and a sense of humor helps in succeeding in the job. I recommend it to people who like to work with ambitious, energetic men and women who are on the "go" much of the time. The chance to see the inside workings of the legal system is another reward in this work.

LETTER CARRIER #1

I have been a letter carrier for the U.S. Postal Service for 22 years because I like this kind of work very much. After graduating from high school and prior to my postal service work I worked as a grocery clerk, clerical supervisor, and as an accounting and finance clerk. I needed a better paying job so I a took the civil service test, passed it, and have been basically satisfied since.

My responsibility is to sort mail and deliver it to 750 families. In order to handle this type of work, you must have reading skills and manual and mental dexterity. You must be quick! This is one part of the job which I don't particularly like because the requirements to sort the vast quantities of mail at such a rapid pace is very stressful. What I do like is the people contact I have with this job. I like the people I work for and the people I work with. I find job satisfaction from making people happy with the mail they receive.

LETTER CARRIER #2

A postal carrier, I spend about three hours in the morning sorting mail and arranging pieces sequentially. In the afternoons, I deliver the mail, which takes approximately five hours. After spending four years in the U.S. Navy, I've been a postal carrier for 18 years. I was out of work for a while after military duty; I took the qualifying test, passed, and accepted employment as a letter carrier.

I like everything about my work: the people, my supervisors, the fact that I can move up in this field, and the postal service itself. I especially enjoy the interaction with the people on my route. Being outdoors most of the day and getting the exercise are two advantages of my job.

I earned an Associates of Science degree with a business concentration, but if you are not able to go to college a degree is not essential for this work. Having had some college experience has helped me in other ways, however.

To do this work, you should have a good memory. Being friendly, along with having a very good attitude toward the public, is very important. A person must not mind wearing a uniform, and must enjoy being in the public eye all day.

LIBRARIAN #1

For the past fourteen years, I have worked as a librarian in a small branch library. My duties include checking out books for library patrons, filing catalogue cards, taking inventory of the books in the library, keeping track of overdue fines and pending charges, attempting to locate missing books or books out on loan, and reading book reviews to help in purchase recommendations. My library also uses a computer to keep track of some of our information.

In addition to attaining a Bachelor of Science degree, a librarian must always remember that the responsibility of a librarian is to help people. A librarian also needs to pay careful attention to details and to conduct oneself in an orderly fashion--a sloppy library cannot be tolerated under any circumstances. A person who enjoys bookkeeping will most likely enjoy the work of a librarian as they require a lot of the same personal qualities and attitudes.

I enjoy my job very much, especially when I know that I have helped a patron find information key to their success on a project. I feel so good when one of my patrons expresses gratitude and appreciation for my efforts and assistance. I like this type of work because of the variety of my daily tasks and the unrushed tempo of my work. I never get bored on my job, especially since our computer system was installed. I find that using a computer makes my job easier, but when the computer system is down, chaos results.

Prior to becoming a librarian, I worked as a secretary/bookkeeper and as a general secretary; I believe these positions helped me develop the necessary people skills and communication skills used in my present work.

I plan to continue my work; there are very few jobs in today's job market that do not require a lot of overtime, or do not have daily crises as a part of the routine.

LIBRARIAN #2

I started my career as an English teacher and then taught drama/debate/speech. While in this position, I was asked to change my occupation to become the librarian of the school/city library. At that time, I had earned a Bachelor of Arts degree in Education, and a Masters in Education. I then returned to school to earn a Masters in Library Science.

As a librarian, my responsibilities include administration of the library, buying, cataloging, reference work, and equipment procurement and maintenance. Some of my typical activities include: ordering books, writing grants, teaching library skills, telling stories, attending meetings, and answering reference questions.

As well as the specialized training in library science, organizational skills, people skills, and teaching skills are essential in order to perform this kind of work.

Although I dislike my salary and the lack of opportunity for advancement, I like the kind of work I do, and the people with whom I work. I find personal satisfaction from this work in filling a need for the community. I am rewarded by seeing results. My future career plans are to continue in library work and to become a district media supervisor.

LIBRARIAN #3

My love of books and reading, from a young age, plus my desire to help others, were the main factors which prompted me to change careers and earn my Masters in Library Science degree in order to become a librarian. Prior to this I worked as an administrative assistant and a private secretary in private industry.

As a librarian in a high school, my responsibilities include selecting and organizing materials, supervising the library, and helping students and faculty learn to appreciate and use library resources.

I think the key attributes which are important to have in order to perform this kind of work well are an appreciation of detail, an inquiring mind, interest in a wide variety of subjects, and the desire to help others.

Having to keep students quiet is the major frustration I must deal with as a school librarian. I would like to spend less time supervising students and more time working with them.

I enjoy the opportunity to find out about a wide assortment of subjects. There is also satisfaction in seeing a student or faculty member find something in the library and gain an appreciation of the resources available and how to use them.

My future career plans are to either continue with this position or to change to a research or university library.

LIBRARIAN #4

For 28 years I've been a librarian in a public school enjoying watching students become successful in research. I love my work, the people with whom I'm involved, and the school. If I could begin again, I'd choose librarianship. If I could improve on this job above the way it is, I'd like to have more assistance in the technical aspects of this job and to have more time to teach.

I am in complete charge of the high school library. I handle mail, answer phones, and order and process books and audio visual materials. I'm in charge of all machines and their maintenance. I supervise students in study halls or teach in class. Skills which are important in my work are the ability to plan and organize, to scan books and professional journals with insight, and to be willing to be available for one-on-one instruction. Being patient and understanding while creating a pleasant environment are important. Earlier I was a secretary and later a business teacher, but I enjoy library work most.

I got into library work after substituting for a librarian while teaching summer school. I earned my Masters in Library Science, was asked to replace a retired librarian, and since I enjoyed the work, I remained in the position. I plan to be here until retirement.

LIBRARIAN #5

I am looking forward to retirement even though I have loved my years as a librarian. (I'll have more time for reading.)

To be an effective librarian you must have good organizational skills. Attention to details, research skills, and a love of books and reading add to your success. A desire to be of service to others, to be willing "to go the extra mile," to assist others, and patience are important traits as well. You need an aesthetic touch too, I believe.

In my work, I catalog and organize materials acquired through orders and gifts, and I assist patrons. Processing periodicals received daily, taking care of the mail, and handling invoices are all part of my duties. I also keep the library attractive by arranging displays and bulletin boards.

I would enjoy my work more if I were able to delegate more of the routine work. Yet, I find much satisfaction in helping others. I find joy in receiving new books ordered and examining them. Working in the "world of books," I am content in an orderly surrounding and in a pleasant, quiet atmosphere. There is a challenge in finding answers to research questions, and making known to others the tools available.

Prior to my library work, I was briefly a Congregational Church secretary and, later, a teacher. As an English teacher, I was automatically given charge of the library in smaller schools before the days of state requirements. As a college student, I also did some work in the college library. I found both experiences very attractive and decided on librarianship as a career.

LIBRARIAN #6

For 13 years, I've been a librarian, handling the responsibilities of the library. Currently, I manage and direct two school libraries. My tasks are to take care of the mail, do statistical reports, write, and plan for the coming year. My job also means keeping the shelves up-to-date with current catalogs, magazines, and books. I take care of study halls and look after audio-visual equipment.

Organizational and clerical skills are needed to be a librarian. Being able to plan is also helpful. You should like kids and have patience. The ability to work well with people is significant as well.

I have a Bachelor of Arts degree in education. When I was in high school, I was a library aide. I enjoyed the work and I liked the field of education; so I decided to put them together.

Formerly, I was a waitress and a hotel maid, both of which I liked. But now, this job appeals to me much more than those earlier ones because I very much like the people I work with and the kind of work I do. What I appreciate about my work is being able to organize and do clerical work. I like working alone, and I like books. I plan to continue my career as a librarian and work in a public or college library.

LIBRARIAN #7

My many years experience as a librarian may be helpful in explaining this job to anyone interested in entering this line of work. The responsibilities differ according to the type of library. In the Order Department of a University library, you look up information on book order requests to determine whether the library already has a copy, what it would cost to buy it, the Library of Congress number, and other such details. After orders are sent out and books come in, there is considerable clerical work to be done: check the invoice, pull the order slip, and indicate necessary information for the catalog department. Sometimes, follow-up correspondence with publishers is necessary.

One position I held was as Reference Librarian in a college library. There you need to know the reference materials thoroughly to help students find what they need. A Lab Technical Librarian, however, might have circulation desk duties, some cataloging, and must be able to find material requested. Sometimes translations must be made or arranged for and bibliographies might need to be produced.

Skills needed for the job are knowledge of a subject, if working in a special library like law or music, interest in working with people, and, depending on the type of library, a knowledge of languages. Typing is required and some knowledge of computers is needed. Being part "detective" helps--in fact, is necessary.

My education as an undergraduate student led to a Bachelor of Arts degree in education, but I never did actually become a teacher. I chose to return to college and get a Bachelor of Science degree in Library Science. That led into my library jobs.

LIBRARIAN, ELEMENTARY & JUNIOR HIGH SCHOOL

In my career you have to like kids and people--even the ones with "warts"! I am a public school librarian shuffling my work time between two schools. On Monday, Wednesday and Friday I am at a K-8 school. Two of those days are spent having classes with students. The third day is spent in consulting, selecting teaching aids, ordering new print and nonprint materials, cataloging them and getting shelves ready. I also help teachers find materials for teaching units and weed out old materials. Tuesday and Thursday are spent at another school K and 4-8. I am responsible for spending the library budget and keeping and updating the collections which are needed for K-8 children.

My previous experience includes work as a church youth director, a career education teacher for 8th graders and as a 3rd and 4th grade teacher. As a teacher I saw a need for enthusiastic people in this field. I love books and wanted to share this with children. I knew it was a poorly-paid field but I wanted weekends, holidays, and summers with my children. I returned to school and earned my master's degree in library science.

The reason I have loved my work as a librarian for the past 20 years is the personal satisfaction I receive when seeing students and teachers get excited about and want to use books and non-print materials. I also enjoy professional meetings. What dissatisfies me is being in more than one school. Also, I would like to have enough paid clerk time so that I could work with students and teachers--not do clerk's work.

After retirement, my husband and I hope to do short term work in other countries (where we are really needed).

LIBRARIAN, HIGH SCHOOL #1

As a high school library media specialist I work with teachers, design library programs, and help and teach kids. On a typical day I might attend a computer/technology meeting, catalog/classify books and other materials, work with kids and teachers and select new materials for purchase for the library. It is also my major overall responsibility to design our library program.

To perform well as a school librarian it is important to have the ability to get along with people. You must like kids, be flexible, have the ability to improvise, and have good communication skills.

I like almost everything about my work and that good feeling includes such factors as the kind of work, the people I work for, and the school district. However, I wish there were less scrambling for materials to work with at my school. I am also feeling a lack of opportunity for advancement in my present position, although I hope to move someday into media planning on a district level.

I got into this occupation after I put myself through a trial term at my college library while earning my bachelor of arts degree. I then continued in school to earn a master's as a specialist in arts.

Because of my love of books and people, this has been a good career for me. If you have similar interests, it will be a good career for you.

LIBRARIAN, HIGH SCHOOL #2

In my role as a high school librarian, I select, purchase, and catalog books, magazines, and audio visual materials for the library collection. I provide a reader advisory service while teaching students how to use the materials. I oversee the circulation of library materials and assist the faculty in the use of the materials.

I've been in library work for 24 years, thirteen in an elementary school library and eleven in a high school. I have found a fascination with knowledge and learning is a trait of a librarian. Other characteristics are a willingness and eagerness to help others, ability to communicate well, and enjoyment in being around teenagers. That includes attending some sports, plays, and other extracurricular activities because they need your support too.

Conducting an effective reference interview can be learned, and the librarian must be able to do that because the patron doesn't always know how to ask for what he or she really wants. Each librarian sets the tone for that area; if you want it to be quiet, you have to have the disciplinary skills to make it so. Persistence is the key. Disciplining students and keeping them on the task is a big part of what I do. Clerical work must be done each day: look through mail, check in the magazines, help students sign out materials, file those cards, etc. Professional journals are read daily--the book reviews in those help in selecting the materials to be added to the collection.

I fell into librarianship because of needing an extra course in college. The introductory course in Library Science was selected to fill that need, but I found it to be very interesting in itself. Later courses led to a Bachelor of Science in Education and then to a Masters of Library Science degree. In college, I worked in the library part-time and I liked it very much.

I like helping people find the information they need. I enjoy purchasing new materials. Reading interesting books, learning, and sharing with others all please me. I dislike the lack of money to buy all the needed library materials, and to increase my paycheck. I'd like to have more students who are quiet and eager to study. I plan to retire in a few years and find a position as a reference librarian at a public library; answering reference questions is the best part of my job.

LIBRARIAN, HIGH SCHOOL #3

As a high school librarian, my job is to select and order books and non-print library materials, to help students find the information they need for schoolwork, and to supervise all the activities of a high school library.

For the past 6 years, I have enjoyed the kind of work involved and especially the independence it allows. Previously, I was an employment counselor, and an elementary teacher. I like the library work more than those jobs, but if I were starting my career over, I think I would like to try something in anthropology or the health field. Working in a book store also appeals to me.

A librarian needs to have a college degree, usually in Library Science. On a daily basis, the librarian sees to tasks such as: supervise library aides to see that books and newspapers are checked in and out accurately and returned to shelves; help individuals find materials and use the CD ROM and copy equipment as needed; make up the budget, keep inventories of print and audio-visual materials, and sometimes catalog books on the computer; create displays to encourage interest in books on a given topic.

To do these things well, you have to have an awareness and interest in news, trends, and current events. You also must pay attention to details, have a knowledge of sources available for reference, and the ability to operate all equipment in the library.

The only negatives to this job are working on a tight budget sometimes and wishing that more people would use all the facilities that are available. Major rewards of library work are having easy access to all kinds of information, getting to read reviews of new books, and the great satisfaction felt in helping students find just what they need for projects and schoolwork as part of their education.

LIBRARIAN, JUNIOR & SENIOR HIGH SCHOOL

I'm a public school librarian presently working in a junior/senior high school. With a Bachelor of Science in education, I worked previously at the elementary school level. Daily, I supervise and discipline the library patrons and those in study hall. I must instruct student librarians as well as order and process new materials. Arranging displays, keeping the premises neat and inviting, and working on updating the card catalog are a few of my responsibilities. Keeping up with the audio-visual equipment use and handling the repairs of this equipment are also part of the job. As the reader's advisor, my work includes giving presentations on book content and helping students to research.

All of my experience in education has been gratifying. Yet, nothing pleases me more than finding books and reading materials, either for assignments or for pleasure, which will excite students. I hope reading will provide them with life-long enjoyment. My plans are to do an even better job at whatever I do.

I'd like to inspire school officials to give more support to school libraries. It would be grand if more school boards and administrators saw the value of well-stocked libraries staffed by trained librarians. Once I entered the library field, I loved it. I've never desired a change. The profession allows me to combine my two favorite things: young people and literature.

A good librarian must genuinely like people and have a desire to work with them. This person must be willing to be of service to the patrons. They must have an interest in literature of all types, the desire to read, and the willingness to share this passion. One must have intellectual curiosity in order to be adept at collection development. This requires open-mindedness to supply the needs of all patrons--not just those with the same interests or philosophy as the librarian.

LIBRARIAN, MEDIA SPECIALIST #1

As a school librarian/media specialist, each day is different--some days I teach, which might include giving book talks, or my duties may include assisting students involved in research projects, repairing media equipment, cataloging new materials, checking on orders, or preparing bibliographies; essentially, the variety of my work day is determined by the demands and needs of the teachers and students using the library services and materials.

My education includes a Bachelor of Arts degree and a Master of Library Science degree. In addition to a solid educational background, my position also requires a good memory, the ability to get along well with others, an inquisitive mind, organizational skills, mechanical aptitude, a high energy level, and a sincere desire to help others.

In the twenty-four years I have served as a librarian, I have at times felt overwhelmed by the demands of my job and I am sure I will never feel that I have enough knowledge. This job requires a great deal of time doing paperwork; good clerical help is as precious as gold in this profession. I believe that some teachers would greatly help their students, and make my job less tedious, if they had more current knowledge of the use of library resources. But there are those times when a teacher or a student really shows appreciation for my efforts, and when I believe I have helped a student or teacher become more successful, and it makes it all worthwhile. I enjoy the interaction with others and the constant mental stimulation that this profession provides.

Before working at a school, I worked in a large public library; I chose to work in a school environment so that I could complete my Master's in Library Science degree during the school summer breaks, but I also found that I really enjoy working with high school students and the greater freedom and challenges of the school library.

I believe I will always be involved with people and information, especially books, even when I reach retirement age.

LIBRARIAN, MEDIA SPECIALIST #2

As a library media specialist in a school environment, I maintain an educational media program for a school setting--grades seven through twelve. For the past fifteen years, I have administered and maintained school library media for the students and staff of my school.

Once completing a Bachelor's degree, the decision to make a career in this area should consider whether you possess the following qualities essential to success in this field: a friendly nature, good organizational skills, flexibility, and the ability to cooperate with others for the benefit of all.

Although there are not many opportunities for advancement, I really like my job. There is great self-satisfaction to be derived from helping others to do well in teaching or assigned school work. I like the people I work with, even though I wish I could hire an assistant.

I became interested in library media work while in college and volunteered to work in the college library. I have always enjoyed reading and spending time in libraries.

Although I have also worked as a teacher, I prefer my present work.

I plan to work at my job for as long as possible and I may return to college and study library science, perhaps on a graduate level of education.

LIBRARIAN, MEDIA SPECIALIST #3

Although there is no typical day in the life of a librarian, there are certain duties to perform. I am responsible for acquiring and maintaining all of the print and non-print materials for an elementary school. As a media specialist, I also keep up with all the audio-visual instructional equipment.

Since my sister was a librarian, I became interested in the field. It seemed to be a happy profession.

I earned a Bachelor of Science degree in library science and a Masters degree in media and related technology. A secretary for a while, I now enjoy helping students grow and would pick the same career again. I appreciate my coworkers, my work, and my superiors.

Librarians must get along with people. They should have people management skills in order to maintain control. Strong verbal skills are essential as well. The only future plan I have is to retire early enough to enjoy life.

LIBRARIAN, MEDIA SPECIALIST #4

My job as the librarian and media specialist in a high school is to organize and direct the activities of the library. I teach research skills as well. I've always been interested in areas of visual and performing arts, radio, TV, and education. Going into library work while combining educational media and technology seemed the perfect career combination.

One specific quality needed to be a good librarian is patience. Liking people and having the desire to help them are both equally important. You should, in addition, be well organized. Having a good sense of judgment is needed as well.

A typical day in the library is quite varied. I might order new materials or teach a class on research skills. Assisting a teacher in preparing a lesson or researching some point or issue myself are possible activities. I usually have to prepare curriculum statistics and keep accounting records. My duties also include processing and cataloging new materials for our library collection. Some days I prepare a display or a bulletin board.

I received my Bachelor of Arts and Master of Arts degree and taught for a while before changing to media specialties. After 20 years in library work, I particularly enjoy working with young people. What is lacking, which would make my work more satisfying, are really outside issues, such as better support for schools and adequate funding. For the future, I want to become better at what I do. I'd like to lead our library and media center into the 21st century.

LIBRARIAN, MEDIA SPECIALIST #5

My decision to become a librarian and media specialist was influenced by early role models and personal interests, such as research. I completed a Bachelor of Science degree with additional hours. Then I worked for a while in sales and as a teacher before accepting a position as school librarian 16 years ago.

Job satisfaction comes in knowing I have influenced a student in some way that will have a positive effect on his or her future. It's rewarding to recognize that I have introduced students to the power of knowledge.

I really enjoy cooperative, appreciative people as much as I dislike uncooperative, demanding ones. My job would be more satisfying if the administration knew more about what librarians do. I'd also like this position to be placed on the school administrative level since the library and media center are at the core of the curriculum. My goal is to move into administration and make positive changes for our library program.

Primary for a librarian are good organizational skills. You must not be over-sensitive, but be flexible and maintain an ability to work with the results of the decisions of others. You must not submit to pressure and overextend yourself. A person in this position must understand that there are many influences that affect the failure or success of a library program. Cooperation with others is important since one person cannot do everything required for an effective program.

I work with students a minimum of four hours per day. As a media specialist, I deal with equipment: checking out, setting up, trouble-shooting, and making minor repairs. I also teach individual students, small groups, and classes. Spending time planning for short and long-term library program goals, ordering materials and equipment, and handling paper work for the program are some of my duties. In addition, I plan the budget as well as process and catalog all materials and equipment for circulation.

LIBRARIAN, MEDIA SPECIALIST #6

In my work as a librarian and media specialist on a campus for eighth graders, I love to find just the right book for someone. I also enjoy the ordering process, reading about all the different materials, then selecting what I feel is best. The only aspects I do not like are the low salary and the lack of advancement opportunity.

After earning a Bachelor of Arts degree, I taught school for 12 years. I decided later to obtain my Masters of Education in counseling and another specializing in learning resources. I've worked as a librarian for eleven years.

To be an effective librarian, you must be very familiar with the curriculum of the school and must know well the book collection. Good communication skills are essential--you must know how to phrase questions to initiate responses and determine how much or what kind of help to give a student. Strong people skills are also important so that you can get along with the entire faculty.

I spend my time in the library ordering and processing materials, weeding the collection, and generating lists, such as bibliographies and overdues. There is a great deal of paperwork. On average, three teachers each week reserve the library for their classes and I help oversee the students as they check out books or do research. Giving lessons on how to use the library efficiently or how to do research are also part of my duties. I enjoy all of those duties.

LIBRARIAN, MEDIA SPECIALIST #7

I enjoy my work as a school librarian so much that I plan to continue working in libraries following my retirement from the school. I've been in this work for 13 years. After going back to school as an adult, I began by studying elementary education and minoring in library science. After substituting in a high school, I decided to become a librarian. I have found it useful to have a sense of humor and the ability to be flexible.

I love discussing books with students. Teaching others to use various sources pleases me. When alumni come back to visit, I am delighted. There's only one thing I don't like about my work--there's no opportunity for advancement.

My duties are cataloging new materials, giving tours of the library, emphasizing subject area materials, and answering questions. I help with book selections, answer the telephone, and attend meetings. Demonstrating the use of equipment, i.e., the computer and the microfiche reader, also occupy my time.

LIBRARIAN, MEDIA SPECIALIST #8

Every day is different in my life as a library media specialist. For 13 years, I've taught, assisted instructional staff, and worked with the administration. I even planned, with the architect, the design of our new media center!

Teaching students, in groups or individually, how to use the media center and its resources is my responsibility. The instructional staff also needs my assistance in using the center productively. I help trouble shoot in maintaining both audio-visual and computer equipment. Working with our staff in ordering, processing, and cataloging audio-visual and library materials is also part of my job. Finally, I assist the teachers in developing the school curriculum.

Seeing friends who were librarians enjoying their work made me look into the library field. I'd earned a Bachelor of Arts degree and I'd always enjoyed research, so I went to graduate school and got a Masters degree in Library Science. I'm glad I did because I like the variety of my work as well as the fact that it takes many different skills.

I also like helping students be better researchers. Assisting teachers with instructional and research techniques is rewarding as well. Even though I don't like the disruptive and disrespectful behavior of some students, I do enjoy keeping up with the variety of challenges associated with learning new technologies. We could use more technical help in this area.

LIBRARIAN, MIDDLE SCHOOL

As a middle school librarian, a typical day includes teaching a sixth grade skills (library) class, one or two booktalks to class(es) of children, helping students and teachers find information, supervising all AV equipment and use, and processing new materials.

Of utmost importance in this profession is skill in story telling. Also necessary are organizational ability, personality with students and teachers, and computer literacy.

I find satisfaction from spellbound children listening to a story. Gratitude from teachers for help is also rewarding. It gives me satisfaction also to weed out and discard junk!

I was a classroom teacher and a part-time private piano lesson teacher for many years. I worked part time in a public library and was urged to get my degree at age 59, and I did it! I have a BS in education and a Master's degree in library science.

Because I enjoy this environment and the children with whom I work, when I retire, I plan to do substitute teaching.

LIBRARIAN, PUBLIC LIBRARY

To make a change from a stressful human services job (also a dead-end one), I went back to graduate school to earn my Master of Library Science degree. I was fortunate to find a job in a library right away, in my town.

I chose library science because it seemed to be a non-stressful occupation and I have had a life-long love of books. As it turns out, there is a bit more to the career than that.

My day is very varied including: selecting books to purchase, setting up work schedules for the staff, cataloging books and other materials, bookkeeping, sorting mail, placing orders for books and materials, attending community and professional meetings, writing articles for newspapers, and supervising staff work.

To perform well as a librarian in a public library, it is important to have a knowledge of books in general and of the specific library collection. You need a strong ability to communicate with people as to their information needs. Patience and willingness to be of service on many different levels is also necessary for a librarian. In my position as director, I need management skills in budget preparation, money management, and personnel management.

I find this work satisfying because I enjoy providing access to information to all kinds of people. I am learning about books on a daily basis. Also, I like the interacting with people about one of my favorite things - books. This work would be even more satisfying with more clerical help.

LIBRARIAN, PUBLIC SCHOOL

My career in library work started out in high school where I worked as a library page, and it has taken a natural progression since then. After earning my college degree in library/educational media, I have been working as a librarian in a public school.

My responsibilities as a school librarian are: handling circulation, reviewing book titles in order to select new material, maintaining reference material, processing new materials, assisting students, and monitoring students.

I like my work but get frustrated at times because of the lack of funds allocated by my school district for the library. There is so much new information generated all the time and I would like to have our school library kept up to date, but it takes money which I never seem to be able to get.

I find job satisfaction in helping students. It is rewarding to be a part of their learning process.

I plan to continue my public school work. However, I am considering becoming a reading teacher or media specialist.

LIBRARIAN, SCHOOL #1

Working as a librarian can be satisfying, particularly when you see children get excited about learning abstract and concrete information and seeing their level of intellect grow.

My basic library duties in the school library are to order and process books and tape instructional television. I too, like the other teachers, must share in other regular school duties like watching the children in study hall.

I like the kind of work I do and the people I work with. However, I am probably better suited to handle children under 12 years old and would be happier doing that.

To qualify for this profession I earned a Bachelor of Science degree and minored in Library Science.

LIBRARIAN, SCHOOL #2

As a school librarian, I manage all aspects of the library program in my school. This includes: managing all personnel--students and staff, ordering books, processing books, managing circulation files and on-line catalog, and developing programs.

The skills and attitudes which I consider most important for a librarian to have are organization, patience, and determination.

I started my career as a social worker, but switched to this library work because I felt I could combine my love of books with my love for assisting people. I started working in the library part-time while I returned to school to earn my Master's degree in Library Science.

The main satisfactions that I find from being a librarian are assisting students and faculty with their work, the order within my workplace, management satisfaction from a "job well done," and seeing the use of the library grow.

LIBRARIAN, SCHOOL #3

I started my career as a commercial credit officer for two local banks. I then left that job to stay home with my newborn son. During that time, I went back to school to earn a Bachelor of Arts in Education, and a Masters of Science in Library Science. I chose a career as a school librarian because it fit with my child's schedule and provided challenges for me.

As a school librarian, I teach 33 classes a week, am responsible for spending the library budget appropriately for books and materials, and help the staff, students, and parents. My classes are for teaching reference skills or literature appreciation.

In order to perform this kind of work well, it is important to be self-motivated, to like detailed work, to be flexible, and have the ability to work with many people (750 students, 40 teachers).

Although I wish I could make my own teaching schedule, and could have the services of a full time clerk, I like most aspects of my work. I particularly like the opportunities I have for advancement, the people I work with, and the kind of work I do. Job satisfaction for me is happy children that like to come to the library. You never get bored because there are always so many things to choose from to do.

In the future, I am considering getting into school/library administration.

LIBRARY ASSISTANT, ELEMENTARY SCHOOL

If I could choose to start over, I would have earned more than a high school education so that I could become a librarian instead of the job of library assistant in a public elementary school that I now hold. As it is, my opportunity for advancement is limited.

Otherwise, the job is very satisfying. For six years I have done all the clerical duties in a library setting, as well as order books and classify and catalog books. Previously I had been an underwriter at an insurance company, a typist, and a receptionist in a large manufacturing company. The receptionist work was enjoyable, but it is more satisfying to see children learn to do research and use books to enrich their lives. On a personal level, the job provides an opportunity to read book reviews and keep current on what is being published.

You have to be skillful at interacting with teachers and the students. Good computer and typing skills and a knowledge of books and literature are essential in going a good job of assisting in research and helping to choose reading material.

I have a great fondness for reading and books, and this school district position makes it possible to combine a career with care of my family.

LIFE INSURANCE AGENT

After many years serving in the U.S. Military, I currently am a general life insurance agent. My work primarily is to train and assist agents in preparing for insurance presentations. I spend a great deal of my time planning for the next client to contact, letters to write, or research to conduct. I am always studying and learning about new insurance products.

I obtained degrees in industrial technology and hotel/motel management. Then, after personal observation of the misfortunes of others, including my own family, I became interested in the insurance field. It is my desire to eventually become a company vice president for my state region in operations and control. I see the power and authority in that position that I need to accomplish my special goal--doing everything I can to rid the industry of all unscrupulous agents who give the insurance business a bad image. I'd very much like for all agents to be required to earn a professional designation in order to work within the industry.

To be an effective insurance agent, you must positively care about people. You should enjoy dealing with the public, be honest, and thoroughly know all the insurance products available. A person must be very empathetic and maintain a professional appearance.

The greatest satisfaction I get from this job is the feeling that I'm filling a very important need for my clients.

LOGISTICS ENGINEER

As a logistics engineer, I am responsible for the details of transport, housing, and supply of new, as well as modified, military weapons systems. I study engineering data, then develop procedures and tasks on how to maintain the missiles, aircraft, and tanks which carry the weaponry for the Armed Forces.

To do this work, you need to be mechanically inclined. Experience in several engineering fields is a must: mechanical, electronic, and hydraulic. Diplomacy is essential since you need to be able to listen politely even when your customer or supervisor is wrong. In my situation, you should be able to work well with egotistical, inflexible people. Finally, good writing skills are very important.

While I don't like my supervisors very much and the fact that they use the intimidation method to motivate, I do appreciate my coworkers and the work I do. I like the personal satisfaction, and that of the customer, from a job well done. The knowledge I gain in the process is valuable as well.

My future plans are uncertain. I'd like to go back to college and get a civil engineering degree in addition to the Bachelor of Arts degree in industrial technology I have now.

LONG RANGE PLANNER

In my career, I am involved in new technology and have the freedom to dream. It was through my educational background and experience in several areas of communications that I was able to land this position as long range planner of transmission equipment. It is my job to study and evaluate new transmission systems in the field of communication and to perform economic analysis. My typical work schedule includes: looking at all alternatives to a solution, studying the alternatives, making an economic analysis on all the alternatives, doing write-ups, presenting plans to upper management, and budget input.

To perform well at this kind of work, it is important to have writing skills, an engineering background, economic analysis skills, and VISION.

Prior to this position, I was a supervisor of operations and maintenance of telephone and communication equipment, and a research and development manager. My educational background includes a Bachelor of Arts degree and a Masters in Business Administration.

The part I like least about my job is completing the write-ups required for my plans. However, I really like having the opportunity to be a part of new technology and find satisfaction in presenting and selling my ideas to a long term solution.

LOSS CONTROL WORKER

To be a loss control representative, I earned an Associates degree in fire protection and a Bachelor of Science degree in arson investigation. My previous job as a safety inspector was enjoyable, but I really like working with my customers in this field. I also like learning about new businesses and visiting different locations.

In my work, I evaluate risks due to lack of safety measures. One of my specific duties is to work on implementing new safety ideas. I make appointments and visit five to six customers a day. Researching code violations and evaluating cases with potential loss are my responsibilities.

A loss control representative must be technically competent in knowing the fire codes. You have to be highly knowledgeable about the Occupational Safety and Health Act (OSHA) and know all about the Environmental Protection Agency (EPA) requirements.

I'm sorry there isn't much chance for advancement in my work. The only other aspect I don't like is the amount of time I have to spend in the office rather than outside. My future plans are to manage a loss control operation on my own.

LOUDSPEAKER ENGINEER

The Chief Loudspeaker Engineer in the component audio division of a major corporation, I supervise engineers and review their progress memos for new products. I direct technicians in building new types of speakers, attend planning meetings, and review project plans. Inventing new loudspeaker technology, standardizing project techniques, along with using computer modeling to investigate possible speaker configurations, are some of my duties. I also conduct engineering manager performance reviews as well as advise on other loudspeaker projects.

Receiving recognition for my contributions is very satisfying. It is rewarding to do something that's never been done before and to be regarded as an innovator. I like making an excellent product and I really enjoy the freedom to do what I think is important.

My work would be more interesting if the engineering department were reorganized to involve new engineers. By not including all engineers within the company's development areas, expertise is lost. I'd like it if the company had smaller divisions, and if there were more time to pursue new speaker technology.

Most important in my work is having knowledge of the company's new product methods. Good listening skills, perseverance, and creativity are also essential. Technical knowledge of loudspeakers and acoustics along with being able to plan well are also important. You must be willing to do anything to overcome obstacles, but it is an interesting challenge to do that.

I got into this job by luck; the only job offer at that time was with a speaker company. Eventually, I was hired by a customer and over 18 years worked into my current position of engineer. I have both a Bachelor's and a Master's in electrical engineering. One day I'd like to meet my goal and become the Director of New Products in this corporation.

MACHINE OPERATOR #1

I have spent the majority of my career life as a machine operator in various manufacturing plants and have been satisfied with this type of work. After six years in the U.S. Navy, I made women's shoes and then car radiators. For the past 18 years, I have been a dough packer operator and biscuit can machine operator.

Typically my work day starts by preparing the biscuit line for operation and starting up the line. Weighing the biscuits, making sure everything is running properly and keeping the production line moving smoothly are my primary duties.

In order to handle this type of work well, it is important to be mechanically inclined and to know very well the manner in which machines operate. Above all, cleanliness is the crucial factor.

I feel fortunate to work for a supervisor who cares for his workers. I like the people I work with, the organization I work for, the opportunity for advancement and the kind of work I do. This work is satisfying to me because I feel that I am involved in making something that is needed.

MACHINE OPERATOR #2

When I got out of high school, I wasn't interested in trying to attend college. I looked for a job and fairly quickly got into the construction business. Not long afterward, I had a chance to run a "detacher," a machine to cut forms. I've been doing that kind of work for 31 years and I guess it is obvious that I like the job. In fact, I find satisfaction in everything about this job.

To do this work, I receive forms to be detached. I check them for print quality before detaching them. Also, it is necessary to print a line-up that accurately reflects the order in which they are to be done. Then I detach the forms by operating a detacher. Next, I make sure they are in the proper sequence, then place them in boxes, and I deliver them to the proper area. I keep a record of the number I detach for each area so that the bookkeeper can bill properly.

To do this job, you must be willing to work at a steady pace all the time. Occasionally, you must increase your pace because of the work load. Also, you must be able to work with people. Mechanical ability is, of course, important. It is important, too, to keep your work area and machine clean and in good repair. Finally, you must be able to communicate well.

Since I like this work, I'll keep at it until I retire.

MACHINIST #1

I have tried out other occupations such as painter and park manager. However, I have found my job as a machinist for a large national manufacturer to be the most satisfying. I do electrical discharge machining, commonly known as ELOX. My particular job activity is to burn dovetail cavities into forge dies.

The skills and attitudes which I find important for this kind of work are: blueprint reading skills, strong math skills, and level-headedness. Computer literacy is helpful but I do not consider it to be essential.

My job as a machinist has some drawbacks because of the hazardous machine fluids you work with and the smell. However, I like this kind of work and the people I work with. I plan to become a tool and die maker, which is a logical step for me to take so I can give myself some potential for advancement in this field.

MACHINIST #2

Since I have always been interested in creating and machinery, I chose to become a machinist and am satisfied with that choice. In fact, I would make the same choice even if offered the opportunity to start over and train for any kind work.

As a machinist, my work tools are a lathe, grinder, millers, and computerized lathes and millers. With this equipment and my skills, I take raw bar stock and produce a finished part to print, always maintaining a high level of quality. During the course of the day, I work on different jobs (products) and various machines.

To perform this kind of work well, I consider the following skills and attitudes to be important: good work ethics and responsibility; understanding of machine tooling, etc.; and good mechanical skills and coordination.

I like the kind of work I do and the organization I work for. If it weren't for some frustrations with fellow workers, I would be even more satisfied. Being a machinist, I find satisfaction from a complete job and viewing the finished end product knowing I have created something from raw material.

My future career plans are to finish my degree in engineering, and delve more into systems for computer design and drafting (CADD).

MACHINIST, REPAIR FUNCTION

I work as a machinist because I enjoy doing what I'm good at and happy doing. I was influenced by my industrial arts teacher in high school to pursue this as an occupation, and I am glad I did.

In my particular machinist job, I build and repair air, gas, and fluid pumping equipment. This involves a lot of one only and prototype work. In this work of fixing and building machines, I make parts which often involves coming up with new ideas and the use of lots of "Yankee ingenuity." My activities also include figuring (math), welding, turning, grinding, painting, bolting, building shipping crates, ordering parts, and talking to customers.

Machine shop skills are necessary, but most important to performing this kind of work well is taking great pride in your workmanship of the finished product.

My pet peeve with my kind of work is having salesmen lie to customers by telling then they can get pumps to them in less time than possible, even though they know we can not do it. It burns me up and causes rushing and unneeded pressure. But, sadly, this problem happens in all fields, not just mine.

Basically, though, I like my work because it is an interesting, low pressure job in a field where I'm well suited.

I find job satisfaction in having taken part in the design and building of machinery and seeing it finished and looking and working as if it were built by a true craftsman.

My future career plans are to just get better at what I'm doing so my pay will increase accordingly.

MACHINIST & FABRICATOR

I worked as a truck driver, millwright, terminal manager, and factory worker before being led into this career by a company engineer. He sought me out for this work and offered to have me learn the skills at work. I am glad he did, because I do think this is the right career for me.

As a machinist/fabricator, I operate the lathes, mills, drills, welders, torch, grinders, etc. to build machines and their parts from prints. I work in a shop that is almost totally self contained. I am the group leader, and as such I get my instructions and then hand out and organize work for others. After I have answered questions from my group, I go ahead on what is left to do. I have certainly found times when I would rather work by myself instead of having to make sure everybody else does their jobs correctly.

To perform this kind of work well, it is important to be a good listener, have good math skills, have patience, have the ability to start over completely without getting angry, and have the ability to see work that needs to be done without being told.

I think that this work appeals to me because it has given me the opportunity to think and act.

What I dislike about this work are those occasions when I see other workers abusing their freedom. I also feel that there may be a lack of opportunity for advancement in this work. Despite these drawbacks, I like my work as a machinist/fabricator and find satisfaction from my accomplishments - seeing something work that I have built. I am fascinated by machines and their applications. Satisfaction is a job well done that not just anyone can do.

In fact, this work has suited me so well, I hope to develop a machine shop business of my own.

MAIL CARRIER

One of the strongest requirements of the postal profession is to always do the best you can. Good interpersonal skills, including enjoying people, along with a consistently positive attitude are essential to the postal worker.

My duties as a postal worker are to sort and deliver the mail. I report to work at 6:15 a.m., pull my mail and begin the 4 to 4 1/2 hours it will take to sort it. After loading my jeep with the mail, I set out to serve my route which takes 3 to 3 1/2 hours. On returning to the post office, I sort my afternoon mail and settle my accountables.

I enjoy my work as a postal employee, but I may not continue in it indefinitely. Prior to this job I was a nurse's assistant which I very much enjoyed also. I'm very satisfied with this work knowing I do my job well with no valid complaints from anyone. The chance to meet people is one of the best parts of this work. My job would be more satisfying if my route were not so large and I could really enjoy being the best I can be.

I was recruited for my job, completed the application, and passed the test. I plan to make a career with the postal service and advance as the opportunities arise.

MAIL CLERK #1

As a mail clerk for two years, I collect, sort, and distribute interoffice mail for my company; I am also involved in quality checking and assisting others with their workload when my other duties are complete.

I enjoy my work; it gives me the ability to do my share as part of a team. I have also worked as a computer operator, but I find that job more solitary in nature--I personally need to be part of a team, so I came back to a job as a mail clerk, a position I held immediately after graduating from high school.

To work as a mail clerk you must be neat, have a degree of manual dexterity, pay attention to detail, and most important have good common sense.

I enjoy working with minimal supervision, being the best at what I do, and the lack of pressure on this job--it makes the day seem to go by faster.

I do not have any immediate or long-range career goals; I am just taking life as it comes--one day at a time.

MAIL CLERK #2

As the mailroom clerk at a college, my major responsibilities are to sort all the mail which is delivered twice a day and to process all the outgoing mail. Basically these tasks are easy, but it is important to have a good memory, basic math skills, and a friendly personality.

I like this kind of work and find my work pleasant because of the people I work with and the organization and people for whom I work. My only complaints with my job are that I dislike the many interruptions. I find satisfaction from knowing a lot about the postal system that most people don't know or that they take for granted.

Although I like this kind of work and have been employed as a mail clerk for 6 years, I do not see it as a permanent occupation. My future career plans are to find employment in the computer field.

MAINTENANCE FOREMAN

My daily work involves all forms of maintenance to keep a hydro- electric plant running.

It is essential to have mechanical skills as well as common sense to perform this job well.

I get satisfaction from my work because I am doing the job well.

My high school training in electronics and the skills and training I got while in the US Air Force helped prepare me for this occupation.

MAINTENANCE LOGISTICS SUPERVISOR

As a maintenance logistics supervisor, I spend a typical day scheduling work, discussing emergency situations involving machinery and vehicles, conferring with outside contractors, and reviewing maintenance work orders received. I am responsible for the upkeep of buildings, transportation, and grounds at an educational facility. I like the people where I work, the work itself, the advancement opportunities, and the variety of challenges that come up from day to day.

In my line of work you need a positive attitude and knowledge of all phases of building maintenance including such details as the structure and function of A/C and heating equipment, proper floor finishes, etc. Being adept and willing to streamline tasks is also important.

Formerly, I enjoyed my work as a construction superintendent, and I've had experience as a purchasing agent. I've also been a carpenter and cabinet maker as well as a factory clerk. Although I very much like the job I have now, I look forward to retirement and working in my own shop.

MAINTENANCE MACHINIST

For many years I have been a maintenance machinist. I repair and make new parts for machinery. I like the people I work with and for and the place I work. I particularly like getting equipment back into production as soon as possible. Sometimes the work is pretty greasy, though. I would like cleaner surroundings. Having no college education, I am lucky to be in this job. It helped to take technical courses in high school.

Being able to work within close quarters is a characteristic needed in this work. A person needs to be calm and not get excited under pressure. Also, no claustrophobia.

I have been a roofer, a house painter, and a small-scale farmer, but maintenance work is my favorite occupation.

I got into this type of work by mere chance. I enjoy life now and will enjoy retirement life when the time comes for me to retire.

MAINTENANCE MECHANIC

It's my job to keep the machinery and mechanical function of the aluminum plant in good running order. To do this, I make or repair all the mechanical equipment at the plant.

To perform this job it is necessary to have a wide variety of mechanical skills. Electrical skills are not as essential in my job.

The pay is what keeps me satisfied with my job. I also like my work, the people I work with, and I like the organization I work for.

I would be more satisfied if I had more shop work, but that is just a personal preference.

My work at a service station and as a wrecker operator provided some of the experience and training I needed to get this job. I graduated from high school but have no college education. It is not needed for success in this job.

MANAGEMENT ANALYST

My career started after graduating from college with a Bachelor of Science in Business Administration degree. I have held jobs as a stocks and bonds salesperson, an office manager, inventory manager and computer programmer. Due to my exposure to the work ethic and after passing entrance examinations, I became a management analyst.

It is my job to develop and implement procedures for office operations, e.g. accounting, purchasing, and technical work. I must innovate new procedures and document them so there is more efficient and effective work flow for different corporate departments.

To perform this work well, it is important to have expertise in the principles of business operations covering the fields of accounting, purchasing and planning, and management practices, plus a positive attitude that your efforts are going to produce the results you anticipate.

From my business experience, I see the need for more open lines of communication between upper and middle management personnel, to obtain a more cohesive movement in pursuit of set goals and objectives.

I like my kind of work very much, the people and organization I work for, the opportunity for advancement, and the people I work with. This is satisfying work for me because it affords me the opportunity to activate my creative and innovative capabilities.

MANAGEMENT CONSULTANT #1

As a management consultant, I provide guidance and make recommendations to work teams. During any week, I attend 2 to 3 meetings, am in the office 35 to 40 hours, and spend 5 to 10 hours studying.

I became interested in this occupation while in school for my B.A. in management. I was exposed to the writings and works of Edward Deming, the esteemed quality expert, and pursued finding a job where I could use what he taught.

The most important skills to have in this job are a very positive attitude, a vision for the future, and the ability to speak in public. My main satisfaction comes from setting goals for myself and organizations and seeing those goals achieved. Greater satisfaction could be attained if I could make more money in this field.

MANAGEMENT CONSULTANT #2

I have a degree in Business Administration and had jobs previously in traffic management and factory management.

I applied for a position with a different consulting firm and later switched to another firm that I found interested me more.

In my job, I work on improving methods, schedules, and program designs for firms that need help. A consultant troubleshoots any problem areas or manufacturing locations.

To do this kind of job well, you have to be a self-starter and have an analytical mind. You need to be systems-oriented and it helps if you are free to travel. An accounting background can be a plus in many consulting jobs.

The main satisfaction of a management consultant's work comes from making things happen. There's a definite sense of accomplishment if you can suggest improvements, and it's very nice if you also get recognition for a job well done.

MANAGEMENT CONSULTANT, LARGE COMPANIES

Typically my work as a manager and consultant involves 20% reading, 15% travel, 15% writing, 10% presentations, 20% talking to coworkers and 20% talking to clients. For my specific job as a solid waste consultant/manager, I analyze solid waste systems and problems, devise plans to solve them and prepare reports on the results of the analysis.

For this type of occupation it is important to have the ability to get along with a wide variety of people, make oral presentations, write well and analyze information mathematically.

I find this work satisfying since, after preparing a report and presenting the results, I receive favorable comments as to its quality and completeness.

If I could change anything about my occupation it would be to get paid more money and have less supervision and oversight of my day to day activities.

This occupation for me was actually chosen by accident. The company I was working for diversified into the field; I needed to find something to do during a downturn in defense activity. As a result, I went into solid waste activities.

Prior to this job, I was a college teacher and did defense work.

In the future I am looking forward to managing some sort of investment after I retire and sell my personal residence.

MANAGEMENT CONSULTANT, NUCLEAR POWER

I am a management consultant for nuclear power plants. I advise senior utility management on organization, staffing and operations. I have been doing this job for fifteen years.

I travel to nuclear plants to meet with vice presidents and senior managers of the plants to discuss staffing, organization, costs and operations. I spend one day reviewing work of others and one day marketing.

Interpersonal skills and the knowledge of power plant operations are important to perform well in this line of work.

The satisfactions that I get out of my job are improving things at the plants, being asked for advice and having people take it, being paid a considerable salary, and being in charge of my life and business. The only thing that I can think of that I don't like is having to figure out how to find more assistants.

I started working with submarines, got out of that due to family separation, went into consulting, then combined nuclear expertise with management consulting and started my own company.

Previous occupations that I have had are a nuclear submarine officer, college faculty, and engineering consultant. My future career plans are to keep my company successful as long as possible, retire early and teach at the college level.

MANAGEMENT, INDUSTRIAL ENGINEER

I discovered early in my life that I had a mechanical aptitude and thus I decided to pursue a career in engineering. In order to also accommodate my interest in capital equipment, I moved into an industrial engineering management position. Prior to this job, I earned my Bachelor of Science in Engineering degree and held a job in marketing and other engineering positions.

I am now responsible for managing people in the engineering department of the industrial manufacturing company for which I work. The other primary duty I perform is to coordinate user needs with company attributes. To accomplish this work, I travel 1 1/2 days a week, do compilations 1 1/2 days, and work on management duties 2 days a week.

Good communication skills and the ability to determine facts are vital attributes to have in order to perform well at this job.

I have liked my engineering career for 30+ years because of the kind of work I have been doing, the opportunities I have had for advancement, and the people I work with. This has indeed been a satisfying career for me because I can find job satisfaction in my accomplishments. I plan to stay in this profession, and to eventually become a consultant.

MANAGEMENT TRAINER & CONSULTANT

Working as a Management Trainer and Organization Development Consultant for ten years has proved to be very rewarding for me. I conduct training seminars for managers to learn more about the interpersonal skills required for their jobs. The training focuses primarily on interpersonal and motivation skills for managers in different areas, so I spend a lot of time traveling. The amount of time spent away from home can be a drawback if you prefer time with family as I do. When I am not involved in presenting a training seminar, I am usually designing other training programs and meeting with potential clients.

I really enjoy the flexibility and autonomy that this job provides as well as the personal satisfaction I derive from empowering others to be more effective in their work.

Management training requires confidence (with the realization that you could never be a real expert in this ever-changing field), some group facilitation skills, training skills, and the ability to work with many different people. All these qualities and skills combined with a good education (I have a Bachelor of Arts degree), can lead to success in this field.

Always interested in the field of training, after considering several options, I decided that adult learning in a corporate environment would be fun, and at times it is.

Previous employment as a high school teacher and as a business system analyst have proven to be valuable experience and very good preparation for my present job.

As a member of a consulting firm, I want to continue to grow with the firm and someday work as a partner of the firm.

MANAGER, ART SALES

I coach and direct managers for a fine arts handling company. Guiding the managers to perform profitably, and to sell properly to major prospects, describes my job. Some of my day is spent in administrative duties, but during the rest of the time I am responding to any one of many problems or I am selling or planning.

With a Bachelor of Arts degree in philosophy and a Master's in business administration (MBA), I've enjoyed previous work as a sales manager, director of training, and a professor in an MBA program. While I was giving a seminar once, I was asked by the president of a struggling company if I would help out. Now I enjoy being the general manager for this company.

To do this work well, you need strong communication skills. A person should be a logical thinker and, in my opinion, you should be well versed in philosophy. A great deal of stamina is needed too.

Seeing results through the efforts of others is very rewarding. The neighborhood where the company is located is most unsatisfactory and we need more capital in the company, but I do enjoy the clients we deal with. My plans are to continue as a manager and maybe one day teach, consult, or both.

MANAGER, AUTO TIRE COMPANY

I very much liked my earlier work in landscaping, but I'm enjoying the very good pay and benefits in my present job as uniformity manager at an auto tire company. I'd like my work more if all of my colleagues would carry their own weight. Because of seniority, some feel they do not have to produce.

As uniformity manager at an auto tire company, I study the way we build tires. I change any process which has a negative effect on the end product. My typical day is to select a problem tire, follow it through each stage of development, trying to figure out which particular process is harming the performance of that tire. Then I recommend changes in procedures or production so the tire will meet our standards.

Effectiveness as an uniformity manager requires good analytical skills and effective communication skills. Even though the job can be very frustrating, you need to maintain a very positive attitude.

I have a Bachelor of Science degree in Political Science. I'd like to pursue a Masters Degree in Human Resources and find employment in personnel work. However, I'll probably continue in my present job because of the pay and benefits, and I do like my work, especially if I could make a few changes.

MANAGER, CHEMICAL TECHNICAL STAFF

After graduating with a Bachelor of Science degree in chemical engineering and a Masters of Science, I began in this company as a chemist. Since there are opportunities for advancement here, I moved up to my present position as manager of the technical staff.

My work involves chemical research and design of products. Review and study of reports made by staff are part of my job. I regularly check the calendar for scheduled meetings. There are many project review meetings to attend. Monitoring and directing technical projects are also my responsibility. I plan for the next day's operations as well.

Knowledge of chemistry is a must in my field. You also should have strong organizational skills as well as the ability to make decisions. Very important is being able to listen to others without interrupting.

I am satisfied with everything about my work. Recognition of work well done is particularly rewarding. Having the respect of peers as well as management is valuable to me. I also like the good salary. My plans are to move up in the company to a senior position, retire early, and go into teaching.

MANAGER, CIVIL SERVICE OFFICE

I am a mid-level manager/program director of quality control for medical claims decisions in a large agency of the federal government. I've served in this capacity for 16 years. I enjoy being the manager, the person who makes the decisions and assumes the responsibility.

Starting as claims examiner, I grew into this position. Desire and youth required me to keep pushing myself toward higher positions. My Bachelor's degree in business administration helps.

For my work to be more enjoyable, several employees would have to leave. Time spent on issues other than work annoys me.

A skill needed for my job is knowing what motivates people to achieve. The capability to understand our program, its needs, and how it can be improved is essential. You must be perceptive to get enough facts to resolve conflicts in the office.

Over a year's time, I deal with the following matters. During the final quarter of most years I am busy planning and assigning department objectives for the next year. I am also pushing employees who haven't yet finished their assignments. During the first 6 or 7 months of each year, I watch objectives form, set dates for completion, implement necessary actions, and prepare program reports.

I am considering retirement and thinking of studying law, perhaps as a hobby. I'd like to earn a law degree, pass a law examination, be licensed, and litigate some issues that "bug" me.

MANAGER, COMMUNITY DEVELOPMENT

As a manager of a community development project, I am responsible for the social service grant programs for low income families and elderly citizens. For the last six years I have directed activities generated by a grant program for low income families by interviewing applicants for housing rehabilitation, arranging appraisals, approving contractors bills, and settling disputes.

Although a college degree is not essential to this position, some formal education beyond high school is necessary; you must be a good listener with good people skills, patience, good communication skills, and a sense of fairness.

Even though the approval procedures can be somewhat tedious, I enjoy my job. I like this kind of work as I believe I can really help people overcome obstacles and resolve problems that cause them to worry. I find that assisting low income families and elderly citizens can hold many personal rewards, as these are the people who really get bogged down by the bureaucracy and red tape; I know that I help them get through the red tape to receive the help that they genuinely deserve.

I have always been involved in management throughout my career; I have held such positions as a claims adjuster and a personnel and training manager.

I plan to continue my work and get involved in volunteer work once I reach the age of mandatory retirement.

MANAGER, COMPUTER SUPPORT SERVICE

I have had a diverse background. I started out as a teacher of English literature after graduating with a bachelors degree in education. I then left the teaching profession and worked as a technical representative, applicators engineer, and executive recruiter.

I found my current position through a client I placed while I was an executive recruiter.

As the National Dealer Support Manager for a company that manufactures and markets a specialty computer printer, I support liaison between factory/dealers and dealers/customers, do industry shows, give seminars, and train dealers. When I am in the office I handle the following duties: telephone contacts with dealer, end-users; identifying, qualifying, recruiting new dealers; and market analysis. I also spend a lot of time outside the office: setting-up, manning, and tearing down of the booth in industrial shows; giving seminars; and training dealers.

To perform well in my position, it is important to have the following skills and attitudes: listening, communicating, patience, letter writing, platform presentation skills, organization, prioritizing, time management, problem solving, and negotiation.

The drawback to this kind of work is the very long "entrepreneurial" hours. However, I particularly enjoy this kind of work, the people I work with, and the opportunity I have to "wear many hats." I find job satisfaction in training dealers to sell successfully, and in solving problems.

I plan to continue with this job to help drive my company to a mature, major market status. It is my intention to grow with the company as it grows.

MANAGER, CONSTRUCTION COMPANY

As the Management Coordinator, I am basically the key person in a medium size design/build remodeling company. My job involves business planning, sales, and business management. I oversee all aspects of the business from office staff to field work (construction personnel). I make decisions on scheduling budgets, payments, equipment, etc. I make sales calls, estimate projects, and make sales presentations. Reviewing potential new suppliers and subcontractors is also my responsibility. I advise the owner of strategic planning decisions. I also troubleshoot.

The skills which I consider important for performing this work well are: computer knowledge, typing, design, people skills, communication skills, management and motivational skills, and negotiation skills. Attitude is another important element in performing this work, and I think the following traits are important: flexibility, open mindedness, honesty, a desire to help others, a desire to make a profit, fairmindedness, and empathy.

I have moved up to this career position mainly through hard work and previous job experience. Previous jobs have been as owner of a motivational company, in real estate sales, and as project planner for a major developer. I was offered my current job because I was referred to the owner as someone who could help him with his business.

It is rewarding to produce projects that work--seeing what I design actually built. It is also satisfying building a successful business, and to continue to learn and grow. My career goal is be a certified kitchen and bath designer, and to be a partner in the company I presently work for.

MANAGER, CORPORATE SPECIAL EVENTS

The best way to describe my work day as an internal communications and special events manager is meetings, meetings, meetings--from 7:30 A.M. to 5:30 P.M. with very little desk time. The meetings are held to conceptualize and to develop detailed planning. Other duties included in my job for this large corporation are managing my staff, coordinating with others in my organization, reading articles, approving videos, generally supervising work, delegating projects, synthesizing ideas plus coming up with creative solutions, and dealing with political realities.

Having a positive, solution-oriented attitude is important to perform this job well. Interpersonal and managerial skills are also necessary. A communications and special events manager must have the ability to conceptualize and then to create and implement detailed plans. Selling ideas and directions is another important ability. Creativity plays a major role in the successful performance of this job.

I find job satisfaction from creating something that shows artistic/creative qualities and meets business needs. It satisfies me to work with a great group of people, break new paths, and the ability to positively impact lives of 10,000+ employees.

Changes in this occupation which I would welcome would be more money, a clearer career path and advancements. Less political realities (or more control over them) would be a good change too.

My occupation evolved from previous positions in marketing and public relations and as a systems and procedures analyst. My mentor, a senior executive, also was involved in my being selected. I chose to accept the job because I like to tackle "never done before" jobs, and I have natural communication abilities.

In the future, I hope to become a Senior Vice President of Corporate Communications.

MANAGER, DATA PROCESSING PROGRAM

I graduated with a Bachelor of Science degree and a Master's in chemistry. In using the computer as a research tool in chemistry, I found the field of computers and data processing much more rewarding. I left chemistry to discover, over the next 20 years, that working with computers made good use of my interest in problem-solving and my creativity.

Managing the staff of data-processing professionals and overseeing computer-related projects describes my job. I meet with staff individually or as a group to suggest or review solutions to our problems. Reviewing the progress of on-going projects is my responsibility along with meeting with clients, planning future projects, and designing networks. Finally, I analyze client requirements and propose solutions to meet these needs.

Working with computers requires good analytical skills and problem-solving abilities. Being able to communicate well, both in writing and speaking, are very important. Strong people skills, especially the ability to listen well, are also valuable. An attitude of service, i.e., "the customer is always right," is pretty much required. You also need to be a creative person to be in computer system design work.

Although I'd like to see more recognition financially for jobs well done, I do enjoy my work. I like seeing computer users more productive because of the computer systems we develop. Watching a design become reality and observing employees grow and mature in their professional skills are very rewarding to me. One day, I'd like to build a department unrivaled in excellence in medical computer applications.

MANAGER, ELECTRIC UTILITY

There is nothing at all I have disliked about being the manager of an electrical utility. After graduation from engineering school with a Bachelor of Science in electrical engineering, I applied for my position, which I have been in for many years.

What I have enjoyed most about my work are the happy employees and satisfied customers. I like the fact there have been opportunities for advancement as well. My coworkers, my supervisors, and the electrical company itself are all part of my job satisfaction.

As the manager, I direct all of the operations needed to provide electrical service to new customers. I also see that a good level of service to existing customers is maintained.

For this work you need the ability to lead a "team of professional people." You must have the necessary technical knowledge for working with an electric company as well as a background in engineering. Finally, you should have good human relations skills to work well with customers and employees.

MANAGER, ELECTRONIC REPAIR COMPANY

As a manager of an electronic repair facility, I supervise the operation of twenty-four technicians, review various job assignments, track job progress, approve fund expenditures, and strive to maintain good communications with my employees.

The role of a manager requires good analytical skills and logical thought processes, the ability to express yourself verbally and in written communication, and the ability to maintain an attitude of fairness with all employees.

I enjoy my work very much, especially when I have the opportunity to share the joy of a job well done with my employees.

In my present position as the boss, there is not much of an opportunity to advance my career, but I would really like to be able to eliminate the bureaucratic nonsense that I believe interferes with managing the personnel and monetary aspects of my job.

I enlisted in the military after completing high school. During my military service,

I attended electronics school; my present job was, in my opinion, the next logical step in my career.

I have been working with electronics for forty years now and look forward to retirement.

MANAGER, ENVIRONMENTAL SERVICE COMPANY

My job as a manager of environmental services is to provide assistance in all environmental areas of the pulp-and-paper industry. I had retired early from my work as a chemist and, with a Ph.D., I wanted a few more years of interesting, personally rewarding work with acceptable pay and without supervision. Fortunately for me, I found this job in management.

It is very satisfying work. Helping make industrial plants meet environmental regulations and being thanked for doing it is highly rewarding. There's less interaction among people than I would like, but I enjoy the people I do get to work with, the management, and what I do. One day I'll retire and do a little consulting.

My work involves some time in my office reviewing the mail and returning phone calls. I check to see if there are any new government regulations I should know about. Responding to state and federal environmental agencies regarding permits, applications, compliance orders and the like is part of my duties. I am responsible for 30 plants, providing them with guidance in meeting environmental standards. Writing reports on the results of environmental audits follows up a trip to one of my plants.

It takes being highly observant as well as having technical competence to do my job. You also have to have persistence and patience. In this job, you must have a lot of common sense to maintain a balance between environmental needs and industry's requirements. A desire to be helpful is useful too.

MANAGER, FIELD DISTRIBUTION

I've worked as a fuel oil field distribution manager for 3 states over a period of 8 years. I particularly enjoy the traveling required, and I enjoy motivating people.

In my case, I have only a high school education so I worked up to this job. Over the years, I have been a farmer, carpenter, and store clerk. With this company I started as a driver delivering fuel oil, then dispatcher, then assistant manager, and eventually manager in one location. From that, I moved up to department manager, overseeing product supplies and delivery in three states involving 200-300 employees.

In my job, I supervise schedules for both receipt and disbursement of products. Part of my duties are to review personnel performance and ratings of people to determine monetary rewards and possible promotions.

Skills needed for my kind of job are knowledge of what is required for the job. You should have the ability to motivate people as well.

MANAGER, FINANCE DEPARTMENT #1

I started as office manager of a small firm and, as the company grew, I grew into my position. Although I have only a high school degree, I have complete responsibility for all bookkeeping functions: accounts payable, accounts receivable, payroll, general ledgers. I generate financial statements based on these functions, and I also handle benefits administration for employees.

You must have a knowledge of accounting principles, bookkeeping, computer application skills and especially organizational skills to do this kind of job well.

I personally like having some control over the financial success of the company and the authority to approve or disapprove financial transactions. I have a certain status and confidence in my own ability.

Although the kind of work I do is fulfilling, I do not especially like the person or company I work for. It would be more satisfying if my superior were more competent and if I had even more decision-making responsibilities and an equal pay structure with fellow male employees.

Ultimately I hope to become a Certified Public Accountant (CPA).

MANAGER, FINANCE DEPARTMENT #2

As the manager of the finance department of a small company, I supervise the accounting aspects of the business along with the cash flow. Handling the many parts of financial controls, the budget, and check processing is my responsibility. I am also in charge of the data processing, personnel, and purchasing in a manufacturing facility.

Using common sense in your actions as well as being practical is important in my work. You need a positive attitude about your job and must realize that what you do affects the growth and profitability of the company. The ability to be fair in the decisions that must be made is essential. The appropriate training is also necessary; I have a Bachelor of Arts degree in math along with a Masters in Business Administration.

It is very satisfying to me being able to train and help fellow workers do their jobs a little bit better every day. Even though there's little opportunity for advancement, I enjoy my work. The daily variety in the job and the challenges are all very rewarding to me. My goal is to stay with this company and continue to improve my performance.

MANAGER, FOOD SERVICE

My choice of a career in food service management was made to a large degree because I enjoy giving parties. I earned a Bachelor of Science in Hotel Administration and have now worked in the field for years.

In my current position as food service manager, I perform administrative and supervisory work for 300 school and college food services. Part of this work includes writing operating procedures and revising corporate regulations. I make visits to the food service units and consult with managers about methods to improve their products, service, efficiency, and, therefore, their profits.

My advice for success in this kind of work is to listen well and understand what motivates individuals in order to attain the best results from them.

There are some things which I would like to see changed in food service. I would like to see a shortening of the extraordinarily long working hours. I also feel that the level of skill of the workers should be raised while increasing their benefits accordingly. My final frustration with this occupation is in dealing with the poor operating procedures.

Because there are so many frustrations and drawbacks in work in the food service industry, it leaves me with much opportunity to improve service and profits. I like the challenge, and am continually striving to make improvements. I find job satisfaction when services are well delivered, food is good, and the unit contributes its share, or more, to corporate profit. I also feel rewarded when customers compliment the results of our work.

MANAGER, GOLF PRO SHOP

Since my business is seasonal, my jobs vary with the season. In the summer we are open 12 hours a day and sometimes 7 days a week. In the spring, most of the time I am inventorying new merchandise. In the summer, I am selling; in fall, I am buying; and in winter we go away for 2 months.

It is important to care about people, understand why people buy and to have good taste to perform this job well. I enjoy people. They come to me for their leisure time, and I help make it enjoyable. I like dressing people to make them look good. I like making a "deal" with an outlet or a company in which they are happy and I make a good profit.

Changes I would like to see in the future would be to have a larger pro-shop and office and better club management.

I got into this job primarily because my husband is a golf pro. The golf business is very seasonal and it is difficult to match time off with other occupations. When he took his current job, we moved and I decided to work with him so we could have similar schedules. I found I enjoyed selling.

Prior to my pro-shop work, I have been a director of religious education, supervisor of a dental clinic, a dental assistant, a bank bookkeeper and a full-time mother.

MANAGER, GOVERNMENT CONTRACTING OFFICE

The job of a government contracting officer requires a number of skills: oral and written communication, listening, and analytical ability. The ability to make independent decisions within the boundaries of laws and regulations is also crucial as is attentiveness to detail. Analyzing processes and procedures, mediating, negotiating, and persuading are all required functions for this work.

Most of my personal work time is spent in meetings or in discussions for planning strategies for up-coming requirements. I receive file documentation from subordinates, handle personnel actions, conduct in-house training, and receive revisions to regulations affecting my division's work. I am responsible for ensuring that my agency's property purchases are conducted in accordance with about 4,000 federal laws. This is a big job considering that my agency is located in 4 states and has approximately 80 field stations.

Finding solutions to difficult problems, such as those relating to schedules and money, is my greatest satisfaction. I enjoy training and developing personnel under my supervision. It also pleases me to act as a team player in supporting the agency mission. What I love about my work is that it is never boring; there are constant changes and challenges.

My job would be far more pleasant if the government contract rules were not so complex and specialized. The public's perception of wasteful spending is not warranted. The processes and procedures required by Congress often produce data which no one uses.

My career aspirations are to improve the quality and timeliness of services provided to our customers while fostering a work environment that attracts the best talent available. I expect to retire from my current position in 5 - 7 years, which is early retirement, but that does not mean that I don't enjoy this work.

MANAGER, GRAPHIC DESIGN DEPARTMENT

My career has been in business management for the last 24 years. My educational background, which prepared me for this type of work, includes a Bachelor of Arts and Master of Arts in Economics. I have held the position of economist with three companies, and now I am a manager of computer operations and graphic design. I was exposed to this position while going through rotational assignments in a management intern program.

As the manager of computer operations and graphic design, I provide management direction to staff, lead a variety of special assignments, and review staff work. On a typical day, I spend four hours in meetings - with my boss, my subordinates, and regular technical meetings on special assignments. Other regular duties include: reading and dealing with mail/paperwork; developing reports; and leading task forces.

My advice for those of you interested in pursuing a career in business management is to be a team player, and support everything your bosses do (at least outwardly). In making decisions and problem solving, you must be willing to negotiate and compromise to win. Understand the in-house political process. Also, as a manager, you must be able to direct and coordinate the work of others.

From my years of experience in the business community, I have observed several problem areas. I would like to initiate several changes in order to make my work more satisfying: have more people sensitive to senior managers, cut out turf battle, enact clear consistent assignments, and be consistent with rules so they are not continually changing.

Although my work has its points of frustration, I basically like the kind of work I do. I like the organization I work for and the people with whom I work. There are several aspects of this occupation that are rewarding: developing people and watching them move up, getting work done well and on schedule, leading new efforts, and the pay received for this job.

MANAGER, HOME-BUILDING COMPANY

My work background is somewhat diverse. Before ending up in a management position for a home building and land development company, I worked in an office supply store and then managed a college bookstore. This was followed by a job as office manager of a manufacturing facility. Academically, I have earned a Bachelor of Arts in Political Science and Economics degree.

As a manager with a home building company, I work with land planners, engineers, and subcontractors, plus various governmental agencies. My typical activities include: meeting with land planners about plans for a new subdivision; reviewing water, sewer, paving, etc., plans with engineers; meeting with municipal staff on zoning problems; calling in subcontractors to review plans for bidding.

It is important to have the following skills and attitudes in order to perform this work well: mathematical ability; imagination to transform two dimensional paper to three dimension reality; diplomacy; and ability to communicate both verbally and in writing.

I enjoy the kind of work I do, except for fighting government bureaucracy.

I find job satisfaction in seeing subordinates grow within their job. The reward from this work is seeing a project reach a successful conclusion.

MANAGER, HOTEL

I like very much being a hotel manager, and I have been one for 17 years. It is my responsibility for the overall operation of a full service hotel including food and beverage service. On a daily basis, I visit all parts/departments within the hotel to ensure policies are adhered to. I also regularly visit with guests.

It's most important to have the ability to get along with varied types of personnel.

My job satisfaction comes from satisfying people. I like the people I work with, the opportunity for advancement, the kind of work I do, and the organization and people I work for. There is nothing I would change about this occupation.

I retired from the military after 20 years (the United States Navy for nine years and the USAF for eleven years) and then attended college to earn my BS in Hotel/Restaurant Management. While in the service I had worked in NCO clubs and restaurants.

I plan to remain at my current position, because I enjoy it very much; I do not plan to move on to other jobs.

MANAGER, INFORMATION SYSTEMS

I am an information systems manager for a clinical laboratory. It is my job, which I've been doing for 5 years, to manage a small mainframe computer in the laboratory of a medical center.

The wonderful part about my job is there are no "typical" days. I may handle the planning and implementation for a large computer information project one day. Another day there are small, yet immediate, problems to be corrected as they occur.

You should have a background in clinical laboratory work to do my job. You need to know all the aspects of the medical business you are computerizing. An even temper is important in this work and a sense of humor is essential.

I worked for 15 years as a laboratory technician. Before, during, and after that period, I earned a Bachelor of Arts degree in mathematics and a Masters of Science in biology. I also have an advanced degree in hospital administration. I became interested in computers and new technologies and joined a professional group who were computerizing the lab.

Even though there is little opportunity for advancement here, the chance to keep learning and working in a challenging environment is fulfilling for me. There's a constant challenge to meet the needs of the computer users as they access information. I also enjoy the people I work with and the administration. One day I'd like to go into business for myself installing laboratory computer systems.

MANAGER, INSURANCE DEPARTMENT

As the risk manager for property-liability insurance, I work for a holding company that has about 100 different companies with 22,000 employees, 1800 offices, and operates in 50 states. My job is to buy and administer all the property-casualty insurance needed to protect the assets of the company. There is no set routine on a day by day basis, but the work volume keeps me busy all the time. Purchase of insurance and allocation of costs and claim handling are the primary functions of the job.

In order to perform this kind of work well, it is important to have a knowledge of many different types of insurance. Knowledge of my company and its needs, the ability to communicate both verbally and in writing, and the ability to work with insurance brokers, insurance companies, lawyers, and people within my company, are all necessary qualities for this job.

I was given the opportunity to advance into this position because of my property--casualty background. Prior to this job, I have been a regional vice president for a major property-casualty company, a vice president of shareholder's relations, and a charitable contributions administrator.

There really isn't anything I dislike about my work. I like the organization I work for, and the people with whom I work. I like the challenge of continually looking for better ways to be more effective and more efficient. I have job satisfaction because I find that my experience and ability have given me sole responsibility for the entire insurance program for which premium dollars have been in the area of $15 million annually.

MANAGER, INTERNAL AUDITING

As manager of internal auditing for an $8 billion manufacturing company, I oversee the corporate auditing program. I supervise the staff of 40+ auditors who are assigned to audit more than 100 company locations. This includes reviewing audit reports and discussing reports with management.

To perform this type of job well, you need accounting and operational experience, plus a college education, including a strong emphasis on reading, writing, and speaking the English language.

My background includes earning a Master of Business Administration degree, and working as an accountant and comptroller. After several years experience in accounting positions, the company management moved me into internal auditing. I enjoyed the work and progressed in it satisfactorily to my present position.

Auditing has been satisfying work for me for the past 22 years because I find this work gives me a sense of accomplishment by enhancing the operational and financial effectiveness of my company.

MANAGER, MANPOWER PLANNING

I have held a number of positions during the course of my career life and, now that I am nearing retirement, I was selected to be a manpower planning manager because of the knowledge and experience I have gained through these various jobs. I have been a high school teacher, advertising writer and manager, sales manager, and sales operation development manager.

In my position as manpower planning manager, I forecast future manpower needs (numbers and skills), and hire and train persons to fill the forecast. This includes organizing studies to be conducted and assigning personnel to carry out the studies. Once the studies are complete, I review them and make suggestions for the next course of action, including setting up training courses. I report to a Board on the programs and needs.

The skills and attitudes which I consider important to perform this kind of work are organizational, analytical, and communication. I would consider building up working relations with experts in the field in other countries to be another asset for this work.

I like almost all aspects of this work.

I find job satisfaction from the development and growth of people with whom I have worked.

MANAGER, MARKETING COMPANY

In my work as a manager for a marketing company, there's total satisfaction when all the representatives have completed their work on time. It is even more satisfying when the main office acknowledges this accomplishment. The aspects of my work that I don't like are the little opportunity for advancement and the inadequate pay.

Between graduating high school and assuming my current position, I was an employment agency counselor, a marketing interviewer, and an executive secretary. I hope to stay with my present job for a while.

My duties are to interview, hire, and train new representatives. Coordinating all the work for a two-state area keeps me busy. I also perform cost and time evaluations on prospective jobs in the field. I make sure that all work is completed on time and ensure that all new work has been received by the reps.

A good manager is self-disciplined, patient, and persistent. Enthusiasm along with a positive attitude are important. Being diplomatic is a must.

MANAGER, MARKETING DIVISION

Being a marketing manager for eleven years has entailed directing a large graphics dept and doing business development and P.R. In addition, I draft major print proposals for new work and supervise a staff of 10.

In the course of a typical day, which starts by being at the office at 7:15, I first plan the day, then I may go through mail, spend one hour scrutinizing invoices, discuss with two employees about how to finalize a project, have meetings, discuss problems, go over work "in house" and work to come. Also on my regular schedule are meetings with a senior vice-president to analyze past projects, calling vendors, finding lost projects, reassuring another vice-president that she will get my full attention, dealing with current projects, plans, and orders, and keeping track of my people.

Attitude is always critical. Be prepared to do everything and not complain. Know your math and how to write good letters. Get a good education and keep learning all your life.

I find job satisfaction from challenges and opportunities to solve problems creatively, working where I can use what I know and the challenges to learn more.

I wish my company had the financial resources to update computers, raise salaries and hire more interns.

I have had many jobs starting at 19 with long hours and lots of work. I received a bachelors degree in fine arts and math and I also have an M.B.A. Previous occupations have been art director, sales manager and food publicity and P.R. My career aspiration is to become the vice-president of the Paris office.

MANAGER, PAROLE OFFICE

In a field with new opportunities for women, I plan to remain with the Department of Corrections for a while. As a district manager in a probation and parole office, I manage an office of 10 people whose positions include supervisors, probation officers, and clerical workers.

Before this position, I had always worked with people who were victims of crimes. Because I wanted to change to working with the offenders, I transferred to the Department of Corrections from the Department of Social Services in Human Services. A child protection worker for 15 years previously, I investigated child abuse or neglect and worked with these children. Someday, I would like to work inside the jails.

There's never a dull moment in this work! My day consists of conducting checks on offenders placed on probation or paroled. We also have the authority to arrest offenders under certain conditions. With the court work involved, writing violations, preparing pre-sentence reports, making recommendations, and testifying, we stay busy.

It's exciting work yet sometimes frustrating. There's not enough money to hire adequate staff to reduce the heavy caseloads. Further, since we are union represented, I have to spend a great deal of time with personnel grievance issues. We also need higher salaries for our staff.

Very satisfying is seeing offenders straighten out their lives; many come back months later just to tell you they're okay. I like working to change the system from incarceration solutions to treatment. There's also a lot of independence in this job.

Strong communication, good listening, and competent decision-making skills are needed in this work. Being able to interact with the public, to be non-judgmental toward offenders, and to treat everyone with respect are all vital. You need to be committed to the belief that people can change.

MANAGER, PERSONNEL DEPARTMENT

As a personnel manager for a major food processing company, my work schedule includes screening and recommending job applicants, setting up orientation and training classes (also adult education courses), records (attendance and absenteeism, exit interviews, job postings), disciplinary problems, policy matters, salary schedules and adjustments, regular visits to all departments, and setting of department objectives and long-range goals.

To perform these tasks well it is important to have a deep interest in the individual employee, enthusiasm, innovative approaches, ability to appreciate and enjoy working relationships, and patience and a bent for problem-solving. Find a need, which is easy--and fill it, which is more difficult.

I like being able to establish programs and practices which contribute to the efficiency and cooperation of all departments. Establishing a new word processing system was interesting and rewarding. I enjoy encouraging a cheerful working atmosphere.

I would like to continue to see more women in responsible positions and to eliminate the resentment that occasionally surfaces from being the only woman on an executive committee.

I started with the company as a clerk/typist through the recommendation of a friend. Prior to that I worked in a welcome-wagon enterprise, was a courthouse clerk, and a secretary to an attorney. I do not have a college degree.

In retirement I plan to assist with local schools and businesses as requested and to pursue the writing I have never taken the time to fully pursue.

MANAGER, PLANNING OFFICE

Supervising writers and automation specialists who develop contingency plans, programs, and procedures describes my job as personnel management specialist. I enjoy my work and receive particular satisfaction from developing a plan or program and then seeing it through to completion. I am interested in a developmental program which allows personnel to become specialists in their field by working at other major headquarters, the objective being to utilize personnel to their full potential (but not beyond it).

Typically, I attend meetings on program design and on administrative work. I read at least 100 documents each week and make assignments. I review the work of senior project officers. My responsibilities include checking electronic mail entries, scheduling work, approving personnel action requests, discussing on-going projects with colleagues in other cities, and monthly travel to conferences.

In the military, I developed the skills needed for this job. My college degrees are helpful but not essential. After I left the service, I applied for a position in civil service and was selected. Some skills needed in my work are reading and writing, computers (word processing and database), oral presentation, and supervisory ability. The flexibility to compromise on issues to develop a working solution to a wide variety of issues is very important. Being able to cope with occupational stress is equally crucial.

My plans are to retire eventually and become a handyman for minor home repairs.

MANAGER, REHABILITATION HOMES PROGRAM

I love my job--the challenge to help the poor help themselves. As program manager for 5 state programs funded by the state or federal government, I am involved with remodeling homes for energy efficiency and reconstruction or remodeling of older homes for low income persons. I interview clients from a 4 county area of 17,000 square miles which includes some Indian reservations. Some of my activities include: interviewing clients; verifying income; writing many memos; inputting clients into computer; reporting to state agency; interviewing contractors; handling bids and proposals for homes to be rehabilitated; negotiating contracts; field visits to monitor work, purchasing material for homes; supervising and scheduling my crew persons; attending at least 2 meetings a week; training office workers on a state program every 6 months. Most of the year, I do the secretarial and receptionist work myself because my program can't afford additional staff.

Good organizational skills are essential for this work. Basically, you have to be a workaholic. I usually work 12-14 hours per day. Some of my travels are to the 4 corners of my area, about 5 1/2 hours from home. Good computer programs and skills are also essential. Good writing ability is important because of the volume of correspondence that must be written. A general happy go lucky attitude is helpful too.

My educational background includes a Bachelor of Science degree. Included in my varied list of previous occupational experiences have been: accountant for a drug company, purchasing agent for an open pit and underground coal mine, personnel manager for the coal mine; and raising thoroughbred horses and racing them. I accidentally got into this career after our mines closed down and I was working for a government agency. Because of my performance record on another project, I was asked to take over this rehab program.

Satisfaction is found in helping an elderly person finally have a warm home, new windows, doors, new roof, siding, and a new furnace; a young family finally being able to help themselves; or the handicapped person able to open his own door and window. This job is a very self- fulfilling and satisfying occupation because of the people contact.

MANAGER, REINSURANCE

There is no typical day in the life of any reinsurance manager I know. (Reinsurance means the sharing of risk and expensive liability by two or more insurance companies.)

Resolving disputes or agreeing to financial settlements with organizations with which our company does, or did, business takes some of the day. Preparation of analyses for management review or for outside related parties, i.e., legal counsel, actuaries, or auditors is also part of my work.

I am happy when I'm able to resolve problems--legal, personal, and communication. Resolving these problems leaves one with a great sense of achievement. In the nine years I've been in this business, I have become very involved in legal disputes, due to the unwillingness of others to do so. I would prefer to be more involved in the financial aspects of the company.

Although I've gained experience in other work areas such as accounting, I'm pleased with my current career, the opportunities for advancement, and the company itself. Flexibility is required to efficiently and effectively handle the changes, such as schedule alterations, which occur in this job. People skills are needed to deal with diverse groups of humanity. I have a Bachelor of Business degree with a major in finance. One day, I'd like to be president of my own insurance business.

MANAGER, REPERTORY COMPANY

Knowing that the work we do makes a difference in our community makes my job as manager of a summer theater repertory company worthwhile. In addition to that, I am convinced that the arts should have an important place in the experiences of the public. I've been a bartender, waiter, and have worked in construction and landscaping, but I enjoy the career I am following now in the theater far more than any of those other jobs.

If I could start over, I'd choose my career in theater again. My degree is a Bachelor of Arts in theater and my plans are to stay with this company and be a part of its success.

My duties are to assist in casting for plays after we have selected the shows for the season. It is my responsibility to look after the daily office administration of the company and keep everything organized. There are no typical days, which is what makes this job interesting. While the details of each season's work change, the main organizational features do not.

To do my job well you need a great sense of humor. You need to be able to listen well, along with being willing to learn. The ability to work with different people with varied levels of experience is very important. Finally, you need to be able to make your own job fun and interesting.

The only thing I don't like about my job is the lack of opportunity for advancement. However, seeing everything about a production come together, knowing that it all started with just an idea, is satisfying to me. I'd like to be paid more, but cash isn't everything.

MANAGER, SOIL TESTING LABORATORY

While working in a lab as an undergraduate, I became fascinated with orchestrating all phases of the operation so that it produced "results" that made everyone else's work easier. I was considering a career as a professor. I now know I would have been a mediocre professor, but I'm a heck of a laboratory manager!

As the manager of a soil testing laboratory at a land grant institution, I oversee all aspects of the laboratory--budgeting, personnel, analysis, etc. My typical duties include running analyses, making recommendations to growers, instructing students in analytical techniques, working on various research projects, managing funding, and interacting with personnel on projects or planning their schedules.

To perform this kind of work well, it is important to have: patience, a math aptitude, and a strong stubborn streak when it comes to doing things right.

I find satisfaction from this kind of work from producing results which can be used by others to produce crops, or to write research papers. A job well done is the satisfaction. I am currently working on my doctorate, but the job will be the same. The Ph.D. is for validity in an academic setting, not a requirement of the position.

MANAGER, TECHNICAL TRAINING

As a manager in a technical training department, I supervise and schedule training for our customers who are employed by the commercial airlines. We teach these employees to maintain or repair the environmental control systems, auxiliary power units, and other components on commercial aircraft. In general, my work requires me to write reports, plan the training, give presentations, and supervise people.

The instructors spend their time presenting training, revising information, or developing new materials. Technical training managers must be able to communicate well with strong oral and written communication skills. You must be able to work well with different types of people and you must have a level of technical expertise. My instructors are subject matter experts who can teach their skills to other employees.

Job satisfaction for me is finding new and creative ways to meet customer demand without an adequate budget. I would like my work more if senior management would manage properly.

I have an Associate's, a Bachelor's Degree, and a Master's Degree in Education. Despite having three college degrees and an excellent work record, I may lose my job in the next round of corporate "downsizing." Career aspirations or plans are on hold while I fight to stay employed at all. I like this work and I will stay with it in this company or some other.

MANAGER, TELEPHONE COMPANY

Manager of telephone operations performance describes my present position at headquarters. I currently supervise 13 management/clerical positions covering 10 states. I review last month's and year-to-date performance for each operation. The job is to analyze internal performance and customer perceptions of quality of service by this telephone company. To do that, I establish standards and then measure and analyze performance results of all operation functions (e.g. operators, repair, billing, etc). Also, I review customer opinion surveys to determine areas needing improvement. Reviewing customer opinion surveys along with previous performance records makes it possible for me to develop a presentation for bettering performance, weaving together the internal and the external results.

The skills needed in my job are broad and are strongly analytical in nature. Adeptness in measurement techniques is vital. Computer and writing skills are also needed. Such skills are required to understand the operational process that is being measured, to develop measures that will capture (measure) performance, and to understand the analytical tools to determine if changes in performance are "statistically significant" or just chance occurrences. In addition, analytical skills are necessary to model the potential change in performance if certain inputs are changed. Lastly, one needs the necessary analytical skills to relate internal performance to external perceptions.

Developing an objective view of the performance based upon a review of results and predicting outcomes is the most satisfying portion of the job. I am paid well for my work. I've also enjoyed all the travel I've had in this job. Occasionally, I've had to educate senior management as to the significance of a change, whether to make it or not, and that is the key. I dislike the stress in getting results together on a monthly basis, but that goes with the job. I chose my current occupation because I wanted to (1) work in a company located in suburbia rather than in the central city, (2) have stability in the chosen industry, and (3) be in a position that would enhance my broad understanding of the telecommunications industry.

MANAGER, TRAVEL SERVICES COMPANY

It was by pure chance that I got into this occupation in the travel industry. Prior to working for this company, I attended college for 2 years, and worked as an office manager and secretary. My work for the travel company started 18 years ago and I have held my present position as Regional Manager for the last 4 years.

The company provides services for European travel products. It is my job to plan budget seminars, develop sales and marketing plans, conduct training sessions, seminars and presentations, and to supervise the regional sales staff. 90% of my work involves making public contact via telephone, and face to face sales calls and presentations. The remaining 10% of my time is spent in planning, supervision and inter-office contact.

The skills and attitudes which I consider important to perform my kind of work well are: interactive people skills, credibility, honesty, a true caring attitude for customers, good listening skills, the ability to make good and quick decisions, and public speaking ability.

I like the kind of work I do, and the people I work with, but, I could use more staff, more room, and more money. There is also some worry now about my job because of the pressure and uncertainty of the travel industry at this time. However, I find satisfaction from my work in seeing regional sales increase due to personal plans and marketing strategies. I also feel a sense of value to my national headquarters because of my input. Positive responses of our customers is also rewarding.

MANUFACTURER & INVENTOR

As an inventor and manufacturer of tension test machines, I enjoy solving problems for people. I got into this work when I saw a niche and decided to fill it.

In the design phase, I draw or review prints that lead to production. We manufacture these test machines that assess tension in equipment. In the sales phase, I follow up by telephone any and all sales leads and coordinate the sales orders. I've also had jobs in industrial sales and construction. I have a Bachelor of Science degree in business administration.

To do this work, you need an inquiring mind with the desire and willingness to find an answer. You should be a persistent and determined person. Being self-motivated is also important as is keeping an open mind to things.

There's opportunity for advancement here. What I don't like is when people don't do their jobs. I'd like more sales orders to relieve the cash flow problems; that would lessen the stress. Even so, I'd choose this work again.

MANUFACTURER & SALESMAN

After graduating from college with a Bachelor of Arts in accounting, I worked with a CPA firm. I decided "the grass looked greener" in sales for a wood box manufacturing company. I also knew about the company, having done their accounting work while still working for the CPA firm. After working in sales for the company for several years, I decided that the real money was in having my own manufacturing business. Having my own wood shipping container manufacturing company and doing the sales, accounting, and managing has been a satisfying experience for me.

My routine duties include: selling to customers, designing or redesigning the product, preparing specifications for manufacturing and supervising manufacturing.

Besides the more technical accounting skills, I consider a sense of humor and common sense to be of utmost importance in running a successful manufacturing operation.

This work is satisfying, because I enjoy getting the job done with satisfied customers.

MANUFACTURER'S REPRESENTATIVE #1

I have held various positions throughout my career and have somewhat enjoyed moving to different companies to add variety and diversity to my life. Prior to my job as a manufacturer's rep., I have been a buyer for a mail order house, a sales manager and president of a small manufacturing firm, and the executive vice president of a national trade association.

As a manufacturer's rep. and co-owner of a firm in the home furnishings field, I sell necessary component materials to special manufacturers in this field. I am on the road selling about 30% of the time, and in the office 70% . My office time includes phone selling and the administrative work of the company.

My advice for success in this kind of work is:
1. Never promise to do something and not do it--be dependable.
2. Enjoy helping a customer solve his problems.
3. Don't let work totally dominate your life.
4. But WORK.
5. Be careful with personal habits and health.
I like almost every aspect of my work, and find satisfaction from earning enough

to live a modestly comfortable life; helping customers; people contact (most of the time!); and most aspects of travel, especially since it is not constant.

MANUFACTURER'S REPRESENTATIVE #2

Working with commercial building materials, I am employed as a manufacturers sales representative. I bid on commercial building projects for sales commissions. I research and follow up on construction news reports in my territory to see if my products are incorporated into the particular project. If so, I purchase plans and specifications. I get those plans and specifications to manufacturers for pricing, and then try to sell the products to the general contractor who is awarded the project.

In addition to an Associate's degree, office organizational skills, aggressiveness, speech articulation, interpersonal skills, and a professional attitude are required for this job.

Although there is generally a lack of opportunity for advancement within this field, I really like my job. This kind of work is very interesting to me, although I have often experienced a lack of funds. This position affords me the opportunity to work for myself, and that gives me a tremendous sense of accomplishment on a personal level; I like being my own boss.

I was drawn to this kind of work in an attempt to follow in my father's footsteps. He worked for thirty-five years for a large company. The main difference between the work that he did and the work that I do is that I work for myself.

I held several other positions in unrelated fields and I did not find real job satisfaction until I decided to work in the same kind of work that my father was in.

I intend to continue in this type of work as long as I can make a living and give to my family all the things I had when I lived with my parents.

MANUFACTURER'S REPRESENTATIVE #3

My career as a manufacturers' representative is very satisfying in that people trust me enough to buy from me. In my work, I make sales and service calls on distributors, retail dealers and growers. Making the sale is most rewarding. I really like being independent, which includes not going to an office every day.

To do this work well, you need good communication skills and the ability to listen well. Enjoying being around people having a "sales" attitude, and the desire to help people are all part of being successful in this field. You need to be positive and to be honest. Being willing and able to follow through on your commitments is essential.

With an agricultural background and a Bachelor of Science degree in animal science, I was previously in a successful retail career in agronomy sales. After being noticed by manufacturers' reps, I interviewed with many major manufacturers. I've been a manufacturers' rep for agricultural chemicals for eight years now.

My usual day is to spend half an hour in the morning making phone calls and checking internal messages. During the rest of the day, I make scheduled and unscheduled visits on customers, positioning company products and answering product inquiries. I spend a small part of the week, perhaps half a day, in my home office doing job-related administrative work. This includes three monthly reports, program administration, and preparation for meetings.

MANUFACTURING ENGINEER

Working as a manufacturing engineer for five years, I study engineering blueprints for new product development and verify hardware designs to ensure manufacturability for release to manufacturing sites.

In addition to a Bachelor's degree in Business Management, my job requires blueprint reading skills, knowledge of CAD/CAM technology, personal computer skills, and an open attitude toward the seemingly impossible tasks at hand.

I like my job; this kind of work is very interesting to me and I believe there are many opportunities for career advancement in this field. I especially enjoy seeing new products complete the manufacturing cycle, which starts with conception of an idea and continues through its manufacture.

Although I have held several other positions within my career, I never felt challenged until I entered into this line of work.

I would like to do something with customer relations and engineering. I plan to start up my own business some day in precision sheet metal fabrication to support metal product needs in markets such as electronics and medical equipment.

MANUFACTURING FOREMAN

I started as an assistant foreman and learned as much as possible about my area of work, which gave me the opportunity to get promoted to manufacturing foreman. As such, I supervise operators and troubleshoot when problems occur on the line in the manufacturing of rigid computer discs. My typical daily schedule includes 2 hours of paperwork from the previous shift and 1 hour at different times for taking audits of a water purification system and pumps and filters. At all times my priority is keeping the 17 machines in my area running well. I trouble shoot problems with the machines and fix them if possible. I am responsible for 13 people working for me.

I consider written and oral communication and mechanical skills to be important in order to perform this kind of work well.

Except for the lack of opportunity for advancement in this job, I like all other aspects of my work.

The pay is excellent and I enjoy the challenges I encounter and the good relationship I have with fellow employees.

MANUFACTURING, OPERATIONS MANAGER

For the past thirty years, I have worked with satisfaction as a Manufacturing/Operations Manager. I plan, direct, and manage the efforts of production workers and staff at my company. I plan workloads for my work force and evaluate performance on a regular basis; I direct the efforts of the management staff and evaluate their day-to-day performance; and I direct special projects and lay the ground work for future projects.

I graduated from college with an industrial engineering degree. In addition to a college education, my job requires a desire to achieve order in the depths of chaos, an optimistic but realistic attitude toward work and people, and a balanced outlook with a strong sense of reality.

Although there is not much of an opportunity for advancement, I enjoy planning and directing a project so I can step back and watch things happen while knowing I played a major part in the final outcome. I like knowing we have all worked together as a team.

I enjoy this type of work. I have always had an interest in the mechanical--how things work. Previously, I worked as a machine operator.

For the future, I plan to stay in my present occupation, but I would like to see the task become a more challenging assignment with a greater degree of difficulty and more responsibility.

MARINE

Being a Marine to me means travel, dedication, and the best of the best, just as the recruiter said. I have now been in for 5 years and I have found that I like this career very much.

My specialty is as a fire direction controlman/surveyor. My work days are different depending on whether I am at the garrison or in the field. At the garrison, my day starts with reveille at 0530 and formation at 0700. My work day is from 0730 to 1630 and includes shop maintenance, equipment maintenance, and weapons cleaning. There is no set time schedule when we are in the field. My field duties are varied and may include firewatch, surveying, guarding, patrolling, camouflaging, digging in, etc.

In order to perform well as a Marine, you must first know the skills which you are taught in boot camp and specialty school. Besides the skills, a "can do" attitude is necessary.

I like almost every aspect of my career as a Marine including the organization I work for, the people I work with, the opportunity for advancement, and the kind of work I do. I find self satisfaction in knowing I accomplished my assigned mission.

I am somewhat undecided as to whether I will reenlist or retire at 20 years. If I retire, I am considering going into the banking industry.

MARINE ENGINEER

My job as a marine engineer was a natural career for me following my career in the U.S. Navy. My job is to inspect ships' equipment, and prepare descriptions of conditions and required repairs. My typical daily activities include: reviewing inspection reports and repair statements for completeness, technical accuracy, and grammatical correctness, and working up time and labor estimates for new jobs to be accomplished.

To perform my job well, it is important to have technical knowledge of marine equipment, writing abilities, and mathematical skills through calculus.

Except for the lack of upward mobility, I am satisfied with this job. I particularly like the people I work with and the fact that I am using my prior training, education and experience. I have earned a Bachelor's and Master's in Science degree. I find satisfaction from this work in completing tasks on time and error free.

MARKET RESEARCH PROJECT DIRECTOR

After earning a Bachelor of Arts degree, I did personnel work for a time. Since my child was born, I have worked as a homemaker/market research project director. The research director's job has allowed me to earn income while staying at home to nurture my child.

As a market research project director, I perform the following tasks: troubleshoot, check deadlines, proofread, juggle several projects at once, meet with people to find out what they want, and answer clients' questions about previously reported work.

To perform this kind of work well, it is important to have the following skills and attitudes: a sense of humor; attention to detail; patience for people changing their minds over and over; a good memory since many projects are just a rehash of other studies, flexibility; and the ability to get along with others.

I am satisfied with my dual career because it allows me the freedom to do or not do what I want on a particular day. As a research director, I find satisfaction in being treated like an expert--my opinions are sought. It give me the opportunity to deal with other people in a business environment which I like and offers me a change of pace from my environment as a homemaker.

MARKETING ASSISTANT

As Marketing Assistant, I work for and assist the Director and Vice President of Marketing. I have been a receptionist and was a secretary when I was promoted to the Marketing department and eventually promoted to Marketing Assistant. When I have been in this latter position for a sufficient time, I eventually hope to become a Marketing Manager myself.

Marketing is the heart of any business and I like the fast pace and challenge. It is never monotonous but you have to be very organized, self-motivated, and able to work without a lot of direction to be successful.

I like playing an important role in organizing and completing business plans and dealing with the sales force. My work usually involves some menial, routine tasks but I like to keep them at a minimum.

I have thought about teaching as a career, but I really enjoy just about every aspect of my present field of employment.

MARKETING COMMUNICATION SPECIALIST

As a marketing communications specialist, it is my job to lead sales generation programs in order to get new prospects to buy my company's products. My typical work day is spent in meetings with advertising agencies, writers, artists, and telemarketing companies in order to come up with new ideas to boost sales. In order to accomplish this goal, it is essential to be detail oriented and to possess a high energy level.

Prior to this position, I worked as a customer service rep. for the same company. My job background also includes work as a graphic artist and production planner.

Despite the lack of opportunity for advancement, I plan to continue with this kind of work because I like the kind of work, the people I work with and the organization and people I work for. I will continue to strive to obtain higher level positions in marketing or sales. I have found satisfaction from this kind of work in the responses received from my sales prospects.

MARKETING CONSULTANT

I now have my own business and am a marketing consultant in the field of publishing and events promotions. I was publisher of a magazine that was acquired by a NY company. I chose not to move to NYC having just moved from there two years prior. With few options in my field, I took a temporary project from a colleague and it led to more work until I realized I could make a living from it. Thus, my company formed. I've been in magazine publishing since college. I began as an assistant to the promotion director in a new magazine and after 12 years was regional sales manager. From there I left and started my own magazine publishing company. I eventually sold that, moved out of NY and was publisher of another magazine until this was bought and moved to NYC.

As marketing consultant, I create sales presentations for magazines, do research surveys, create marketing plans, and run sales training courses. I have different projects for each of my retainer clients. I will plan to spend usually 2 days on one and 2 days on the other. I reserve one day a week (if possible) for non-billable work--prospecting for new business, in-house business accounting and paperwork.

The skills and attitudes important for my kind of consulting work are: ability to listen to clients and ask questions about their goals and objectives; help them understand what they need to do to achieve their goals. This is true for sales presentations I write, for long term strategy projects, and for creating useful research projects. You must be able to get all the data from clients and mold it into a concise plan.

What I don't like about my work is seeing things that could be run better, but which I can't change because I'm an outside contractor. Also, I don't like prospecting for new business (cold calls), but I love presentations. I also am not completely at ease with the insecurity that an independent service business person has. I'd like to be more certain about my income--and long term security. However, I like the variety of clients I have, and freedom of time. I have found satisfaction when the projects I design have resulted in measurable increases in ad sales or in gate sales, and when clients call me back or refer others to me.

MARKETING EXECUTIVE

I got started in my occupation as a photojournalist with the U.S. Navy. I consider those three years of intense daily work-training to be the best in the world. Since that time, I have held positions in sales, advertising, publishing, and public relations. My background also includes an associate degree in marketing.

Now, as a marketing communications executive, I have the responsibility for creative advertising and sales promotion programs. My typical day includes: 100's of phone calls from salesmen and suppliers; 3-4 meetings with internal marketing people; and sessions with the advertising agency concerning current projects and future work.

To perform marketing communications work well, the following skills and attitudes are important: budgeting of time and monies, marketing/sales training, heavy people skills, good positive attitude, keeping an open mind, and respect for other people and their opinions.

When asked what I would change in my occupation, I would say, "Not much." However, I would like to change the attitude of other people toward the importance of this profession in contributing to the accomplishment of corporate business goals.

I would definitely choose to go into this career even if given the opportunity to start over and prepare for any kind of work. I like the kind of work I do very much. I find job satisfaction from my work because it is challenging, diversified, and creative.

My future career plan is to stay in the corporate environment doing communications related work.

MARKETING REPRESENTATIVE & CUSTOMER SERVICE

I am very people oriented and with the flexibility of hours, salary, and product lines available, my career as a marketing representative is ideal for me. My previous job experience, which has helped in various ways to prepare me for my current work, includes work in product engineering, in production control, in customer service/public relations, and as a nurse's aide. I am now close to earning an Associate degree in Marketing and Business to help advance my career further.

As a marketing representative, I seek out target markets for various products, create new and update current products, design packaging, and handle advertising through various media. This work is carried out by analyzing research data and statistical plotting in order to forecast future product area strengths, weaknesses, and stable markets. My work also involves testing various markets and direct selling.

In order to perform this kind of work well, it is necessary to have motivation, assertiveness, confidence, a good attitude, good delivery, precise speaking, and a knowledge and backup of product(s). SMILES never hurt! A businesslike manner is also important.

Working with people is the primary reason I find this work so satisfying. I also find satisfaction from standing behind a product I feel good about. Another major plus to my career as a marketing rep is the ability to set my own goals, hours, and salary.

I would like to expand my work internationally with an emphasis on Japan and Australia. My future plans are to further pursue my career in marketing research, design, and international marketing, and build an excellent business rapport with people.

MARKETING SPECIALIST

I started working for my present employer as secretary 3 years prior to taking on my current position of marketing specialist. During those three years, I took on responsibilities that were not mine. I learned as much as I could about software and hardware. I applied for the position I am currently in and got the job. Prior to this work, my job background includes work as a daycare assistant, home health aide, travel agent, sales clerk, telemarketer and switchboard operator. I feel that I have now found the right avenue toward a successful career, and I have done it with little formal education.

As a marketing specialist, I manage a software catalog and report financials from the sale of catalog items. As a project manager for the company's software products in the catalog, I track sales and analyze results in order to see how the products and software are selling. The catalogs are done 2 times per year.

This kind of work requires a person who is very detail oriented, organized, can communicate with others, can learn computer software, is a good public speaker, and has the ability to handle several tasks at one time.

I like most aspects of my work.

I would be even more satisfied if I could have more training, and if I were given more freedom with some decisions. What I do find satisfaction in is seeing the finished product (the catalog), working and being part of a team, and hearing positive feedback from customers.

MASON CONTRACTOR

As a stone mason contractor, I supply and install granite, marble, limestone, and precast panels. For 10 years I've bought, sold, and placed natural quarried stone. My family is in construction and bricklaying. So after high school, when I had a chance for a job with a stone mason, I took it and have enjoyed setting stone ever since.

Job satisfaction for me is looking at a job before I start, sometimes taking pictures, and then seeing the finished product. Being able to go with my children past a building I've worked on, and feeling the pride that I've contributed something permanent, is very fulfilling. I enjoy the opportunity to meet many different people in the construction field. The people I work with and the opportunity for advancement are also important to me.

I don't like it when other companies bid at cost or low-bid and unfairly compete. Then they do a poor quality job at that low cost. I say, "Quality first."

I get to the office early to beat the office worker traffic. Working mostly outdoors, I spend my day estimating and bidding jobs. I handle materials quarried from all around the world. Making decisions on the job when required is also part of my job.

A stone mason needs to be able to work both with the hands and the mind. You must have the ability and willingness to listen and learn, realizing there is always someone out there who may have useful ideas. My creed is to always give 8 hours work for 8 hours pay. Be sure not to rush a job; it costs 3 times as much to take something down and rebuild it right.

I own a small yet productive company which I'd like to grow large enough so that I can live comfortably. One day I'd like to build an ice rink for youth hockey.

MASTER CHIEF, U.S. NAVY SEABEES

I got into this line of work because I like construction and travel. As a Master Chief with the U.S. Navy Seabees, I joined the Navy when construction in the States hit a low point 21 years ago. I found a career in the Navy the only way I could satisfy both my love of travel and construction.

In my work, each day is completely different. I am responsible for the operations of a 650-man construction battalion. My involvement with the battalion is from the top level to bottom. I manage the equipment, the manpower, and the resources. We also plan for operations up to a year in advance.

The skills required in my work are many. You have to have the ability to lead and to manage well. Motivation and self-discipline are key qualities in this line of work. Being able to think logically is also very important.

Before joining the Navy I worked as a pipefitter, as a vocational education instructor, and did some sheet metal work. I like everything about my work in the Navy except that I have a little difficulty with some of my superiors. But, I especially enjoy the travel involved. Even though I am satisfied with my job, one day when I retire, I'd like to be a high school teacher and handle the shop courses. A high school graduate now, I plan to finish college.

MASTER SCHEDULER

After graduating from college with a Bachelor of Science degree, I began my career in business as a cost estimator. The position worked into becoming a make/buy specialist and then into my present position as a master scheduler. I instruct the helicopter manufacturing shop when to build major items. I then track them through the manufacturing process. In looking for the creating of new parts and where they will be sourced, I read new engineering reports daily. My tracking, scheduling, and reporting are done on the computer. It is also my responsibility to plan starts for the manufacturing of spare parts. Ultimately, I try to expedite parts for early delivery.

Attention to detail, timeliness, and the ability to handle mental constructs are important abilities to have in order to perform well in this kind of work.

I have encountered some frustration with this work because I am not given the authority to control some of the details which are a part of my assembly. I would also like to receive more recognition/ acknowledgement from management. However, I do like the kind of work I do and the people I work with. I find personal satisfaction in doing a job well and satisfying internal customers' needs.

My future career plans include pursuing a career in production control or purchasing.

MATERIALS ENGINEER

In my work as materials manager at a major corporation, I meet with people who are having problems with materials, such as plastics or adhesives, or with applications of those materials. I devise plans to satisfy their needs. Using chemical selection, applications, processes, and analysis I am able to solve their problems.

First, you need broad knowledge in the field to be a materials engineering manager. My degree is a Bachelor of Science in chemistry. You have to listen well with comprehension to determine people's precise requests. Being able to plan for cost-effective solutions to find quality resolutions to problems is very important. You also need strong communication skills.

I enjoy the successful solutions to problems and the interaction with people. I hate the bureaucracy in the company, but I enjoy my fellow workers, my work, and the challenges in the field.

Future plans include eventual retirement when I can sharpen up on my golf game.

MATHEMATICS PROFESSOR

To be a mathematics professor, you need curiosity, persistence, and intelligence. Certainly, math and science skills are important, but writing skills are as well. I've found tolerance of incompetence is necessary for me. Having an imagination is helpful as well.

My work involves preparing for classes, teaching, and grading papers. My education includes a Bachelor of Science degree, a Master of Arts, and a Ph.D.

I get personal satisfaction from solving difficult, unsolved problems and reporting my results to colleagues internationally through conferences and journal articles. I also find it rewarding to help the rare students who really want to learn all they can. I've always studied my favorite subjects, and, since it's so much fun, I haven't quit yet. The university environment is the best place for extended learning. I'd like to continue a successful academic career, solve some additional unsolved problems, and help a few more students realize what mathematics is really about. I'd like my profession even more if the pay were better and the benefits were increased. Raising the standards and expectations of students would help as well. I've held summer positions with a power company doing rate analysis and load research, as well as on the highway maintenance crew, but nothing is as satisfying as mathematics.

MECHANIC, BUS SERVICE

For seventeen years I've worked as a mechanic on school and transit buses. I enjoy just about everything in my job: the work itself, the people I work with and for, and the company. My only regret is that there is little opportunity for advancement.

My work requires strong mechanical ability along with the desire to learn. It is equally important to be able to get along with others. You have to be capable of performing any necessary mechanical service on school and transit buses which need attention. It makes me feel good to see a bus operate after I've finished working on it. I also like the good people who are my coworkers.

My college degree is a Bachelor of Arts in theology. I pastored in small churches for years; I guess you could say I am multi-vocational. I was a school bus driver, had a paper route, and worked in a large machine shop while attending college. Although I enjoy this job and its rewards, I'm looking forward to retirement eventually.

MECHANIC, COAL MINE

I must honestly say that the prime motivation for having this job as a mechanic in a coal mine is for the money and the medical insurance benefits it provides. However, I do like this kind of work and it is also the kind of work you can leave behind and don't take home with you mentally.

As a mechanic in a coal mine, I am responsible for repairing the large machines and doing the electrical repairs in the mine. I work from 3 p.m. to 1 a.m. 6 days per week. This adds up to 60 hours and is mandatory for this position. A 40 hour week with a flexible schedule would be nice.

I consider mechanical skills, flexibility, and ingenuity to be important requirements for accomplishing these tasks.

My educational background includes a Bachelor of Science and Master of Science degrees. Prior to working in the mine, I had jobs as a machinist and an educator. I have now been working as the coal mine mechanic for 15 years and plan to continue until I am able to find a means of being financially independent.

MECHANICAL ASSEMBLER

Because I find satisfaction from building things, my machine assembly job suits me well. My particular task is to make and test thermal night sights.

This kind of assembly work requires the ability to read blueprints and to work well with your hands.

It is not my intention to continue in this career for an extended time; however, until I find another career path, I am basically satisfied as an assembler.

MECHANICAL DESIGNER #1

My career started upon graduating from high school by my utilizing the mechanical drafting skills I acquired during high school. My initial job was as a draftsman and I am now working as a designer.

As a mechanical designer, my particular job is to design mechanical devices to hold work pieces for manufacturing. In order to perform this kind of work, you need technical drafting skills, math skills, and imagination.

I like the kind of work I do, the people I work with, and the pay. I do, however, find there to be a lack of opportunity for advancement for me.

Therefore, I intend to learn computer-aided design in order to open up more opportunities for myself. I plan to continue in mechanical design work because I find it satisfying to see my design built and functional.

MECHANICAL DESIGNER #2

Going on to vocational school to get an associate degree in drafting was critical to my success as a mechanical designer. I chose this field because I enjoyed drafting in high school. I have held jobs as a brick layer, carpenter and laborer in a factory prior to my design work.

As a mechanical designer, I normally perform the following activities: layout and design of mechanical components; making schedules for upcoming jobs; fixing problems that may arise from designs that don't work properly; and attending meetings.

This kind of work as a mechanical designer requires organizational skills, imagination, and confidence that the work is correct with the ability to back it up. You must know what you are talking about in this precise type of work.

I have been satisfied in this career for 10 years because I like this kind of work very much. I find satisfaction in new designs that perform well and are incorporated into future orders. My future career plans are certainly to teach, possibly drafting, in a technical college.

MECHANICAL ENGINEER #1

I have spent a good many years as a mechanical engineer after earning my Bachelor of Science in Mechanical Engineering degree, and I am glad I have. If I were given the opportunity to start my career life over, I would again choose this occupation. Prior to working for a mechanical contractor, I worked in research and development and as an automobile mechanic.

As a mechanical engineer, I design mechanical facilities for commercial and public buildings. This involves conceptualizing, making calculations, selecting equipment, writing specifications, and inspecting contractors' work.

To perform this kind of work well, it is important to have the knowledge of physical laws and mathematics, the ability to plan work for a group, and skill in organizing group efforts.

I like almost every aspect of my work.

This job gives me a feeling of accomplishment and contribution. It is also financially satisfying.

MECHANICAL ENGINEER #2

One of the functions of a mechanical engineer is to design production equipment; another is to review design and layout prints.

I have a Bachelor of Science degree in Engineering and in addition to this degree my job requires mechanical aptitude; the ability to take on responsibilities; the motivation to find information and make deductions, not assumptions; and good communication skills to explain the conceptual part of my job to others.

My main job satisfaction is derived from teaching other engineers how to do my job, but I would like to see more input from the engineering group affect management decisions.

I like my job. I progressed through the organization over the course of fifteen years to my present position.

In the future, I would like to complete a Master's degree in Business Administration and take on the responsibility of a larger group, overseeing more people and handling projects on a larger monetary scale.

MECHANICAL ENGINEER #3

I am a mechanical engineer who evaluates performance assessment used by various organizations. Writing and reading are essential skills in my line of work. I have found that many people cannot even write simple reports without errors in grammar. Many young students think that makes no difference, but inability in English does work against you. You really need at least an undergraduate college degree to do this work well. I consider my BS in Mechanical Engineering to be very important for my job.

My main satisfactions derive from causing improvements in established processes which increase efficiency and save money. It would be more satisfying if computers and more up-to-date technology were available in this organization.

I was recruited for this job in college. I accepted the offer because of the location which met my personal needs both then and now, ten years later. I'm not a "ladder climber"; the family is more important to me. I'll continue to work hard and take things as they come. I'm not on any kind of career plan; I don't have specific career aspirations--I just enjoy doing what I'm doing.

MECHANICAL ENGINEER #4

In my 20 years as a mechanical engineer, I've designed, tested and evaluated new mechanical equipment. My undergraduate degree is in mechanical engineering and mining. I also have a Ph.D. in mechanical engineering. My previous work was in research, which I enjoyed.

Part of my day is spent in small meetings with co-workers discussing that day's plan. Keeping up with new developments by reading the most recent technical magazines is also important. A mechanical engineer must, of course, have knowledge of mechanics and dynamics. They should be responsible and be able to stay focused. The ability to work with people is also very important.

Job satisfaction comes from being able to see the results of my work. The work would be easier, and I'd be happier, if the math courses in the engineering schedule were improved. Sadly, there's not much opportunity for advancement in this field, but I like the people in my work, the work itself, and the people I work for. My plans are to increase my responsibility for projects.

MECHANICAL ENGINEER #5

My career of 30 years has been as a mechanical engineer. In my work, I plan and direct research on new projects, as well as direct development projects already in process.

Through simple hard work, I've reached this level in my career. You need training in engineering to do this job along with the ability to work well with people. I'd been interested in engineering since junior high school, so I earned a Bachelor of Science degree in industrial engineering.

I'm not crazy about my boss, but I enjoy my work and the satisfaction of completing a project. I'd choose engineering again, but my job would be more rewarding if there were less supervision from the top. Also, decreasing the amount of status reporting we have to do would leave more time to carry out projects. Some day I'd like to own my own business.

MECHANICAL ENGINEER #6

Graduating with a Bachelor of Science degree in mechanical engineering 33 years ago, I've been in the field ever since. My primary task is to provide consulting services on machine design. I work with machine tools and in product development.

My work requires that I judge machine designs and evaluate conclusions which have been drawn. I do this by performing engineering calculations, often times using the computer. I am called upon by several groups: the people who design, the manufacturing division, the branch of employees who assemble the machines, and the sales engineers.

I entered the engineering field because a high school teacher encouraged me to apply for a particular college scholarship. After winning the scholarship and graduating from college, I went to work for the company who sponsored that scholarship!

Good communication skills are very important in my work. You have to be proficient in math and have strong problem-solving skills. Certainly, you must know the engineering field, but you must be adept at using the computer as well.

If I had the chance to start over, I'd again choose the engineering field. I really enjoy being able to solve problems. I like coming up with machine concepts, and I take pride in doing it quickly. My relationships with my coworkers and with management are very rewarding to me. I particularly like this company. My work would be more satisfying if I knew I could advance and if there were more latitude in obtaining machine design computer software and hardware. I'd also like to be able to travel more.

When I retire, traveling will be a major activity for me. In the meantime, I will continue to enjoy my work; the satisfactions I receive far outweigh my relatively minor complaints about this field.

When I eventually retire, in addition to traveling, I might like to run a small business as an entrepreneur.

MECHANICAL ENGINEER, NUCLEAR POWER

As a mechanical engineer I generally investigate, solve, and report on mechanical problems and specifications. For the past 18 years I have worked on nuclear power solenoid valves. My day-to-day duties now are writing or dictating reports on problems/solutions, supervising draftsmen and designers on changes and new designs, writing test procedures and specifications, working with manufacturing or performance, consulting with vendors and customers on problems and making improvements.

I find satisfaction in contributing to the success of the department and finding that my work is important, appreciated, and challenging.

I was always interested in the technical aspect of things. A friend and mentor urged me to enter college, earn my degree in mechanical engineering. Prior to my present job I have been a machinist, tool maker, designer, technical salesman, and staff engineer on physical research.

I like the kind of work I do very much and the people I work with but I'm looking forward to an active retirement including traveling, sailing, reading, singing, folk dancing, choral singing, and volunteering for cancer care, the local power squadron, and at a music and art school. I may also try writing.

MECHANICAL ENGINEER, PROFESSOR OF MECHANICAL ENGINEERING

I am very much enjoying my profession as a mechanical engineer and professor of mechanical engineering. My work can be described as designing, building, and testing machinery. I also teach these skills to students.

Preparing for lectures and lab classes, instructing in labs and classrooms, and grading students' work keep me busy. I meet with several committees dealing with improving instruction techniques and I review the scholarly work of others. Additionally, my work includes planning and actually doing experimental research on engines as well as consulting as an engineer.

Completing a project which functions well is rewarding. It is also satisfying to observe students learning as well as growing, and knowing I have contributed to this growth. I have had, and do have, a major impact on the lives of many of my students. There is nothing significant to complain about in my work. Most problems are people problems which will be there no matter what the occupation.

An engineer should have the desire to solve problems. A strong interest in math and science along with solid organizational skills are also important. You must enjoy working with people and want to construct--have the desire to be a builder. My educational preparation includes a Bachelor of Science, a Master of Engineering, a Master of Science in mechanical engineering, and a Ph.D. degree in mechanical engineering.

MECHANICAL ENGINEERING STUDENT

For the last six years, I worked as a mechanical engineer in a research facility that studies automated control of welding; in this capacity, I read technical papers and books and collect data for my research project.

I addition to completing a Bachelor of Science degree in Mechanical Engineering, my job requires an intensive comprehension of mathematical theory and persistence.

I really like this type of work, especially learning new material and discovering new ideas and relationships that are useful to industry.

I find that an engineer's work is so independent in nature that it is difficult at times to promote team projects.

I previously worked as a process engineer which I also enjoyed.

I plan to return to the classroom, earn my Ph.D., and continue in technical research.

MECHANICAL ENGINEERING TECHNICIAN

I really can't imagine anything being more satisfying than what I do now. Making a machine come together from your own ideas without any criticism from anyone is the best way anyone could want it. I have the freedom to do what works for the machine and the company without limitations.

I became involved in making machines run from the time I saw my first water pump for a 1949 Ford truck. I helped repair it along with my brother. This magic of making something run intrigued me. I began fixing car motors at 14. When I first left school, I worked at fixing sewing machines. Then industrial machines came in my path, and I learned I could quickly assemble one without much trouble. I went to school and then worked for a company fixing and repairing their equipment. Unfortunately, the company went under. I was told by my boss that he knew someone who would need my repair knowledge, and gave me a way into where I am now. Being a woman, I had to prove myself of course. As you can see, it worked out.

As a mechanical engineering technician, my main job is to design and maintain the production equipment I design. I research the best way to process the product, and design equipment accordingly. I also am constantly looking for easier ways to do something, or more efficient ways of doing it. This is also accomplished by keeping data on the machine's process.

It is important to maintain a flexible attitude, whether you are designing machines or working directly with the people operating the machines. Sometimes things do not operate the way they are supposed to, and when this occurs, you look at what does work right, and try to focus on that to maintain a good attitude. Skills needed to perform this job may vary depending on the machinery. I have good machine and math skills and knowledge of cost-saving ideas which come from doing the job. It is also helpful to have computer design (CAD) knowledge to draw out the idea first. Part of my knowledge has been gained by earning an associate degree in mechanical engineering as well as from all of my work experience.

I enjoy making machines that make work easier and more satisfying. It is nice to build something from the bottom up, and have it work. If it needs extra help or new ideas to make it work, it is gratifying to know you can think beyond your original idea without feeling you have failed.

MEDICAL ASSISTANT #1

For the past nine years, I have worked as a medical assistant in a doctor's office. My responsibilities are to assist the doctor with patients, perform administrative duties for the doctor's medical practice, and perform certain nursing duties.

After graduating from high school, I enrolled in a certificate program in college, and upon completion I was qualified to work as a medical assistant. In addition to this certification, my job requires strong organizational skills, patience, tolerance, a friendly nature, and an attitude that conveys caring and compassion.

Although there is no opportunity for career advancement from my present position, I like my job. I enjoy the people in my office, the doctor I work for, and this kind of work; I like being a part of the medical profession. Being a naturally organized person, I enjoy keeping the office in order; I also enjoy helping the patients that come into the office.

I chose this job because I wanted to get into a people organization and I wanted to do something in the health care profession.

I plan to continue my educational studies in the health care field, perhaps I will study nursing, and work in a hospital someday.

MEDICAL ASSISTANT #2

Working with the female patients in the obstetrics-gynecology department, my job title is medical assistant. My work involves checking in patients as they arrive in the office, assisting the doctor, and helping in any way I can with patient education.

To be successful in this line of work, you must work well with people, have some experience and knowledge of the responsibilities of medical assisting, and have the ability to both give and take orders.

Although there are not many opportunities for career advancement within this organization, I really like the people I work with, the doctor I work for, and this kind of work. I feel really good about my job when I know that I have helped a patient that is ill, or when I have used my skills to make them comfortable or more relaxed. I also really enjoy the people I meet as a result of my work. I enjoy meeting new people.

I previously worked as a surgical technician, and I have been in the medical field for 10 years.

I plan to stay in my current position for several more years. I enjoy it and I like to use my skills to help people.

MEDICAL ASSISTANT #3

I went back to school because I got sick of working in a factory and not getting anywhere. I went to a technical school to become a medical assistant.

As a medical assistant for a doctor of obstetrics and gynecology, I am always busy, preparing the patients, and assisting the doctor. I must get the patients weight and blood pressure, and assist the doctor with medical treatment or preparations.

Although you need technical training, usually at a technical school, many of the skills must be learned on the job. It is important to have a good attitude toward the patient and everyone else with whom or for whom you work.

I enjoy this work very much and the people I work with. However, the salary is lower than I would like and the job is more stressful than I anticipated. In spite of these factors, I plan to stay with this career until it gets too routine and I see the need to go back to school for more training.

MEDICAL CASE WORKER

I spent 11 years as a caseworker in the state department of welfare and Medicaid. In my work I determined the eligibility for people needing medical assistance. Criteria were financial need, old age, and/or disability. This involved interviewing people after establishing rapport with them. Through interview, I obtain information pertaining to their income, health, and degree of and length of time of incapacitation.

Even though some of the supervisors were not considerate of the applicants, I enjoyed my work helping people in need. Little opportunity for advancement and lack of adequate time to spend with the clients were offset by being able to help those who couldn't help themselves.

I found being able to converse with people helpful in my work. Compassion and understanding were valuable as well. Although I attended college for only 3 years, I would say a college education, or the equivalent, is needed.

This job offers security in that I work for a state department, and it offers opportunity to interact with and help needy people. I enjoyed the five years I served as an officer in the U.S. Army. I also chose to stay home for 20 years to raise my family. My future plans are to retire eventually, spend some time with my grandchildren, and travel.

MEDICAL DOCTOR

I've practiced family medicine for 39 years. After deciding to retire from general medicine, I began my practice specializing in geriatric psychiatry. For the past 16 years, I have diagnosed and treated mental disorders in people over 60 years old.

There is nothing I dislike about my profession. I enjoy my colleagues, my staff, and my patients. I chose medicine as a career while a young man in college and I've had no regrets through the years of practice. Specifically, it gives me a great deal of joy to see hurting people find relief. If there weren't so much paperwork required, I'd be totally happy.

To be a good doctor, one must be a caring person. One needs to "know people" and have the ability to relate warmly to them. Being sensitive to patients' needs is very important. Certainly, a thorough knowledge of geriatric psychiatry is essential.

In my work, I spend my mornings caring for in-patients at a small psychiatric hospital of 100 beds. During the afternoons, I see out-patients. I also spend time doing hospital and nursing home consultations.

When I finally retire from medicine entirely, I plan to become more involved in our local church and its ministry. I've pursued no other careers. Since obtaining my M.D. degree, medicine has been my only career interest.

MEDICAL DOCTOR (RADIOLOGIST)

As a Medical Doctor specializing in X-ray diagnostics, or Radiology, I analyze X-ray films of patients' bodies, ultra-sound scans, or nuclear medicine scans, in order to diagnose disease processes.

As well as the education and certification to become a Medical Doctor, you need the ability to think logically and arrive at logical deductions from gathering scientific data, organization, and the ability to methodically follow up on data to ensure the best care for each patient.

Although I believe there are too many rules and regulations in this field, I really love my work. I enjoy the professional interaction with my colleagues and fellow physicians on staff and the thrill of correctly diagnosing and curing a patient of his/her ills; I imagine that this is the same thrill that a detective must feel in solving a criminal case of a baffling nature.

At about the age of eight years old, I decided I was interested in the field of medicine and, to my good fortune, my parents encouraged and fostered that interest over the years; I believe I could not have made it this far without their loving support.

I plan to stay in the field of medicine, and keep current with medical breakthroughs in technology.

MEDICAL LIBRARIAN

My work as a medical librarian of three years involves obtaining, organizing, and making available information in a medical library. This work entails answering reference questions, performing on-line searches for information on the library computer, purchasing books that fulfill the mission of the institution, processing books, shelving books and journals after use, conducting user surveys, writing reports, completing applications for grants, giving orientation talks, finding books and journals through other sources so we may borrow those articles that our users need, and helping researchers prepare projects.

I have completed studies and have earned both the Bachelor of Science in Biology and Master of Science in Library Science degrees. In addition to education, you need the ability to interact with all kinds of people, the ability to approach a problem from many directions, persistence to keep searching until an answer to an inquiry is found, and the ability to pay close attention to details.

Although I was previously employed as a scientist, I enjoy this kind of work; I find the chase for elusive bits of information to be particularly rewarding. I enjoy the people that I have contact with on a regular basis; they really make my day. I only wish that the position of a librarian was perceived to be that of a professional; many people still hold the idea that librarians are old maids--we are not!

The work of a librarian affords me a great deal of time to spend with my family, which is important to me since I have small children.

Next, I would like to move on to manage a small hospital library while my children are at home, and then I would like to go on to a larger academic library with more responsibility and a larger time commitment.

MEDICAL SECRETARY #1

My work of eight years as a medical secretary involves working as a receptionist, answering telephones and greeting patients; and various office duties such as scheduling patients, bookkeeping, billing, typing correspondence, filing, and using the office computer.

After graduating from high school, I attended a business school for one year to earn a certificate which qualified me as a medical secretary. In addition to this certification and possessing good typing skills, good interpersonal skills, and extensive knowledge of office functions, you must be patient, kind, and understanding when dealing with patients. You must also possess the ability to work alone without supervision to complete assigned duties.

Although there are personality differences within the office staff, I like the office I work in and the doctor I work for. Satisfaction comes from the knowledge that I perform my job well and work accurately, meeting people, and getting to know the regular patients.

Although I previously worked as a typist at the telephone company and at a publishing company, I did not enjoy either of those office environments, so I decided to enroll in business school to train as a medical secretary. I have never regretted that decision; I love my job.

Because of family considerations, I plan to work on a part-time basis for now; this position offers the perfect schedule for me.

MEDICAL SECRETARY #2

Even though I have an associate's degree in computer work, I left the field seeking a more people-oriented career. Now a medical secretary in a clinic, I help people get the services they need, and it is very rewarding to me.

I enjoy seeing people leave satisfied with their medical treatment and knowing that they are happy they came to us for help. It's important to me to give people the positive attitude they need to beat their sickness. I say, "Mind leaps, body follows."

I'm sorry there isn't an opportunity to advance here and I'm not crazy about the people I work for, but I love working with the patients. My coworkers are delightful as well. I'd be happier if the multiple layers of management that are dead weight could be eliminated. We need more people, who actually work, to help with the patients' care.

My job is to book appointments, answer phones, and check to see that the patient has completed the forms correctly. I solve problems for the patients, doctors, and nurses. It's my responsibility to keep things running smoothly and efficiently.

The ability to prioritize is very important in this medical setting. You should be very familiar with the office's procedures. You have to be able to do multiple tasks at the same time without losing track of any of them and a good sense of humor is another essential. In other words, a positive attitude as you face the workload, and the daily negative aspects associated with medical problems, is critical to being happy in this field.

MEDICAL TRANSCRIPTIONIST #1

I was working in a hospital in the Department of Family Practice, which bored me. I transferred into the Department of Pathology for the challenge and found my niche. My previous business experience includes processing credit applications for a large department store, and general and legal secretarial work.

As a medical transcriptionist, I transcribe pathology diagnoses for dermatology clients. My typical daily activities consists of transcribing using a dictaphone and word processor terminal. I transcribe the descriptions and diagnoses from the pathologists on between 150 to 200 patients a day.

To perform this kind of work well, it is critical to have proficiency in typing, spelling and grammar. Good telephone manners, organizational skills, and flexibility are also important. To be cheerful under pressure, and have a calm, even disposition and sense of humor are all helpful attributes. A willingness to work hard is a necessity.

Pathology is a fascinating facet of medicine--not glamorous like "Quincy," but always a learning experience and the terminology is a real challenge, even after 8 years.

In the future, I would like to be an office manager for my present employer; otherwise, stay right where I am. I truly love what I do. No two days are the same, and although much is routine, it's never totally boring, and pays me well.

MEDICAL TRANSCRIPTIONIST #2

In my work as a medical transcriptionist, I listen to a doctor dictate the history of a patient's illness and treatment and enter the information in a word processor. I attempt to type 120 lines per hour each day. Being computer friendly and having excellent spelling, punctuation, and typing skills are necessary for my work. Just as important is being able to understand a broken accent and understanding medical terms.

I love everything about my work: the people I work for and with, the organization, and the fact that there is opportunity for advancement. Even if I could choose any other work, I'd choose this work I've been doing for 15 years.

Learning new medical terms and gaining an understanding of different treatments for various diseases are what I enjoy most. My work would be easier and more satisfying if some of the doctors wouldn't speak so fast, slur their words, or have very heavy accents.

I got into this work after taking a civil service exam. I was offered a job as a medical transcriptionist. The government taught me medical transcription since I did not have a previous medical background.

My future plans are to continue in this job indefinitely since I find it very satisfying. In addition, at some time I would like to sell some of the handicrafts that I produce as a hobby.

MENTAL HEALTH TECHNICIAN

I work on an inpatient psychiatric unit. I run different group therapies, have one to one therapy with clients, and offer care as a nurse's aide. My typical work schedule consists of waking the patients up, getting their vital signs, blood pressure, temperature, and helping them get ready for the day. After that I'm involved with the group and individual therapies.

To perform well in this profession, you must be open minded and have a very good understanding of mental illness and its treatment. You must have a secure, mature understanding of self. Academically, you need at least a Bachelor's degree in psychology.

I find this work satisfying by being able to get on the same wave length as a patient and really getting "in there" to help them. There is great satisfaction seeing a patient coming in crisis to our unit and then leaving, stable and ready to face their problem.

The problem with my job is that I am required to offer care as a nurses aide. I would be much more satisfied if I had less or no nursing care duties and I could spend all my time in psychotherapy with patients.

I started as a receptionist in the mental health center where I work, and when a position opened up I applied and got in. I chose being a mental health technician because of my Bachelor's degree in psychology. I used it for experience and as a stepping stone. I am currently looking for an advanced position since I have recently earned my Master's degree.

My future plans are to obtain my Ph.D. in psychology and open a private practice as well as work in a hospital setting which would keep me in touch with up-to-date therapies, techniques, etc..

MERCHANDISE SYSTEMS ANALYST

As merchandise systems analyst, I work with the merchandise assistant making sure the stores which our company owns are well stocked but not overstocked. My activities vary from day to day. Since one of my main functions is trouble shooting, no two days are the same. There is no set pattern. I am responsible for the creation and maintenance of records, initiating price changes, and answering questions and solving problems for 105 retail stores.

In this job, dealing with pressure and being accurate are essential to your personal success as well as the company's. Being able to deal with constant interruptions and having to stop one project to start another is also vital. A sense of humor doesn't hurt either.

I earned a Bachelor of Arts in communications and found it very difficult to find a job in this field. After spending several years searching for a communications-related job, I answered a newspaper ad for this job and have found that I like this kind of work. In fact, I plan to go back to school to learn more about computers to equip myself better for this career.

I like the organization I work for, and the people I work with. I find job satisfaction in making customers happy!

MERCHANDISING SUPERVISOR

The work of a merchandising supervisor is supervising all employees in sales and inventory control; this includes making sure all merchandise is in stock, keeping main or popular items on back order, selling and presenting merchandise in a positive manner, handling bank audits, and keeping track of the bank account's daily balance.

In addition to a good education, to work as a merchandising supervisor, you must be able to work with the public and convey a positive attitude, while handling large sums of money.

Although I would prefer to be steadily busy, I like my job; I enjoy meeting people and generally working with the public. I especially enjoy being able to find exactly what a customer is looking to buy; I know that I have satisfied their need when they come back to my store and show their appreciation.

I have been working in this position for over four years. I feel fortunate to have found this position through a temporary agency. I previously worked as a bookkeeper, but I prefer to work more with people than figures.

Eventually, I plan to go back to college in order to advance my career in this field.

METALLURGICAL ENGINEER

As a metallurgical engineer, I am involved in mineral processing and plant design. In a nutshell, my job is to supervise other metallurgical engineers who decide what processes and equipment are needed to treat different mineral ore; this involves preparing estimates of resources available to get the job done, specifically man-hours and personnel available for scheduled work. I monitor work progress and update the scheduled plan of action for each individual on a daily and weekly basis, prepare preliminary schematic drawings detailing the project with necessary revisions entered as they arise, and then issue the schematic drawings of comments and suggestions for overall improvement.

In addition to a Bachelor of Science in Metallurgical Engineering, to work as a metallurgical engineer requires a detailed knowledge of mineral ore characteristics, potential uses, processes, equipment, and testwork needed to define the way the ore will react. It is also important to have the ability to work in an accurate and efficient manner; and the appreciation for the need to, and be willing to, check assumptions with qualified colleagues, listen to criticisms and ideas for improvement, and support your own ideas if they are indeed the best approach to the solution.

I appreciate that my job provides me the opportunity to make others aware of the importance of my field and the potential uses for knowledge gained from research in my field. Many times using this knowledge can result in a better design for a new plant, making money for the investors, safer and more jobs available for workers, and valuable products for society as a whole.

Due to the nature of an engineer's work, each is easily boxed in to his or her specific aspect of the job; and I believe that all should be encouraged to get more involved with the overall picture of the business in an attempt to generate a greater team spirit in the work environment.

I became interested in metallurgy through an expansion of my aptitude and interest in math and science; I am very pleased with my decision to devote my life's work to this field; I have no regrets.

MICROELECTRONICS ASSEMBLER & INSPECTOR

I assemble and inspect electrical circuits for different companies and for military government equipment. The pressure is always on to fill orders by certain dates, pushing for quality and quantity at the same time. It seems everyone has a different opinion on how to accomplish this goal.

Manual dexterity and eye coordination is a must as a semiconductor assembler. Specifications of the product must be followed to the letter. There is always someone out there who thinks they know better.

I have found my job satisfying for 16 years. I take pride in my work knowing that, when I do it, I know it's done correctly.

This type of work is a roller coaster ride. There's no telling if you'll have a job tomorrow. In my opinion, this type of work is very discriminating against women. More women lose their job in this field before men will. Men will also be paid more. I would like to open the minds of men in this field to see that women are equal and as intelligent as men are.

I was forced to go to work after high school and not able to go to college. I found I had a natural talent for this kind of work so I stayed with what I found to be comfortable.

I would like to continue to work in the field as a source inspection person going from company to company to buy products or to evaluate them in terms of quality control or quality assurance.

MICROELECTRONICS ENGINEERING TECHNICIAN

As a micro-electronics engineering technician, I am responsible for all diffusion steps in processing integrated circuits on silicon wafers. Most of my day is spent in a laboratory clean room, insuring that all equipment and room supports are operating correctly. If there is a problem with the equipment, I must troubleshoot the problem and solve the problem if the repair is within my realm of expertise. I follow a tight schedule of integrated circuit processing and I use a wide range of equipment from test stations to microscopes. When I'm not in the laboratory clean room, I am either at a meeting with other staff members or tackling the vast amount of paperwork ever present in my office.

In addition to a good training program for this type of work, I earned a certificate in electronic technology from a technical institute. This type of work requires a strong electronics background, safe and organized laboratory skills, a lot of patience, good task organization skills, and the desire to perform research as a part of the job.

I like everything about my job, especially the people I work with, my boss, this kind of work, and the company I work for. I believe there are many opportunities for career advancement within this company. My work is at times so enjoyable the I tend to look at it as though it were a game I am playing. In the five years I have worked in this job, I have found the most job satisfaction comes from obtaining good yields from device work and from overcoming the problem blocks encountered with research work on first-time devices. Also, successful completion of government projects usually leads to a large group celebration.

I plan to continue my education and work very hard to obtain a full staff position in the laboratory.

MIDDLE MANAGER, PERSONNEL

As overseer of a small workforce, my responsibilities include employee hiring, employee services, and benefits and training. I enjoy my work, the people I work with, my supervisors, and the company. I appreciate the satisfaction of accomplishment and the opportunity for advancement in my field.

After 15 years in my present work, my ability to appreciate and recognize a job well done and delivered on time has assisted in developing a high-performance staff. If I could change anything in my occupation, I'd share work requirements with those who doubt the effort and amount of preparation needed to do this job.

My promotion to this position was due to prior relationships and accomplishments, and being in the right place at the right time without benefit of higher education or degree in this field. My previous experience has been as a customer representative, a warehouseman, a department store troubleshooter, an employment officer, and state president of a supervisory association.

At this point in my midlife, I'd choose the job I have now over any other. But if I could start over again, I'd choose a career in the legal profession or an advocacy position, perhaps labor law. As I approach retirement, I'd like to be self-employed in sales or in service work.

MILITARY, MARINE CORPS

I desired to be "the best of the best" and the Marine Corps appealed to me as a place to show my stuff. The challenge and the chance of unlimited horizons also attracted me to a military profession. Prior to enlisting, I worked as an electrician and a security guard. Currently I am a college student and have thus left active duty temporarily.

As a marine, I led individuals in the accomplishment of training and exercises to prepare them for combat. Typical days varied depending on the training schedule. The variety of the training days is good so that activities don't become too repetitious and boring. The one thing, however, that does not vary is rising early and physical fitness training. My days are divided between conducting field training and classroom training and dealing with administrative problems.

A positive attitude is definitely an attribute for a marine. It is not essential to have specific skills in order to join the marines but an aptitude for learning and willingness to learn are important for training. An enjoyment of changing conditions and for meeting new people should be part of your character when considering a career in the military.

One of the main reasons I like the military is the challenge and the variety of the work. However, I found that educational opportunities were limited. Therefore, I left active duty to seek an education in order to strive for my personal goals. I plan to continue my military career as an officer upon completion of college.

I find satisfaction in my work from seeing a group work together in the accomplishment of the mission under an effective leader. It is pleasing to see a group of individuals operate as one body and know that I had a part in developing the teamwork.

MINE SUPERINTENDENT

My career has followed a normal progression in a large company. I started as a mucker (laborer in a small gold mine) and have progressed to mine superintendent. My intermediate steps have included metallurgical accounting for a small contractor, test work in metallurgical ore dressing, mine engineering doing surveying, operational studies and mine planning, assistant shift foreman, drilling and blasting foreman, and general mine foreman. My educational background includes a Bachelor of Science in Metallurgical Engineering.

My typical duties as a mine superintendent include: meetings with supervisors, reporting to management, interviewing employees, meeting with equipment sales people, and meeting with union representatives concerning arbitration of union disputes.

In order to perform this kind of work well, it is necessary that you have a knowledge of mine operations and equipment. Also, you need to develop skills in dealing with and supervising employees.

I am satisfied with my career because it provides me with a feeling of accomplishment.

If given the opportunity to start over again and prepare for any kind of work, I would again choose to be in metallurgical engineering.

MINISTER #1

As a minister, I have the satisfaction of making a difference in people's lives. I felt compelled morally and spiritually to make a difference in people's hurts. Using Biblical terminology, it was the "call of God."

I consider my basic responsibilities as a minister to be building people's emotional, spiritual, mental, social, and physical health. My routine activities in order to perform these functions are: office work, writing administration work, preparation work, studying, visitations of those in crisis and transition, counseling, attending planning meetings, conducting counseling sessions, and leading studies of various kinds. My work hours are typically from 8:30 to 5:30, plus 2 to 3 hours of meetings or other sessions 3 or 4 times a week. I also must be available most anytime for crisis situations.

People/relationships, discernment, and psychology skills are important in order to perform well as a minister. Flexibility, a positive but realistic outlook, and faith are the necessary attitudes required for this kind of work. Educational requirements includes a bachelor's degree and a master's in divinity.

There really isn't anything I dislike about my occupation. In addition to the spiritual gratification I find from this work, I also have the joy of relationships and the satisfaction that derives from helping people.

My major aspiration is to train others to effectively carry out ministry, not professionally, but in all of daily living.

MINISTER #2

I grew up in the church, observed my minister, and had the desire to serve Christ and people. Thus, I became a minister. As such, I tell others about God and Jesus Christ, organize committees, recruit volunteers, and visit members. On a typical day, my mornings are spent in the office. During the afternoons, I visit members in the hospital and/or nursing home and make other visits to members homes. Many evenings are spent attending committee meetings.

To be a minister, it is important to be flexible, caring, and personable. Some organizational skills are necessary.

Aside from my dislike for the administrative work involved with my career as a minister, I like the other aspects of the job very much.

I would again choose to be a minister even if given the opportunity to start over with training provided for any kind of work. There is satisfaction for me in my work from helping people with crises in their lives. Seeing people grow in the their understanding of the meaning of life is my reward. My plans are to continue to serve in a local congregation.

MINISTER #3

I have been a minister for 26 years. My interest early on stemmed from a desire to be in a singing ministry. Music is an important part of ministry and it was my link to my ministerial position. I am involved now in the part-time coordination of a ministry, and I continue my intense interest in the field.

A typical day is as follows: mornings spent at the church studying, planning, and phoning people. My afternoons center around visitations. In the evenings I conduct a church service, visit, attend board or committee meetings, and/or attend school functions.

To be a minister, you must have the conviction that what you're doing is the right thing. You must have a desire to help people and a sincere concern for them. Furthermore, you must have the ability to lead as well as get along with people.

My satisfaction derives from helping people and sensing their gratitude. Also, there is satisfaction in the conviction of fulfilling destiny and from seeing others find their destiny.

To make the ministry more satisfying, I would have to change human nature. I spent several years as a teacher, and I have a Masters in education, but the Bachelor of Arts in religion, of course, is the more important degree for me.

MINISTER #4

What satisfies me most as a Catholic Minister is that I can make a difference in people's lives. I truly believe I help people gain insight into what life is about.

Previously, I was into agronomic (the theory and practice of field-crop production and soil management) crop development and research. With a Master of Science degree in plant genetics, I worked as a research geneticist for a seed corn company. When I decided to become a minister, I returned to school for a Master of Arts in theology.

In my ministry I teach, preach, and visit people, such as shut-ins or patients. I organize church activities and coordinate volunteers in their work. My time is further spent in meetings and doing office work. I also prepare presentations, either a class or lesson or a homily, which is a persuasive little sermon.

A minister needs to be very patient with people. You also need to be committed to self-education and be open-minded. Good communication skills along with the willingness to grow and adapt are important.

While there are no limits to the amount needed to be done, I love the diversity in the work I do. I enjoy the people around me, the other ministers, and the church. If I could start over, I'd choose the ministry again.

MISSILE GUIDANCE PROGRAMMER

Working with the Patriot missile, my job title is a patriot logistic. This means that my job is to program the guidance system for the Patriot missiles used in military applications.

Although my job involves travel, since I jump around from plant to plant in completing my work, I like very much the company I work for.

It was my interest in computers that got me into this line of work. I have had the opportunity to work with other military systems during my career and I believe that the same work on different projects in commercial applications may hold more of a challenge for me. The military has a tremendous amount of paperwork associated with any project.

I honestly believe that I got my job by being in the right place at the right time. I had no previous experience, I formerly worked as a waiter, a stockboy, and an accountant.

To go any further within my career, I must return to college. I only have a high school education so far. More than likely, I will pursue an undergraduate degree in computers and put my experience to the test in a commercial position within the computer industry.

MISSIONARY PHARMACIST

I like my work and the location of my work in India. My parents were missionaries. My dad was an M.D. and started the pharmaceutical plant in India. I earned my Ph.D. in pharmacy at a college in the United States and then went back to work in the pharmacy with the Methodist Church in India.

I am a superintendent of the small plant and as such I have managerial, secretarial, typist, mechanical, and pharmaceutical duties to perform. The day starts with prayers with the factory staff. Routine morning chores include: opening the mail(post), entering orders, accounting of checks received, paying bills by check, processing receipts of money orders and posting the mail. After our noon lunch, office work is done until 4P.M. tea. Tennis is at 5P.M. and sometimes there is also pigeon racing. Evening is family-time.

To perform well in my career, it is important to have office and typing skills, and understanding of personnel management, knowledge of the local language(Karuada) and the customers, and pharmaceutical training.

Except for too many government rules and too much government interference, I like almost every aspect of my career; the people, the peace, and the kind of work. The location of my work is good, because it is within the same compound with my home and hobbies. The atmosphere is personal and friendly. We provide a good service, which is supplying pharmaceuticals at cost to many Indian hospitals, dispensaries and schools. As a side note, I must add that the weather is beautiful in this area.

MISSIONARY, PROTESTANT

The tasks of a protestant missionary vary immensely, but the most important part of this life endeavor is sharing my love for Jesus with others all over the world. As a missionary, I travel extensively and have the unique opportunity to serve God in a very special way. The life of a missionary is one of sacrifice--you must have an abiding love of God and be willing to suffer anything for Him, even jail if necessary, as I did while in Turkey.

I was drawn to commit my life's work to sharing my love for Jesus from reading the Bible.

The people that I work with are great! We are like a family. I derive so much satisfaction seeing people gain eternal life and serving the Lord; this work has changed my life, although I confess I still do have some bad attitudes that I am striving to change.

I am studying to be a nurse so that I can use that knowledge and skill in my missionary work in Turkey and other foreign countries of this world.

MONEY MANAGER, INVESTOR

Six years ago, after having worked as a teacher of the hearing impaired, I inherited some money and had to learn how to deal with it. I have a Bachelor of Science and Master of Education degree. I study the stock market, buy and sell stocks, bonds, real estate, and keep up with current financial trends through reading and research.

You need a basic understanding of how money works, tax liabilities of various investments, and a financial strategy. Good organizing skills, patience, and learning what resources are available to answer your questions are very important to success. One negative is being dependent on others to do their part correctly - such as stock brokers, title companies, etc. It would be helpful to have someone do my clerical work such as filing, but that would require supervision by me so I have not moved in that direction.

I have doubled the investment I originally made and hope to triple what I started with. The satisfactions are the increase in my income as a result of making my own decisions and achieving respect from trained professionals in the field.

MORTGAGE LOAN PROCESSOR

As a residential mortgage loan processor, it is my job to make up a complete credit file for loan applicants. I must do employment, banking, and credit verifications. The process of registering a new mortgage application involves sending out the necessary documentation for the verifications, and taking measures to obtain any other information pertinent to loan approval. I also handle many inquiry calls daily on the status of certain files.

To qualify for this kind of work, it is important to have good communication (speaking and writing) skills, a positive and enthusiastic attitude, and the ability to solve problem situations and think reasonably.

Prior to this occupation, I worked as a customer relations manager, and a sales associate. I took this job which I found through a personnel agency because it offers me a chance to work with people constantly and to learn a new business. I do not have a college degree. I plan to keep working and moving my way up in the business world with future aspirations of owning my own network of a personal shopping service and/or party planning service. I would also like to pursue fashion design or advertising.

I get satisfaction from my job as residential mortgage loan processor in knowing that I took part in making someone's life a little better by their being approved for a mortgage on a new home.

MORTICIAN

I own and operate a one person mortuary so I do everything: embalm, prepare, arrange funerals, and conduct funerals.

Some days begin with going to work at unusual hours, traveling to a hospital, followed by embalming. During that day arrangements are made with families, clergy, cemetery, etc. Obituaries are taken care of, further preparation on the remains are completed. The following day the funeral home is readied and a visitation is held, the next day a funeral is conducted. During off days, paperwork is completed.

The most important quality for a person to have to perform well in this career is a desire to help people during a difficult time. You must be able to work with these people and help them. You must also be skilled in preparation.

This has been a satisfying profession for me. I derive satisfaction from knowing that I can be helpful when that help is needed badly.

There really isn't any part of the job I dislike but, if I were to start again, I would find a way to allow more dependable time off. Perhaps I would share weekends and holidays with a neighboring mortician.

I am a third generation mortician. To prepare for this occupation I earned a bachelor of science degree in psychology and a master's in mortuary science. Prior to this I was a furniture retailer for a brief period of time.

MOVIE THEATER MANAGER

Because it involves an industry I am interested in, I have stayed in this business, working up from usher, projectionist, assistant manager, and now manager of a movie theater.

I have the basic managerial responsibilities of hiring, firing, training and payroll. I oversee ticket sales, concession sales, cleaning, deposits, and merchandise ordering, and I deal with customer complaints or comments.

Good math and social skills and knowledge of projection are important. As a manager, employee control is essential. I would like to have more money allotted for renovations and improvements and more control over advertising and marketing. Overall, I like the job fairly well but have a desire eventually to get into production and/or performance in theater or movies and to continue my interest in music.

MUSEUM EDUCATOR

As a museum educator, I coordinate youth programs and oversee school group visits at a botanic garden. My duties are to design and deliver programs on plant science topics, direct volunteers and instructors who are on contract to teach programs, and maintain supplies and records for the programs.

Listening to others' ideas, especially those of the audience, helps me do my job better and is essential in this work. Having a feeling for how people learn and what factors influence learning is important. Being creative with people and with ideas while applying strong presentation skills is also very important. You should be able to combine knowledge about the museum's collection, continuous group feedback, and educational learning theory into an educational experience for the audience.

My work would be more satisfying if inconveniences which inhibit instruction could be eliminated, such as equipment that doesn't function or inability to acquire supplies except during limited hours. Having to plan very far in advance, without knowing for sure if planned events will happen, is also very frustrating.

My work day involves assembling materials for the programs of the day, talking with other personnel to make sure things go smoothly, and greeting volunteers. If the volunteers can't cover all the programs of the day, then I teach one or two. After lunch with coworkers or at my desk, I prepare for the next day's events, complete reports for files, attend meetings, and order supplies. I also might plan events for the next season.

Future plans include moving into a management position in this same field. I'd like to do some freelance writing about educational experiences which would be curriculum-related. I'd also like to design educational kits for sale. I have a Bachelor of Fine Arts and my M.A.T. in the field of museum education. In addition to my current position, I've worked briefly as a receptionist, lifeguard, and as a copy shop sales clerk.

MUSIC PUBLISHER & OFFICE MANAGER

In my career, I "wear many hats": music publisher, song plugger, office manager, publishing administrator. What I do is evaluate and cast the compositions for the artists. This involves developing relationships with record producers, artists, record representatives, and record company executives, so they will be aware of our work and record the material. I also manage a music publishing office's day to day operations and develop new programs. Additionally, I administer the copyrights of the music we publish.

My daily activities are so varied and numerous, it is hard to list them. Some of them are such as calling to follow up on songs pitched, labeling copy information, negotiating contracts both foreign and domestic; meeting with writers, developing ideas to help advance each writer's career, casting material, making up the tapes, delivering the tapes, paying bills, keeping up with mountains of royalty accounting forms, and answering requests and questions.

I believe you have to have a great love of music and art of all kinds. However, I think it is very important not to aspire personally to becoming either a singer or a songwriter in order to be effective as a music publisher. I believe you have to be a liaison between them and the business of music.

If given the opportunity to make changes in my occupation, I would change many things I believe are detrimental, or at best unfair, regarding the creators of the music we all listen to. I would somehow balance the scale of power/money and the creators. I would allow the creators and artists more of the profits gained by sales of popular music. I would also find a way to let the American public determine what it wants to hear and buy instead of a few record personnel having that power.

I was always a music lover and have enjoyed performing myself since childhood. I admired a singer/songwriter in the small town where I grew up and followed his career. My fascination grew for the way in which this performer earned his money. Some years later a company he was associated with offered me a position and I started there.

I like this career very much because it is always changing. The music is a continuing source of inspiration and amazement. I am challenged constantly both in the business aspects and creatively.

MUSICIAN, SINGER #1

My day as a musician, guitarist, and singer consists of learning new songs at home as well as at group rehearsals. Much of my time is spent practicing. I perform in night clubs, hotels, or parties. In an effort to obtain a recording contract, I write and record original songs.

The primary satisfaction I've found in my 30 years in the music business is performing to the best of my ability. It is also great to be liked by the audience. Sometimes I get to travel to exciting places. With low pay and no benefits in this work, musicians need a stronger union with health and retirement benefits. The only other drawback is that fellow workers and employers are sometimes unreliable.

A musician must be proficient on the instrument of choice as well as creative and original. Getting along with coworkers and behaving professionally are also important. The music business is best approached as a business--not as a party.

As for the future, I'd like to get a recording contract, which is very difficult to do and is expensive. I'm writing songs now in hopes of being published.

A high school graduate, I've worked in telemarketing, in construction, and in sales while pursuing my music career.

MUSICIAN, SINGER #2

A vocal soloist, I also play an orchestral French horn. I rehearse with the orchestra on Mondays and with a brass ensemble on Saturdays. During the rest of the days I rehearse voice an average of two hours a day. I love music more than anything, but the pay is low and there are not enough opportunities to perform.

To be a musician, it is important to practice a lot. Practice helps develop extended concentration and the ability to learn new and difficult pieces. Good coordination, precision and a love for music are helpful.

The feeling you get from making good music is beyond comparison. I especially enjoy the camaraderie from making music with other people, the satisfaction of hard work, and then a job well done. And I love being challenged. The objective is to be entertaining to an audience. I am happiest when playing--I can't help it. My regret is that I don't have enough time to practice, more occasions to perform, and enough pay to enable me to pursue music full time.

Currently, I'm working on a Ph.D. in pharmacology. My undergraduate degree is also in science. I have worked in several laboratories. I plan to continue taking singing lessons and hope to have more opportunities to sing in recitals. I'd love to play French horn in a professional orchestra full time. Perhaps, one day, I might like to lead a choir.

MUSICIAN, SYMPHONY ORCHESTRA

As a professional orchestra musician, I play the double bass in a regional orchestra. I also teach private lessons on bass. My schedule varies quite a bit as most musicians' schedules do but, roughly, I have an average of 7 services per week (a service being a rehearsal or concert) usually in the evenings. During the day, I try to practice a few hours and teach 1 or 2 private lessons of 1 hour each.

I earned a bachelor's and master's degree in music and was a public school music teacher for 4 years. I continued playing the bass while teaching full-time and thought I'd enjoy full-time performing more than the tightly structured teaching world. Music was something I always did for enjoyment, but when I entered college, I found it was something I excelled at enough to make a living.

You must be highly skilled on your chosen instrument. Most professional musicians have at least a bachelor's degree in music; many have gone on to a master's degree. An ability to work in a group as large as 85 people all under the direction one person (conductor) is a requirement in this kind of career. Good listening skills, and the ability to work unusual hours like nights, weekends, and holidays, are also part of the job.

The major drawback to this career is the amount I am paid for what I do as a professional. Regional orchestras, like the one I am in, are only now beginning to pay a decent wage. I would like to have more professional players in our orchestra and do more performing/touring. In this way, we could hopefully generate more income. We now work a 36 week season as opposed to a major orchestra that has a 52-week contract.

Despite the fact that I dislike the low pay, I stay with it because I like the kind of work I do so well. I find great satisfaction in playing the greatest music written over the past 400 years by masters like Bach, Beethoven, Mozart, and also brand-new works. It is a very satisfying sensation to turn in a good performance in front of 2,800 people. I also enjoy playing in my own combo.

NAVAL OFFICER

I joined the Navy ROTC program because it was a good way to get a college education. The Navy turned out to be my career which I like very much. If I could start over, and prepare for any kind of work, I would still choose this. I continued my education after receiving my bachelor of science degree in electronics engineering to get my master's in aeronautical engineering.

My job for the Navy is to administer naval aviation procurement and maintenance programs. I have 8-10 hours of office work per day, five days a week. I direct efforts of technical, financial and administrative workers on a program basis. Traveling to military commands and private industry is also necessary to do my work.

In order to perform well at my job it is important to have problem solving and analysis abilities, people and program managerial skills and technical and administrative knowledge.

I like the people I work with, the kind of work I do and the organization, the U.S. Navy. I particularly like the individual responsibility I have. I receive job satisfaction from my work because I enjoy the responsibility for successful completion of programs and projects. I would like to see more responsibility at lower levels of the organizational structure and more authority in personnel hiring and firing.

I look forward to retirement to pursue my many hobbies but I like my work and I feel I found the right career for me in the Navy.

NAVAL PILOT OFFICER

I followed in my father's footsteps when I joined the Navy 13 1/2 years ago. My work allows me to fly A-6 jet aircraft for the Navy. I also serve as department head of certain personnel.

In my work, you need the ability to assimilate lots of data and to make decisions quickly. Strong interpersonal skills are highly recommended.

With a Bachelor of Science Degree in Mechanical Engineering and a Masters of Science in Management, I spend a typical day making personnel, supply, and management decisions for a 14-aircraft, 250-man department. I interact with the personnel, and I usually fly the Navy A-6 jet 3 times a week.

I most enjoy the personal feeling that I've done an honest day's work keeping a large department running smoothly. My only regret is the time I have to spend away from my home and my family.

In approximately seven years, I plan to retire. I will have 20 years of service at that point. My plans then are to begin a teaching career.

NEWSPAPER EDITOR

As a newspaper editor, I spend my day discussing ideas with reporters, editing news and feature stories, selecting photographs, and helping design news pages. Job satisfaction means informing the public as well as watching news develop from the front row.

I like the people I work with and the kind of work I do. I'd be happier if the workload were reduced and work days were shorter. But, if I could start over, I'd choose this occupation again. In my case, it took a few years for me to get over shyness so I could be an effective reporter, but that was accomplished. I became very successful, first as a reporter and then as an editor.

Foremost in this job are communication skills and insatiable curiosity. The ability to read and write well and to critique without insulting are also essential. I began as a reporter and my future aspiration is to stay employed in this work indefinitely because I like it!

NEWSPAPER REPORTER

After earning a Bachelor of Science degree in public administration and receiving a teaching diploma, I taught for a while and did some editing before becoming a reporter for a daily paper. I'd like one day to write editorials, but, for now, I enjoy reporting on educational issues.

I particularly like publishing reports and meeting important people. I feel rewarded when my supervisor appreciates my work. Admiration from my family and friends is also important to me. My work would be more satisfying if supervisors had less say on how reports are written, especially headlines. I'd also like more pay since money is relatively low in journalism.

The ability to listen well--and take quick notes--is essential in my work. You need to feel comfortable approaching strangers as well. Solid language skills are basic to the job.

In my work as a reporter on educational matters, I interview people who are involved in education. Some of those with whom I speak are students, principals, teachers, and university presidents. I very much enjoy my work and would chose this field again. My only regret is that there are few career growth opportunities.

NUCLEAR PHYSICIST

In my work as a nuclear physicist, I analyze the effects of weapons, including laser and nuclear, on space craft. Part of my work is reading reports and proposal requests. I attend and participate in meetings and consult with people by phone. Traveling to technical meetings, and writing reports and sections of proposals, are also required in my job. It is evident that my work is heavily literary--both reading and writing in the field of nuclear physics--rather than laboratory or field work. About half my time is spent reading reports and proposals and talking with people on the telephone. Another quarter of my time is used to write reports and proposals. It is a job involving much evaluation of others' ideas.

I entered this field primarily because I found physics and math easy. There were a lot of technical jobs in this field when I became associated with it. I plan to (or at least I would like to) teach college part-time as I once did, if the economy improves.

Job satisfaction for me is producing a good report as well as making a good presentation. I'd like my work better if there were fewer meetings, especially the non-technical ones, and if I could have more control over my own time. (About 50% of those meetings are worth the time; the other half are not.)

Skills required in my work are the ability to read and analyze technical reports. The ability to write technical material and to make technical presentations are also required. My degrees are a Masters of Science and a Ph.D.

NUCLEAR POWER PLANT OPERATOR

I went into the US Navy after high school and enrolled in their Naval Nuclear Power Program because of the opportunity it provided for me to get a good education and good pay advancement potential. Because of this training, I have held jobs as an instrumentation and control technician, power plant electrician, and now nuclear power plant operator. I have also had experience working for McDonald's and found it to be a great place to work because, even though the pay was low, there were good advancement opportunities if you worked hard.

I do like working in the hi-tech environment as a nuclear power plant operator. It is my responsibility to manipulate plant components, monitor plant operations, and monitor maintenance. My typical day includes: the shift changeover briefing, operating valves/equipment, logging operating parameters, monitoring equipment, tagging out equipment for maintenance, and sitting around about 25% of the time.

For this kind of work, it is important to pay attention to detail, have troubleshooting and problems solving skills, and patience.

Although I like most aspects of my work, I would like to see a change in management/employee relations. In my opinion, management doesn't listen to front line employees. I do like the people I work with, the opportunity for advancement, and the kind of work I do. I find this work satisfying because of the pay, and the friends I have at work. I find that this job gives me a sense of duty towards the public and makes me feel good about performing this job well.

My future plans include earning a reactor operator's license with the NRC (Nuclear Regulatory Commission) and becoming plant supervisor/manager.

NURSE #1

After spending 10 years as a housewife, including child care and farmhand work, I wanted extra income for the children's education and other needs. Because of my childbirth experiences and other medical problems which I encountered over the past years, I learned to like the "ladies in white." I wanted to do human services work and to make a salary too, so I earned my license in nursing.

I now work in a hospital where I am on 10 hour shifts. My duties include: reading charts, taking orders, taking care of the various patients' needs, dispensing medications, and talking with patients and their families. Although there are many daily routine tasks, every day is different.

I consider the following skills and abilities to be important in order to perform well as a nurse: reading, writing, mathematics, listening, knowledge of nutrition and medications, public relations, and patience. You should also have a pleasant and cheerful personality.

Except for the frustration of not having enough supplies, I am very satisfied with every aspect of my work as a nurse. I particularly like working with patients and seeing the progress they make. It is satisfying work because I feel I am needed. Although the pay is fair, I could always use more salary.

NURSE #2

For twenty-eight years, I have been working in the medical profession as a Nurse; currently I review medical records with close attention to quality.

I have a Bachelor of Science in Health Science and a Master's in Health Education.

My job requires basic nursing skills and compassion. In this field you see a lot of pain and suffering. Also needed are good judgment skills to react to critical situations and a high physical energy level. The medical profession, in general, requires personal sacrifices, but it is satisfying to contribute to the health and comfort of sick people. I personally enjoy this kind of work.

Because health care requires team work, I strive to encourage more mutual respect among the individual patients and the medical professionals working together.

The decision to become a nurse came at an early age for me and all my professional working life I have been a nurse; one position in which I was employed was in a critical care nursery. I responded to a newspaper advertisement to obtain employment in my present position.

As far as the future is concerned, perhaps I will move into some avant garde health-related occupation.

NURSE #3

I am a Nursing Supervisor who also gets involved in individual patient care. My duties range from scheduling the other nurses' shifts and evaluation of patient care, to cleaning up when patients get sick and we are short staffed; I do it all.

To be a good nurse, you must complete at least a Bachelor of Science degree in Nursing, possess good to superior interpersonal skills because of the nature of this work, and have an excellent memory to be able to react with skill to any situation.

Although I do not enjoy the great amount paperwork my job involves, I realize that it is necessary.

I find great satisfaction seeing patients relieved of pain and it is particularly satisfying to see patients get better and no longer need my care or services.

I have worked as a nurse for six years and enjoyed it immensely. I always knew I would be happy working in the field of medicine.

My next career step is to earn a doctorate degree in nursing, but even if I do not pursue that and just continue as I am, that will be very satisfactory to me.

NURSE #4

Specifically, I am a pediatric nurse, taking care of sick babies and young children, and I have been doing that for 13 years. I also have ownership in a small business on the side, but I consider myself to be primarily a nurse. I am more interested in my nursing activities than I am in the business. My comments will pertain to my work as a nurse.

There is no typical day in nursing--each day is different from all the others. To describe my day, I will take one example. I might be called to help a teenager who is in diabetic shock--who is almost dead--in a small community hospital. I transported her to our medical center, thus bringing her to a more stable, though still critical, condition. Eventually, she recovers, and that makes this profession one of the most satisfying you can enter--at least, it is for me. Even when the final outcome is not known or is not as fortunate, it is rewarding to know I have helped a patient feel better than before.

One of the basic requirements for nursing is education; I have a Bachelor of Science degree in Nursing from college. When I went to college, I figured out that I would enjoy nursing and that I could do it well, so I took the appropriate course sequence.

As to the personal characteristics that are needed for success in nursing, I would say: intelligent judgment in pressure situations, sometimes in life-threatening situations; patience; medical knowledge; and medical skills. If you have all these abilities, you may find it a bit frustrating that the nurse does not have more freedom than he or she does. It would be better if nurses were allowed to act more on the basis of their own judgment. In spite of these complaints, this is the right profession for me.

In the future, even if my business grows, I will not leave nursing. The reason: It is very satisfying to administer to the sick and cause them to feel better.

NURSE (LPN) #1

I always knew I would like nursing, but I did not start my schooling for it until I was in my late thirties. Now that I have my license as a practical nurse and have worked for three years in the field, I am so satisfied with the profession that I want to continue my education and earn a nursing degree.

My patient care duties at a rural hospital include bathing, feeding, giving medications, charting, giving treatments, etc. per doctor's orders. To perform well at this work you must like people and be able to work well with others. You must keep on learning. There is always another class to take, etc. It seems that you are in demand to do a dozen things at the same time, so you need to organize your time to accomplish everything. I consider going to a good nursing school where they demand lots of clinical experience a must.

The downside in this profession are the low wages, long hours, working holidays and weekends, and the large patient load.

The positive side of nursing and the reasons I plan to stay with this career is partly because it is satisfying to work with people who have common goals. I know that what I do each shift does make a difference, and I am always learning something new and interesting.

NURSE (LPN) #2

Although I wanted to be a nurse since early childhood, I was not able to go to nursing school because of the financial situation of my family. It was after my husband died, and I knew that I must find employment to support myself and two young sons, that I finally was given an opportunity to enter nursing school. I went to nursing school for one year to become a licensed practical nurse and have now been in this career for 23 years. It has indeed been satisfying work for me.

A brief description of my work is that I give medications, do prescribed treatments to open areas on extremities, and keep written records of what has been done. More specifically, my day to day activities include: getting a report from charge nurse of previous shift-- news of any changes, mishaps or worsening of condition of any patient; performing the shift count of narcotics; doing med prep work on patients for tests assigned that day; checking if new antibiotics have been ordered for a patient or if some have been discontinued; starting medications and signing off on medications as per doctors' orders; and administering after meal time treatments.

Attitude is very important. A nurse must have love for people first. Other important skills and attitudes are: a good grasp of medical terms for parts of the body and abbreviations of medical terms; math skills for measuring dosage of medications; a background in Latin.

It is satisfying to make a patient comfortable and feel good about himself or herself, which encourages early recovery from surgery. Tender loving care is a potent medicine.

NURSE (LPN) #3

After graduating from high school, I worked at various jobs such as waitressing, bartending, and as a service station attendant before finding out from my nurse's aide job that nursing would be a satisfying career for me.

I went back to school and earned a license to be a practical nurse. As such, I work in a hospital taking care of patients by dispersing medication and giving shots and treatments per doctor's orders.

Since this work is primarily service and people oriented, you must enjoy working with and caring for others. I have found this to be very rewarding, and that is the primary reason why I am satisfied with my career in nursing. I plan to further my career by continuing my education in this field and becoming a registered nurse.

NURSE (LPN) #4

I am a nurse because I want to make the old people's last days happy, to help the sick get well, or give the dying the support, care, and love they need.

As a licensed practical nurse (L.P.N.), I hold the position of Charge Nurse for 60 patients in the long term care unit. My typical duties include: passing medication; doing treatments; calling doctors for orders when needed or reporting on patients' conditions; supervising patient care and assisting when needed; giving patients support when needed.

As a nurse, you must be willing to work hard and do anything to make the patients happy and feel better physically and mentally. In order to do this, proper training is essential. In fact, I would like to see mandatory requirements initiated for updating nursing skills before a nursing license can be renewed. Another key factor for good work performance is to have a loving and caring attitude.

Although I like my career as a nurse, I am somewhat frustrated with some of my co-workers. I think more practical training should be required before entering the field, and that only caring people should be licensed. I think the abundance of government regulations, and the continually rising cost of malpractice insurance, are other negative factors affecting the medical field.

However, I don't want to paint a negative image about this career. I like my work very much and plan to continue . I find job satisfaction from making patients feel good about themselves, know we care and love them, and easing them when they are hurt and suffering. Nursing to me means giving love to my patients.

My career plans are to further my nursing skills by continuing my education, in order to give the best care possible.

NURSE (LPN) #5

I mainly care for home-bound patients, such as the 4-yr old child born blind and unable to walk or talk, who is my current case (for 8 hours daily and 5 days weekly). I do pediatric nursing, but also Ob/Gyn hospital and private duty nursing as well.

One needs a calm, caring, supportive attitude for this work in order to help alleviate the normal stress of illness in the patients you care for.

I am well satisfied with my occupation and the rewards I receive from helping people who develop a trust in me.

I got into this occupation after being tested by a Technical School on three choices of courses they offered. I scored high on the LPN course and attended while I was married with two young children. I have been extremely pleased with my choice for the past nine years.

NURSE (RN) #1

I have always been interested in nursing, and now after working in the field for 10 years, I am happy to say that I am glad I went into this profession.

I work on a cancer unit. I am responsible for total patient care, including: bathing, administering medications, giving a lot of emotional support to both the patient and family, and giving chemotherapy to the cancer patients.

To perform well as a nurse on a cancer unit, you need patience, understanding, a "big shoulder," and the ability to talk honestly and frankly to a family while being sympathetic with what they are going through. You also need good skills with intravenous lines and chemotherapy. The main satisfaction I find from this work is that patients and families appreciate even the smallest things I do for them. I only wish we had more staff so we could do more.

NURSE (RN) #2

My interest in nursing started at a very early age while watching my aunt who was a nurse. In order to practice in the profession, I earned my Bachelor of Science in Nursing degree. I have now been working as a nurse for 11 years and have definitely found this to be the right career choice for me.

My basic responsibilities are to give care to ill people, and help the doctors in treatments. As the night charge nurse of the medical/psych/pediatric floor at a medical center, my normal activities include getting the shift report when I report for duty; checking all patients; checking, charting and administering IV's and medications to be given; checking condition of any unstable patients; making up lab slips; making up dietary lists; and giving the shift report to incoming nurse.

As well as the scientific knowledge and procedures training which is required to perform the nursing duties, the correct attitude is very important. A nurse must remember that the patient is sick and may be low in patience and scared. Every patient must be treated with kindness and respect.

If I could initiate any changes in my occupation, it would be for more cooperation between doctors and nurses, and between nurses and administration. I would also like to have a smaller patient load so I could give better and fuller attention to those for whom I am caring.

Despite these frustrations, I am satisfied with my career and plan to continue in nursing, doing the best I can. I find satisfaction in knowing that I helped a person get well, comforted them when they were scared. As a nurse I help the families get through a trying time. My reward is that I can be there when someone needs me.

NURSE (RN) #3

I have wanted to be a nurse since age 5 and have never had another career. In order to become a registered nurse, I earned a 3 year diploma from a nursing school. I have now worked in the field for 18 years.

My current assignment includes patient care in the emergency room setting and patient and family teaching. Upon arrival at work, I get a report from the off-going RNs on patients present in the emergency room. My next duties are to count narcotics, check equipment and restock as needed. The rest of my duty time includes: implementing emergency room doctor's orders, doing on-going patient assessments, teaching, performing physical care and reassurance till disposition--admission to hospital vs. discharge home. Patients may also be discharged to social services agencies as needed.

To perform this kind of work well, it is important to have excellent assessment skills; a calm attitude and ability to cope with the unexpected; good "people" skills like tact, caring, and a professional attitude; and the ability to work well with others--ERMD, LVN's, paramedics.

I have liked most aspects of my career as a nurse. However, I am concerned about the increase of social problems which are complicating the delivery of health care efficiency. I would also like to see better staffing of assisting personnel to eliminate non-nursing tasks. The positive aspects of my career are the attractive salary, the job security, and the work schedule--12 hour shifts, 3 day work week. I like the kind of work I do, and the people I work with. Another benefit to the nursing profession is that there are many options for other jobs within the nursing area if desired or needed .I find job satisfaction from knowing that what I do every day makes a difference--sometimes life and death.

Since I may not be able to keep up the physical pace of the emergency room for many more years, I plan to take courses in critical care for neonatal intensive care.

NURSE (RN) #4

I work as a Registered Nurse in Orthopedics at an outpatient clinic with nine Medical Doctors. Among my many involvements, I teach patients scheduled for surgery about pre-operative procedures; assist post-operative patients by giving them advice, over the phone after their discharge if they become anxious or nervous about their recovery; assist the doctors during minor surgical procedures; change dressings; remove sutures; assist with joint injections and casting; and document all of these tasks accurately and as briefly as possible, which is not always an easy task.

Education is a major prerequisite to becoming a nurse; I have a Bachelor of Science degree in Nursing. Other skills needed are accuracy; the ability to report in a clear and concise manner; the ability to make decisions quickly; an even temperament; and ability to enjoy dealing with, and caring for, many different types of people.

There are many personal rewards to a career in nursing, but there are also some drawbacks. There is a high level of stress and never enough time to do it all. The workload can be overwhelming at times. I believe that raising the pay level of the support staff would attract more qualified people to those positions and, in turn, that would relieve the heavy burden of paperwork that has become a big part of a nurse's duties.

I have also worked as a dental assistant among various other positions.

Over the years I have found that someone involved in nursing needs a creative outlet to offset the stress of this profession; for me that outlet is silk flower arranging and interior decorating.

NURSE (RN) #5

I was challenged by a friend to go to nursing school. I did not really think I was intelligent enough, but I accepted the challenge and won! Prior to earning my Bachelor of Science in Nursing and becoming a registered nurse, I was an elementary school teacher, secretary, receptionist, and in cosmetic sales. I am now happy that I made this career change.

As a registered nurse, I take care of growing premature babies. My typical activities include: getting reports on infants; monitoring heart rates; doing physical assessments every 2, 3, or 4 hours; feeding infants every 2, 3, or 4 hours either with nasagastric tube, gastrostomy tube, or by mouth; giving ordered medications; starting intravenous lines; monitoring IV lines and fluids.

To be a pediatrics nurse, you must be comfortable with and care about babies. You must know how to care for all their physical needs. Knowledge about medications and how they are given and their effects is also an important requirement for a nurse. Additional skills in working with the medical/mechanical equipment is necessary.

I would like to see better hours, better pay, and better benefits for nurses. There is also a need for more coordination between schools of nursing to accept credits from one school to another. Assistance to get a higher degree would be a good benefit.

Despite these drawbacks to this career, I like the kind of work I do very much. I find job satisfaction in caring for premature babies to whom I can give all the love and care I have. It is also satisfying to help teach parents how to best care for growing prematures. The reward is seeing them return for visits as a "normal" child.

I am considering going back to school to earn my Masters in Health Care with an emphasis on "special children."

NURSE (RN) #6

I didn't go to nursing school until I was in my late 20's because I was raising a family before then. I had wanted to be a nurse as a child but didn't verbalize it until I was about 25. My husband is a diabetic, and as I nursed him through many illnesses, I found that caring for people in a nursing capacity fulfilled many of my needs. I'm a nurturing, task-oriented, people person, and nursing gives me a chance to "do my thing"! I was a secretary-receptionist prior to returning to college. I didn't mind it, but I found the "sameness" of the days (same people, same tasks, same hours, same days of the weeks) to be tiresome. I also worked as a salesclerk all through high school, and I loved it.

I work from 11 a.m. to 11:30 p.m., 3 days per week, including every other weekend. I take care of 5-6 mother/infant couplets in a multi-cultural, inner-city, socioeconomically-diversified city hospital. My responsibilities include hands-on care of low- and high-risk post-partum patients, all teaching regarding self and infant care, assessment of physical, psychological, social, and emotional needs, and management of personnel and staffing needs.

To perform this kind of work well, it is important to have organization, the ability to handle constant interruptions and changes, the ability to work with and respect many different kinds of people, the ability to make quick, appropriate decisions, and a strong base of knowledge.

My wish list concerning my occupation includes more time with each patient to teach and assess, better equipment so that not so much time is wasted searching out usable equipment.

Despite my frustration with the particular hospital and manager I work for, I like my work and the variety of cultural and socioeconomic backgrounds of patients and co-workers. I find satisfaction from enabling a mother and/or father to grow in knowledge, skill, and confidence as a parent. I also find satisfaction from working as an effective team member/leader. Working 3 days a week gives me 4 days of my own, so my life is well-balanced. The fact that I chose this career as an adult, I believe, makes me more contented--I know that the grass isn't always greener elsewhere. I'm very happy doing exactly what I'm doing.

NURSE (RN) #7

I chose nursing because I wanted a people-oriented job. I studied three years to earn my diploma as a registered nurse and have now practiced this profession for 25 years.

As a registered nurse in a hospital, I plan and assess the health care needs of individuals, carry out the plan, and supervise and correlate the work of others. My typical schedule includes: reporting on (being briefed on the condition of patients); planning day's care; conferring with doctors, nurses, aides, and supervisors; providing patient care; charting; and reporting off (briefing incoming shift).

I consider intelligence, the ability to listen and articulate, compassion, and tolerance to be critical attributes for a person in this career.

I am somewhat dissatisfied with the hours and the pay scale, although I plan to stay with my nursing career because I find satisfaction in seeing others become well or adjusted to their situation.

NURSE (USN)

I am a nurse in the US Navy and work in a hospital which cares for patients with post-operative needs. I administer health care and assist with orthopedic and surgical patients. My routine responsibilities include organizing work for 3 to 4 other nurses and corpsmen, assessing patient problems, dealing effectively with other problems, assessing personnel problems, maintaining the uptake and structural integrity of the ward and updating policy manuals.

To perform well as a nurse it is important to have health assessment skills, motivation, people-organizing skills, and writing and math skills.

I like my work because of the people I work with, the organization I work for (USN), and the opportunity for advancement. At the present time I am not particularly satisfied with my pay, my boss, or my personal work schedule. However, I am still satisfied with the kind of work I do when patients leave the hospital alive and healthy due to my direct intervention.

I have this job mainly because I have earned my bachelor of science degree in nursing. If I have the opportunity to return to school, I aspire to become an MD or nurse anesthetist.

NURSE ADMINISTRATOR

I have been working as a nurse administrator for 20 years, and that is the career I studied for in college. I first earned a Bachelor of Science in Nursing, and then a Masters in Arts in Child Psychiatric Nursing. Once in the field, I got raised quickly after graduating to management positions.

As a nurse administrator, I direct a psychiatric unit in a community hospital as department head. My typical duties include overseeing patient care, counseling staff, planning programs, adjusting schedules, and solving problems.

I have found communication skills and intervention with good problem solving skills to be critical to performing my job well. It is also important to have empathy with the staff, patients and the public.

If I could initiate any changes in my occupation, I would have the program I am currently working with a little more developed. Aside from that drawback, I like the kind of work I do very much.

There is job satisfaction for me in being able to help run the unit and stabilize the system.

My future career goals are to become Director of Nursing or possible an Executive Director of a clinic.

NURSE (RN) & SECTION MANAGER

I was born a nurse! I feel fortunate I always wanted to be a nurse and that I am doing it. During my years of nursing, I have spent 13 years in labor and delivery, as an operating nurse, and 5 years as director of nursing services. For the last 2 years I have been the registered nurse manager of a surgical center. My background includes earning a bachelors in nursing, pursuing graduate studies, and being a wife and mother of six children.

As registered nurse manager, my 10 to 12 hour days start at 6:45 a.m. My duties in this position include: doing time sheets for payroll, writing patient's medical reports, writing up quality assurance reports, admitting patients, starting I.V.'s, and scrubbing and assisting physicians doing surgery.

In order to perform your work well as a nurse, you must enjoy and love what you do and be happy doing it. It also requires knowledge, flexibility, friendliness, caring about people as a total person, compassion, and honesty. A willingness to make sacrifices to meet the needs of your co-workers as well as patients and physicians is important. Lastly, I consider loyalty to your employer to be a necessary asset for this work.

Except for my dislike for the long hours and my desire for more pay, I like this work very much. I particularly like working with the patients. I find it satisfying to help other people in their time of need. My future career plans are to continue to be the best person and nurse I am capable of being.

NURSE ASSISTANT

As a nurse assistant, I feed and bathe mentally-handicapped children. I got into this work because a friend thought I would be good at it. I tried it and like it.

When I arrive at work at 7:00 a.m., I bathe and dress six mentally handicapped children. I then feed them between 8:30 and 9:00 a.m. Before lunch, I exercise three of the children. I then feed all six, change their diapers, and exercise the other three before feeding them dinner between 5:30 and 6:00 p.m. Before I leave work, I change them and get them ready for bed.

I have not had any previous experience in this field, but the most important attributes for this work are not something that is usually learned through school or job experience. To perform this kind of work well, you have to be very gentle and loving.

I like the kind of work I do, the organization and people I work for, and the people I work with. I am planning to become a registered nurse and continue working with mentally-handicapped children. This will also provide me with more opportunity for advancement. It is indeed satisfying to use my abilities to help someone else.

NURSE, GERIATRICS

I always wanted to be a nurse since childhood, and it has indeed proved to be a satisfying profession for me. There have been periods of time when I was not practicing nursing because I was called in as the cook and baker in the restaurant that my husband and I own. However, I have always gone back to it.

As a registered nurse, I have had a variety of positions: personal care, skilled nursing, emergency, private duty, and general duty. I am now a general duty nurse in the geriatrics unit of a hospital. As such, I provide morning care and medicines, check old and new orders, administer treatments, communicate with the family of patients, and generally provide help and care as needed.

In order to perform well as a nurse, it is important to have an interest in people and their care and treatment, know what to do and how to do it, be informed of new medicines and treatments, and be able to function well in emergency situations.

I have enjoyed being a nurse because of the kind of work I do, the people I work for, and the people I work with. I find job satisfaction in my work because I am appreciated for helping people in some way. I feel needed.

NURSE (RN), INTENSIVE CARE

As a Registered Nurse specializing in the areas of medical intensive care, cardiac care, and trauma, I care for and coordinate care for critically ill patients in a hospital environment. My shifts rotate, so I work on a different hourly schedule almost every day of the week; working such a schedule can make for some very long days. The field of medicine requires teamwork; I work very closely with the physicians in the care of all my assigned patients.

This position requires a minimum education of a Bachelor of Science in Nursing degree, and some very special skills, which can be learned. Among the required abilities are an investigative approach to health care; a team spirit; a sense of humor, and the ability to keep control of the situation, especially since the patient is usually frightened. It is a nurse's duty to help the patient confront and cope with those fears.

Nursing is a very rewarding and demanding field. I enjoy the respect of my co-workers and colleagues; my position enables me to feel that "I can" in any situation. I know that my work effects change in the lives of my patients, especially those who get well, but also in the lives of those that are allowed to die peacefully. There are continuing opportunities to learn. The field of medicine is very challenging. I must point out, however, that although the required education for a nurse is on the same level as for an engineer or an accountant, the pay level is not on the same or even close to the same level; this can cause great frustration. Another source of frustration in this line of work can be working on holidays, because illness does not take a holiday.

I always knew that I would someday become a nurse, but I held other positions before enrolling in and while attending college.

For the future, I plan to become certified in critical care. I would also like to teach the young or nurses who are new to the field those fundamentals of good patient care that I have learned from experience. I do not feel that this is a sufficient part of the college curricula at this time.

NURSE, NEONATAL INTENSIVE CARE

I went directly into nursing school after high school. Then I found I liked new born and mother care, so I decided to specialize. As well as my nursing diploma, I have a Bachelor of Arts in Administration degree with a major in human resources. Prior to my neonatal intensive care nursing job, I taught computer literacy as a nurse to other nurses and health care personnel.

As a neonatal intensive care nurse, I take care of sick and premature newborn infants. I also assist in the transport of babies from one hospital to another via helicopter, ambulance, and plane. More specifically, I help other nurses with the care of the infants, and attend infant deliveries and Caesarean sections with doctors and other nurses. If a transport call is received, I change clothes and travel via helicopter, ambulance or plane to pick up the infant and return it to our facility if the other facility cannot care for it.

Sometimes, we must go to a hospital other than the one I work in if we are full or if my hospital cannot treat the infant.

To perform well as a nurse, it is important to have patience, common sense, good technical skills (such as to start i.v.'s, intubating babies, etc.), compassion, and the gift of communication with those that are not medical personnel.

I like my kind of work very much, but am somewhat frustrated with the organization (hospital) for whom I work. After holding this position for 13 years, I would also like to eliminate the transport part of my job so I could have my own patient load. What gives me satisfaction from my work, though, is being able to work with people and know that I have been effective and made a difference.

In the future, I plan to go back to business management and to continue my education toward a graduate degree in business.

NURSE, PEDIATRIC INTENSIVE CARE

I have kind of a unique work schedule now as a traveling nurse. I contract to work at teaching hospitals for 3 months at a time enabling me to see the country and to learn different techniques of medical and nursing care. My current assignment is as a pediatric intensive care nurse. As such, I take care of physical, emotional, and spiritual needs of children and their parents.

In order to perform this kind of work well, it is important to be flexible, open-minded, compassionate, and knowledgeable about drugs, equipment, human anatomy/ physiology, etc.

My father was a physician and encouraged me into my career in medicine by taking me with him on patient rounds. This taught me a great deal which I was later able to use in school and on the job. I prefer nursing to being a physician due to more direct patient contact.

I like most aspects of my work as a registered nurse except for the long hours involved (often 7 p.m. to 7 a.m.) and the lack of opportunity for advancement. I would also like to see more operable equipment available so less time is spent tracking down needed equipment. Aside from these concerns and dislikes, I like the kind of work I do very much. There is a great deal of instant gratification in a pediatric intensive care unit; the vast majority of these patients respond quickly, get better and go home.

NURSE PRACTITIONER

As a nurse practitioner, I enjoy helping others get well and stay well. I have multiple roles to play in my work, one of which is caring for young women in a college setting. My work includes nursing, treating patients, teaching, and prescribing medications for patients. Underlying these multiple roles is decision making. Conditions would be more satisfying if we had more help on a dependable basis.

While serving as a medic in the Army, I admired the Registered Nurses. So, after leaving the Army, I attended school to become a Licensed Practical Nurse. The field of nurse practitioner appealed to me. I earned my Registered Nurse Associate's degree, a Bachelor's degree, and finally a Master of Science degree in nursing for Adult Nurse Practitioner.

Qualities needed in my work are self-motivation and self-esteem. You should have solid clinical knowledge. Flexibility is very important. The desire to learn and to keep learning plus a sense of maturity are also needed. Being a good decision maker is equally important.

I am responsible for ambulatory patient care which includes making appointments and dealing with walk-in patients. My job involves charting, following up on phone calls, and informing patients about test results. I attend meetings, teach, and supervise part-time assistants.

When my children are older, I would like to be more involved in nursing organizations, to travel, and to teach more. I even think of starting my own consulting business in nursing.

NURSE, PRIVATE DUTY HOME CARE

I always wanted to be a nurse, but spent many years employed in other jobs before finding the opportunity to go to school for my nursing degree. These previous jobs included IBM key punch operator, making airplane fuel tanks, garment factory worker, assembly line work in an auto plant, janitress in missile plant, department store clerk, painter, and seamstress. I finally got the opportunity to attend nursing school and, after earning my degree in geriatrics and becoming a registered nurse, I tried nursing home work but found that I tired of all the paperwork and had a desire for more patient care. This is why I decided to work on my own as a private duty home care nurse.

I have the daily responsibility of taking care of an elderly person in her home. I am with her from 8 a.m. until 4 p.m. tending to her needs. My job includes housekeeping responsibilities as well as caring for her medically. This kind of work requires patience, good observation skills, and good listening skills as well as nursing skills. You must be able to observe habits and look for signs of changes in habits in order to anticipate and know the patient's condition.

My kind of work gives me the satisfaction of helping persons who can't do for themselves. It is satisfying to work on my own for the patient's well being--physical, spiritual, emotional, and environmental. I listen and learn.

NURSE, PSYCHIATRIC

I work with homeless and mentally ill patients as a psychiatric nurse (RN). It involves social work, evaluations, and assessment of needs. I help clients engage back into the system. This includes helping with food, shelter, finances, etc. I work out of a mental health clinic and evaluate the homeless mentally ill for treatment.

To perform this work well it is important to have analytic ability, to be street savvy and to have a nonjudgmental attitude.

I find this work satisfying because you see clients go from point A to point B and feel you had a part in the improvement of their quality of life.

I would like to see the clinics hire quality workers with more professionalism. I would be more satisfied too if, in this occupation, people were promoted only by quality of work rather than seniority.

Before I entered this field I was a waitress, secretary, and salesperson. However, I had an interest in the homeless and since I feel psychiatric nursing evaluates the individual holistically I studied this area of nursing as a means of helping these people. I earned a bachelor of science degree in nursing.

I plan to return to school, get a master's degree, and work in a third world country.

NURSE, WALK-IN CENTER

As a licensed practical nurse, I work in a corporate owned medical walk-in center. I have held this job for only 3 years; however, I have been practicing nursing for the past 20 years. I like this profession very much; however, I also found out from another previous job as an interviewer for a marketing firm that I really enjoy doing political interviews.

As a nurse in the medical clinic, I perform basic office nursing, i.e. EKG's, handle paper work, and perform lab tests. I greet the people when they come in the center, assessing the urgency of the medical needs and then possibly getting vital signs. Some of my other duties include taking payments from people, instructing the patients on the care for their illness, answering telephone calls, booking appointments, and making calls to people with followup care.

Basic nursing skills are required for this kind of position. Being pleasant and understanding with the people who come in is important in order to perform this job well.

Although I like nursing very much, I do not like working for a large corporation. Despite this, I like the people I work with and the people for whom I work. I find satisfaction in seeing different people every day in a wide variety of age groups and in different jobs. I also like being involved in performing physicals.

NURSING AIDE

As a collection agent for a hospital, I write letters, make phone calls, look up addresses, and contact patients' relatives. I track down people whose bills haven't been paid.

It's important to have good communication skills and nice phone manners. Listening skills are also important in collections. You must be accurate in conveying instructions to nurses' aides and in transcribing doctor's instructions to patient care sheets.

My main satisfaction comes from pleasing the patients and the doctors. I could get more satisfaction from the job if doctors could write and spell better.

My entry into collections came through another hospital channel. I applied for a nurses' aide job after taking a nurses' aide course. I was put into a position as ward clerk and later into collections by the hospital administrator. For 12 years I served as the nurses' aide and ward clerk and have been in the collection job now for 5 years.

NURSING HOME ADMINISTRATOR #1

As nursing home administrator, I direct the overall operations and supervise care of individuals residing in a skilled nursing facility. The typical day or week consists of usual business operating decisions. However, since health care is ever changing, staying abreast of these changes occupies a lot of time. Also, since patients and staff come and go frequently, supervising the care given occupies considerable time.

To perform this kind of work well, it is important to have general business management skills; knowledge of federal/state regulations, knowledge of medical and nursing protocols, knowledge of plant operations, marketing, and community/public relations, the ability to deal with all kinds of people--especially doctors, nurses, and other professionals.

My educational background includes a Bachelor of Science in Health Services Management degree. Prior to becoming the nursing home administrator 16 years ago, I was an intelligence officer in the U.S. Army for 8 years. It was through coaxing by a long-time friend, who is now a business partner, that I got into this field.

If given the opportunity to make changes in my area of health care, I would propose less government regulations. I would also like to see more reasonable reimbursement for care services. Being able to pay employees what they are really worth is another important change I would initiate.

I find job satisfaction in having a clean inspection report, being envied by peers for operating a good facility, and watching a patient improve from being total care to being discharged back home.

My future career aspirations include owning my own skilled nursing facility.

NURSING HOME ADMINISTRATOR #2

Being the administrator of a nursing home is like being the father of a very large family. Nursing home residents are either old or sick, so you are in full charge of their daily care, overseeing all aspects of their lives. It is very satisfying work to help those in need while still making a decent living.

I got into this work because, with my degree in public accounting, I was the bookkeeper for the former owner of the nursing home, a 17-bed facility. After I bought the institution, I eventually expanded it to 126 beds.

I can say I truly enjoy my career and the people involved. If I had the chance to start over, I'd choose this occupation again. However, it would be even more pleasant if there were fewer governmental regulations and less bureaucracy.

To do this work you need to know about medicines as well as have an accounting background. A love for the elderly is very important and a great deal of patience is essential.

NUTRITIONAL SCIENTIST

With a Master of Science degree in nutrition and food science, I am a nutrition scientist for a major food company. I research and develop new, healthier food products. I also conduct nutritional analysis. For the company, my colleagues and I develop new ideas, which may begin in the test kitchens and continue to the marketing phase of the product.

I very much enjoyed my position earlier as a researcher and faculty member at a leading university. But I am glad now that I can help the population toward improving their dietary patterns and, therefore, their health. I like developing new products, but I'd like to see more projects come to fruition. If I could start over, I would have earned a Ph.D. degree so I could have advanced further in my career.

My work requires a background in nutritional education, both with foods and in laboratory skills. You should have research talent, too. Determination, with a stick-to-it attitude, is also necessary. You must be able to work independently as well.

Since I've been in my position, I have so many things I want to do. I'd particularly like to help educate the consumer, on a large scale, on health improvement topics. One day, I'd like to write a book.

OBSTETRICIAN/GYNECOLOGIST

There is no typical day for an obstetrician/gynecologist, except for the typically long hours. My schedule for the past eleven years has been unpredictable, with a mixture of surgery, deliveries and patient visits.

In my profession, communication skills, the ability to adapt to constantly changing situations, to make decisions quickly, and motivate others are important.

I like my career because it is never boring. There is a good balance between human interaction, working with your hands and intellectual challenge.

However, this occupation would be more satisfying if the malpractice crisis could be lessened.

OCCUPATIONAL THERAPIST #1

My career as an occupational therapist is very rewarding because of the feeling of accomplishment I get in working with people to minimize their disabilities. I give exercise through activity, teach easier ways of caring for self, and test abilities. My typical activities include: testing new patients for their abilities and weaknesses, giving range of motion and muscle strength tests and exercises, testing and training in self care, taking activities to ward for graded activity for heart, surgery, orthopedics, psychiatric, geriatric, and reality orientation to confused patients, and fashioning splints for orthopedic or stroke patients.

To perform well as an occupational therapist, it is important to be interested in people, have good dexterity and strength, have an interest in a variety of activities and crafts, be knowledgeable about adapted equipment available and/or have the ability to make your own if not available, have the ability to motivate many types of people, be able to teach the value of activity, and retest to show improvement.

I have been interested in this profession since a very early age. In high school, I volunteered at a veterans administration hospital and made my first contact with the occupational therapy department. This career satisfies my interest in people, arts and crafts, and medicine. To prepare for this career, I earned a Bachelor of Arts in art degree and then did post degree work to obtain my Certificate in Occupational Therapy.

As well as liking almost every aspect of my work, except for feeling pushed because of the heavy patient load, I am rewarded when I see mental and physical improvements in my patients. It is satisfying to find the activity a patient likes and may continue to do after being discharged: silversmith, artist, leather craftsmen, ceramics, author, etc. I like being able to help patients realize the beneficial use of forced inactivity and seeing the gradual increase in their interest as they see the benefits of what they learn from my therapy.

OCCUPATIONAL THERAPIST #2

For fifteen years, I have been working as a Registered Occupational Therapist on a contract basis in several different psychiatric facilities; I consult with various psychiatric facilities, usually no more than two per day, assessing patients for independent living, developing treatment programs, running patient groups, conducting staff functions, working on proposals, or meeting with department heads and administrators to discuss work-related issues.

I have completed the program of study leading to a Bachelor of Science in Occupational Therapy degree; in addition, my work requires good interpersonal skills, creativity, problem solving skills, a professional attitude, flexibility, objectivity, a good sense of humor, high energy, self-discipline, good written skills, good organizational skills, common sense, and for one to be a self-starter.

Although there are some hospitals with which I contract that I don't particularly like, which is mainly because of my personal differences with the owners of those institutions, I really enjoy this kind of work and the majority of people with whom I have contact. I hold a high degree of enthusiasm for my work especially since I am my own boss and I have the opportunity to be self-employed. Job satisfaction comes to me in the form of contributing to quality treatment of my patients, the flexibility of my schedule, and the independence I enjoy as a result of my work.

Prior to graduation from college, I worked part-time in retail sales and food service; a summer job while in college first exposed me to the field of Occupational Therapy.

My work is very rewarding and I plan to continue helping others with my work; I am currently enrolled in graduate school. I plan to complete my graduate studies and earn a Master of Science in Counseling very soon. I believe that the work I do is very important and I hope that I can continue to convey my enthusiasm to those I work with as well as the patients whose lives I strive to improve.

OFFICE ASSISTANT & RECEPTIONIST

I work as an Office Assistant and Receptionist for the health department. For three years, my duties have involved handling of the phones; accepting water samples to be passed on to the environmental health department; making appointments for various clinics run by the physicians for whom I work; readying patients for X-rays; helping to dispense medications; filling out forms for clinics; collecting money from patients; acting as a local registrar, signing off death certificates and burial permits; assisting the nurses by taking care of the office dictation and transcription; interpreting for nurses if there is a patient who does not understand English; and handling bank deposits. The health department also runs various clinics with which I assist: immunization, tuberculosis testing, pregnancy testing, and children's physicals.

With so many varied tasks, my job requires a lot of patience, the ability to deal with the public, basic skills as an interpreter, a good memory, and the ability to handle more than one task at a time--several projects are always going on simultaneously.

I especially enjoy working with the young children and infants brought here for care, the variety of interesting work, and knowing that I deal well with patients by the way they respond to me and the way that they treat me.

I like my job very much, but I would like to go out on more home visits with the nurses to occasionally get out of the office.

I have also worked as a printing apprentice, legal office assistant, insurance secretary, real estate secretary, road yard assistant, and a volunteer office worker.

As soon as my children are old enough to attend school all day, I would like to take medical classes at the local college to further my career in the medical field.

OFFICE MANAGER #1

As office manager of a small business, I manage the accounting and bookkeeping department. I start work each day by getting organized and making assignments to the other employees. During the course of the day I assist where my help and advice is needed and compile reports for my employer.

To perform this work well you should have good accounting skills, always do the best you can, and be positive but accept wise criticism.

I always try to do the best I can at my work so that I can be proud of it. I also get satisfaction from being liked as a boss and a person.

When I got out of high school, I was planning to be a beautician. However, I started working as a bookkeeper to earn money for beauty school. I advanced so quickly in the job because I seemed to have the right characteristics, so I gave up the thought of beauty school and took more accounting courses. I have interrupted my career as office manager several times in the course of my life to raise four children.

OFFICE MANAGER #2

I have designed my job to fit my personality and my business needs. I was an English literature teacher but found that I liked the auto business better. I enjoy being my own boss.

Each day I supervise the cash flow for all the departments of our business. I make sure that all the rather complicated clerical work is accurate and legal. I also do computer input as well as supervising payroll preparation.

To be an effective office manager you must be an independent and persevering type of person and have a sense of humor. You must be knowledgeable about your company and the office procedures.

I receive job satisfaction from the accomplishment of work well done. In hard economic times it's satisfying to keep a large business going despite some bad sales months.

It was happenstance which got me into this business. My family owns this business but I was not planning to be a part of it. I changed my mind after working at the auto business part time while still teaching. I have been working at the dealership for 25 years, and plan to continue there in my present position.

OFFICE MANAGER #3

As the office manager in a university linguistics department, I handle correspondence, organize semester deadlines, and generally help the faculty and students in the department. My typical day might include writing letters, keeping department chairman's calendar, answering questions and problems from visitors or telephone calls, making sure deadlines are met, filling out forms, and taking minutes of meetings.

To perform this kind of work well, it is important to have the ability to deal with all types of people, ages, and personalities; a good education to be able to converse with them; good writing skills; computer knowledge; shorthand skills (helpful but not essential); typing skills; and some bookkeeping skills.

Prior to being promoted to this position from department secretary, I had a diverse background. I received a certificate in England from a 2 year post high school program. I have been a bookstore manager for 6 years; a secretary to an antique book dealer, book publisher, and airline manager; and in public relations for an airline, writing feature articles.

I like this job because of the people I work with, and find satisfaction in using my skills and abilities to help people work together as a department.

My future plans are to become a freelance feature article writer upon retirement.

OFFICE MANAGER #4

My job at a medical clinic started as just a job for extra income 15 years ago and has now become my career. When I started, I was a clinic clerk, and although I still perform the tasks of that job, I now have the added authority of office manager.

As the office manager/medical billing clerk, I prepare charges, billings to patients, and claims to insurance companies. In addition, I collect money and generally run the office. My typical day-to-day activities include preparing data for computer input, inputting data and charges to generate claim forms, processing claims, posting payments and preparing deposits, processing mail, preparing and sending statements, ordering supplies, and meeting and talking with salespersons. To perform these kind of tasks well, I have found that I need to be organized and efficient. Despite this, I still find there are many projects which I just do not have time for and would welcome another employee so more projects could be accomplished.

I find job satisfaction in this work through knowing I did as much as I could as well as I could. However, I am feeling that there is a lack of opportunity for advancement. Therefore, I am planning to finish college in order to qualify for higher medical management positions.

OFFICE MANAGER #5

My personal suggestion to anyone in search of a career is keep in mind that many opportunities may come to a person, and it is wise to stay open to these, even if it means starting a different career. This is based on my own experience with ending up as an office manager. After 20+ years as a mechanical designer and 9 years in my present. department, I was asked to fill a vacancy in the administrative area. I accepted and started a brand new career at the age of 46. I took computer courses and went to workshops and symposiums to bring myself up to speed. I have found that my mechanical design background has been very helpful.

My background is diverse with many jobs from high school on including heavy construction, housebuilding, blueprint and photostat operator, draftsman, and shipping clerk. As a designer, I worked on the navigation unit for a bomber and helped design the hatches for a lunar module, plus many other interesting research programs.

As office manager, I basically respond to the needs and problems of 150 scientists. This can be anything from a non-functioning telephone to setting up automated equipment, computers, etc. It means making sure our scientific community is properly assisted by my support group and keeping people, in general, productive and happy.

My only complaint about this position is the general bad rap that office managers get from the rest of the community. I would like to have the office manager regarded as equal to the scientist in decision-making.

Communication skills are very necessary for this kind of work, particularly listening. An openness to others' problems, and a willingness to cooperate with the requester as well as with those who must eventually do the work needed are important. Patience and flexibility are also very necessary. Saying "I can" more often than "I can't" is a helpful attitude.

Despite a problem I have with one person whom I believe to be insensitive toward people and, therefore, the who makes it difficult for me to provide the support and acknowledgement for my people, I like my work very much. Satisfaction from my job comes in helping people and accomplishing a task, particularly a difficult one. It is rewarding knowing people come to me because "you're a doer" (their words) and feeling I help the scientist accomplish his/her research.

OFFICE MANAGER #6

Working as an office manager of a water utility plant, I am responsible for the billing and all cash receipts for the 20,000 customers in my service area, all public relations with the customers, the functions of the human resources effort within the company, and the supervision of five people. I work with the employees regarding their questions about company benefits; I maintain the service contracts for the office equipment and the cleaning contract for the building; I order all office supplies for my plant and two other offices; I handle all written and oral correspondence on behalf of my company; and I resolve customer problems if possible. If unable to help a customer with a problem, I have direct contact with the Public Utilities Commission, but I only direct a customer to them if I can't solve the problem on my own.

I earned an Associate degree in Business Administration and I found this position through a temporary employment agency. In addition to a business degree, to do this kind of work you also need good communication skills to handle the demands of all written and verbal correspondence; the ability to deal with people for interaction with staff and customers; knowledge of office procedures and operation of a computer; experience or knowledge of federal and state laws, procedures, and policies; experience in benefits administration; and knowledge of budgets and cost containment.

I really like my job; I take pride in an efficient well-functioning department and a staff of satisfied employees; I enjoy helping employees and contributing to their development. I really like the people I work with, my boss, and company I work for; I see many opportunities for advancement within my organization.

I intend to return to college and complete an undergraduate degree; then I plan to specialize in the area of human resources within this organization or something closely related to my present work.

OFFICE MANAGER #7

I served as a U.S. Army officer for 21 years with a variety of management and technical assignments. I learned the Defense Department procedures for acquiring new weapon systems along with technical and management skills. At the time I retired from the Army, I used the skills which I knew best and found a job as manager of an office providing management and engineering services to the U.S. Army.

As office manager, I provide administrative and technical supervision of computer science, electrical engineering, and management personnel. My typical work activities include reviewing technical papers prepared by staff, planning work efforts for staff and providing guidance, attending meetings with clients and providing technical and procedural management advice, resolving conflicts and identifying issues, researching regulations and providing interpretations to staff and clients, preparing and presenting briefings on a variety of technical issues and management approaches, training staff to handle bureaucratic procedures, counselling, hiring, and firing staff, and providing assistance with personal problems.

My advice for those interested in pursuing this kind of career is to remember that, although the customer isn't always right, he is right because he is the customer. You need strong interpersonal skills, verbal skills, and the ability to stand up and be counted. In my opinion, people are people and basically good, but view them differently depending on their background and the position they are in. HONESTY in day to day relations with EVERYONE is the key to success.

I like most aspects of my job, except for the government bureaucracy with which I must work. I would like to do a job from start to finish without being restricted by a minor bureaucrat! What I like about being an office manager is being in charge and responsible for what is done well. I find satisfaction in being able to provide what I have learned from my experience to my staff and the younger members of the client staff--being asked for what I think and being in charge. In the future I would like to conduct seminars dealing with bureaucracies.

OFFICE MANAGER #8

A great deal of what I do in a small office setting is bookkeeping and accounting. I had been a shipping/receiving clerk, word processor, file clerk and then secretary without being very happy with it. The opportunity came along to manage this office and I decided to try it. For 6 years, I have been very satisfied and so have picked up student accounting and am obtaining a degree in that area.

I record accounts payable and receivable, do payroll, and manage personnel.

Being organized and detail-oriented is essential as is being fair and consistent in describing rules and regulations to employees.

I plan to continue to improve my accounting skills and become a CPA eventually because I do like the work very much. However, if I could start completely over in a career, a paralegal or legal function is appealing.

OFFICE MANAGER, AUTO DEALER

I most enjoy the respect I receive from my coworkers in my occupation as a business and office manager. I appreciate the fact that my work performance pleases the owner and general manager. When each month ends and all the accounts balance, when the bottom line is healthy, I get a big boost to my self esteem. I enjoy most of the people I work with; working well with all the employees is very satisfying, but I do dislike the disparity in salaries.

You need, for my line of work, a background in computers. Problem solving skills along with patience and tolerance are very important. Also needed are a strong accounting background to reconcile accounts, the ability to run all office equipment, and compassionate counseling to assist in working with others. Getting along with diverse employees is challenging.

After college, I started my career as the treasurer and manager of a federal credit union and then moved to become a bank teller. My promotion to loan officer brought me in contact with many businesses. A new Honda outlet was built in the community, and I knew the owner through banking. He offered me the opportunity to work for him as office manager, and I chose to accept. I have now advanced to comptroller of the company.

My daily activities include approval of all contracts, supervision of the staff, and overseeing payables and receivables. As the compliance officer for the firm, I maintain all federal and state reporting, and tax liabilities. I am also payroll officer. Eventually, I hope to become a finance and insurance manager for a megadealer.

OFFICE MANAGER, FINANCE COMPANY

Working for a finance company for six and one-half years as an office manager, I direct personnel, develop the overall business plan, approve loans, collect on delinquent accounts, and interact with customers on behalf of the company. I may accept loan applications or credit inquiries in reference to the unsecured loans or second mortgage equity loans that I service, answer customer's questions, fill out reports as requested by my peers or required by upper management; but mainly I oversee the branch operations, reviewing collection efforts and loans made by my staff.

Although my boss can make my job difficult, I do enjoy my job and I like this kind of work. I find the most job satisfaction comes through helping my customers through financial difficulties, reaching corporate objectives, and attaining goals for the growth of the business--which means growth in loans outstanding with reductions in the number of delinquencies.

I excelled in business courses while in high school; my interest in the field of banking led me to a part-time job in a bank while attending high school. Once I started working in the field of banking, I liked it so much that I decided to work full-time after high school graduation and attend college on a part-time basis. Prior to working my way into this management position, I worked as a loan preparation clerk, a customer service representative, an accounting representative, and the assistant manager.

As I have reached my goal of becoming branch manager, I now want to continue with my Associate's degree program and go on to earn a Bachelor's degree. I am seriously considering returning to college on a full-time schedule. I believe I could rearrange my work schedule to make time during the work day for classes while keeping up with my responsibilities. If I had the opportunity, I would change the decision I made in high school; I would have attended full-time college and only worked part-time. On the other hand, perhaps I would not have been able to achieve the success I now enjoy--one never knows.

OFFICE MANAGER, PERSONNEL OFFICE

In applying for my current position, I was looking for a job with more challenges than my previous job, and I found it. For the past seven years I have worked as an office manager/personnel manager/advertising coordinator/administrative assistant. My previous job experience has included the following positions: customer service rep, sales clerk, accounting clerk, relocation coordinator, mortgage underwriter, and secondary mortgage market assistant. For the last several years, I have been working on earning a college degree and should be receiving a Bachelor of Science in Business Management next year.

My job definitely has diversity which is one of the reasons I like it. My various duties and responsibilities include managing the building, making major purchases, supervising maintenance and tenants, writing copy for employment and retail advertising, handling personnel records and the policy manual, enforcing the policies, screening job applicants, performing secretarial duties for the C.E.O., and planning social functions. A typical day could include seeing to problems that crop up such as ice in the parking lot, dealing with vendors that call or pop in, answering personnel questions, clarifying and enforcing company policies, attending manager's meetings, writing ads and coordinating with newspapers, writing and disbursing memos to employees regarding coming events, policy changes, etc., performing some secretarial functions, and answering phones for three executives.

In order to perform well at this job, you should have versatility, writing skills, independent thinking, a take-charge attitude, resourcefulness, good listening skills, work processing skills, the ability to make decisions, inquisitiveness, boldness, sensitivity, and a thick skin.

I find satisfaction from this job because it allows me an opportunity to express my talents. It is also gratifying to have the respect from my employer and co-workers. Making decisions that are right is also satisfying. I would be more satisfied, however, if I could eliminate the secretarial functions of my job and concentrate more on the human resource aspects of this position.

OFFICE MANAGER, SECRETARY

I am the office manager/secretary in an office where the boss is gone roughly 275 days per year. Therefore, I have the major responsibility for keeping the home office operational. Much of my job involves phone work in the United States, Canada, Asia, and Europe. Other typical activities are: typing quotes, invoices, etc.; ordering supplies; making travel arrangements for trade shows; promotional and sales work; preparing monthly financial statements; and keeping the schedule of the boss.

To perform this kind of work well, it is important to be good with people, self disciplined, articulate, and a self-starter.

I have done paste-up in a printshop and handled advertising for a newspaper prior to this position, but I definitely like this kind of work better. I like the organization and people I work for.

If I could start again and choose any career, I would again choose this kind of work. Job satisfaction for me is found from recognition of my work by my employer, by fellow employees, and by clients.

OFFICE SUPERVISOR

I had definite career goals when I was searching out my present job. I wanted to work in management and supervision in an agency which provided public service. As Supervisor for the Social Security Office, this is what I do. It is my responsibility to supervise personnel and operations in this government office which administers entitlement programs. A more specific list of daily and weekly duties is: conducting meetings on new procedures with staff, analyzing statistics to determine ways to improve productivity, discussing employee performance and writing performance evaluations, auditing interviews of new trainees, and supervising office operations.

To perform well in this supervisory capacity, I think it is important to have communication skills, analytical skills, writing skills, team playing, and a positive attitude.

After graduating from college with a Bachelor of Arts degree, I have had various other careers as an art teacher, administrative assistant, and bookkeeper. I have been at my present job for 15 years and I plan to continue in this field. However, I plan to progress to positions with more responsibility and compensation and ones that will offer me career growth.

My job satisfaction comes from improving employee performance and recognition of success from my superiors.

OFFICE SUPPORT CLERK

Working in an office since high school, my position for the last nine years has been office support clerk in an agency that handles child protective services. I type, file, answer phones, answer questions, talk with clients, and sometimes look after children for a short time.

In addition to a Bachelor of Business Administration degree, my job requires patience, tolerance, diplomacy, typing skills, experience with assorted office equipment, filing skills, and people skills.

Although I don't think there are any career advancement opportunities from my present position, I like my job. I have always enjoyed this kind of work and I enjoy working with children. The people I work with make my job enjoyable, and I hope I do the same for them.

While enlisted in the Army, I was placed in an office job because I had experience in bookkeeping and typing skills. I have remained in this field because I truly like this type of work. I also previously worked for a car company as a receptionist and "Girl Friday."

I plan to return to college to learn about computers and perhaps pursue a degree in the field of computers.

OFFICE WORKER, CLERICAL

I work four jobs and am happy to be doing what I can despite a learning disability. I do clerical office work, clean offices, care for older people, and pet sit.

My office work consists of filing, operating the mailing/stuffing machine, answering the phone, running copies, making coffee, opening and distributing the mail, and generally helping where I can.

My work gives me satisfaction because I do it to the best of my ability. My advice is to always do the best you can, be attentive to directions and add input where needed, and be on time and ready to work. I think it has been my good work habits that have been responsible for having been called back to work three times after being laid off previously because of work slowdown.

I am continually striving to learn despite my learning problems. It is my aspiration to learn good writing skills in order to write children's books. I would also like to learn to paint.

OIL BUYER & SELLER

As a broker I buy and sell crude oil. After determining the needs of a refinery, I purchase enough crude oil to satisfy their requirements. I've enjoyed my work so much that if I could start over, I'd choose this occupation again.

To do this work, you need to have a good rapport with your clients. Developing a personal relationship is very important in any sales work. You also need to always be honest and fair in any negotiations.

A high school graduate, I began as a sales clerk with an oil company and worked up to my present position. I like the fact that there are opportunities for advancement in this field. I also like being able to accomplish my objectives on a daily basis.

OIL EXPLORATIONIST

I found this career through a college job interview just prior to graduating with a Bachelor of Science in Math degree. I knew very little geology and nothing about geophysics, but at the time, the industry was expanding faster than the schools were graduating in geophysics. I have found my math background to be very beneficial in this field, because of the skills in logic which are derived from studies in math.

As a oil explorationist, I perform geological and geophysical interpretations of data to determine where to drill for oil. My typical activities include: reviewing studies of junior professionals; discussing interpretations of results; providing recommendations to management of exact location of areas to drill for hydrocarbons.

As well as needing logic (best derived from studies of math and physics), it is also important to have an open mind, and to be artistic, creative, and perceptive, in order to perform this kind of work well.

I have worked in this career for 20 years, and have found my work to be very satisfying. In fact, if given a chance to choose any career, I would choose to again be in oil exploration. I like the people I work with, and the opportunity for advancement. I find job satisfaction in my work because there are direct results, positive or negative, based on my work.

OIL FIELD MAINTENANCE

As a maintenance worker in an oil field, I am responsible for preserving and repairing pipe lines and pump stations. My territory covers several miles for which I am totally responsible. I have to respond immediately to a malfunction in the pipe lines or stations in order to keep oil flowing through the pipes.

To do my job and to do it well, you have to know engines. You also have to understand pumps and electrical components. I got a lot of my training after high school when I was serving in the Navy.

I enjoy my work in the oil fields because I like building something and seeing it perform like it's supposed to. I really like repairing a pipe and putting it back in operation. While I don't particularly like some aspects of our administrative structure, I do like the work itself. I'd like it even more if I could get some more training on some of the equipment. I also wish I had continued my education. However, if I could start over, I'd choose my occupation all over again.

OPERATING ROOM NURSE

I like my career as a nurse very much and have been in the profession for 24 years. I became a registered nurse by earning a diploma in nursing.

My current duty is in the operating room where I care for anesthetized persons during surgery. I participate in 3 to 4 surgical procedures per day in which one of the most critical skills necessary is the aptitude to handle sterile instruments. In fact, the procedures in sterile techniques is a skill which I feel is not being adequately taught in the nursing schools today. Assisting with operations also takes the physical and mental endurance to withstand long hours of intense work.

I like almost every aspect of my work, except for the lack of opportunity for advancement.

If I were given the opportunity to start again and choose any career, I would again choose nursing. It has been satisfying to me knowing that I help people get well.

OPERATIONS COORDINATOR

It is my job as operations coordinator for an agriculture product manufacturer to handle the various behind-the-scenes projects to make the manufacturing process operate more smoothly. My daily activities depend upon the phone calls I receive and the time of the month. At the beginning of the month, I make shipping forecasts and make other production decisions. I am the troubleshooter whose major objective is to have a smooth running shop. In order to do this, it is necessary to be knowledgeable in all shop operations, and to have the ability to work well with people.

My career in manufacturing management started 27 years ago after earning my

Bachelor of Science in Business Administration. Prior to the company's reorganization and downsizing, I was a supervisor in production control.

I like almost every aspect of my work including the people I work for and the people with whom I work. The only major drawback to this career for me has been the lack of opportunity for advancement. Despite this, I plan to stay in this career. I find that it offers me job satisfaction from seeing forecasts met and a factory running smoothly.

OPERATIONS RESEARCH ANALYST

With a Bachelor of Arts degree in mathematics and physics and a Masters of Science in operations research, I am now an Operations Research Analyst. In the past, I worked as a volunteer EMT, a weight loss clinic receptionist, and have done some tutoring. In my current work, I plan future test programs for Department of Defense projects.

After meeting with my customer and discussing test requirements, we consider necessary resources and plan analysis methods. One day we hope to run tests, collect data, and compress that information using the capability of the computer. We will analyze the data and report on the test results.

After an undergraduate course, I became interested in operations research. I like it because it particularly applies a mathematical basis to problem-solving. I enjoy working with others in my job and being part of the team who will design the tests. Using my mental expertise to solve problems gives me much satisfaction. I like my work so much that I'd choose this field again if I could start over.

It is frustrating, however, that we haven't had the satisfaction of actually conducting the tests of my current project yet. Until that time, we will not able to do any analysis. My plans are to become more and more involved in the applications of operations research. I am particularly interested in the area of transportation.

OPERATOR, HOT METAL CRANE

Delivering molten iron at 2600 degrees to foundry lines to make engine blocks is what I do as a hot metal crane operator in the central foundry of an automobile manufacturing company. During my 8 hour shift, I get totally filthy. One of my primary concerns in performing my work is not to get burned. This requires a respect for the molten iron and a good safety attitude. It is also necessary to have skill in operating heavy equipment.

I was provided a transfer into this job through my union, and I accepted because I liked the challenge it offered. After 15 years on the job, I have found that I like most aspects of the work.

I like having the skills it takes to handle molten iron properly, and I am fascinated with the nature and characteristics of molten iron.

If given the opportunity in the future, I would like to become involved in some way in the field of environmental law in order to have some influence on the laws governing the handling of hazardous materials. I would work toward making the air and materials that people work with completely safe to breathe and handle.

OPERATOR, SCHOOL BUS & COMPUTER

Working at two jobs for the past five years has been an interesting experience. I work for the school system as both a school bus driver and a data processing clerk. As school bus driver, my day starts very early. First I pick up my bus, perform a daily inspection, drive to the high school, and park the bus. Then I go to the data processing department and check my schedule for the day. Then I start my six bus runs for the morning. After my morning bus runs are completed, I supervise approximately one thousand students in the school cafeteria during the lunch period and then make two more bus runs. Next, my schedule requires that I return to the high school to my second job in data processing to finish my work day, updating school records on the computer.

As you may have guessed, it takes being very well organized to juggle this daily work schedule, and my jobs also require accuracy, punctuality, the ability to handle students, special training to become a school bus driver, a good driving record, and basic computer skills.

I enjoy working with the students and working on the computer; it makes me feel good when the information sheets come back with few or no errors.

I fell into my current position after moving to a new area of the country; I was unable to gain employment similar to that in which I was previously qualified as a medical receptionist.

I enjoy working with people and plan to enroll in nursing school in the near future.

OPERATOR, WATER SYSTEM

As a water systems operator for eight years, I am responsible for the production, treatment, and distribution of water. I enjoy my work which includes checking plants, taking water samples, and trouble shooting problems. There are new challenges every day.

I am a high school graduate who worked as a brick mason for 17 years. I find my present work much easier. There's more free time, I can pretty much work at my own pace, plus I meet all kinds of people, since everyone drinks water.

In the future, I'll probably stay with this job and try to change the more unsatisfactory elements. What I don't like is what I consider an unprofessional board of directors who are not paid and are, therefore, disinterested. I don't like it when a person's water is turned off for non-payment. I'd also like better pay myself and more back up when there are emergencies and during the weekends.

I've found in my job that a good water systems operator should have mechanical ability. Being very observant as well as having a good sense of humor are important. The willingness to get up and go out at any hour of the day or night, since water systems never break down at a convenient time, is also necessary.

OPHTHALMOLOGIST

After high school, I wanted to do something I felt was worthwhile. Ophthalmology was my choice because I wanted to specialize. I earned a Bachelor of Arts and an M.D. degree and have been in practice for 10 years.

An ophthalmologist should be a caring person. You have to be thoughtful and considerate of the patient. The profession requires 4 years of training after medical school to deal with eye problems exclusively.

Examining patients' eyes and treating diseases of the eye is what I do. Once a week I perform surgery on patients who need that attention. Each day in my office I see 20 to 30 patients with eye problems.

There's a great deal of satisfaction in my work from helping people keep their vision. I get personal pleasure from doing a good job. On the downside, the hours are extremely long and there's stress in the feeling that I'm not doing my best, even if it is the very best treatment that can be provided now to a patient. I plan to continue keeping up with the advances and changes in my chosen career.

OPTOMETRIC ASSISTANT

I've been an optometric assistant for eight years and enjoy my work very much. The only part I dislike is the lack of opportunity for advancement. I very much enjoy helping patients choose frames and lenses pleasing to them. Finding the best lenses for a person with a strong prescription is difficult and rewarding at the same time.

In the past I worked as a sales clerk and a waitress. I got into my present occupation accidentally. My husband is an optometrist; while he was interviewing for additional staff, I helped out in the office for a week. I've been here ever since.

An optometric assistant must be knowledgeable about fashion. You should be able to get along and enjoy people. Organization and precision are also helpful. I have a Bachelor of Science degree, but that is not required for my job.

In my work, I help people pick out glasses, fit contact lenses, and assist the optometrist any way I can. I discuss with patients the options available for the best visual acuity with their prescription. My duties include ordering patients' glasses from an optical laboratory and checking work orders received from a lab. I also adjust the glasses and make repairs.

ORGANIZATIONAL PSYCHOLOGIST

As an organizational psychologist, I'm involved in strategic planning, productivity studies, and training. Teaching, as well as conducting attitude surveys, are part of my work. I plan to continue in my field, writing, teaching, and sharing knowledge.

The very early part of my day is spent reading articles and business journals. I check my electronic mail (E-mail) on the computer for messages and make or return phone calls. Depending on the project I'm working on, I meet with clients from 9:00-12:00 and 1:00-2:00. In between and after 2:00 I reserve for project development, phone calls, and writing.

To be an organizational psychologist, you need adequate education. I have a Bachelor's degree and a Master of Arts as well as a Ph.D. degree. You must have good interpersonal skills to be able to deal with people. A burning curiosity, along with the willingness to try new things, and a hunger for knowledge are also important.

I've been in this work for many years and enjoy it. I'd choose this field again. Although I don't feel that there are opportunities for advancement, the opportunity to learn and apply what I've learned is rewarding to me.

ORTHODONTIST

Unlike a general dentist who helps patients with preventative problems, an orthodontist is a dentist who helps people improve their appearance. It's quite satisfying to help in such a personal way by straightening their teeth. Patients like to come to my office.

I first explored the field of orthodontia for two reasons: every interest survey I took suggested I become a dentist, and I tried what I initially wanted to be--a research biologist--and hated it, so I obtained my Bachelors and Masters of Science degrees and a D.D.S. Orthodontics was the field for me. I enjoy the life style and the satisfaction I get.

My plans are to work as an independent orthodontist for the remainder of my career. I have many years ahead of me and I plan to grow professionally and develop the practice during these years.

When I arrive at the office each day, I take care of administrative details, checking the mail and messages, and addressing any concerns of the staff. My day is spent in appointments with patients with various kinds of treatments. At the end of the day, I process financial information and deposit income. I also send letters to communicate with referrals, patients, and other doctors. During the week, I may have lunch visits with general dentists, promotional lunches or buffets in the office or at Chamber of Commerce meetings.

To be a good orthodontist, you must have strong problem-solving abilities in case diagnoses. Solid communication skills are necessary in dealing with patients and staff. Good manual dexterity along with attention to detail--perfectionism--are vital to this work. Reliable business sense helps, but this area can be handled by others.

ORTHOPEDIC SURGEON #1

In my medical speciality of orthopedic surgery, I treat and operate on injuries, diseases and abnormalities of the musculoskeletal system. My work days are a combination of doing surgery, examining hospital and office patients, and covering the emergency room.

The skills and attitudes which I find are most important to perform well as an orthopedic surgeon are desire to do the best you can for other people, good eye-hand coordination, being mechanically inclined, having a curious-probing mind, energy, knowing and accepting your limitations, and having a strong faith.

I like my profession because it gives me the satisfaction of contributing to good results. I also find satisfaction from assisting people in their recovery to good health. I feel rewarded from making a horrendous situation turn out well. It is also gratifying to know that I have special skills and abilities to help others. The only major item which I dislike about this occupation is the amount of paper work.

Orthopedics appealed to me even as a teenager. I'm mechanically inclined, and have always loved science and physiology which are great prerequisites for this profession.

I have been in practice for 15 years and cannot think of another career I would like better. I plan to continue to deliver quality community care.

ORTHOPEDIC SURGEON #2

Because I've always liked "mechanical things," I studied to become an orthopedic surgeon earning my Bachelor of Science and my M.D. In my work, I do reconstructive bone surgery. For two days each week I perform surgery to insert artificial joints or repair fractures. I'm in the clinic for two and a half days weekly where my attention is on fractures and other clinical work.

It's most gratifying to see people get better. I'd like my work more if we could rid our profession of governmental intervention. I also dislike the fact that we have unethical physicians in the medical field. However, I like the work I do very much and I enjoy the people with whom I work and those I serve.

Being a successful orthopedic surgeon demands great attention to detail. Things must be done right the first time.

A surgeon for fourteen years, I'd choose my career all over again. My plans are to continue in my practice.

OWNER, ANTIQUE & GUN SHOP

After retiring from the U.S. Army as a First Sergeant, I am now self employed as the owner/operator of a small antique and gun shop. I chose the business because I have always loved antiques and guns.

Not only do I buy and sell, but I also restore antiques and guns. This requires knowledge about these items as well as carpentry, gunsmithing, and various other skills to do the restoration work. As a retailer, I find good communication skills are important.

I like this kind of work very much. I find job satisfaction from the good hours, good pay, and being my own boss.

OWNER, AUTO PARTS STORE

I started in the automobile parts business as a young man and never left. Now, as owner of an auto parts store, I am involved in sales, billing, payables, ordering, and receiving for the store. When I arrive at the store in the morning, I check in the goods received. During the course of the day, I answer phone calls for orders to be shipped, wait on over-the-counter sales, check all previous day's receipts, enter all charges in ledger and file, write orders for the next day, and answer correspondence. The key to accomplishing all these duties is a well organized mental process.

I have been in this career for 25 years. I find job satisfaction in keeping busy and helping solve peoples' mechanical problems. However, I was an officer in the US Army, and sometimes think that I would choose a career in the Army if given the chance to start over.

OWNER, CONVENIENCE STORE

With a Bachelor of Science in education, I was an elementary and junior high teacher for a period. I then spent some time as a stock broker and financial consultant. With the opportunity to own my own business and avoid traveling long distances to work, I bought a convenience store from friends. I've been involved in this work for four and a half years.

As a business owner, I am "the management." I am responsible for hiring and firing employees, ordering merchandise, keeping the books, plus waiting on customers. My day, beginning around 4:00 a.m., starts with doing paper work in the office without disturbances. The store opens at 7:00 a.m. and I spend the day as described above in addition to making deposits and meeting sales representatives. When the next shift comes on, I continue working in my office doing whatever needs to be done until sometimes 10:00 p.m.

My life would be great if there were less paper work required. I'd also like the customers to be more considerate to the help. But I love meeting people and working with young people as well as the adult public. Working for myself makes it all worthwhile as I build equity in my own business. The challenge of staying up with a continuously changing world is very satisfying to me. Eventually, when the store is paid for, I'll remodel and expand to make my business even more prosperous.

Strong people skills are needed in this business. It's important to be able to meet, welcome, and talk with customers of all levels. A positive attitude, good selling skills, and some mechanical ability are all necessary. You should be able to mentally calculate mathematically, to think quickly, and make decisions. Computer literacy and knowing accounting procedures are a must in this business. You also must keep up with economic trends as well as marketing and business affairs.

OWNER, EQUIPMENT SALES COMPANY

I'm self-employed. I do it all!!! I handle all design/engineering, buying, bookkeeping, etc. for my materials handling equipment and conveyor systems company. A major part of my work day is spent contacting customers and potential customers to show them how I can solve their materials handling problems. I must identify customer wants versus needs. It is essential to determine the amount of money the customer can/will spend for my service/equipment. Writing letters and proposals and phone or in-person customer contacts are a major part of my work.

I receive satisfaction from my work because I am utilizing my mechanical/spatial skills. I enjoy designing workable solutions. This job is also satisfying for me because it is financially rewarding.

I would like to have two or three sales employees to make more money and make my company grow to the $1-2 million level.

I chose this occupation because I enjoy mechanical equipment. I also like selling (although not my strong point). I have worked for two "majors" in my field and felt it would be less restrictive and more rewarding to do it on my own.

Prior to my work in the materials handling industry I was a US Army helicopter pilot/soldier and in retail sales.

I hope that my company stays strong and becomes well known enough to eventually give it to my two sons so they can have fun, make money, and do things their way and on their terms!

OWNER, FURNITURE REFINISHING COMPANY

Having my own business gives me the privilege of controlling my own schedule. When I get there I stand around drinking coffee with the employees and discussing the work for the day. Once we are set up, we work very hard at stripping and refinishing furniture for individual homeowners with only a quick lunch break. At the end of the day I make phone calls for people to come pick up their furniture and to give estimates on new jobs.

To do well in a business like this you must be diligent in getting work done. Being extremely courteous and understanding of customers who don't know anything about furniture is also part of doing this job well. As an employer, you should be sympathetic to employees' needs and desires--you take care of them and they'll take care of you.

I like having my own business because I go in when I want and leave when I want. Most customers are extremely satisfied with the quality of our work which is very rewarding to me. I feel I'm in control of how good or bad my business is run. There is of course always room for some changes in some areas of how we do our work to improve things.

My parents offered to teach me the business and then sell it to me. Before that I did construction and office work. I also earned a BA degree in English literature.

I hope to train people to entirely run the day-to-day operations of the business so I can do just the management work.

OWNER, MACHINE SHOP

Upon finishing high school, there was an opening in an apprentice program for toolmaking, and, considering my fascination with machines and how they operate, I thought this would be right for me. I have in fact found design engineering to be the right career for me. Prior to owning my own shop, I was in sales and engineering and managed people in other machine shops.

Now as the shop owner and machine operator of machines which make metal details, I transfer raw metal into finished details usually per drawings. The work day can vary greatly each day since the needs of customers are usually spontaneous. By this I mean you start performing one task and, within the hour, you can be doing something entirely different. One of the most important abilities I must have to operate my business successfully is to decide the best and quickest way the machine can make the metal detail so the job gets completed and is done properly.

I like the kind of work I do very much. In fact, if given a chance to start over and the opportunity to prepare for any kind of work, I would again choose design engineering. My job satisfaction comes when a job is completed and I can watch it perform the way I expected it to. I plan to continue in this work and possibly expand the shop.

OWNER, MOTEL/RESTAURANT

After getting home from the Vietnam war as a 1st Lieutenant, I didn't want to go back to school for a Masters degree. So, I leased, then bought, a motel which I've run for 20 years.

My work is doing anything it takes to run a motel and restaurant. There are many different jobs to do and long hours involved. Some of the tasks I do are helping to cook, cleaning rooms, and making repairs.

While I don't like the hassles of bookkeeping, I love being able to be my own boss. It would be great if someone else did all the book work. I enjoy all the people involved--from the guests to the employees. This is one of the requirements of running a motel; you need to get along well with the public. I'll continue operating the business until I sell it some day and retire.

OWNER, NURSERY SCHOOL & TEACHER

As the owner of a nursery school, I also am a teacher there. I plan and implement lessons for 3-5 year olds. I love kids, so I've been a camp counselor, a mom, and I've earned a Bachelor of Science degree in child development. Now I have my own preschool!

A great deal of patience is needed in my work of 7 years. You should be a person who cares about life and about children. A warm, positive attitude is important. One must be a consistent, fair disciplinarian and, above all, be a good teacher.

My mornings, from 9:00-11:30, are for 4 year olds. The afternoons, from 12:30-3:00 are for 5 year olds. My time with each group is spent pretty much the same way. There are projects to do, snacks to eat, and songs to sing. I particularly enjoy reading stories to the children. I also zip coats, tie shoes, and give hugs.

The only drawback to this work is the shortage of money. Otherwise, I love working for myself, the job itself, and I love happy children! I plan to teach until my own children are out of school. Possibly then, I'll open an educational toy store.

OWNER, PLUMBING COMPANY

I am the owner of a small business that performs plumbing repairs and installation in new construction and remodeling projects. I also have a physical disability. As a sole proprietor in business less than one year, I do it all--estimating jobs, keeping the books, scheduling work, performing the scheduled work, handling advertising and public relations functions, and keeping current inventory. I would really like to do more, but I just do not have enough time. Working for myself, each job is different, and that constant challenge really keeps me going; I love my job. I worked in some related jobs for fifteen years before starting my own company: rod buster, carpenter, electrician, roofer, brick mason, fertilizer salesman, sheet rock installer, tapper, heating and air conditioning installer, painter, and sand-blaster.

Preparation for employment in plumbing repair requires a journeyman plumbing skill level with a good measure of common sense, the drive or motivation to get the job done the right way in as short a time as possible, and good people skills. I have found that customers are willing to pay for a job well done by a person they can communicate with--my motto is Keep It Simple Stupid, otherwise known as the KISS principle. When presenting a quote to a customer, you must be able to justify all costs. This is a key to customer satisfaction--I believe that a quality job done today, completed to the customer's satisfaction, is almost guaranteed repeat business; and the repeat customer is the foundation of a good solid business reputation.

Each challenging job successfully completed, is like a trophy for me to remember with pride; I really enjoy providing a necessary service to the public. Being my own boss, I set and accomplish my goals--I do not have another person constantly looking over my shoulder. It is uniquely rewarding for me to be able to perform these tasks; after five years of total disability, still partially disabled, having the ability to be productive again is my greatest satisfaction.

My only complaint is that there are never enough hours in a day.

OWNER, PRINTING COMPANY

It takes a great deal of energy to run a small printing company. As a business owner, I've found you need to be able to handle multiple tasks at the same time. You also must be willing to work well with people even when they are not sure what they want or need.

In my work, there is a lot of contact with customers in sales and delivery. I deal with vendors as well as with the government and its regulations. There is much paper work to do in the office as well as printing products to produce. Problem solving is a great part of my job as well. In general, as a small business owner, you have to wear many hats and you have to do many jobs.

Job satisfaction for me comes in finishing a project and doing it well. I enjoy everything about my work: the customers, the help, the opportunity for advancement, and the work itself. I'd prefer that there not be so much stress and that there be more free time. It would be easier, too, if I didn't have to deal with others' mistakes and if I had better financial backing.

My father was a printer; going into the business seemed like a great opportunity for me. I earned a Bachelor of Arts degree in journalism and, after working as a manager in customer service and as an inventory auditor, I've been in printing for 13 years. My plans are to continue with this work but to diversify into non-related business areas. I'd like to have some financial options available to me should technology change the printing domain too quickly.

OWNER, PROPERTY MANAGEMENT COMPANY

I presently spend a typical day as the owner of a property management firm answering questions for a younger administrator who will eventually take over the company. Although I am soon going to be nearing retirement, I still enjoy making and closing deals on properties. It's a delight when I can make a client happy.

After earning a Bachelor's degree in business administration, I used my accounting and tax background to package and sell real estate. Being a Certified Public

Accountant and working in real estate syndication has been helpful to me in my work, which primarily involves multi-family rentals. I have as my goal now to guide and direct my company and the employees to ensure that good performance will continue, with less of my own direct involvement.

Very important for a property manager is the ability to listen well. You must be able to keep an open mind. The abilities to do financial analysis and handle administrative tasks are also essential if you are to be successful in this kind of work.

OWNER, RETAIL CHAIN

I own and operate a retail chain of stores selling home products and pianos. I also consider myself a financier because I assist my customers in financing the purchase of these high ticket items. My typical responsibilities include balancing the inventory, planning advertising and promotions, and rating the progress of the various stores.

To perform well as a retailer it is important to understand the markets in which you are dealing. You must know what products to supply and what motivates people to buy.

I like this work because of the people I work with and the opportunities I have had for advancement. I have the opportunity to sell the same kind of products or to change my product lines, which makes the work interesting. I receive satisfaction from my work when the products I sell produce pleasure for the owners. The dissatisfying aspect of this business has been dealing with the dishonest segment of the public.

I did not plan for this career but rather entered it by chance. However, after 40 years in the retail business, I can still say I like this kind of work very much.

OWNER, RETAIL HARDWARE STORE

My husband and I own and operate a small retail hardware store. Although I cherish my years as a high school registrar and as a church organist, I've liked the work in retail and I've enjoyed the customers. Given a choice, I'd choose retail again, but would like to have more help. There is too much to do for so few people and not enough volume to warrant hiring adequate assistance. My life would be more enjoyable with a few less hours and an occasional day off.

To be in a retail hardware franchise business, you need common sense. Being able to make decisions, listen patiently to what the customer is asking, or saying, and pleasantly interview the customer to determine needs are essential to running this business. Basic math and reading skills along with a legible handwriting, especially with numbers, are all needed.

My responsibilities are to handle the money and all banking transactions. Once a week I determine inventory needs, then order goods, receive and price merchandise, and stock shelves. I assist our customers with their shopping, handle complaints and other occurrences as necessary. My duties include dealing with the janitorial work while, at the same time, keeping all office records and managing correspondence.

Pleasure has come from working with figures and financial records. Being a neighborhood "mom and pop" type store, we like being able to help shoppers and have them become "repeat customers." I also receive a great deal of pleasure from constructing good-looking merchandise displays. It has been satisfying to produce neat and accurate tax and payroll reports as well as bank deposits. Yet, even though I've enjoyed my years in retail hardware, I think I would have also been interested in being a pianist or organist.

As I look forward to retirement some years from now, I hope to learn to use my computer for accounting and word processing along with doing some volunteer work, i.e., literacy programs or senior activities.

OWNER, WELDING SUPPLY COMPANY

What appeals to me in my work as the owner of a welding supply distributorship are the people involved, the compensation, and the opportunities for advancement. There is a great deal of diversification in the job requirements and I like that. If I had the chance to start over again after these years, I'd definitely choose this work.

Running a welding supply distributorship involves selling welding supplies, purchasing materials, repairing equipment, and scheduling deliveries. Customer and employee satisfaction are very important.

Qualities needed in my work are the ability to get along with people as well as be mechanically minded. Because much of my work involves sales, enthusiasm is critical.

Although a college degree is not a "must" for this work, I am glad I obtained a Bachelor's degree. I got into the welding business without experience, learned as I went along, liked it, and stayed in the business. Now I'm an owner, and I like that too.

OWNER/MANAGER, MAIL ORDER COMPANY

I employ and manage 20 people at my mail order company. On a regular basis I communicate via FAX with Europe and the Orient to discuss new products and designs. As business manager I do the detail work like purchasing and accounting.

To own and manage a business, you should have organizational skills, leadership skills, respect and trust of people and a knowledge of the market.

Feeling the sense of accomplishment or growth, survival, and respect from the market is satisfying to me. I also like the problem solving aspect of my work.

I got into this occupation by turning my hobby into a business. Prior to this business, I was a university physics professor.

OWNER/MANAGER, MANUFACTURING COMPANY

I attribute an inventive mind and a willingness to take a risk as the reasons I am now manager/owner of a manufacturing business. Since this is a small operation, I handle almost all the management functions. My typical activities include reviewing incoming orders, requests, and correspondence; reviewing and signing outgoing correspondence and purchase orders; reviewing backorders, accounts receivable and payable and cash on hand; visiting the manufacturing area, and meeting with department heads and office staff.

As well as inventiveness and willingness to take a risk, I consider multi-disciplined experience, knowledge and mathematical skills to be important to performing this kind of work well. Accepting priority status for business matters, fairness, and humanity are necessary attitudes for operating a successful business. My multi-disciplined experiences includes work as an airplane inspector, a watch and instrument maker, and credit manager.

I find satisfaction from my work, having earned a profit by serving customers well while treating employees fairly.

OWNER/MANAGER, PRINTING FIRM

I like "running my own show" as the owner/manager of a reprographic printing firm (blue prints). I am the second generation of my family to own and operate this business. I appreciate the opportunity it affords me to do my own thing. The drawback for me is the environment I work in is that it is New York City.

My day starts with a one hour commute to work. Once there, my responsibilities include: administering, supervising, selling, negotiating, and representing the firm. I basically divide my time into three segments: one-third customer contact (consultive sales): one-third internal meeting, employee reviews, sales meetings, etc.; and one-third external affairs--meeting vendors, accountants, bankers, attorneys, etc.

The important skills and attitudes for my kind of work are keeping people working together, good communication with employees and outsiders, and fairness.

Prior to taking over the family business, I earned a Bachelor of Science in Business Administration and was a naval officer.

As the owner/manager I do get frustrated at times with the large number of non-productive details I must do. I also would like a change at times so I would be dealing with a higher level of basic employee. Despite these frustration, I like my work and find satisfaction in having the option to try different ideas and succeed or fail because of them.

OWNER/MANAGER, RESTAURANT

I chose to buy into a restaurant because it was the only business I found that I could get into for a small capital investment which allowed me to be my own boss. Prior to this career, I earned my bachelor's degree in economics, and worked as a bookkeeper, translator, and correspondent in different languages.

As the part owner/manager/bookkeeper of a deli restaurant, I work six days a week preparing and serving breakfast and lunch. My typical daily schedule is: waiting on people for breakfast, preparing for lunch, waiting on customers again at lunch; preparing for the next morning, cleaning, and doing the paperwork.

To perform this kind of work well, you have be well organized, friendly and very patient. It is also very important to be quick enough to efficiently handle any problem that might arise. The physical capacity to stand on your feet all day long is another requirement for this work.

The one aspect of my business that I would like to change would be in the number of items served. I would like to cut down on the items offered, thus requiring less storage space, less time for inventories, and less preparation.

My job satisfaction comes from contact with people--mostly professionals in my case. It is rewarding to hear all the nice things they say about the deli, the food, and us.

Although I like my work, I do get impatient sometimes because this is not a fast money business. I am tempted at times to give this up for a job in commerce where I think I could make more money faster.

PARALEGAL #1

I have been a homemaker for years but have recently become a paralegal after taking the appropriate training. Other previous careers have been as a flight attendant, a real estate sales and marketing person, and a legal secretary. It was from my work as a legal secretary that I developed an interest in pursuing a career as a paralegal.

I attend 3 hour classes several days a week, and spend approximately 15 to 20 hours a week studying at home or doing research in a law library. When I am not studying or researching law, my time is spent running a household.

I feel a personal sense of accomplishment from the knowledge I am gaining from my studies and research. I have found it absolutely necessary to develop concentration skills and to have perseverance to achieve my goal of becoming a paralegal. My plan is to work for a mid-size law firm in a large city.

PARALEGAL #2

As a paralegal, I provide assistance to the attorney in preparation of cases, conduct client interviews, and attend court or other meetings with the attorney. In general, I act as a buffer between the attorney and the client. I also handle the attorney's paperwork--typing, word processing, filing, and conducting research on behalf of the attorney, both in books and through people.

In my two years in this position, I have found the skills necessary to perform my job are knowledge of the legal system, the ability to work well with people, the ability to get and stay organized, and the ability to meet deadlines and work under pressure. I have completed a Bachelor of Science in Paralegal Studies.

Although hectic at times, my work is very rewarding. I have always wanted to work in the legal field. I enjoy helping the attorney solve or rectify people's problems, seeing the legal system work, and knowing I am a part of it.

The field of paralegal is so new that most people do not understand it or are misinformed of the importance of this kind of work. I would like to see more general awareness of the importance of my job; perhaps then I could enjoy more of a leadership role in the firm.

I have also worked as a secretary to a Vice President, as office assistant to a placement agency, and as office helper at a hardware store.

I like this kind of work, especially having the opportunity to help people with a problem. Eventually, I would like to establish my own firm of paralegals to assist attorneys and I may even try free-lancing.

PARAPROFESSIONAL BOOKKEEPER

I am a self-taught paraprofessional bookkeeper. I have always liked working with numbers and, after graduating from high school, I started working my way up in this profession. I now work for an accounting firm writing up accounts payable, the general ledger, cash/disbursement, and cash/receipts for various clients.

To perform this kind of accounting work, it is important that you have mathematical and problem-solving skills. Having a positive attitude, knowing there is an answer, and searching out that answer are also necessary for this job. You must be able to take something with less than perfect information and make it all become meaningful.

There is not anything I dislike about my work; what I particularly do like is that way the elements fit together. That is the satisfying part of my job--to do the work correctly.

My plans for the future? These include earning a college degree in accounting in order to continue to advance in this field.

PASTOR

As the pastor of a church, it is highly gratifying to me to see people change and grow spiritually. It is rewarding to watch the church increase in numbers and to watch people increasing the depth of their conviction.

In my work, I preach, teach, counsel, administer, and motivate. My week is planned so that Mondays are spent doing administrative paperwork. Tuesdays through Thursdays I prepare for Sunday's sermon, meet appointments, and work in the church office. There are evening services Wednesdays. Friday is my day off. Saturdays I work with volunteers around the church and Sunday is spent in services.

Although there is too much time required for administrative work and I'd rather work in a larger church, I've enjoyed my 16 years in the pulpit. After earning my Bachelor of Arts degree and my Masters in education, I was recruited into the ministry by a church pastor. I'm glad that happened because I like my work and I enjoy all the people with whom I am involved. My plans, of course, are to continue in the ministerial field.

A pastor needs strong skills in dealing with people. The abilities to communicate well and to motivate people are essential. Of course, you must have the appropriate theological and counseling training. A positive attitude with a "can do" mind-set has been valuable to me.

PASTOR, PROTESTANT EVANGELICAL

After 32 years in the ministry, I can say that I like it very much and would not choose another career even if given the opportunity to make another choice and start again. I cannot readily identify anything I dislike about pastoring.

As a senior pastor of a Protestant Evangelical congregation, my time is divided between studying, preaching, teaching, staff supervision, administration work, attending meetings, pastoral care, counselling, and visitations.

As well as the education background necessary to become a pastor, I think it is important to have the following skills and attitudes: public speaking, writing, organization, optimism, reading, relational skills, and to feel comfortable with people.

It was with a sense of divine calling and encouragement of those who knew me that led me into this career. Except for feeling sometimes that there are nebulous indicators of my effectiveness as a pastor, I do find satisfaction from preaching a well prepared sermon and pointing others to a more satisfying or meaningful life.

PATIENT COORDINATOR

As a Patient Coordinator in the office of an orthodontist, I work as both a certified dental assistant and an office manager; I have worked in a dental office for the last twelve years. Overall, I ensure the proper function of the office--sorting mail, posting payment checks to the proper accounts, handling new patient interviews and current patient examinations, updating dental charts, handling of public relations, answering phones, and making and rescheduling appointments.

Although there is not much opportunity for advancement, I do like the people I work with, the dentist I work for, and the kind of work I do. If I had it to do over again, I would still choose this job.

I enjoy knowing that I am contributing to peoples' dental health. I have always worked in a position that deals with people.

I possess an Associate in Science degree in dental assisting. Also required for this position are superior people skills, office skills, and some technical knowledge of dentistry.

I would like to see more automation in the field of dental assisting. My future goals are to return to school part time and keep this same job.

PAYROLL & BENEFITS COORDINATOR

By volunteering to do my church's books, I discovered my natural ability to work with numbers which led me into pursuing my current job as a payroll and benefits coordinator. Prior to this I had numerous other jobs including salesperson in a department store, doctor's assistant, claims adjustor, insurance salesperson and secretary, which were not particularly satisfying to me. However, I am now more satisfied with my work because of the accounting responsibilities.

As a payroll and benefits coordinator, I process the payroll biweekly, administer and monitor benefits, and maintain employee records. More specifically, my day might include some or all of the following activities: talking with new employees, maintaining employee records, processing payroll for 200 employees, answering questions about benefits, doing various payroll and benefit reports, paying insurance bills, and/or handling workman's compensation claims.

This kind of work requires a very well organized and detail-inclined person. It is also important to be good with numbers and accurate in order to perform well at this job. Working well with people is also an important requirement.

Except for the lack of opportunity for advancement, I like every aspect of my work. I find my work satisfying because I love working with numbers.

My educational background includes a Bachelor of Science degree in Home Economics. I have now decided to return to school in order to earn a degree in accounting. My future career plans are to become an accountant for a non-profit organization.

PAYROLL/BILLING SUPERVISOR

As a Payroll/Billing Supervisor and Accounts Receivable Representative, I key in time slips to the computer for payroll processing and billing, call on people whose payments are past due, prepare bills for outgoing mail pick up, handle all filing for my group, answer all phone calls, and pass out payroll checks to employees--the one time in a week that I can depend on everyone being happy to see me.

To work in this field, you must have a positive attitude, good communication skills, good people skills, a mathematical background, and computer experience.

In the one and one-half years I have been employed in this position, I have enjoyed the challenge of collecting bad debts--I know that it is considered a bad debt only because someone else gave up; I do not give up.

I have always worked in a job dealing with people and I would like to continue to be able to help others.

I plan to pursue a degree in nursing at night school while still working at my present job.

PEDIATRIC NURSE PRACTITIONER

I have several jobs all within the nursing profession. As a registered nurse, I work in the hospital in obstetrics, but I also contract to write nursing programs and new in-service staff programs. As a pediatric nurse practitioner, I work in an office and take care of well and ill children.

My work days are different. Some days I do consulting and writing, and other days I work a 12 hour shift in the OB department of the hospital. My P.N.P. work is done on alternate days.

I got into the nursing profession because of my co-dependency (father was alcoholic). I wanted to be needed. So, I attended college and earned my Bachelor of Science in nursing degree and also became a Pediatric Nurse Practitioner. My first job was as a public health nurse.

To perform well in my kind of work, I think the most important skills and attitude are: caring, common sense, good communication skills, and a desire to help people to help themselves.

The things I would like to see changed with my profession is the salary level which I would like raised, and more professionalism among nurses. A change in the nurses' attitude may result in a more professional attitude toward nurses by doctors and other lay people.

Nursing has been satisfying for me when I am helping people to help themselves to gain their independence by my teaching them to take responsibility for their health.

PEDIATRIC REGISTERED NURSE

I always wanted to go into pediatric nursing, and worked to support myself through school to earn an Associate of Science in Nursing degree and then became a registered nurse. As such, I give comfort and medical care to children and their families.

As a pediatric nurse, I have charge of 4 to 5 children, mostly under 2 years old. My duties include assessing the condition and needs of the children, then giving then their medication, and feeding, bathing and comforting them. I also have the responsibility to chart the evening activities and to process the unit paperwork.

My evaluation of the skills and attitudes which are important for performing this kind of work well are to be a team player, to have empathy, and to have a knowledge of nursing and medical technology and the biopsychosocial development of all age groups.

The major frustration I face with my job is that of being understaffed. I would definitely like to have more nurses recruited at my facility. I also see a need for an increase in interaction between the different disciplines involved in providing medical care. This occupation would also benefit from an increase in the powers of interpersonal communication.

Despite these frustrations, I like most aspects of my work. I like the people I work for, the people I work with, the opportunity for advancement, and the kind of work I do. I find job satisfaction in knowing that I am doing my best to help a child and his family to achieve optimal health; giving a child a chance for a quality life.

I plan to continue with my career in nursing and aspire to become a pediatric clinical nurse specialist.

PEDIATRICIAN

As a pediatrician I provide preventive, anticipatory and emergency health care for children and adolescents. My typical daily work hours are from 8:00 am to 6:00 pm and then I am on call from 6:00 pm on. I make hospital rounds from 8:00 to 9:00 am and do examinations and treatment of patients from 9:00 am to 6:00 pm.

To perform well in this profession it is important to relate well to people, be analytical and be an easy learner.

The reward I receive from being a pediatrician is that I have the sense of accomplishment and the personal satisfaction of helping others. My profession would be more satisfying if there were less demands from patients and the financial rewards were greater as in other medical specialties. I would also like more free time.

I became a pediatrician because I enjoyed this medical specialty more than the others which were presented in medical school.

PERSONNEL CONSULTANT

After graduating from college with a Bachelor of Arts degree, I went to an employment service for their assistance in finding a career spot dealing with the public. I liked what I saw in the consultant I had at the employment agency, and ended up becoming a personnel consultant myself for a private employment service.

My responsibilities as a personnel consultant include: placement of clients in jobs, marketing to company's clients, writing advertisements, negotiating salaries and placement, and scheduling interviews.

To perform this kind of work well, it is important to have a high energy level, sense of urgency, intuition, empathy, and a desire to win.

Aside from my dislike for writing advertising, and my frustrations with getting employers to understand the need for our services, I think I have a great job.

For the past 15 years my satisfactions have come in finding careers for clients, negotiating salaries, the repeating business over the years, and the variety of people changes.

PERSONNEL DIRECTOR, PUBLIC SCHOOL

For 5 years, I've been Director of Non-instructional Personnel for a large school district. My duties are to interview applicants, handle the telephone and paperwork, and attend meetings. In addition, I spend some time on the computer.

For this kind of job, it is critical to have solid interpersonal skills. There is a large amount of interaction with other people and you should be skillful at that if you are to be fully successful.

I have held several other jobs prior to this one: welfare visitor, teacher, job placement counselor, and sales. Of these, selling was most interesting to me; however, my present work in the personnel department of a large school district has been and will continue to be my favorite occupation.

I feel satisfaction when I've done a good, productive job. My plans are to continue in my present occupation. I am happy in my work; if I could begin again, I'd choose the same work. Yet, my work would be more interesting if there were more positions available for the many applicants we have; the lack of opportunities for advancement is also a bit discouraging. My education includes Bachelor of Arts and Master of Arts degrees.

PERSONNEL MANAGEMENT CONSULTANT

I chose personnel work more than 30 years ago because it sounded more interesting than inventory control, which seemed to be my other option at that point in my life. It has indeed turned out to be the right career choice for me because of my successes in being promoted from the clerical ranks through management positions. Now I hold the position as Personnel Management Consultant.

I now work on project type assignments, advising managers on their human resources to effect more efficient organizations. Although my work is somewhat sporadic at this point, when I am working on an assignment, I am often involved in my work for 12+ hours daily.

To perform this kind of work well, it is important to have planning and organizing skills, a positive can-do attitude, and the ability to translate clients' problems into practical action plans and finished products.

What I most like about my work is the people I work with. People contact, wonderful surroundings, unlimited funding, travel, travel, and recognition lead to satisfaction too.

PERSONNEL OFFICER

After graduating from college with an anthropology major and working for a recruitment ad agency as their advertising-client liaison, I again moved into another unrelated field as a personnel officer. Although my educational background and previous job experience did not point me toward this career, I have found that I like this kind of work.

As the personnel officer in an ad agency, my responsibilities include: interviewing prospective employees, conducting salary surveys, handling safety issues and employee relations, writing the company newsletter, administering various programs, writing policy manuals, taking photos, administering the transportation program, and writing job descriptions.

To perform this kind of work well as a personnel officer, it is important to have: excellent verbal and written communication skills, good judgment, the ability to make decisions, the ability to perform a variety of tasks and prioritize them, and the ability to counsel people and remain impartial.

Although I am somewhat frustrated with my job because I do not feel the management of the company for which I work is receptive to change, I like the kind of work I do and the people I work with. I find job satisfaction from helping people. It is also satisfying following a project from start to finish. I like working independently - setting my own priorities and introducing new programs. Another asset to my job is the variety of work.

I plan to build on my experiences in this line of work pursuing one of the following options: management in human relations field, corporate communications, or employee training.

PETROLEUM ENGINEER #1

I have been a petroleum engineer for all of my adult life. I started out in this career immediately after earning a Bachelor of Science in Petroleum Engineering degree.

It was through discussions with friends that my interest in this career was developed. I have liked my work very much and would choose this occupation again even if given the chance to start again.

The major objective of my work is to drill and produce oil and gas at a profit. As an engineer, I assist and advise staff in drilling and producing oil and gas wells. To perform well at this job, I have found it important to have communication skills, to foster cooperation, have an analytical mind, and to be a good decision-maker.

If I could initiate any changes in this occupation, it would be to have more intelligent and cooperative relations with governmental institutions.

Job satisfaction comes from my work as a petroleum engineer in getting an essential resource into practical application and use.

PETROLEUM ENGINEER #2

I've been a petroleum engineer working in reservoirs and drilling for many years. Enjoying every minute, I really have no complaints.

I earned a Bachelor of Science degree in engineering, and have always been interested in the field. Deciding on the petroleum area was primarily because it was the most popular at the time of my graduation. I have had no other career except this one, which has been all spent overseas.

My earlier days were spent primarily in hands-on engineering work with emphasis on field work, drilling for oil, and petroleum storage. Assignments were highly results-oriented. We determined where petroleum reserves were located and prepared drilling programs. Later in my career I found myself more involved in planning and working very closely with other engineers out of the field. I am involved in the development and implementation of ideas. Training additional engineers is also part of my job.

What I have enjoyed most about my career is the good friends and relationships I've had. Financial security is wonderful, too. I have also found great satisfaction in the work itself.

PETROLEUM ENGINEER & CONSULTANT

The key components for a career as a petroleum engineer are education, and possessing a temperament and personal ideals that are compatible with the work. You should be inquisitive, persistent, and have a positive attitude. Knowledge of basic math, chemistry, physics, mechanical engineering, petroleum engineering and economics are important for this kind of work.

I earned a Bachelor of Science in Chemistry and became a registered professional petroleum engineer. I worked my way up the ladder to senior production engineer and petroleum consultant. As such, I evaluate, design and calculate costs and payout for drilling and production engineering projects. I also act as the oil and gas project manager when the projects are under construction, setting up the drilling equipment.

Although I have enjoyed my many years in this occupation, I have been frustrated with the politics which seem to interfere in this industry. I would like to see politics and politicians removed from scientific projects. Politics and personal opinions should not override facts.

I receive personal satisfaction, like climbing a mountain, from this kind of work. The money I have earned through this occupation is another good feature. Satisfaction also comes from making a contribution to society from my work--development of natural resources and environmental protection.

PETROLEUM GEOLOGIST

I think I can trace back the reason why I chose a career in geology to my childhood and my fascination with fossils and rocks. After 32 years as a geologist I am still fascinated with this field. Except for 2 years of active duty as an Army Lt., I have always been involved in this career. I have worked as an exploration geologist, and an exploration manager for two different companies before going off on my own as a petroleum geologist consultant.

In this capacity, I generate prospects for drilling by oil and gas explorations for production companies. The first step is to gather subsurface data from the library such as logs, scout data, production data. This data is then organized and posted to maps for the purpose of generating drilling prospects for sale to the industry.

To perform this kind of work well, you must have a willingness to work hard and pay attention to detail. You must also have the ability to project from the known producing areas and use this information to project into the lesser drilled areas to predict the location of new fields.

This work is affected by poor business conditions, but aside from that, I like most aspects of the occupation. I particularly like the challenges involved in this kind of work. My ultimate satisfaction is in having wells drilled on my prospects that are economical productions. There are also many intermediate satisfactions such as selling my ideas, acreage being bought on my prospects, etc.

My career plans are to find enough oil or gas so that royalty income will allow for adequate retirement in the future.

PHARMACEUTICAL SALESMAN

To be successful in pharmaceutical sales, a positive attitude and a great deal of salesmanship ability are needed. Also needed is a firm knowledge of the qualities of your medical products. Although it is not entirely necessary, you will be helped by having a college degree. The job can be done with only a high school education; however, I have a Bachelor of Arts degree in economics. While that degree does not directly affect my work, somehow the college background gives me a self-confidence and general foundation that is helpful. Before becoming a pharmaceutical salesman four years ago, I worked as a bank manager. In my present job, I particularly like the people I work for and with, the sales work itself, and the organization. I go to doctors' offices, attempt to see them, and I persuade them to write prescriptions for my products.

I got into this work by answering an ad in the newspaper. I find satisfaction meeting goals and expectations. It is also good to know that the products I sell may be helpful to many people that I'll never see. Unfortunately, I don't believe there is much opportunity for advancement in this field. If I could, I would also move the central office of my company closer to where I live. My plans include continuing in what I'm presently doing because I like it; later I expect to become a trainer or recruiter, still in this area of work.

PHARMACIST #1

As a teenager, I worked in a pharmacy delivering prescriptions and was drawn to the field. I've spent 30 years as a pharmacist in the hospitals and clinics of the Veterans'

Administration system.

Pharmacists need people skills, for we deal with many different kinds of people. Solid skills in science and arithmetic, along with a strong ability to communicate, are all necessary. My degree is a Bachelor of Science in pharmacy, which is needed along with registration as a pharmacist. You must be dedicated to accuracy and committed to the best health interests of the patient.

Knowing that my work helps people is job satisfaction enough for me. I would be more gratified if our profession were able to consult more with patients.

My usual day is to review projects pending from the previous day, to check the clinic activity schedule, and to dispense prescriptions to patients at the pharmacy window of the institution. It is also my responsibility to prepare prescriptions to be mailed to patients. I must prepare unit doses for patients and bulk doses for large volume use. It is important to consult with the staff of medical and dental offices, nurses, social services, and other institutions.

PHARMACIST #2

At an interview with the Dean of the College, the field of pharmacy was suggested to me. I earned a Bachelor of Science degree in pharmacy and have now spent many years in work I thoroughly enjoy. If I could start over, I'd choose being a pharmacist again!

As a pharmacist, I run a pharmacy as well as sell drugs to physicians and hospitals. I call on physicians to market my products and also make appointments with hospital administrators. Visiting retail drug stores takes my time as well.

I have enjoyed just about everything about my work: the people with whom I am involved, the opportunity for advancement, my customers, and the company. I particularly like the freedom I have in my work.

A pharmacist needs a great deal of knowledge about pharmaceutical products. You should be detail-oriented and very precise in order to keep all the records that are necessary. You should be able to make sales presentations as well if you are going to call on physicians and market the pharmaceutical products as I do.

PHARMACIST, HOSPITAL STAFF

I enjoy math and the sciences and helping others so pharmacy has been the right choice for me for the past 13 years.

My daily schedule usually includes interpreting physicians' orders, filling such medication orders, doing quality assurance checks, checking any work done by technicians, preparing IV's, doing pharmacokinetic monitoring, and patient education as well as education of other professionals.

To perform well as a pharmacist it is important to have a high degree of professionalism. It is imperative that you are accurate which means triple checking.

What I find satisfying about my career is that I am assisting in health care, some education of others, and am using math and sciences. If I could initiate any changes in this occupation, it would be to have more professional leadership and better hours.

To prepare for this profession, I graduated after a 5 year program to earn my bachelor of science degree in pharmacy. I like this kind of work and plan to continue in the field. I think I would choose this career again even if I were given the chance to start again.

PHOTOGRAPHER #1

I am a photographer for the United States Department of Agriculture Soil Conservation Service. As such, I photograph conservation practices or events related to conservation. My photo assignments are obviously done in the field, and then I do the processing of my work at the state office. My photography is used for articles, brochures and other printed publications pertaining to conservation issues.

I have an associate degree in electronics although I did not work in that field. My prior jobs have been as procurement agent, and civil engineering technician. I started at my present occupation because someone knew of my skills at my photography hobby and offered me the job.

Despite the low pay and lack of opportunity for advancement, I like this kind of work very much. I find satisfaction from this work and from the decisions that I have the freedom to make in order to carry out my assignments.

To perform well at this kind of work, it is important to: improvise as you go along; adapt to changes in schedules and plans; think for yourself as changes unfold.

PHOTOGRAPHER #2

As a commercial photographer for the past six years, I make photographs for editorials in magazines or for corporate publications. Getting work takes up more time than one would imagine. I spend a lot of my time on the telephone trying to get work; there are also business skills involved, so a college education is very helpful. I have completed an Associate in Science degree in addition to specialized training in my field and an apprenticeship with an experienced photographer.

Working as a photographer involves so much more than taking pictures; good people skills, patience, and a good working knowledge of photography and the industry in general; hence, the need to serve as an apprentice before launching a career as a photographer.

Although it is tough to get work in order to keep busy, I enjoy my work and the people I meet. My greatest satisfaction comes from making beautiful pictures that satisfy my clients. The only change I would make to derive greater satisfaction from my work is to decrease the ratio of sales to creative photography--there is too much time spent in the sales effort of my business.

I previously worked as a waitress and as a cashier, which helped me to develop good people skills.

For the future, I may decide to seek full-time employment at a company that provides benefits. Unfortunately, that might take some of the creative aspects away from the job, and it will probably restrict my freedom as an artist. You have to weigh the factors involved in this or any decision.

PHYSICAL THERAPIST #1

The key attributes for work as a physical therapist are liking people and patience. I work with crippled children and the progress is most often very slow. However, it is seeing improvement, no matter how small, that has provided me with job satisfaction and kept me working in this field for 20 years.

As a physical therapist, it is my job to set up an exercise program on an individual basis in order to eliminate a handicap or to learn how to function better despite the handicap. I work on the muscles primarily. Therapy sessions are usually on a one-to-one basis several days per week. It could also be just a single session to teach the patient how to perform exercises on their own. With most of my patients who are handicapped children, I work with them to exercise their body and try to build up the muscles that are still functional.

I decided on this profession because of my interest in medicine and my desire to help others. In order to practice, a bachelor degree and certification are necessary. I am glad I chose this career and if given the opportunity to start over and choose any career, I would again choose physical therapy.

PHYSICAL THERAPIST #2

Over 20 years ago, I saw a physical therapist in a dramatic program on television. The role caught my attention and I explored further, eventually going to college and attaining a Bachelor of Science degree in Physical Therapy.

For 19 years I have been able to help people regain their independence through exercise and rehabilitation.

I spend early mornings in an office doing paper work on progress notes and business forms. I wish there were less paper work! I schedule patients for the day and start out to see them in their homes by about 9:30 a.m. I work with patients for approximately 45 minutes each and see between 5 to 8 patients each day.

I enjoy my work but wish doctors and the physical therapist had more say in determining the number of treatments a patient should have. Currently, insurance companies have too much control.

Success in this job takes patience, tact, friendliness, the ability to relate to all kinds of people, and, of course, a thorough knowledge of physical therapy skills.

I plan to continue in this work until my retirement many years down the road.

PHYSICAL THERAPIST #3

I've been a physical therapist for 20 years, and I got into this work because of answering a questionnaire just like this when I was in Junior High School. My work takes me daily to four or five patients' own homes, usually the elderly and usually after hospitalization. I help rehabilitate the patient, teaching how to improve physical function through exercise, adaptations to the environment, and training.

Having an understanding of normal physical movement, the physiology and kinesiology of the body, and the effect of many diseases is important in a physical therapist's work. People skills are essential in helping patients set goals for treatment and in motivating the patient to see the benefits of establishing and maintaining a therapeutic regimen.

I do not like the governmental regulations in this field or some of the organizational policies. I delight in helping people feel better physically, gain more independence, achieve their goals. One day I'd like to be a manager in the profession of physical therapy.

PHYSICAL THERAPIST #4

As a physical therapist, my day is spent scheduling, making phone calls, taking notes (or documenting), and attending conferences. I also see patients for evaluation and treatment. In patient meetings, I make assessments and teach the patients what they need to know about their therapy. In addition, I do research for information which might help with patient care. In a word, I help people regain or achieve their maximum level of physical independence.

Although I like the people I work with, the work itself, and the patients, I don't enjoy the politics in health care. As administration has needed to streamline health care into a more conventional business, the fact that we are working with people in crisis is sometimes lost. Our time cannot always be clocked as if we are doing piece work in a production business.

I like the considerable choice one has in a physical therapist's working environment. The hours are good, there are always "new" things to learn, and new challenges.

When I was in college before I'd decided to earn my Bachelor of Science degree in physical therapy, I knew I wanted a career in the medical field. After talking with a guidance counselor who told me about physical therapy work, I volunteered at a school for the developmentally disabled; I was fascinated by the field. The work is challenging intellectually, physically, and emotionally. As a therapist, I help people, and my work makes a difference in someone's life.

Good listening skills are the key in my profession. One also needs an open, caring attitude as well as respect for others. Flexibility along with the ability to improvise and adapt are very important. It helps to be perceptive, particularly when working with family groups related to an individual patient. Patience is also a necessary strength.

PHYSICIAN #1

I have now worked as a physician for 9 years after completing my internship and other doctorate degree work. I like taking care of the sick, but find that the long hours and pressure of work being in private practice have become somewhat frustrating. If there are no emergencies, I work at the hospital from 8 a.m. to 12 noon and then at the office from 1 to 6 p.m.. At night I make house calls. Of course, emergencies can occur any hour of the day or night, so it is basically a 24 hour a day job. There is also the pressure of malpractice suits which has me somewhat dissatisfied. I am seriously thinking about using my educational background and experience in the medical field to go into teaching medicine and/or missionary work.

As well as the medical education necessary for entering this profession, I consider patience to be the most important attribute you can have to perform well.

I like the people I work with and the kind of work I do. My main satisfaction as a physician comes from patient gratitude.

PHYSICIAN #2

As a 14 year old, I was a victim of an auto/bicycle accident and was hospitalized. As a result, I was inspired by the hospital and the doctors and nurses, and told my parents at that time that I was going to be a doctor. Now after years of practice as a physician, I can evaluate my career by saying that I have no major dislikes about my career, and I like almost every aspect of my work.

My typical schedule is to see hospital patients in the mornings and to have office hours at other times. In order to do this kind of work, and do it well, I consider understanding and compassion to be the key attributes.

The main satisfaction I derive from serving in this profession is from my interaction with people and helping them achieve good health.

I plan to continue in this career for as long as I am physically able. Medicine is a very satisfying career.

PHYSICIAN #3

For forty years I have been a physician. As a child, I wanted to be a doctor. If I had the opportunity to begin again, I would certainly choose medicine as I very much enjoy my work. I'd have enjoyed it more without the interference of the government. I think the government's becoming involved too much in medicine is a mistake.

I found school very easy and entered medical school after college. Being a good physician requires a solid education, the willingness to listen, patience, and setting aside enough time for the patient. Honesty and sincerity are also crucial.

The physician receives much satisfaction from the gratitude of patients and their families, and I find it rewarding to be highly regarded in the community and to have a special kind of favorable reputation.

Other than medicine, I have had virtually no jobs except for a short while I worked in my father's bank. I hated banking and would have been most dissatisfied with my occupation if I had remained in that.

I practice general medicine, treating colds, aches, pains, cuts, and bruises. I diagnose problems, both physical and personal. I have spoken at local clubs and at medical meetings. I have also served as an expert witness in court. I will enjoy peace of mind in my retirement, but I have always enjoyed this work too and will continue to do so for some years to come.

PHYSICIAN, GENERAL PRACTICE

Coming from a family of physicians, I decided on the medical profession myself. I've been a family doctor for nine years after graduating with a Bachelor of Arts and an M.D. degree.

In my work, I evaluate and treat sick people. The result is that they are either cured or their discomfort is relieved. I visit patients in the hospital or see them in my office. Patients and pharmacists call in for information and I return their calls. I also review lab reports and consultants' letters.

Helping people is very satisfying to me. The problem-solving aspect of medicine also fascinates me. I very much enjoy the people I work with and my practice.

My life would be easier if government and third-party interference in the practice of medicine could be eliminated. I'd also like to see the risk of lawsuits reduced.

A physician must enjoy problem-solving, based on training, knowledge, and experience. It helps to have strong interpersonal skills and be a good communicator. A pleasant appearance and good grooming are important. Being well organized and having perseverance are also significant attributes.

PHYSICIAN, GENERAL PRACTICE--STUDENT HEALTH

I started my career as a physician in general practice and later became the administrator of a student health program in a private college. In this position I diagnose and treat patients in both my office and at hospitals. I must also handle the administrative duties of the program which involves coordinating the work with my associates in the health care program.

To perform well in this profession it is important to have the ability to interact with associates as well as patients. You must also have the desire to help people.

I have always been a physician, and I like it very much. I like it because I find satisfaction in a job well done. I also think I might also enjoy medical teaching. In this profession I have enjoyed the people I work with, the opportunity for advancement, and the people and organization for which I work. I would choose the career of a physician again if I had chance to start over. However, I wish there were some way to change this occupation to provide more time to spend with the family.

My interest in medicine started early in childhood. I never intended or was never interested in any other career.

When I retire from my job in academic medicine my plans are to have a refinishing and reupholstering of furniture business.

PHYSICIAN, INTERNAL MEDICINE

I have been a physician for 35 years and plan to continue practice as long as I am healthy. I like this kind of work particularly because I like dealing with medical problems.

I have a solo private practice of internal medicine. On a typical work day I make hospital rounds, which usually take about 30 minutes, then I have office hours for 4 to 5 hours a day. Much time is spent dealing with the health insurance industry and handling financial matters.

To perform well as a physician it is important to seek the best possible medical knowledge in the specialty which you practice. You must have the ability to deal with people who vary in intelligence, income, and mental health.

I got into this profession primarily because of my exposure to the medical field as I was growing up. My father was an M.D. If I could start over and prepare for any career, I would again choose medicine but probably a different specialty. Also, I would select a practice setting which would eliminate dealing with financial matters, possibly a salaried position.

The main satisfaction I find from my work is problem solving and helping people.

PHYSICIAN, INTERNIST

I finally ended the search for the right career for me when I became a physician internist. Prior to that I was a research chemist, pharmaceutical manufacturer, and tool and die maker. It was while working as a biochemist and because of an association I developed with a medical doctor, that I decided on a new career for myself as an internist. I decided what he did was interesting and had great potential for "good."

I try to keep myself to a somewhat set work schedule although you can never anticipate emergencies. I go to the hospital at 7:30 a.m. to examine patients, consult, and evaluate test results. I am in my office at 11:00 a.m. to see patients for examinations and consultations, reviewing case histories, interpreting lab reports (EKG's, chest x-rays, etc.), and to counsel patients. At 4:30 p.m. I return to the hospital to see the sicker patients, and evaluate proper change therapies. Evenings are spent studying and reading.

To perform this kind of work well, it is important to like people, be able to communicate, have a basic background knowledge, and have the ability to read and assimilate medical terms so that information gained can be used in day to day care of patients.

I am somewhat apprehensive about recommending my career to young people now, because I am growing particularly frustrated with some changes that have occurred since I entered the profession. One factor is the interference by "third party" persons in my care of patients. I am referring to government and insurance company intervention. I am also frustrated with the malpractice dilemma.

Despite these drawbacks, I like my career very much, and my son has also entered this field and become a successful internist. I have stayed with it because of the satisfaction I receive when patients respond to my therapies. There is indeed a personal reward in helping others.

PHYSICIAN, MEDICAL SCHOOL PROFESSOR

I am a professor of endocrinology (glands and secretion) and internal medicine, along with my responsibilities as a physician. Being a physician takes energy, intelligence, and a strong desire to help people. As for teaching, I enjoy instructing, reading, and discussing the fine points with students and colleagues.

My degrees are a Bachelor of Arts, an M.D., and a Ph.D. My career plans are to become involved in administration and serve on an academic medical faculty.

Satisfaction for me is when I can use my intelligence and my appetite for incessant reading to make a difference. Helping people and developing better ways to do things gratifies me. The only thing I'd change about my profession is the institution and its location.

I chose my work because I wanted to be both a professor and a physician. In the morning, I see patients in a clinic. In the afternoon, I spend time doing research in the library, writing, and reviewing data. I also plan my experiments.

PHYSICIAN, SURGEON

I was a pilot and flight surgeon in the U.S. Air Force before opening my own practice as a physician and surgeon. It's been a very happy choice. If I could start over, I'd choose a medical career again.

In my work, I treat patients for allergies and skin diseases. It's my job to read pathology (science of treating diseases, their nature, and cause) reports and determine treatment procedures. I perform cosmetic surgery as well as make surgical repairs.

A competent physician/surgeon needs a great deal of training and experience. I have undergraduate degrees as well as several graduate degrees in medicine. You should have a great interest in the sciences--natural, physical, chemical, and mechanical. I, myself, am interested in human beings in general. You also need excellent vision as well as good hand coordination for surgery.

I really enjoy curing people of their ills. It also pleases me being able to improve my patients' appearance. In addition to enjoying the people I work with, it is very rewarding to know that my knowledge and skills can be of value to my fellow man. My plans are to continue to practice medicine until I decide to retire.

Unfortunately, the fear of legal liability, governmental control and restrictions, and patient hostility are dampening the effectiveness of medical practice. I'd like more freedom to treat and manage my patients' health to the best of my ability and skills. I hope these negative trends can be reversed.

PHYSICIST

I work for an Air Force laboratory as a physicist. Part of my job is to conduct research and experiments in space physics and the other part involves managing the space division. I conduct laboratory research on atomic and molecular structure and field experiments using rockets to study earth's upper atmosphere and solar ultraviolet emissions.

To perform this work well it is important to have an interest in and enjoy science, have a good academic background, be inquisitive, enjoy studying, and be persistent--research results may be a long time in coming.

This has been satisfying work for me because I am discovering new knowledge, learning more about our existence and working with interesting people. I am only dissatisfied with the low salary.

I had always enjoyed physics, chemistry and math in high school. In college I started in electrical engineering. After one year I switched to physics because I enjoyed the basic knowledge, experiments and broadness of that field. I have earned my Master's degree, plus I have taken additional courses. After more than 30 years in this profession, I would still choose this work again if I could start over.

Upon retirement, I plan to do management consulting.

PHYSICIST, NATIONAL LABORATORY

For eighteen years I have worked as a physicist in a national laboratory. In addition to the supervision of ten other physicists, I perform basic research and experiments in fundamental plasma physics. This sometimes involves planning an experiment which I believe will answer a fundamental physics question; then discussing the proposed experiment with colleagues and considering their suggestions for improvements to my original plan. Obtaining the equipment for the experiment may take some time, especially if we need to borrow equipment--a common practice in this profession. Once we have the equipment, we usually need to reconfigure or modify the equipment to suit our needs. I supervise the technicians and students as they set up the equipment, take the data, and interpret the results; when complete, I give a few talks describing the results and write a paper for publication in a professional journal, documenting the experiment and the knowledge we gained.

The work of a physicist requires a broad background in math, physics, electronics, and material sciences; I also completed a graduate degree and doctoral thesis work. In addition to the proper background studies, you must be creative as often times it is necessary to change the approach in the face of surprising, or disappointing, results or progress. You must also have the ability to work productively with a wide variety of people and enjoy working as part of a team.

The rewards of my endeavors are outstanding--I have the opportunity to learn something that no one else knows, to discover first hand a fact of nature, and then be privileged to present my discoveries to the world! It is always a pleasure to share new and creative ideas with my colleagues and co-workers and to see students plan and execute the experiments better than I planned; there are great rewards in working with young, fresh minds--it gives me renewed vitality for my work.

Frustration arises often times around the issue of funding, and much time and effort is spent convincing sponsors that requests for resources are not extravagant or inflated. I believe that poor training and a lack of insight and vision among those who make important funding decisions leads to the high degree of scrutiny and cutting of funds.

I have a natural ability in physics; I have always identified with role models engaged in this kind of work and followed their examples.

PHYSICIST, SPACE SCIENCE & PROFESSOR

I have been interested in science since childhood. One of the major influences leading me into this career was my enrollment in a very good summer program in atmospheric science while I was in high school. I worked my way through school to earn my doctorate and have worked as a scientist for 25 years.

As a physicist/space scientist/professor, I research and teach at a university. My typical activities include: writing, making sense of data, reading research papers, teaching class, and interacting with graduate students.

To perform this kind of work, it is important to have an analytic approach to your work, logical reasoning, communication skills, and sales abilities.

I like this kind of work very much, and if given the opportunity to start over and choose any career, I would again choose this. I find job satisfaction in understanding something new/difficult, and in seeing students learn.

PHYSIOLOGIST

I investigated all of the life sciences and found physiology to be the most challenging. To qualify for teaching and research work, I earned a Masters in Science, and then my Ph.D. degree. I have always had an occupation relating to physiology and after 20 years in this field I would still choose this career even if given the chance to start again.

I teach physiology and do research in cell physiology. On a typical work day, I give one or two lectures to dental or nursing students. Several hours are spent in the laboratory designing or doing experiments. For the remainder of the day, I do paper work or prepare for other lectures.

I like the organization I work for and the people I work with. I have found opportunity for advancement in this occupation. I find great satisfaction in teaching young people about the excitement of the life process.

PIANO TUNER

I am self-employed as a piano technician, tuning and rebuilding them. My typical work schedule includes checking my appointment calendar and scheduling my work for the day. Since my town has a population of 40,000, I have not had to go out of town to work for the last 30 years, which is how long I have been in this business. I go to my client's house to tune or I do work for visiting artists or the symphony. If I have a rebuilding job, I usually do that work in my shop. Piano tuning and rebuilding involves woodworking skills and dexterity, patience, self-control, and integrity.

During high school and over the summers while in college for 2 years I did ornamental wood-carving. I attended a vocational school at a music conservatory. While working in a music store, I decided there would be a need for a new piano tuner serving the community some time within the next few years. That proved to be correct.

If I could change anything about my occupation, it would be to have better quality pianos in large numbers here and to have more knowledgeable clients. However, I enjoy the results of my work when I get the thanks and gratitude for my quality efforts from the many trained musicians in the area and from those who occasionally pass through this community.

PICTURE RESEARCHER & PUBLISHER

In working for a publisher of a social studies textbook, I must find interesting, effective and perhaps unknown images to illustrate a given point. For instance, perhaps an historical society or private collector has a good civil war photo to be used, or I go on location with a photographer and have something photographed, or track down a work of art.

To do this job well you should have good "people" skills on the phone. You are trying to convince them to give you something. An art history and American history background are important for this job.

I find this job exciting and satisfying because I am uncovering or finding new images, meeting tight deadlines and photographing new subjects.

However, I would like it more if I were paid better.

I have earned a B.A. and M.A. degree and taught art for 20 years. I was ready to try something new when my neighbor, who had this visual research business, asked me to join her.

PILOT

After 35 years as a pilot, I still like my work very much and if given the chance to start over and the option to choose any career, I would again choose to be a pilot. I started out through R.O.T.C. and the Air Force while in college. I figured that since I was going to have to serve in the Korean War, I would choose the lesser of two evils--flying over Korea as opposed to walking through it.

As a pilot for a commercial airline, I fly to a variety of locations about 3-4 days a week. My schedule changes every month. To perform this kind of work well, it is important to have good motor skills, coordination, a cool head and a good sense of humor. It also takes many hours of training to qualify for the various types of aircraft licenses.

The one drawback to my career is the labor/management relations problems that sometimes plague the airlines. Aside from the frustrations I have because of this, I like my job very much. I primarily like it because of the people I work with. I find satisfaction in bringing people together.

PIPE FITTER/WELDER

It's hard work, both physically and mentally, as a pipefitter welder on large industrial projects, and especially so when I am top supervisor as I often am. The people you work with are often very independent, and it is indeed a challenge to organize and direct the jobs and keep everyone on schedule.

I worked in a steel mill and hated it. Time magazine carried an article on plumbing-pipefitting which sparked my interest. I quit the steel mill and went to a technical school to earn an associate degree in hydronic engineering. After I left school, I got into the pipefitters' union. I have now handled union work for 22 years with a couple of hundred different companies. I build mechanical installations for refineries and other industries as well as heating installations on commercial jobs.

If I am not in charge of the job, I will work from drawings and fit and weld the piping. I will also rig and lift all pipe with heavy rigs. If I am in charge, I will plan and direct the entire job, including correcting engineering mistakes. This kind of work requires mechanical ability and a no-nonsense approach to leadership. You must have self-confidence.

Although I like the kind of work I do, there are several drawbacks. I would prefer to work for one company full time and receive paid benefits. I also would like a safer work area. My work situation is very dangerous.

There is, however, job satisfaction from this hard labor. I like the hands-on work. I could do with less supervision and more just ordinary fitter-welder work. When I am in charge, though, it is rewarding to organize and direct a job which gets finished on schedule.

PLANT MAINTENANCE ENGINEER

To be a plant maintenance engineer, you need good interpersonal skills along with a high level of organization and ability to observe. I enjoy my work coordinating maintenance activities with available resources. Sometimes I act as a project manager for new construction and remodeling. I survey a job site, develop and select alternatives, generate and implement the plan, and complete the project.

I began as a clerk in a maintenance office. Thinking the work the engineers did looked interesting, I went back to school to earn a Bachelor of Science degree in engineering. I like control over a project. Developing a concept and following it through to completion also pleases me. However, I'd like it if there were more opportunities for advancement in my company.

If I could begin again, I'd choose this occupation which I've been in for three years. In the future, I plan to move on into facilities management or into building construction.

PLANT MANAGER #1

As a plant manager, I am responsible for an $85 million per year operation with 500 people employed. I obtained this position through a series of technical job experiences and as a result of my record of getting things done. Prior to this position, I worked as an engineer, teacher, and machinist.

In the capacity of plant manager, I spend all of my time communicating to members of the staff, plant people, sales and corporate office employees. I work a great deal on future plans--3 to 6 months in advance.

To perform this kind of work well, it is important to be a good communicator both orally and written. You must also be a good listener to receive ideas from above and below you.

I like most aspects of my work. I would like to have more exposure to field sales in order to find out more about the customers and in what direction the plant should be going in the future. Despite this frustration, I like very much the kind of work I do.

There are new challenges in the position each day. I like not having a direct supervisor looking over my shoulder. I find satisfaction from having the flexibility to get things done.

PLANT MANAGER #2

Starting out as an industrial engineer with a large manufacturing company, I am now a plant manager overseeing the assembly of heavy machinery. I'm not particularly fond of this company, but I do enjoy my work, the people, and the fact that there are opportunities for advancement. One day I'd like to be a Director of Operations or a General Manager.

To be a plant manager, one must have strong communication skills and an understanding of the plant's technical processes. Being able to work well with people and to value customers are very important in this occupation. One also needs an education; my college degrees are a Bachelors in industrial engineering and a Masters in business administration.

What I enjoy most in my career is working with people. Improving customer satisfaction is very rewarding. I'd like my job more if there were less bureaucracy and if we had a better educated work force. We also need to work with less expensive overhead.

My job is to coach teams of people to produce a product of good quality, on time, and at the lowest cost. I review the status of the factory, coordinate meetings, and handle personnel issues. Analyzing information on employee performance and planning for the short and long term are part of my duties. In general, my job is to provide vision, direction, feedback, and counsel.

PLANT MANAGER, QUALITY CONTROL

I got into my career as a Quality Control Manager when a new plant, which makes large steel castings, was built in the area where I wanted to live. After being hired as an hourly laborer, I worked very hard, earning a reputation as a person who could get the job done and done well. I became a supervisor, then a manager. A high school graduate, I've been with this plant for many years. I'm now in middle management; at my age, I have no higher aspirations. I'll continue here until retirement.

The most important skills you need as a manager of quality control are verbal and analytical skills. A positive attitude and leadership skills, along with the ability to be sensitive to people's needs, also help. It's very important to be accomplished in math and to be computer-literate.

My daily duties include going through the mail, responding to any requests for information, and visiting the various inspection stations to keep in contact with what's going on. I must attend production meetings and make and receive customer telephone calls. I review sales orders, work on various inspection procedures, and plan customer visits. Writing inspection instructions and training inspectors are also part of my responsibilities.

I especially like the opportunity this job has provided for travel to different companies enabling me to meet their people. I particularly enjoy helping people perform well. Meeting and exceeding customer expectations gives me a great deal of satisfaction. I have only one dissatisfaction--I'd prefer that employees would take more interest in their work and be better prepared to meet the requirements of their jobs.

PLANT MECHANIC/PIPEFITTER/WELDER

I've worked as an apprentice electrician, and in an auto repair shop, but, as a power plant mechanic, I feel useful to the general public by helping to supply a product as necessary as electrical power.

If I were given more of the latest tools to perform my work, my work life would be easier. I also regret the lack of opportunity for advancement. I do enjoy the steady employment and the regular pay increases. My work itself is great as are the people I work with and the company.

My training for my work came from attending classes at trade schools and doing the same type of work while I was in the Navy during World War II. My job requires that I work as a pipefitter as I install piping in pumps, radiators, and cooling towers. I make repairs on diesel engines and do some welding as well.

You have to have a fair understanding of math to do my job. Being handy with tools is also helpful. You should have the desire to arrange machine piping and see the satisfaction of a completed project.

PLANT NURSERY CO-OWNER

Although I am in my present occupation as a co-owner of a plant nursery because I married into it, it is a natural job for me because I lived on a farm and loved it. Prior to the job at the nursery, I worked as a secretary, reports analyst, and circulation manager. I have now been with the nursery for 30 years and prefer this kind of work.

As the co-owner, I am involved in growing plants, selling them, and keeping the books. My typical daily activities include: opening the business, selling plants, caring for the plants, filling displays, waiting on customers, keeping the employees working, answering questions regarding plants, and landscaping.

To do this kind of work, you must be a dedicated worker and one who can work well on your own with no supervision. A knowledge of math and about plants is necessary. You should also have a pleasant attitude toward people in order to be a successful salesperson.

Aside from wanting to cut out a few of my responsibilities so I would not have so much stress, I like the kind of work I do. What keeps me going is the satisfaction I find in seeing a well grown plant and all the satisfied customers.

PLANT OPERATOR/MECHANIC

I had tried several other occupations including dairy farmer, textile factory work, and scheduling clerk, before I was introduced to this line of work by a friend. One of the main reasons this work, as a wastewater treatment plant operator/mechanic, attracted me was that I can work outdoors and do different things every day.

The plant operator/mechanic keeps the treatment plant and collection system operative by operating, repairing and maintaining equipment. This involves turning valves, pushing switches, collecting samples, lubricating equipment, reading gauges, recording data, performing lab tests, and dealing with the public. The major objective of all these operations is to maintain the water quality.

The skills and attitudes which are important to perform this kind of work well is dependent on the size of the plant. Small plants require a "Jack of All Trades." In large plants, you will specialize in a certain phase of operation. Generally, you should like the work and have skills including: supervisory, public relations, laboratory, trades, truck driving, mathematics, and English.

Although I like this kind of work very much, and the people with whom I work, I dislike the fact that a political committee oversees the plant operation accounting for some decisions to be politically motivated. If I could make changes in this occupation, it would be to find ways of making the job safer.

I find job satisfaction in doing my job well, the outcome of which is a community service--good water quality. Job satisfaction though, depends on the gauge you use to measure it and what you make of the job. If you want dollars, then work for a large city. If you want prestige and/or job satisfaction, than a small municipal operation is probably your ticket.

PLANT SUPERINTENDENT

I have worked hard learning the manufacturing business doing whatever was asked of me. I started as a machine operator, then moved up to assistant supervisor, supervisor of quality control and now plant superintendent. As such, I am responsible for all the day-to-day production operations, as well as plant maintenance. I start at 7:00 a.m. by taking a walk through the plant, checking quality from the previous day. I then schedule the equipment for what is to be printed and converted. As superintendent, I supervise the supervisors to ensure they are doing their jobs. Filling out production reports, interviewing job applicants, and dealing with the union on grievance matters are also my responsibility.

I consider 80% of the reason for performing well in this kind of work is dependent on caring about your job, wanting to learn the business, and having a positive attitude. The other 20% is dependent on having basic high school skills and common sense.

I like every aspect of my job.

If given the opportunity to start my career over and prepare for any occupation, I would again choose manufacturing. I find job satisfaction, knowing that I have moved up the company ladder and that I have been told that I have a bright future. I am hoping that the future promotion will be to vice president of production.

PLAYWRIGHT/NOVELIST

I am now doing what I have always wanted to do as a playwright and novelist. I have always enjoyed writing and have done this throughout my life. I have combined this career with homemaking for the past 10 years and have found this to be very satisfying.

My work is done on a personal computer on which I try to work every day. The amount of time I spend on my writing depends on how I am inspired. As well as inspirations and creativity, I have found patience, independence and concentration to be important for this occupation.

In order to support myself prior to having my work published, I have had to take jobs as limo chauffeur, telephone operator, accounting clerk, receptionist, and security guard. Since being published, I have been able to do writing on my novels and plays full time. It is difficult to find a publisher and I would like to find a reliable agent who could handle the job of selling my work for me.

I like this kind of work for its creative aspect and its diversity. My career aspiration is to have my new novel published with much success.

PLUMBER

My career as a plumber started while I was in the U.S. Navy. Training for the job involved 3 years of school and 1,000 hours of work in the field to qualify for a license. Personally, I think there should be a higher pay scale for plumbers because of all the training involved.

As a plumber, I install all phases of plumbing in big commercial buildings. This may include the heating system too. To perform my job I must be able to read a blueprint. Knowing how to solder copper pipes and fittings is necessary to perform this type of work. You must also have skills in using a transit for shooting grades and elevations. On the large commercial projects that I work on, physical strength is also required in working with very large pipes.

I like this kind of work very much. I think there is opportunity for advancement. I enjoy the people I work with. I am not particularly satisfied with the people I work for and the amount of travel involved in getting to the job sites. However, I do plan to stay with this career and hope to own my own business someday. I find satisfaction from my work in seeing a big building go from start to finish.

PLUMBING CONTRACTOR

For all these years, I have worked in the plumbing business. I came into the plumbing arena not by design. Due to family health problems, I had to leave New York University after only two years; I went into the business although I had very little knowledge of the requirements. I was able to learn what I needed and eventually I ended up owning a plumbing contracting concern.

A multifaceted business, plumbing is difficult to describe. Meeting the customer, estimating cost, and ordering materials are only part of the work. Making a comfortable living is job satisfaction for me.

I began as a helper and worked up to mechanic. A typical day for me as an owner of the company would be to designate the work assignments to the men I have hired. I plan schedules, sending my employees to various sites. If there is a complaint from a customer or if one of my employees has a question, I have to deal with those on an individual basis. It is a challenge, but I am managing to do it satisfactorily.

PODIATRIST

For the last two years, I have worked as a podiatrist; a typical week involves seeing twenty to twenty-five patients a day, with scheduled foot or ankle surgery one day a week.

While still completing a Bachelor of Science degree, a recruiter from a school of Podiatry came to my college and got me interested in Podiatry. The field of medicine was always of interest to me and this recruiter inspired me to visit several podiatrists' offices; that was how I got started in this medical field. I currently work for a large HMO.

A Podiatrist is one who diagnoses problems of the feet and ankles, and performs surgery for those problems that do not respond to other forms of therapy. To be successful as a Podiatrist, one must work well with people on a one-on-one basis, have an interest in helping people, and an aptitude toward medical science.

My greatest satisfaction comes from helping others.

The field of medicine can be very demanding. There is considerable politics connected with working for an HMO; along with practicing any form of medicine, there is a constant awareness and fear of medical malpractice suits; and I do not enjoy the hassle of handling insurance paperwork.

Those considerations aside, I really like working with people in a medical environment; podiatry is a very interesting field; I am glad I chose this as my career.

I plan to build my practice and stay associated with the HMO for the present.

POLARIZER, CERAMIC CRYSTALS

I perform an electro-chemical process called polarization on ceramic crystal. My specific task in this process is to polarize, check the parameters and then box the crystals for shipment. I arrive at 7:45, get a morning and afternoon break for 15 minutes each, lunch out, and then leave at 4:45.

To perform my job well you must be able to handle delicate pieces, be careful and alert with the electrical machinery, and adaptable with the equipment and the new developments in the job and product.

There is job satisfaction for me from producing a part that has so many useful applications. I take pride in producing a product that is almost exclusive to our company. I also find satisfaction from getting something very small and delicate to work for the customer like they want it to.

My job would be more satisfying if we as employees were more aware of what is happening with the success of our company. I would like to know if we are doing good or if we need to really work harder on something. I would also like to be shown more appreciation.

I was told by a friend that the company was hiring. I applied, got the job, have now been here 13 years, and plan to continue in this job. It was small company of eight people; now there are 18 people and it has moved to a large town. I have a high school degree and have had previous work experience as a postal carrier and office worker, telephone switchboard operator, and a supply department clerk for an insurance company.

POLICE CAPTAIN

During the course of a day's work as a police captain, almost anything that can happen, WILL! In the 33 years I have worked for the police department I have learned to expect almost everything.

The skills and attitudes which are most important in order to perform this job well are an even temper (be able to take abuse without violent reaction), understanding, intelligence, honesty, helpfulness, and physical and emotional strength. I like my job very much and would go into police work again even if I had the chance to start over. However, I am opposed to Affirmative Action because I have observed unqualified people getting hired and promoted for the wrong reasons.

I became a police officer for no particular reason other than the need for a steady job, after being home from Korea for 18 months.

I have found satisfaction from helping people in trouble, finding lost children, and locking up the criminals.

My future plans are to retire eventually and spend all of my time fishing, visiting relatives, friends, and just plain traveling. I want to let someone else go after the fruitcakes and put up with the politics and government regulations.

POLICE OFFICER #1

For twenty-five years, I have worked in law enforcement as a police officer; presently I hold the position of desk sergeant. I supervise junior officers, monitor the police radio, handle complaints, and dispatch officers to handle problems within the community. Basically I monitor all the activities at the police station, with the added responsibility of being the day shift supervisor.

Although I have no college degree, I have advanced in my career by accepting any training offered in connection with my job. The work of a police officer requires being able to make quick, honest and righteous decisions, possess the desire to help people, and basically be able to tell the difference between right and wrong.

I like police work and law enforcement very much; I am a person who likes to know that I am doing the right thing. I like the people in the community where I work; I enjoy the camaraderie of my fellow officers and I believe that my department is run in an efficient and proper manner.

It was a boyhood dream for me to become a police officer; after spending twenty years in the Air Force performing similar duties, I realized this dream and enrolled in the police training academy.

I believe that this is where I will spend the remainder of my professional working life; I may move up in rank, but if I don't, I know that I will be happy as long as I am involved in police work.

POLICE OFFICER #2

I have always wanted to be a police officer ever since I was a small child. I have a college degree--business administration, criminal justice. Five years ago I passed the test in a local town, went to the Police Academy for 10 weeks, and then was certified by the state as a full-time officer.

I was firefighter for 5 years, a certified EMT Ambulance driver for 5 years, and taught CPR and first aid all while attending college.

In general I enforce traffic laws, transport prisoners to and from court, and respond to a variety of calls. Some are medical emergencies, domestic disputes, motorist aid, motor vehicle accidents, destroyed property, and sudden deaths.

You must be very level-headed in a crisis and have a good attitude. It could cost you your life if you lose your temper or fail to think clearly. It is also important to be in excellent physical condition.

It is satisfying to have people look to you for help or protection. On the down side, statistics are very much a reality in police work: there is pressure for arrests and tickets. Another negative is a lot of favoritism within departments.

Students should get degrees that will enable them to prepare for a career after police work. My own plans are to obtain a job in the FBI eventually.

POSTAL CLERK

Although my educational background is not reflected in the work I am doing, I have found that I like my occupation as a postal clerk. I earned a Bachelor of Arts in psychology and worked as a teacher and tutor for several years. However, I found that postal service work offered me a higher pay scale, a more convenient schedule, and job security. To get this job, I applied to the U.S. Postal Service, took the postal service exam, and then went through training to qualify for my job as postal clerk/letter-sorting machine operator.

It is my job to sort mail at a rate of one per second on a machine that sorts first-class letters. As the machine operator, I sit at the 20-key console to key in the zip codes which allows the machine to sort. I also load ledges of mail to be sorted and clear bins of mail to be dispatched.

To perform this kind of work well, it is important to have good hand-eye coordination, a good memory, and speed and accuracy.

I like this kind of work because I find satisfaction from the large amount of letters sorted in a day, and being able to sort mail accurately with a low error rate. I also like the people I work for, the people I work with, and the opportunities I have for advancement. It is my intention to move into a supervisory position.

POSTAL WORKER

I have been a postal worker for several decades and the job has been very satisfying to me for I enjoy just being with people. I like talking to them and getting their thoughts on various things. There is nothing I can think of that I don't like about my career

A postal worker must be accurate and dependable. You should be able to get along with all kinds of people. The ability to get your work done fast is necessary. It's nice, too, if you like the job.

For a brief period early in my life, I did a little bookkeeping and also worked as a grocery clerk, but the post office job was my real calling. With 2 years of college, I got my job after taking a qualifying examination. For the next 31 years, my mornings have consisted of putting the daily mail in cases for delivery. It takes me 2 and one half hours to case the mail for a city of 500 houses. For the rest of the day, approximately 5 and one half hours, I deliver that mail.

POSTMASTER

Helping people solve their mail problems is what I most enjoy as postmaster. My work would be happier if John Doe Public realized it takes time to distribute mail, and how important it is to use post office numbers. I wish we could somehow educate the public on how important it is to address mail correctly. Everyone should work in the post office at least 3 weeks, just to see how much work goes on behind the scenes.

I got into this work because I was job-hunting, and this position came to my attention. I applied, passed the test, and have enjoyed a secure, rewarding position ever since. This kind of situation is far better (for me) than the jobs I had before as a sales clerk, a supply sergeant in the U.S. Air Force, and a librarian. If you are unable to go to college, this is a very good way of making your living.

In my work I sort mail, sell postal products, and distribute the mail. I handle window transactions and keep up with the bookkeeping. Reporting to superior officers and supervising a clerk and a custodial person are also part of my work.

Skills which are important in a postmaster's position are good communication, reading, and solving problems. Adeptness at quickly grasping and remedying a problem is necessary. You must like people and empathize with their wants and needs. Physical fitness for heavy lifting is also needed.

I enjoy this work, but when I finally retire on a pension, I probably will become a land/building developer because I like the thought of doing that work too.

POTTER

I was working as a bank teller and waitress before I found my love for working with clay and went into business for myself. As a potter, I make functional ware which I sell.

The work is done in cycles rather than doing all the processes on each piece before starting another piece. In other words, I will work on the wheel throwing many pots, then do the trimming on this group of items. The firing, in turn, is only done when there is a sufficient quantity of pieces for it to be economically feasible to start up the kiln and fire them. Glazing is the last step in the manufacturing process.

I have found that this type of work requires discipline in keeping to these independent tasks and skills in throwing. This work is done in an isolated setting which you must be able to tolerate.

Despite the fact that I do not foresee many opportunities for advancement in this occupation, I like the kind of work I am doing so much that I hope to be able to continue. I find satisfaction in owning my own company, working on my own terms, and creating the products.

PRACTICAL NURSE

To earn my license as a practical nurse, I went to school for one year. I must then attend in-service seminars to keep updated. I really found the right career for myself when I went into nursing because I still like this kind of work after practicing for 25 years. Prior to this I worked for a number of years in the mail order department of a large retailer and as a potato processing plant worker.

As a licensed practical nurse, I am the charge nurse. The duties I perform on my 8-12 hour shifts are: giving medication to patients, doing treatments, assisting in patient care, charting, giving oxygen as ordered, and calling the doctors if necessary.

To perform this kind of work well, it is important to have skills in how to deal with family members of patients and skills in getting co-workers to do good patient care. You obviously also need to have the knowledge necessary to care for the patients and to administer medication and treatments.

Although I have found my job to have a lack of opportunity for advancement, this is outweighed by my like for the kind of work I do.

I basically enjoy personal contact and people. I find satisfaction from the appreciation I receive from the patients I take care of.

PRESIDENT, DECISION SCIENCE FIRM

After earning a Bachelor of Science and a Ph.D. in physics, I taught nuclear physics in college and was an experimental physicist for a while. Later, I founded my own company because I wanted to pursue opportunities for research in areas of personal interest. For 30 years, I've been president and chief executive officer for a firm concerned with decision science applications and processes.

To do this work you should be interested in problem-solving. Regard for the welfare of employees is important as well. Also essential is concern for the needs and goals of the customer.

I've enjoyed the challenge of problem-solving in my career. Working with my colleagues is also very rewarding. I've found the enticement of innovation particularly satisfying. The requirement of too much time spent on marketing and financial management is less enjoyable. When I retire, I will continue my research in economics and in the decision processes.

I coordinate research activities along with marketing endeavors in my work. Fortunately, the days are usually unplanned for they are filled with interruptions, particularly as I try to write reports. There are many meetings with clients, and meetings with individual members of my staff, dealing with specific research and marketing problems.

PRESIDENT, DISTRIBUTION COMPANY

The core of my occupation as the president of an international luxury products distributing company is to make sure every aspect of the work to be performed in the company is fully understood and carried out. That involves many contacts with the staff and with outside companies.

As company president the most important skill is the training of other people, ie:

understand their problems and help find solutions. You should have an open mind. Get clear goals for the company and individuals.

I find satisfaction in running a successful company and developing good relations with others.

I would be more satisfied with my job if I could simplify the operating methods, mainly government and legal red tape.

I have always wanted to have my own company. I trained for it, worked for it and paid for it. Other occupations which helped train me for this were sales area manager, export manager and general manager.

I will continue to work to develop my company to become a holding with several different types of activities to minimize work.

PRESIDENT, ELECTRONIC BANKING COMPANY

As president and chief executive officer of an electronic banking concern I manage, plan and administer all company functions and supervise personnel. On a day-to-day basis I meet with personnel or clients, administer policies, and make plans for the company.

To perform well at my kind of work it is important to have communications, planning and decision-making skills.

There really isn't anything I can readily think of that I dislike about my work. I like the people I work with, the opportunity I have for advancement, and the kind of work I do. I like the opportunity we create. I derive satisfaction from success, achievement and building relationships. One thing I would change about my company is that I would like to see an increase in the capitalization to reduce the stress.

I have been in the field of banking for 25 years and started my own firm. I earned my master's degree from a graduate school of banking to help prepare me for this career. All my occupations have been related to banking.

PRESIDENT, LARGE MANUFACTURING COMPANY

As president of a large manufacturing company which employs over 6000 people, I am the chief overseer. I monitor the cost as compared to selling price of our product, our joint venture, and our company divisions. I serve as the company's entrepreneur, evaluating new ideas.

To perform this kind of work well it is important to have a solid background in finance, sales, manufacturing and legal matters. To prepare myself for a career I earned a bachelor of science degree in finance and a juris doctor. However, you do not need a doctorate to perform this work.

I like my kind of work, because I have a good organization and I find satisfaction from the growth of activities, employment, and net worth. However, I would prefer to be involved with products which do not tend to become "commodities," but rather have their exclusive market position. I would also like to work for less powerful customers.

As well as my formal education which helped prepare me for this job, my prior work experience as buyer, salesman, vice president of planning, executive vice president, and legal training also helped open up this opportunity.

PRESIDENT, MOUNTAIN-CLIMBING SCHOOL

This occupation, as the president of a mountain climbing school and guide service, chose me. Prior to this career move, I was in competitive ski racing and entertaining.

I handle all of the office work; the secretarial, planning, and promotional work. I also actively teach and guide. There is no typical day or week. I sometimes work locally outside the office during the day, and at night catch up on the office paperwork. Often, I am in another part of the world for 1 to 3 months.

The skills and attitudes which are important to perform well at this job are being direct and friendly, enjoying people, and paying attention.

The dissatisfying aspect of my job is that I have all the administrative work and the field work to do. I would like to be able to focus on one or the other without having to do both. I feel I could then achieve the standards I want for the school.

Despite this, however, I very much like the kind of work I do, the people I work with, and the opportunity for advancement. I receive satisfaction from my work from taking people to places, either geographical or intellectual places, they never dreamed they could go to or accomplish.

My future career plans include more writing and developing an educational facility to train guides.

PRESIDENT, RETAIL CORPORATION

I am the president of a retail corporation which my father first owned. I've worked in the business since I was seven years old. Now, my duties are to oversee the buying and the financial aspects of the business. I am also responsible for advertising.

Job satisfaction is having sales go well. I enjoy this work and the people involved with the business, but it would be great if I could just have more control over the results of our efforts. I'd like to be more efficient and to be more forceful. Having more time off would be outstanding. One day I'll retire and, perhaps, open a small shop specializing in Christmas things.

The primary skill needed to do my job is accounting. You must also have the ability to motivate salespeople. In addition, it is necessary to know and be able to keep up with the financial side of the business. My degree is a Bachelor of Science in business administration.

My job is essentially that of supervisor. Monitoring the purchasing, the financial, and the advertising efforts of my employees takes a lot of my time. I also review the merchandise displays and make recommendations. Talking with salespeople in my two stores takes my time as well.

PRESIDENT, RUBBER COMPANY

I am my own boss. I oversee all operations of a rubber factory employing 50 people. In addition to the rubber company, I am a real estate investor of a family trust. After 21 years, I am still the first one at work. I start the day by reading papers, sort all papers on the desk, making decisions what to do on each and going over the day's scheduled production with the plant foreman. My responsibilities include pricing any new formulas and putting them in the computer, checking accounts receivable and payable. I talk to customers and salespeople trying to sell the plant manager at our other factory and me, and we go over problems we might have. Also, I talk with lawyers and accountants about finances and investments. I am the last person to leave for the day.

To perform well at this job you must have honesty with your customers, and be happy with most people. My word is my bond and everyone knows this. I am well liked by most people I do business with, and I personally guarantee all of our work.

My career gives me happiness with my life. I feel an importance in my work because of the fact that I am responsible for the lives of all my employees and their families. I find satisfaction because I satisfy most of my customers all the time. I have built a trust for my children and my wife and don't have to worry about money.

This occupation chose me in 1963. I was running my own landscape business when winter set in and I needed a job to tide me over. I took a job as a mill man in a rubber factory and was promoted to foreman in one day. I liked it, so I did landscaping days and worked nights in the factory. Six years later I couldn't pay a hospital bill for my wife so I left that job to manage a rubber company. Six years later I bought the company and expanded it to doing seven million dollars a year. I also built a real estate trust.

I went back to school several years ago to study anthropology, archeology, psychology, and went on an expedition to Zaire, Africa with Earthwatch. I would like to do more expeditions.

PRESIDENT, SOFTWARE COMPANY

My company develops and sells computer software to orthodontists. To summarize my job description as owner/president, I make sales presentations, teach seminars, consult with doctors on practice management and design new systems. To be more specific in describing a typical work schedule, I take phone calls from customers with concerns about the product and service we deliver and calls from new prospects. I prepare proposals and follow up on earlier calls. Overseeing customer service, and administrative and accounting personnel is my responsibility. Reviewing ads and articles on new hardware developments is another routine activity.

You always have to have an optimistic attitude. You must look at every potential problem to find the opportunity in it. Attention to detail and complete follow through is also essential.

I find satisfaction from establishing a good relationship quickly with new customers and prospects. Solving problems for prospects and customers is rewarding. I feel I have succeeded when I keep our development, administrative and customer support teams running smoothly.

I would like to increase my profit margin to enable me to have more staff and more management help.

My strong business management experiences prepared me for this work. These previous positions were systems programmer for a major computer manufacturer, regional manager of a technical marketing company, a management consultant for a leading consulting firm, and a director of another management consulting service.

I plan to continue to run this business at a profit and to continue to grow.

PRESIDENT, SOFTWARE DEVELOPMENT COMPANY

I started out as a programmer, worked hard, was as helpful as possible, and did as many tasks as possible, and just flowed with the opportunities I encountered. I am now the president of this company.

As president of the software development firm, I set objectives for upper management, oversee running of the company, write software, and fix problems in all software. A typical work day for me might include: talking with the vice president of sales about prospects, talking with development people about projects in the works, signing checks, checking financial records, reading The Wall Street Journal, and answering questions from customers.

I think the important attributes which got me from programmer to president are listening, thinking and smiling. My educational background has also been a contributing factor. I have a Bachelor of Science in Math and a Bachelor of Science in Computer Science degree.

I like everything about my job, the kind of work I do, the organization and people I work for, the opportunities for advancement, and the people I work with. Most of all, I like the varied opportunities I have. Satisfaction comes to me when I sign up new customers, have a profitable month, have old customers call up to say thank you, and in creating new products.

My career plans for the future are to continue to build up the company.

PRIEST

Immediately after I rise every morning, I pray. While sipping coffee and juice, I handle a few routine office matters. I conduct Saturday 9:00 a.m. Mass in church. Other regular duties include organizing homilies, conducting funeral liturgies in church and burial services. I make phone calls and visit people who need help because of serious illness of themselves or in the family or because of a death in the family.

A priest must have compassion, patience, endurance, and strong development of one's personal life and spirituality.

My main satisfaction as a priest is a realization of aiding those in some way or another who have a need.

I would like to have a competent lay person to take charge of parish finances and other important but material needs.

I felt called to the priesthood while in high school and responded. After graduating from college, I spent 4 years training in the seminary. Since responding to my personal call, I have experienced gradual fulfillment.

As I continue to grow older and can see retirement approaching in the future, I am not pleased. I plan to continue in parish work and help in some modified way even after I have passed the age for regular, active involvement in this work--that's how much I like it.

PRIEST AND PROFESSOR

My career as a priest and professor has given me a sense of purpose in life. I became a priest/professor out of obedience to the wish of my Bishop, and am very satisfied with this position. During the week, I teach undergraduate courses, and on weekends I assist in a parish by preaching.

My day starts early with mass and morning prayers. I teach from 9 a.m. to 12 noon, and 1 to 2 p.m. The rest of the afternoon is spent on paperwork and attending meetings as scheduled. My schedule also regularly includes visiting the sick in hospitals, and speaking to various groups.

In order to perform this kind of work well, the following skills and attitudes are important: good public speaking ability; a generous attitude of understanding others and not sitting in judgment of them; desire to do the will of God each day.

I have liked almost every aspect of my career.

My satisfaction comes from the responses of appreciation and love I get from those I have tried to help by teaching and pastoral ministry.

PRINCIPAL, HIGH SCHOOL

I've spent most of my career in education as the principal of an inner-city secondary school (I was a teacher for 12 years). For everything involved in operating a high school, in particular establishing school programs, I've had full responsibility.

There is a thrill in creating educational programs which affect the lives of the students. I like coordinating the energies of 150 teachers to serve 3,000 students as we work together to solve problems. It is very rewarding to help these thousands of students attain adulthood and, we hope, successful lives.

In the inner-city high school, there are all types of problems to be handled with students, staff, or parents. Problem resolution comes before administrative details and before demands from central and district offices. There are many conferences, spontaneous as well as scheduled. There certainly is no typical day.

To be a successful principal, you need to have a sense of fairness in working with students. Educational background is also important; my degrees are a Bachelor of Science, a Master of Science, and a Master's in Education. Strong people skills and the ability to listen well are equally necessary. You must often hear a point of view without showing personal bias.

Indispensable to this work is the tremendous amount of courage it takes to make decisions that you know are right but that are not acceptable to a loud vocal group.

I chose the field of education as a career following military service. After being a teacher for a few years, I completed the required competitive examinations and was assigned a position as a principal.

PRINT SHOP OWNER

While I was the editor of my college newspaper, I became very interested in printing. I also like being in charge. So, my decision to own my own print shop fits my interest and personality.

As print shop owner, I take customer orders and follow through with production plans. My duties also include purchasing materials for printing, scheduling deliveries, instructing press and other production people, estimating jobs, and guiding customers in stock/ink selections.

To perform my job well, you must be detail oriented, be able to deal with hourly deadlines, and have the ability to adjust schedules. This job also requires much patience.

In spite of frustration caused by demanding customers and being somewhat short staffed, I like my work very much. It provides me with an opportunity to call the shots and make changes in the company as needed. It would be very difficult for me to work under an employer's direction. I enjoy seeing jobs from the beginning to end, and, of course, depositing the check.

My future career plan is to maintain and expand somewhat on the print shop that I have now.

PRINTING COMPOSITOR

I entered the printing field after high school graduation through the influence of my father who was a printing compositor. I directed my high school education in order to pursue this career, and I am proud to say that I was awarded the printing award in industrial arts and the journalism award from the English department because of the quality of my work. When I entered the printing field, I was a keyliner and plate-maker. Now, because of the effects of the computer and copier to the printing industry, I deal more in the marking products field. I am basically a printing compositor, now doing computer processing for rubber stamp making for marking products.

My typical daily activities include: making up layout for a proof from computer typesetting galleries; making a reversal negative; processing a photo polymer plate which is used to make a board for processing rubber for rubber stamp making; and making copies of signatures and artwork. This kind of work requires not only printing skills, but a positive creative attitude.

I like the kind of work I do very much. This is an occupation I have aspired to since watching my dad work as a printing pressman. It allows creativity and the opportunity to have a direct input into the product produced. I find satisfaction in helping others, and through satisfying the customers needs. I also like the teamwork involved in this job.

Even though I have worked in the printing field for many years, I am still learning and am currently enrolled in a keylining and platemaking college course to gain additional skills. I also want to learn more about cameras. My future plans also include earning a Bachelor of Arts degree.

PRODUCE MANAGER

I like my work as a produce manager because I do it alone and I do it well. My job is to check and package produce to be shipped to rigs. As the orders come in to be filled, I break down the larger units and put the produce in boxes to be shipped out.

Prior to this occupation, I was a factory worker, and an aide to the elderly. Although I like the kind of work I am now doing as a produce manager, selling offshore, I find that there is a lack of opportunity for advancement which might mean that I will eventually search out another occupation.

My work philosophy is to have a good attitude and not be lazy.

PRODUCE RETAILER

I tried work in a printing shop, a collision shop, and the jewelry retail business, but I went back to my roots. I learned the produce business from my father and went on my own 5 years ago. I am very satisfied I did.

As a produce retailer, my job involves buying, displaying, and selling produce, and dealing with people and the competition. I wake up at 4:00 a.m. and go to the produce terminal to buy produce for that day. I then take it to the store and set up the display. The rest of the day is spent dealing with employees and customers until 8 p.m. It obviously takes good physical endurance and energy to perform this kind of work. Math skills, patience, and practice are also key ingredients.

In spite of the many hours, 80 to 90 hour per week, I love my work. I like dealing with people, using my mind and learning. I find satisfaction from dealing with people, earning money, and putting in a full day's work. My future career plans are to open a large produce store.

PRODUCT MANAGER

I love the challenge and the variety of my work as a product manager for a medical supply company. When I started college, I was majoring in nursing. I switched to business and graduated with a bachelors degree in marketing management. I have also become a registered nurse and have worked in this capacity for several years. I then made a career change and worked in pharmaceutical/medical sales for 5 years, which led me to my current position as product manager for a biosensor, specifically a cholesterol sensor. In this way, I am fully utilizing my medical and business background.

As a product manager, I am responsible for coordinating production, manufacturing, design, advertising, and marketing, and for development of training and promotional sales programs. I work as the "hub" in a wheel. I work daily with the engineers, designers, sales managers, production/manufacturing staff, customer/technical services, international managers, and others in marketing to guide my product. Demands of the position change daily based on changes in product demands.

To perform this kind of work well, it is important to have flexibility, to delegate authority, be a quick decision maker, have a positive attitude, have financial savvy (stay with budget), be a leader and negotiator, and to be innovative.

The major drawback to my work is the long hours. In response to the question about how I would change my occupation to make it more satisfying, I would like there to be better communication between the U.S. and the U.K, to have a bigger budget, and to have a higher salary. Although I can think of a few frustrations and drawbacks to my job, I am very satisfied. I like the kind of work I do and the opportunity for advancement. I find job satisfaction from the challenge, working with great people, and traveling. I am always learning, and my work is never boring. My future career plans include working on my Masters in Business Administration, and coordinating the sales training program for the sales force.

PRODUCTION CONTROL PLANNER

I have worked up the corporate ladder because I like the idea of being responsible. As a production control planner, it is my responsibility to commit when orders will be ready, expedite materials, and tell assembly what they will build daily. More specifically, my work activities include: daily meetings on how to improve production; moving materials through the building to be fitted into a production order; making commitments when various jobs will ship; and making judgment calls on stock to carry and how and when things will happen.

In order to perform this kind of work well, you must be able to work well with all people at all levels of the organization. It is also important to be organized and to pay attention to detail.

I like the kind of work I do and having responsibilities, but I would like to change the idea that the planner is totally responsible to see that jobs are on time and of high quality; that should belong to all people in the company. I like the organization I work for and the people with whom I work. I mainly feel satisfied when jobs ship as I quoted, when my product lines remain 100% on time, and when people like to deal with me.

My future career plans are to manage a group of people at the company for which I presently work.

PRODUCTION MANAGER, TELEPHONE COMPANY

As production manager for a telephone company, I am responsible for the quantity, quality and accuracy of over 2,500 telephone operators. On a daily or weekly basis, I study and analyze performance results, attend and hold meetings, and visit various work locations.

The skills and attitudes which I consider important to perform this job well are: a sincere interest in people, a good memory, to be comfortable with people, an innate but controlled competitiveness, and a leadership instinct.

I do not have an explanation as to how I got into this line of work after receiving my Bachelor of Arts degree. However, I have liked it for the more than 30 years I have been doing it, and would choose it again if given the chance to start over. I particularly like the "family" aspects of the organization for which I work.

PRODUCTION MANAGER, STEEL MANUFACTURING

I was born and raised in the Pittsburgh area and grew up around steel mills all my life. Each summer, while in college earning my Bachelor of Arts in Business Administration and studying mechanical engineering for 2 years, I worked in the steel mills. I tried work in other fields of manufacturing such as clothing, railroad car building, graphite machining, and paper products, plus work as a safety consultant for an insurance company and heating, ventilating and air conditioning salesman. However, I have now come back to steel work as the production manager/assistant plant manager in a steel grinding shop. My responsibilities include supervising production, planning work, training employees, dealing with government regulations, and supervising people. My day-to-day activities are: determining what orders of production jobs need to be done that day and arranging for them to be done; looking at future production demands and organizing the men and material so that those future demands/orders can be met also.

To perform this kind of work well, it is important to have common sense, organizational skills, planning ability, leadership qualities, the ability to work with people, an even temper, clear thinking, creativity, imagination, confidence, a friendly personality, fairness, and honesty.

The small size of the company I work for has its advantages and disadvantages. I find advancement is limited, but I am included in decisions. I have the feeling that I am a real part of the organization.

Job satisfaction comes from the sense of accomplishment I feel when the work is completed "on time." Knowing I help create an environment in which people are able to complete the work and in which they enjoy working is also satisfying. I like being "in charge" but being "a part" also.

Since I am not a part of the family that owns this small privately held company, I may find promotion to company president to be a difficult road to travel. This is my goal, but at least I hope to become plant manager.

PRODUCTION SUPERVISOR, SILK SCREEN

As the production supervisor, I oversee quality control in finished products. My particular job is working 2nd shift in a silk screen company. I didn't choose this job, rather they chose me, and I am glad they did. I am very satisfied with almost all aspects of this work: the kind of work I do, the people I work with, the opportunity for advancement, and the person and organization I work for. I have also worked as a banquet waitress and cook , and housewife, all jobs which I also liked.

My work day starts by communicating with the 1st shift supervisors on the workload for the 2nd shift. During my shift, I oversee workers' accuracy with numbers and quality control and keep 14 people busy and productive. I work with shipping department heads to insure that the product is out in time for delivery. Dealing with workers' questions or attitudes or work performance is also my responsibility.

In order to perform this kind of work well, you must have good communications skills, a positive attitude toward work and workers, organizational skills, common sense, and excellent work habits.

Job satisfaction for me is found in total team effort--maximum productivity from all workers.

PROFESSIONAL SECRETARY

As a professional secretary for over twenty-five years, I answer and route all incoming telephone calls, and transcribe correspondence using a word processor for nine executives and engineers. As I am the only secretary in my company, my work is varied and anticipating the needs of the persons I report to can be somewhat challenging. I also edit the company's monthly newsletter and serve as the chairperson on the committee that plans our company summer outings and Christmas party.

In order to be successful in the secretarial field, you need good communication skills, both written and verbal, an interest in people, and the ability to remain courteous to others no matter how the day is going--since my position is the initial contact for people with the company. The ability to type at the speed of ninety words per minute, a thorough knowledge of grammar, punctuation, and spelling, time management skills, and the ability to work well under pressure are important skills as well.

Although at present there is no opportunity for career advancement, I enjoy the work I do.

Upon graduation from high school, I worked as a production assistant, a media director, and for an advertising agency. Although I entered this field with no specific training, I have since passed the examinations for the Certified Professional Secretary program.

I am currently studying for my Associate's degree and plan to continue in the pursuit of a Bachelor's degree. I am mapping out a career path that I believe will lead to a position in business management.

PROFESSOR #1

I very much like what I do. As a university professor, I teach German, read a lot, and write articles and books on literature and language. My job also involves some administrative work.

The skills and attitudes which I consider important for a teacher are: patience, a thorough knowledge of the subject taught, frequent visits abroad for a language teacher, good speaking abilities, well organized, and a like of young people. A researcher needs an ongoing commitment and keen intellect.

I have always wanted to teach and so to prepare myself to become a professor, I earned the B.A., M.A., and Ph.D. degrees, and these are very important if you plan to be a college professor.

I would be more satisfied with my occupation if less bureaucratic things were due all the time so there would be more time for reading and traveling.

However, I have taught because of the satisfaction I find in teaching young people and seeing a new world open up before their eyes. I am also satisfied because I am helping others.

PROFESSOR #2

To become a college professor was definitely a planned career move for me and one which I diligently sought out. I am still very satisfied with my decision which I made over 20 years ago after previously pursuing careers as a manager/baker, entrepreneur, consultant and traveler. My educational background includes a Bachelor of Science in

Business Administration and a Masters in Business Administration.

My 20 to 25 classroom hours per week including days, evenings and weekends requires me to have a good attitude, patience and understanding, and an expertise in the subject matter.

I am so satisfied with my career that if given the opportunity to start over and prepare for any kind of work, I would again choose to be a college professor. I like the people I work with and the people and organization for whom I work. I find satisfaction from my work by seeing my students succeed in their chosen careers. My future career plans are to continue with what I am now doing.

PROFESSOR & ADMINISTRATOR

Having always enjoyed the academic atmosphere, I planned to become a teacher from early childhood. With Bachelor of Arts and Master of Arts degrees, I serve as a college professor and administrator. I enjoy the interaction with students and colleagues. Although my earlier work was as a dental assistant, I particularly like the sense of accomplishment when working with students and seeing them improve and then advance.

My administrative duties take place in a learning center where I write articles, seek grants, and organize meetings. As a professor I teach classes and write lesson plans. Coordinating activities with colleagues and working individually with students are also some of my responsibilities.

Success as a college professor requires sound knowledge of the subject matter, the ability to get along with others, and creativity. I find ambition as well as sincerity to be helpful.

It would be preferable if there were better funding and more flexibility in scheduling, but, other than that, I enjoy everything about my work.

PROFESSOR & PROFESSIONAL ACTOR

I have the Bachelor's, Master's and Ph.D. degrees in geology. I enjoy that field, but I love the theatre more. I've always wanted to perform. My acting career started in undergraduate school. Because I also find satisfaction in helping students improve and learn, I have combined my interests into a career as a teacher/actor. Actually, they are separate occupations, but I spend almost everyday doing both. I teach one 50 minute class on Monday, Wednesday, and Friday, and two 75 minute classes on Tuesday and Thursday. On Tuesday through Sunday from 2:00-10:30 p.m., I have rehearsal/performances. I have the additional school duty of interviewing high school students applying for admission.

In order to manage this kind of career, I have found it important to have energy, talent, concentration, the ability to listen, and vocal-movement-acting training.

Aside from the fact that I rarely get a complete day off, I like what I am doing very much. It's challenging, and I find that every day is different--never the same twice. I have job satisfaction because I take pride in my work. I have enjoyment of my colleagues. Basically, I am a teacher/actor because it's fun to do!

My future career plans are to do occasional jobs with other theatres and some film work.

PROFESSOR, BIOLOGY

For 27 years, I've been a university professor who has taught, done some research, and served as an administrator. I've earned 3 degrees: a Bachelor of Arts, a Master of Arts, and a Ph.D. My field is biology.

With my biology major, my career choice was between medicine and the academic realm. I elected the stimulation of the academic over the pragmatism of medicine.

My work is made up of lecturing, instructing graduate seminars, spending office hours with students, and teaching in labs. I do research whenever I can. There are committee meetings with major departmental, university, and professional personnel as well as international committee work.

For work in the classroom you need to know what is involved in teaching. You also must know diverse research techniques. A person should have leadership qualities and be creative administratively.

If I haven't liked all the organizations for which I've worked, I have enjoyed the people. I appreciate good students. The accomplishments made in my research gratify me. I'd be happier in my work if there were more feedback and more interaction among colleagues. One day I plan a "benevolent retirement" which may include another career.

PROFESSOR, BUSINESS

Upon graduating from college with a Bachelor of Science degree, serving as an officer in the military, and then working in retail sales, I enrolled in graduate school to earn a Masters in Business Administration. During my course of study, I made the decision to work as a college teacher, and I have been pleased I did.

As a college teacher, I give business topic lectures and prepare and grade tests. A typical day includes preparing lecture material, conducting one or more classes, making and grading assignments, attending administrative meetings, reading, and communicating with colleagues.

To perform well as a college teacher, it is important to have the ability to communicate for comprehension. A teacher should also have confidence in his or her own ability to present useful information in an up-beat manner. You also need patience and the ability to see problems from a variety of positions.

Although I dislike the large workload for the money, there are more aspects to the job that I like. I find satisfaction from control of the requirements of the job and from time management and the flow of responsibility. I like the fact that much time is spent alone reading. It is also satisfying to me to be in a position of being the major force in the classroom environment.

My plans are to continue my education and to earn a Ph.D. which is needed for continued promotion. I will also be searching for advancement through job changes within this teaching profession.

PROFESSOR, BUSINESS ADMINISTRATION

I've been a professor of business administration at a state affiliated community college for 24 years. Not only do I teach, but I also serve on three different committees and advise students. I like the people I work with and for, the type of work involved, and the organization itself.

Over the years, I've learned that this is a dynamic field which mandates heavy reading. Furthermore, to be successful in the field, one must be creative and patient. The payoffs for doing the job well are earning a respectable living and watching my students become successful.

Although I have always greatly enjoyed my work, it would be more satisfying if I could reduce the course load and the amount of bureaucratic paperwork. The ultimate goal for the most satisfying job possible is to spend more time with the students.

I chose a career in teaching because of my love of academic life. In the first grade, I liked school and decided never to leave it. Academic preparation has included a college degree and a Masters in Business Administration. Although I've completed the course work for a Ph.D., I haven't yet finished my dissertation.

In addition to working as an academic, I have also held jobs as a deputy sheriff, a bar manager, and an accountant. As for the future, I have a desire to develop real estate and to retire. Were I to start all over again in choosing an occupation, I would definitely choose the same one.

PROFESSOR, CHEMISTRY & CHAIR

I like teaching very much and have been doing it for many years. The contact with students is exhilarating. What has kept me satisfied for so many years is seeing students learn and grow and the student friendships that have developed.

I am a college professor of organic chemistry and department chairman. My responsibilities for this position include lecturing, conducting labs, attending department and committee meetings, and student advising.

If I could change anything about my college teaching and chairmanship it would be to lessen the administrative duties. I would particularly like to see students better prepared and motivated.

Initially in my career I was a research director of a small chemical company. However, my memory of and admiration for some excellent teachers in the prep school, college, and grade school I attended were motivation for my entering the field of teaching.

PROFESSOR, COMMUNICATION #1

I have taught classes in communication, conducted research for publications, prepared papers for conventions, met and worked with students, and served on committees for many years.

Of particular pleasure to me has been interacting with and working with young adults. I've enjoyed the freedom and flexibility of my position. I would like to see a more equitable and effective way created to evaluate work, and higher compensation would have made me happier, but the job setting in a college is ideal for a person of my interests. It is the freedom and the opportunity for research that pleased me most.

To be an effective professor of communications, you must have excellent communication skills. There must be a firm foundation of understanding the bases of effective means of communication and interacting with others. Of course, a professor must have at least two college degrees, the Bachelor's and the Master's. I have three; the Ph.D. in hand avoids your hitting the ceiling in promotions in college as you might with only two degrees. Strong interpersonal skills along with an open mind are needed in this job as in many others. A good sense of humor and broad interests are also very important.

I have been invited to teach in a university in Russia, and I will probably accept that invitation.

PROFESSOR, COMMUNICATION #2

With a Bachelor of Arts, a Master of Arts and a Ph.D., I am a professor at the university level. My field is communication. Success as a teacher requires creativity and a great deal of patience. You must be able to explain concepts and processes. High verbal aptitude, scientific curiosity, self-motivation, and self-direction are essential.

My daily activities include class preparation and instruction, and conferences with students and advisees on projects and careers. I also spend time conducting research. I particularly enjoy the sense of discovery in my work. I like helping others understand things. The flexibility of my work schedule is very nice. To be more satisfied in this work I like so much, I would like more immediate and tangible rewards for my efforts.

While working toward my degrees, I spent time as a bus driver and in insurance sales. Although I enjoy teaching and research, I'd like to know more about meteorology and aviation. Some day I'd like to learn to fly a fixed-wing aircraft.

PROFESSOR, COMPUTER SCIENCE

I went to college to earn a bachelors, masters, and doctorate in computer science and have remained in the academic community for my career. I had a good research programming job as an undergraduate, which developed my interest to go on to graduate school. When I interviewed after my Ph.D., academic positions seemed to allow me to set my own research directions better than industry. I might someday do industry research instead of academic (development rather than basic research), but I would never leave computer science.

I work from 10 a.m. to 12 midnight, Monday through Thursday, 10 a.m. to 7 p.m., Friday, and 2 to 10 p.m. on Sunday. Sometimes I start work earlier due to meetings. I teach about 3 class hours per week, attend group meetings about 10 hours per week, and most of the rest of the time is research and administration. I travel about one week per month.

In order to enter this career, you must be highly skilled at scientific research, and have the ability to do oral and written presentations. I publish about ten major papers per year, and write about ten proposals for grants. A lot of my time is management and training of graduate student researchers. You must be able to deal with stress well in this career.

Although I like my work and wouldn't change careers, there are frustrations involved in research work, primarily in obtaining funding. I would like to see more emphasis in the U.S. government and industry on basic research funding. I would also welcome less pressure to be a superstar in order to get tenure, and more free time.

What keeps me going is the frequent rewards in the form of recognitions from scientific colleagues nationally and internationally. The work itself is extremely interesting because you are finding answers to questions not previously known--and even finding new questions.

My career aspirations/plans are to get tenure, to be well known and respected in my research field, and to produce many good Ph.D. students.

PROFESSOR, ECONOMICS

It is useful to me as a college professor in the field of economics that I am a perfectionist and have a sense of humor. I also find it helpful to have an inquisitive mind and be able to think abstractly. Additionally, enjoying problem solving and being patient are most helpful.

After obtaining a Bachelor's degree and a Master's degree, I earned a Ph.D. I am an instructor at the college level because I like the flexibility plus the freedom university teaching offers. The economics field interested me as much as the college scheduling.

For 20 years, I've enjoyed helping my students develop analytical skills. Learning something new myself every day also pleases me. While I'm not fond of my superior and think the salaries should be higher, I do enjoy my colleagues, my teaching and research duties, and the college atmosphere. My plans are to continue my instruction and research responsibilities at the college.

My obligations include teaching three classes of 30 students each. I am in constant contact with students, meeting them formally in class and during office hours as well as casually in the hallways. In my work, I read, write and perform statistical tests as I manage research projects.

PROFESSOR, ENGINEERING

I am a college professor teaching courses in industrial engineering. I've also taught classes in the science and technology of metals and their properties--known as metallurgy. For the years I've taught these courses as well as classes in engineering drawing and in the manufacturing process, I have enjoyed many aspects of the job.

A professor must thoroughly know the subject matter. Being patient is also necessary, and you should have a good sense of humor.

My teaching days are spent either lecturing or conducting labs. I also have time in my office from 7:30 to 8:30 a.m. In the late afternoon, I correct students' work and prepare for the next day.

I've found great satisfaction in seeing my students learn, and the success of former students has been rewarding as well. I enjoy everything about my career: my colleagues, the school, teaching, the administration, and the opportunity for advancement. I'd earned a Bachelor of Science degree in mechanical engineering and I'm glad I applied for the teaching position when there was a vacancy. Although I've previously spent some time as an experimental engineer, I'd choose teaching all over again because of its rewards.

PROFESSOR, ENGLISH #1

As a college professor of English, I lecture, read papers, and perform research in literature. My schedule has been to meet with my scheduled classes and hold conferences with students enrolled in those classes.

For anyone considering a career as a professor of English, I recommend a great deal of formal education--I completed both a Bachelor of Arts degree and a Master of Literature degree. You must have an interest in working with the public.

My greatest personal satisfaction is derived from the opportunity to share knowledge with others.

I chose my present occupation because of my love of literature; I have never regretted my choice.

I believe there is plenty of opportunity for advancement in the field of education and I wholeheartedly encourage the pursuit of knowledge. I enjoy working in a college atmosphere because there is always the challenge of new students with the opportunity to shed new light upon my lecture material.

Upon retirement, I plan to continue sharing the wealth of knowledge I have accumulated over the years and work part time as a lecturer.

PROFESSOR, ENGLISH #2

As a college English teacher, I teach four sections of thirty students each, three times per week; the areas in which I specialize as a teacher of English are advanced composition, remedial English basic skills, and introduction to literature classes.

I have been teaching on a college level for quite a few years and in that time I have found the most important preparation of this job to be a solid education; I have earned an Associate in Arts degree, a Bachelor of Arts degree, and a Master of Arts degree. In addition, an English teacher must be well read, be able to write and speak accurately, and possess physical and mental stamina, a sense of humor, and great patience.

I love my job; I derive great personal satisfaction from my efforts, especially when I see students, who were previously floundering, actually improve their skills and mastery of the English language. I enjoy my interaction with the students and my fellow colleagues on the faculty. A college environment is intellectually stimulating and I particularly enjoy the institution for which I work.

Although I have the highest enthusiasm for my job in general, I would prefer not to be required to serve on, what I believe to be, "do nothing" committees.

I decided to become an English teacher when I was in the fifth grade. Years later, during my freshman year in college, I told the President of the college that I wanted to teach at that institution, and he responded, "Get your Master's." I did just that and, four years later, he hired me; I have served on that same faculty ever since.

I intend to teach for the rest of my natural life; I believe each new day is an opportunity to teach as well as to learn.

PROFESSOR, ENGLISH #3

I enjoy my career as a university professor, teaching English. The intellectual growth of my students, along with my own scholarly development, has always given me great satisfaction. I enjoy my students and the pleasant anticipation of seeing them in class. The contact with people and my professional associations also mean a great deal to me.

Since I always knew I was going to be a teacher--even when I was very young--I earned my Bachelor of Science degree, a Master of Arts, and an Education Specialist certification. Besides appropriate training, I found thorough preparation to be essential for success in the classroom. Enthusiasm for the material being taught, along with a good sense of humor, are very important as well.

I also devote time to research and class presentations. Evaluating individual students and their response as well as their grades are part of my work. No day is typical; there are always new challenges. My job would be even more pleasant if I had more time for students.

I also own and operate a farm. When I eventually retire, I will devote myself to the management of the farm and to doing volunteer work in the community--particularly in the hospital and nursing home.

PROFESSOR, GEOPHYSICS

A professor in a university, I've been teaching geophysics and geology for seven years. My duties include instructing, doing research and attending committees. I also supervise other researchers.

To do my work, you must have strong math skills and should be an organized person who has the capability of completing tasks. You also need advanced education. I, myself, have a Ph.D. degree.

To teach at a college, you do not have to have a "terminal degree," but you very quickly reach a ceiling, especially at a university, and you cannot move to a higher position without the needed "credentials."

I particularly enjoy working with students. The research process also is very rewarding to me. Further, my colleagues and my work give me a great deal of pleasure. If I could start over, I'd again choose my field, but I'd like the salaries to be higher.

PROFESSOR, GOVERNMENT & TECHNOLOGY

Presently employed as a professor of government and technology at a major university, I direct a research center, teach post graduate courses, conduct conferences with the students in my classes, prepare for lectures to be given outside the university, and attend meetings at a company where I am a member of the Board of Directors.

Besides completion of several degrees (a Bachelor's, a Master's, and a Doctorate), you must be intelligent, altruistic, with good communication skills, and proficient in several intellectual disciplines.

I enjoy the fact that my position gives me the opportunity to learn something new every day and influence world events. My only complaint is that there are not enough hours in the day!

My field of interest is science because I consider science to be the most intellectually challenging subject and I have an older brother who became a physician. I chose the field of government and technology, partly because of my interest in science but mostly because of strong encouragement I received from my parents and other helpful adults who were influential in my life.

I am in an excellent position, careerwise, so I have no plans to move on to something else. I find teaching to be intellectually stimulating, so I intend to teach and learn as much as I can throughout my life.

PROFESSOR, HISTORY

I have taught history at the college level for many years. I'd earned a Bachelor of Arts degree and a Master's and a Ph.D. in history, which equipped me to chair our department at this religious college.

In my work, I schedule history classes for each semester. During my free period, I see students who come for academic or personal counseling. Attending committee meetings as well as planning meetings are part of my responsibilities. I also spend time preparing for and presenting my lectures.

The fruits of my labors give me great job satisfaction. Producing thinking, productive, truthful adults is very rewarding to me. I really appreciate the gratitude and love returned to me. The students, my peers, our superiors, and the college itself all mean a great deal to me. There's nothing I would change except to do my work better. I'd choose teaching all over again.

An effective teacher respects the dignity of others. You should trust students and others. One must have strong speaking skills and healthy study skills. The ability to have good rapport with people is helpful.

I've taught successfully all my life. When I retire, I might teach in a preaching context for a while. Eventually, I plan to go back to the elementary schools and offer to teach history to all grades. Maybe I'll write my memoirs or the history of the church.

PROFESSOR, HISTORY & DEAN

I teach History and Sociology and was at one time a College Dean. A college professor conducts classes and meets with students from those classes during the day, attends departmental or committee meetings, prepares for the next day's classes, grades papers and assigns grades, studies to keep ahead of the subject material for the upcoming lessons, and reads because there is always something to be read in this line of work.

This profession requires the ability to teach the subject material to the students, genuinely like students in general, have the ability to get along with others, and possess the enthusiasm to motivate the students to learn. Education is a key factor in success as a professor; you must enjoy studying and researching material enough to earn a college degree at the doctorate level. I have a doctorate degree in history.

I love to teach! I enjoy the interaction with my associates and the thrill of seeing young people take an interest in my subjects. It is a wonderful occupation. A faculty member is respected, and my work as a professor has led me to become involved in interesting sidelines of my work, such as administration of the institution and advising or counseling students. In my years of working at a college, I have only had a few bosses that were not to my liking and there are few, if any, aspects of teaching that I would change.

My father was a high school principal. I always assumed I would become a high school teacher, but once I completed my undergraduate degree, I had trouble finding employment at a high school as there were many graduates and few openings. So I decided to continue my education through graduate school to a doctorate level. I was pleased to find that this did qualify me for a position as a part of a college faculty at the college level. You do not encounter the problems with discipline found at the high school level; the majority of students are in college because they want to be there.

My career has also given me the opportunity to teach overseas which was one of the most enriching experiences of my life.

PROFESSOR, JUNIOR COLLEGE

I analyzed my career choices, taking into account my interests, abilities, and potential for earning a living and was then left with teaching . My father, aunt, and uncle were also teachers, and I am sure that was an influencing factor. I enjoy reading and studying. Over my 40 year career history, I have taught in 5th grade, graduate school, honors classes, remedial classes, reformatory, and jail. The last 14 years have been at a junior college. To prepare myself for teaching, I earned the equivalent of a doctor's degree in education.

As a professor at a junior college, my typical activities include lecturing for 3 hours a day, preparing lectures, counseling students, reading sociology, and supervising students doing volunteer social service.

To be a teacher, you should believe in education, social service, volunteerism, people, pupils, and organizing content in "logical sequences."What I don't think is needed is all the professional courses in theory; more practice teaching would be better to prepare for the occupation.

My long years of satisfaction from teaching have come from the friends on the faculty, the students, social service, and social service boards on which I have served. I hardly go anyplace now without seeing someone I know. It's a real ego booster.

PROFESSOR, LANGUAGE ARTS METHODS

There are numerous experiences which have led up to my present position as professor of language arts methods. I taught elementary school for 14 years. While doing that, I was invited to teach methods classes at a local university on a fellowship. I then began my doctoral studies and was hired as continuing faculty at the local university.

As a professor of language arts methods, I prepare for classes, design in-service programs, and write for professional journals. On a weekly basis, I teach 3 sections of language arts methods, direct a National Writing Project Site, advise master's degree students, and plan and present in-service programs for teachers.

The skill and attitudes which I consider important for performing my work well are: enthusiasm, flexibility, a good sense of humor, public speaking ability, a solid knowledge base, and a like for people.

I like almost every aspect of my work: the people I work with, the opportunity for advancement, the people and organizations I work for, and the kind of work I do. I particularly like my flexible and varied work schedule. If I could change anything about my occupation, I would have fewer advisees and less "publish or perish" pressure.

My future career goals include: reaching the rank of full professor, publishing several articles a year, and publishing a book on composition methods or children's literature.

PROFESSOR, MATHEMATICS #1

I was always good at mathematics and chose it as a college major because it was the subject which was easiest for me. I went to graduate school because I didn't want to get a job in the business community but rather in the academic world. To qualify for this work, I have earned a B.S., M.S., and a Ph.D. While going to school, I worked as a research assistant and computer programmer.

As a professor of mathematics, I do research in mathematics and teach. My typical work week includes: approximately 30 hours teaching, grading, preparing lectures, and seeing students, 10-15 hours of research, and 5 hours of administrative duties.

To perform well as a professor and do research, I think it is important to have patience, intuitiveness, and good communication skills.

I like the kind of work I am doing very much but would prefer to have less grading, and less of other administrative paperwork. I find it thrilling when I figure out something new or see a student "get" something.

My plans for the future are to continue doing research, publish papers, and get tenure.

PROFESSOR, MATHEMATICS #2

A teacher of mathematics at a religious college is involved in more than teaching a class--you must prepare for each class, carry out research perform committee work, know word processing of reports and articles, advise students when needed, and pray in the college chapel. I also took on the responsibility of publishing the campus journal.

In the time I have been teaching I have found the most important quality is a professional and academic background; classroom showmanship is also important; and the work I perform also requires a religious vocation.

Teaching affords you the luxury of long vacations, but I enjoy more the public esteem and sense of community spirit I have encountered, and the intellectual stimulation of working in the field of education.

I was inspired to this profession by the impression left on me by others before me who set good examples; also by the expectations of religious satisfaction and intellectual stimulation. These expectations have more than been fulfilled, making this the best choice for me.

My schooling includes Bachelor of Science, Master of Science and Master of Arts degrees; I also taught previously at a secondary school.

I love this profession and, except for grading papers and disciplining students, this does not seem like a job; it's a lifestyle.

PROFESSOR, PHYSICS & HISTORY

Preparing and presenting physical science and history lectures to college students summarizes my typical work activity. To do this work it is important to have a high level of concentration and interest in the fields of study.

I planned for many years to become a professor. I spent many years as a special agent for the FBI and during that time I attended night classes in graduate school to earn the credits I needed to qualify for a professorship: a BA, MA, and partial credits toward a Ph.D. degree.

I want to continue teaching and hope to fit a full time slot at the college level.

PROFESSOR, POLITICAL SCIENCE

Teaching political science on a college level includes reading, teaching classes and discussing various issues with students.

It is essential to have an interest in the field. It is important to have patience.

I enjoy engaging in debate on substantial questions. I also enjoy reading.

I would like to see the pay tripled for this profession. However, I am doing what I really always wanted to do and plan to continue.

PROFESSOR, PSYCHOLOGY

I am a professor of psychology. I teach college students, do child development research, and write. I have been in this line of work for 14 years.

Various aspects of this occupation include working with graduate and undergraduate students on research projects, teaching class, reading journal articles, writing papers, talking with colleagues about department policy, and carrying out research.

Some important skills you have to have to be a professor are writing ability, self-discipline and analytical skills.

Satisfactions that I find from my work are completed research writing projects, working with students, giving a lecture to students that is received well, and doing a variety of tasks on my own schedule in a given day. Two things that I would like to change about my job are to have a greater income and guaranteed financial support over the summers.

I had initially planned to be a clinical psychologist, but, late in my senior year, I discovered I didn't like clinical psychology. I entered a Master of Arts program in psychology and developed an interest in developmental psychology. Previous occupations that I have had are part-time work during college, and bank teller.

My future career aspirations are to continue in my present occupation and position. I have no aspirations to move into administration (Dean, vice president, etc.). I may like to spend more time writing, but basically I plan to continue to do the same types of work I do now: teaching, research, and writing. I like the variation.

PROFESSOR, THEOLOGY

With a Bachelor of Arts degree and a Master's in Divinity, I worked as a parish minister and a missionary. Then, after earning a Ph.D. degree, I found myself teaching and liked it. After 17 years in teaching, I plan to continue to improve myself and to write more.

Teaching theology and courses on global focus at the graduate level in a denominational seminary, I must keep up with theology, politics, society, and economics around the world. I also do consulting outside of the seminary venue.

I spend my day checking the computer, cable news, and newspapers for the latest information. Additionally, I study in the library and in the office, attend too many meetings, prepare course materials, and read students' papers. My work requires some international travel for research and some U.S. travel for speaking engagements, conferences, and more meetings. I write articles and other materials for publication.

My work gives me great satisfaction in watching people transform and grow. An eternal learner, I find international perspectives, plus continually facing new challenges, new ideas and materials, and new possibilities to be very rewarding. It disturbs me that teaching is valued too little. At the top of the teaching profession at a young age, I have no advancement opportunities except to leave the classroom. I also see the administrative level emerging with more power and less wisdom.

To do my job, you must be self-sufficient, work with little supervision or accountability, and be a self-starter. Also vital in teaching at the graduate level are high intelligence, an open mind, and flexibility. Good people skills along with diplomacy are necessary. With few external rewards, you must be able to live on internal satisfactions, finding joy in learning and in aiding others in their efforts to learn.

PROFESSOR/DEAN

I never had any doubt that I would go into teaching at the advanced level along with biological research. In order to pursue this career, I started by earning my Bachelor of Arts degree and eventually my Ph.D. My field of teaching is medical education. After working as a professor and biomedical researcher for many years, I was promoted to dean of the medical school.

As the dean, I am responsible for many administrative and management functions. I oversee the educational quality and continually work to upgrade our teaching and research programs.

To perform this kind of work well, it is important to have imagination, perseverance, command of the spoken word, and clarity in writing and speaking.

I like almost every aspect of my work and am very glad that I went into the teaching profession. However, I would like to see less paper work involved in this job and also greater public support for education. It has indeed been satisfying work interacting with young minds.

PROGRAM ANALYST & CONSULTANT

I have always been intrigued by new avenues as they have appeared in my career life: always looking for challenges. That is why I made a change from teaching and have become a program analyst. I earned my masters in curriculum development which led to writing curriculum for a technical manual. It was a natural lead in from teaching. As my abilities surfaced, many opportunities presented themselves, and I have moved up the ladder to my current position.

As a program analyst, I am a consultant on government and private contracts. Everyday is somewhat different. Some of the more typical daily work tasks are: budget activities relating to the formulation and execution of the budget; editorial work on manuals utilized for training classes; writing papers and responses for daily needs of the office related to program and strategies planning. I basically do whatever it takes to make the office run smoothly and have the proper materials to go forward to the top level managers.

In order to perform this kind of work well, it is important to have accuracy, editorial skills, prompt response, writing capability, and the ability to recognize and perceive needs of the office.

My biggest frustration now is a lack of respect for professional women. Also, government contracting isn't the easiest because of all the bureaucracy involved. Despite these frustrations, I like the kind of work I do. Another positive aspect is that there appears to be opportunity for advancement. Job satisfaction for me is found in being able to satisfy the needs of the office and being challenged by the opportunities of new tasks.

My career plans for the future are to continue up the management chain within the current structure in pursuit of new challenges.

PROGRAM COORDINATOR

What started out as a temporary job after I was graduated with a Masters of Science degree from the University of London, has turned into a career position for me for the past 16 years. I had planned to find a teaching job, but they were very hard to obtain at the time I graduated. I took the job of program coordinator at a sports center and have been basically satisfied with it. Prior to this work, I had done some coaching and teaching.

As Program Coordinator, I work out the program for sporting and recreational activities in a college campus facility. My daily routine includes cleaning the pool area and bleeding tanks, answering questions about programs 50% of the day, working on programs 25% of the day, setting up programs 10% of the day, and personnel and scheduling duties 15% of the day.

To perform this kind of work well, it is important to be open minded and patient. You must have the ability to perform many different jobs such as office procedures, pool maintenance, rules of athletic competitions, and cleaning up and setting up for programs and function.

I like the kind of work I do and the people with whom I work. I find job satisfaction in knowing that students are joining in an exercise program.

I plan to continue working at the sports center and work toward becoming the Recreation Manager.

PROGRAM DIRECTOR #1

As the program director for a karate academy, I teach karate, review memberships, start new students, and monitor progress. I compile statistics to monitor my progress and those that I oversee. There is paperwork to do and conferences with parents and students regarding the progress and what their children or they are trying to develop from karate.

To perform well as a martial arts director it is important to be open minded, to be a good example to others, and to be motivational and supportive.

I like my kind of work very much, the people I work with, the opportunity I have for advancement and the people I work for. The main satisfactions I find from my work are seeing people develop, reach their potential, achieve their goals, and have fun.

I earned a bachelor of science degree in mathematics, health and physical education. It was because of my education and my previous involvement in the martial arts that made this job opportunity available to me.

I plan to keep doing what I am doing and to promote the martial arts. I aspire to show people the benefits of karate--that it's not just kicking and punching.

PROGRAM DIRECTOR #2

I am an employee program specialist for employee volunteerism, events, self-development, and recreation. I am responsible for organizing cultural awareness events, coordinating employee involvement in the community, and supervising a recreational facility. There is no typical day or week in my kind of work. My schedule depends on the project or events that are currently taking place or being planned for the future. Most events and projects require finding volunteers, and scheduling and coordinating them. Making all necessary arrangements for publicity, site, food, entertainment, etc., is part of the job. Publicity includes creating posters, flyers, and publishing a monthly newsletter.

My career background includes the following positions: pension trust reviewer, computer programmer, management consultant, and life insurance trainer. My educational background includes a bachelors degree in sociology/English, and an associate degree in TV production.

To perform this kind of work well, it is important to like people and have the ability to motivate them. Excellent organizational and writing skills are also necessary.

I like this kind of work very much. I like the organization I work for and the people I work with. If I had the chance to choose a career again and start over, I would choose this. I find job satisfaction from employees learning and/or experiencing things that they had not known before.

I see the possibility of having this job and my experience lead to other career opportunities in public affairs or human resources work.

PROGRAM MANAGER

On a daily and/or weekly basis, I prepare schedules, attend meetings, prepare reports and program computers. I manage aerospace/defense contracts and develop management systems.

To prepare for this occupation it is necessary to have a background in statistics, electronics engineering, computer science, management, accounting, personnel and law.

I get satisfaction from having things work out precisely.

My job would be more satisfying if I could be assured there would be constant allocation of government funding.

I am working in the defense industry because I watched too many WWII movies which showed the "romance" of the war. Also, my father was an engineer which helped push me toward a technical field.

Past work experience has been as a scheduling engineer and systems analyst.

PROGRAMMER

I have been programming for more than 20 years. Currently I am the lead technical person for all phases of development for a relatively large licensed program. It is my job to evaluate requests for additional functions and to recommend action to be taken, review and control design code and publications, and the preparation of media for shipment to customers. No day is typical, except for long hours. The variety of work is what makes it so interesting. Activities include: review of hardware specifications to determine programming support required, work with planners to determine what can be done, review and approval of design, code, and schedules, documentation (internal and customer), packaging, trips to customer sites to better understand customers needs or to resolve problems, and the list goes on.

To perform well as a programmer it is important to be logical, analytical, and dedicated to the tasks and the problem solving. You must definitely have writing skills. Also it is important to have the ability to get along with people.

I have stayed with this career for so long because I like this kind of work and the opportunities it has given me for advancement. I derive satisfaction from satisfying the customers' needs. I enjoy finding good solutions to problems, respect of peers, and feeling that I have been able to make a significant contribution. This occupation has also afforded me a reasonably good salary. I would be even more satisfied if I did not have to process so much red tape.

As well as a bachelors of arts degree, my background includes work as a research assistant in medical research and work in the accounting division of an insurance company. While I was working for the insurance company I was introduced to computer processing and discovered that this really interested me. I'm still interested in it, and I expect my work will lead to a promotion within the next two years.

PROGRAMMER/ANALYST #1

Working in an MIS department, I write software for my company. For the past five years I have worked as a Programmer Analyst. Basically, I maintain, support, and develop software in an MIS environment. I write software for users of all levels of ability and computer skills; I also perform analysis and design in conjunction with developing the software.

I received some training in programming while in high school; I took a course in basic programming language and I was hooked--I knew then that I wanted to write software in a business environment after I graduated from high school.

In addition to training in programming, the work I do requires analytical skills, people skills, creativity, design skills, and knowledge of the computer software available in today's market.

I like working in a job that has clearly defined opportunities for advancement; it really makes me want to achieve superior results for my company. I enjoy this kind of work. Programming provides me with a lot of challenges on a daily basis and allows me to make the most of my creative talents. The part I enjoy most about my job is working with people; I like the interaction I have with my customers or system users.

Prior to working as a programmer/analyst, I was employed as a clerk in a finance department coordinating the billing activities; I also worked as a secretary for a test engineering group in a high tech company.

I plan to become a group manager; I believe I could excel in the role of a project leader.

PROGRAMMER/ANALYST #2

I graduated from college with a Bachelor of Science degree in Business Management, and worked as a computer operator. I was promoted to programmer/analyst on the computer system. It is my job to create and modify programs, and train users. My typical day is spent on many maintenance projects on current existing software, occasionally on some new development work, some "fire-fighting," performing software quick fixes, and creating reports.

To perform well as a programmer/analyst, I think it is important to have good system skills, the ability to work well with internal people, and some knowledge of the corporate ladder.

If I could change anything about my occupation, I would create a more structured environment. There should be a more disciplined attitude toward prioritizing and sticking to task priority. There are sometimes too many interruptions.

However, I do like the work very much, the people and organization I work for, and the people I work with. I find job satisfaction with completed tasks and satisfied customers.

PROGRAMMER/ANALYST #3

Shortly after getting a job in the computer industry and finding out that I was fascinated with computers, I started taking courses towards a computer engineering degree. Having taken some programming courses, I managed to find a job programming which has since led to my present job as a programmer/analyst for business applications. I am still working at earning my degree, which I hope will enable me to get a job as a software engineer.

In my current position as programmer/analyst, I analyze clients' needs and develop automated solutions to meet those needs. The tasks associated with this job are not typical over the course of a day or a week. They are typical over the course of a project to develop a new application. At the beginning of a project, much time will be spent with clients defining what the new application will do. After defining this, the bulk of the project time will be spent designing the system. After more meetings with the client to go over the design and get their approval, another large amount of time will be spent programming. Then comes implementation including testing, software installation, documenting application, and user training. The projects I have worked on usually take several months, but some have gone on as long as 2 years.

To perform this kind of work well, you must be able to: listen to and understand client's needs; be very organized, thorough, practical and good with details; able to examine complex problems and foresee potential difficulties and be proactive in preventing them; have skills necessary to implement solutions (or have enough sense to know when to delegate and to whom to delegate) and be good at communicating ideas to peers, management, and users.

I like my work best when I am designing and developing new computer applications instead of just supporting applications. I like the fact that there are always new things to know and keep my interest. Job satisfaction for me is seeing a system or sub-system I have designed and (at least partly) programmed being used to its full potential.

My future career plans are to work as a software engineer on basic technologies in any of the following areas: graphics, graphical user interfaces, relational databases, or distributed computing.

PROJECT MANAGER, CONSTRUCTION

I was interested in construction as a child and therefore pursued this career. I earned a Bachelor of Science in Construction Management degree as one of the "building blocks" which got me into the construction industry.

As a project manager, I am responsible for all the work associated with a commercial construction project. I am at the job site daily, resolving technical and personnel problems. It is my responsibility to expedite the project and ensure progress.

To perform this kind of work well, it is important to have common sense, the ability to change direction, the ability to secure respect, and the ability to get along with others.

This has indeed been the right career for me, and I can say after working in this field for 18 years, if given the opportunity to start over and prepare for any work, I would again choose construction management. It is satisfying for me to see progress and results from the efforts and energy expended on the projects. I plan to continue in this field and to advance in higher level management.

PROJECT MANAGER, DESIGN ENGINEER

I am a project manager for a design engineering group. After working as an engineer for four and a half years, I was a manager for six months. I began in engineering right after receiving my Bachelor of Science degree in electrical engineering. My career goals are to enter the senior management level of a successful corporation.

As a youngster, my hobbies were ham radio and electronics. During high school, I worked in a grocery store as a stockman and as a construction worker, but I decided at age 14 to be an electrical engineer. My job satisfaction comes in the creation of products from conception through production in the factory. Working with leading edge technologies is particularly enjoyable to me. I am pleased that I can contribute to the business success of this company and my own rapid career advancement.

In my work, I manage engineers who design fiber optic communications equipment. Attending meetings to plan projects and meeting with engineers to review the status of various projects are some of my tasks. Further, I help engineers and manufacturing personnel solve technical problems. Handling personnel problems and meeting with customers to discuss technical capabilities are also part of my job description.

To be a manager, you must have strong analytical skills and be organized. You must have very good people skills. Having good technical skills related to the engineering field is also necessary.

My job would be more satisfying if the company were better organized. I'd like the products to be of higher quality as well. More competent employees would also make my job more pleasant.

PROOFREADER

My career life has taken several turns over the years. I started out in the Air Force as a Company Commander. I changed careers and spent many years teaching in the New York City schools. After retiring from the public school system, I taught in a school for missionaries' children. Now that I am retired from that, I volunteer at the mission headquarters to help in the office.

I work as a proofreader which involves reading and correcting articles about missionary work. I receive the manuscripts for editing. After I have edited them and they are typed, I then read them again carefully for errors. This kind of work requires that you be a good speller and have grammar knowledge.

I have been very satisfied with my career life and presently have no dislikes concerning my present work.

Job satisfaction for me is seeing the final field paper!

My plan is to continue helping as long as I can.

PROPERTY MANAGER

To be an effective property manager, you should have strong people skills. Dealing successfully with tenants requires the ability to work well with individuals. To maintain equipment, you need good mechanical skills. You also need bookkeeping ability plus you should be familiar with contracts and laws.

I spend a lot of my day responding to maintenance requests. Collecting, tabulating, and recording rent receipts are also my duties. Further, I act as the leasing agent and I interview prospective tenants.

For the past six years in this job, satisfaction for me has been the diversity of the work. I enjoy all the different aspects of my job, but I don't like the periods of inactivity. I'd like to stay busy on a regular basis.

A high school graduate, I got into this work because I used to renovate homes for resale. Because of the slump in house sales, I began to rent these homes. I hope one day to enlarge the operation, adding more units or more houses.

PROPERTY TAX CONSULTANT

I formerly worked as a deputy county assessor in the real estate division. I then decided to become a contractor of single family homes, but returned to appraising when there was a real estate recession. Since I would have had to start at the lowest level with the county, having been away for more than one year, I decided to use my knowledge for the benefit of the taxpayer. It was the right decision.

As a self-employed property tax consultant, I offer assistance at a taxpayer's request for help to resolve a valuation dispute with the County Assessor's office. Most of my clients are companies. An analysis is made of the books and records of the company, and the assessor's appraisal reviewed. Then an independent appraisal of the taxpayer's property is made and presented to the deputy assessor. Differences are noted and an effort is made to resolve the differences. If a resolution is not arrived at, I then make an appearance before the Assessment Appeal Board where evidence is presented to support the new appraisal.

I feel I have incorporated both my educational background and job experience into this work. I have a Bachelor of Science in Real Estate/Finance. The following skills and abilities which I have built up from previous work experience and which I consider important for this kind of work are the ability to analyze data (i.e., accounting ability and appraisal skills for both real and personal property), and the legal skills to review legality of assessment procedures employed.

I have liked almost every aspect of this career. I like the kind of work I do, and the people I work with. Because my clientele is so diverse, I have the opportunity to analyze various businesses, which I consider very interesting. I have had the opportunity to be involved in industries such as motion picture studios, T.V. broadcasting, hotels, marinas, defense contractors, newsprint manufacturers, newspapers, outdoor advertising, etc. I find considerable satisfaction in problem solving and in being reasonably well compensated for my services.

PROTESTANT PASTOR

I was urged by my friends and other pastors, and felt called by God to enter this profession. In order to become a pastor, I earned a Bachelor of Arts degree and then a Bachelor of Divinity degree before working in this capacity for the Protestant church for 39 years.

My work includes preaching, counseling, teaching, making visitations, administrating, and performing weddings, baptisms, and funerals. My day starts with devotions and studying. I work at the office in the morning making plans and meeting with staff. After lunch, I make hospital calls and home visits to sick members and other calls to people in need of pastoring. At least three nights a week I attend church committee meetings or make more visitations to members or prospects. Saturdays can be my day off, but is often spent performing weddings or funerals.

To be a pastor, it is important to have a healthy mind and attitudes. You must love God's kingdom and His people. Common sense and wisdom are also necessary attributes for this career. To perform well you must work hard, study and be diligent in your work.

The reward to me for all my years as a pastor has been the satisfaction of my effect on people's lives. They have been changed, blessed, and encouraged.

PSYCHOLOGIST

Solid people skills are needed to be a competent psychologist. Balancing this ability to get along with people with other interests makes a more well-rounded professional.

My degree is a Ph.D., which is needed to do the counseling in psychiatric work. I also conduct educational evaluations. Consultation sessions with my patients are part of my practice as well.

I've been an Air Force navigator and a special education administrator and, as a psychologist, I like most everything about my current work. I especially enjoy helping others. The people with whom I'm involved, the work itself, and my associates make my job rewarding. If I were able to limit commitments, my work would be more satisfying. One day I'll retire and travel.

PSYCHOLOGIST, SCHOOL

I became bored with my job as a school nurse at age 53 and went back to school to earn two master's degrees, one in counseling and the other in educational psychology, so I could become a school psychologist. I basically like everything about my new profession in which I assess and counsel learning-disabled and handicapped high school students.

I work three days a week. One day I do psychological assessments and evaluations of the students. The second day is spent meeting with parents and staff, and the third day I conduct group and individual counseling sessions.

To do well as a psychologist it is important to have intelligence, empathy, diplomacy, tact and initiative.

I find this career satisfying because of the intellectual challenge of assessment and the opportunity for problem-solving.

PSYCHOLOGIST, WRITER & COUNSELOR

My career started in advertising as a space salesman for a major national magazine. I spent several years in the military where I advanced in rank to Lt. Colonel. Then I went back to advertising, working for an agency in copy, research and contact. When I eventually returned to college I expected to become a dean of students. However, I found counseling was more interesting and creative and eventually earned my Ph.D. in order to practice psychology. If you enter this field, you must have at least two college degrees and, preferably, you should earn a doctorate degree as I did.

As a counseling psychologist, it is important to be able to listen intently and empathetically. You must learn how to relieve stress and the restraint on the client. Honesty, consistency, and sincerity are also important. You must have the diagnostic ability to detect the kinds of blocks or neuroses present. To provide treatment, you must have the courage to communicate ways of solving the problems WITHOUT IMPOSING solutions.

If given the chance to change anything in my occupation, it would be to be entirely free of any pressures from what I consider hard-boiled and self-assured officials. I particularly like this kind of work. I enjoy the variety and the chance to help individuals develop their own resources. I feel it is creative to help another person build self-esteem, strengths, and resources to adjust more effectively to life's challenges. Every day is different, so is every client, and so are his or her particular situations. I also like having work that comes to me, rather than me going after it. It is a very satisfying occupation.

PSYCHOLOGY RESEARCH MANAGER

I like the independence and the responsibilities of being a research manager. My field is cognitive psychology. In general, I handle large and complex federally-funded psychology research projects. I'm glad the results of the research I carry out will improve the quality of life for many people. It will make a difference in people's lives.

My usual day consists of attending meetings, analyzing data, writing, and presenting results. I handle some clerical work and create work procedures and systems. I delegate tasks, monitor the work of others, and give feedback.

The skills important to this work are leadership and the ability to work well with people and computers. Open-mindedness, a sense of fairness, and people and organizational skills are essential. Being able to work independently is important.

I got into this work after studying psychology in college. I took a course in psychology with a professor and worked with the professor after graduation. I like the variety of challenges I handle in this job. My future plans are to continue doing this work since I like it very much.

PUBLIC RELATIONS & ADVERTISING MANAGER

As a Public Relations and Advertising Manager for eighteen years, I interface with the media, handle community relations, plan and execute advertising campaigns for my company, and spearhead transit development and land use education within the community. I scan the media and survey articles for local stories, prepare press releases, and handle media inquiries that may impact my job.

As a part of community relations, I handle customer complaints, work with community outreach programs, and handle the printing of community maps. I work with our management staff on decisions that may affect the future of our company and work on our marketing plan with advertising agencies. I work with city and county staff on pending land use decisions affecting the public transit system for my community and consult with officials in a position to offer guidance in community funding programs.

In addition to a Bachelor of Science degree and a Master of Public Administration degree, my job requires an in-depth knowledge of working with the press, the ability to judge people fairly and correctly, the ability to change direction when needed, detailed knowledge of resources available to get the job done, strong networking skills within the community and the industry, and experience in writing, editing and printing.

Though demanding at times, my job can be very rewarding; for example, I like discovering that what I do or say to do works, getting the praise from others for work accomplishments, or producing programs that provide very positive results for the community.

For me this job was a natural evolution from newspaper work into public relations. I was previously employed as office manager, newspaper editor (news and copy), publications specialist, and public and government affairs adviser. My future plans are to stay in the field of public relations; perhaps I will move into media relations for a larger firm and continue my studies in Public Administration on the Doctorate level.

PUBLIC RELATIONS & MEDIA SPECIALIST

I like what I am doing now as a public relations/ media relations specialist for a regional water authority, and plan to continue doing this work for a long time. After earning my Bachelor of Arts in journalism degree, I began my career as a photographer and reporter for a hometown newspaper. I then was a radio reporter/anchor, and then a television reporter/producer.

I serve as the spokesman for my agency and design and implement public awareness campaigns. My regular job activities include talking with program managers to determine public relations needs of specific programs, working with writers and artists on a variety of media campaigns, working with senior staff to ascertain public relations needs and objectives, and determining what is realistic and financially prudent.

The keys to success in this kind of work are listening skills, negotiation skills, and an ability to know what is realistic.

I like almost every aspect of my work.

I find satisfaction from the independence I have in doing my job. I enjoy the teamwork in working with my co-workers in meeting goals, and influencing and changing public opinion.

PUBLIC RELATIONS CONSULTANT

A brief description of my public relations consulting work would be writing, making decisions, coordination with clients (mainly corporate) and thinking of ideas. This is never done by a routine schedule. There is no typical day, ever! My work does include many meetings, phone calls to deal with, delegation and supervision of projects, training of younger people, much writing, and numerous crises to settle.

The skills and abilities important to perform my work well are good writing abilities, initiative, poise and self confidence, versatility and flexibility and a broad background--educationally and job-wise.

Job satisfaction for me is the enjoyment of writing, experiencing teamwork on projects, and the ability to reach superior decisions through discussion with trusted and intelligent colleagues. I also like my work because I have a client base which broadens my horizons continually and offers me a variety of projects to work on.

A problem I am having is finding a means of keeping good people for a long time. This work depends on good people. One other drawback of this career for me is that I never feel that I am caught up.

This occupation seemed a natural profession for me. All the various jobs I have had have provided some background for this job. Ability to write well is a strong factor in public relations.

My various other jobs were in marketing research, advertising, as an airline attendant, as a reporter, in corporate public relations, and as a librarian.

I plan to build up my business, sell out, and continue traveling, reading, and enjoying a life style that is relaxed and rewarding.

PUBLIC RELATIONS OFFICER

For three years, I have been employed as a Public Relations Officer. My work involves writing press releases, speeches, and newsletter articles and supervising the printing and advertising departments. I clip newspaper articles, prepare copy and layouts for a newsletter, arrange photography for newspaper articles, get involved in desktop publishing, attend job related events, and plan and attend meetings.

Although a college degree is not required to perform these duties, you must have some formal training in journalism. Essential ingredients for success in this field are good writing and communication skills, open- mindedness, creativity, and political savvy.

I enjoy this kind of work because I enjoy working alone; independence has always been my strongest personality trait; I love being my own boss. I believe my position also gives me a certain sense of social status and I take great pride in the finished product.

I studied journalism in college and got the opportunity to work at a major daily newspaper. I then chose Public Relations because it was most like the newspaper business.

I plan to finish college and earn at least a Bachelor's degree, then continue in Public Relations with a concentration in Public Affairs and Crisis Management.

PUBLIC UTILITY TECHNICAL ASSISTANT

I like my job because I am learning about computers. When I graduated from high school I worked construction, was a salesperson, and then got a customer service job with the public utility. This job as a computer technical assistant was made available from an internal posting of the opening. Prior to this, I have not had any computer experience. I assist the electronics engineers with their work on the personal computers (pc) and the computer software.

To perform well at this job, it is important to have computer literacy or have the aptitude for learning it quickly. Mathematic skills and an eye for detail are also important. I have found patience and good humor to be another useful asset for this job.

PUBLIC WATER SYSTEM OPERATOR

Operating the public water system is the basic responsibility of my job. Daily, I check all the equipment for proper operation, and if I detect any problems, I perform the maintenance on the equipment. The water quality must be checked every day. As well as maintaining the system, I also am involved in building additions to the system. My job also includes handling problems and complaints, and checking work in progress.

In order to perform this kind of work well, a positive, can-do attitude is important. You should be good with your hands, have mechanical skills, and be able to solve problems.

This work as a public water system operator has many positive aspects for me. First, I like being my own boss. Working outdoors is also appealing to me. In this kind of work, I am meeting and helping people which I find satisfying.

The major drawback, however, is the lack of opportunity for advancement. There is also some politics involved in this public service work which I could do without. I plan to get more training in order to put myself in a better position for advancement. Meanwhile, I will continue to do the best I can to maintain the good water quality for my community.

PUBLIC WELFARE ADMINISTRATOR

My career background includes working as a salesperson of insurance and investments, and as a social worker. I have earned a Bachelor of Science in Psychology, and a Masters in Social Work. I was solicited for my present job as Public Welfare Administrator by a state agency recruiter.

In my position as Public Welfare Administrator, I direct policy development and program planning for adult social services. My typical work activities include: planning and carrying out staff meetings on policy issues and program development, reviewing final and draft copies of written materials, meeting with executive and legislative persons/groups, and coordinating my policy/program products with other administrators in different program areas.

To perform this kind of work well, it is important to have knowledge of the field of work, knowledge of the government executive/legislative process, the ability to assimilate and synthesize diverse material, the ability to communicate well with staff at all levels, and the ability to coordinate input from users of my services.

I do like the kind of work I do very much; however, I am somewhat frustrated by the legal and legislative structure which I feel is more politically motivated than socially responsive. However, I do derive satisfaction from my work when I achieve the goals set for human services and especially for the people they impact. It is also rewarding to have the respect and acceptance by my peers and subordinate staff. Satisfaction for me is also the recognition of achievements.

When I retire, I plan to teach in a junior college or some type of college.

PURCHASING AGENT #1

As a purchasing agent, I manage a special purchase program involving over 50 suppliers. My major responsibilities involve establishing consistent programs and monitoring the activity of the various accounts. More specifically, my routine activities include developing monitoring programs and reviewing existing monitoring activity, reviewing suppliers' activity and performance, developing and monitoring budget, and working with others to rescue program problems.

To perform this kind of work well, the skills and attitudes that are important are a clear understanding of program objectives, good listening skills, good analytical skills, and good interpersonal skills.

To prepare myself for this position, I earned a bachelor's degree in business administration. Prior to this position, I worked in production planning and capital project material planning. I have had an interest in planning and materials procurement for sometime, so when I received a request from management to work in this specific area, I welcomed the opportunity. This kind of work appeals to me because I find satisfaction in problem solving. I also am satisfied that I am working with competent people. My plan is to remain in material planning and procurement.

PURCHASING AGENT #2

I like every aspect of my work which I happened across by chance. I started out at an entry-level position. Due to my performance and growth of the company, I was promoted quickly into management. My current position is as purchasing manager for administrative goods and services. Prior to that I was an office manager/bookkeeper, logistics supervisor, systems business analyst, and project manager.

As the purchasing manager, I manage 18 people, communicate with customers, solve problems, prepare metrics and reports, do special projects and attend many meetings. I am in constant communication with customers and employees. You must know who your resources are to get things done, and do not be afraid to approach higher levels of management. I am extremely busy and often need to work extra hours to catch up.

The skills and attitudes which I consider important to perform this kind of work well are: being organized, being able to handle many things at once, being responsive and following through on issues, having excellent oral and written skills, having a positive and cheerful attitude, knowing how to motivate, train and discipline people, and knowing how to delegate.

I find satisfaction from my work by keeping my customers and employees happy and being able to solve problems quickly. Being recognized as a highly motivated individual also pleases me. When one of my employees gets a "thank you" note for a job well done, it makes me feel good.

I want to earn a bachelor's degree in business management and continue to advance in management, specifically within purchasing, for the computer company for which I work.

PURCHASING AGENT #3

Being a purchasing agent requires honesty and patience. Analytical and organizational skills are also needed. With my Bachelor's degree in Business Administration, I've worked in this profession happily and successfully. I'd choose the same work if I could start over.

Getting a job done on a timely basis pleases me. I like satisfying my client with the service and price they desire. I'd be happier if I could get some relief from the telephone and if I could do this same job with a change of institutions. Otherwise, I like my coworkers and supervisors.

In my work as a purchasing agent, I ascertain where needed materials can be found and I place orders with vendors. I look for distributors who will give my firm the choicest products or services for the best price.

PURCHASING AGENT, CUSTOMER SERVICE

I am still in the process of developing my career and, although I like the kind of work I do now fairly well, it is somewhat of an interim position while I prepare for a career in energy conservation. I am studying engineering now, and next I plan to study business. Then I'd like to go to work in the energy field for a utility company developing new conservation and efficiency technologies.

My previous job experience includes work in metal fabrication, solar systems installer and service representative, construction site clerk, and research and development technician. I was hired for my present job as purchasing agent and customer service representative for a variety of factors; I have had some nontraditional duties in small companies with broad responsibilities and exposure which made me a good candidate and afforded me this opportunity.

As a purchasing agent and customer service rep., I place orders for goods to be manufactured by the company and orders for service repair work on our products. I take calls from customers with machine problems, answer questions and make arrangements to get products repaired.

The various skills and attitudes which I consider important in order to perform this kind of work well are: general ability to comprehend what is necessary to accomplish various results; comparative ability to choose between alternatives; basic math; good language skills; low error rate; ability to anticipate and avoid problems; and electrical, mechanical and service skills.

Although I like the kind of work I am now doing, I would like to have clearer goal-setting and more help from my supervisors in evaluating tasks and methods--in short, more direction. I do find, however, that this job gives me job satisfaction from being in a position to delegate menial and repetitive tasks, from being trusted to use sound judgment when making purchases, from the varied tasks which break up the monotony, and from the wide contacts I have outside the office.

PURCHASING AGENT, PAINT MANUFACTURER

I got into my occupation as purchasing agent kind of by accident. My first job after high school was with this company, and opportunities just became available. I have been with them for 17 years, during which time I did go back to school to earn my Associates of Arts in Business Administration degree.

It is my job to buy the chemicals used in manufacturing paint. This involves determining what to order, placing orders, following up on orders, and maintaining records. The one frustration I have with my work is with the amount of manual record keeping. I would like more computer assistance. My experience with this kind of work has made me realize the importance of math and communication skills to perform this work well.

Although I dislike the lack of opportunity for advancement with my job, I like the people and organization I work for, the people I work with, and the kind of work I do. It is satisfying for me to obtain lower prices in order to help keep the plant profitable.

PURCHASING ASSOCIATE

As a purchasing associate for two years, I buy products and services that help people solve their problems. I use the telephone to place and process orders and handle problems that arise with the orders; I process all orders on the computer system which makes them easier to track.

In addition to a good education, my work requires good communication skills, an understanding of people and how each person reacts differently to the same situation, and knowledge of purchasing.

I like the people I work with and I believe there are many opportunities for career advancement within my present company. I enjoy solving problems and dealing with people. I chose my present job as I believed this was a good stepping stone for my career and it has proven to be a good opportunity to learn as well.

Previously, I worked in construction and held such positions as a part-time salesperson and a restaurant manager.

I plan to continue to study at an undergraduate level, and I may return to the field of sales after completing a degree program. In any event I have gained valuable experience in my current work which I have also enjoyed very much.

PURCHASING ASSOCIATE & BUYER

As a purchasing associate and buyer, I place orders, handle price negotiations, prepare quotes for competitive bidding, work with accounts payable issues, answer telephones, handle daily filing, and process orders.

I have an Associate degree in business. My work also requires careful negotiation skills, good phone skills, and a thorough knowledge of the commodities for which I buy.

I really like this kind of work and the people I work with, especially because I work with many different groups of people.

Other previous employment has been in sales or an office environment as a secretary.

Currently, I am enrolled in a Bachelor's degree program with a minor in Finance and Accounting; I plan to work my way into the world of finance and become a financial analyst.

PURCHASING OFFICE MANAGER

As a Purchasing Office Manager for an electronics company, I generally coordinate the workflow in the clerical section of my department. The clerical section consists of printing, separating and mailing of purchase orders, handling data entry and maintenance, writing correspondence using word processing equipment, and developing Lotus spreadsheets.

For the last nine years, my responsibilities included organizing priorities, delegating responsibilities, and supervising various projects.

My background includes an Associate's degree and I have developed supervisory skills. You will need to have an understanding of department procedures as well as word processing skills, which I acquired in previous positions as a secretary and clerk typist, and an understanding of Lotus. This position also requires patience and diplomacy.

I derive satisfaction in this job when goals are met or I learn something new. Although my job provides some self satisfaction, I would like to know more about our computer system and I would like to work toward improved communications throughout the entire organization.

Eventually, I would like to work in a quieter atmosphere, perhaps my own office where I believe I could really make a difference.

PURCHASING MANAGER

Skills involved in being a purchasing manager are varied. Critical thinking, problem-solving, and decision-making are three very important ones. You also need to be able to organize, plan, coordinate, and implement. Cooperation, adaptability, and dependability are needed as well. Strong communication skills, both oral and written, along with being a person with vision and foresight are equally important.

I've been in this position 22 years and I've enjoyed helping others maximize their potential. I like saving the company money while making the best buys of computer hardware and related mechanical parts. My work will be more enjoyable if efforts to minimize the volume of paperwork continue. It would also be an improvement if incompetence were not tolerated.

I left a previous career in marketing because I didn't want to live out of a suitcase. I still wanted to maintain some outside contacts, so I entered this field. While I like my job, having earned a Bachelor of Science in mathematics, I may one day want to teach math in the classroom.

My duties are to supervise employees while making sure prioritized tasks are accomplished. At the same time, I must maintain flexibility for emergencies. My work involves attending conferences and meetings, evaluating employee performance, and making plans for employee development as well as conducting periodic reviews and appraisals. I answer a great number of questions from employees, other departments, and from suppliers regarding problems and/or solutions.

QUALITY ASSURANCE ENGINEER #1

Involved in nuclear power plant construction for sixteen years, I currently work as a senior quality assurance engineer. My job is to ensure the plant under construction is built to the specifications spelled out in the drawings and to the requirements of the government agencies that hold authority over these plants. It is critical that the work be done right the first time. Dealing with nuclear power plants, we may not get the chance to redo the job.

I enjoy seeing the construction is done right by craftspeople who are interested in quality and safety, not hourly production.

Although I like my job, I would prefer to be working for a third party concern; I believe the necessary quality level would be easier to achieve if the quality assurance program were conducted through a third party instead of being a representative of the construction company or plant owner. I also find it discouraging that the future of nuclear power plants is uncertain; this may force me to pursue other interests.

Previously, I worked for the U.S. Navy as a chief engineering officer and a marine engineering surveyor; the training I received qualified me for my present job.

My job's future is uncertain in my present field of endeavor. I may enroll in a college engineering degree to advance my career into other engineering disciplines.

QUALITY ASSURANCE ENGINEER #2

As a quality assurance engineer in the computer/electronics industry, I plan, direct, make decisions, evaluate, and sell ideas, and work with many people of different levels and backgrounds--all of which is done to assure the production of a quality product. My typical work activities include going to meetings, directing inspection, reviewing new designs, researching problems, preparing data presentations, and writing procedures.

In order to perform this kind of work well, the following factors are important: open mindedness, fairness, good math, personal skills, and short- and long-term goal orientations.

I like almost every aspect of my work. In fact, I accepted this job after working in sales, in landscaping, and as an inspector because I was "made an offer I couldn't refuse." I like the variety in my work activities, and the organization and people I work for and with. It is satisfying when other people make transitions to my way of operating (control), and to see the company's product improve over time and to feel a part of that. I like working with people for a common goal.

QUALITY ASSURANCE ENGINEER #3

My work for six and one-half years has been in an engineering department as a quality assurance technician. My job is to ensure the quality of the plating process by examining cross-sections of commercial and military printed circuit boards at different stages of the plating process. After this, I examine the data I collected during the plating process. Next, I examine one final cross-section of these printed circuit boards, then chart and graph the results combined with results obtained from previous data recently taken, to show the trend of quality.

Although there is a great deal of repetition, I like this type of work, especially the many opportunities for advancement within my department. I really enjoy seeing the detail and workmanship that goes into the building of just one circuit board. It gives my work a sense of purpose, knowing that I am an important part of the manufacturing team.

In addition to a good education and some technical training, my work requires the ability to read and understand military specifications and apply them to the cross-sections of the printed circuit boards. It takes the ability to adapt to change and the patience to deal with military specifications as these change constantly.

In the future, I plan to continue working within this engineering department and learn as much as I can about the manufacturing process and the engineering concepts involved. I also plan to take some classes and work toward a degree in engineering as I find the field of engineering fascinating.

QUALITY ASSURANCE LABORATORY TECHNICIAN

My job as a chemical quality assurance lab technician is as follows: get passdown from previous technician about how the plant is running, prepare lab for my shift, receive samples every two hours, run tests, compute results, clean-up, give passdown to next technician.

To perform this job well it is important to have the ability to work and to do problem-solving alone, a math and science aptitude, and ability to work with precision.

I get satisfaction from this job in being accurate. I also like playing with chemicals and recording the numbers and plugging them into equations. What I don't like is the lack of upward mobility. Without a chemistry degree I could spend 15 to 20 years doing the same job. I have to wait on seniority to get promoted.

I got into this occupation when I dropped out of college at age 19. I had three semesters of college. I needed to get a job so I decided to work at the mines. When I was interviewed I was informed that I wasn't big enough to work as a laborer. I was asked if anything else interested me. I said laboratory work; suffice to say, I was hired.

My previous occupations are in various fields. I have been an Aviation Electronics Technician in the United States Navy, sales clerk, homemaker, outdoor laborer and hostess/cashier.

I like my present occupation and feel it is necessary to further my education in order to advance in it. I plan to go back to college to earn my Bachelor of Science degree in medical technology or biochemistry.

QUALITY ASSURANCE SUPERVISOR

I kind of fell into my present occupation. After starting college with the original goal of graduating with a computer science degree, I soon realized that this was not the right avenue for me. I got a job as a quality control inspector and have worked my way through and up the ladder.

As the quality assurance supervisor in the manufacturing of printed circuit boards, I supervise three separate areas in the quality assurance department. I also do some engineering and project management. A daily responsibility is to organize the work flow through the department. In the course of my work, I often deal with "fires" resulting from department rejections, customer rejections, process problems, or interpersonal problems. Conducting meetings is also sometimes part of my job.

A quality assurance supervisor needs good organizational skills and the ability to motivate people. Improvisation is a must in this kind of work. Having the ability to think logically through problems as opposed to reacting with emotion is another important attribute for a person in this job.

I like the kind of work I do very much and find it exciting working in this extremely high tech and fast paced industry. As a supervisor, I love it when I can praise the performance of employees and am able to reward them. I only wish that I could remove the "fires" and allow more time for objective problem solving.

As far as future plans are concerned, I intend to complete my college education.

QUALITY CONTROL & PRODUCTION CONSULTANT

My job as quality control and production consultant allows me to use a combination of lifetime experiences. Without a college degree, I worked as a microbiologist for a major food company. I worked to finance my college education and planned to major in education. However, due to medical problems, I was unable to teach, so I stayed in quality control. I set up control systems in several plants and advanced rapidly to plant manager. Other diverse occupations have been: operating and instructing a music conservatory, and inspecting and assembling automotive parts.

As a consultant for a packer and wholesaler of produce, I advise changes in methods of production, grading and standards. My regular duties include: confirming incoming produce, confirming inventory and orders, planning and ordering the production schedule with supervisors, meeting other daily appointments with personnel from quality control and insurance, interviewing applicants, and coordinating packing with loading and shipping departments.

To perform well at my kind of work, it is important to have: a general knowledge about crops, specific understanding of U.S.D.A. and Food and Drug Standards, a background in quality control or microbiology or entomology, and last but most important, an ability to use employees' talents for both their and the company's success.

If I could change anything in my occupation, I would like to have more input in company policy regarding employee benefits and more flexibility in working hours. However, I do like this kind of work, the people I work for and the people I work with. My job satisfaction comes from meeting the challenge of using the variables inherent in growing, packing, and shipping field produce. I also feel rewarded in seeing diverse personnel work together to help a fledgling company succeed.

QUALITY CONTROL MANAGER

As a quality control manager for a medical corporation, I oversee the day to day quality of production as well as all incoming and outgoing parts and products. As my company manufactures disposable surgical products, another important part of my job is to maintain the quality assurance records for the federal Food and Drug Administration. I meet with vendors to address quality problems and keep extremely close track of all paperwork and quality records.

In addition to a high school education, this job requires an eye for detail, the ability to operate various testing equipment, and the desire to learn and solve problems with the skills acquired in performing a job on a daily basis.

I really like my job. I absolutely love this kind of work. I enjoy the idea of working with something used in saving lives, and I find my work very interesting. I like the fact that I am always busy, although at times I would like to have more time to get my job done. I work for a really great company and I believe in the work that we do; I also feel fortunate to work for a boss that I like. I get along very well with my co-workers and that gives my job a real team orientation.

As there are tuition reimbursement benefits available to me through my company, I plan to return to college and earn a degree in a discipline that combines working with people and medicine. I would like to move up within my present organization.

QUALITY CONTROL SUPERVISOR

As a supervisor of surface mines for the past 29 years, I've found the knowledge of geology very important in my work. Comprehension of legal standards and finances are needed as well. Being skillful in the field of public relations is also very useful.

After graduating from high school, I became involved in dairy farming for a while before being attracted to my present job. I am also looking forward to eventual retirement and pursuing interests in travel, charity work, gardening, and community service.

As a supervisor, I've enjoyed watching my skills improve over the years. My relationships with others are rewarding, along with the pay. If I could start over, I'd choose this field again for I enjoy the people, the chance to grow in my career, my work, the supervisors, and the company. My job would be even more satisfying if we didn't have to deal so much with used equipment.

A mine supervisor is responsible for overseeing the washing process of state-approved aggregates for construction of buildings. It is my job to order supplies and see that plant and mobile equipment is maintained. My responsibilities include quality control and preserving safety standards. Sales is also a part of my duties.

RADIATION PROTECTION TECHNICIAN

As a radiation protection technician, I calibrate, or systematically adjust, portable radiation detection instruments. My work requires that I use devices to check radiation contamination levels, then brief workers of any hazards. After that, I observe workers to ensure instructions are followed.

I got into this work through a company-sponsored program. All expenses to a local junior college were paid in return for at least one year of employment. My training is as an Associate of Applied Science and as a nuclear technician. My plans are to return to college for a Bachelor of Science degree in, perhaps, accounting.

To do this work, things have to be done right the first time. You have to have the capability to follow procedures and to mentally perform calculations. You must be able to work with others to make sure the job is done safely. Since the purpose of this job is to warn people of radiation hazards and advise them on methods for minimizing exposure, good communication skills are required.

Job satisfaction for me is accomplishing something, like calibrating instruments, and providing a service, such as processing dosimetry (measuring and indicating the amount of x-rays or radioactivity which has been absorbed). I'd like my job more if technicians could be allowed to be dedicated to particular jobs on a long-term basis. Cross training between very different job areas should be lessened in my opinion.

RADIO STATION OFFICE MANAGER

A typical day in my office includes general office work like answering the phone, sending out catalogues, scheduling people for interviews, and sending out enrollment contracts.

An office manager should be very professional on the phone, have good typing skills, and be friendly to people who contact the company whether in person or over the telephone.

My daily contact with people makes my job satisfying. I am very satisfied with my occupation, and would not change a thing at all.

The job was listed in our local newspaper, and I applied for the job. It seemed to be interesting. I come in contact with people in the broadcasting profession. I previously worked as a billing clerk for several local trucking firms, and have always done office work. I hope to continue working as an office manager in the radio broadcasting field.

RADIOLOGIST #1

I enjoy the daily challenge with each case I study. I perform diagnostic radiology with interventional procedures. I'm at work in the hospital by 7:30 a.m. I begin fluoroscopy; read films between handling fluoro patients, consult with referring physicians, perform interventional studies like abscess drainage, arteriograms, needle biopsies, breast lesian localization for surgery, kidney drainage, catheter procedures and angioplasty procedures. I then go to the clinic at 11:00 a.m. and read films on fluoro patients and go back to the hospital to finish up. My work day ends at the office where I do routine work.

To be qualified for this profession you must earn an MD degree to obtain knowledge of the fields of diagnostic imaging and expertise in needle and catheter procedures. A positive attitude is important. Do not hesitate to admit you don't know everything. Have courage to resist performing exams that you do not feel will benefit the patient. Treat each patient as you would like to be treated. Be sympathetic and explain all procedures to the patient.

I enjoy working with and helping patients. I like my hospital, the clinic and office. I feel that I can contribute something to others. I also enjoy my standard of living.

I would prefer to limit my performance of those procedures which require prolonged standing. I would like to be able to spend more time on routine diagnostic exams and particularly mammography.

I have wanted to be a physician since early childhood, probably because my grandfather and uncle both were physicians. I chose radiology over pathology and urology because I would have had to take two extra years of surgery for urology, and I disliked prolonged microscopic examinations.

Radiology has been my profession for 27 years and I am glad that it has been. If I had a choice to start over again, I would still choose this career.

RADIOLOGIST #2

No two days are the same as a radiologist. It is a rare day that I do not see something new. This career allows me to be on the cutting edge of medicine.

I chose radiology as a specialty because of what I consider superior input while I was in medical school. Although it was somewhat of a spur of the moment decision and opportunity, it was obviously the correct one because I have been immensely satisfied with this profession.

As a radiologist, I interpret x-rays, nuclear scans, CT scans, ultrasound images, etc. In the process of doing this, I am in constant interaction with other doctors. I am the "medical detective."

To perform this kind of work well, it is important to be able to work under stress, meet deadlines, and have the correct attitude and skills to respond to emergencies.

The one thing that I wish I could change in my occupation would be to remove instigators of malpractice suits. Their existence has caused many undesirable changes to my profession. My career plans for the future are to stay with the profession but to reduce the number of days I work per week.

RADIOLOGIST #3

As a radiologist, I begin the day by reading and interpreting radiographs done overnight in the hospital and in the emergency department. Throughout the day as each procedure is done, I read and interpret x-rays, cat scans, ultrasound, and MRI scans. I perform on patients invasive interventional techniques: angiography, angioplasty, nephrostomes, nuclear medicine, and biopsies. Consulting with the referring physicians on their cases, I explain the techniques used, the findings, and suggest diagnoses.

In order to be a radiologist you must have a thorough and meticulous approach to problem solving. You should meet each case as a mystery, seeking the clues and their meanings. A certain amount of manual dexterity is valuable. A person should have strong eye/hand coordination. You must have a surgeon's "bold," aggressive attitude and be quite decisive. As they say, "I may not always be right, but I am never undecided." Basic to this occupation is following the sequence in college that leads to the M.D.

My work is very fulfilling; I enjoy the people with whom I work and the daily challenges; there's something new every day. I find great reward in solving a mystery or finding a clue that helped determine what is wrong with a patient. With the invasive/interventional techniques, being able to do something for a patient that will either cure a problem or give him temporary or permanent relief is highly satisfying to me. I'd enjoy my profession more if there were less governmental intrusion and third party paperwork. My plans are to keep on learning something new each day, each week, each month.

Radiology is a fine specialty for "who-dun-it" fans!

RADIOLOGY FILE CLERK

I have spent most of my adult life working with my parents in the grocery store which they owned and operated. My parents were tragically killed by holdup men and due to the deteriorating conditions of the neighborhood where the business was located, I was forced to close the store. I am also a first generation American and since English was not the language spoken in my home, I had to learn it on my own. Despite these setbacks, I am a hard worker and developed some skills which I have been able to use to procure employment since closing the store. I always had a strong interest in photography and had a business in this field.

I now work as a radiology file clerk in a Veterans Hospital. I prepare the films for the radiologists, set them up on the viewer, and file the reports and films. To do a proper job, you must know how to read the films by being able to distinguish the different parts of the body and know their names. There are also special procedures depending on the type of x-ray that is being taken. Although this might be considered remedial work, I take pride in a job properly done knowing it is the first real step in helping a patient on a sometimes long road to recovery. It is rewarding work for me when the radiologist says, "You were a great help."After retiring from my job at the VA hospital, I plan to have my own furniture-making business. I have developed carpentry and cabinet-making skills which I would like to use.

RAILROAD SUPERVISOR

My work as a railroad supervisor of twelve years is to supervise the tradespeople who work with the railroad company. The people I supervise are carpenters, pipers, and mechanics for the most part. I plan and direct work for ten different crews daily, trying to keep a yearly planned maintenance schedule and juggling many emergencies and requests; I act as the head of meetings and employee councils; I attend seminars; and I instruct employees and contractors on safety procedures.

Needed to succeed as a railroad supervisor: first of all, a good education; secondly, good people skills; thirdly, the ability to motivate others in a positive way; next, good communication skills; and, of course, thorough knowledge of and experience in safety procedures.

Although at times I don't agree with the union way of getting the job done or their treatment of workers, I like this kind of work. I find job satisfaction in seeing the results of my work, in the knowledge that I have helped to solve my workers' problems, and in the feeling that I am appreciated by others.

I previously worked as a salesperson and as a photographer, which I also enjoyed.

I look forward to improving my supervisory and management skills by attending some college classes and perhaps earning a degree in the field of business management. I believe that furthering my education may help me in negotiations with the unions.

RAMP SERVICEMAN--AIRCRAFT

I have spent 22 years as a ramp serviceman for an aircraft ground operation. I like this kind of work very much because there is a lot of action to it with constant movement and deadlines. At the time I started work in this occupation, it was considered a good paying position and a secure job. Times are now different in airline work, and I can't recommend this career for its security. However, I still consider it to pay well.

As a ramp serviceman, I am part of the ground operations loading and unloading freight and baggage from aircraft which requires knowledge of weight and balance. This kind of work involves lots of hard physical labor, deadlines, and it includes much mandatory overtime.

To get this work done properly, it is important to be able to work well with others because much of the work can only be done by teamwork. The other critical factor about this job is that safety is paramount--you must be attentive to your work at all times to avoid accidents.

I find job satisfaction from getting the job done properly and in the good pay.

RANCHER, INVESTOR, AVIATOR

I have been fortunate to do what I wanted to do almost all my life. I inherited assets, primarily the ranch with oil fields, from a successful father. The military portion of my life, as a military aviator, was my choice. Other careers which I have pursued are: oil field roustabout, airplane salesman, life insurance salesman, and accounting work. Now that I am retired from the military, my day is spent looking after 100+ head of cattle and investing in stocks and bonds. On a typical day I will read the local newspaper and the Wall Street Journal. I will discuss investments with one or two brokers. Two days a week I will drive 45 miles to the ranch to check the cattle. Other days, I enjoy playing golf.

I'm a conservative investor, mainly in municipal bonds and blue chip stocks. I try to consider the down side of investment more than possible profits.

I truly loved flying before my military retirement. Now I like to observe the cattle and their growth.

RANGER, U.S. NATIONAL PARKS

As a government employee for the U.S. National Park Service, I work as a Park Ranger. For the past thirty-four years, my activities have ranged from the basic park ranger duties of law enforcement, forestry, fire control, and wildlife conservation, to park management and administration.

While in college, I studied plant ecology and forest ranger management. In addition to a good education and the completion of the training program, a park ranger must have a positive attitude, the ability to interpret and relate park values to the public, and some accumulated experience in wildlife management, forestry, fire control, and law enforcement.

I love my job; I know a great many people dream of having a job like mine--having the opportunity to work outdoors and in a peaceful, but solitary, forest environment. Working for the National Park Service provides a type of satisfaction that money can't buy, and that is good because, in my opinion, the monetary compensation is not the reason to devote your life to this kind of work. I would not change anything; I have lived in eight different states in some of the most beautiful and fascinating places in the world--such places as Yellowstone National Park, Glacier National Park, and Death Valley.

I plan to stay in my chosen field; I am working toward a promotion to Superintendent. It is my belief that there is no other career that can compare to mine for personal rewards.

REAL ESTATE BROKER #1

I am very glad I changed my occupation and got into real estate. I had been a legal secretary and property manager. My previous boss convinced me that I would be good at real estate sales. I decided I did not want an 8-5, 5 day a week job and that I wanted to be somewhat my own boss.

Basically, as a real estate broker, I list and sell houses and vacant land. I arrive at the office between 8 and 10 a.m., and work until 5 or 6 p.m. I sometimes show property after 6 p.m. or on weekends, plus I usually have one open house per month.

To perform this work well, it is important to have self motivation and an outgoing personality. You have to like doing your job and meeting new people. Knowledge of financing and the market are also important.

What I most like about my career is the person and organization I work for, the people I work with, and the kind of work. As I mentioned before, I like the flexible hours, despite all the extra time that is often necessary. The drawback to this kind of work, however, is the sporadic market and income. I have also been frustrated at times because of the number of agents in the field that are not professional and competent. I continue to work at building up my knowledge by attending classes and seminars, and wish more agents did. I find satisfaction as a real estate broker in having buyers and sellers appreciative of what I do for them. Also, I love those commission checks! I plan to continue in this profession, building up my designations and reputation as a competent broker.

REAL ESTATE BROKER #2

The work of a real estate broker involves marketing, sales, and the opportunity to work directly with people. For the past twelve years, I have worked as a real estate broker; I enjoy the flexible schedule and a good income as well. In addition to showing and listing properties, I write contracts and follow up on dates to be met, or requirements to be met, in order to fulfill those contracts. There is a large amount of paperwork and correspondence with strict deadlines associated with my job, and these deadlines must be met.

In order to succeed as a real estate broker you must enjoy meeting and dealing with the public, possess good communication skills, and have the ability to cope with a somewhat erratic schedule.

I work with and have met, over the years, some very nice and interesting people; that gives me great personal satisfaction. I enjoy real estate sales. The only real drawback to this profession is the uncertainty of remuneration; a broker may at times work diligently to put a deal together only to have it fall through--there are so many uncertain factors connected to this line of work. This profession is a direct barometer of the economy which can cause great stress since the economy cannot be accurately predicted. If I could, I would change this job to make my work hours more regular, but that is impossible. A broker must always be ready to show a property or be available to answer questions and address problems, almost immediately, to avoid future obstructions to the deals I work so hard to put together.

Previously, I enjoyed working as a secretary and as a teacher; I was drawn to this profession by the flexibility of a broker's schedule.

My background includes a Bachelor of Arts degree in education.

My future plans are to stay in the real estate business in some capacity.

REAL ESTATE BROKER #3

A usual day for me, as a real estate broker, is working with people involved in a foreclosure which might be the owner of the property in jeopardy, a lender, a contractor repairing foreclosed property, or a real estate agent. I manage and market foreclosed properties for a mortgage loan broker. Another task might be dealing with the details of a loan.

A real estate broker should be flexible, thoroughly knowledgeable of real estate law as well as commercial law and real estate itself. Competency in title and escrow practices along with dealing with appraisals are also vital. You need also to be able to deal forthrightly and sympathetically with both the lender and borrower in the foreclosure.

There is nothing I dislike about my work. Helping people out of a distressful situation is job satisfaction for me. I enjoy the people, the institution, the advancement opportunities, and all aspects of my work.

Fortunately, I was offered by a friend the opportunity to enter this line of work. Earlier, I had a successful career as a life insurance salesman. I'd made several real estate investments when a client/friend offered me the job. I've been involved in this work for 10 years and hope to retire in a year or so.

REAL ESTATE BROKER #4

I've been a real estate broker for 20 years. Not only do I buy and sell homes, but I also fix them up. The work I do is very exciting and challenging.

It's necessary that you be able to "go with the flow" of what's happening. You can't plan too far in advance and you must remain flexible. A typical day doesn't exist in this work--you never know what's going to happen next. That suits me very well.

I receive satisfaction from my accomplishments and can't think of anything I'd change to make the job more satisfying.

I chose this job because I like people, enjoy selling and like helping people develop under me by teaching them better sales techniques. I did not attend college, nor did I finish high school. Previous jobs included supermarket manager, and then supermarket supervisor, and finally, operations manager.

REAL ESTATE CONSULTANT & BROKER

I'm an apartment complex investment consultant for the owners of the structures. I also act as their independent real estate broker. The independence, the pay, and the location all make my work very satisfying. I like the creativity involved in identifying potential clients and developing successful deals in their investment medium--apartment buildings. The only downside is that there is little security in this field.

To be a successful real estate investment consultant, you need the proper training. My college degrees are a Bachelor of Science in industrial engineering followed by a Bachelor of Science in real estate. You should be well trained in investment economics, in demographic trend analysis (study of the characteristics of the human population), and in counseling sophisticated people. The ability to analyze using computations, as well as maintain the integrity of numbers used, is vital. You must also have a positive, "can do" attitude. In addition, you must want to continue learning and be adept at using high-technology equipment, especially the computer.

In 21 years, I've found no typical day. My client base and investment deals are developed over 3-6 months. Much is involved: locating clients, identifying their needs, matching the client with investment property, making transactions, and getting the transaction completed. My pay is commission based, ranging from five to six figures, which is paid only upon completion of an investment deal.

Prior positions I've held have included being an industrial management engineer and a corporate real estate manager. Some day I'd like to start a small brokerage operation with seven or eight agents. I could use the work systems which I've developed, my databank of investors, and my management skills. After making it highly profitable, I'd sell all the stock and retire to a life on an alpine ranch.

REAL ESTATE DEVELOPER #1

I wear two hats. As a commercial real estate developer I buy, design, and build leased buildings. As the chief executive officer of a coin laundry chain, I operate four laundries. My work usually includes going to the office, meeting with general manager and maintenance manager, visiting stores three days a week, and working on real estate deals. A more detailed list of my real estate tasks are meetings with bankers, realtors and tenants, planning designs and handling paper work.

To perform well in this type of work you should have a positive attitude and common sense.

I particularly like being self-employed. It gives me a feeling of accomplishment to have developed these businesses. My career would be more satisfying, however, with less government interference.

I got into the real estate business when a big oil company gave me a job as a real estate representative. Prior to that I had been employed as a salesman, sales manager, bus boy, dishwasher, and glazier. I have an Associate Degree in Business.

REAL ESTATE DEVELOPER #2

Knowing I have created an economically viable project gives me a lot of satisfaction as a real estate developer. I particularly enjoy the freedom to make choices as well as mistakes. If I had to start over, I'd choose real estate developing all over again. My plans are to continue developing industrial sites.

I got into this work about 9 years ago after acquiring some real estate. I learned carpentry, plumbing, and proficiency with electricity on the job. Then, I began to hire contractors to do the work. On the side, I also lobbied in the state legislature concerning land use legislation.

My work also involves drafting building plans, reviewing city building standards codes, and meetings with contractors, bankers, and attorneys. I work with city planners, working out compromises, and solving problems. If it is necessary, I'll drop a building project if it doesn't "pencil out."I've found having a salesman's friendly characteristics and personality useful in my job. Also, being able to be an economic forecaster is helpful. You should like building and engineering projects. You need to be decisive, like to be in control, and be realistic. Being a risk-taker with good planning and scheduling skills is important to a builder. I learned some of these skills while earning a Bachelor of Arts in business administration.

REAL ESTATE ESCROW CLOSER

My job as a real estate escrow closer is an on-the-job training position. I started out as a receptionist in a small real estate company after graduating from high school. Since I found that job boring, I kept asking for different things to do to help out. I learned a bit at that company. I moved to a large real estate company, did the same thing, someone noticed, and I was promoted into training very quickly.

In a week's time, I handle approximately 10 closings. I have numerous conversations with both buyers and sellers of a property to make sure all requirements of the contract are met. I draw up closing statements, working with the buyer's new lender to make sure the seller's loan gets paid off. Dealing with title problems is a major part of my work. I have to know a lot of real estate law to do this.

This is detail work involving math, legal issues, financial matters and a lot of interaction with people. To do this work well, it is important to have a positive, helpful, intelligent attitude.

Time is of the essence with my job, making it very stressful. However, I find it satisfying when someone calls and tells me they have a problem as to how to work out a closing with a deceased owner's estate, or an incompetent owner, or an impossible time frame, or a difficult personality, and I get it all working smoothly. I know I've really helped and I feel a great sense of accomplishment.

My job qualifications aren't transferable to any other field really, at least not in my income range. I find, though, that the longer I do this, the easier it is because I can remember other situations that are similar and how I worked them out. Management of the entire escrow department is my goal, and I should reach that within two to three years.

REAL ESTATE FINDER, DRUG CHAIN

My title indicates that I am a real estate representative for a very successful national discount drug store chain. As such, I evaluate sites for potential new drug store locations. If the decision is made to follow up on some of my favorable recommendations, then I become involved in negotiation of leases or property purchases. Since "location, location, location" are often mentioned as the three most important considerations in the success of a business, this job is pivotal to the profitability of the individual units and is thus clearly important to the company. That gives you security in the job as long as your recommendations are sound.

Obviously, you need to get technical knowledge about the characteristics of a good location and about real estate, legal forms, closing procedures, etc. For a national firm, these might differ from state to state. A college degree is needed, and I have a B.S.B.A. with areas of concentration that helped prepare me for this job. A high level of energy is needed too. My personal belief is that integrity is important--knowing right from wrong, believing that we are responsible for our own lot in life, self-discipline, willingness to work hard, and persistence. As a reward for work in this field, you get job security and a satisfying sense of accomplishment.

My employment background extends to only one other job that I have had--I was area manager for a photo developing corporation. The present job, which I have had for 16 years, is much the more satisfying to me. Plans? Continue doing this work because I enjoy it.

REAL ESTATE SALES AND ANTIQUES

For the past fifteen years, my work in real estate sales and dealings in the antique business have been extremely rewarding. I set up meetings, organize negotiations, and maintain my contacts in real estate sales and I also load, organize, set up, and establish contacts in my dealings with antiques. In addition to training and acquired experience in the real estate business and knowledge in the antique market, my work requires a lot of physical energy, self discipline, an appreciation for the power of positive thinking, and organizing my time to be able to do it all.

I like everything I do; I enjoy the people I meet and I have established several long-term friendships through my work. Although I work independently in both of my jobs, I enjoy the people I work with in the real estate office and the firm that I work for. I believe I have dedicated my life's work to some very positive ventures.

I have always chosen to work in positions that gave me the chance to work with people - in retail sales, modeling, and as a ski instructor.

I plan to take some college courses so I can learn more about financing real estate and investments.

REAL ESTATE SALESPERSON #1

I sell about 35% residential and 65% commercial real estate. Typical duties involved in selling and listing real estate are contacting prospects and updating them with information about progress in connection with their transaction, recommending actions to clients, coordinating the process of decision making on the property, and advising and informing.

To be a successful agent you must be a personable kind of individual. It is also very important to have the knowledge and organizational skills to prepare the data needed to support the sales and listings.

I chose this career because I was involved in the construction of properties for sale and envied the sales person who handled the sale. I made this decision 22 years ago and have been satisfied since. I like the flexibility of the hours, the work methods and the pay when the market is good. I would, however, like to see this occupation become harder to enter so that there would be a reduction in incompetent competition.

I have earned a bachelors of arts degree and have also passed the realtor licensing board exams.

My plans for the future include putting my learned skills in the profession to use to develop more properties that satisfy specific needs, by bringing capable people together in a development ownership deal.

REAL ESTATE SALESPERSON #2

After serving as a U.S. Army Officer, I entered the field of real estate. I wanted the independence of working for myself and I did not want to be tied to an office. My goal is to make my business grow.

It would be easier for me if I were in a larger city. Still, I find that doing research to locate a site for a business, and then finding the site, to be very satisfying. I appreciate the respect I get from being a business owner and being a professional. Particularly, I enjoy having the opportunity to solve problems and to be an expert in my field.

During my day as a real estate agent and manager, I show property, write leases and sales contracts, and collect rents. I conduct site searches for businesses as I develop relationships (networking) to be used for help when needed. Part of my job is to make proposals to manage or sell property.

A successful real estate person listens well, has integrity, and is flexible. You must be able to do a "quick study" and understand what the customer wants and needs. A positive attitude and a strong belief in yourself are crucial to being happy in this field. I have a Bachelor of Science Degree and a Masters in Business Administration, and I find this education to be helpful in this business.

REAL ESTATE SALESPERSON #3

Involved in real estate sales for eighteen years, specifically with multi-family housing or apartments, I strive to provide the best compromise for the buyer, seller, and broker. That is not always an easy task.

Success in the buying and selling of real estate is dependent upon somewhat aggressive behavior; you must find people who want to sell their property and match them with those who want to buy the property. Most of the time neither party is aware of their need, so I search records and find those who have lost their tax advantage or those who have too much equity in the property to be receiving an adequate return on invested equity. Once these parties have been identified, I convince them that they need to sell what they have or acquire something else. This job also requires knowledge of and skill in applying the tax laws relative to real estate. The constant goal in this profession is to ensure that at the conclusion, each of the parties--buyer, seller, and broker--is better off than before the transaction takes place.

I believe I have achieved a higher level of success than most in my field because I have a solid educational background; in addition to the aforementioned skills, I earned both a Bachelor of Science and a Master of Science degrees.

Aside from the financial satisfaction of closing the deal, I derive a lot of satisfaction in accomplishing the task.

I would like to see the licensing laws changed, in an attempt to discourage those who are only in this business for the cash gains and not the desire to be the best; I believe this change would make the term "real estate broker" sufficient evidence of competency.

For quite some time during my selling career, it has been my goal to shift into a different area of selling that would allow me to have more control over all the elements involved in a sale; I believe I could then achieve greater satisfaction for all parties involved.

REAL ESTATE SALESPERSON #4

I sell commercial investment real estate. For the last fifteen years, I have located buyers and sellers of investment properties and put them together. This work involves a great deal of time on the phone, either seeking new prospects or staying on top of current negotiations; constantly looking at properties for sale to keep abreast of the current market; and spending considerable time on paperwork.

The advantages of commercial investment real estate are a good income, a flexible schedule which affords me a high degree of freedom, and the benefit that most business is conducted during a normal working day-- this contrasts greatly with residential real estate in which you are called upon to work evenings and weekends.

The disadvantage of being involved in any aspect of the real estate business is that this profession directly reflects the ups and downs of the economy.

Basically commercial investment real estate requires the ability to analyze investments and the ability to communicate with people; I also have a Bachelor of Science degree.

Previously, I managed an insurance agency; that experience prepared me for many of the aspects of my present work.

Commercial investment real estate is a challenging and interesting career choice; I recommend it highly.

REALTOR #1

I have been selling real estate for twenty years and like it very much. Prior to this career, I earned my bachelor of arts degree and substitute taught for two to three years. I have also written a 1300 page book.

I became a realtor because I wanted a flexible occupation. There is no set schedule, but regular responsibilities include making calls to customers, other realtors, bankers, title companies, etc. I use the computer for new offerings. Sometimes, not everyday of course, I show property and write contracts.

To perform this job well, you must be consistent and punctual and do what you say you'll do-don't promise what you can't do. You must be willing to follow a project to completion-even longer than planned.

The main satisfaction I derive from this career is helping people find property which suits their needs. I enjoy solving problems with loans, properties, and timing. I find satisfaction in earning the money to support myself and help my grown children with their special wants and needs.

If I could change anything about my occupation it would be to make customers more flexible and other realtors more problem-solving oriented rather than shrill or bossy.

In the future, I plan to invest proceeds of "fat" years to retire completely and be able to travel and to follow other ventures of an entrepreneurial sort.

REALTOR #2

A high school graduate, I own my own real estate agency where I train salespeople and sell properties. I supervise the salespeople, hold short, motivational meetings, and follow up on sales made. Contacting people regarding the sale of properties is also part of my day.

I got involved in this work after deciding to try the sales field. Starting out as a real estate salesperson, I progressed to having my own office. Previously, I've enjoyed being a die maker and an insurance salesman. After 19 years, I can say there's nothing I dislike about the real estate business.

A successful realtor must have a good attitude. This person must want to be "Number One" in any business venture. I really enjoy dealing with people in my work. My future plans are to be the best at what I currently do, or the best whatever else I decide to do.

RECEPTIONIST

This has been the right job for me. I have been here or a receptionist/insurance clerk for the last 20 years. Basically, I greet customers and salespeople, answer the telephone, do insurance, and process final bill letters. When I arrive at work, I open the vault and set up the telephone and computer for the day. I do the insurance work and final bill letters and follow-ups for the company. I am the first person on the phone at all times. Greeting and routing the people who come into the office is, of course, part of my receptionist duties.

To perform my kind of work well, it is important to know office procedures and how to get along with people. A receptionist must be friendly at all times. You do not need a college degree.

This job suits me and gives me satisfaction because I like people and I like to talk with them. Also, my job has a lot of variety and that makes it exciting. The only thing that I would change is the work load.

I live just a block away from this office and I needed work so I applied and was hired right away. The only other job that I have had was as a waitress. I plan to stay with this company for 10 more years until it is time for retirement.

RECEPTIONIST & ACCOUNTS PAYABLE CLERK

Working as a receptionist and an accounts payable clerk, I am involved in many different tasks, usually at the same time. I answer the telephone and greet visitors as a part of my duties as a receptionist; I match invoices with packing lists and input the data into a computer system as a part of my duties as an accounts payable clerk.

My work requires a high school education with some exposure to accounts payable, patience, a pleasant attitude, and typing skills as well as interpersonal skills--and the ability to handle several tasks at one time.

I like the company I work for and the person I work for. I enjoy the fact that my job gives me the chance to learn new skills and interact with many different types of people.

Although I have had previous experience as a receptionist, I also have worked as a waitress and as a cashier.

I plan to get involved in raising a family in the near future, but I know that the experience I have gained over the years will be valuable, especially if I find a way to balance a family and a career.

RECEPTIONIST, DENTAL OFFICE

As a receptionist at a dental office, I answer the office telephone, book appointments, confirm appointments, file patient folders, set up the patient folders for the next day, enter treatments performed or prescribed in the computer, post payments in the computerized accounting system, enter insurance payments, greet patients upon arrival, and escort patients to the dentist's work chair and seat them, making sure they are as relaxed and as comfortable as possible.

In addition to an Associate in Science in Business Administration degree, my job requires typing skills, good phone manners, a positive and cheerful attitude toward my work, a professional appearance, and the knowledge of the billing procedures to calculate the cost of dental treatments and services.

I like my work because I enjoy meeting people and helping them. My job makes me feel that I have accomplished something when I set up a day's schedule and filing and balance my payments at the end of the day; my job also provides me with the opportunity to work in a clean environment with a good schedule and no weekend work required, as I have encountered in other positions. There is one aspect of my work that I would change. I wish patients were more aware of the havoc they cause when they cancel appointments; it would make my job much easier if patients planned their time so it would be unnecessary to cancel an appointment, especially at the last minute.

Previously, I have worked as a credit investigator, a cashier, a secretary, and a waitress.

I plan to go back to school to complete my Bachelor's degree program, and then I expect I will look for more challenging work that provides me with a greater feeling of importance.

RECREATION THERAPIST

As a recreation therapist for chemically-dependent teenagers, I spend my mornings in staff meetings, make phone calls, and deal with paper work. In the afternoons, I am involved in group and individual therapy sessions.

I like the work I do because I receive personal satisfaction in watching people learn about themselves as a result of the therapy sessions. I don't enjoy the unvarying routine and the fact that there is little opportunity for advancement.

To be a therapist, you need people skills, creativity, and education at the college level. Open-mindedness and a non-judgmental attitude are also valuable. You need also to understand your own personal characteristics. I began as a recreation major in college and specialized in various populations during my junior and senior years. Then I settled on this therapy line of work, but my future plans are to return to general recreation programs. Although I am quite satisfied with this line of work, if I could start over, I think I would go into something in the business world, outside of health care.

REFERENCE LIBRARIAN, PUBLIC LIBRARY

With my Bachelor of Arts degree and my Masters of Library Science, I find it pleasant to work in the reference section of a public library. Helping the public identify their needs, find information, and/or interpret that information is part of my work. I select material to add to the collection, and I keep the collection updated by weeding materials out of the collection. There's a great deal of paperwork in making schedules, time sheets, and reports. I also do some public speaking at meetings and on TV.

In my work one needs a lot of general knowledge along with a good memory. Strong people skills with all age groups are important. One needs tolerance, patience, enthusiasm, and flexibility. Computer skills are needed as well. A high energy level and "good feet" are advisable. A reference librarian must answer a wide range of questions as well as give instruction on research. This person must also give instruction on research, be able to select materials, and frequently write book reviews.

I love the work I do and the people involved. I most enjoy helping the public learn about new things, and I love ordering new books. If I could make any changes, I'd lessen the paperwork and hire more co-workers for this chronically understaffed profession.

After working in a library in high school, I chose not to enter the field. Although I did not pursue it then, I later returned and earned a Master's Degree in Library Science. I would suggest that anyone considering library work try it on a volunteer or part-time basis before going to graduate school. Just liking books is not enough. I plan to continue as a librarian as long as it stays fresh and provides a challenge.

REFORM RABBI

I chose this career as a Reform Rabbi after a diverse work background. I have been a social case worker, construction laborer, construction estimator, life and health insurance salesman, and a newspaper copyboy. While I was a social worker, I was influenced by a friend, who was in the seminary ahead of me, to consider this career. Before being ordained as a rabbi, I completed 4 years of college and 5 years of seminary. I have now been a rabbi for two decades.

On any given day, I am up by seven. My typical activities include: communicating with people by phone; visiting the sick; officiating at funerals and weddings, teaching children and/or adults; counseling people; and attending committee meetings at night. I get home for the balance of the night at 10 or 11 o'clock.

In order to handle the responsibilities as a rabbi, decision-making and social skills are very important. You also have to like to read a great deal of material.

This is a very demanding job, and I would welcome an assistant rabbi in my medium-size urban congregation, so that I could get some time off. Aside from wanting some time off and feeling that there is a lack of opportunity for advancement, I like my career very much. I would choose this occupation again even if given the chance to start over. My main satisfaction is in helping other people. I also enjoy seeing students grasp an idea and take off with it.

I plan to remain a rabbi, and even when I retire I want to pastor part-time to a small congregation and do some research and writing.

REGISTERED NURSE #1

I work 12 hour shifts in the critical care unit (intensive care unit) of a hospital. Because I'm a manager, I'm responsible for the organization and policies and procedures in my department. These duties are in addition to my usual work of bedside nursing care.

You need to be in good health mentally and physically to perform well as a nurse. You need to be comfortable with people in distress. Good problem-solving skills are essential.

I like nursing because I feel I am making a difference in other people's lives. I would like the profession better if there were an increase in professional autonomy with less reliance on doctors.

I was inspired to pursue nursing by friends, a nurse, and a physician while they were talking about the contributions of nurses. Prior to nursing I taught physical education in a private school.

I plan to continue in my present role until retirement.

REGISTERED NURSE #2

I've always wanted to be a nurse. I just pursued my dreams and goals. I did try secretarial work for a while but was not satisfied.

My day consists of caring for the sick. I do what I can to ensure a speedy recovery and make things a little easier for people staying in the hospital. Mentally and physically I care for the well being of people.

To perform well as a nurse, it is important to have a positive attitude toward people and confidence in yourself. Caring is definitely the trait to have if you plan to choose this career.

The most difficult part of my occupation is dealing with death. It is so evident in my career. I just wish there was some easier way to handle it, for my sake and the sake of families and loved ones everywhere.

I do like my work as a nurse because of the people I work with and the kind of work it is. The satisfaction I receive is seeing that one patient smile again, walk again, or even talk again. Knowing my patients are happy makes me happy.

I plan to continue nursing and I may become more specialized--perhaps in the area of trauma nursing.

REGISTERED NURSE #3

As a Registered Nurse for five and one-half years, I have also worked as the clinical educator for our hospital's emergency department. I take care of sick and injured people, trying to save lives or helping people die comfortably with dignity; my duties as clinical educator are to train other nurses in emergency procedures.

I have a Bachelor of Science and a Master of Science, both degrees in nursing. Working as a nurse also requires good judgment, the ability to relate well to people, compassion, and the ability to function well under stress.

I like my job as it gives me the opportunity to help others and to make a difference in the lives of my patients. I enjoy the staff that I work with, the hospital I work for, and the field of nursing in general.

The only frustration that I find in being a nurse is that medical technology has not advanced far enough to alleviate all suffering.

I have always held positions where I dealt with people--as a waitress, a child care worker, and a salesclerk. Being a nurse is best.

I plan to stay in the nursing field, study further in this field, and some day earn a doctorate degree in nursing. Perhaps then I will move into a more academic environment to teach nursing at a university.

REGISTERED NURSE #4

Part of the reason I became a registered nurse was because I thought nursing would be an extremely practical way of helping others. A doctor I worked for in high school (as a receptionist) encouraged me to pursue a medical career, and I am glad he did.

As a nurse, I prepare people for surgery, help them recover from surgery, and teach people about health. My typical daily activities often include taking vital signs, doing a medical physical assessment, preping people, monitoring post-surgery patients, giving I.V.'s, replacing dressings on surgical incisions, watching for complications of surgery or disease, giving medications, and teaching patients about their surgery, diet, medications, and other necessary factors relating to their recovery.

In order to perform the duties and responsibilities of a nurse well, the following factors are important: the ability to accomplish duties with exact precision--i.e., administering medications promptly, properly, and accurately; good observational skills; the ability to function independently to perform accurate nursing assessment, diagnosis and intervention; the ability and willingness to work with and assist all different types of people; and willingness to function as a patient advocate.

I find nursing to be emotionally, mentally, and physically demanding at times. In spite of this, I like what I do because of the satisfaction I have from helping others return to health. Grateful patients are my reward. It is gratifying to realize that my skills can greatly improve a person's health and chances for recovery and that I have acquired a high degree of professionalism and dedication. Professionalism, dedication, and caring are indeed satisfying qualities to possess.

As far as future plans, they include being a full-time homemaker when my children are young (the most important job I will ever have) and then returning to nursing or pursuing an advanced degree possibly in a nursing or related field such as physician's assistant or nurse practitioner.

REGISTERED NURSE #5

As a Registered Nurse, I chose to work for an insurance company after 18 years in a hospital setting. The hours are more reasonable for me and there is no weekend work.

My work involves pre-certifying patients for hospital visits. This means I determine the medical necessity of a hospital stay for inpatients. Through contact with the insurance provider and the hospital staff, I make my assessment. Sometimes I can accomplish this over the telephone; sometimes I make on-site visits to the hospitals. I review charts of patients for further assessment of the medical necessity for a prolonged hospital stay.

I have a college degree in nursing and would like to go back to school and get a degree related to health care management. I would also like to work in preventive care, perhaps for patients in a rural setting, and would like to do volunteer work with the Red Cross Disaster Team.

My work would be more satisfying if there were more personal contact with the patients and less emphasis on production. The pay is low and the work is routine; therefore, I'd like more varied assignments and duties. The lack of opportunity for advancement, the predictability of the duties, and my particular organization are drawbacks to this type of work.

Requirements for being a nurse for an insurance company are, above all, patience and assertiveness. One needs a thorough knowledge of both the field of nursing and medical practice norms for patient hospitalization.

REGISTERED NURSE #6

I am a Registered Nurse who works in the field of obstetrical nursing--from labor to delivery. I made the decision to go into nursing right out of high school where I enjoyed the sciences and the contact with people. After earning a Bachelor of Science degree in nursing, I entered the field and still like the interaction with people. I enjoy the technology and skills involved in the delivering of babies.

Future career goals for me are to earn an advanced degree in nursing. I'd like to be a clinical specialist with a Master of Science in Nursing (MSN).

A good obstetrics nurse must have excellent communication skills and lots of patience in dealing with new mothers. A good memory and the ability to reason logically are both very important. Being able to "think on your feet" is a requirement.

I like my profession and would choose it again, but the lack of advancement opportunities is discouraging. Further, hospitals typically undervalue their nurses and do not treat them as respected professionals.

My shift begins either at 6:30 a.m. or at 11:00 p.m. In my care of infants and their mothers, I must document the care provided as well as assess their status and provide for their needs. I conduct patient education programs and teach parenting skills to new mothers; therefore, teaching skills are important. Additionally, there is special equipment you need to know how to operate.

REGISTERED NURSE #7

I am a registered nurse in a nursing home. I make work schedules for our employees as well as supervise and evaluate their work because I am the nursing director as well.

Further, all departments report to me. I am liaison for the doctors, families, patients, and employees. There are conferences regarding the patient's care held with the resident and/or the family. Supervising a resident's daily care and treatment as well as advising families of any new concerns about the patient are my duties. I also call doctors with any new medical problems, arrange appointments, and coordinate transportation for the residents. I'm always revising schedules and informing employees of new hours. There's a great deal of paperwork, particularly that involved in employee references, hiring, and firing.

It pleases me that the elderly who have multiple problems are cared for. It's good, too, that local people can be given jobs here which carry respectable benefits. I like trying to schedule our employees around their needs, such as their schooling or their children.

What I don't like are the conflicting state and federal rules and regulations. If there were less paperwork, leaving more hands-on time for the professionals, I would like my work even better. Yet I enjoy my work and, if I could begin again, I'd choose nursing as an occupation.

Nursing and supervising in a nursing home requires good communication skills, both oral and written. You need to take the time to listen and praise as often as you criticize. You should be able to evaluate your employees objectively. Finally, you must continue to read professional materials to keep current on new developments.

REGISTERED NURSE, HOME CARE

As a Registered Nurse, I specialize in home care, which means that I manage a caseload of patients, coordinate their care, see my patients in their homes, assess each patient's condition after visiting with them and examining them, and keep up with all the paperwork. I also have to communicate my findings, over the phone and in written report form, to the necessary medical doctors and clinics to whom the patient is assigned. I order supplies, answer questions from both the patients and doctors, and handle the budget for my service. Usually, I have a pretty hectic schedule, as I see my patients three to five times per week.

In addition to a Bachelor of Science degree in Nursing, my job requires the ability to get along with various types of people, the ability to make efficient use of one's time, and good communication skills. One must be self directed, well organized, calm, patient, focused, and tolerant.

In my twenty-three years as a nurse, I have most enjoyed helping other people and improving my patients' lives. I believe that it is my duty to be an advocate for people unable to help themselves.

The field of nursing could be improved, in my opinion, with greater use of computers in reporting back to the doctors. I do not like all the paperwork the present system generates.

Eventually, I plan to get involved in private practice which would give me greater independence and the opportunity to set up my own system.

REGISTERED NURSE, OBSTETRICS #1

I work in a large university hospital as an obstetric nurse. I have been a registered nurse for 28 years so I am now doing managerial work more than patient care. I manage the nursing staff and the obstetric department. My work typically includes making sure the unit is equipped and has enough staff to provide good nursing care, consulting with the staff, attending meetings, and communicating with physicians and patients.

To perform well as a managing nurse, it is important to have organizational skills and be able to prioritize. Communication and time management skills are also important. You must be able to handle stress.

I always wanted to be a nurse and also I felt I only had a few choices open to me (nursing, teaching, secretary) at the time I entered the work force.

Except for dealing with the staffing schedule and negative people sometimes, I like my work very much. I would again choose nursing as my career even if I were given the chance to start again. I receive satisfaction from doing a good job and making sure that our patients have a good birth experience.

REGISTERED NURSE, OBSTETRICS #2

I have been a registered nurse for 13 years. My specialties are obstetrics and public health. I work part-time--two 12 hour shifts--because of my family requirements. A major part of obstetrics is teaching self and infant care to patients. I assess the patient physically and then evaluate the patient. I also administer medication.

In nursing, self-confidence and patience are both very important. Staying current in your knowledge base is necessary since more of the public is becoming informed. Then you should not be hesitant to speak up.

Making a difference by teaching people how to care for themselves is very satisfying. I enjoy the people I work with, my work itself, and a moderate level of autonomy. I dislike the excessive paperwork. I think the public image of nursing merits improvement. We need more recognition for nurses from the public.

I've been interested in medicine since high school and became a nurse since more schooling is needed for the physician's assistant than for nursing. My future may lie in nurse practitioner school, or perhaps taking the necessary courses to become a physician's assistant.

REGISTERED NURSE, STAFF DEVELOPMENT

I have been in the nursing profession for 20 years, serving in staff development for the last 2 years. In my work I interview graduate nurses for their first positions, and I conduct nursing orientation courses. I travel to schools and community events, making presentations about my field. In overseeing our "Medication Occurrence" program, I help nurses who have made medication errors.

Some of the skills necessary in my work are good speaking skills, a friendly, firm manner, and intelligence. Physical strength and dexterity, as well as keen hearing and eyesight, are also valuable.

Although I have a B.S. in Nursing and an M.S. in Management, I might choose a career in engineering if I could start over. On the other hand, I like the work I do and the autonomy, but I dislike the people I work with and the organization's politics. I've been a cashier in both a fabric store and a grocery store. I've also been a counter person in a fast food restaurant.

If I had lots of money, I'd move to the country and have a rescue shelter for dogs. Since I don't, I'd like to get a Masters Degree in Nursing, become an adult nurse practitioner, and open my own practice in Alaska or Montana.

RESEARCH AGRONOMIST

My job as research agronomist is to plan research projects. For 32 years, I have discussed project plans with colleagues and reviewed scientific literature applicable to the field of agronomy. Agriculture testing and evaluating fertilizer materials on forages and field crops to increase and improve production are also part of my work.

My degrees are a Bachelor of Science in agricultural education, a Masters of Science in agronomy, and a Ph.D. in agronomy. A person in my work should have a good working knowledge of plant nutrients and their function in plant nutrition. You also need the ability to read well and comprehend. Being able to write clearly and concisely is very important.

Previously, I was a farmer. I got into this work because the head of the Agronomy Department at our state university advised me to do so. In my work, I most enjoy obtaining expected results. I like it when results turn out well. It's great when superiors show appreciation for work well done. My job would be more satisfying if I had more time to spend studying computers. I'd like to know how computers may be applied in agronomic research.

RESEARCH & DEVELOPMENT ASSISTANT

The best word to describe why I like my job is that it is challenging. My previous work as sales clerk, file clerk, and elevator operator can not compare to this work. I consider myself fortunate to have found this job.

As an assistant in research and development in chemical etching, I find the best way to etch small parts from metal, using various chemicals. When we receive blueprint drawings of small parts, usually from the medical industries, we determine how to etch them out of various metals, using various procedures.

In order to perform this kind of work well, it is important to have concentration, precision, and a desire to perform in a quality way.

I like every aspect of work including the organization and people I work for, the people I work with, the opportunity for advancement, and the kind of work I do. In fact, I like this work so well, that given the chance to start over and prepare for any kind of work, I would again choose this. I find job satisfaction from the challenge, and having a job well done.

RESEARCH ENGINEER

I've enjoyed everything about my work over the past 15 years. A research engineer since earning a Bachelor of Science in electrical engineering, I feel rewarded when I produce solutions a sponsor likes and uses. I particularly appreciate peer approval and recognition. Even though I don't enjoy the government bureaucracy, I'd choose this occupation again.

My work involves designing and conducting analysis of civilian and military electrical optical systems. We also test these systems. Staff meetings and briefings with sponsors are part of my duties, too. There is some travel in my work as well as budget planning and writing proposals. In the future, I'd like to pursue a career in management, perhaps at a government post.

To do this work, one must have a solid grasp of physics and math. My job also requires management skills and an understanding of personnel needs. Strong communication skills are very important as well.

RESEARCHER, LANGUAGE DEVELOPMENT

I have combined my lifelong interests in both language and medicine into my career as a medical language development researcher. As such, I study the impact on children's language development/skills of various chronic illnesses. I am utilizing my educational background and prior job experience in this position. I have earned the Master of Art, Master of Public Health, and the Ph.D. degrees. My previous jobs were as a graduate school teacher, a college teacher, and a clinical language diagnostician.

My typical job activities include: seeing patients for language testing; explaining testing and overall program to parents; scoring and interpreting test information; writing reports; attending clinical case conferences; meeting with associate research investigators; writing grant applications for research projects.

In order to perform this kind of work well, it is important to have a basic knowledge of language development, general linguistics, and child development; writing skills; analytical skills; "diplomacy"; good communication and organizational skills.

Although I like most aspects of my work, I do not like the fact that many of my patients will die young. However, I find many things about my work to be satisfying, including parents who gain information; children who progress/get appropriate treatment based on my work; getting grants funded; getting articles published; feeling I have written well or given a good presentation.

RESEARCHER, MOLECULAR BIOLOGY

I was always interested in biology. It started with plants and insects when I was a toddler, and went from there. I hated biology in high school (doesn't everyone?), but majored in it in college anyway. (Math was my best subject and could have led to a more profitable career, but it wasn't challenging). I spent one year on a Caribbean Island as a marine biologist--no salary, just room and board; then settled down as a molecular biologist. I have had a variety of other occupations over the years in order to support myself. I ran a small business full time while I was in college full time. I was good at it, and it was fun, but very hard. I taught gifted children in special Saturday science classes. I worked in a clinical lab--boring, too routine. I did underwater modeling with sharks (briefly)! I've taught high school, college, medical school, and graduate school classes, and elderhostels.

My salary is extremely low--especially for the level of education required. In fact, I now still work two part-time jobs to make up the difference; teaching biology at a university and doing word processing at home. Our government cut a lot of funding of basic science research, but I think it should be better supported. Advances in science and technology make our country stronger.

As a medical research/molecular biologist in a big university, I use recombinant DNA techniques to study cell-to-cell communication. I work on several experiments at once. I begin with whatever will take longest and organize my time to prepare solutions or get supplies during long incubation times. At the end of each day I record what I did and my result.

It is very challenging, and stimulating work. I work with fascinating people from all over the world--the best and the brightest! It is a big thrill to publish your work (I still love to see my name in print). It is like a little piece of immortality. My time is flexible-- I make my own schedule and work independently. Research is a method of study--pursuit of knowledge. Learning is what life is all about. If you stop learning, you may as well be dead. Most things in life are cyclical. Teaching is the other side of the circle of learning. Careers that allow for learning and growth are always rewarding.

RESEARCHER, PHARMACEUTICALS

I retired after 36 years in chemical research and research management applied to drug discovery. Getting into consulting after that was easy because of extensive contacts in the pharmaceutical industry. As a side note, I would like to interject my opinion that consultants are a bargain considering they don't get fringe benefits.

As a consultant for chemical research in the pharmaceutical industry, I advise on project management, and on strategy in organic chemical synthesis. I prepare for my work day by reading monthly progress reports written by group members. I then have 1/2 hour sessions with individual researchers to discuss what they are doing and their future plans. Answering questions about chemical synthesis as they arise is also part of my work.

In order to pursue a career as a consultant, you need long experience in research management, an aptitude and strong liking for problem solving, and the ability to think on your feet. In short, consulting takes stamina and experience.

The major drawback to my consulting business is the insecurity--one year contracts which may or may not be renewed. I only wish I could negotiate longer term contracts. Aside from that, I like this kind of work very much.

The work is high-level problem solving and non-repetitive, which is the feature I most like. Research is exciting! Helping other people plan and execute good research is very rewarding.

RESOURCE SPECIALIST, K-6

As a resource specialist at an elementary school where I deal with children in grades K-6 who have learning disabilities, I remediate learning disabilities exhibited in scholastic settings. I go to several different classrooms during the day, working with children and teachers, and, at times, children come to my classroom for one-on-one remediation. I also prepare academic assignments on a weekly basis.

I have completed both a Bachelor of Arts degree and a Master of Arts degree. In addition, my job requires flexibility, acceptance, patience, self-direction, dedication, and good organizational skills. You must enjoy dealing with special children to work at the level I have chosen.

I enjoy great emotional validation from my work because I know that I have been helpful to these very special children, and hopefully, I have made a difference in these children's lives. I believe that my work is extremely important.

I have been working in this field for eleven years; previously, I held such positions as a secretary and a social worker. The only area of improvement that I could suggest is to reduce the size of the classes and provide for more special educational tools, making it possible to give each child more individual attention and guidance on a regular basis.

I enjoy my job so much that I plan to stay with my present job and improve my interpersonal skills; there is always something to be learned when working in the education field, especially with children.

RESPIRATORY THERAPIST

Respiratory therapists are part of a specialized field of nursing. They treat patients with lung disease and must, therefore, be able to work calmly in traumatic situations.

They also must have the ability to work well with people.

I've worked as a medical assistant, dental assistant, and as a secretary, but became a respiratory therapist because I always liked the medical field. There was a training program available at the community college, so I studied there, earning an Associates degree in applied science. Since I'm a wife and mother, I took advantage of the two-year program. Also, the pay from my new career is enough to allow me to work part-time.

One of my duties is to spend one day a week doing diagnostic tests on patients' lungs. The other therapists and I are responsible for the ventilator care of our patients. We answer immediately any codes or traumas that come into the hospital.

My reward comes when I'm able to make breathing and, therefore, life, easier for people. Visiting with patients is also a joy. I'm pleased with my job, coworkers, superiors, and the hospital. There is nothing I can honestly say I dislike about my situation. In the future, I plan to continue what I'm doing.

RESTAURANT & DRESS SHOP OWNER

As the owner and operator of a restaurant and the owner and buyer for a dress shop for the past forty years, most of my time is spent in planning and management of these endeavors. I have to work seven days a week due to the nature of my work.

I have completed an Associate degree in Business, but this work also requires good health, flexibility, imagination, and, most important, the willingness to work hard for what seems at times to be inadequate monetary compensation.

The rewards of my hard work come from my interaction with others, my patrons and regular customers; I enjoy seeing them come in, especially my "regulars." It is also rewarding for me to watch my businesses grow, for I know that my hard work is the main ingredient that has led to success.

I believe that there is too much government interference with the business of the restauranteur and retailer. I would like to see fewer Federal and State Laws that restrict the profits to be made in businesses dealing with the public.

Future plans are to hire and train a good management team for each of my businesses, so that I can enjoy more leisure time with my family.

RESTAURANT HELPER

A typical day for me as a restaurant helper includes setting up for luncheons, wedding breakfasts, or meetings. During the summer I prepare the outside area for meals. When needed, I do general janitorial duties such as sweep the walk, change light bulbs, remove garbage, collect laundry, or wash dishes. I also assist in the preparation of food on occasion.

What you needed for this work is the willingness to work. You need to have communication skills to please the customer and be able to work without supervision. I am pleased when the customer is happy with the design of the room, the food, and the service. There is nothing I dislike about my work; I particularly like the people and organization I work for.

My education did not extend through high school. I attended no college, but no college education is needed for this kind of work.

I found this work through a referral from someone who was working here. Other jobs I've had were in fast food and in janitorial work. Those jobs and my current work are not sufficiently challenging, so some change will be sought at a later time. My plans are to work eventually in the criminal justice system, in civil service, or the postal service. If I follow the criminal justice line, some college education would be very helpful if not essential.

RESTAURANT MANAGER #1

I would say that the restaurant I manage is nice but not an elegant establishment. On a routine day I start by talking with the manager from the previous shift to find out the events of that shift. I must be sure that everything is set up for my shift. Once the work is underway I talk with, observe and direct others as they work. I try to foresee problem areas and correct them. At the end of the shift I must check to see that each person cleans up as they should, count the money, and close up the building.

To perform well as a restaurant manager, it is important to have people skills. A positive attitude is a must.

The main satisfaction I find from this type of work is hearing from happy customers and employees. I like managing a restaurant. However, I am occasionally dissatisfied with the people with whom I work when they are unreasonable or have a "don't care" attitude.

I got my job somewhat accidentally. My college degree is Bachelor of Science in communications, which is not really related. Prior to that, my summer jobs while going to school were varied, including factory work, sales, cook, waiter, gas station attendant, and life guard. I think that all these experiences have helped me be aware of and to understand work situations and problems and therefore have made me a better manager.

Although I did not initially seek this kind of work, I find that I now like it and I plan to continue. I hope to advance to district manager for my company eventually.

RESTAURANT MANAGER #2

I started at the bottom working in a fast food restaurant, and have moved up to restaurant manager. As a manager, I am responsible for the preparation and serving of food, managing workers, and scheduling prep work, employees and maintenance. My typical daily activities include making a prep schedule, checking over night's work and figures, preparing food, setting up serving area, serving customers, cleaning up the dining room after lunch, taking a break for lunch, doing a special project such as dusting or scouring pans and pots, restocking food for supper, and serving customers.

In order to perform this kind of work well, it is important to have a positive attitude. You must get along with people and be flexible enough to see different points of view.

There is a lack of opportunity for advancement for me now that I have reached this position as manager. Aside from this, I find job satisfaction from meeting and beating the every day challenges of the job. It is also satisfying to train people to do a good job. They know it and take pride in the work they do.

In the future, I would like my work to be more focused on the training of employees and management in the restaurant job, rather than continuing with all the other duties such as preparation and serving of food.

RESTAURANT OWNER/OPERATOR

Making daily menus, shopping and helping with the cooking describe my work as a restaurant owner and operator. For 22 years I've enjoyed the challenge, the people, and being my own boss. I like greeting customers and supervising employees. As the owner, I have to make sure each person is properly doing his or her job. The work does require a great number of hours; I'd like to train someone to cover me for days off. My plans for the future include continuing to grow and polish my skills in the restaurant business.

Requirements involved in restaurant work are the ability to work with your hands, being creative, and being willing to do whatever needs doing. Flexibility and an attitude of service are crucial. Customers like it if you are a bit obsequious, but it is worth it to be your own boss. In addition, this kind of work does not require any college education. Although I finished high school, it is possible to get by without so much formal training. I learned from my father who was also in the restaurant business. I have been a hospital worker and a construction worker, but owning and operating a restaurant is by far the best of those jobs.

RETAIL MERCHANDISE MANAGER

I always enjoyed selling because I found it challenging. However, I don't like commission sales or pressure to sell as in insurance and auto sales. So, having my own retail sales business worked out well for awhile, except that I didn't own the property on which my outdoor sports and marine equipment sales store was located. The land was sold and I didn't relocate and reopen. Instead, I was hired by a good friend as manager at a large chain store.

As a merchandise manager in a large retail store, I oversee operations/merchandising of a group of departments. The duties and activities which are usually part of my daily and/or weekly schedule are corporate office follow-ups, inventory control, customer complaints, special assistance for problem customers, smoothing ruffled feathers of employees, and some of the following items--training, ordering, scheduling, budgeting, meetings, interviews, pep talks, and planning; answering phone calls and questions. Never a dull moment!

Relative to the skills and attitudes necessary for success in retailing, you need an iron will, patience, desire to overcome any obstacle, desire to please, thinking before speaking and knowing when to keep your mouth shut, mastering Murphy's Law, and a sense of humor. I have witnessed many changes in the retail industry and am finding that computerization has closed many doors for advancement, and the soft retail market has eliminated many positions. My advice, therefore, is you must be determined if you really want to make it in this industry.

When I first started in retail sales, I found satisfaction from pleasing people and doing the job as best I could. Now, I am finding that my satisfaction comes from getting a regular pay check, vacation time, insurance, and the retirement plan.

RETAIL OWNER/SALESPERSON

I taught piano for 20 years and also did cashier work, but I gave that up and bought my own tanning business. I am glad I did.

It is a one person operation. I do everything from greeting clients, to selling products, making appointments, and scrubbing floors. My daily routine is to open the store, count the money, answer the phone, make appointments, greet clients, take money, show new products, listen to client problems, clean, count money, balance the books, and close the store.

To be successful in this type of business, I think it is important to have the gift of gab, a bubbly personality, a positive attitude, and to be friendly.

I love my kind of work and receive satisfaction from happy customers. However, I would be more satisfied with more customers. I plan to continue to build up this business and work for many years to come.

RETAIL PHARMACIST

My sole occupation has been involved in retail drugstores, from clerk to pharmacist, to manager. I admired the local drugstore in the community I lived in while growing up. I had even chosen pharmacy for an occupation when I was in seventh grade. My career started with working at the soda fountain. After earning my Bachelor of Science in Pharmacy degree, I moved behind the drug counter. I took on the job as manager/pharmacist for 5 years, but was happy to return to staff pharmacist when so much attention was placed on merchandising.

As the staff pharmacist, I prepare prescriptions, and supervise other clerks. My daily activities include greeting and waiting on customers, filling their prescriptions, consulting the customers on how to take their medication, answering questions, demonstrating various appliances, general cashiering, and supervising other clerks.

To perform this kind of work well, it is important to have: a scientific knowledge, accuracy, a willingness to help others, and patience.

I basically have been very satisfied with my career.

There are usually some frustrations with a job, and mine are dealing with complaining customers, not having enough time to spend with the patients, and the constant emphasis on price of goods, rather than the service obtained. Aside from these frustrations, I find job satisfaction in helping others, a smiling child, and having a respected profession.

RETAIL SALESPERSON #1

I work as a salesperson in a retail clothing store. A salesperson spends almost the entire time while on duty on your feet! Fortunately, I work part time; I do not believe I would enjoy spending an entire eight-hour day standing up. This does not mean that I do not like my job; quite to the contrary, I really enjoy it a lot, especially having the opportunity to interact with many interesting people.

I believe that a positive attitude and a pleasant disposition are the essential ingredients to success as a salesperson; you also must not allow yourself to be influenced by the mood of others.

I enjoy the people I work with and I am fortunate to have a great boss. I believe in the company I work for and the products we sell. That makes my job so much easier.

Even though there is opportunity for advancement at this store, I plan to work in this position for only a short time. My aspirations are to attend college to earn a Bachelor's or higher level degree in Electrical Engineering.

I believe that, eventually, my present position will certainly enable me to accomplish my goal of becoming an Electrical Engineer, and the experience and interpersonal skills I acquire will not be wasted.

RETAIL SALESPERSON #2

I have been employed as a salesclerk for thirty years; I currently sell gifts and housewares. My duties are to assist customers to find certain items and answer their questions about the merchandise; to keep the merchandise in presentable condition by straightening up, dusting displays, and sweeping the floor; to rearrange merchandise as the seasons change; and giftwrapping items when requested by the customer.

Although there is no opportunity for advancement, I really like having the opportunity to meet people. I appreciate that my shop still keeps an uncomplicated cash register as I do not have the experience to work with a computer.

The atmosphere in the shop where I work is rather informal and I believe that allows people to relax when they shop here.

I started at my job as a teenager, hired as Christmas extra help, but I have enjoyed this job more than any of the other positions I have held over the years. Those were receptionist, waitress, dance instructor, and director of a youth center. As you can see, I have always been drawn to jobs where I deal directly with people.

Family considerations are probably the biggest reason that I would leave this profession, but I quite honestly would miss this job.

If I had the chance to do something else with my career, the only change I would make is to be the owner of the shop.

RETAIL SALESPERSON, HARDWARE

In the field of hardware and home improvement, I have worked as a salesperson for several years now. I receive freight, stock the shelves with merchandise, and help customers with home improvement projects by giving them advice and selling them the tools needed to get the job done.

I received extensive training in my twenty years of service in the U.S. Marine Corps. To do this job well, you must know of the products, their uses and practical applications, and have a sensitivity for the feelings of people.

I believe there are many opportunities available to me for advancement beyond my present position. I enjoy my job, especially when I have helped a customer who really needed direction in a project. I know that I send my customers home with the tools and knowledge they need to do the job right.

After twenty years in the Marine Corps, this job seems like fun to me. I plan to work at this job for a few more years and after that I will probably travel and start a more entrepreneurial venture.

RETAIL STORE DEPARTMENT MANAGER

If you analyzed my educational background and most of my previous work experience, you would probably not predict what I do now. I am very satisfied in this career as a department manager in a retail store. I earned a Bachelor of Arts in sociology with a minor in psychology and emphasis in group dynamics. Previous job experience includes work as a machine operator, security guard and church youth worker.

As a department manager in a large drug store, it is my responsibility to order softgoods, food, hard goods, photo supplies and equipment, and cosmetics; help customers; do checking; count money; stock shelves; supervise personnel; and open and close the store. I am scheduled for 10-hour shifts (includes a 1 hour lunch), and I usually work 1-2 hours more. I either work a 7-5 shift or a 12-10 shift which means I either open or close the store. My typical daily activities include assigning work to the clerks and checkers, approving returns and overrings, ordering merchandise, setting up merchandise for the season, filling shelves, dealing with emergencies, and helping customers (nice ones and upset ones).

To perform this kind of work well, it is important to have patience, the ability to work unsupervised, accuracy (particularly when working with money), a lot of energy to work long hours, and the ability to direct others as a supervisor without being an over-lord. My basic overriding working philosophy is to always treat fellow employees and customers the same way you would like to be treated and to always do a job you can be proud of. Except for the long hours, 53+ hours per week, I like almost every aspect of my work.

The satisfactions from my work are great customers, great fellow employees, a great boss, and working for a great company. I plan to continue with this company for 5-10 years and then to manage a small store or boutique of my own.

REVENUE ANALYST, ELECTRIC COMPANY

My job for an electric utility company as a senior revenue requirements analyst entails preparing analysis and reports which are filed with the public utilities commission to substantiate requested rate increases. I help to determine when rate changes are needed. My day to day schedule includes data gathering, running computer models, verifying and interpreting results, writing reports explaining results, creating exhibits and training junior level persons.

To perform this job well you need strong mathematical skills, to be good at analysis, good project management skills, always question reasonability and correctness of data and analysis results and be able to work under tight deadlines when necessary.

I find satisfaction in solving mathematical problems. I enjoy the opportunity to be involved in the issues and helping to think of solutions rather than doing routine clerical work where no analysis is necessary.

After graduating with a B.A. in Business and Math, my first job was as a financial analyst for this utility. I applied for this position because it was analytical work with some regard for detail, good people to work for(supervisor, etc.), and better exposure to management and issues.

ROBOTICS TECHNICIAN

I find satisfaction in my work when I am able to take a broken down piece of equipment, figure out what is wrong with it, and am able to repair it. That also describes my job function as a robotics technician. I am part of a support group waiting for the robots and automated arms in the production line to break down. When they do, we go to work to repair them. If no machines are broken, preventive maintenance will be conducted.

In order to perform this kind of work well, it is important to be able to work by yourself, to make decisions which control production, and have mechanical and electrical aptitudes and the ability to work under pressure. I was going to college working on an associate degree in electronics when the company I was working for as a factory worker had this position open. I have now worked as a robotic technician as a member of the technical support group for 4 years and plan to move up to group leader. Prior to working for this manufacturing company, I worked as a carpenter's laborer and construction worker. I prefer the kind of work I am doing now but would welcome the chance to learn more about engineering to better understand the background of robotics.

ROMAN CATHOLIC PRIEST #1

Each morning begins with prayer and celebration of liturgy with people. I then have meetings with staff to plan the day or week. I meet people as they come for counseling or go out to homes to serve peoples' various needs. Visiting school to meet with students and teachers, reading, studying, writing and visiting sick in hospitals and nursing homes are regular activities. To manage the office and buildings, prepare budgets, pay bills, raise money, celebrate funerals, weddings, etc are all my responsibility.

To perform well as a priest you should be patient, have a love for people, be tolerant and have kindness toward everyone. Clear thinking and speaking and love for continuing to learn are important skills. You should be flexible and yet firm to be a good guide.

I like the priesthood because I find satisfaction from helping people in times of need--especially emotional, familial and spiritual needs. Presiding at worship and preaching and teaching children and adults is also satisfying work for me.

It would make my job more satisfying if it were possible to remove the administrative duties and financial responsibilities for the church from me.

I became a priest after much reflection and prayer, and the example of other priests who inspired me as I was growing up. I sought counseling, and advice in college from teachers, priests, friends and family. My degree was a BA in Philosophy. Prior to these 21 years I have now been a priest, I worked in the family construction business and also for an insurance company. I also worked as a church organist.

I would like to continue what I'm doing. My satisfaction comes from being available to people and that's ongoing.

ROMAN CATHOLIC PRIEST #2

I cannot even imagine how happy being a priest has made me. There is always meaningful work to do! I chose this career through seeing "first hand" what a church situation was like from my college years. I was a music major and worked at a large Catholic church as their Director/Organist. Being involved with people and seeing how priests really lived and worked enabled me to realize my vocation. I then applied to my Diocese, went through the screening process, was accepted, and then was sent to Graduate Studies in Theology at a Seminary for Roman Catholic Candidates for the Priesthood. My background also includes working as a music director for an elementary school in college and working on the boardwalk operating amusement rides at the seashore throughout my summers in high school.

As Roman Catholic Priest and Pastor of a large parish church, I handle the administration of the parish and related elementary school. I also provide for the spiritual welfare of our 2,455 families through outreach, worship, etc. Although there are set things to do each day (celebrate Mass, moderate organizations, visit our school, visit the sick/homebound, counsel), each day is filled with the unexpected-- special occasions in parishioners' life, deaths, or funerals--people with special needs, repairs to the buildings, and personnel situations. It is the unexpected things that make my life and vocation extremely interesting.

One must be a "people person" to be a good priest. I think a genuine concern with the people entrusted to your care is extremely important. Yet, underlying this would be a solid prayer life and time taken each day for spiritual reflection. I would not have the strength to function were it not for this.

Although I like being a priest/pastor very much, living "on the job" and being always accessible sometimes can be stressful. When asked what I would change about my occupation, the question for me would be what things in me would I change to find my occupation more satisfying. This would include taking continuing education for administration and church management. Job satisfaction for me is that the work of the Church (and Christ) is assisted through my actions. Being able to minister to people in extreme situations of life is fulfilling in a very profound way. My plans for the future are to be a good pastor to the people.

RURAL MAIL CARRIER

For twenty-five years, I have worked as a rural mail carrier, sorting and delivering mail for the U.S. Postal Service. A usual day starts very early and varies in length; my work day is considered complete when I have finished delivering the mail to the postal customers on my assigned route. In sorting the mail for my route, I rack the mail, then remove the mail from the rack, fill my vehicle with the mail, and go out and deliver the mail to the intended destinations. While delivering mail, I also collect the mail left to be picked up by me and returned to the post office.

Although personal differences arise that make some people difficult to work with, I enjoy the people that I get along with at work. I like this kind of work, the people I work for, and working for the postal service in general; I have the opportunity to meet some very nice people and I find that each day brings new challenges; I would not still be working at this job if I didn't enjoy it.

In my job, you need to keep simple records, possess a good memory, maintain a good driving record, be outgoing and caring, strive to be easy to get along with, and have the ability to read the public.

Although I held several other jobs as a factory worker, a taxi driver, a dog groomer, and the owner and operator of an upholstery shop, this is the work that I enjoy. I plan to work in this position for as long as possible. The fringe benefits are great.

RUSSIAN TRANSLATOR

My work involves translating Russian texts in various scientific and technical fields into English. This has worked out well for me because I can do this work while I stay at home to raise my children, and I am utilizing the skills and knowledge which I have acquired. I do much of my work after the children go to bed.

In order to do translation work, you must have reading fluency in the language. In my particular case, I have Russian reading fluency. Also, I need the knowledge of science and technology because I do scientific and technical translations.

This is a satisfying job for me for many reasons. I like working alone and working with language, and I enjoy the feeling of accomplishment I get from working with a difficult language like Russian. I would be more satisfied if there were more relaxed deadlines and higher pay. However, I plan to continue this kind of work while raising my children.

I earned my bachelor of arts degree and was recruited into this field while I was at college.

SALES ACCOUNT MANAGER

The responsibilities of a Sales Account Manager are to: present sales programs to the corporate headquarters of the retail chain for which I work; assist sales representatives in the retail stores; call on district managers to sell them on the sales programs already accepted by headquarters; call on individual stores in the chain to follow up on calls made by salespersons; and work with individuals to prepare new presentations.

The skills necessary to work as a Sales Account Manager are product knowledge; knowledge of customers' business needs and the overall corporate profit picture; and a thorough understanding of the concepts of product mark-up, pricing, and profits. In addition to these skills you need to be enthusiastic and possess the ability to work with people. I previously worked as a corporate buyer, which I believe contributes to my success. Education is an important factor in my preparation for this career. I have completed a Bachelor of Science degree in Business Administration.

I find it particularly satisfying when corporate headquarters decides to run with a program that I have researched and presented to them. It makes me believe that my contribution plays an important part in the company profits. I also like to see the salespersons follow up on leads or problems.

SALES COORDINATOR, POSTAL SERVICE

I am a high school graduate and have been a letter carrier for 10 years. Recently, I've been given the opportunity to act as sales coordinator at our post office. This will mean participation in sales and customer relations to restructure the present system. My mission will be to develop a more competitive and professional approach to the mail services, such as organizing and dispatching overnight mail.

Three days a week I deliver mail. During the rest of the time, I try to direct a more professional sales approach to the present governmental system. I supervise and assist in sales while developing and following up on leads. Conducting research and developing advertising strategies for more competitive customer-oriented procedures are also part of the job.

I would like to see my ideas and plans reach all post offices. Perhaps even my place of employment would improve. I enjoy the challenge of improving the system. Customer contact and the excitement of experimenting make my work enjoyable. Everything about my job pleases me except the inability of those higher up to improve things.

SALES EXECUTIVE, INSURANCE

I very much enjoy my job as a sales executive for a retail insurance broker. I sell commercial insurance to companies. Typically, my day involves gathering information from clients and deciding what type of insurance they need. I then obtain alternatives to fill this insurance need and present my proposal to the client.

To perform well in sales, particularly my type of sales, it is necessary to pay attention to detail. As with most sales jobs, interpersonal communication is essential.

The main satisfaction I find from my work is solving problems for my clients and providing a service and product they need, thus satisfying my clients. It would be more satisfying, however, if I did not have to rely on other people to make sure they do their job properly.

I earned my bachelor of science degree in business administration and got my first job as a sales rep for an industrial packaging company. I was able to advance myself professionally into my current position because I knew some people in the business. As previously mentioned, I like this work and plan to stay with this career. I feel there are opportunities for advancement. It is possible that I may get into sales management at a later time.

SALES MANAGER #1

I like people, and I like to sell. I began my sales career early as a teenager selling "stuff." I always tried to outsell my buddies. It was a game--still is!

Now as the sales manager for a large national food and beverage company, I work with local marketing sales representatives and help them sell "national accounts" on their brands. I act as an adviser/consultant to the salesmen. I also have my own "personal" accounts.

To be an effective salesperson, it is important to have sincerity, honesty, ENTHUSIASM, "people skills," modesty, desire to help, and the ability to LISTEN.

My background includes a Bachelor of Science in Business Administration and military service as a Navy officer. I have now been in sales full time for 23 years and plan to continue selling. There is not much I dislike about my job. I am very satisfied.

I find satisfaction in making a sale, particularly one that has taken awhile to make. I also find satisfaction in being well-paid.

SALES MANAGER #2

I started working in the cosmetics department of a large department store while in college. Since that start of working behind the counter, I have managed a cosmetic department and bought and merchandised cosmetics for a small department store. Now as a territory manager for a national brand of fragrances, I service and sell to the person in the position which I used to have. I don't consider this to be a career which I exactly chose; it's what I fell into and have enjoyed thus far.

As territory manager, I visit area department stores who carry our fragrances. I write their basic and promotional orders, negotiate for store-paid advertising, and I try for in-store placement of our brands.

My job requires excellent communication and organizational skills. You have to be self-confident and comfortable negotiating with the stores/accounts.

I like almost every aspect of my work including the people and organization I work for.

However, I sometimes think I am in a very superficial industry and feel I could contribute more to society elsewhere. Despite this, my work is satisfying to me because I am doing something I am good at! Also, the pay and benefits are quite good--company car, bonus pay, etc.

My future career will probably take one of two directions: work towards becoming a regional manager over several territory managers like me, or go to grad school and continue my education to earn my master's degree in philosophy or English.

SALES MANAGER #3

I am a sales manager with a company which makes corrugated containers. In my work I design and sell boxes, but as required by my major responsibilities, I service existing accounts in the company, seek potential accounts, and make sales presentations. I work with four sales people to help them promote more sales.

The qualities a sales manager needs are honesty, commitment, and product knowledge. A strong work ethic is also important.

Problem solving for regular and potential customers is a primary satisfaction for me. I've been involved for many years in this business, even as a youth helping my father who was in sales as well. It would be even more satisfying if there were more commitment from others. I try to encourage people to build lasting business and personal relationships and not let greed and self-satisfaction guide them.

My future plans are to teach and to encourage young people to accept responsibility for themselves. I'd teach them to reach out to others and bring about a better society.

SALES MANAGER #4

A high school graduate, I've been a sales manager for 16 years. My sales territory is the state of Hawaii. As a printer and as a department store manager, I enjoyed my work, but now I plan to continue with my sales career.

It's very satisfying to help people solve cargo transportation problems. There is nothing I dislike about my work; I'd choose it again if I could start over. I arrive at the office around 6:30 in the morning to send faxes to the Hawaiian Islands. The time difference helps the faxes transmit faster. My work involves a great deal of phone solicitation to seek cargo transportation. I try to reach old customers as well as new ones. Often there are lunch meetings with customers.

You need to have excellent people skills to be a good salesman. Both a positive attitude and the ability to put yourself in the customer's shoes go a long way toward being happy and successful in sales.

SALES MANAGER #5

A regional sales manager for a long distance telephone service needs technical product knowledge. It is necessary to be familiar with business applications and have the ability to communicate well with customers. Good people skills for customer service is very important.

I get satisfaction in this job because of my successful performance and the recognition I receive. I like the work I do and the people involved. I'd be happier in my work if upper management would be more respectful of their human resources. They'd also do well to ask employees for more input on how to help the business run smoother.

This was my first job out of college where I earned a Bachelor of Arts degree in political science. I direct and manage all sales and customer service activity for a large geographic territory. One day I hope to own my own business.

SALES MANAGER, FARM MACHINERY

For 29 years I have marketed farm machinery as territory manager and factory sales manager--promoting and selling and working with others to do the same. If I could start over, I would do exactly the same job with the same people and organization.

My educational background was a Bachelor of Science in Business Administration. I met the Branch Manager of John Deere while doing a college survey and liked the company atmosphere.

Typically, I study economic conditions worldwide. That involves continuous awareness of market and inventory levels, any sales promotion results, new programs, and tests and evaluations and market input on new products.

It is important to be a self-starter, aggressive, and knowledgeable about your product line and your competition. It is also very helpful to be a good listener.

It is a great satisfaction when you are No. 1 in a business, especially if you enjoy selling and working with people.

I hope to improve my foreign language capability and would like to become an international marketing consultant in farm machinery. The need is great worldwide.

SALES REPRESENTATIVE

My work as a sales representative is satisfying in that I enjoy being on my own. Calling on supermarket retail chains and selling grocery products is what my kind of sales representative does.

Previously, I was a personnel interviewer, but I like the freedom of travel and the accompanying benefits of this job. Through networking, I found my work five years ago. I like all aspects of the job except the lack of opportunity for advancement and the salary. I'd like to make more money through commission selling of these products. My future plans are to remain in sales--maybe go into real estate sales--and start a business of my own.

Good communication skills are needed in my occupation. A sales rep also needs a positive attitude along with a strong inner drive. My education is a Bachelor of Arts degree in business.

SALES REPRESENTATIVE, HMO

Although I do not like the person I work for, I do enjoy my coworkers in my position as sales representative for a health maintenance organization. I came to this fine company through an agency who provided temporary help. When my temp job was over, I submitted my resume for this job. My job satisfaction comes from the commission I receive. It helps me live my life in a comfortable manner.

To do my job, you need the ability to handle difficult people. Math skills, the ability to sell, and a good personality all help in performance and success in this job. It's very important to be able to explain health plan eligibility rules to people who have a limited understanding of the product.

My college major was marketing and I have used some of what I learned in my sales work. My day begins with visits to account holders and many phone calls. There are new accounts to be sent to enrollment, to underwriting, and to employer groups. Maintaining existing accounts and working on opening new accounts in all our different health packages keeps me busy. My plans for the future include owning my own business in my home town.

SALES, COMPUTER SOFTWARE

After working as a bank teller and doing some automotive sales work, I've very happily been in computer software sales for a year now. After answering an advertisement in the newspaper, I interviewed with several people in this company, talked to their customers, and decided to accept the job.

A positive, confident attitude helps the most in my position. In addition to the necessary training, a friendly voice is particularly important in sales.

There is nothing I dislike about my current career. I enjoy my coworkers, the customers, the company's positive attitude, and the work itself. That there are opportunities for promotion is a benefit. I get great satisfaction helping customers find computer programs which serve their needs.

In my work, I deal with customers and their computer software needs. I answer their questions as I help them find appropriate software for their requirements. Further, I check existing merchandise orders as well as any backorders.

My plans are to continue to grow with the company. I want to expand my horizons and get a Master's degree in business in addition to my Bachelor of Science degree in management. Working in human resources might be of future interest.

SALES, INTERNATIONAL AIR FREIGHT

I am into sales for the challenge and the money. I earned a Bachelor of Science degree before starting my career and have now been involved in selling for 17 years. For a time I was in pharmaceutical sales, and now I sell international air freight service.

It is my job to convince companies to use my firm to ship their international commodities. My typical duties include: contacting prospective new customers (by appointment only!); visiting new and old customers; and doing paperwork in the office including proposals, price charts, sales reports, etc.

To perform this kind of work well, it is important to have good verbal and written communications skills, the ability to listen and understand body language, and the belief in your product or service.

I like my sales job because of the people and the organization I work for and I feel I meet the challenges of the job, have the very considerable satisfaction of receiving good money for my services, and I look forward to a comfortable retirement.

SALES, NEWSPAPER ADVERTISING

Salesmen of newspaper advertising make daily contact with their clients. They're busy creating advertisements and writing copy for the newspaper. I, additionally, supervise other ad salesmen.

While I don't enjoy my supervisor, I love my work generating sales for retail advertisers. I particularly appreciate the humor I find out in the main streets of the retail markets.

I regret that the life of an ad salesman in the retail markets has changed so. Once there was creative interaction with independent owners and decisions were made locally. This all changed with the growth of national and regional chain stores.

Strong people skills are needed in my line of work. Dealing with retail store managers and owners takes good interpersonal skills. You need a positive attitude along with familiarity and understanding of the retail market.

SALES, REAL ESTATE

As a retirement community counselor and salesperson, I call and interview clients, mail brochures, help clients with their plans, and receive calls of inquiry; the main objective of my work is to encourage clients to buy property in our community.

To succeed in this line of work, you better have a good knowledge of the program, good communication skills, interpersonal skills, and the ability to convince clients that the program would be suitable for their retirement needs.

Although there can be many conditions that hinder a sale, I like my job. I believe in this community and enjoy selling a product that I believe in. I find this to be satisfying work. I have the opportunity to meet some really great people, make friends, and gain the confidence of the people I deal with because they realize that I am helpful to them while also satisfying their needs.

Prior to this job, I was employed in retail grocery sales and also served as a Merchant Seaman for several years.

I have high enthusiasm for the project I am currently involved in; I look forward to seeing this project through to completion.

SALESPERSON #1

I have been selling construction materials for 11 years and like it very much. To summarize what I do, I solve problems on distribution or technical problems, make sales calls, and develop new markets and uses for our product.

To do well as a salesman you should be skilled in sales techniques, and have problem solving, decision making and analysis skills.

I find job satisfaction because of the daily variation and people contact. Making a sale and solving a problem also contribute to the reason why I like my job. I would like it more with less paperwork and less corporate interference.

I quit college at age 21 and found a job through an employment agency with this company as repairman/technician. Prior to that I worked in a factory and construction. While working I have also returned to college to earn my B.S. and B.A. degrees.

SALESPERSON #2

My present job actually evolved from my job as a truck driver while in college. I have gone from unloading trucks, to tractor trailer driver, to dispatcher, and now to sales representative. I make sales calls on traffic managers to obtain the business by telling of my company's service. It is my job to sell the transportation service. It is an intangible item, nothing to see or touch. You must first sell yourself to people that you are honest and truthful. Most work days are spent making sales calls on active and prospective customers, doing telemarketing, problem solving, and working up transportation quotes.

To be successful as a service salesman, I think it is important to have a level personality, understanding, communication skills. and prompt answers to questions and problems.

I like this very much because of the organization and people I work for, the people I work with, and the kind of work I do. My job satisfaction comes from being able to meet and interact with all types of people and from knowing that I am doing the best for both my customer and my company.

SALESPERSON #3

My career has basically been sales oriented and has included selling insurance and shoes. My background also includes a Bachelor of Science in Psychology. I started by being a sales clerk at a shoe store. I was good at selling and enjoyed telling management what needed to be reordered or marked down. After a year, I was employed by another company as an assistant buyer and merchandiser for a group of 18 stores. I came into contact with the shoe sales representative, and after four years, decided I wanted to try that aspect of the business. My retail and buying background has been of tremendous help to me, making me more credible with my customers and giving me much insight into their business.

I work out of my house selling women's shoes to retail stores in a tristate area. I visit retail stores about 4 times a year to sell them the next season's goods, make reorders on current goods, and help to plan promotions for my merchandise. I make my appointments with existing customers, leaving a little time every week to prospect for new ones. I drive to my customers, show them my goods, and try to sell them as many as I believe they can retail (not as many as possible). I see approximately 2 to 3 people a day. Each presentation takes about 3 hours. Much of the day is spent in the car driving.

To work in sales, you must be self motivated, and care about people. Enthusiasm and an optimistic attitude are very important. People like to buy from an "up" person.

Although I like most aspects of my work, there are a few changes I would like to make. I would like to be able to input more information to our line builder and designer as to what my customers needs are. Having less paperwork (many of our reports are redundant) would be another positive change. On the other hand, what I particularly like about my work is the freedom to plan my own daily schedule. As long as I make my quota, I can do pretty much as I please (taking a day off to play golf, etc.). I find job satisfaction in having my accounts trust and value my opinion; being considered an expert professional in my field. I aspire to a larger territory or possibly a sales manager position.

SALESPERSON #4

I've been an insurance salesman for many years. My area of concentration is selling deferred compensation plans to clients who want to have some money withheld from their salaries for later use, such as retirement. I also sell a variety of specialized plans, such as insurance for parachutists or unique medical plans.

Good communication skills are needed in sales work. You also need to be a considerate listener. Having an inquiring nature along with joy in finding solutions is important. You have to be motivated to influence and encourage.

I spend my day, which begins at 7:00 a.m., making appointments with or meeting new clients or potential clients. Since my time is my own, I spend some of the afternoons in volunteer work. One day soon I'd like to retire and fill my time doing my volunteer work.

After earning a Masters in Business Administration in the field of industrial relations, I owned and operated several restaurants. I also built a few. But I particularly enjoy, in my insurance work, finding good solutions to business problems. I also enjoy the income. I would like to have more time for recruiting. I'm not crazy about my coworkers, but I do like the fact that there are opportunities for advancement in this work.

SALESPERSON #5

I enjoyed my time in the U.S. Navy, yet I really like my work in sales. Exploring different methods of merchandising and seeing if they work better than present methods is very satisfying to me. I also like working pretty much on my own.

While working in a retail drug chain, I was offered a salesman's job by one of our vendors. I've been in sales for 10 years now. Although I don't like the lack of communication in the particular company I represent, I would choose sales over any other career.

A salesman must have a very positive attitude at all times and strong communication skills in interacting with prospective buyers.

During the week I visit 40-50 stores and shops. I introduce new products for the owners to sell to their customers. Writing orders for current products they carry is also my responsibility. Finally, I inform them of other advertising and merchandising ideas to help make them and myself more successful. There is freedom in being out of an office, but you have to get the orders.

SALESPERSON #6

I like my work as a salesman for contract furniture enormously. Right out of college, where my major was general studies, I met the owner of a company that sold contract furniture and went to work for him.

I call on architects, designers, and people who will use the furniture--end users--to educate them on why my product is best. As a salesman, I try to get these people to buy or to use our products. I also call on a furniture dealer network to help sell to the end users. Job satisfaction for me is the "rush" I get from a sale. I enjoy the freedom I have in doing my job, also. It's a commission-pay basis, which means the more I sell, the more I earn.

The downside is that there's little opportunity for advancement. I'd also like to see a better commission rate or pay scale, which would mean higher commissions paid.

My plans for the future are to stay in sales. I want to make money while developing a profitable sales territory. Making as much success as possible for myself and for others is my goal.

SALESPERSON #7

I am presently attending college and majoring in engineering. For the last 3 1/2 years I have been working as a salesperson at a sporting goods store. I have found that I like this work because I enjoy sports. I worked as a salesperson in a computer software store prior to this sales position and did not enjoy that work.

I usually work the night shift. I work in the shoe department, helping people decide on the right sports shoe for their needs. After closing, I clean up the store and make sure the displays are ready for the next day.

As a salesperson, it is important to have good rapport with the customers. Your personality and knowledge of the product you are selling affects the customer's opinion of the store.

The most frustrating aspect of retail sales for me has been that there seem to be some customers that are impossible to satisfy no matter what, and they tend to take their poor attitude out on you. However, there is the other side, which is the satisfaction I find from knowing that I have aided a person in choosing a comfortable, reliable sports shoe. I also like the people for whom I work, which makes a big difference in my opinion of this work.

SALESPERSON #8

After earning a Bachelor's degree in Business Administration, I chose sales because it has the most potential for the most money in the shortest time. Prior to my current sales position, I was an insurance salesperson, and in retail sales management.

In my current sales position, I contact businesses in the Southeast by the telemarketing strategy for repairs of their hydraulic components and press rebuilds. This work, and sales in general, takes sales skills, a positive attitude, and persistence.

Although I have had to deal with some discrimination because I am a woman in a primarily male sales field, I like the kind of work I do and the people I work with. Job satisfaction for me is getting the sale.

SALESPERSON #9

I enjoy working six days a week in my jewelry sales position. One of my duties is to sell class rings to schools. In that capacity, I visit classes, measure, and place orders for rings. Attending sports gatherings and delivering awards donated by my employers to colleges and high schools are my duties as well. I also handle gifts for weddings and anniversaries.

Honesty and fairness are very important in my sales work. I've also found that, if you enjoy what you do and do your best, you'll succeed. A good personality and a neat, pleasant appearance take you far in sales. You also need to have respect for others.

I enjoy my coworkers and sales work itself. My supervisor and the company have added to my job satisfaction. Working with people has always been rewarding to me, and I'd choose a sales career again.

When I was nineteen, fresh out of high school, I answered an ad in the newspaper. A young, bright, eager learner, I absorbed all the information and experience I could get from my employers; they were good teachers and I worked hard. I have no future plans other than to continue in my current position.

SALESPERSON, AUTOMATED MATERIAL

I sell automated material handling systems now. I have previously sold other products and worked as an industrial engineer. This job seems to utilize all my job experience as well as my education. I earned a Bachelor of Arts degree in math/physics.

Monday is spent generally arranging appointments with clients in the territory. Tuesday through Friday, I make sales presentations, and work with inside engineers on system design and proposal preparation.

To perform well as a salesman, it is important to have good communication skills. Most important is the ability to read (understand) clients and establish trust. Most of my customers are spending from $100K to $1 to $2 million. They must respect my ability.

It is my personal commitment to increase product knowledge. I feel I must continue to train my mind to analyze problems faster. Sales requires a constant mind set on positive conditions. You can never allow a lost order to overwhelm your attitude.

My job satisfaction comes from the repeat business with customers and closing orders. I also like the people I work with, and the organization and people I work for.

Some day I plan to run my own rep. operation. However, sales now are good which allows me to stay with this business and invest in other outside ventures.

SALESPERSON, FLOOR SUPERVISOR

I decided to try working in a retail sports store because of the love I have for the type of things sold at this store. I started out part-time and found that I enjoyed so much the work and, most important, the company I work for that I gave up my restaurant work and now work full time as a floor supervisor/manager.

My responsibilities are selling outdoor sports equipment to customers, supervising salespeople, merchandising the selling floor, and handling daily operations. A typical day begins with some office work to open the store including making a deposit and doing some sales audit paperwork. The day progresses by assigning jobs to specific salespeople and following up to make sure the work is done right. Throughout the day the most important thing is to make sure the customers are being helped and your employees are doing their jobs.

To perform this job well, you need to be outgoing and friendly with the customers and get along well with people. You need to be able to put matters in priority and get things done. Following up is very important, whether it's on the employees or the customers. The biggest satisfaction I get from my job is when a customer comes back just to thank me for helping them pick out the appropriate item for their trip or vacation. The only thing I would change in my occupation is the way some of the other people handle problems. Occasionally problems become greater because they were not taken care of in the beginning, and this makes everyone upset. I would like eventually to work in the corporate office as a buyer or in the advertising department.

SALESPERSON, JEWELRY

When I started in the jewelry sales field, I had no experience in sales or in jewelry. I had to learn both from the ground up by myself. I would have gotten farther faster if I had taken a job with a company that offered both training and mentors. I was burned out working in personnel so I started looking for another job/career. The person I now work with asked me to run his business while he went on vacation. I did and found I loved the work, so I continued with it.

My educational background includes earning a Bachelor of Science in Business Administration. My previous job experience includes work as a human resources manager, a personnel, administration and facilities manager, an office manager, and a secretary.

My typical activities in wholesale jewelry sales to retail stores include: going into the office to restock merchandise; setting up sales week; making appointments as necessary; driving to retail stores to sell merchandise from stock in case; returning invoices and payments to office; mailing out any telephone orders; and assisting in buying and in running office.

To perform this kind of work well, it is important to have excellent sales ability, strong self-motivation, good discipline, some product knowledge (very easy to learn), positive thinking, skill in setting and achieving goals, and ability to establish rapport and build an ongoing relationship with customers.

I find job satisfaction from the "high" I feel when I've had a great sale, day, week, month. Reward is based solely on my effort and ability. I can always give myself a raise by selling more. I work entirely on my own which provides me the opportunity to choose when to work and to set my own hours.

I plan to continue in sales, to look for jewelry lines that pay better commissions or to find another product with a better profit margin. If I stay with jewelry, I plan to continue to increase my sales 50% over the same period one year ago. Jewelry is very seasonal--I need a product to fill in slow periods. In a few years, I want to get into real estate.

SALESPERSON, LEATHER PRODUCTS

My job is selling many different kinds of leather products. I classify the merchandise according to the type of leather and where the products are made; I also keep the stock current and clean the products when there are no customers in my store.

Although there is not much opportunity for advancement, I like my job.

I have been employed in this job for three years. I have also worked as a janitor, a bartender, and a grocery store clerk.

I believe the most important characteristics for a person to have in this job are politeness, willingness to be courteous to the customers, a good personality, good communication skills, and some knowledge of the product.

I find considerable satisfaction when I meet nice people who appreciate the products I sell. They are usually the ones that I like to spend the most time with.

I am working as a salesperson for a friend who owns the business; I believe I am fortunate to be working for him and really appreciate the opportunity to work here.

I plan to pursue a career in business administration and I believe this job is a good starting point in that direction.

SALESPERSON, MORTGAGE FIRM

I am a salesperson for a mortgage loan audit firm. I solicit mortgage bankers, savings and loans, and commercial banks to use the services of the company. I do 98% of my sales efforts over the phone. I prospect for new customers 1-2 hours. I send letters to all prospects and then follow up with a phone call. I also control our advertising efforts in national public relations. When I am waiting for calls back, I help the clerical staff.

To perform well at this type of work you need a thorough knowledge of mortgage lending, and sales ability in knowing how to get to the decision maker, how to handle objections, and how to ask for the business.

The service we provide is needed and appreciated by our customers. It is not nearly as stressful as other work I have done. Since I am on straight commission, I have the freedom to schedule my own time.

Given another chance to choose a career, I would choose this again.

I would find my job more satisfying if I owned a portion of the company (with other employees), so that I could be involved in decision making.

After graduating from college with a bachelor of science degree, I started my career in the group health claims business. I have also sold real estate. I had this experience in real estate and insurance when an old friend offered me a job as a mortgage guaranty insurance salesman. I then worked for a number of mortgage companies as a loan officer and as branch manager.

I would like to continue my career in the mortgage lending business. I regularly attend courses and take new courses in the general area of real estate finance to broaden my knowledge.

SALESPERSON, NATURAL FOOD PRODUCTS

While working in an administrative position in a sales group, I found I had a knack for dealing with people. I applied to a firm looking for entry level sales people and got my start in this career.

As a salesperson handling natural food products, I sell to manufacturers, distributors and retailers. Part of the process of selling the product is turning up the leads and qualifying the potential buyers. My kind of sales work is very hectic. I must continually make new contacts and remain enthusiastic and optimistic. It is also important to be detail-oriented, organized, and self-motivated in order to perform well as a salesperson.

I am so confident that sales work is the ideal career for me that even if given the opportunity to start over and prepare for any kind of work, I would again choose this.

I am not satisfied with the people and organization I work for, but I definitely like the kind of work, the people I work with and the opportunity for advancement. I enjoy working with people and view sales as "helping" people to fulfill their needs.

My future career plans are to stay in sales and eventually manage a sales group.

SALESPERSON, OFFICE EQUIPMENT & SYSTEMS

As a salesman of office equipment/systems/supplies I call on and service accounts. Another basic responsibility is developing new accounts.

I am used to working hard. Prior to this job, I was a soldier, truck driver, and dock worker. I did not have any educational training for this position other than a high school diploma. I was offered this job because it is part of a family business, and I have found it to be the kind of work I like.

The skills and attitudes which I consider important for a sales job of the kind I have are: speech and memory skills, self motivation, and the ability to work well with people. I get a good feeling from my work by helping people. It also is monetarily rewarding.

SALESPERSON, PRINT ADVERTISING

As a print advertising salesperson, I sell advertisements to companies. Actually, my philosophy is that I sell ads to companies "wishing to grow." I work for a magazine publisher and sell ad space. My typical activities include making phone calls to clients, problem solving pertaining to ads and invoices, letter writing, personal sales calls, and prospecting.

My educational background includes a bachelor's degree in agriculture and business. Prior to my advertising sales job, I worked as a truck driver and for the family retail business. I landed this job 5 years ago and have found it to be very satisfying work.

The qualities which I find necessary to perform this kind of work well are listening skills, verbal communication skills, a positive attitude, patience, and the ability to see the big picture.

I like almost every aspect of this work.

I find that this work meets my own needs because I am helping other people succeed and I am making friends. I am also living comfortably because of this work.

My future career plans are to move into sales management and eventually to become publisher of my own periodical.

SCHOOL ADMINISTRATOR #1

After nine years of teaching I moved into administration as school district administrator and coordinator of curriculum and instruction. My typical duties now include meeting with the district superintendent and other administrators for planning, implementation and evaluation, meeting with groups of teachers, acting on meeting outcomes. The job basically involves much planning, putting out "fires" and handling problems.

To perform well in this kind of work it is important to have a positive attitude about people's ability to perform. You should have a belief that change is important and know how to foster it. Focus on optimism and have a can-do attitude.

It is rewarding to feel that I can make a difference in education today through my work. I get satisfaction from helping teachers and therefore students succeed in their educational process. I feel good about promoting positive change in education.

I need more hours in the day! I am almost too busy with much pressure and feel frustrated sometimes because I feel the superintendent is not decisive enough. However, basically I'm satisfied and like my work very much.

To become a teacher I earned a bachelor of science degree in education. I have also earned my master's in education. I decided to become a certified administrator after taking on leadership roles while teaching.

I am unsure of my future career plans although I feel there are opportunities for advancement for me. Perhaps I will become a principal so I will have more single building involvement or become an assistant superintendent for curriculum and instruction.

SCHOOL ADMINISTRATOR #2

I started out my career in education as a teacher and have worked my way up through education and job experience to independent school administrator. I have earned two bachelor's degrees and a Masters in Education degree. Before teaching, I was in business as a trainee.

It is my responsibility as school administrator to administer programs, facilities, and employees for a 1200 student school. Thirty percent of my time is spent handling personnel issues. Forty percent of my work day involves paperwork, and the remaining thirty percent is spent doing public relations work.

For this kind of work, it is important to have balance, perspective, and judgment.

I like almost every aspect of my work, including the organization I work for, the people I work with, the opportunity for advancement, and the kind of work I do. If given a chance to start over and again choose a career, I would again choose school administration as my occupation. I find satisfaction in being a part of the growth of an individual.

SCHOOL COUNSELOR, HIGH SCHOOL

Every day is different in my job as a school counselor. I hold group counseling sessions, conduct testing, and keep records. I attend many kinds of meetings comprised of administrators, individual students, parents, and teachers. In group testing, I evaluate the results and report these results to students, teachers, the administration, and to the public. I also plan various activities for groups.

A school counselor must be a very patient and caring person. You need strong listening skills and solid communication skills. It's also very important to be knowledgeable about tests and about how to apply their results.

In my work, I most like helping others. I enjoy the people and the school together with the work itself. I do not like all the paperwork and the fact that there is little opportunity for advancement.

I've done restaurant work and I've taught. After teaching a few years, I realized the need for student counseling in the school system. I earned a Master of Arts degree in counseling and have been in the field for 14 years.

SCHOOL DISTRICT ADMINISTRATOR

Involved in the field of education for thirteen years, I now work as Administrator in a school district central office; I am the Director of Special Projects. My work encompasses many areas: coordinator of the at-risk program, coordinator of the business partnership program, planning new schools, parent and staff development, and coordinator of the volunteer program. I accomplish many of my tasks using the phone; written documents for planning , grants, reports, and budget articles; and meetings with staff, community members, or other administrators.

To succeed in my profession you must be creative, flexible, visionary, and giving; must care about kids and education; and have some form of administrative experience--I have eight years experience as a high school principal. Of course, education is an essential element in your background; my credentials include Bachelor of Arts in Business Education, Master of Arts in Educational Administration, and Doctor of Education in Educational Leadership.

I enjoy the autonomy, chance for creativity, and opportunity to help others succeed; I love everything about my job, especially helping children and parents plan for the future.

I was inspired to pursue a career in education by a high school teacher who gave me the opportunity to teach the class.

I plan to remain in school administration and I would perhaps like to write a book at some time in the near future.

SCHOOL LIBRARIAN #1

As a child, I lived only one block away from a very good public library which became my second home. I learned a great deal there, was allowed to help out and eventually "worked" there. I worked in my college library, too, and was fortunate to have a cousin who was a librarian and who encouraged me. My mother read to me a great deal and both of my parents revered "learning."

My work as a school librarian, media specialist, and teacher involves helping people locate information; being a source of information; working with all forms of recorded knowledge and AV equipment; constant selection and organization of program materials, budget work, publicity, decorations and displays; teaching library skills; relations and responsibilities as a faculty member; constant interchange with students, faculty, staff, and parents; organization and administration of department and program; working with people and "things."

You must enjoy working with people and enjoy helping them. Attention to detail and organizational ability are very important. A good background in the library and AV field (including computers and latest technology) is necessary. Also, a school librarian should have a sense of service and accountability to the taxpayers, and a professional attitude, as well as an inquisitive nature and knowing where to find information.

If I could change anything about this occupation, it would be to have more budget money, more paid help, and more hours in a day!

I particularly enjoy the challenges of my work. It is satisfying to be able to help others. I enjoy the friendliness and warm rapport with students, staff, and community. The sense of accomplishment at the close of the day is truly gratifying as well as the feeling that I have returned to others what has been so freely given to me.

SCHOOL LIBRARIAN #2

I started out my career in education as a classroom teacher. After receiving my Masters in Library Science degree, I have worked as a bookmobile librarian, a public library librarian, and an academic librarian. I am now continuing my studies in order to qualify for library administration work.

As a school librarian, I instruct students in library use, act as reader's advisor, and administer all aspects of library operations. A typical work day includes: recording the previous days stats, coding new books, shelving and processing books, monitoring study halls, assisting students in research, recommending reading to students, teaching library skills lessons, delivering AV equipment, taping off educational T.V., filing catalog cards, etc.

As well as the education background required for this profession, I consider patience and organizational skills to be the most important in order to perform this work well.

My major frustration as a school librarian is with other school personnel who allow the library area to be used as a holding area when no substitute or teacher is available. I would also like to see more money spent on library needs.

I like my occupation because of the person I work for, the kind of work I do, and the people I work with. It is satisfying for me when I am creating lessons that students enjoy and in finding information to fit the needs of students and staff.

SCHOOL LIBRARY MEDIA SPECIALIST

I love my work as a school library media specialist! My interest in this field started when I worked in a public library during high school. I earned my Bachelor of Science in Elementary Education degree and worked as a school teacher for several years. I left teaching to become a full-time homemaker while my children were small. I then earned my Masters in Library Science degree and finally started to work in the career which I knew I would like.

As a media specialist, I manage, teach, work with faculty and students, support curriculum, make book selections, do inventories, and manage computers. I serve the library and audiovisual needs for a faculty of 56 and student body of 654, including computer use. My routine activities include: answering reference questions, giving assistance when needed, maintaining records, teaching library skills, and troubleshooting machines.

To perform well at this library work, you must be service-oriented, organized but flexible, pay attention to details, have computer skills, have verbal and written communication skills, and have people skills.

The most frustrating part of my work has been the serious budget constraints under which I must work. I always need more help and am always running out of time to do all that I want to do. Because more information is generated all the time and technology is constantly changing, it is very hard to keep on top of things.

I like almost every aspect of this work which I have been doing for 18 years. I find it satisfying helping both adults and students. I do not anticipate making any career changes. I do plan to keep learning how to do my job better and to continue to learn new technologies.

SCHOOL PRINCIPAL

With an Associate degree in liberal arts, a Bachelor of Science, and a Master of Arts, I serve as a school principal in an elementary school. I set goals and make and implement plans for long-range improvement. My duties include resolving conflict as well as evaluating and supervising teachers.

Reward for my work comes with affirmation from the school community when a job has been done well. I particularly enjoy seeing "the light go on" for students and active, enlightening discussion with my peers is a source of pleasure. I also enjoy the opportunities to identify new ways to teach.

A school principal must be an effective communicator. Competency, flexibility, and an open mind are essential to this job. One also must be a visionary and a risk-taker who is able to set goals. Being a hard-working, organized person who has high values and a commitment to his calling is very important. This work requires a caring person who has strong interpersonal skills.

I came into this profession because of my parents who thoroughly enjoyed their teaching careers. I like my work, but it would be more rewarding if there were less criticism from outside forces and more commitment from society regarding the importance of education. Having more time to contemplate problems and determine their solutions would make my work more satisfying. My plans are to move into district or county administration where there is more control, or "voice," in achieving educational goals.

My work includes observing instructional practices and students. I resolve faculty and student conflict as well as manage maintenance of the facility. I'm responsible for fiscal planning, budgeting, and expenses. Working with colleagues, planning for school improvement, and devising activities to enhance involvement of the school committee are part of my duties. There is also a great deal of paperwork in my job.

SCIENTIST & ENGINEER

As a scientist/engineer I organize and manage a small highly-skilled technical group to perform energy research and development. There is no typical day. In fact, I find it annoying at times to justify my activities and account for my time because in research you don't know where your work will lead you.

I got into this profession 14 years ago because I studied physics while in college. I have earned both the bachelor's and the master's degrees.

To do well in research and development, it is important to have perseverance, patience, and the ability to concentrate and work with constant interruptions and background noises.

Except for some personality conflicts and shortage of funding, I like most things about my work which I have been doing for 14 years.

Accomplishing new state-of-the-art advances and presenting the completed research at technical meetings are the rewards of my profession.

SECRETARY #1

I like the kind of work I do as a secretary for a lumber company. I keep the inventory of the lumber and handle shipping, invoices, barge shipments and the telephone. On a typical work day, I input the previous day's inventory, answer the phones, make coffee, do invoices, put inventory tickets away, type letters, and clean up the kitchen.

To perform well at this kind of secretarial work, it is important to have a good attitude, phone ability and computer skills.

Other jobs I have had since graduating from high school have been as a fast food worker, housewife, and secretary.

I like this kind of work. I enjoy the people I work with and the organization and people I work for. However, I do feel there is a lack of opportunity for advancement. I intend to continue to work in an office and eventually to gain the skills necessary for a bookkeeping position.

SECRETARY #2

I am a civil service secretary with an additional title of chairman of a technical board. I started out as a temporary secretary for a government contractor and learned as I went along about the program. I was then hired by the Air Force to work with this same job assignment. I have worked my way up from secretary to the chairman job. As such, I organize and identify software problems and manage a database of them. I am a communication link between the Air Force and contractor.

Although I have not found it necessary to have a college degree or formal technical training for my work, you must develop computer skills. I consider organizational and communication skills to be also very necessary. You must have a secret clearance with the government as well. Confidence is another requirement.

I like almost everything about my work, the people and organization I work for, the kind of work, the opportunity for advancement, and the people I work with. It is excellent to be appreciated for what I accomplish, and that is so with this job. It is also extremely interesting to me.

I plan to stay in my current field, but switch back to working for the contractor when the project gets turned over to him. I would like to become a software engineer and continue running the software reporting and database management.

SECRETARY #3

I basically like to work and have demonstrated this to my employers. My initial job after graduating from high school was as a manager of a video store. After several years, I had been promoted to executive manager of seven video stores. I then moved out of state and found a job as a telemarketer. This company took notice of my industriousness and I was promoted to secretary.

My basic responsibilities as the secretary of a telemarketing company are to do typing, filing, and answering the front office phone. My typical day starts at 9:00 a.m. and includes: sending information to clients, calling clients, preparing a recap record of what programs were worked on the previous day, and answering the phone. I try to do what is expected of me in order to help the office function smoothly.

To perform secretarial work well, the following skills and attitudes are important: be pleasant, have good English and spelling, good typing, and familiarity with Word Perfect and Lotus.

Aside from disliking to deal with unhappy clients, I like this kind of work very much.

I find satisfaction from this work when my boss says, "Thank you." I also find satisfaction in helping someone with their job.

SECRETARY #4

As a copier sales secretary for three and one-half years, I type sales proposals, handle general correspondence with the aid of a computer, answer sales lead calls, and perform other miscellaneous office duties.

To be successful in my position, you should have a high school education and be capable of very good English and grammar usage. In addition, you must have typing skills and all around good clerical skills, the ability to get along with many types of people, good phone skills, and some basic computer skills.

I like most of the people I work with. I take pride in knowing I am good at what I do. I really enjoy working for a well-known, reputable company; we sell reliable equipment and it is easy for me to believe in our product.

I chose to work in a sales environment because I enjoy the fast pace of a sales department.

I plan to remain in the secretarial field, perhaps working in an art department, where I believe more of my creative talents would be utilized.

SECRETARY #5

I find that my job as a secretary offers me the satisfaction of helping people and doing a job well. I took secretarial courses in high school because I knew at that time that this was the career field I was interested in. I have worked at other jobs such as hostessing in a restaurant, seamstress work, supervising children in school, and as a telephone operator, but secretarial work seems to suit me best.

As a secretary, I handle clerical duties, answer the phone and do word processing. I also act as the receptionist, greeting people as they enter the company office. In order to perform this kind of work well, it is important to have accuracy and neatness in your work, a pleasant personality, dependability, and to be trustworthy.

Although I like most aspects of my work, I have found there to be a lack of opportunity for advancement. I do like the organization and people I work for and the kind of work I do.

Because I also have an interest in various arts and crafts, I am considering trying to find a job at some point in my career where I can pursue these interests and use my acquired skills.

SECRETARY #6

I have found that I like secretarial work and particularly my current position as secretary to a college vice president of finance and operations. I chose this job because I enjoy working with students, I had the skills necessary for the position from previous job experience, and the school offers excellent educational benefits for me and my family.

As a secretary, I do typing, answer the telephone, handle billing, and work with students, parents, faculty and staff. My primary responsibility is to address the immediate needs of my boss. Beyond these duties, I also work with the rest of the staff in the finance and operations department in a team effort to keep the school running smoothly.

As well as office skills, it is important to have good interpersonal skills and a professional telephone manner in order to perform well in this secretarial position.

I like almost every aspect of my working including the kind of work I do, the people I work with, and the people and organization I work for. The only major drawback is the lack of opportunity for advancement. There is satisfaction for me in this work when I see that the college is running successfully. I feel part of this success. Having students satisfied with the job performance of the staff is also gratifying.

SECRETARY AND INVENTORY CLERK

For the past two years, I have been in charge of stock received, payments for invoices related to stock, and the input of purchase orders. My job titles are secretary , inventory clerk, accounts payable clerk, and purchasing clerk.

Although there are not many opportunities for advancement within this organization, I like the company I work for, my boss, and this kind of work.

In addition to at least an Associate degree in Accounting, my job requires good communication skills, math skills and the desire to work with numbers, plus self-motivation.

I like my job very much, and I believe that enjoying a job is the best reason to do it.

Previously, I worked as a supervisor in a factory environment and as a trainer in quality control.

The aspects of my job that have involved training others have been so rewarding for me that I may return to college to earn the certification to teach. If I change my career direction to the field of education, I will most likely get involved in teaching math.

SECRETARY, COLLEGE DEPARTMENT

I went to business school and learned basic skills. With that I have advanced myself professionally and have always been recommended for all positions I have had. My philosophy has always been to do a good job at whatever task I tackle, which seems to be the key for a satisfying career life. I have always liked whatever position I've been in.

As the administrative assistant/executive secretary in the psychology department of a college, I handle various administrative and secretarial duties. More specifically my job involves: being in close contact with students for things like academic advising; arranging conferences; supervising graduate assists; secretarial duties like correspondence and organizing paperwork; budgeting for the department (travel, equipment, supplies, etc.)

Administrative and secretarial skills are necessary for the work that I do. I also think it is necessary to like the academic world, be able to work at a fast pace, and like people.

I like almost every aspect of my work.

I find it particularly enjoyable to work in the academic environment and to work with college students.

SECRETARY, MEDICAL

As the secretary in a medical office, it is my job to greet the patients, pull their charts and log them in. I handle filling out and submitting of insurance forms. It is also my responsibility to set up the office schedule including making the patient's appointments.

After graduating from high school, I did general office work in the accounting department of a bank and also was a keypunch operator. My job as a secretary in a medical office started out as a part-time Saturday job, and I was then asked to work full-time.

I like this kind of work very much, the doctor I work for, and the people I work with. However, there is generally a lack of opportunity for advancement. I do have the opportunity to become an ophthalmic assistant, but I am satisfied with the managerial part of my current job. I receive satisfaction from satisfied patients and always doing my job well.

SECRETARY, OFFICE CLERK

In my three years as a secretary/clerk, I have found that I do not always have enough to keep me busy, perhaps because I have learned my job so well. My primary responsibilities are typing and filing, data entry, sending faxes, answering phones, and designing computer spreadsheets.

I like my job very much and if I could go back in time, I would choose this job again.

My position requires a high school education and good secretarial and people skills. This position requires a good knowledge of computers, adequate filing system knowledge, and the ability to concentrate with people all around in a sometimes hectic work environment.

I enjoy the people I work with and the whole organization of the company I work for; I work for a nice boss and I believe when one is working for the right person, it makes all the difference. I like secretarial work and I can see many opportunities for future advancement within this company. My boss gives me a lot of opportunity to learn more about the company. I get involved in presentations, and accomplishing a task for a presentation gives me a lot of job satisfaction. There is a real sense of team spirit in my department--we all try to make the boss look good, because we all know that when we make the boss look good, it makes the entire group look good, too.

I plan to further my education and gain more knowledge of computers and then maybe I can grow into a position where I deal with more computers.

SECRETARY/RECEPTIONIST #1

I actually consider myself having two jobs, one paid and one unpaid. I am paid to be a secretary/receptionist and unpaid for my wife and mother job. A friend recommended me for the job at the doctor's office because she realized I had office experience as administrative assistant to the manager of a health and welfare fund. As my daughter has grown, so do my hours at work. Actually, I like both jobs very much.

The doctors I work for see approximately 36 patients or more a day. The phones ring constantly and the Medicare paperwork is relentless. The office is really too busy for just one person but too small physically to accommodate more than one.

I like my hectic job because I like 98% of the patients, the doctors I work for, and the kind of work I do. I am very happy when a patient who has been very ill makes a complete recovery.

SECRETARY/RECEPTIONIST #2

I had selected my career path early in life and took the business classes in high school to prepare me for secretarial/office/computer work. I chose it because I consider it to be a very stable occupation. There is always a need for secretaries and computer operators.

As a secretary/computer operator, I handle general office work, data entry and operate the computer. It is very hectic work because of all the deadlines which must be met. My work also requires me to juggle several tasks at once. In order to perform this kind of work well, it is important to have accuracy, confidentiality, patience, knowledge of computers, good typing speed, and the ability to work well with others.

I have been in this occupation for 12 years and have found that I like my job very much in general. However, I am dissatisfied with the people I work for, and the lack of opportunity for advancement. Despite these drawbacks, I do derive satisfaction from the good pay, fair medical insurance, and seeing the good results due to my hard work and excellent skills.

Someday I hope to work up to a managerial level position.

SECRETARY/TECHNICAL ASSISTANT

I always thought I wanted to do secretarial work, and after working in this occupation for 9 years I have found that this is indeed the right kind of work for me.

As a secretary/technical assistant, I do typing, plot graphs and charts on the computer, and procure authorizations on various properties for approval to do work. My daily activities include: distributing and forwarding the mail; sending letters to property owners; logging in approved and disapproved work orders; answering the telephone; handling inquiries; running plots and graphs; and recording sick time and vacation days for all office employees. I consider it my prime responsibility to be always available.

To perform secretarial work well, you should have a willingness to change from one job to another even though the first task is not complete. Having P.C. (personal computer) skills is also necessary for this kind of work.

I have worked at other jobs such as sales, manufacturing, and answering service work, and have found secretarial work satisfies me the most. I like the people I work for, the people I work with, the opportunity for advancement, and the kind of work I do. I find satisfaction from obtaining approvals for work which shows that I have done my job and now the rest of the work can proceed.

I plan to stay in this career and work up to a higher secretarial level, and eventually to the managerial level.

SECURITIES BROKER

I've been working in securities for 25 years, which has provided me with much experience. Currently, I am a securities broker specializing in syndicate-underwriting operations.

My job includes working with corporate finance associates to structure new securities underwritings. I interact with legal counsel, banks, and other brokerage firms. I assist syndicate trading desks to monitor trading as well as to balance security positions and profit and loss.

A strong knowledge of the securities industry and the rules and regulations is essential. A clear understanding of the end result and ways to achieve same is essential. Contacts with other professionals and keeping up with changing products is very important. You must be able to adapt to pressure situations, keep others calm, and put the work in order of appropriate priorities.

Job satisfaction for me is successfully closing and underwriting millions of dollars worth of business with the least possible problem. I'm pretty much in charge of the whole process; it is for me alone to succeed or fail. Actually, I'm very satisfied with my job. But, sometimes, I think my work is so good people expect the excellence and take my talent for granted. Everybody wants a pat on the back. I have not found that my lack of a college degree is a problem; I entered low in a brokerage and worked my way up by getting experience.

Eventually, I would like to be in charge of a group of professionals whom I have selected. Together, we'd develop the ultimate syndicated operations department on Wall Street and use state-of-the-art tracking systems.

SEISMOLOGIST/GEOPHYSICIST

I have spent 40+ years in my career as a seismologist/geophysicist primarily in basic research and teaching. I started out as a physics major in college, but wanted to branch off from pure physics, so I went into geophysics. I continued my studies in this field and have obtained my Ph.D.

My work now is quite varied and depends to a large degree on the funds I am able to obtain for research. I no longer do teaching. Rather, my time is spent on research and different projects, in meetings, consulting, and some work at sea.

To perform my type of work well, you need adequate professional training, the ability to make decisions, good health, and the ability to work well with others.

The major frustration I am now dealing with is that research funding is tight and economic rewards could be better. A great deal of effort goes into obtaining funds rather than into the research itself. This does not deter me, however, because this is the kind of work I like to do. I have found this challenging and interesting especially when I obtain a new insight into the phenomena being studied.

SENIOR DATA TERMINAL OPERATOR

The work of a senior data terminal operator is to ensure that the computer system is working, to print out work schedules, and assist users with computer and material problems. For seven years, my daily schedule has included opening the computer room, making sure all communication lines are up and running, running reports, and delivering those reports to the intended persons.

Although I recommend some formal training in computers, to be successful in this kind of work, you must also possess good communication skills, accuracy, the ability to work well with a variety of different people, and the ability to function independently and make decisions.

Even though I don't see many opportunities for career advancement within this organization, I like my job and the kind of work I do. Most of all, I find satisfaction comes from completing my work and helping others.

I first became interested in computers from a high school teacher. My first job after graduating from high school was in the file department of this company; after six months and much persistence, I was promoted to my current position.

I am planning to return to school eventually and further my education in the field of business and computers.

SENIOR DESIGN ENGINEER

My career started while serving as an electrician apprentice in a shipyard in the U.S. Navy. After leaving the service, I attended college and earned a Bachelor of Science in Electrical Engineering degree. Now in industry, I work as a senior design engineer.

My responsibilities include designing capacitors to customers' specifications, resolving field problems, and working with sales in product development and promotion. Typically, my daily/weekly activities are: going through the incoming mail; selecting the programming to be done to prepare rough designs; making cost estimates and giving necessary information to sales for response for quotation to customers' specification; working with manufacturing in problems arising during construction of a new design; working with quality control on test specifications and allowable tolerances; telling the boss why the product development report isn't ready; attending meetings to determine the design and cost of a new unit for a multi-million dollar quotation, etc.

A good working relation with all personnel involved in the product, sales, manufacturing, quality control, production control, engineering, etc. is critical to performing this kind of work well. You should also have a good working knowledge of the various fields and skills involved in the product. I am primarily in electrical engineering, but I must be well versed in mechanical and chemical matters. I must also have knowledge of manufacturing methods and what can be made with our existing facilities. I have liked my career and still do, and that includes especially the people with whom I work. I get my satisfaction from this work by contributing to advances in state-of-the-art in my field.

SENIOR PERSONNEL ASSISTANT

I think that my enjoyment of people has led me into this career in personnel work. Prior to this I was a nurse's aide. I started as a secretary for the company I am now with and transferred into personnel.

As the senior personnel assistant, I administer various insurance, savings and pension plans. My work also includes counseling employees.

Except for the lack of opportunity for advancement, I like every aspect of my job including the people I work with, the kind of work I do, and the people and organization for whom I work. I have found that in order to perform well in personnel work it is essential to have the ability to deal well with people and to have a positive attitude.

My career plans for the future are to move into human services work.

SENIOR PROGRAM DIRECTOR

With experience teaching at the college level plus package goods production management, I was the perfect candidate for a job combining both abilities. I found this position by pursuing a lead in The New York Times. Having earned my M.A. and M.B.A. degrees was also important. As a senior program director of a management association, I conduct seminars for executives in strategic planning. I develop, write and teach general management seminars to middle and senior managers of major corporations. In addition, I have a faculty of 25 facilitators who work for me teaching my seminars all over the country. Needless to say, problems involving all these factors are dealt with daily.

To perform my kind of work, it is important to have interpersonal and intellectual ability, and a genuine altruism toward wanting others to be more educated and skilled at their jobs. Also, excellent public speaking skills are essential.

My job satisfaction comes from knowing that I am making a difference in terms of job performance by these executives. I plan to grow and advance vertically with my company and to continue teaching as an adjunct marketing professor.

SENIOR PROGRAMMER/ANALYST

I enjoy the sense of accomplishment I have from acquiring the technical skills and achieving success as a programmer/analyst. I have gone to night school to become educated in this field. Prior to this kind of work, I was in farming and in the Air Force. I got my start in the computer industry as an analyst for a Department of Defense firm after being discharged from the Air Force. As a senior programmer/analyst, I do computer analysis and design programs. It is a multistage process starting with determining the output specifications upon receiving the project/program assignment. Analyzing available data, usually with the end-user is also part of the initial phase. The middle phase is to code the program(s), followed by testing. The final step is to install/deliver the completed program(s) to the end-user(s).

Good communication skills are imperative for this kind of work, as well as good working technical knowledge. I believe an upbeat, confident attitude helps instill confidence in your users.

In addition to the satisfaction I get from producing a program, I also enjoy my job because I enjoy working with people (corny as that sounds).

I like the basic job, but could be more satisfied if I had a better working relationship with management. I feel that management sometimes gets in the way of good project design development.

I am as ambitious as the next guy. One of the problems with a technical career path is that you reach a pinnacle. Once this is reached, technical advancement ends. Hence, management must become your career path if you wish to continue upward.

SENIOR PROJECT ENGINEER/PROJECT MANAGER

As a Senior Project Engineer/Project Manager for testing and evaluation of military systems, I develop test concepts, oversee test planning, and manage task resources. This involves the review of military system employment concepts, system requirements and specifications, operating environments, and operating procedures. I develop test and evaluation concepts, designs, and test plans. The assessment of threat system, instrumentation, data processing, analytical techniques, and player force requirements for testing are also part of my responsibilities. I also write plans, progress reports, and studies.

Work of this nature requires a sound engineering background, experience using military systems, writing skills, computer literacy, interpersonal skills, and an objective attitude. I have also earned Master of Science and Bachelor of Science degrees. My background includes twenty-seven years as an Air Force Officer and two and one-half years as a management consultant.

My rewards are derived from the development of tests for complex systems that evaluate their effectiveness. Providing the necessary information and participating in the improvement of military systems is also satisfying. I know my work is worthwhile.

I would like to get more involved with clients to gain a better understanding of the projects from their point of view.

I plan to stay on this career path and gain more responsibility and experience in my present position.

SENIOR QUALITY ENGINEER

I have found my career to be satisfying as it has developed through various promotional stages. I earned a Bachelor of Science in Biology and a Masters of Science in Chemistry. With this educational background, I obtained a chemist position in a corporate research and development department. Because of my math/statistics background, I was promoted to the corporate quality department to plan and implement long term goals and programs for chemical water treatment. I moved to another company and became the senior quality engineer involved in the manufacturing of circuit boards.

As a quality engineer, it is my responsibility to do the long term quality plans, quality administration, and administer returns and customer service. The majority of my work week (70%) is spent interacting with my staff to develop a quality program. Ten percent of my time is devoted to customer returns and twenty percent to a variety of other duties including meetings with other departments.

This kind of work requires a strong educational background with a minimum of a bachelor's degree in statistics, math and technical training.

I enjoy my job very much. I feel productive being able to see the final outcome of my projects. Job satisfaction for me is seeing positive results and comments from customers.

My plans for the future include obtaining a Masters in Business Administration within the next two years. I then hope to assume a position in management requiring a technology/management degree and then to a higher level position in a new technology type department in quality/engineering.

SENIOR TECHNICAL WRITER

I wanted to be a journalist but fell into job training at the organization where I worked part-time during college. This job evolved into computer systems design and implementation. Both positions required a great deal of writing; training manuals, procedural and system documentation, which I enjoyed. Given a choice now between journalist and technical writer I would now choose technical writer.

As senior technical writer, I plan, develop, create and implement various written materials (manuals, promotional materials, etc.). I am currently working on 6 projects. Therefore, I need to decide, based on deadlines, which project to work on. It also depends on the stage each project is in. I may spend a whole day writing or the next in meetings analyzing procedures or work flow.

To perform well as a technical writer, it is necessary to have research, analysis, and interviewing skills. You must be very organized. It is essential that you are able to write clearly based on the target audience. Editing is an important skill. Additionally, you must be able to look at things in various lights.

If I were given the chance to change something about my occupation to make it more satisfying, it would be to increase the level of corporate commitment to spending time and money for quality documentation. Aside from this frustration, I like my kind of work very much, the people I work for, and the people I work with. I find job satisfaction in creating something useful that did not previously exist and working closely and independently with diverse occupations. In fact, someday I plan to work freelance.

SERVICE REPRESENTATIVE

I enrolled in business classes in high school where I gained the skills which I needed to start my career in business. As a customer service representative for an insurance company, my major responsibility is helping customers with their insurance questions or problems. I also am given some bookkeeping tasks. Much of my work is performed by telephone communication or by sending letters.

Typing and math skills are required for this type of work. Because the nature of this job is interacting with people, good communication and people skills are necessary. Also, having a good attitude toward your work is a key to performing well.

I like the kind of work I do and find job satisfaction from helping other people with their problems. Because I like the people I work with and the organization I work for, I plan to stay with the company. However, I would like more variety and challenge in the work I do, so I am hoping for an advancement.

SHIPPER

As a shipper, I package, palletize, and ship 45,000 lbs. of utility hardware every day all over the U.S.A. Eighty percent of my day is spent assembling, packaging, and loading this hardware into the trailer trucks; the rest of the day I assemble export orders. Most of the cartons weigh from 65 to 140 lbs, although some of the hardware, such as the steel rods, may weigh up to 1,000 lbs. It takes some engineering to get these 12-24 feet hardware items on the 8 feet wide trailers. The export orders going to South America or the Middle East must be assembled, crated, secured, identified, weighed, and dimensioned.

The skills that are important for performing this kind of work are knowledge of driving, balancing the weight in the trailer, and math. You have to work carefully because you are working around 15 other drivers. Being familiar with the complete product line and identifying the products by identification codes is necessary. I consider it important to know what the boss wants and to try to do the work even better than he/she expects. You should be willing to assist other co-workers when help is needed. The No. 1 priority is safety in this very fast-paced working area.

I have worked at other jobs with the U.S. Post Office, a pharmaceutical distributor, newspaper, musical instrument factory, but found more satisfaction in being the third generation to work at this company. It is also gratifying to earn a good hourly wage; working with good co-workers, bosses, and office staff; 3-weeks of vacation; and double time pay when called for emergency shipments.

I enjoy traveling, and the good thing about this job is that it provides the money and vacation time to continue to pursue traveling and photography which is "in my blood," and makes possible return trips to Australia, New Zealand, Norway, and Finland.

I received some of my training for this work while in the military, and perhaps that is where I got the travel bug.

SHIPPING CLERK

For 18 years, I've been a shipping clerk in a furniture factory. Previously, after high school, I worked several jobs, including being a self-employed truck driver, which I also enjoyed very much. But, as a shipping clerk, I like meeting people, the customers, and the drivers who bring in the freight.

My job is to organize, supervise, and help load furniture cargo into boxcars and trailers. I am responsible for billing as well as seeing that the furniture gets where it is supposed to go. It is my job to fill orders from the warehouse or from the production line. I calculate weights for the crates of furniture and make out bills of lading for them as they are being loaded.

It is a rewarding job because it gives me a sense of accomplishment at the end of the day. I do regret there are no opportunities for advancement. Also, it would be easier and more pleasurable if there were enough mechanical equipment to help with the heavy lifting.

A shipping clerk needs substantial knowledge of geography. You also need strong mathematical skills. Physical fitness, of course, is essential with all the lifting.

SKI RACER AND COACH

I was a successful ski racer, and after my days on the U.S. Team were over, I was chosen to coach at a well established ski academy in the East. After 4 years there, I moved to another academy in the mountains of Idaho where I now coach elite juniors (12 to 18 years old) in cross-country skiing.

My background includes a bachelor's degree in exercise physiology, and work as a teacher at a private boarding school teaching biology, physiology, and photography. I have also worked as a camp counselor teaching horseback riding, and as a sporting goods salesperson.

As a ski coach, my responsibilities include working out and teaching techniques to the students, ordering ski equipment, and organizing trips to races. My day starts early in order for me to have time to work out myself. After my work out, I go to the office to make phone calls, order equipment, and do the necessary work to organize the trips. In the afternoon, I work out with the juniors I am coaching.

To perform this kind of work well, it is important to have insight, patience, a desire to teach and learn, and the ability to pick out flaws and good parts of technique.

I like the kind of work I do very much. The only drawback is the lack of opportunity for advancement. Aside from that, I like the organization and people I work for, the people I work with, and the work itself. I find job satisfaction in happy skiers, improving in technique, and in getting the jobs done.

I plan to continue coaching youngsters and adults for the U.S. Ski Team, as well as doing some personal coaching. I also foresee a time when I might want to settle down with a more professional, thinking-type job, but I will not do that for quite a while into the future.

SMALL BUSINESS OWNER AND CO-EDITOR, NEWSPAPER

I am the owner of a small business and co-editor of a local newspaper.

A typical day includes answering phone calls, scheduling appointments, paying bills and performing bookkeeping tasks for my small business. As a co-editor of a newspaper, a day might include covering local events, typing up copy, making phone calls, checking facts, taking photographs, and helping with new advertising copy and lay-out.

It is important that I have diplomacy, creativity, and lots of energy to perform my jobs well. As an outcome of my efforts, I am building a good reputation for my business with return customers. Seeing the finished newspaper and receiving community support is a satisfying aspect of my newspaper work.

I would like to have more part-time help rather than my having to do everything involved in this job. (I also run a small business out of my house involving scheduling and bookkeeping.) My spouse helps me, but still more help is needed.

SOCIAL GERONTOLOGIST

I've always loved being around old people, especially my grandparents. So I earned my Bachelor of Science degree in social rehabilitation and a Master of Arts degree in social gerontology and became a social gerontologist. I am the director of social services in a home health agency.

I enjoyed previous occupations as a secretary, an administrative assistant, and a psych/geriatric ward clerk. Now, and for the past 8 years, I've liked working on my own with minimal supervision. I share the management philosophy of my group and I appreciate my coworkers, particularly the forward thinking owner of the agency. There are opportunities for advancement for which I'm glad.

This work requires skills in problem-solving, training, organization, and good written and verbal communication. Computer skills are a plus. A person must enjoy the elderly, be adaptable, and like performing a variety of duties.

I'd like to be able to become more organized and better handle constant interruptions. Eventually, I'd like to study marketing and also take computer classes. I want to study photography and do a photo book featuring old people.

SOCIAL SERVICES ADMINISTRATOR

I am now a social service administrator for a state department of children and youth services. Prior to this I had a variety of other career experiences as a marketing consultant, a retail cosmetic salesperson, and a military police officer. I have received my Bachelor of Arts in Communications degree and am now a candidate for my Masters of Art in Religious Studies degree.

A basic job description for my social services administrator position is that I develop programs and services for children and families, and manage foster care and adoption for our region. My daily schedule usually includes reading mail, going to meetings, returning phone calls, planning events/programs, handling crises, listening to folks' problems, and writing memoranda.

I consider the following skills and attitudes important for this social service position: flexibility, good reading, writing and speaking skills, a sense of humor, a positive attitude, patience, the ability to organize people, activities and self, self-direction/discipline, sensitivity to the oppressed, and good people skills.

I am sometimes dissatisfied because of the lack of resources, money and staff and the red tape. I would like to see more sensitivity from other people within the system for the oppressed. I keep working because I find satisfaction from the work I do in making the social service system more responsive to people who are in need. I am personally rewarded by knowing that I can improve services and can help children and families.

My future career aspirations and plans are extensive. I want to write essays on women's issues and have them published. I would like to be a professional public speaker. Other aspirations are to travel extensively, speak French, and get my Ph.D.

SOCIAL WORKER #1

As a social worker for refugees in the health profession, I evaluate available documents or photocopies and ascertain the best sites of resettlement.

An excellent memory is helpful in performing this job well. Other personal characteristics which I found useful are tact, the ability to use my imagination and a sense of humor.

I find this work to be very satisfying and am particularly pleased at having the ability to do this work even though I do not have a degree in social work. I received much on-the-job training from my sister to qualify me to handle this particular job. I do, however, recommend entering this field after obtaining a masters degree in social work. After that, there is no substitute for experience which you can only receive from working with the clients.

SOCIAL WORKER #2

In my position as a social worker, I have worked with the elderly and teenagers for three years. As an advocate for my clients, I counsel, advise, and in other ways help my clients by making phone calls, writing reports, traveling to their homes to see some of them, render assistance, and attend meetings to sell the agency on funding for their programs.

The role of a social worker has many facets, and there are unique characteristics that make for a good social worker. Among these are being socially active, enjoying one-on-one personal contact with others, enjoying (often with very little monetary compensation) helping people less fortunate than oneself, having strong feelings for pertinent social causes, being organized and goal oriented, and possessing strong communication skills--written, oral, and listening. One must also be satisfied with small gains for great efforts and one must possess a college education, at least a Bachelor's degree in social work.

Social work can be very satisfying as a way to contribute to changing the social system toward more humanistic goals and values. A social worker may at times see a client function better as a result of his or her efforts and at such times the social worker learns to appreciate even the smallest steps in an individual's progress.

If I could change anything, I would reduce the amount of paperwork this position requires, cut out the red tape, and increase the monetary compensation for this work--a social worker is notoriously underpaid and overworked. A social worker's case load usually increases with a downturn in the economy and, ironically, that is the time when the payroll budget gets reduced, leaving you to work longer hours with less compensation.

I believe my career path will soon lead more in the direction of a consultant's role; perhaps I will start my own referral and counseling agency to assist the elderly in the search for nursing homes and retirement communities that will meet their individual needs.

SOCIAL WORKER #3

I came into contact with social workers for the first time while a student in college, and I was very impressed by their knowledge and ability to be effective with persons in need. After receiving my bachelor's in sociology, I earned a Master's in Social Work. I have now practiced social work over the years in different capacities.

At present, as a clinical social worker in a chronic disease hospital, I work with the staff, patient, family, and community for the benefit of the patient. My typical daily activities include meeting with staff regarding patient's needs, telephoning family or resources, sending out letters regarding patients, talking with patients about discharge or current need/problems or just checking to see how they are, and interacting with administrative staff.

In order to perform this kind of work well, it is important to have the following: a knowledge of social work principles, knowledge of the availability of resources, tact, common sense, and the ability to listen to what isn't being said in a conversation.

Although I like my work, I do get frustrated because of the lack of funding for this very vital service. I would like to have less worry about funding my salary and the resources needed to do my job well. A more kindly attitude toward welfare persons so that services will be paid for through necessary taxes would be a welcome change to this occupation.

I like the kind of work I do, the organization and people I work for, and the people with whom I work. I also have the added benefit of working at a facility located on the water with a beautiful view. My social work gives me satisfaction from seeing the patients and families less troubled or worried about issues/problems. I also find satisfaction from working with dedicated staff, and from feeling I have accomplished something every day in one way or the other.

SOCIAL WORKER #4

I have spent my career in the social work field in several capacities, as an assistant professor at two colleges and now as a counselor. As a social worker I am the supervisor of a therapy program for severely emotionally disabled children and adolescents and their parents. This kind of work requires the knowledge usually gained while earning a

Masters in Social Work plus something which cannot be learned--a caring attitude to help others.

I like the kind of work I am now doing as a social worker, particularly working with the clients. I like the organization and people I work for and the people with whom I work. I also find there to be an opportunity for advancement in this field. I find satisfaction from putting therapy programs together which create the positive effects desired on the clients.

My career plan is to spend some additional time working as a therapist/supervisor, and then to return to college teaching.

SOCIAL WORKER #5

Because of my interest in elder care and related problems, I became a volunteer in the field. My volunteer work opened a door into a career with the Department of Human Services. As a social worker, I am involved with adult protective services.

To do this work, one needs a great deal of patience. Self-discipline along with a positive attitude are extremely important. I find strong people skills, as well as having respect for clients, to be essential.

It is rewarding to me to be able to improve living conditions for clients. Providing the means for the elderly and the incapacitated to be independent is so satisfying. I'm happy to be able to contribute to the quality of life for my clients. In my particular office, I enjoy the freedom to help my clients as individuals.

I'd like my work even more if there were less paperwork. It would be far better if the law and other policy makers had more personal information about the people who are impacted by their decisions. I am concerned that the laws made from good intentions may infringe on the rights of the elderly.

My education includes a Bachelor of Arts degree. I intend to remain in my current position until retirement.

SOCIAL WORKER #6

I've been a resident director of a female dorm on a college campus for six years. As a child, I read "Twenty Years at Hull House" by Jane Adams and decided I wanted a similar career. I trained to become a social group worker in an inner city community center, a settlement house. I've also been an administrator of a social service agency. My educational background is a Bachelor of Arts degree in religion and a Master of Science degree in social work.

In the dormitory, there are 150 young women with whom I live. From 9:00 a.m. until 12:30 at night I'm available to assist them with any problems, either personal or housing-related. I also enforce the college's policies regarding areas such as safety and discipline.

Knowing that what I do has helped someone improve the quality of her life is very satisfying. I very much enjoy my work, the people involved, and the college and I'd choose this career again. My only complaint is the excessively long hours. I think this aspect is the central cause of burnout among resident directors. Even though I enjoy everything else about my work, I plan one day, when I retire, to work in my family's pottery shop. I'll also be an active volunteer in the Peace Movement.

To do this work, you first must have the ability to listen well. A genuine desire to help others along with a good sense of humor is needed as well. You must be flexible, and you must be willing to let others take any and all credit for success.

SOCIAL WORKER, HEALTH CARE

As a social worker in health care, I assist people with issues of loss, and advocate for patient rights. I counsel mostly crisis situations. The advocacy part of my job usually pertains to patient care planning. I handle paperwork and then more paperwork. I do resource, referral and personal directive counseling, and discharge/admission planning.

To prepare for this occupation, I earned a bachelor's degree in social work. Prior to my employment as a social worker in health care, I have been an occupational therapy aide in institutional settings, an interior decorator for several years, manager of a leather craft shop, and an office worker.

The skills and attitudes which I consider important to have in order to perform well as a social worker are: respect for individual needs and quality of life and death; interpersonal skills to deal effectively with staff, patients, and family; assertiveness, gentleness, and ego strength; knowledge of laws, resources, human development and potential, and medical information.

The frustration I face with my work is the amount of time I must spend doing paperwork, and the limited money and resources available to provide the services needed by the patients. Despite these frustrations, I like my kind of work and the people I work with. My job satisfaction is found in seeing people satisfy their own quality of life goals, and dying with control and dignity.

SOFTWARE ENGINEER #1

My career as a technician started while I was in the US Navy and was trained as a sonar technician. After my tour of duty, I worked as a test technician on computer hardware. For the last 24 years, I have been employed as a software engineer. As such, I test software written by software developers.

To perform this work well, you must first think logically and then also think like a customer or end user. This requires you to be an aggressive tester.

Satisfaction to me from this kind of work is finding problems. If I can find the problems and get them resolved before the customer gets the product, I will have done my job well.

I like almost every aspect of my work including the people I work with, the kind of work I do and the people for whom I work. I would, however, be more satisfied if the work was less driven by schedules and more driven by quality.

My future career plans are to continue in this field and to become a software test manager.

SOFTWARE ENGINEER #2

I have liked all my jobs and feel that they have followed in a logical progression to get me to a satisfying point in my career. I started out as a phototypographer. This was a job that I enjoyed a lot but I leaned toward the more technical side. I eventually became a systems analyst working on a software documentation product. Although I enjoyed this position, it was somewhat frustrating to be a middleman between users and developers. I am very happy now working on the development team.

As a software engineer, working on a software documentation product, I write programs, test and modify software. I attend quite a few meetings in a week. Some are brainstorming sessions, and some project status. There are many projects in the works at the same time. This job involves working together with lots of people--each person with his or her own personal responsibilities but all with the responsibility for the final project--making the process work together. There is also a wide diversity of personalities.

In this kind of work, you need to like a mix of working alone, as well as working with others. You should be open to other people's ideas and suggestions, but have confidence in your own ideas and abilities. I have found the need to be able to function under stress and deadlines. A major key to performing well in this kind of work is to have a strong team attitude.

Although I like the people I work for and the people I work with, there is a problem within my organization concerning some groups' respect for other groups. I see a need for a better idea of "company." There are, however, many satisfying aspects to my work. I enjoy working alone, which I do perhaps 60% of the time. I enjoy the brainstorming sessions-- you need many differing views to mold the final product into something that is useful. I enjoy the freedom I am allowed for creativity.

SOFTWARE ENGINEER #3

My career path has taken and continues to take many different avenues with a primary goal of retiring at the age of 45. I currently work as a software engineer, instructor, entrepreneur of a Christmas tree farm, breeder of Siberian huskies, financial planner, tax accountant, and apartment building owner. My educational background includes a Bachelor's and Master in Computer Science, a Bachelor of Science in Accounting and work toward a Ph.D.

I was introduced to computers 14 years ago while in college and liked it so much I changed my major from electrical engineering to computer science. I'm glad I did! I have now been working as a software engineer for a major chemical company for 11 years, writing programs and managing people. My work day starts at 7:00 a.m. More specifically, my duties include putting computer systems together, installing software, solving computer system problems, writing programs, generating scripts, making decisions on hardware and software releases, and system administration. My day as software engineer ends at 6:00 p.m. after which I teach college courses till 10:35 p.m.

The abilities I consider necessary to do the kind of work I do are to work well with people, have a systems knowledge, and be patient, adaptable and flexible.

I find satisfaction from my job as a software engineer knowing I am the only one in the entire company that is capable of doing my job. I replaced three people's jobs when I was hired and have been rewarded as such for a job very well done.

With 9 years to go before I plan to retire, I will continue to follow my plan for success and that is to spread my eggs out and not put them all in the same basket. I invested heavily in real-estate in the late 70's and early 80's. I have sold many buildings since then and have profited quite well from my ventures. I plan to continue building on this nest egg and retire in my large expensive home on 19 acres with my wife and 3 daughters.

SOFTWARE ENGINEER #4

I started working at a computer facility in college and enjoyed it. The course work came easy to me, and I found that I could make a good living doing it. I earned a Bachelor of Science in Computer Science degree in order to pursue my career in this field.

As a software engineer, I design and write computer software. I maintain a segment of the operating system that stores and retrieves information from disks. There are two main parts to my job: designing and writing improvements, and hearing about problems customers have encountered with this software.

In order to perform this kind of work well, it is important to be able to understand how this large and complex machine, the computer, operates. Having logical thought processes and problem-solving skills is also necessary for this occupation. You must have the ability to limit the scope and complexity of the problem in order to come up with a solution quickly. Since some of the problems can be tedious, patience and attention to detail are also essential attributes for the job.

I like my occupation as a software engineer for many reasons: the flexible hours, the sense of accomplishment, the good pay, and the sense of contributing. It is satisfying for me to be part of a team that is building the most wonderful tool since the lever.

Computers are used in nearly every occupation. The work I do makes the computer a better tool for everyone else to use.

I plan to continue working where I am, becoming a more senior engineer to eventually become more involved in the future directions and strategies for my company's products.

SOFTWARE ENGINEER #5

As a Software Engineer for three years, I write and test software for printing systems. In charge of many projects involving testing postscript laser printer software, I organize and keep track of the work that gets done on those projects and who does it. After verifying the testing results, I spend a lot of time in meetings reporting those results. That requires organization, good communication skills, and logical thought processes for these technical procedures and reports.

I could have more control over product specifications if I could make more people understand the need for quality in these products. I really enjoy determining when a product is of good quality and then recommending that it is ready to ship to customers. I know then they will be satisfied; I have found major bugs that would hamper use, and I am the person that stops those products from being shipped.

I like this job and this kind of work, the company I work for, and the people I work with. I am really glad I got this job as a co-op student while in school; after completing my Bachelor of Science degree in Computer Engineering Technology, I was hired right away by the same group I had worked for while in the co-op program.

Future aspirations include getting involved in the development of products similar to those I currently test.

SOUS CHEF, KITCHEN SUPERVISOR

I am a sous chef because, when I needed a job, I found an opening at the bottom of the ladder in a restaurant. Rather than staying a peon, I worked my way up. Prior to restaurant work, I was a house painter and mechanic.

My job description states that I must know every aspect of kitchen work: sauces, specials, supervising, light maintenance, food costs, dishwashing, banquets, etc. My daily activities include: checking prep lists and organizing prep cooks, setting up nightly specials and costing them out, supervising setting up of line and waitress set up, expediting line through rush, working on prep list whenever possible, supervising closing of line and clean up of kitchen, and locking up of the kitchen.

To be a chef, you must be able to work well with people and have a mellow temperament. You will find yourself repeating directions continually. There is a lot of stress working a line. You must be able to deal with cooking 40 dinners at once, plus answering questions at the same time.

I like this kind of work very much. However, I do not like the fact that the hours can change at a moment's notice. You cannot make plans if you are in this occupation. I have also found this work to be very stressful. In spite of these drawbacks, I like my work and get satisfaction from creating new dishes and flavors. In fact, I plan to open my own restaurant or bed and breakfast someday.

SPACE SYSTEMS ENGINEER ANALYST

I've been a meteorologist, a research director in meteorology, a meteorological research investigator, and now I work as a space systems engineer and analyst. I gather, analyze, and report data from space systems which are used in developing improved operating procedures. Drawing conclusions or making inferences from the analyses and developing analyses, plans, schedules, and procedures are all part of work.

I like doing something unique and important which will have significant impact if the results are successful. I'd be more satisfied if I had a better work environment which would mean giving me privacy and a larger work area. Lack of downward information makes my work more difficult, but overall I like this job.

Characteristics needed in my field are math and physics proficiency, high quantitative aptitude and interest, curiosity, and versatility. Computer skills as well as a broad background in and knowledge of space systems are also required.

From past work and experience I found greatest satisfaction in data assimilation and analysis tasks. So, I sought work with that emphasis, selecting and seeking opportunities to get where I am. My career plans are to achieve optimum success in my current work.

SPECIAL EDUCATION AIDE, ELEMENTARY

Two of my children were grown-up and my third was in sixth grade when it became necessary for me to contribute to our family income by finding a paying job. I was informed of the opening for an aide in the elementary school, so I applied and got the job. I had stayed home with the children until then, thinking that a mother's place is with the children.

As an elementary classroom special education aide, I provide one on one subject help, substitute K-3, prepare materials, give tests, grade papers, and record grades. I also have recess and lunch hour duty, and sometimes early morning bus duty. I listen to students' problems and apply band aids, etc.

To perform well as a teacher's aide, you must be able to follow directions or do it on your own. Caring, compassion, and understanding are necessary.

Despite the low pay for the vast number of duties which you are expected to perform, I like my job very much. When my children were younger, I could be home with them during the summer months. I like the school and people I work for, the people I work with, and the kind of work. Aside from the satisfaction I find from contributing monetarily to our income, I hope that I've made a positive difference in a young life.

SPECIALTY CANDY BROKER

Although I am now a specialty candy broker because I married into the business, rather than having made an individual decision, I can say, after working in it for 15 years, that it has proved to be a job which I like very much.

As a candy broker I represent manufacturers and importers of specialty candy and sell to wholesalers and retailers. My typical work activities include: taking and tracking orders by phone, making suggestions as to what sells and what is slow, suggesting ways to merchandise the products, taking part in conventions or shows, making calls on existing and new customers, follow-up paper work, general office work like answering letters, filing and organization, and helping others to succeed.

To perform well in this job, it is important to have general office knowledge. You should have the ability to talk to people and hear what they are and are not saying. Have confidence in yourself and your product. The ability to think quickly and find answers to problems is also important. You should have a general "up" attitude and positive approach to life, the ability to handle rejection, and be able to convince people that they need your product and why.

I have a very diverse occupational background which I feel has helped me in this position. Previous jobs have included: fast food restaurant manager, department store clerk, factory assembly line and quality assurance testing worker, housewife, and telephone answering service operator.

The part of my job which I least like is having to police payments and untruthful retailers. However, this dislike is outweighed by the many things I like about my job: the people I work with and for, and the daily changes in my work activity and the travel. This is satisfying work for me because I enjoy watching others succeed, especially when they try something I suggest.

SPEECH-LANGUAGE PATHOLOGIST #1

My time as a speech-language pathologist is basically divided up with 30% diagnostic evaluations, 20% meetings, 40% therapy and 10% parent/teacher/phone consultations.

Important skills and attitudes for this profession are: patience, flexibility and desire to help others; thorough knowledge of disability characteristics and remediation techniques; tactful, though direct presentation of findings; empathy toward client and family; consideration of other aspects of individual intelligence and emotional factors.

My job satisfaction comes from helping to resolve questions/issues concerning disabilities by finding concrete, productive ways to help. Seeing people comforted by my results is indeed gratifying.

I would be more satisfied if I had a more supportive salary, increased third party reimbursement for services and greater public knowledge of what I do. I do see, however, that increased public knowledge about this profession is occurring.

I became aware of this occupation when a close relative had a stroke. The more I found out about speech pathology the more I liked it. My previous business experience has been as Assistant Bank Manager and Production Control Planner.

I have a variety of future career aspirations or plans. The various options I see now are staying with the same job or setting up my own private practice, becoming a supervisor/head of a speech department, university teaching, or special education administration.

SPEECH-LANGUAGE PATHOLOGIST #2

As a sophomore in college I went to the Career Center for Counseling. Speech pathology was one of the options which came up on a "test" I took. I looked into it as there was a department of speech pathology at my university. After talking to the head of the department at length, I began the course work necessary to graduate with a Bachelor of Arts. Then immediately, I went on to get my Masters of Arts in Speech Pathology. I initially started my career in pathology as a speech-language therapist. Now as a speech-language pathologist I supervise undergraduate university students.

My primary job responsibilities are to coordinate all clinical activities, schedule all clients, and supervise students and give feedback. Each day of supervision is different depending on the schedule of clients coming in for therapy. They are seen by student clinicians on Monday and Wednesday or Tuesday and Thursday for an hour each session. I supervise all or part of each session depending on whether it is a first semester student or a second semester student. One day a week the students and I have a scheduled two hour diagnostic (evaluation) session. Clinic meetings are held on Fridays.

Professional writing skills, flexibility and creativity are important requirements for a speech-language pathologist, However, the most critical skill is in interpersonal communications.

I am satisfied with my career decision. I have found job satisfaction from my current position because of the flexibility of the job, and from working with undergraduate students and faculty members. Although I like the academic environment, my future plans are to go into private practice. I also will possibly pursue a Ph.D. degree.

SPEECH-LANGUAGE PATHOLOGIST #3

Evaluating and treating children and adults with communication disorders describes my work as a speech pathologist, an occupation I have followed enthusiastically for eight years. I deal with group and individual therapy. My day is also filled with a variety of conferences--with families, physicians, and case teams.

The person who would enjoy this work is flexible and creative. Good interpersonal skills and the ability to work as a team member are also needed. To succeed in this field, you must be a person dedicated to the work.

I've earned a Bachelor of Science Degree in Speech and a Master of Arts in Communication Disorders. I like everything about my job except the case loads need to be limited. The people with and for whom I work, the institution, and the fact that there are chances for advancement make my work enjoyable.

Originally, I was interested in educating the deaf, but I realized that a speech pathologist would deal with a greater variety of disorders (thus the need to be flexible). The settings, too, vary--hospitals, schools, private clinics, nursing homes, etc.

Job satisfaction comes when someone who is non-verbal learns to communicate. I'm also pleased to be working with people who are professional and dedicated to their work. I'd like it if the public were aware that all different types of populations can be treated by a speech pathologist. A few of these are victims of stroke, head injuries, cerebral palsy, head or neck cancer, and even AIDS victims.

In addition to continuing the work I'm doing now, I hope to expand my own private practice to some extent.

SPRINKLER FITTER

A sprinkler fitter installs fire protection systems and sees that these systems are maintained to ensure they function properly. I usually work 11 to 12 hours a day traveling a 5-state area. After finishing high school, I farmed for a while and enjoyed it. I moved into the sprinkler field with the help of a friend in an attempt to better my standard of living.

It pleases me to install a system without any leaks. In my work, I have the opportunity to meet different people, which is an aspect I like. I'd like better working conditions, but other than that, I enjoy just about everything in my work and would choose this occupation again.

To be a sprinkler fitter you have to have a basic knowledge of math. You have to have people skills and know how to work with contractors or owners. Currently, my future plan is eventual retirement.

STAFF ACCOUNTANT

In my position as a staff accountant I report to the controller of my company. I deal with many different reports and postings related to the monthly closing of the books, on and off the computer. I gather information about monthly expenses for the controller. The skills most important to a staff accountant are: math, computer knowledge, and accounting skills. Debit and credit know-how and analytical skills for detailing the accounts are especially important.

During the two years in this position, I find that learning and verifying reports give me great satisfaction. I like the fact that my job enables me to help other workers with information they need. I would like to learn more about the preparation involved in the controller's reports.

I have an Associate's degree in accounting.

Previously, I worked as a payroll administrator/coordinator and was promoted to staff accountant while attending classes.

I plan to continue my education and learn about tax accounting, perhaps leading to a Bachelor's degree that will significantly increase the ceiling of jobs for which I can then qualify.

I believe this type of work gives me opportunity for advancement. I have always liked math. I like my boss and the people I work with although at times I have felt I was working alone, as an accountant often does. Overall, I like this organization and would not change anything about my job.

STATE TROOPER

There has not been one day since I've been a state trooper that I did not want to go to work. There are things I don't like such as bad accidents, high speed chases, etc., but overall I enjoy my work very much. Some one once told me that he thought I would make a good police officer, so I put in an application at the local police department. I was accepted, trained, and worked there for 7 years before becoming a state trooper. I have spent 17 years in law enforcement. My background includes earning a Bachelor of Arts degree in Criminal Justice and Philosophy, and working as a mechanic.

As a state trooper, my work includes: routine traffic patrol, dealing with citizens, instructing various courses, preparing court cases, investigating accidents, responding to emergency calls, and being a role model. When you go to work, you must be self-motivated. The job is as boring or exciting as you make it. You have personal priorities you work with, as well as personal goals. You start with routine patrol activities and enforcement that are important to you and consistent with the goals of the organization. Every traffic stop involves salesmanship, selling the law, and enforcement. It is also educational, and you are the teacher. It is professionalism at an accident scene and in the preparation of court cases.

To perform this kind of work well, communication skills are perhaps the most important. Self confidence is also important, and that is gained in part through education. Grammar is valuable, but obviously not required. Prejudice must be set aside as much as possible. A good sense of fair play, and a generally good outlook on life is important. Not everyone is a dirt bag and not everyone is as innocent as they would like you to believe. It doesn't hurt to have a good vocabulary and spelling skills too.

Although I like my work very much, I could stand a higher salary. I wish there could be promotions without becoming a supervisor. Job satisfaction for me is dealing with people from all walks of life; making a difference on an individual basis;

responsibility and trust. Some day I hope to be chief, but if I retire as a road trooper, I will still view my career as a success.

STATISTICAL PROCESS COORDINATOR

Basically my job includes training people, building teams and taking an active role in problem-solving. My eight-hour work day may include facilitating 2-3 hours worth of meetings used to problem-solve sources of variation. Preparing for and conducting training sessions also constitutes a major portion of my work day.

People and communication skills are of utmost importance for this type of work. Also necessary skills are public-speaking abilities, organizational skills, knowledge of basic statistical tools and team-building skills.

I am satisfied with my work when I get the opportunity to get others excited about problem-solving and reducing waste. I find satisfaction from the opportunity to do a job right.

I do not feel the compensation fits the job. I would be more satisfied too if there were better support from the real upper management.

I was utilizing basic trouble-shooting tools as a machine operator. I decided to get training in statistical process control and when a job came in the plant I bid on it and got it. My previous employment as a saw operator in a mill, a farm laborer, and paper mill laborer have given me valuable experience and insight into the problems I deal with and help to solve.

I plan to continue to do this job the best I possibly can.

STEAMFITTER SUPERINTENDENT

I tried out many jobs before settling in my occupation as a steamfitter. My previous work has included: working with a produce huckster, delivering papers, working in a sandwich shop, sailing in the merchant marine, shipyard worker, and part-time clothing salesperson. A good friend recommended this occupation as a steamfitter to me, so I took the test for the apprenticeship and have gone on from there for the last 20 years. I always enjoyed some sort of physical work, and construction fit the bill.

As a steamfitter superintendent for a large mechanical construction firm, I do estimating, layout, planning and implement startup on the heating, ventilating, refrigeration, and air conditioning projects for which my company has contracts. Included in these responsibilities are staying on top of deadlines, meetings, ordering materials, making schedules, and coordination of subcontractors.

In order to perform this kind of work, it is important to have mechanical skills. Common sense, dedication, and fairness are attitudes that are important in the job. I am very satisfied with my work as a steamfitter superintendent. In fact, if given the chance to start over and prepare for any kind of work, I would again choose this occupation.

The accomplishment of completing a project and seeing the customers satisfied with my ability to perform is rewarding to me.

As far as future career plans, my career has basically peaked. Not too many people advance to superintendent of a firm this size. My plans are to try and get even better at my job. I want to constantly learn and be of greater assistance to the company and industry.

STORE MANAGER

I manage a family owned grocery store with three other sisters. I do the computer work and all types of office work like paying taxes, bills and working with the accountant. I also do baking, cashiering, liquor stocking and pricing, and ordering for all departments. As can be imagined from this list of responsibilities, I spend many long hours at the store. It would be nice to have backup personnel so that I am not constantly interrupted. I could perform better without the many long hours I put in. In spite of this, I still like my work very much primarily because of the challenge involved in running a business. The work continues to be interesting because every day it is different. As well as my own particular responsibilities, I often fill in for people who are out sick or out on emergency.

To be successful in the grocery store business, I think you must be able to listen to customer complaints, and work with employees without criticism. Being creative, thinking up ways of improvement, keeps the business viable. It is important to continually analyze the business to find out what is needed.

As previously mentioned, I like this kind of work very much. I like the people I work with. I find satisfaction from improvements in the store. I feel rewarded when we are positively recognized by our customers for the personalized catering we do.

STRUCTURAL ENGINEER

For 7 years I've been a structural engineer inspecting houses for their structural preciseness. I also design the various structural components for new houses, such as their foundations.

In my work, I investigate the structure of houses for 4 or 5 hours each day. Then, I make verbal and written reports which include drawings and specifications for repair procedures. In addition, I oversee the repair work as it's being done.

I find great satisfaction in my ability to help people determine what repairs need to be done to their houses. What follows is that buyers are willing to buy and lenders will lend. I enjoy my coworkers, my clients, and the company. I least like collecting delinquent accounts from customers. My future plans are to continue to build my business.

All of my previous education, my Bachelor of Science degree in civil engineering, and my experience qualified me to do what I'm doing. I was unemployed and looking for something to do when I began this work. It's a great job; if I had to start again, I'd choose this occupation again.

You need adequate knowledge of housing construction to do this work. You should have a good background in structural design and analysis. Also necessary are strong oral and written communication skills. A desire to help people and the courage to report the truth are both essential.

STRUCTURAL ENGINEER, CHIEF EXECUTIVE

As a chief executive and the structural engineer for a concrete products company for thirty years, I direct management personnel in the direction of their respective companies, monitor expenditure decisions, and direct company policy.

I have a Bachelor of Science degree in Structural Engineering and I believe the most important characteristics to do my job are the ability to handle and motivate people and a genuine concern for both the company and its personnel.

I enjoy my work and the responsibilities that I hold; I believe that the results of my efforts create a more acceptable bottom line for myself and the people I direct.

Following in my brother's footsteps, I began my career shortly after graduation from college.

My plans include making my business and clients as successful as possible for as long as possible.

STUDENT, HISTORY

I am now in the process of starting over as far as my career is concerned. I have held various office jobs over the past 10 years: church secretary for 6 years, administrative assistant for 2 years, fiscal/policy analyst for 1 year, and material planner for 1 year. I have decided to make a switch to the academic community and am in the process of earning my Ph.D. in American and Women's History. I have always enjoyed reading history monographs, and I started taking night courses in history while in my previous jobs.

As a history graduate student, I teach and attend classes. Other regular activities include: reading books and articles; writing/editing papers; and communicating with fellow graduate students.

I consider the following skills and attitudes to be important as a graduate student: analytical and synthesis skills, writing well, love of reading, willingness to work long hours for little pay, enjoyment of libraries and archives, public speaking ability, flexibility and responsibility, and willingness to work hard and be self-motivated.

Despite the low pay, I am very satisfied with my plans to change my career and am enjoying my work as a graduate student. I like the college and people I work for, and the people with whom I work. I find satisfaction in discovering new knowledge, transmitting it to students, and talking with other historians. My future career plans are to work toward a tenure-track faculty position in a research university.

STUDENT, LAW

I tried out various careers, as a research assistant for a drug company, a media planner for an advertising agency, and a realtor, before deciding that I really wanted to practice law. It was indeed exciting when I got admitted to law school and I will of course be more excited when I receive my J.D. in six months. One of the reasons I think this career interests me is that I enjoy service-oriented jobs which this will be. My biggest frustration with law school is the lack of time to complete projects. I only wish there was less work so I would have time to do my work more thoroughly. My classes run from 8:45 to 5:30 except for two hours during which I work for the legal aid officer for one hour and prepare my opening statement for the mock trials during the other hour. My classes now include: Debtor-Creditor, Commercial Paper, Trial Advocacy, and the mock trial. My work at the legal aid office includes returning client calls, getting needed subpoenas from the sheriff, and preparing questions for hearings.

To perform well as a law student, it is important to have a good memory, to think quickly on your feet, and have good knowledge of rules of evidence.

I find satisfaction as a student from the praises for my well-done work and as a student legal aide from the gratitude from my clients. Now I am looking forward to the satisfaction of graduating and passing the bar.

STUDENT, MUSIC (VOICE)

After graduating from high school, I worked as a filing clerk, cashier, and assistant secretary, until I received what I regard to be a calling, through prayer, into the music field. I enrolled in college and have spent the last three years studying music.

As a music student, I study, do research, read, memorize music, practice singing and piano, and attend classes. A major portion of my time is spent practicing. In order to get in the practice and homework required as a music student, it is important to set up a schedule which you must, at times, force yourself to follow. It also helps to receive encouragement .

Despite the fact that I miss having some time for myself, and would like fewer reports assigned, I am glad that I am pursuing my studies. I like the school and professors, and my fellow students. It is satisfying when I see improvement in my performance, and when I gain more understanding. It is also exciting meeting people of importance in the music field.

My plans for the future are to sing with a traveling contemporary Christian group, as a traveling-singing couple, or as a song/worship leader in a church.

SUBSTITUTE TEACHER

I did clerical and bookkeeping work for many years, but decided to change occupations and do substitute teaching work. As a substitute teacher, I oversee and teach classes and overall maintain control of the classroom. The critical skills, which I find necessary for being an effective substitute teacher and controlling the students, are tact and patience.

Except for the low pay and lack of opportunity for advancement in this occupation, I like this kind of work. I also like the organization and people I work for, and the people with whom I work. I started in this field fairly late in my career life. I only wish I had tried it sooner. It is indeed satisfying for me to see young people learn and grow. I too am planning to learn more by returning to school and taking education courses.

SUBSTITUTE TEACHER, K-12

For many years I have taught school as a substitute teacher serving six towns. I often teach a different subject and grade level each day. I love teaching and would choose this occupation again if I could start over. Yet, I have also enjoyed working as a grocery clerk, a caretaker of children, and a full-time teacher.

For me, job satisfaction consists of the smiles and comments from students when I see them outside of school, or when I have them in class again. I love to see them grasp a concept and "learn" the lesson I'm teaching. Unfortunately, since I am a substitute on a part-time basis, I receive no benefits, get low pay, and have little warning when I'll be needed. I decided to leave full-time teaching when my children were born.

For this work, you must like working with children and young people. You must be even-tempered, intelligent, adaptable, and self-confident. A pleasant personality, good physical condition, and the ability to improvise are also important.

One of the advantages of substitute teaching, as we have moved to three different towns, is that I have always been able to "find a job."

A usual day includes identifying my new classroom, developing rapport with my new students, and following the lesson plan left by the regular teacher. At the close of the day, I write a summary of the progress and events, including any disciplinary problems of the day. I'd like to continue substitute teaching until I'm too old to crawl around with the kindergartners!

SUPERINTENDENT, MINING OPERATIONS

To be a miner of uranium, you must pay a great deal of attention to safety. Being aware of the cleanliness of the air and the roof support are really necessary. A good knowledge of mining equipment is also important. Some familiarity with minerals and gemology helps.

A high school graduate, I've been a sanitation engineer, a soldier in World War II, a musician and I've enjoyed all of them. As a miner of uranium and silver, I've found excitement in anticipating what I might find. There are also benefits to be gained in what is found. I got into this work because I'd known about this particular property for many years. Then, at 60 years of age, I took advantage of the mistakes of others and began mining it. Besides uranium and silver, there are other minerals on the property such as copper, zinc, and lead, but no gold.

My goals are to retire, travel a bit in my motor home, and continue with my music hobby. Also I own half interest in a silver mine which I'm trying to sell.

SUPERINTENDENT OF SCHOOLS #1

After 28 very happy years as Superintendent of Schools, I plan to retire in 3-4 years and pursue my hobbies, including traveling. For now, I continue to enjoy seeing the success of former students as well as watching employees grow and develop in their jobs. It is meaningful to me to observe students becoming successful in their school activities and in academics. If I could start all over again, I'd choose the same career path.

My responsibilities as a school administrator have been the supervision of principals, the overseeing of transportation, managing custodial care, and being accountable for cafeteria service. I've prepared many reports and attended many professional meetings. Attending school activities, hiring professional personnel and capable staff, and working with the Board of Education have been some of my pleasant tasks.

Once a teacher and always a principal, I've particularly enjoyed being the chief administrator and supervisor of a K-12 school district. Having all students and staff be more interested in the educational activities, along with personally having more time for planning and thinking, would have made my job even more gratifying. I also wish funding to provide educational opportunities were adequate.

The position of Superintendent of Schools requires that I be a good listener and a very understanding person. You must maintain a good sense of humor and get along well with a wide variety of people. Advanced degrees are also necessary. I have a Bachelor of Science degree and a Masters in education and special education.

SUPERINTENDENT OF SCHOOLS #2

As superintendent of schools, I generally have a 60-to-80 hour work week. I manage the schools in our school district, providing leadership and direction for our personnel. My responsibilities include overseeing the budget, finances, training, and curriculum development.

My work week is filled with numerous meetings and constant interruptions.

Human resource management and staff development all fall under my charge. My work also involves a great deal of strategic planning.

To be an effective superintendent, you must have strong people skills. You should have a good speaking presence, both in the verbal presentation and in speech content. You need to be optimistic and enthusiastic, with an intense interest in and aptitude for learning. The ability to deal with stress and a tolerance for vagueness are both very necessary. Being politically astute is critical to survival as a school superintendent.

Although I'm not fond of everyone on the Board of Education, I do very much like my colleagues, the schools, and my work. It is rewarding to me to generate changes in instructional practices or organizational patterns. When these changes result in improved student performance as well as a feeling of pride in the school district from community, students, and staff, I'm satisfied.

If I had it to do all over again, I'd choose the educational field and being a superintendent. On the other hand, it would be far more enjoyable if the size and the authority of school boards could be limited. All board members should be required to be trained in group dynamics and in team work as well.

I wanted to teach when I entered college because of the influence of teachers upon my life. After earning a Bachelor of Arts degree and graduate degrees, I taught for a while, was an elementary school principal, and served as the director of special education. I became an administrator to have a wider effect in education. My plans are to stay in my current position until retirement. Then, I'd like to start a new career, possibly in sales.

SUPERINTENDENT, PRODUCTION

Through a series of promotions and some planned career choices, I am now Superintendent of Production for an automotive assembly plant. I started out as a line worker, moved up to a first level supervisor, and now a superintendent. In this position, I am responsible for the activities and financial planning of 29 supervisors and 650 line workers. My typical work activities include: attending meetings, monitoring outgoing quality, monitoring financial performance, coaching counseling subordinates, and interacting with people of all levels of responsibility.

As well as my work experience, my educational background has also contributed to my promotions to this position. I have a Bachelors of Industrial Administration degree and a Masters of Science in Manufacturing Management. The important skills and attitudes which I have been able to acquire through this background and which I consider necessary for this job are: financial judgment, decision making, interactive people skills, and logic.

I like almost everything about my job including the organization and people I work for, the people I work with, the kind of work, and the opportunity for advancement. I also consider the pay and benefits to be good. My only major frustration with my work is that I do not have enough time to spend with the people I supervise. My job satisfaction comes from delivering a good product on schedule at a reasonable cost, a satisfied work force, and my own internal feeling of well-being.

My future career plans are to keep being promoted to upper level management positions.

SUPERVISOR, BUILDING & GROUNDS

After earning an Associate degree in liberal arts, I began my work as the Supervisor of Building and Grounds. My duties are to supervise 18 custodians doing office and warehouse cleaning. I like everything about my work except I'd like to eliminate all the unnecessary paperwork.

My job requires good communication skills and the ability to supervise well. You must be able to set high standards of achievement for the crew to follow. Very important, also, is maintaining a positive attitude.

Usually, when I come to work, I first check out messages and then give daily briefings to the crew. I walk through areas to talk with employees, perform quality checks, and handle any problems or emergencies which arise. My job is also to follow up on work being done.

It is rewarding to know my crew has performed well and that everything has been accomplished. I enjoy working with my people as well. I've been a baker's assistant and a gas station attendant in the past, but part of my job satisfaction now comes from working for a great company. My plans are to continue gaining knowledge about my field and learn to be an even better supervisor.

SUPERVISOR, CONSTRUCTION

I'm on the road to work by 5:30. Before actual work starts, I look over the job site for safety and construction problems and set completion goals for the day. During the day I check on materials, equipment, and personnel; assign work to crews; check on subcontractors' work progress; coordinate work areas to be completed in sequence; go over prints change orders; lay out surveying for the next day's work; inspect crew's work; and keep daily records.

It is important to be able to think on your feet. Solving construction problems is a daily occurrence. Be willing to listen to ideas, but time is money so use your best judgment and go with it. Look ahead to the work coming up in the next few weeks or months. Studying the plans now may help you and the owner save time and money when it comes to building it. Also, self-motivation is a necessary skill for performing this job well.

My satisfaction in this work is great when I have completed an important project that will last for years, such as a water treatment or power plant or a school; doing the best job I can and getting it done on time and under budget; discovering new and better methods of construction; being free to make my own decisions and manage time.

To qualify for this job, I earned a BS in Construction Management and a minor in Business. I was offered this job after my college internship with the same company. I had previously been employed as a carpenter, welder, draftsman and estimator.

I feel best suited to continue in the field that I have chosen although, with my experience, I also feel I can offer useful ideas in the design of projects. I would like eventually to earn my degree in architecture and go into consulting.

SUPERVISOR, ELECTRICAL POWER DEPARTMENT

I work in a large factory, originally on the production line, now as an electrical manager. In the position of electrical manager, I supervise the electricians and their work. I am responsible for overseeing all the electrical power and the electrical control equipment in this company.

After I finished high school, I joined the Air Force. I enjoyed electronics and learned my trade while serving. Vocational schools also provided some of my training. My work is so satisfactory to me that if I had to start over, I'd choose the same career. Now I try to keep current on electronic developments.

To be a manager of an electrical power division, you certainly have to know a great deal about electricity. You also need to know how to be a supervisor and be able to manage people.

I have spent my time at work with good people and I enjoy it. Job satisfaction also comes in keeping all equipment in good working order. It is nice, too, to have appreciation for a job well done.

SUPERVISOR, ELECTRIC UTILITY

I've been a Department Supervisor for a municipal electric utility for many years. While I also enjoyed being a truck driver while serving in the military, as well as janitorial work in a local high school, I find my current work particularly rewarding.

The challenges in each of the new projects, along with getting to know new people, make my job great. I like the salary as well. Being able to see technology change our everyday lives is further compensation. Almost everything about my work is enjoyable: my coworkers, the chance for advancement, and the people I work for.

I would like to see the utility business taken completely out of the control of the city politicians. It should be governed by a utility board who would oversee its operation. That way political decisions which affect the utility could be avoided.

My work day consists of directing the activities of 3 department sections in the area of maintenance, repair, and buildings. I am responsible for assigning new projects, managing the status of projects in development, and reporting the progress to my supervisors. Writing reports, attending meetings or seminars, and counseling employees are part of my duties. I decide on disciplinary action for policy infractions as well as evaluate and recommend employees for promotion or salary increase. Customer service is also my responsibility.

Being able to place the success of the utility above personal goals is important in my work. I also have to be very knowledgeable in electronics and have strong organizational skills. Being able to deal with varied personalities, attitudes, and cultures is vital to supervisory work.

I'm very satisfied with my present position and status. However, if there were an opportunity to be a member of a supervisory body of a utility board, I would consider a career change. Otherwise, I will stay in this line of work and with this company indefinitely.

SUPERVISOR, ELECTRONICS ENGINEERS #1

My career path was changed after I was assigned to the Army Specialized Training Program. I had intended to be a secondary school teacher of chemistry. Instead, I went into electronics engineering. I have been an instructor in two colleges on a part-time basis, but my major career has been in electronics engineering.

I supervise a crew of electronic engineers, who design, develop, produce, and test state-of-the-art radar transmitters. My crew and I are involved in experimentation, drafting, contracts, production liaison and testing, both in the plant and the field.

To perform this kind of work well, you must have a knowledge of electronic design and be motivated by the desire to advance the state of the art. Your goal is to build a product that is efficient and cost effective and still of high quality.

I have spent more that 30 years in this industry and have found it very satisfying. I like the people I work with and the kind of work I do. In fact, if given the chance to start over again and choose any career, I would again choose electronics engineering. My job satisfaction comes from completing a successful product. It is also rewarding to receive acknowledgement of my talents by my peers.

Although I have liked electronics as a career, I plan to do social studies research when I retire.

SUPERVISOR, ELECTRONICS ENGINEERS #2

I chose to major in electrical engineering because I found it interesting, financially rewarding, and challenging. I have managed to pursue this career along with raising two children.

As a supervisor of electronics engineers, I coach other engineers on the job: answering questions, allocating resources, prioritizing work, setting up time schedules, and reporting on progress. My typical daily activities may include: reading many draft documents, marking comments and returning to originator; developing schedules; tracking progress of work; motivating people to meet commitments; writing memos; answering many questions; writing reports on group activities; locating and obtaining needed materials for group use; calling meetings and soliciting discussion and suggestions.

To perform this kind of work well, it is important to have diplomacy, tact, a positive attitude, good verbal and written communication skills, technical knowledge, computer literacy, persistence, and organizational skills.

There is always too much work and too little time to complete it but, in spite of that, I like my work very much. I enjoy the people I work with and the kind of work I do. Also, the salary is good. I find job satisfaction in seeing other people develop skills and advance in knowledge; getting work completed successfully; achieving goals. I have personal satisfaction of a job well done.

In the future, I plan to continue to develop my skills and keep up with rapid changes in technology. I may possibly work for myself eventually rather than for a medium-sized corporation.

SUPERVISOR, ELECTRONICS INSTALLATIONS

For many years, I have worked at various levels as a supervisor of electronic operations. In my job, I directly supervise personnel during the installation and operation of electronic equipment. My crews, which range from 3 to 25 employees, are often involved in trouble-shooting electronic problems as well.

To do this work, you must have thorough knowledge of how to manage people. Getting the maximum work from employees is the goal. You must always remember that an employee is a tool for his supervisor or manager. The supervisor should be capable of keeping the worker sharp, just as you would keep a cutting tool sharp. Encouragement of employees is important in helping them become as efficient as they can.

I learned electronics and got my experience in this field while in the U.S. Marine Corps. After leaving the Corps, I applied for a job in the aircraft industry in electronics. Through various levels of promotion, I reached the position of supervisor.

Job satisfaction for me is completing a task or an assignment on schedule and within budgeted cost. This is the most rewarding part of all. My only regret is that I waited so long to get a college degree. I was in supervision for 10 years before beginning my studies. I have now earned a Bachelor of Science degree in business administration, with a major in management.

SUPERVISOR, FOOD LABORATORY

While I enjoyed also my time as a postal employee after high school, I really like being the lab supervisor at a frozen food company. I came to this job when my manager asked me if I would take the position; I accepted enthusiastically.

It is my job to keep all the quality control records on the computer and provide any necessary computer reports for my manager. Along with updating manuals and attending meetings, I order equipment and supplies for the lab.

It is great knowing everything is in order at the end of a work day. I also enjoy making plans to complete assignments in a timely manner. I'd choose this work again because I've enjoyed my colleagues, my supervisors, the company, and the pay.

Accuracy and attention to detail are of utmost importance in quality control. You also need to be orderly. Being able to work well with others has been very helpful to me.

SUPERVISOR, HOSPITAL PBX

Because I love working with the public, my job as PBX supervisor for the local hospital is the right kind of work for me. I also am the emergency room secretary.

My duties include: answering incoming calls, paging doctors and other employees, filling out emergency room records, copying insurance cards, and admitting patients in and out when the admitting clerk is out.

To perform well at this job, it is important to be able to work well with the public, have good rapport with doctors, nurses and the general public. Good telephone manners are also essential.

I have had a number of jobs since graduating from high school, such as: factory worker, salesperson, cashier and stock manager. I have held this job the longest and like it very much, except for the lack of opportunity for advancement, and the pay scale. I also am somewhat dissatisfied with the morale of some of the other employees. I tend to overlook these dislikes, however, because I like most of the people I work with, the hospital I work for and the kind of work I do. It gives me satisfaction to help people and know that I have done a service for my community and fellow man through my work.

SUPERVISOR, HUMAN RESOURCES

I've worked as a production supervisor and planning supervisor, both of which I enjoyed. Yet, as a general supervisor of human resources for 24 years, I've found great satisfaction identifying and selecting good candidates for employment. It's rewarding to efficiently "put out fires" in labor relations, in the area of safety, and in the benefits department. I enjoy helping solve others' problems, forming better benefits packages, and improving working conditions. Interceding in employee and manager relations is challenging.

In this field, you must be honest and ethical. Speaking effectively before groups or individuals is very important. Being a good listener, "soothing wounded egos," or helping people get their problem into focus are significant. Compassion, diplomacy and calmness are three particular traits needed. You must also be able to prepare good reports and cost studies as well as be able to write sound personnel policies.

I never dreamed I'd go into personnel work. After earning a Bachelor of Science degree, I had several positions in the production field. When I became dissatisfied and began seeking other employment, I was recruited by a division personnel manager who wanted my "floor" experience and my varied background.

To describe a typical day is difficult because my priorities are set by others' requirements. Every day is an adventure. My work includes recruiting employees, preparing for labor negotiations, and setting up salary recommendations by classifying new ranges of job responsibilities. Safety and security review is on-going as is benefits administration. Training is done on an "as needed" basis.

I'd choose this job again, but with some changes. I would like for the employees to be given opportunity to have their "say" on benefits and policies. I'd prefer the corporate attitude toward personnel be more sympathetic--just being given major changes, and then being told to implement them, does not make for a stable personnel staff. I wish we had more autonomy for our employees.

SUPERVISOR, IRS ANALYSTS

I am a first-line supervisor of national analysts at the Internal Revenue Service. My job is to answer telephone calls to resolve problems, issue memos to disseminate information nationwide, and analyze data to determine the status of implementation. Further, I meet with colleagues to discuss strategies and to plan ways to improve work processes and procedures.

My job requires strong people skills. Well-honed communications skills, both written and oral, are necessary. To be able to negotiate effectively is also important.

I worked my way up to my present position from a clerical job. This was the route to take because I have no college degree. For this work, however, a high school diploma is essential. My plans are to move up into middle and upper management. I am gratified when I receive appreciation for helping others. It also pleases me to find solutions to correct work procedures which have failed.

I'd like my work more if the politics were eliminated. The excessive levels of management and the bureaucracy should be reduced.

SUPERVISOR, MANUFACTURING ENGINEERING

As the supervisor of manufacturing engineering, I supervise a group of engineers in a company that manufactures medical diagnostic instruments. My supervisory functions include keeping close contact with my subordinates for problem solving and project updates, attending daily production status meetings, and personally inspecting the production area to see if any problems need my attention. I also perform certain engineering tasks such as tooling design and setting up tooling methods.

This kind of work requires good mechanical and electrical engineering skills and the ability to communicate with all levels of personnel in an effective manner.

I like my job. I enjoy bringing engineering problems to a satisfactory resolution and the responsibility and prestige involved in leading a group of professionals. I like the people I work with and the many opportunities for advancement within this organizational structure. Overall, I like this company, and I believe we make quality products.

Prior to this job, I worked as an assistant manager at an equipment rental company.

I plan to continue in my present position, working with the manufacturing engineering group.

SUPERVISOR, MANUFACTURING LINE

I am a line supervisor in the manufacture of industrial fabric. I supervise the weaving, seaming and finishing of fabric, that is like the "screen" used on a paper machine to form a sheet of paper. I have been doing this job for 12 years.

My day starts with a review of things that have happened in the last 16 hours of operation since I left. I go out on the floor and review progress and problems with operators and maintenance personnel, help determine solutions, plan changes in product, evaluate quality problems etc. The job involves a lot of walking and thinking on your feet, lots of irons in the fire and a minimum of paperwork.

Basic science in practical application and ability to deal with people in long term relationships are two very important skills that this job takes. However, you also have to have a lot of tolerance, patience, and an even temperament.

Bringing a work group to the point that they can do their jobs with confidence, efficiently, and still enjoy their work is my main satisfaction with my job. It would be even more satisfying if I received more pay and had to make less decisions by myself.

Part-time jobs in manufacturing got me interested in this job. Some other occupations that I have had previous to this job are such things as being a mechanic in the Air Force, department head of quality control at a yarn manufacturing plant, line supervision in other textile plants, insurance sales, and operating a carpet cleaning business.

My future career aspirations are to move up to a position where I would supervise people doing jobs similar to the one I am doing.

SUPERVISOR, METAL INSPECTORS

Being a supervisor of inspectors requires becoming involved in the processes to examine heavy metal industry machinery for flaws. To accomplish this, we use a variety of nondestructive means, such as radiography, ultrasonic, magnetic particles, visual, penetrant, and gamma probe. We inspect welds, castings, forgings, plates, pipes, and pumps. Our territory includes the civilian as well as the Navy nuclear arena. We also inspect space age rocket casings.

My duties as supervisor are to review the unfinished work of the two previous shifts. I assign inspectors to jobs for which their expertise qualifies them. Checking the darkroom as well as radiography areas for hazards are part of my responsibilities. My job ranges from ordering supplies to reviewing completed radiographs and sending them to quality assessment. I check instruments to make certain each is precisely tuned and dated, check production control for new inspection needs, and study quality control for new information.

After graduating high school, I worked for a while as a fire fighter and then as a boilermaker. I've enjoyed everything about my 29 years in this work except the gross amount of paperwork. We badly need computer assistance. Yet, I am always happy to get a better, defect-free product in use. I'd choose this work again, perhaps because of the mere challenge of examining different materials, shapes and sizes.

An inspector needs a great deal of patience. You should have good communication skills, ask questions, and cooperate with coworkers. Working in a field with radiation hazards, you need to be able to faithfully carry out all requirements.

SUPERVISOR, NAVY AIR LOGISTICS

After earning my associate degree in history, I took a civil service test in order to qualify for employment with the federal government. I have now been doing civil service work for 26 years and have the current position as Supervisor in Navy Air Logistics.

It is my responsibility to supervise, determine procurement quantities, and monitor and expedite contracts. More specifically, I ensure that employees finish projects on a timely basis, monitor and expedite key contract, receive external requests for assistance, and engage in problem resolution with internal and external organizations.

To perform this kind of work well, it is important to have the ability to: motivate others to assist you, develop ideas verbally and in writing, analyze, organize, and prioritize.

I like most aspects of my work, except the supervisory function. I also feel somewhat encumbered with the government system for procuring personnel, and the way we are being governed by computer-driven statistical goals. In spite of these frustrations, I like the people I work with, the kind of work I do, and the opportunity to work independently. I have the job satisfaction of changing policy and solving problems. I also find it satisfying to provide encouragement to employees.

SUPERVISOR, NURSING HOME LPN'S

I always wanted to be nurse. I grew up in a family of medical professionals and saw the enjoyment they received from their work. I have now been working in this profession for 40 years, and I still like nursing very much. In fact, if given the opportunity to start over and prepare for any kind of work, I would again choose nursing.

As a R.N. (Registered Nurse) Supervisor, I oversee the care of the elderly in a nursing home. I supervise L.P.N.s (licensed practical nurses) and nursing assistants. My normal daily work involves preparing reports, writing up employee evaluations, and handling the other required paper work relevant to the job.

To perform this kind of work well, it is important to have compassion for the elderly, good interpersonal relationships, and adequate education in nursing. Aside from my frustrations with management and my desire for them to be more responsive to the problems of the nursing staff, I am satisfied with my work. It is indeed satisfying knowing that what I do helps the elderly have a more comfortable meaningful life.

SUPERVISOR, POWER PLANT

My work day begins at 6 A.M. when I review and assign work requests and consult with operations people on any problems. The rest of the day, from 7 A.M., is spent coordinating the work of various maintenance departments and attending to personnel and equipment problems as they occur. Each Friday, the next week's work is planned. I am usually home by 4:30 P.M.

A high school education and considerable (at least 10 years) experience is required to get to my level in this business since a thorough understanding of power plant operation and theory is necessary. I was a meter reader, cable splicer, equipment operator, and control operations foreman previously and enjoyed all of them except meter reading. Have been in this business 18 years, with four in my present job.

The rewards of my work are a higher than average salary and a sense of accomplishment in a job well done.

The major frustrations are having to deal with unions and the need to be on call constantly for emergencies. Because of the nature of the work, you have to have a positive attitude about problem-solving to keep from getting discouraged when problems pile up some days or when things can go wrong in a split second. It is not boring.

I didn't select this occupation exactly but needed work at 18 and did not want to go to college. Once I'd invested several years, I decided to apply myself to earn advancement. If I could start over, I would get an engineering or medical degree, but at the moment I plan to continue to advance to higher levels of management and perhaps go back to school for a degree at the same time.

SUPERVISOR, PRINTING OPERATORS

It was through a high school friend who worked in his father's print shop that my interest in the printing profession was sparked. After high school graduation, I applied to and was accepted at a large, well-respected technical school where I studied the printing profession and confirmed that I liked the field. After that, I was in the Army doing the work that I trained for. Upon separation from the service 17 years ago, I started working at my present occupation.

I am the supervisor in a large graphics department for an insurance company. On a daily basis, I will discuss with the production coordinator the status of projects in the system and what time frame to expect for their timely completion. Next, I will discuss job problems or concerns with the other members of the management team and work on solutions that are equitable to all concerned. Lastly, I will greet all employees that report to me at the beginning of their shift and lay out a schedule for them to follow to achieve the goals set up by the management group.

I consider the most important attribute for this kind of work to be commitment. I am very big on this. I go by the principle that if a job is worth doing, then it should be done right. The other skills and abilities which I consider important are high motivation, attention to details, knowledge of equipment and operators (their strengths and weaknesses), crisis prevention (ability to turn a project around in a short time), and organization.

If given the chance to change something in printing, I would like to train our clients in the methods of our operations and give them a better sense of what we do and how we go about doing their printing. Once you see what it takes to do a project (not just printing), you have a greater respect for the talents and abilities required. I am also somewhat frustrated with the unmotivated and poorly-trained work force I sometimes have to work with. Aside from these frustrations, however, I like the sense of accomplishment I feel in turning out quality printed materials.

SUPERVISOR, RETAIL DRUGSTORE

When I took a job as a clerk in a drugstore, I thought it would be temporary. I found that I liked it and that I could move up in the company on the basis of my dedication and performance. I have been at it for four years now.

At present I handle paperwork and supervise the other employees, scheduling their hours and breaks, and overseeing the stocking and pricing of merchandise. I also work on the cash deposits, and help customers when the need arises. Doing the latter and having the figures look good on the business end are the main satisfactions of this work. I enjoy knowing I have played a part in the success of the business. Sometimes the work can be uneventful and boring. My career goal is to move up into the advertising and marketing areas of this business with the company I presently work for.

SUPERVISOR, SOCIAL SERVICE DEPARTMENT

After spending some years in education as a music teacher and a school administrator, I chose to switch careers and work as a supervisor helping the indigent, or needy, of our area. I am a supervisor of a program called TWP. In this program, we spend our time doing whatever we must to help people in need. Every case is different and every day is unique, depending on the number of people to be seen. We contact various agencies to secure any help that is needed for the assorted problems which arise.

Being able to help people in difficulty, whatever the magnitude, is rewarding. I've been in this work now for 13 years and like just about everything except I'd like to see more time and money available to help people in need. Nevertheless, I would choose this work again. My future plans are to continue in my present job.

In this field, you must have a great deal of compassion for people. You have to be able to distinguish between the "needy" and the "greedy." Being able to make decisions according to the rules of the agency is also necessary. Even though I have a Bachelor of Science degree in education and a Masters of Science, I don't think advanced education is needed for this job.

SUPERVISOR, TRAVEL MANAGEMENT

I have been involved in travel management as a supervisor of customer services, as a tester (software), as a systems analyst, and finally as a supervisor. My jobs have been progressive through a company and I have been successful because I have been willing and able to learn the business and apply it to computer systems. I originally went to school and became certified in travel management. I was then involved in developing specifications for a reservation system to automate most of these functions. Then I was promoted to test the programs developed for the system. Thus my interest in computer science began and has continued. I have also earned an associate degree in computer science to better qualify myself for my job.

As a supervisor of software quality assurance (QA), I am responsible for the supervisory functions for the software test and QA staff. I supervise 10 people and interface with management of all levels. My typical activities include: reviewing my staffs written work (i.e., test plans); developing work schedules and quality assurance audit plans delivery schedules; troubleshooting system problems; and working with the business analysts and programmers on system changes required by the use.

I consider the following skills and attitudes important for this kind of work: good knowledge of the business; good written and communication skills; ability to work with other people; and ability to compromise and negotiate deadlines and problem resolutions.

Although I like my work very much, I do get frustrated because of unreasonable deadlines imposed on my department to deliver software products to production. Aside from this frustration, I like the kind of work I do and the people with whom I work. I find job satisfaction from the accomplishment of completing a project according to the deadlines, from solving user problems, and from developing a team of people that are productive and happy in their work.

SUPERVISOR, TRUCK DRIVERS

I enjoy interacting with employees and customers in my job as a supervisor of the routes for truck drivers.

My job involves overseeing the pick up of raw milk from farms. The milk routes usually begin around 5:30 a.m. I supervise the truck drivers who are routed to the different farms to collect the milk and deliver it to receiving stations. The work day is between 11 to 14 hours long, but we work only 4 days each week.

The ability to work well with people is important since this job involves contact with dairy producers. You also have to be able to direct the drivers and plan their routes, so you have to be really good at organizing.

Earlier I had a job in insurance sales, but I like this job quite well. I have a Bachelor of Science degree, but you don't need a college education to do this work. You do in order to advance in the workplace, though. There's not much opportunity for promotion unless I buy and run this trucking company, as I eventually plan to do.

SUPPLY CLERK, MANUFACTURING COMPANY

As a supply clerk in a furniture manufacturing plant, it is my job to see that the upholsterers have all the supplies they need to do their work. I write up orders for the tools and products needed for the upholstered furniture.

My prior work experience has been as an electrician and store operator. I have graduated from high school but have not attended college.

Although I like the kind of work I do and the people I work with, I dislike the lack of opportunity for advancement and the pressure of the job.

The main satisfaction I get from my work is that each day I do my work so that the other people that rely on me can build their quota.

SURGEON & PHYSICIAN

As an ear, nose, and throat physician and surgeon, I spend my day making hospital rounds or visits to my surgery patients. I also see patients in my office in the mornings and in the afternoons. In addition to examining patients, some days I perform surgery.

In my senior year in high school, I got interested in medicine because of my local doctor. I earned my Bachelor of Arts degree and then my medical degree. For 30 years I've practiced medicine, finding satisfaction in solving problems and in the independence. I also find my work very interesting.

I very much dislike the excessive government rules and regulations in the medical profession. The insurance companies have extreme requirements as well. There are so many time-consuming and unnecessary things you have to do to protect yourself against malpractice suits.

A physician must be able to ask enough questions to determine a good diagnosis and not miss anything. The ability to handle hostile patients is also important. You have to avoid becoming too self-confident and have respect for other people. Manual dexterity is essential for a surgeon. Continuing your education is a must. A good doctor must be able to figure out what patients mean, not just what they say.

SWITCHING TECHNICIAN TELEPHONE

As a telephone switching technician, I check trunk lines for routing and directing telephone calls. This involves repairing equipment when problems arise and returning service to customers who have temporarily lost service. I've been involved with telephone repair for 28 years.

Job satisfaction for me is knowing that customers have been helped. They are pleased when telephone service is returned to them. I realized I liked this kind of work when I took technical training in the U.S. Navy.

Characteristics important to my line of work are proficiency in digital electronics and high motivation to provide good customer service. Treating people as if they were you yourself is my working philosophy. While I like my work, fellow employees, customers, and the company itself, my job would be more satisfying if communication within the company improved. On the whole, however, I am satisfied with this work and plan to continue in it for years to come.

SYSTEMS ANALYST #1

Having earned an Associate degree in Computer Science and from my experience with data entry, I moved into my present position as systems analyst. My job is to solve problems with the computer system used in my workplace. More specifically, this entails overseeing the software package on the computer system, answering questions, doing research and solving problems, and doing projects associated with maintaining, amending and upgrading the system software.

As a systems analyst, it is important to have the ability to make decisions, and the ability to deal with people to analyze and solve problems. This, of course, is in addition to the computer technology skills which are essential for this kind of work.

I do like the kind of work I do, but I am very undecided about my future career plans. At the present time I also have a second job as a church organist. I don't know if I will pursue more of this kind of work or take off in another direction. I mostly want to be happy at what I do, and climbing the corporate ladder and money are not particularly important.

SYSTEMS ANALYST #2

My career started by my working in an assembly line of a large manufacturer of computers. This led into my next position with this company as a computer operator on their night shift. Following that I was able to move into my current position as systems analyst. As such, I install operating systems on computers and work with users to help install their products. My typical work schedule is as follows: checking phone messages; logging into system and reading my electronic messages; taking care of problems or issues related to these messages; and then working in the lab on installation of operating systems or at a job site.

Communication skills are very important for this kind of work because you are dealing with customers in order to help them out with their problems. Aside from the personal skills, technical skills are of course necessary.

I like most aspects of my work, although I now feel I have reached a level where it has become difficult to find an opportunity for advancement. I do, however, like the kind of work I do.

Once each task/problem of the day is complete, it makes me feel good to know I have helped out with a problem.

SYSTEMS ANALYST #3

Although the term systems analyst is difficult to define specifically and covers many kinds of jobs, I refer to my occupation as a data systems analyst, which means that I work with computers and the handling of data that go into and come out of those machines.

I work for a company that needs data, and the needs change from time to time. It is my job to modify computer programs as required by management's needs, produce reports for management, be sure that the data in the computer system are accurately maintained, arrange for system back-ups (so that data will not be lost if anything goes wrong), and, when records are outdated, purge them.

To do this job effectively, you need to have a general knowledge of computer operating systems, a high degree of accuracy in doing what you do, and the ability to follow up on programs with memory of and understanding of functions so that changes can be made if needed.

There are many satisfactions to be derived from this work: a sense of accomplishment when a program works the correct way, acknowledgement from management for a job well done, and usually the organizations that have this kind of position are good to work for. However, I find the people I work with are in some cases a negative in the job, and I would like to be in a position to do more writing of programs. Personally, I would like the job better if there were less debugging of programs; however, I still like this job quite well overall.

If someone gets into this work the way I did without formal education beyond high school, you would start as a data entry clerk and work your way up. I hope eventually to become a systems programmer or applications programmer or become a software development engineer.

SYSTEMS ANALYST #4

As a systems analyst I design, write, test, and implement data processing systems. For 10 years I have enjoyed the work I do, the people I work with and work for, and the organization. I graduated from college with a B.A. degree and have earned a Masters of Arts degree.

Skills of organization, concentration, communication, and flexibility are needed in my occupation. I particularly enjoy the feeling of accomplishment when a computer system works; I like dealing with problems and fixing them.

Previously, I was in the teaching profession; I retrained and worked my way into my present job as a systems analyst. I'd enjoy my current work more if the pay were higher and more vacation time were allowed. I regret the lack of opportunity for advancement in my work. In the future, I'd like to advance in this or other organizations and improve at what I do in my work.

SYSTEMS ENGINEER #1

Because of my interest in math and machinery, I engaged in the field of aero engineering. I earned both a bachelor's and master's degree in aero engineering before starting my career.

I am currently Systems Engineer for a company doing government contract work. It is my responsibility to define requirements and/or the approach to solving new problems by the use of our company's equipment. My regular activities include meetings with people to define problems, planning the approach to problems, working with and/or directing people involved with these efforts, and reporting on the progress of our problem solving.

To perform this kind of work well, it is important to have verbal communication skills, writing skills, good people relations skills, and honesty.

The only problem with my current work is that it is associated with the military. I would prefer work which is not part of war. What does give me satisfaction is solving problems and/or developing approaches to solving problems and working/guiding people working to solve problems.

My future career plans are to work as a consultant to engineering companies. I also aspire to establish a bed-and-breakfast service.

SYSTEMS ENGINEER #2

Working as a systems engineer for process and control systems, I program and troubleshoot computer systems that control paper machines. Although I have been working in this position for over ten years and enjoying it, I will never get used to the number of reports I must prepare or the amount of time I have to travel for my job. Traveling to customer sites, I evaluate the performance of our equipment that was purchased by the customers. Some of the procedures that are a regular part of product maintenance are tuning process control loops, modifying software to meet customer expectations, training system operators, and following up with results in the form of reports.

I have an Associate degree in Computer Science. In addition, my job requires both oral and written communication skills, programming skills, electrical engineering skills, troubleshooting skills, and problem solving skills.

I like this kind of work and customer satisfaction brings me a lot of job satisfaction. I enjoy the problem solving aspects of my work, the communication I have with the customers, and the opportunity to teach operators to get the most out of their equipment.

Although I have held several other positions in unrelated fields, no other work gives me the same feeling of accomplishment.

I plan to remain in my present job. I am happy with it and there are many advantages to working at my present company.

SYSTEMS PROGRAMMER

As a systems programmer for seven years, I perform total systems integration of different computer systems by setting up network data communications connections, writing programs to integrate different protocols for hardware platform communications, working on improving overall computer system performance, maintaining and improving security on the computer system, and handling all administrative tasks for the system.

In addition to experience in computer programming and some technical training on computer systems, you must be self-motivated and possess the ability to work alone with minimal supervision. It is also necessary to prefer working with computers over working with people as there is not much interaction with any person other than my boss. I received my training on computer systems while serving in the U.S. Air Force; I opted for this training program because computers have always held high interest for me.

Although there is not much of an opportunity for advancement in my present position, I really like this type of work and I enjoy my job, especially when I have accomplished the successful implementation of a computer system. My interaction with system users is satisfying, especially when they express their appreciation for a very useful system upgrade or the overall system improvements that I provide.

I would like to see my work get higher visibility and more credit from the upper management level within my company, I feel many times that I am working very much behind the scenes; this is frustrating because the work I do has front line implications for the entire system.

I would like to return to school and apply the training and knowledge I have gained in work experience toward an undergraduate degree in computers; I believe that the experience I have gained may be applied to earn several college credits in lieu of attending classes. Meanwhile I would like to move on to design a computer system for a software company to be sold as a profitable software package for business or scientific applications.

TAX MAPPER, ASSESSMENT OFFICE

A tax mapper works on maps to describe property from deed descriptions. I have worked as a tax mapper for 20 plus years in a county tax assessment office. I read property deeds for information to put on the map for proper taxation of that property.

To do my job, I have to know about the laws pertaining to transfers of the sale of properties, a process called conveyance, or conveying property from one owner to another. I have to know about, as well as how to use, drafting equipment, such as plotters which are printed copies of computer-generated maps. Knowledge of photogrammetrical (use of aerial photography) techniques is also necessary. Finally, getting along with people as well as having a great deal of patience is useful.

What I like most about my job is meeting the public. I don't much like the person I work for, but I do enjoy my coworkers and knowing that I am doing my job well. One challenge is getting my work done, plus keeping up with the latest developments or techniques in this line of work.

I got into this work after the factory I'd worked in was closed. I'd had about 2 years of college and my background in math was good, so I applied to the county mapping office and was hired.

TEACHER #1

My day starts early, since I must be prepared by 7:25 when my fifth- grade students arrive. I teach classes all day and attend meetings after school.

The most important skill for a teacher is the ability to deal with and communicate with children in an effective way.

I find it rewarding to help students gain knowledge and life skills. It is pleasant to work with young people. This position can lead to a position in school administration, and that is one of my own career objectives. I have had experience in sales and as a law clerk, and I like teaching much more than either of those jobs.

Before entering this field, I taught on a part-time basis and I visited classes, all of which helped me to make the decision. It has been the right one for me.

TEACHER #2

My typical day includes: bus duty, teaching and discussing social studies, some free time while students go to art, music or gym, recess duty, teaching math, science and language arts including spelling, grammar, reading and writing, and bus duty again.

A positive, encouraging attitude is important. A teacher must have the ability to work with children and find something likeable about each one. Also important is the ability to deal with parents and the public.

I find satisfaction as a teacher when students learn to be independent and take on responsibility.

I would like to see public opinion of the profession and funding for education changed.

TEACHER #3

I've always wanted to be a teacher and that is why I have been teaching for 35 years. My duties can be described in basic terms. I teach five classes, correct papers and have duties like study hall monitoring.

The most important factor in performing well as a teacher is to like what you do. You will probably find, as I have, satisfaction from this work of watching the children learn and progress. The most dissatisfying part of teaching for me has been the enormous amount of paperwork and the lack of opportunity for advancement.

Before becoming a teacher I was a factory worker. I found ways to get myself through college to earn my teaching degree and later also managed to earn an M.A. degree.

TEACHER #4

I have been a teacher for many years and, if I were to start over again and could prepare for any kind of work, I would again choose teaching. Since you have all been in elementary school you know basically what I do on a day to day and week to week basis. The routine duties include preparing all the lessons, teaching them, and grading papers. There are always extra duties, too, like lunch room or bus duty. There is a certain amount of structure and bureaucratic control that you might find unpleasant--for example, too many reports--but there are many compensating advantages and satisfactions in this work too. Although you might think that this kind of work would get boring, I want to emphasize that I have always found it challenging because there is always new information to learn and teach and new methods to try. The main reason I have been teaching so long and have found it so satisfying is that look on the face of a child when there is understanding. If you love and understand children, this job will be rewarding for you and for your pupils.

TEACHER #5

To describe my work briefly, I would say I instruct 6th graders by responding to their academic, personal, and social needs. In more specific terms my work hours are from 8:00-4:00 (usually until 5:00). I instruct 30 sixth graders in math, social studies, science, spelling, and a whole-language approach to reading and language skills which includes writing, speaking, and listening.

I consider classroom management to be the most important skill to have to perform well as a teacher. Students now are difficult to motivate, stimulate, and discipline for learning. Also important are communication skills and subject matter knowledge.

I find my work satisfying when I am teaching students new things. It is also rewarding to give them tools to cope. Because many of my students come from very troubled homes, I feel good about providing them with a safe/stable environment.

I would like to see a reduction in class size so I could give each child the individual time/attention each one needs and deserves. Also, cut out "fluff" from the curriculum; too much is expected of us and we cannot teach everything.

Before I started teaching, I was at home with my five children for 15 years until my youngest entered school. During some of that time I was going to college to earn my degree in elementary education. My credentials now include the B.A., B.S., and M.A. degrees.

I plan to retire eventually. Although I would again choose teaching if I had the opportunity to start over, it is beginning to wear a little thin after 22 years on the job. Teaching is so much more difficult now--all my colleagues agree.

TEACHER #6

I have taught school for many years and would still choose teaching if I could start over again. I have primarily taught English. As an example of the structure of this work, my weekly schedule is as follows: Monday/Wednesday/Friday, I have 3 hours of classes, 2-6 hours grading papers, preparing lessons, and student counseling. Tuesday/Thursday, I have 2 hours of classes, 4-6 hours grading, preparing, having conferences, etc.

The skills which I find important for a teacher are the ability to express ideas clearly and the ability to hold the attention of the class. The attitudes which I find important are command of subject matter, obvious interest in other people, kindness, and understanding of differences in people.

Knowing I have made a difference by helping someone is rewarding. I enjoy receiving respect and appreciation from students. Teaching is just doing something I love.

One thing that I would change in my occupation would be to provide teachers with more time for personal study and development. I would also like to work with less pressure. Originally, I never wanted to do anything but teach. Perhaps my mother's influence as a teacher, my love of books, and the fact that when I was growing up there were not too many careers open for women led to my choosing teaching.

TEACHER #7

It is my continuing goal to increase my skills as a teacher so I can better teach my children. Actually, I think that education involves and concerns everyone: parents, businesses, teachers, and children. Because of my personal convictions, I knew early in life that I wanted to be a teacher. I worked my way through college as a mill worker and bank teller to earn my Bachelor of Arts in Education degree to accomplish this goal, and I am glad I did.

I teach all academic areas to my class of 2nd graders. In the morning, I teach math, spelling, phonics, language arts, literature and reading. After lunch, we work on a class newspaper, I read to the children, and we do whole language activity.

To perform well as a teacher, it is important to have a positive and caring attitude. You must have full academic knowledge and the ability to increase your skills and knowledge in order to update your curriculum.

I like my job very much because of the people I work with, the kind of work I do, and the school and people I work for. I receive satisfaction from having a part in helping a person learn a skill and feel success on the way to adulthood.

TEACHER #8

I like teaching and have done so intermittently for 30 years. Primarily, I teach 7th through 12th graders because I enjoy this age group.

I teach four to six classes per day in English and social studies. I would describe my typical day by saying that it involves teaching and preparation in various subject matters.

To perform well as a teacher, it is most important to have a knowledge of the subject matter. It is equally important to have respect for the dignity of the student as an individual--for his or her abilities and potential. You need to respect the student as a person.

Prior to earning my Bachelor of Science degree, I had office jobs which involved training others. This is probably what led me into teaching as a career. Even when I retire I plan to be involved in teaching or training.

TEACHER #9

My decision to become a teacher just seemed to grow out of finding satisfaction in working with young people. After many years in this work, I can still say that I like very much.

I am a teacher of electronics, math, and general sciences, and I am a counselor. I don't think it is necessary to describe my daily activities since you have all watched educators work.

To perform well as a teacher, it is important to know your subject matter and be fair and firm to all your students.

TEACHER #10

As a teacher, I expect my students to progress and continue to grow in knowledge and abilities, and I too have continued to work on this. I first earned a Bachelor of Arts degree in order to quality for teaching and I have continued going to college every semester to help me in my "lifelong learning" process.

Every day is busy and presents new challenges to a teacher. No two days are alike. Therefore, it is important to be flexible. In fact, I think flexibility is the key attribute for a good teacher. Also, you have to master the basic skills in math, reading, language arts, music, science, social studies, and arts and crafts yourself before you can teach others. Love of children is, of course, necessary for teachers.

It has been my strong conviction to emphasize the basics: reading, math, and composition skills. I also try to emphasize patriotism.

My job satisfaction as a teacher has been found in seeing progress in the skills of a child, the progress in social areas, and progress in individual growth and abilities.

I hope I can continue in education until I am at least 90!

TEACHER #11

I retired from school teaching after 25 years, but couldn't get myself away from the profession because of my love for children. I now teach remedial reading on a one-to-one basis. This not only involves instruction, but diagnosing disabilities and counseling as well.

I prepared for my career in education by earning a Bachelor of Arts in Elementary Education degree and also by continuing my education throughout my career by taking postgraduate courses.

I think the key to this profession is liking children. I know I do. I also have liked the organization and people I have worked for. Ultimately, it is the gratification of seeing children improve and grow as good citizens that has kept me dedicated to this occupation.

TEACHER #12

A good knowledge is critical, of course, for this occupation; but two other factors are especially important to do the job well: a) an interest in young people and b) the ability to impart your knowledge as you motivate the students to learn. It has been a great satisfaction in my career to observe the development of young minds for the fifteen years I have been in teaching. Making a difference in a youngster's whole attitude can provide a sense of pride that few occupations offer. A college degree is required.

The only changes that would improve teaching as a career are more support from administrators in dealing with behavior problems of students, and reducing many of the extra duties that teachers are called on to perform.

TEACHER #13

Being a high school teacher may seem self-explanatory, but I'm a teacher first--social studies just happens to be my field. A "typical" day is both predictable and unpredictable--and it's that duality I enjoy. The schedule is so rigid--yet the problems that come up are different every day. To be a teacher, you MUST be able to make instantaneous decisions. Consider EACH student's needs and personalities--make the tough choices, and bear the repetition. It's ENDLESS paperwork, and being sensitive, but not taking things too personally.

You must WANT to be a teacher--not want just to study history or English or math, or teach because you can't think of what else to do. You must always have a sense of humor, but know when to be firm. Obviously, you must also be skilled in your field--not use it for another primary goal (i.e. to coach athletics).

I originally planned to go to law school (all the way to taking the LSAT). But after taking some education courses in college and seeing the cynical attitude many teachers had--I suddenly felt a social responsibility to pursue teaching. After all, this is OUR future! I couldn't then believe people's attitude. I was stunned! Everyone (family and friends) thought I was crazy--that teaching was "inferior" as a career choice. The lack of respect is something you just can't take seriously. You have to look beyond it.

After working in this occupation for 9 years, there are definitely things which I have observed about teaching which I would change to make it more satisfying. Teachers should be treated, and paid, as professionals. Administrators should be promoted after appropriate training and not because of "politics." (Not just ex-teachers looking for more money.) There should be less paper work, or at least assistance with it. More involvement by parents is needed--education as a priority, not just a warehouse to "keep the kids." Change the way schools are funded. Despite all these concerns, teaching for me is amazingly rewarding AND occasionally frustrating. Money is NOT a satisfaction! There's stress from a myriad of demands on time and physical energy. But to have the opportunity to touch SO MANY lives is an awesome responsibility. What a reward to have that chance AND to find you have made a difference in someone's life!

TEACHER #14

As a special education teacher, I teach a group of 9 behaviorally disordered adolescent boys. I work in a self contained class in a residential intermediate treatment facility, teaching them all subjects. All the boys have been in trouble with the law or have been abused.

I find this kind of work very rewarding. It is not, however, the kind of special education I was trained for. I earned a Bachelor of Arts in Deaf Education, and a Master of Arts in Education. Prior to this teaching position, I worked as an audiologist, and a teacher of the deaf.

In order to perform this kind of work well, the following attributes are important: patience, consistency, structure, love of children, and knowledge of the subject matter.

I like the work very much. I have been doing it for 15 years and I plan to continue. I like the organization and people for whom I work. I have job satisfaction because the kids are learning. I am making a small impact on their lives.

TEACHER #15

I always enjoyed school. I admired several teachers and thought it would be wonderful if I could influence some children as I thought these teachers had influenced me. I have now taught for 20 years and have indeed found this to be a rewarding career.

My goal and responsibility as a 4th grade teacher is simple--to teach children. My day is spent working with approximately 22 children in the usual areas of reading, writing and arithmetic. In order to do this effectively, you need patience and enthusiasm.

I have found several things that seem to obstruct me in accomplishing my goals in the best way I know how. As a teacher, there is a lack of input into the curriculum. I feel I could be more effective if I were given more freedom in developing the curriculum as I evaluate the needs in my particular class. I would like to have more control over scheduling for this same reason. Additionally, I would schedule my school day with fewer interruptions.

Aside from these frustration, I like being a teacher, and would again choose this occupation, even if given the opportunity to start over and train for any kind of work.

Watching children learn skills, develop reasoning, and come to understand cause and effect is stimulating and satisfying to me.

TEACHER #16

I have always wanted to be a teacher. Now that I am a teacher, I certainly can see the pros and cons to this profession. However, I still can say that I like the kind of work I do very much. I have good days and bad days. On the good days, I envision myself teaching faithfully for years to come (until a school is named for me!) I have no aspirations to become an administrator. On the bad days, I think about joining a hip young advertising agency, going to law school, or opening a bookstore of exclusively children's books and games. The latter is the most appealing.

As a 4th grade teacher, with a class of 22 upper-middle class 9 and 10 year olds,

I teach all subjects, with the exceptions of science and music. I teach reading, English (language arts), spelling, social studies (Texas history), math, current events, computers, and art. I make lessons plans for each day, but I must also deal with many unexpected events and things like discipline, illness, and fire drills. There is no such thing as a "typical"day or week in my occupation.

You must be DEVOTED to both the idea of teaching and to children. Flexibility and independence are both useful, also. It helps to be diplomatic, to be confident and to be creative. You MUST be patient, and above all else you must be FAIR--you MUST tolerate intolerable children.

I think it is unfortunate that teachers work so hard, work such long hours, do so much and make very little money. We are shaping the minds of the future and make less money than many people with no college degree selling shoes at Macy's.

Despite this drawback, I still find satisfaction in so many ways from teaching. The children view me as a special person. I am near godlike in their eyes! Some see me as a hero and emulate me. I am a role model and I like it. I taught in an underprivileged area last year where this was all very obvious. When I left, I knew some children would always remember and use the values and ideas I gave them.

TEACHER #17

Business communication and management are the courses I teach in a technical college. I love my work and would choose education again.

After earning a Bachelor and a Master of Science degree, I started out wanting to be a coach. I did coach several sports for a while, but found the classroom to be more rewarding. Working with great colleagues and helping young people develop the necessary skills to succeed in the business world are very satisfying to me. I plan to stay in education until I retire.

To be an effective teacher, you need strong communication skills and must be able to work well with people.

Each day I spend 4 or 5 hours teaching business communication classes in the office management program. Many hours are spent in preparation for classes and in grading papers. I also spend time with students helping them on an individual basis.

TEACHER, ACCOUNTING

As a teacher of accounting in the public schools, grades 9-12, I've enjoyed helping students prepare for careers in business. It's been very gratifying to watch students learn and mature. I've also enjoyed helping them work on selecting career paths.

My responsibilities include conducting a homeroom, teaching five classes, and supervising study hall. I frequently work with students during my lunch break. Meetings take a lot of time in my teaching life: with students for extra help or for make-up work, with guidance counselors or the school nurse, in faculty meetings or in department meetings after school. I also supervise extra-curricular activities. There is a great deal of preparation in teaching: formulating lesson plans, planning field trips, composing tests and grading them. We also must cover other teachers' classes when there is an emergency.

Requirements for a good teacher are patience and perseverance. A positive attitude toward children, toward work, and toward life in general is very important. Knowledge of the subject matter is essential as is being informed on teaching methodology and techniques. Using practical psychology in dealing with the great variety of students and their often difficult family situations is helpful to me. A teacher also needs good health and a high energy level. An open mind along with a disciplined lifestyle, dedication, and inquisitiveness make a successful teacher.

With my Associates degree in accounting, Bachelor of Science in business education, and a Master of Arts degree in business education, I very much enjoy the teaching aspect of education. But, I do not like the many non-professional jobs that are required of teachers, i.e., study hall and lunch duty. These duties should be assigned to support staff. Then, more time during the school day would be available for teachers to meet with individual students about classwork and personal career or college plans, and for colleagues to discuss possible improvements in education.

I look forward to retirement so I can catch up on business reading, especially about national corporations. I also may travel or tutor.

TEACHER AIDE/TEACHER

Working as a teacher's aide in a high school, I run four study halls with approximately twenty-five to thirty students in each and, during two class periods per day, I work one-on-one as a tutor with students needing extra help.

In addition to a Bachelor's degree in the field of education, this job requires patience, flexibility, persistence, discipline, skills in classroom management, fairness, a sense of humor, organizational skills, and people skills.

I can honestly say without a doubt that the main satisfaction of my work is the students and the time that I have with them; I love to see their creativity come to life. I am currently enrolled in graduate school to complete a Master's degree in Education. Then I plan to become certified in Business Education and Social Studies. Once I have accumulated enough experience, I plan to work with "at-risk" behavioral, emotionally handicapped high school students.

TEACHER AND HOMEMAKER

I didn't think about job opportunities when starting in my career. I followed my inner voice, and then teaching naturally followed my theater career. I educated myself in the area I loved, receiving a Bachelor of Arts degree in Theater. Along my varied career path, I have also worked as an elementary teacher, bartender, waitress, cab driver, secretary, and trophy assembler.

Now, I am a homemaker, teacher, actress, writer, and director. I care for two children and my husband. I teach high school and college writing, direct children's theater, and perform in various plays and original work. Because of my home responsibilities, I am unable to pursue my career in the theater and writing fully. During the course of a day/week, I engage in the following activities: cook, clean, wash, counsel, hug, kiss and generally be of service to my family, plan lessons for my classes, teach classes with enthusiasm for the subject and the students, shop, drop off, pick up, worry, and read the papers.

In order for me to accomplish all these tasks and responsibilities, I find it necessary to have patience, high energy, genuine interest and concern for my students, and a belief that I am working to my fullest capacity and that I make a difference. I must love, even to the extent of being passionate about, the subject I teach.

I like what I am doing; however, I would prefer someday to do less teaching and more acting, writing, and directing. On the other hand, I do find satisfaction in what I do as a homemaker and teacher in observing the growth in others and knowing that I helped to further that growth.

TEACHER ASSISTANT

My job as a 1st grade teacher assistant is like being a mom for children at school. I assist with the paper work and work closely with the children. I listen to the children read and am able to take over the class if needed.

I earned an associate degree in human services, and worked as a church secretary, gymnastics instructor and waitress prior to starting in this career. In order to qualify for this work, I completed a continuing education program.

To perform this kind of work, it is important to have the skills to run office equipment, have lots of patience, and to have a positive, healthy attitude and outlook on life.

What I dislike about this job is the lack of opportunity for advancement. However, I like almost every other aspect of being a teacher assistant: the kind of work, the organization and people I work for, and the people I work with. I find job satisfaction in seeing children learn, making their day with me a good one, and working with good people knowing I do a good job.

TEACHER, BIOLOGY & CHEMISTRY

Although I was in pre-med in college and earned a Bachelor of Science in natural sciences and Master of Science in biology, I began my career after college by teaching nursery school. I found that I enjoyed working with parents and children. I also enjoyed the independence. I loved science and wanted to do something in the field, but had trouble finding a laboratory position. A science teaching opportunity arose in a private school and I decided to try it. I have now been in this position for 5 years and have found that I like it very much. My background also includes work as a shoe salesperson, nurses aide, nursery school teacher/director, live-in mother's helper while in college, and musical performer. For my various musical performance work, I played clubs and engagements while in college.

As the biology and chemistry teacher in a private school, my major responsibilities are to plan lessons, teach, and work with students and their parents. My typical activities include: teaching and preparation of lessons and laboratory assignments; testing and evaluation of progress; and contact with parents and tutorial work with some students. I consider patience to be the quality which is of utmost importance as a teacher. You must not mind putting in long hours of preparation time. Teaching is not good for someone interested in a "9 to 5 job and then leave it behind you" kind of job. My major frustration with my career is the salary level. I also would like to change society's view of teachers. Despite these drawbacks, I like teaching very much.

I particularly like working independently and feeling that I make a difference. I find satisfaction in being able to help students and to help them enjoy success.

I plan to continue my education and possibly work towards a Ph.D. in environmental biology. After that, I might try college teaching.

TEACHER, BUSINESS & MUSIC

In my work as a teacher of both music and business, I enjoy working with young people. Academically stimulating and motivating youth to achieve has been very rewarding. I appreciate their progress and enjoy measuring that achievement over given periods of time.

My greatest motivation in entering the field of music instruction was probably having musical talent as a child. The security in the teaching profession was also an incentive. In these 35 years, I would have liked to have more time to do my job and less interference from the bureaucracy. A more helpful administration and more opportunities for advancement would have made things happier. But, I very much enjoy my work, the people, and my superiors.

I hold a Bachelor of Science degree, a Bachelor of Arts in business administration, and a Masters in education. My work has included teaching vocal and instrumental music. I've also taught social studies, word processing, and business subjects; plus I once tuned and repaired pianos.

To be a successful teacher, I've found you need the ability to work with and motivate students. Being able to cooperate with colleagues to improve educational programs and the educational environment is essential. Certainly, teaching skills are very important. You need to maintain a positive attitude every day regardless of tensions and pressures.

A great deal of my time is spent planning and scheduling programs for the day, the week, and for the year. There is also preparation for professional meetings. It is important to me to maintain a pleasant environment. I also try to teach the value of discipline to all students.

TEACHER, BUSINESS EDUCATION & DIRECTOR, ADULT EDUCATION

My daily responsibilities as a teacher include planning material for and teaching classes, correcting and grading papers, keeping accurate records, dealing with individual differences and problems. As the director of adult education, I am meeting with faculty and students, scheduling classes, ordering materials, advertising programs, recruiting students and teachers, attending professional training, evaluating + supervising staff, and evaluating programs.

Educators need enthusiasm, energy, organizational skills, communication skills, and interpersonal skills. An overall belief in the ability of everyone to learn and a basic respect for people and their dignity is an important attitude to perform this job well.

Teaching has been my occupation for 26 years, because I get satisfaction from seeing people learn, building confidence in themselves and knowing I have been able to help them.

I would be more satisfied if I could work less hours. I now work 60-70 hours a week. I start at 9:30 A.M. in my teaching position and leave my adult education director position at 9:30 P.M.

I took an interest test in high school that indicated I would be good as a teacher or in business. It was the first time I thought I could be good at anything, so I decided to follow the test results. The adult education was a move I made, because my teaching job was being partially eliminated and I needed another avenue to pursue. It turns out that I love being "in charge" and have increased the program size over 600%.

In 3 weeks I will become the principal of a prison school. I would like to concentrate on developing teaching strategies that work with a population which has previously failed to learn using traditional methods.

Good luck! My life was pretty much planned as a result of a test such as you seem to be working on now.

TEACHER, CHEMISTRY

To be a teacher of chemistry you must have a passionate curiosity. Patience and an imaginative approach in comparing chemical theory to practical applications are both necessary. A penchant for accurate communication is also important.

I've been a chemistry teacher for a significant number of years. Always curious about "the way things work," I was blessed by a junior high school science teacher who appreciated my inquisitiveness. I also took the Kuder Test in about 1956; it helped confirm my career choice.

My goal is to help my students learn how to think with discernment and with logic. I love giving students confidence. Enabling them to learn, understand, and appreciate the beauty and the utility of the natural sciences is my intent. I very much like the results of my work and the endless variety in new scientific developments, as well as the charming wonder of my students.

Even when I retire, I'll return to teaching part-time. I'll also work on my new business as an environmental analyst inspecting and auditing residential real estate.

TEACHER, COMPUTER APPLICATIONS

I teach people of all ages how to use computers.

Typically, I leave home at 6:30 and open the computer room at 7:25. I usually have duty until 8:00, after which I teach classes. My at-school hours are also spent solving teacher and student computer problems, on lunch duty, and eating lunch while catching up on paper work (20 min.). School is finished at 2:15 but work on computer related problems is usually done until 4:00 or 5:00. I pack my briefcase and go home for supper. After I do dishes I correct papers, except for one night a week when I teach teachers. Even Sunday evenings are spent doing school work.

To do this work you must love people, especially teenagers. It is essential to know how to communicate and to have the knowledge of educational practices. I must know what is learning, etc.

My satisfaction comes from knowing that I am doing my job well and that others have benefited from what I have done.

There are indeed some changes I would like to see in my occupation. First, I would like the public that I work for to realize how much time teachers spend on their "job." Second, that the public realize that education must change in what we teach and how we teach it. I feel the public community only wants schools to be as they were 100 years ago and just as cheap.

I got into teaching because in every job I have held I ended up being the instructor. These previous jobs included construction, sales and the military.

Some day I will transfer to the private sector and work for a company teaching the same stuff I do now for 3-4 times as much money and get the respect of doing the job.

TEACHER, DAY CARE CENTER

I work from 8-5:30 every day with young children who require constant attention and care. In the mornings and evenings, I talk with the parents. As an assistant, I help implement lessons, take the children to the bathroom, pass out the snacks, get supplies, read aloud, help settle the children down for nap-time, prepare activities for the next day, put items in bed folders, etc.

To perform the job well, you must be attentive, loving, and a very patient person who is willing to spend your entire day with young children. You must be consistent and communicate well. Creativity is a fundamental requirement!

I find my work satisfying when a child finally understands a problem or overcomes one with my help. The love and affection received from the children is wonderful. The joy of watching children interacting with each other and with their environment is also gratifying.

A better salary, shorter hours, and more support from others, especially parents and the directors, would make this job even more satisfying.

I graduated from college without any marketable skills except that I had worked with kids in the past. I decided on teaching, so I started to work in day care. Meanwhile, I am in the process of getting K-6 certified. In the future, I plan to be a high school science teacher, or go back to school for an M.A. degree in psychology (my undergraduate major) in order to be a guidance counselor.

TEACHER, ELEMENTARY & LIBRARIAN

I teach 14 kindergarten children for half of the day and run the library the other half. I also run the library two evenings a week and on Saturdays. My duties as a teacher are the familiar ones such as lesson planning, teaching, grading papers and having recess duty, to name a few. As school librarian I must keep the library in order and make sure we have the appropriate materials available for the teachers and students.

To do my kind of work well it is important to have patience, a sense of humor, firmness, tolerance, and office skills such as typing, filing, and writing (for reports). A knowledge about purchasing and budgeting is also necessary because as a librarian I am in charge of ordering materials.

I decided to become a teacher and librarian because I find satisfaction in serving others. I first earned an associates of arts degree and later a bachelor of arts with teaching credentials and have previously used these degrees to qualify as a high school teacher and an ESL (English as a second language) teacher. Someday I plan to earn my master's degree in library science or education.

TEACHER, ELEMENTARY & SPECIAL EDUCATION

I plan sequential learning activities for wonderful youngsters and evaluate the success of them. I listen to and learn from children.

On a typical day I begin by exercising, either running or swimming. I plan the day in detail before I greet the children and listen to them. During the course of the day I work with groups on basics, organized peer tutoring and work with individual students myself. I help children plan projects, field trips, murals, special events and activities, perform required supervisory duties on playground or in school library, plan units of instruction with weekly goals and make daily revisions.

My main satisfaction is good relationships with wonderful children, whom I genuinely enjoy.

I would change the structure for the school district from one TOP HEAVY with highly paid administrative staff to one BALANCED with well-paid, competent, sensitive administrators who help teachers be the best they can be and who always have students' needs uppermost in planning.

I needed to work to support my family, sought employment, and found that teaching was the only reasonably well-paid occupation available to me. I, therefore, chose it of necessity and as my only option, and am glad now.

Some of my other occupations have been: store clerk, baby-sitter, homemaker, mother, church organist, news-column writer, typist, secretary, bookkeeper, tour bus driver/lecturer, volunteer campaigner.

I would like, eventually, to write, possibly fiction articles for children's publications.

TEACHER, ELEMENTARY #1

I work as a teacher of the fifth grade at an elementary school, with a usual class size of thirty students. Teaching a class involves a lot of preparation and enormous amounts of paperwork; I always review the lesson plan each day before I teach the class and there are always papers to be corrected and graded. I teach social studies, science, reading, and math, all on the fifth grade level. I have found that working with the class divided into smaller groups is a more effective teaching method for my students; I introduce math and reading assignments to the entire class, then work with each group one at a time, while the remainder of the class works on written or reading assignments.

My education includes a Master of Arts degree in school administration. Besides education, the work of a teacher requires the ability to exercise good group control, the ability to lead the students to stay with the task at hand, the ability to recognize needs and plan diagnostic instruction accordingly, a desire to and enjoyment of working with kids, and an interest in continual self-discovery.

Although lack of adequate monetary compensation is a perpetual complaint in this field, teaching is a rewarding field; I know that I am helping others. Among the numerous rewards derived from teaching, I am especially grateful for the opportunity to see enthusiasm and success in my pupils, the opportunity to praise my pupils for work accomplished, the ability to stay in a leadership role, and the opportunity to try several methods of teaching and uses for curriculum materials.

I love to teach; I enjoy the interaction with both the students and my fellow colleagues. I have a deep-seated love of learning and have enjoyed success in school situations in my past.

Although I was inspired a great deal by my college professors, my primary source of inspiration and encouragement is my father.

As the schedule of an elementary school teacher affords a great deal of time off, I plan to do more traveling in the next few years.

TEACHER, ELEMENTARY #2

In a typical day, I arrive at school about 7:45 and prepare work sheets or materials needed. I correct papers and share developments with my fellow teachers. At 8:50 the students arrive and we go through the morning schedule. I have one break at 10:10 for 40 minutes. Lunch is at 12:37 for 30 minutes. I teach lessons in spelling, math, writing, reading, and science. There is little variety in the planned activities except for an hour in the afternoon which is left flexible. At 3:15, the students leave. I work in my room or discuss the day until 4:30-5:00. I often spend additional time working in the evening at home.

In this work, you must be able to communicate with children and relate to their problems. You must be able to organize a day for the children and know the curriculum to be taught. You must be able to think of several ways to do things and to explain concepts to young minds.

The main satisfactions come when they finally "see" what you want them to see. Sometimes the satisfactions come years later when you find out they really appreciated what you did. In teaching, the satisfactions are sometimes hard to catch and explain. It's a kind of feeling.

I would like to make teaching less frustrating by reducing the number of students and by providing more outside references to help teachers deal with the problems we have today. I was never trained to deal with the emotional problems I have to deal with in young children. I am dissatisfied with the lack of money to fund the schools in the proper way.

I come from a long line of teachers. My mother and aunt were teachers; my father's father and uncle were teachers. It was in my blood. I cannot remember not wanting to be a teacher and have taught for 24 years.

TEACHER, ELEMENTARY #3

My motto as a teacher is "have patience and expect good from every child." You must understand a lot about child development. You must feel that all people are important and each child in your class is a "most important person." Be willing to do lots of planning so that groups will run smoothly.

I look forward to getting to school and work nearly every day. I try to give the children chances for "hands on" activities that would give them a basis to build up skills in reading, math, science, art, music, etc.

In this work I greet children, solve any problem I can, and provide activities to build academic and physical skills. In addition, I try to offer chances to learn to live together in harmony and build good health habits, and I regularly provide opportunities for creative activities.

The most difficult part of teaching for me has been working with parents. Otherwise, my 22 years in education has been a wonderful career for me.

My advice for those going into the teaching profession is not to expect children to be in the same place in the book at the same time; in other words, plan time to follow children individually.

My mother was a teacher and I helped with her classes. I was interested in art, and teaching was a good job you could get if you were trained in art.

As well as teaching kindergarten for 22 years, I own and operate a nursery school. In addition, I am part owner of an orange grove and help to take care of it.

Teaching has been a career which has satisfied me because I find rewards in seeing children grow and develop skills. It's fun to watch as they progress through school. Their success is your success.

TEACHER, ELEMENTARY #4

Patience is the key word for succeeding at my job as an elementary school teacher of socially disadvantaged children--children from government projects. Teaching socially and financially disadvantaged students involves many unique problems. I try to get parents interested in their child's work. I am a counselor, mediator, teacher, record keeper, nurse, and sometimes parent.

I have worked as a teacher for 22 years. To prepare myself for this work, I have earned a Bachelor of Science in Biology and a Master of Arts in Teaching. I am currently working on Montessori certification.

I like this kind of work very much, and the people I work with. If given the chance to start over and choose a career, I would again choose teaching. I find satisfaction when a child's face lights up because she/he understands how to solve a problem.

TEACHER, ELEMENTARY #5

I have worked with children since I was in junior high, teaching Sunday School, giving swimming lessons, babysitting, etc. I found that teaching elementary children was an appropriate career for me because of my natural interest in children. I earned a Bachelor of Science in Elementary Education degree and have been very satisfied teaching for the past 10 years. In fact, if given the opportunity to start over again and prepare for any kind of work, I would again choose teaching.

I teach a transition class from kindergarten to 1st grade for developmentally-delayed children. I arrive at school at 7:15 a.m. to prepare for the day. I teach from 8:00 to 2:30. I remain at school until 4:00 to clean-up and to do advance preparation.

As well as the academic knowledge and training in teaching methods which are required for teaching, I consider patience and love of children to be the most necessary attributes for an elementary teacher.

If I was given the opportunity to make a change in my occupation to make it more satisfying, I would eliminate the amount of bureaucratic interference.

I plan to continue teaching because I find it personally rewarding to see the gains children have made.

TEACHER, ELEMENTARY #6

After graduating from college with a Bachelor of Arts in Sociology, and finding out that I didn't meet the residency requirement in the state I was living in for a job in this field, I turned to teaching. I have now been teaching inner city children for 20 years and find this work very rewarding. During this time, I have returned to college and earned a Masters in Education.

Teaching for me is finding passages in the story to answer a question, support a theme, characterize a person, etc.; introducing vocabulary for a reading lesson; teaching math; teaching about the states through maps, research, etc.; and studying water animals in science. I further see my role as requiring the ability to know and care about people, being fair to the best of my ability, knowing where to "seat" children in a given classroom; being a strong disciplinarian (this does not mean being unkind--it means no nonsense); giving praise and raising self-esteem.

I have found job satisfaction from: children who are "problems" who learn that "fairness" works and is a two-way stream; sharing my enthusiasm for education; watching children become equally enthused in the process; seeing day to day progress of each child, as well as yearly progress. The most rewarding of all is watching children change--"problems" who turn around and begin to like learning.

My future plans are to continue teaching, to incorporate new learning ideas into my curriculum--science and whole learning, whole language reading approach, computers as tools to create and feel successful, and continued cooperative learning activities. My aspirations are for an optimum environment where all teachers and students share mutual respect.

TEACHER, ELEMENTARY #7

An elementary school teacher teaches all subjects; I teach the third grade and specialize in Reading. In my career of fifteen years, I have found the primary tasks of a third grade teacher are preparing the subject material and activities for the day's presentation and reviewing the work of the students by going over their papers every day. Although I specialize in reading, I also teach language, art, math, and science.

My educational background is a Bachelor of Science degree in Elementary Education and a Master of Science degree in Reading Education. In addition to the required education and certification, one must be mature, patient, cheerful, have a positive mental attitude, and take joy in children and seeing them gain confidence.

Although I don't enjoy record keeping and filling out report cards, I do find my job challenging and different everyday. It has been my experience that children are basically very funny; I enjoy talking with them and being in their company; I love to see the "light" come on when they learn something new; I especially enjoy their perspective on things. They make me laugh when they are happy and cry when I know that their lives are rough. It is easy for me to become very attached emotionally to my students; it also part of the success I have with them.

As a child I always enjoyed school. It was a comfortable place for me. Respect for teachers ran high in my family and still does.

I will eventually return to college to complete a post-graduate degree. I have considered moving into the field of school administration, but I believe I would really miss the one-on-one interaction I now enjoy with the children. It has always also been my secret ambition to become an author; perhaps I will write novels for children and young adults.

TEACHER, ELEMENTARY #8

I decided to become a teacher in the 4th grade and followed that course until I completed college. Having now taught for 16 years, I have found that I like this career very much.

I am a first grade teacher, teaching 6 and 7 year old children basic reading, language arts, math, and science/social studies skills. I arrive at school at 8:00 a.m. The children come in at 8:25 and start the day by eating breakfast. The daily schedule then typically includes the reading lessons, math lessons, lunch, a special such as art or music, and the science/social studies lessons. At 2:00 the bus students leave, and at 2:25 the walkers leave. Later in the day I do lesson plans, correct papers and confer with parents, etc.

To be an effective teacher, you need good judgment skills and genuine concern for the children. Academic training and good undergraduate grades are secondary to a real feeling for the children.

If given a chance to change some things in the teaching occupation, I would allow teachers more control over curriculum and more input regarding decisions of policy. I would encourage more creativity among teachers and reward outstanding teachers. Paying teachers a salary that is more competitive with business and industry is also on my wish list.

Despite the low salary, I have continued to teach for so many years because I find job satisfaction from this career. Being able to identify problems early and begin intervention is a rewarding experience. It is also satisfying to see children progress from non-readers to fluent readers.

My future career plans are to finish my Master's degree in English as a Second Language by next year and then to look for a job involving teacher training workshops.

TEACHER, ELEMENTARY #9

After various previous jobs, I found that I really wanted to teach so I went back to school at age 27 and got another degree. I have now earned a bachelor of science degree in biology, a master's in zoology and a bachelor's of arts in education. Prior to my teaching job, I was lab director at an electron microscope center and a curator of science in a natural history museum.

My typical duties as a 4th grade teacher include planning course work, special programs, replacing bulletin boards, teaching, counseling children, reporting progress to parents and committee work. The skills and attitudes I consider important for a teacher are a positive, optimistic attitude, ability to handle any situation that arises in a calm way, extreme patience and understanding and flexibility.

I particularly like this kind of work because it is rewarding to watch children respond, grow, and develop. It's just too bad that the salary is so low. However, my future plans continue to be to teach for many years to come.

TEACHER, ELEMENTARY #10

Ever since I was myself an elementary school child, I knew I wanted to teach. I was particularly inspired by my fourth-grade teacher. In order to pursue this occupation, I earned my Bachelor of Arts in Elementary Education degree. I have now been very satisfied with my career choice for the 11 years that I have been teaching.

As a kindergarten teacher, I teach all subject areas including reading readiness, math, health, art, music, and social sciences. My school day begins at 8:40 and includes 2 half-day sessions. My typical daily schedule includes the following activities: class groupings for reading readiness, large muscle activities, phonics and/or handwriting readiness, music/art, math, and recess.

To perform well as an elementary level teacher, it is important to have the following skills and attitudes: flexibility, organization, creativeness, firmness, a positive attitude, and predictability.

I like most aspects of my work except for the lack of opportunity for advancement and some current problems I am now having with my school administration. Aside from that, I like my kind of work very much, particularly the children I teach. I find job satisfaction in seeing the educational growth of children. My future career plans include completing a graduate degree in educational administration.

TEACHER, ELEMENTARY #11

For twenty-one years, I have taught reading and language arts to accelerated and gifted students in the fifth grade level of elementary school. I create activities and prepare presentation of my ideas in addition to grading papers and preparing daily lessons.

In addition to scholastic achievement, I have completed a Master of Science degree in Elementary Education. A teacher must keep up with current research in education; must be willing to try new methods; must love children, be kind to them, be understanding, and treat them with respect; and must be knowledgeable in many subjects, especially computers.

I love my job; I believe I have found a good school system in which to teach. I love working with children everyday and becoming a part of their lives. I have the rare opportunity to see these gifted children become more proficient and excited about learning.

I would like to get rid of the grading policy and just guide the children in reading and learning for the love of it; I would like to have more time in a day, too. I believe that the educational system would be more effective if school was in session throughout the entire year.

I was inspired to pursue a career in teaching by my aunt, who is a teacher. I also had some favorite teachers over the years who knew their subjects and led me to question--one of the key factors, I believe, to learning.

I plan to continue teaching, and I aspire to become more knowledgeable. I wish I could return to being a full time college student at some time in the future, but it is unlikely that I will earn a doctorate.

TEACHER, ELEMENTARY #12

I went to college not knowing what I wanted to pursue. By chance, I enrolled in an education class working in an elementary school for one month (mini-term session) for all day and decided to investigate this avenue. I must add that I was also born into a family of educators.

I started in teaching as 1st and 2nd grade teacher. I then switched my teaching position to teaching remedial reading. Now that my children are young, I do this work part-time. My day starts at 8 a.m., at which time I do planning, updating and preparation for the day or week. I teach 5 separate groups of students (25-30) during the course of the morning. I also travel to some of the classrooms to work with some groups within the classroom.

My advice for the kind of skills and attitudes which are important for teaching are: a basic understanding of the material being taught; a love and respect of children; and a positive attitude.

At this time, I am basically satisfied with my career as a teacher, except for the pay scale. At times, I feel I would like to find a career with better pay, benefits, less work to bring home, but--I enjoy being home in the afternoons and summer's off (unpaid!) with my family. I find a great deal of satisfaction in helping children who need extra attention or enrichment.

TEACHER, ELEMENTARY #13

In the past, I've worked as a real estate salesman and vineyard manager. For the past 6 years, I've been an elementary school teacher for 5 to 10 year olds. I love seeing children grow in self esteem and knowledge. In the future, my plans are to become a school counselor in a public school system.

On a usual day, I teach reading and mathematics in the morning. Then I supervise lunch and/or the playground. In the afternoon I teach social studies, spelling, and health. There is also a science unit taught daily in the afternoon. After school hours, I'm involved in conferences, bus duty, lesson planning, and arranging for the following day.

Good organizational skills are needed to be a teacher. The ability to adjust to momentary changes, to listen and observe, and to express yourself clearly, perhaps in different ways, are all immeasurably important. Getting along with co-workers helps as well.

I'd like my work more if there were fewer paperwork requirements and less record keeping. Furthermore, I'd like this career better if non-teaching duties in the lunchroom and playground were eliminated. I also regret that there is little opportunity for advancement here.

My education led to a general Bachelor of Arts degree, but to teach you need certification. I returned to college to become certified because I had always wanted to teach. In addition to teaching, my experience includes working in a flowers and plant nursery, managing a vineyard, and selling real estate. I liked all these jobs, but teaching is my favorite. Eventually I want to become a school counselor in a public school system.

TEACHER, ELEMENTARY #14

I'm very happy as an elementary teacher of 4th graders. Watching kids go from hating school to becoming eager learners is so gratifying to me. When children's faces light up as they begin to understand a topic, I'm delighted. Hearing from former students that I was a force in their success makes my years as a teacher worthwhile.

Although I enjoyed my previous work as a groundskeeper and as a gardener, I love teaching. I'd be happier if some of the administrators were more cooperative. If parents could become enlightened so they would not hurt their children through their own ignorance, I'd be more encouraged. Since I'm content with my profession, my career goals are to continue teaching in the same position.

I was half way through college when I found I could begin teaching with a two-year certificate and earn money. I began teaching but continued to earn my Bachelor of Arts Degree.

An educator must be empathetic, willing to try new methods, and be flexible in thinking and planning. To be successful, you must like children and be knowledgeable in many areas. Having an understanding of the culture of the area in which you work is very important.

As a teacher, I roughly follow a schedule which best enables kids to learn both factual information and how to cope with problems. On the weekends, I plan activities for the week. I attend training sessions occasionally.

TEACHER, ELEMENTARY #15

I've spent many happy years seeing children succeed in learning subject matter as well as learning to "get along" with each other. I thoroughly enjoy being busy five days a week with my assigned group of children. I appreciate my coworkers, my work, the school, and the supervisors. There is nothing I dislike about my job. However, I would like more time for working with the children and less time devoted to required paperwork.

My day consists of a variety of activities: greet the children as they arrive, take attendance, prepare the lunch report, and listen to announcements from the principal's office. Then I proceed with the planned schedule for the day. This continues until the bell rings for dismissal at the end of the school day.

I was influenced to enter the teaching profession by my two older sisters who were teachers themselves. The planned schedule for the day is worked out in advance of the next day's work and is fairly detailed. You will need to have that plan clear in your mind or on paper, then follow it fairly closely.

To be an effective teacher, you must first have knowledge of the subjects to instruct. Patience and understanding are essential in dealing with children as individuals. Cooperation with colleagues is also very important. You have to have an interest in children and a strong desire to see each child succeed. A teaching degree is also required. I have a Bachelor of Science in secondary education although I have taught most of my career at the elementary level.

TEACHER, ELEMENTARY #16

I keep very busy juggling my dual teaching roles at every level of elementary school from kindergarten to sixth grade. My work as the physical education teacher as well as work in the library have me busy conducting 6 classes per day. My biggest frustration is that there is not enough time.

In my opinion, there is one basic requirement in order to perform well as a teacher, and that is to have the ability to get along with people.

I chose the teaching profession when I was in elementary school, and have now been in the field for 17 years. I have earned a bachelor's and master's degree in education. I am so satisfied with my choice of a career, that even if given the opportunity to choose another occupation, I would still choose teaching. I find job satisfaction in children!

TEACHER, ENGINEERING

I have had a variety of jobs as an engineer including sheetmetal fabricator, tool and die maker, tool design engineer, packaging engineer, and aerospace equipment designer. I am now bringing my experience in the field into the classroom as an engineering instructor in a community college.

My daily teaching schedule includes three hours of lecture and three hours of lab. I also teach a night class which meets for two hours, two nights per week. In between my class time, I meet with students and handle the reams of manual paperwork involved in this kind of work.

To perform well as a teacher, it is important to have public speaking abilities, an in-depth knowledge of the subject you are teaching, positive self motivating "up front" integrity, and the desire to help.

Although I like my work very much, I do not like all the hand record keeping which is involved. However, I do like the teaching aspect and my contact with the students and other teachers. It is satisfying work for me in seeing young people improve, learn and get ahead.

TEACHER, ENGLISH #1

I'm self-employed as a teacher of English as a second language. I give one-to-one tutoring sessions to many who have professional occupations. I make my own hours. I work for major corporations and charge their clients 25-50 dollars per hour (which is considered inexpensive--most contract employees charge upwards of 100 dollars per hour). My courses are 20 hours each (two times a week--two hours each). I also do at least one student per week gratis through church or community service. These people quite often have given me names of paying clientele.

To perform well at this job it is important to have a desire to help people who are struggling to attain what is rightfully theirs. A basic knowledge of the English language is the skill needed for the type of work I do.

Seeing my pupils attain levels of achievement in their specific line of work, that they had never dreamed they could accomplish, is very satisfying.

I am completely happy as a part-time employee. It does hurt me that some employers do not appreciate the good verbal skills of their foreign employees but, overall, I am satisfied with my arrangement here.

A friend ran an ESL (English as a second language) Company and asked me to work for her; I did that and struck out on my own three years later. Prior to this I taught third and fifth grade and was a permanent substitute after receiving my BS in Education.

I have always enjoyed seeing people come to their full potential because of the small part I played in their lives. I do not wish to start a major company where I must lead others. I love being self- employed, setting my hours, and feeling good about the work I do. The money is o.k. for ESL, but the satisfaction is excellent!

TEACHER, ENGLISH #2

I instruct college freshmen in grammar, but especially essay writing. Much time is spent in preparing lessons and correcting essays and book reports as well as term papers. Office hours are hours that are held regularly to answer questions and give special instructions to students.

Knowledge of and liking for people is as important as being well-versed in the subject of English and literature. You must also be lively and interesting in order to retain the attention of the students.

Teaching was chosen early in my life. My aunt was a teacher. I obtained my position through a teaching scholarship, and it went on from there. Prior to teaching, I held a number of secretarial positions-- culminating in an executive secretary job in which I was a minor "boss." That was one of my favorite positions outside of teaching.

I like teaching very much. By and large, the pupils are great. Occasionally as a teacher I have had to deal with the indolence of youth, which I dislike.

If I could change something in my occupation it would be to allow teachers more flexibility in teaching material. I want to choose what I teach.

Of course, there is satisfaction in knowing that information has been learned and retained; but personal feedback from students is probably the most gratifying aspect of this work.

TEACHER, GIFTED & TALENTED

As a teacher of the gifted and talented students in my school district, I work with all the gifted and talented students at the junior high and high school levels. In addition to both Bachelor's and Master's degrees, work in this field requires a positive attitude, enthusiasm, a willingness to work many long hours, the ability to communicate well with parents, good oral and written communication skills, an understanding of group dynamics, and the confidence to be at ease in front of large groups.

I like the kind of work that I do. I believe my work is important, and I enjoy working with children and seeing them grow in many ways. I also like the fact that teaching gives me the summers off. Although I sense a general lack of respect within the community, I believe that mine is an isolated complaint. The teaching profession holds high esteem in our society. I always wanted to be a teacher, and it was my major in college. I worked as a teacher's aide before accepting my present job.

I am currently studying to learn more about the education of gifted and talented students. Education for me is and will continue to be an ongoing process.

TEACHER, GRADE SEVEN SCIENCE

As a seventh grade science teacher, I spend my day teaching 11-13 year olds basic science principles. I use various techniques such as lectures, lab work, and student projects to teach effectively.

I've been teaching for 27 years. If I could start over, I'd still choose this occupation I'm in. I love the kind of work I do and the people with whom I work. However, I regret the lack of opportunity for advancement and I have difficulty with the attitude of some administrators.

You should be aware that the hours are long, the pay is low, and really, you get little respect and appreciation for the work you do. On the other hand, it is very satisfying to see a student "get it." I enjoy observing how a twelve-year-old's mind works and I like to hear their logic. Many of these young people also have a sense of humor.

To be a good teacher, you need a sense of humor yourself. You need to be able to teach--to listen, to question, and to let the students work out the answers. Teaching is more than just "showing how."

I got into the field by accident. I wanted to be in retailing, but I took a course for fun, got "hooked" on teaching, and followed that first course with many more. I plan to continue teaching until I retire.

TEACHER, HIGH SCHOOL

I teach world history and government to advanced placement students as well as to regular students. As a child I was mistreated by a teacher and decided no youngster should have that kind of experience. Determined I could do better, I later earned a Bachelor of Science degree and a Master of Arts, both in education. I've been teaching now for over 20 years. Relative to requirements for a job such as this, obviously a teacher needs to be knowledgeable in the courses being taught. A great deal of stamina and patience is necessary. Actually liking students and having empathy with them is important. Finally, you need to have a positive attitude.

My teaching schedule consists of 3 preparations, 6 classes, and 1 study hall. I'm also responsible now for planning a trip for the students to Washington, DC. Additionally, I am the student council adviser. After school, I'm involved with our Intervention Team meetings as well as those of the Education Association. I'd like one day to supervise student teachers.

I experience satisfaction and it is rewarding when students succeed or become motivated. Knowing you've made a difference makes everything worthwhile. It is also very satisfying when you know a student trusts you. Finally, I enjoy my fellow teachers, the administration, and the school. My only regret is I see little opportunity for advancement. There also is not enough time for teaching, planning, and for interacting with colleagues; but, overall, it is an excellent profession.

TEACHER, HIGH SCHOOL (PRIVATE)

A high school teacher, I am chairperson of the religion department at a private high school. Teaching courses about religions and about religious faith and life is what

I do. I also counsel our students.

To teach in secondary school, besides training and education, you need patience and understanding. Being a warm-hearted person helps. You also need an open and honest relationship with your students.

Although I've always wanted to teach, and earned my Bachelor of Arts degree in education as well as a Master of Arts degree, it wasn't until about 12 years ago that I realized I wanted to do counseling. High school students need someone they can talk to and learn from, in addition to their peers and busy parents. I love my work; I'd choose it again if I could start over. My plans are to continue in my career trying to reach more kids who need help.

I am most rewarded when a student feels good about himself. It is so satisfying when a student decides life itself, and especially his/her own life, is precious. When I see someone realize their self-worth, I am gratified. In addition, while I don't like everyone in administration, I do so enjoy my colleagues, the school, and my work of the past ten years.

TEACHER, HIGH SCHOOL ACCOUNTING

I took a vocational business program while in high school and I loved it. I decided in my senior year I wanted business education as a career. To be a teacher, at least one college degree is needed. I have two, a Bachelor of Science and a Masters degree. I enjoyed my previous work as a legal secretary, but job satisfaction for me now is knowing I am positively influencing the lives of my students. I am delighted when they return years after graduation to thank me.

As a teacher of business education, I teach accounting to high school students. I teach two beginning accounting classes and two advanced accounting classes each day. In addition, I also supervise students who are enrolled in an on-the-job training program.

In dealing with teenagers, you must first establish a rapport with them. You must be positive and caring. As the saying goes, "No one cares how much you know until they know how much you care!" You must be understanding, alert, and firm but fair. You must also be flexible and adaptable.

I'd like my profession much better if the unnecessary paperwork were eliminated. My plans are to be a stay-at-home parent when I have a family. I'd like to work part-time at home doing freelance secretarial and bookkeeping work.

TEACHER, HIGH SCHOOL ART

For 18 years now, I've been an art teacher at the secondary school level. It's my job to teach art education to young people. My responsibility is to encourage them to see and think visually as well.

To be an artist and an art teacher you need good hand-and-eye coordination. Self-esteem, along with self-discipline, are important qualities to have. Being willing to experiment with new materials in an individualistic, creative manner is also necessary.

In my work I introduce new problems, also called areas of design, to my students. To solve these problems, they experiment with art materials or with visual aids to inspire them. During the class I allow my students to complete the area of design in their own way.

I have a Bachelor of Arts and secondary education accreditation. I've worked in health care as a dental assistant and lab assistant, but I find I enjoy the diversity in my current work. There are different situations every day. The creativity in my job is very satisfying to me. I also like the person I work for as well as being my own boss in the classroom.

My future plans are to stay in my current profession and, in my spare time, participate in a hospital board contributing toward health care reform.

TEACHER, HIGH SCHOOL CHEMISTRY

I look back over a meaningful and enjoyable life in formal educational settings as a chemistry teacher. I have taught regular and advanced placement chemistry at the secondary school level. Some of my duties are preparing lessons, demonstrations, and laboratory investigations. Routinely I set up and dismantle lab equipment, advise students on topics related to chemistry, and spend at least 2 days each week in lab exercises for "hands on" experience.

Weekends require time for grading papers and planning the next week's schedule. Daily lessons include making reading assignments and selecting problems to be solved, developing demonstrations that help by dramatic means to establish concepts or lead students to "try their hand" at explaining or deducing principles from their observations.

Solid mathematical skills along with adeptness at problem solving are necessary in my field. Above all, one must enjoy people and their differences. One needs a good memory, basic computer literacy, and analytical skills. My education includes a Bachelor of Arts degree and a Masters in Education.

I've done a variety of jobs before teaching, i.e., U.S. Naval Officer, house painter, and manager of an amusement park and gift stores. I've liked all my work opportunities; even jobs that became repetitive offered time for thinking.

I have been allowed, and enjoy, almost complete independence in my teaching methods. Seeing students "catch on" to concepts that earlier eluded them has been most rewarding for me. My only dislike is the lack of adequate one-on-one time with my students. If schools could afford paid assistants for lab courses, then teachers would have more time for teaching and being innovative.

I am sure my association with young people has helped me stay young mentally and physically. My hobbies are traveling with my wife, sailing, golfing, hiking, and reading. I'm also a clarinetist in an orchestra.

TEACHER, HIGH SCHOOL ENGLISH #1

Although I enjoyed the time I spent in retail sales and as a secretary, I've loved interacting with students as a high school English teacher for 19 years. I like the autonomy of the classroom teacher as well as the hours which are the same as my children's. Having similar schedules enables me to spend more time with them.

My profession would be more satisfying if parents became more involved and if they showed more concern for their children. Higher salaries and more respect for the profession would help as well.

My day includes teaching one gifted and talented 10th grade class, 2 regular 10th grade classes, and 2 remedial reading/writing senior classes. My duties include posting the daily schedule for the students, gathering supplies, and completing a great deal of administrative paperwork. I prepare lessons, grade, and evaluate student products. And there are students' questions to answer all day.

Teaching requires a great deal of patience. Nurturing, clerical, and counseling skills are important. A coordinator for numerous activities, a teacher should be able to lecture and entertain as well. I have earned a Bachelor's degree in English and a Master of Arts degree as a Reading Specialist.

TEACHER, HIGH SCHOOL ENGLISH #2

I teach the English curriculum, mainly skills, to adolescents. Typically my day includes planning and preparation for five classes a day, instruction, evaluation, routine record keeping related to classroom duties and administrative request, and counseling of students.

To perform well as a teacher, it is important to have intellectual curiosity, the ability to motivate and regulate groups, and the skills to organize materials and keep good records.

I have been satisfied with my career because I have enjoyed stimulating students' interest and helping the students feel better about themselves.

If I could change anything about the profession it would be to have teachers themselves be in charge of curriculum and their own standards of performance. I would find alternate educational routes for those: (1) more inclined to mechanical and technical interests, and (2) truly socially disruptive.

I chose teaching, because I liked college work and liked writing. I knew teachers were needed, and so I became certified in English and social science. In addition to my B.A., I have an M.A.. I have had no other major jobs outside of teaching.

I am presently writing a novel. I may also consider private school teaching or some other work which might be stimulating socially and intellectually.

TEACHER, HIGH SCHOOL ENGLISH #3

As a high school English teacher I lecture, lead discussions, grade homework, proofread student's work and introduce and examine concepts. In my present position, I prepare three class schedules and teach six class hours.

To perform well as a teacher it is important to have strong organizational skills. You also need to administer strong discipline to enforce rules in the classroom. Adapting easily to ever-changing situations is an asset as a teacher.

I enjoy the spontaneity and class discussion. It is personally rewarding. I would be more satisfied if my school had a broader educated staff and there were more parental involvement. I have always wanted to teach since I was a child. My major in college was secondary education. I am still attending school while teaching in order to earn my masters. My future career aspirations are to teach college or to attend law school and go into private practice.

TEACHER, HIGH SCHOOL ENGLISH #4

I feel I was called to be an English teacher and have really enjoyed my career in this profession. I teach a variety of grade levels and a variety of ability groupings. Before school I check supplies and get my lessons ready. During school, I teach 5 classes which involves 3 to 4 preparations, and 1 planning period. After school, I grade tests and papers, work with students on make-up work or help students having difficulty.

As well as the educational background necessary for this career, I feel it is important to have flexibility, a sense of humor, knowledge of the subject matter, and the ability to plan and organize to be a good teacher.

If I could change anything about my occupation, I would like to see fewer idiotic rulings from a state legislature which does not understand the educational process. I am for full funding for programs, adequate funding for enough teachers, and a proper teacher pupil ratio.

Aside from these frustrations, I like my work very much. I particularly like working with all types of people. It is satisfying to watch children improve in knowledge and skill and helping them to feel good about themselves. I plan to continue teaching. I have no ambitions to move from the classroom.

TEACHER, HIGH SCHOOL ENGLISH & SOCIAL STUDIES

I'd earned a Bachelor of Arts degree, majoring in history, and didn't know what to do with it. Finally, I got my certification in teaching and became a high school social studies teacher.

What I have liked about my career is the pleasure of seeing people learn. I enjoy teaching and working with the administration. What I don't like are the discipline problems and the extra duties we teachers have to perform.

I teach 5 classes a day, some good, some terrible, depending on the discipline problems. The thrill of seeing someone "catch on" doesn't lessen with age.

It's very important for a teacher to like young people and want to help them. You need a thorough knowledge of the subject matter along with the ability to convey that in an understandable, interesting manner. Also, if I knew how to type, preparing written materials, such as tests and handouts, would be easier. Prior to entering the teaching profession I was in the U.S. Navy. I have no further plans other than to continue teaching.

TEACHER, HIGH SCHOOL EQUIVALENCY PROGRAM

I began teaching two years ago and I am now an instructor for a high school equivalency program. My present class load is to teach math and grammar to four groups of ten to twelve students. I prepare class plans, give lectures, correct homework, and give extra help to those in need of it.

I graduated from college with a diploma in nutrition and have been involved in the field of education for quite some time as an assistant coach. My work requires that I be prepared, that I especially try to motivate the students to learn, and that I be able to identify different learning styles.

I enjoy teaching and working in a learning environment; I especially enjoy the people I work with, the students who attend the classes, and the opportunity to communicate and exchange knowledge.

In my present position there is not much opportunity for advancement, so I plan to return to college and get the certification needed to become a bilingual instructor.

TEACHER, HIGH SCHOOL FRENCH & SPANISH

It took me half a lifetime to finally find what I wanted to do. Prior to becoming a high school teacher, I worked as a preschool teacher and secretary. While raising my children, I decided to get my degree in French since I already spoke it fluently having lived in Europe for 4 years. Because I had taught pre-school, I knew I liked teaching, but I felt a desire to really impart to others the knowledge I had acquired, by teaching at a higher level.

I teach level 4 French and level 1 and 2 Spanish. My work/school day runs from 7:00 a.m. to 3:00 p.m. I remain at school until 5:00 preparing for the next day classes. Evenings are often spent correcting papers.

To perform this kind of work well, you should be highly organized to reduce stress. Teachers must like children and adults and be personable. Patience and understanding are also important attributes for this career. You need to be highly knowledgeable in your teaching area too.

If given the opportunity to change something in my occupation, I would reduce classroom size in the foreign language classroom from around 30 in the lower levels to under 20. With as many as 30, teachers cannot teach foreign language effectively and that is why, I think, our country is in the state it is concerning second language learning. I would also hire people from the outside for extra-curricular foreign language activities.

My teaching gives me satisfaction because I know that what I do and how I do it could change a young person's life (even if slightly) and can affect his attitudes by the study of languages, by learning about people in other cultures, and those cultures themselves can affect the student's outlook and development.

If I were younger, I would continue my education with the prospect of teaching at the university level. As it is, I will continue taking courses because I love learning. For the moment I am satisfied doing what I am doing, but could conceivably see myself in another area using my foreign language skills some day.

TEACHER, HIGH SCHOOL JOURNALISM

After many years as an educator, public speaker, and journalist, I am still pleasantly satisfied with my work and still making future career plans. Prior to my current position as high school journalism teacher and publications advisor, I was in elementary school administration, and was a public speaker. My educational background includes a Bachelor of Arts, a Bachelor in Secondary Education, and a Master of Arts degree.

I teach 6 out of 7 class periods daily, Monday through Friday. On weekends, I usually spend 3 to 4 hours with students on school publications.

To perform this kind of work well, it is important to be well-read, have a positive attitude towards teens, and be open to change.

I like almost every aspect of my career.

I only wish I could find ways to obtain grants to further the opportunities for my students. The only major frustration I have is with the stress of deadlines. Aside from this, I find my work very satisfying because of the number of students I have had that have gone on to major in journalism in college, and the number of awards won by my students for their publications.

In the future, I may work into a service career in order to further utilize my talents and skills. Being enthusiastic by nature, I want to keep sharing with others.

TEACHER, HIGH SCHOOL MATH

As a high school teacher of history and mathematics, I start my work day at 7:30. I work with about 140 students each day in two or three different classes of 25-35. Some students are of general ability; some are college bound and are in advanced placement classes. Any time I am not in the classroom, I'm preparing for class, i.e., typing, copying, and correcting, or I'm at committee meetings. I might also be working with students on National Honor Society projects. Two or three nights each week I do about three hours of school work at home.

I like the independence in my work in that I can do what I think best in my classes. Job satisfaction comes in seeing students comprehend what they are studying or finally "getting it" after they have struggled to understand. I enjoy seeing students' pleasure when they have done something well. What I don't like about my work is the large classes and the lack of technical equipment. Also, the time schedule is so restricted; more time with students is needed rather than spending it doing paperwork.

The qualities a teacher needs is to be organized, flexible, and enthusiastic. A good sense of humor and patience are valuable. You should enjoy working with others and have an interest in continuing to learn for yourself.

I have always wanted to be teacher; I've been in the teaching profession for 21 years. In the future I'd like to continue teaching. Perhaps I'll be a college supervisor of student teaching, working with students who plan to be teachers.

TEACHER, HIGH SCHOOL MATH & JOURNALISM

To perform well as a high school teacher, you must have a great deal of stamina. A desire to help others rise to their full potential and enjoying people are musts. Also, a person must be able to function without much sleep.

My education includes a Bachelor of Science degree and a Master of Science degree in education. Math and journalism are the courses I teach. As an adviser, I help students with the school newspaper and with their yearbook. For the future, I might earn my administrative credentials or, perhaps, work as an information officer in a public school.

There's a great deal of paperwork in teaching as well as a lot of planning and organization. Often, time must be spent on school work after school hours. Much interaction with people on many different levels takes place in education.

Before this job, I was a reporter for the local newspaper, a preschool teacher, and a secretary. I chose teaching because I found mathematics and its logic very interesting. I always liked "playing school" as a child and seeing someone perfect new skills gives me a great deal of joy in teaching. I only wish so many hours were not required.

TEACHER, HIGH SCHOOL REMEDIAL READING

As a secondary reading instructor with a Bachelor of Science and a Master in Arts, I teach developmental and remedial reading to junior high students. My day includes classes, lesson preparation, and informal conferencing with other teachers. Meeting with students is also an essential part of my work.

I've worked as a secretary, a waitress and a clerk, but my chief pleasure has been in seeing students develop and learn. When they find understanding of the subject matter and of themselves, I am gratified. I would like my work more if there were fewer state regulations. Also, the concern about lawsuits inhibits the behavior of faculty. Further, I would prefer that we not have to deal with so many social issues that affect learning and that physical facilities be improved.

To be successful in my line of work, you need to be flexible and be understanding of adolescents. You should have a strong work ethic and a commitment to life-long learning. Knowledge of your subject area, along with patience and a sense of humor, are essential.

TEACHER, HIGH SCHOOL SOCIAL STUDIES

Earlier in my lifetime I've worked in a factory and a grocery store. I'm now teaching and have been in that field for 25 years. My subject is high school social studies which I teach to students in grades 7 through 12. I also do many volunteer jobs with senior groups. Satisfaction for me is in the appreciation students show for what was taught to them. The joy of becoming well-informed in current governmental affairs has made my work pleasurable.

Actually, I chose teaching on sort of a trial basis. I found I enjoyed it and now I can't think of what else I might have done as a career. I've liked the places and the people--well, most of them--where I've taught. My wife was a teacher, and I found "book learning" was easy for me. My degrees are a Bachelor of Arts and a Master of Science.

I'd enjoy my work more if others would realize there's a need to adapt to a changing world and we need to keep informed of these changes. It is easy to become static by doing the same thing over and over.

My usual day consists of a class schedule of 5 classes in social studies. I generally teach 1 or 2 sections of American history to grade 7. There'll be 1 class of geography in grade 8 and 1 or 2 sections of American history for grade 10. I have several quarter-long classes in local history which are elective for the 11th and 12th graders.

To teach well, you need to be interested in, as well as know, the material. Being able to read well and being familiar with audio visual resources to make the teaching more interesting and informative are also necessary. It helps to know how to deal with students.

TEACHER, HISTORY

I have taught history at a private high school for over 30 years. Of primary importance to teaching history is first to study and present the historical information and then to explain and examine the understanding and knowledge.

I consider long hours after school, and boring committee and faculty meetings, to be the downside of teaching. However, I would still choose this as my career if I could start again.

Having a knowledge of the field of study which you teach is the first and most important requirement for teaching. It has been satisfying to teach because I learned and learned. I loved (still do) my field of study, and became both tolerant and skeptical which I consider to be great attributes for a human being.

The changes I would like to see in this occupation is for more serious public support for education and a return to teaching of subjects, not students. Also, the education of teachers, especially school teachers, must become more demanding so that we will have the best, rather than the worst, college students teaching in the future!

As I mentioned before I love to learn, so while I taught I was also earning my MA from Harvard and graduate studies Certificates in International Relations. I also worked for a brief time as a propaganda analyst for the State Department.

TEACHER, HOMEBOUND STUDENTS

I have been a teacher of home or hospital bound high school students for 18 years. It is my privilege to tutor my students to maintain their achievement at an appropriate class level. The required subject matter is that which is adaptable to the home or hospital, i.e., no lab courses.

For one hour on alternate days, I visit 5 high school students. On the other days, I teach 5 more students, all of them having up to four required courses. It is very rewarding to me to watch most of my students do so well on a one-to-one basis. Their work is very good, plus they gain much self confidence. I like it that they look forward to my next visit. This work is never routine.

All of my work is not pleasurable. I miss the students who die, and I dislike losing contact with the students when they are able to return to their regular classrooms. I would like to have been able to screen out and dismiss the few students who refused to profit from the program. Those students frequently failed to keep appointments, or they put forth almost no effort to learn.

A visiting teacher needs teaching skills in a variety of subjects: language arts, social studies, and mathematics, in particular. You must be able to motivate to help students want to keep up with their school work. Helping the young people develop self-confidence is also important. You must understand their handicaps without letting these students use them as an excuse to underachieve. Certainly, knowing that expectations vary with each student is essential.

TEACHER, JUNIOR HIGH #1

For the past twenty years, I have been involved in teaching English classes on the seventh and eighth grade levels. I teach classes in English literature, grammar, writing, and speech to students with different levels of ability.

Besides at least a Bachelor's degree in English, one must have patience, understanding, and the ability to generate an environment of cooperation, equity, and fairness among the students.

I really enjoy my work; I find I derive the greatest satisfaction from seeing growth in my students over the course of the school year. I like the school system of which I am a part and the faculty at the school where I teach.

I have always been interested in writing and I love to read; I have a natural appreciation for the English language.

I also research local history on a part-time basis in addition to teaching my classes.

I intend to return to college to complete graduate studies and obtain a Master's degree.

TEACHER, JUNIOR HIGH #2

I have been in education 35 years. It has always been very gratifying to me to see my students both succeed in school and be satisfied with what we had learned at the end of each school year. The only aspect I do not enjoy are the duties unrelated to teaching, i.e., yard supervision. Also, I'd like to see more support services for youngsters with severe psychological problems.

I teach a variety of 7th through 9th grade courses: general science, biology, physical science, reading, math, science, art, social studies and writing. For 17 years I was a teacher in special education classes. For 6 years, I was a resource teacher. I enjoy piloting new programs for the school or the district.

My responsibilities as a teacher are preparing lessons, teaching 5 periods a day, meeting with departmental teams, and correcting papers. I read a great deal and do research through trade journals.

A good teacher has strong interpersonal skills, is organized, and is able to manage people. A solid grasp of the subject matter, as well as being able to listen well, are both essential. A caring, nonjudgmental attitude along with a good sense of humor and sense of honesty and fairness are important. Being flexible and open-minded helps also.

Prior to teaching I was a field laborer and a factory worker. I returned to college and earned a Bachelor of Education and a Master of Arts degree. I became an interviewer with the Labor Department, and I enjoyed that work, but upon entering the teaching profession, I found my niche!

TEACHER, JUNIOR HIGH ENGLISH #1

The teaching profession seemed to be a logical choice for me since I loved school, received awards for my work there, and liked to study. After earning my Bachelor of Arts degree in English, later my Master of Arts in Education, and now teaching for 16 years, I can still say I love school.

As a junior high English/reading teacher, I work approximately 60 hours a week at my career. Time is spent in preparation for six 50 minute class periods of teaching a day, then in instruction and grading papers from these classes. I teach grammar, spelling, reading, and composition.

I consider the most important attribute for a teacher to have is patience. Also, preparation in the field well beyond degrees and credentials is vitally important to be a good teacher.

There are a few areas of frustration which I have encountered over my years in teaching. I have found there to be a lack of opportunity for advancement. The public attitude about today's schools, and the way education is being used as a political issue are disturbing concerns of mine. I would also like to see a realistic evaluation of the effect modern values are having on the learning process and our young people. In spite of these frustrations, I continue to teach and like it very much because I find satisfaction in seeing my students learn and grow. I like the school and people I work for, and the people I work with. As a teacher, I am also learning new skills as I work.

TEACHER, JUNIOR HIGH ENGLISH #2

I've been a junior high English teacher and a teacher of talented, or gifted, students for eight years since leaving my previous occupation in sales. Job satisfaction for me is knowing my work has meaning. Relationships with students can be uplifting and knowing I can make a difference is gratifying.

I'd like my work more if there were less paper work. I also believe that, with the disintegration of the American family, the state of American schools is in deterioration. Students lack motivation. I'd like to see more hope for the future of America and American education. One needs a great deal of patience in teaching. Strong communication skills and the ability to be flexible are extremely important.

There are generally 30 students in each of my two 7th grade English classes. I work with a smaller number of the talented students. Communicating clearly with the staff and with the administration is very important. Frequently, I bring in community members to enrich the curriculum.

My career plans are to take an extended leave and do one or more of the following: further pursue graduate education (I have a Bachelor of Arts degree and a Masters in education), travel, write young adult fiction, or teach high school instead of junior high English.

TEACHER, JUNIOR HIGH HISTORY

As a social studies teacher at the secondary school level, I teach American history and global studies to 7th - 9th graders. I find most of our young people are fun to work with; and it's a great pleasure to watch students learn and "grow" as individuals.

I've wanted to be a teacher from the time I was 10 years old. I would like to continue to teach for 7 more years. Then, I'd like to retire to enjoy some leisure time activities.

I am not pleased with some of the conditions where I work, but I am pleased with the people I work with, and I love my work itself. But it's frightening to see the year by year increase in the numbers of students who are totally unmotivated to learn. I would feel fulfilled if there were something I could do to change that.

My work day, generally, starts early. I arrive at 7:00 in the morning. The students begin to arrive at 7:45. I teach until 2:50 with 8-minute breaks between 76-minute classes. There are 30 minutes free for lunch. If there are no after school meetings, I stay to help students, correct papers, or plan the next day's work. After school, I may need to stay to attend meetings.

You must be well-organized, yet be able to adjust to unexpected changes or new activity requirements which can occur. You must be prepared for the classes you teach. Patience, humor, and friendliness are also helpful in dealing with teenagers. You must be firm, fair, and consistent with students as well. There has to be a commitment to your profession despite much negativism from the community, the Board of Education and, at times, the administration.

In spite of my complaints in these comments, I have enjoyed teaching, and I plan to continue this occupation until I retire.

TEACHER, JUNIOR HIGH SCIENCE/HEALTH

Teaching requires strong people skills. You must be a good communicator. You must be organized and be very knowledgeable in your subject area. You should be able to work with many different kinds of people.

I teach science to 7th and 8th graders and health at the high school level. Many members of my family have been teachers, so I grew up around the profession. My interests were directed toward the teaching and I earned a Master of Science degree in education. I don't like the low pay for teachers, and I would like to see improved physical conditions, more respect from the public, and more cooperation from parents. In spite of these points, I love the people, the work, and the school. If I could start over, I'd choose teaching again. I am pleased when I can teach children to think and to take care of themselves.

My regular day will include arrival shortly after 7:00 a.m. I spend the time before school starts preparing for class. I leave at 4:00 p.m. perhaps returning in the evening for school functions. One to two hours each week night are spent working on school work; Sundays usually 5 hours are given in preparation for school, so it is time consuming but enjoyable.

I have an ambition to be associated with a college by supervising student teachers. My degrees are sufficient for that, and I hope to have that experience soon.

TEACHER, JUNIOR HIGH SOCIAL STUDIES

Watching the growth and expansion of young, bright minds is most rewarding to me as a teacher of 12 and 13 year old gifted children. For 15 years, I've taught 7th and 8th grade social studies and history. The challenge of working with some incredible young people, and knowing that I make a difference in their lives, makes my work so satisfying.

Teaching is always what I've wanted to do. The fact that I'm working with gifted children is pure luck. I'm very content doing what I'm doing and have no plans to do otherwise. I would be happier in my work, though, if the school administration had any idea about what I do.

A teacher needs, foremost, to like working with young people. Having the ability to plan ahead, knowing the subject matter, and being willing to say, "I don't know," are all very important. One needs strong problem-solving skills as well as the ability to be flexible and to be diplomatic. I've also found my work requires the capability of working at the highest level of critical thinking. My training is a Bachelor of Arts degree plus 60 units toward a Masters degree.

My typical day starts at 7:30 a.m. and lasts until at least 4:30 p.m. with maybe 35 minutes for lunch. Because I work with gifted children, I must do a lot of preparation and a lot of reading of the work papers they generate. I also make several parent contacts during the week and serve on several school and district committees, all requiring meetings after school. In the evenings and on weekends, I have an additional one to three hours of work.

TEACHER, KINDERGARTEN

As a kindergarten teacher, I find satisfaction in reaching the unreachable; in my attempting to teach those who don't want to learn and being successful in reaching them. On the other hand, it is discouraging being unable to reach children in need to make an effective change.

I have been a teacher in a large city school system for 18 years; 12 have been as a kindergarten teacher. I see my work as a kindergarten teacher to be to socialize young people and give them the foundations for later learning.

When asked to describe a typical day, these images and words come to mind: runny noses, chatty children, interest, apathy, laughing, crying, needy children, damaged children, happy children, a circus, a library, an infirmary, a nursery, caring, taking care, giving love, and discipline. When asked for the skills and attitudes which I consider important for performing well as a teacher, I would suggest tolerance, patience, and a sense of humor.

I must admit that I am somewhat disappointed in the trends I see in today's children. I only hope that I can continue doing my part as a teacher and still find the satisfaction of seeing the children's knowledge grow.

TEACHER, LIBRARY MEDIA SPECIALIST

My daily routine as a library media specialist is to oversee the school library for patrons. This includes turning in circulation statistics, dating return-due slips, shelving books, etc. I also review or develop my lesson plans. It is my responsibility to teach research techniques to the students, read stories, and generally to help in finding and sorting materials with the students.

To perform well as a library media specialist you need to understand the Dewey decimal system, computer systems related to the library, and understand and use good teaching skills. Also important is lots of personnel understanding, to be friendly and helpful.

I find this work satisfying because I feel I am helping students discover new information and find a book they enjoy reading. I am really just working hard for my own satisfaction.

I got into this profession after my children were in school. I volunteered at my children's school library, enjoyed the work very much, and decided to go back to school to earn my degree. I now have a Bachelor of science degree and a Master's in education. Prior to this, I had no special training and so I worked as a waitress and hotel maid. I am somewhat discouraged by the lack of opportunity for advancement in my present school, but I intend to keep working in the field and hopefully the opportunities will present themselves.

TEACHER, MONTESSORI

I think my primary reason for being a teacher is because I love children. As a Montessori school teacher with children between three and six years old, I teach so as to allow the children to reach their full potential; prepare a learning environment to assist the children to experience confidence and joy of learning. In the course of a teaching day, I prepare lessons in reading and math readiness, observe children using sensorial and manipulative materials, read to the children, have circle time which includes introducing new work, songs, calendar, finger play and games.

A teacher should be well adjusted--calm, consistent, empathetic and sympathetic. It is essential to approve and like children, to be flexible, able to observe, patient, and able to listen to children. You should have an enthusiasm for life and should be able to motivate. A professional attitude and a respect for children is also important.

I was a public school teacher, but after substituting in a Montessori classroom, I was asked by the school's superintendent if I was willing to take courses in Montessori training. I have found that I like this kind of teaching very much. I like the organization and people I work for, and the people I work with. The one thing I wish I could change about my occupation is the pay scale. I do not think teachers receive the salaries they deserve. In spite of this, I plan to stay in this occupation. I love the children and their parents. I am rewarded by the satisfaction of knowing I am laying the foundation for learning. I see teaching as an opportunity to watch and guide children as they grow so they realize their full potential.

TEACHER, MUSIC

As a music teacher, I enjoy seeing my students as they musically progress. I've taught all aspects of music education to teachers new to the field. I've also enjoyed performing great music as a conductor of a large musical organization. There isn't much in the way of advancement opportunities, but I love my work and the people.

A good musician must have an "ear" for music. Honed instrumental skills, an understanding of the piano with minimum skills at the keyboard are all essential in my work. One must also be a good vocalist.

Before becoming a teacher, I was a professional singer and as a factory worker. My family encouraged me to teach. My degrees are a Masters and an Education Specialist.

TEACHER, NURSERY SCHOOL

I teach at a nursery school. My day starts early, as I plan the day's activities for the children before the children arrive at the school. The average age of the children at my school is four years old. At that age, they mostly learn through playing and repeating simple tasks. An average day consists of free choice, circle time, art activity, outdoor play, snack lesson, free play, dramatics, science, or reading time, during which I read a story to the children. We occasionally take the children on field trips to places that have relevance to the concepts we teach. I love my job! I especially enjoy working with the children and getting to know their parents; children give instant gratification for one's efforts. I feel fortunate to have some very good people as members of my staff.

The work of a nursery school teacher requires a warm and caring nature, the ability to listen to each child and respond accordingly to their concerns or questions, the ability to treat all the children with fairness, the ability to discipline a child in an appropriate manner, and self-sacrifice since a teacher must always put the child first.

I started in this field on a part-time basis as an assistant in a nursery school after the last of my children started in grammar school. I took a couple of courses to qualify to teach nursery school.

I enjoy my work so much that I intend to keep teaching for as long as possible; I may return to college to complete the certification process to teach in elementary school.

TEACHER, PHYSICAL EDUCATION

I have always been interested in sports. My first desire was to be a high school teacher and coach. I fell in love with elementary age students during my student teaching experience. Now after 17 years of teaching physical education at the elementary level, I still like this kind of work and working with this age group.

As a physical education teacher, I teach basic skills such as locomotion, nonlocomotion, games, ball handling, and rhythm. I arrive at school around at 8 a.m. Once a week I have playground duty before school in the morning. My typical morning schedule is to teach two classes, then have recess, followed by 2 more teaching sessions. Lunch and planning session is next during which time I usually take a walk too. I then teach three classes in the afternoon. There are usually two or three meetings a week after normal school hours. My school work day ends around 3:30 after which I work at a part-time job for a couple of hours.

Patience is extremely important for this kind of work. A teacher needs to be able to work with a variety of skills and abilities within the class. It is also important to have a positive attitude. Kids need to feel good about themselves.

If I could change anything in order to make my work more satisfying, I would demand all children participate in daily physical education class. I would also require all parents and school board members to work in the school for a month. This would enable people to see how difficult teaching and working with children can be. I would hope this would give teachers and the teaching profession more respect.

I do find satisfaction from my work particularly when I experience the thrill of connecting with a student. The connection can be involved with learning or perfecting a skill or it can be on a personal level. Giving or getting a hug or smile is indeed gratifying. I also find satisfaction in knowing I made a difference in a kid's life. My future career plans are to be an old gym teacher and still be effective.

TEACHER, PRESCHOOL & DIRECTOR

As the director of a pre-school, I operate an educational pre-school program, handling the budgets and curriculum planning. In addition, I am a pre-school teacher and a part-time instructor of college writing. As the director, I plan lessons for the week/month and then make sure that we have all the necessary materials for our program; as a pre-school teacher, I supervise a group of students, assist them when necessary, and evaluate their individual progress.

In addition to both Bachelor's and Master's degrees in the field of education, this job requires truly liking children. It is necessary to be patient, with a good sense of humor, and to have the ability to explain the assigned lessons to children at different learning and understanding levels--that is not always an easy task!

I really like this kind of work very much, especially the people I work with and the organization I work for. I am glad to say that my work affords me the opportunity to learn on a daily basis. One of the main satisfactions I derive from my work is the knowledge that I have helped a child reach a new level of exploration of his or her world; each new skill a child acquires will help that child through life.

It would be so nice for me to have some way of knowing the progress of each child throughout his or her educational career.

At present I am doing what I have always wanted to do; I consider myself a very lucky individual. Future plans include publishing a pre-school curriculum for other centers to use.

TEACHER & PRINCIPAL

It was a childhood dream to be a teacher, and that is what I have done. I spent 10 years as an elementary school teacher, 10 years as a college professor, and 15 years as a principal. In order to educate others, I have pursued an extensive education myself. I have earned a Bachelor of Science, a Master's degree, and a Doctorate in Education.

As an elementary school principal/teacher, I work with teachers, parents, and students to help students learn. I arrive at school at 7:30, unlock the office and other buildings, check the grounds, and greet the teachers, students, and parents. As the day progresses, my activities include performing administrative tasks; counseling with teachers, students, and parents; and teaching one math class.

To perform this kind of work well, it is important to relate positively to all kinds of people, know teaching methods and skills as well as the curriculum, have the ability to manage details, and be able to make long range plans.

Although I like my career very much, and would again choose this career even if given the chance to start over, there are some changes I would like to see in this occupation. There should be better time management, and less interruptions and idle talk allowed. I would like to see a better pay scale, and more resources to assist people in growth.

The greatest satisfaction I have enjoyed from teaching and my job as principal has been in seeing others grow in knowledge.

TEACHER, PRIVATE ELEMENTARY SCHOOL

Teaching, I believe, cannot be taught. Some can, some can't. I saw this in college and believe it today. Attitudes must ALWAYS be positive.

I chose teaching because I love children and thought this work would be fulfilling. I have been very satisfied with my current position as a teacher in a private school. I enjoy the private school climate, as I am given considerable freedom as long as I produce results with my ideas. I teach a class of first graders in a daycare/school situation. The children are of mixed ability, so my curriculum must be varied enough to meet their varied needs.

Except for my very low pay scale, I like almost everything about my career. I find teaching to be alternately hectic, rewarding, joyful, hard, fulfilling, and frustrating--it seems to bring out the best and the worst in everyone. The satisfactions come infrequently, but the rewards are worth the other times when someone sees the light, when someone reacts effectively in a way that you feel you caused, when you get great feedback from parents, or when parents insist their child have you as the teacher.

TEACHER, SCIENCE/ART/SOCIAL STUDIES

I have taught science, art, and social studies from the elementary school level through college. I enjoy my work, the people, and the organizations with which I've worked. I particularly enjoy watching young people succeed.

Good health, patience, understanding, subject knowledge, and neatness of appearance are needed in teaching. I have been a farmer, worked as a forest fire fighter, and a cosmetologist, as well as served in the military. It was in the military that I was asked to teach electronics and there I found I enjoyed teaching. Afterwards, I attended college and became a teacher. Ever since, I've loved helping young people.

This job requires you to be reliable, to enjoy helping young people, and to have achieved at least a bachelor's degree or, better, a Master of Arts degree.

If I started over again, I'd still be a teacher. Except for the interference from government, I've enjoyed my work. When I retire, I intend to travel. I will lecture at schools and to community and service clubs about my travels.

TEACHER, SOCIAL STUDIES #1

In the field of social studies, I teach history, civics, and free enterprise. In the time I have been teaching, seventeen years, I have found that the day-in, day-out duties of a teacher are preparation and evaluation.

In addition to a Master's degree in education, the job of a teacher requires motivational, organizational, and supervisory skills; patience; and the attitude that everyone can learn and succeed if they try.

Although I do not enjoy the vast amount of paperwork involved in my job, I love teaching; I find gratification in knowing that I help students learn and use their potential to the fullest. I enjoy being a part of a faculty and my fellow teachers are just as dedicated as I.

I have always been interested in history and teaching on the secondary level, but my main inspiration came from a college history teacher that I had the privilege to know and learn from.

I plan to learn more about teaching the adult learner and disadvantaged adults and perhaps direct an educational program for such individuals.

TEACHER, SOCIAL STUDIES #2

After a short stint as a caseworker for the Red Cross, I became a teacher at the 5th grade level. I'd finished college with a Bachelor of Arts degree in sociology, minoring in psychology and economics. I took education courses to upgrade my teaching certificate. I've spent a total of 25 years in education and am now teaching 7th grade social studies.

My work consists of preparing all materials needed--maps, films, study units--before classes start. During class I review all concepts studied the previous day and check homework. I introduce our new lesson, involving the students in class discussion and classwork. The class ends with assigning homework.

Job satisfaction comes in interacting with young people. I enjoy helping them learn concepts which give them a better understanding of their world. My work itself and my colleagues are delightful, but it all would be easier if there were fewer students to teach per class. With so many students, record keeping becomes a burden. It is also sad to see students who are disinterested and lack self-discipline. The principal could be of more help in this area.

A good teacher must know the subject matter well. You must have a good sense of humor and have confidence in yourself. It is very important to be accepting of individual differences in the students. Being able to maintain discipline along with motivating students is also critical.

TEACHER, SPECIAL EDUCATION #1

I have worked for twenty-five years as a teacher of special education classes. I utilize creative teaching methods designed to educate children for whom the traditional curriculum has failed. These methods involve exploring lessons that attract the interest of these special students; we then expand on these interests to create this experimental approach to education.

I have a Bachelor of Science degree. Anyone considering this type of work must possess the ability to observe and listen, then disregard traditional academic goals and substitute the practical everyday needs of children.

I enjoy this kind of work; I believe the children enjoy the unconventional approach to learning. I succeed because I am willing to take on the cast-offs that other educational professionals have given up on and help them achieve a measure of learning; I feel I have to succeed because I am their last resort.

My work could be made easier with cooperation from more academically oriented administrators--I believe most administrators worry too much about money and not enough about the children in the school system.

My next major undertaking will be to complete a novel based on my life experiences.

TEACHER, SPECIAL EDUCATION #2

A high school counselor suggested special education teaching as a good career choice for me, but I did not take it into consideration. Being a bored high school senior,

I signed up for a volunteer program. The supervisor was "supposedly" taking me to help a 7th and 8th grade P.E. teacher, but left me in a special ed. classroom for 2 weeks. By the time I saw the supervisor again, I was hooked! I seem to be oriented toward service jobs. Prior work experience has included: aide in an institution for the handicapped, babysitting, bartending and waitressing, respite care, and life guarding. My educational background includes a Bachelor of Science in Education for the Emotionally Handicapped, and a Masters of Arts in Learning Disabilities.

As a cross-categorical resource teacher, currently teaching 7th and 8th graders, I design individual educational programs for each student and then teach to the objectives outlined. A typical day begins at 7:15 where I double check to make sure all materials are prepared, grade papers, talk to students who are early, etc. Then I teach following our district's "Teaching Edge." As students are individualized, I am always working with someone and get few papers graded. During my prep period, I either test or write individual evaluation programs for new placements for the program. At 2:30, I hand in a correctives list, etc. At 3:00 I pick up my 3-year-old and return home to work from 4:30 to 6:00 to grade and prepare for the next day.

In order to perform this kind of work well, it is important to stay positive and caring about the people you work with. It is also of utmost importance not to fall behind.

Although I do like the kind of work I do, there are several frustrations I have to deal with in this teaching position. There is far too much paperwork and testing to do the best teaching I am capable of. I could use an aide to help with the testing and writing the individual programs. However, I do find satisfaction from my work, and enjoy it the most when a person who has given 100% and really struggled, suddenly "gets it" and never forgets that information again!

TEACHER, SUBSTITUTE

As a teacher for ten years, I have been involved with a few different areas of education--substitute teaching on a part-time basis and teaching basic skills to children in the K-6 grade level. I also specialize in the area of English as a Second Language (ESL). My educational background is in the field of education; I have a Bachelor of Science degree. I work half days four days per week teaching children who have academic difficulties, usually in small groups--one to eight children per group-- giving them the individual help they need. Sometimes I work with children for whom English is a second language. I consider myself to be an advocate for these children; I plan academic work for them as well as help them acquire English-speaking skills.

This job demands a high physical energy level, a good understanding of child development and knowledge of curriculum for grades K-6, good organizational and planning skills, the ability to remain clear headed under stress, patience, a good sense of humor, intellectual curiosity, and good physical and mental health.

It gives me great pleasure to know that I can help a child who may seem, in a regular classroom, to be disruptive or slow to learn; being a part of a faculty also is rewarding for me. The only aspects of my job that I would like to see handled differently are a smaller student to teacher ratio, to allow for more quality, individual time with each student; the funding for more positions like mine in the school system; and relief from some of the paperwork and clerical duties associated with my job. I would like to see teachers, in general, have more time to teach.

Teaching was a natural career choice for me, I have always wanted to be a teacher! School was always a very happy place for me to be. Before finishing my Bachelor's degree, I worked in clerical/secretarial positions and as a tour guide.

I plan to teach as long as my health and energy level allows, and at that time I will consider retirement.

TEACHER, THEOLOGY (PRIVATE SCHOOL)

A teacher prepares lessons, teaches classes, and reports on progress of enrolled students. My background in education includes a Bachelor's degree in Religious Education; I teach the history of religion and theology courses at a private religious school. A career in education also requires that one enjoy teaching the selected subject matter, have good communication skills, a sense of humor, and in my particular job, the enjoyment of traveling.

I believe the major satisfaction of teaching is watching the progress of students and meeting them several years later to find they are still interested in the subject you teach or are using the knowledge you personally imparted to them for the benefit of others.

In addition to my role as school teacher, I tutor students and help in literacy programs.

I expect to remain active as a tutor and community volunteer well into my retirement years.

TECHNICAL ILLUSTRATOR

I have always drawn since childhood. As I got older, my skills improved. Also, I have always been interested in science and technology. I didn't choose my career; it chose me. I have earned a bachelor and master's degree in architecture, and I worked as an architect for several years, but I did not like that job. I have chosen to use my talents and skills in the graphic design field as a technical illustrator/art director.

My job involves drawing pictures of technical things and then painting them realistically. I also design magazines. Each day is a mixture of working as an illustrator, getting phone calls, going to meetings, and organizing the work to be done. Design projects take a lot of organization. Therefore, one of the key skills you must have to perform well in this kind of work is organizational skills. Creativity, the ability to communicate, and an open mind with a sense of humor are also important attributes.

The biggest complaint I have about my work is the lack of free time. I would like to see some changes made in my occupation so that there was better scheduling of project deadlines, although this is many times out of our hands as artists. I wish artists/designers had more rights. I would also like there to be less running around involved with our projects.

Despite these frustrations, this job is satisfying because I am always learning new things, particularly about the technical things I illustrate. I also find satisfaction from my accomplishments and helping people.

TECHNICAL WRITER #1

The work that I do is almost entirely for health care systems. Usually, there are several people working together to develop a large or extensive guide for use of newly-developed computer materials, and I am one of those who writes and edits several chapters of these guides. The work involves writing, editing, word processing, and ability to get along with others. You need to have a desire to do a good job and provide good documentation so that others can effectively apply the materials about which the writing is being done.

There is a great deal of satisfaction in completing a book that people will use, will like, and will be able to enjoy or gain from effectively.

Since my organization works primarily with health care systems, the material frequently has important applications in the health field. Hospital employees use the guide to implement a health care system. I like this work very much, and I find that a college education is an important part of my background. I have a Bachelor of Science degree. At thirty, I have had mainly this job for the eight years since completing college. I became interested in this kind of work while in college and, upon graduation, was offered a job as a writer for a company that at that time had no documentation department. During the eight years that I have been with them, there was been a satisfying amount of expansion. There are some frustrations in the job; the major problem, perhaps, is that it does not pay extremely well. Also, I wish I were a technical specialist in one of the health fields for which I am doing this writing. Nevertheless, I like the job I have now and recommend it highly for those who are qualified to do this kind of work.

TECHNICAL WRITER #2

As a Technical Writer for computer systems, I am involved in writing and documenting processes and training others on the use of computer systems. Part of my job is that of a resource person, providing phone access for the computer system; another aspect of my job is that of legal expert on the subject of unemployment insurance laws and instructor in this area of expertise for other professionals at my company. Either by management request or my own decision, I document the system revisions for computer screens and user features; I am currently preparing for a major rewrite project on our computer system.

My educational credentials include both a Bachelor of Arts and a Master of Arts degrees. In addition to a good education, my job requires certain skills and personal attitudes. Among these skills and attitudes are: tact, diplomacy, working well with people, analytical skills, independence, motivation, the ability to make decisions, a strong command of written communication skills, extensive knowledge of the computer system that I write about, and knowledge of unemployment laws and policies.

Although there is not much of an opportunity to advance in my career through my present job, I like this kind of work. In the six years I have been employed at this company, I find that documenting and defining the unemployment laws as they pertain to my present company provide me with a great deal of satisfaction and even enjoyment in this job.

Even though I would really appreciate more help in typing manuals and correspondences, I manage very well and, with difficulty, I can stay on top of this job; the only thing that I would change about my job is the addition of another technical writer to help with the work load.

I have held several other positions that involved working with people and I believe those positions helped me acquire the necessary interpersonal skills I use in my present work.

Someday I will work as the head of a large group of writers involved in writing and revising manuals for a state office.

TECHNICAL WRITER #3

I entered the career of technical writing because this kind of work was readily available and I had the skills necessary to do the work. The thing I most like about this field is the security of the business; there seems to be a continuous need for people qualified in this area.

My educational background includes an Associate of Science degree in Business Administration. Prior to my present occupation, I have been employed as a retail sales clerk, reports clerk, office manager, assistant motor vehicle manager, and motor vehicle supervisor.

As a technical writer/editor, I prepare documentation and arrange for distribution. My typical work day is spent inputting information to the computer which is provided to me by the subject matter expert, following through on the procedures for distribution, and interfacing with the experts as required. In order to perform this work, it is necessary to have typing skills, good understanding of English grammar and good oral and written communication skills.

Although I am basically satisfied with this kind of work, I would prefer to have supervisory responsibilities where I would be more challenged and have less routine work. However, I do find satisfaction in the completion of projects.

TECHNICIAN

For eight years, I have been employed as a Pharmacy Technician. My duties are varied; I use the computer, perform the bookkeeping functions, serve as a sales clerk, and order medications and medical supplies.

The computer is used to print labels for medications and process charge payments to the customers. As a bookkeeper, I handle bank deposits and balance the monthly bank statement.

In addition to computer entry skills and bookkeeping skills, working in a pharmacy with the public requires a positive outlook; I also graduated from a technical college.

I enjoy helping people and I believe our customers would be better served if we could avoid the rushes inherent in any customer service business; a better customer flow pattern may help somewhat, but it will not eliminate the problem altogether.

My future plans include raising a family; I may choose to become a full time homemaker.

TECHNICIAN, AIR DEFENSE SYSTEM

After previous jobs as an electronics technician and technical writer, I have had the title of Logistician for the PATRIOT air defense system for five years. The title is misleading, however. What I really do is research the current and proposed configuration changes to a missile radar system. I maintain all the records [a material change management data package] and shepherd the reports through publication.

I do not have a college education, but was a technical writer and was offered this job based on my ability to think logically and use a computer. An openness to ideas, dedication, and perseverance are important qualities.

Satisfaction in this career comes from solving a problem and seeing it through to implementation. I would prefer to see more immediate results for my efforts, but overall I am extremely well satisfied and hope to reach the highest level possible in my profession.

TELEMARKETER, CUSTOMER SERVICE

I have spent most of my career time in retail sales, either as a telemarketer or at the catalog desk. I managed a telemarketing group for 12 years, but now that the program is canceled, I work "out front." In customer service, I now am speaking face to face with customers, which has been a transition for me from telephone work. I handle order taking, check cashing, ticket sales, and repair work orders.

My advice for you if you enter this field is to have confidence in yourself. "Go with the flow," yet question tactfully any company changes. Compromise, if necessary, but remember you face the customer. I further recommend: learn to type, whether male or female; read the papers and magazines; know your state, your county, and city/town; treat all customers as you wish to be treated; take a course or two in bookkeeping both for your job and personal life.

I like my work and derive satisfaction from it. Meeting people (customers) from the states and foreign countries has always been an enjoyable part of my job. I feel very good when problems have been settled.

TELEPHONE INSTALLER

Each day is different in my work as a telephone installer. This is one of the things I like about installing and repairing telephone lines and cables. One day I could be repairing a data line for a business, and the next I could be installing 1 to 100 telephone lines.

To work as a telephone installer, you must know electronics, color coding, and rules of safety. Your knowledge of telephone lines must be extensive, from repairing a simple problem at a residence to fixing complex data-line problems. Since I am a representative of my company, my attitude is very important. In my work, I find that a happy customer makes me happy. Customers are so pleased when I repair their phone and get it working again.

I finished high school and spent some time in the Navy before joining the telephone company. The independence of working by myself without a boss breathing down my neck, the fact that I work outside most of the time, and the opportunity to meet a lot of people are reasons I like my job. The pay is substantial, there are opportunities for advancement, and climbing telephone poles is good exercise. I started out as a telephone operator, moved up to a lineman's job for 7 years, and now I install and repair lines.

My career plans are to try to get a network maintenance position. The skills are broader, which will allow me to repair anything in a plant and get the customer back in service.

TELEPHONE SERVICE TECHNICIAN

For four and one-half years, I have been working in the field of telephone service and maintenance, installing and repairing telephone system lines as a service splice technician. Installing telephone lines into businesses and residential homes, I also repair existing telephone lines when there is trouble in my service area. Although I start each day in much the same fashion, meeting with my boss for daily assignments, each job that I am assigned is different, so there is a lot of variety to my work. The company provides me with any tools necessary to get the job done properly, and I had extensive company training to ensure that the customer gets the highest quality work in the shortest amount of time. My boss is always available to offer advice if there is a really unique task to be done; but besides that, I work on my own once I leave the office.

This type of work requires many unique individual qualities. You must be comfortable with heights, and any person with a fear of heights should not consider this type of work. You must master and respect specific safety procedures at all times on every job, keep an "on-call" schedule since emergency telephone service problems give no advanced warning, retain knowledge of a technical nature as the training program is very extensive, and be able to interface with people well without losing your patience. As this is a community service, diplomacy is extremely important.

I really like my job; as I stated before, there is a lot of variety to my job assignments and I particularly enjoy working on my own in a very large corporate organization. I have met some very nice people during my career so far and I have enjoyed helping them with their service problems.

At the moment I'm working on a Bachelor's degree in Business; if all goes well with my present employer, I hope to make it into a management position after completion of that degree program. Although I love climbing poles, I believe I would be better off, career-wise, climbing a corporate ladder versus the ladder I now climb.

TEMPORARY OFFICE PERSON, DRAFTSMAN

Working for a temporary service, I work in either an office environment or in a drafting room, depending on the work available. For office work, I perform ordinary office work tasks such as written communications, filing, office organization, and data entry on the computer. In a drafting environment, I work at a drafting table to prepare drawings for various engineering projects. My work requires computer skills, organizational skills, the willingness to work at several different tasks, motivation, math skills, experience in the field of drafting, and some training in the field of drafting. I have a certificate in proficiency in architectural and structural drafting and five years of experience in this field.

During the summer months, I also work as the camp crafts director at a boys' summer camp; this work requires an interest in kids and camping, experience in arts and crafts, and patience.

I find that I am rarely bored, and the schedule I keep does not allow me to get into a career rut, as is common in some professions. I really enjoy the variety of my jobs--the people, working with computers and utilizing my problem solving skills, and helping a child learn a creative skill that is new. I also like the positive feedback I get from my supervisors.

I started in temporary office work because I enjoy working at the summer camp but I need to work all year round. I previously worked in several jobs that were not very gratifying.

My future plans include spending more time with my family and to continue working in a temporary position after I return to college in a few years.

TEST PILOT

After some years in the Air Force, I obtained my Bachelor of Science in industrial engineering and became a field marketing rep for a major aerospace firm. Then I joined an aircraft company as an experimental test pilot. For 16 years, I have also been the Director of Test Programs.

Job satisfaction for me is the joy of precision flying. I like gathering accurate data during the engineering test flights. I do not enjoy the micro-management by outsiders and bosses. It would also be better if we could stop the instant visibility of test programs by Congress and the news media. Yet, I enjoy my work very much and would choose it again, if I could start over.

My job is to fly seven different types of aircraft being used in a very diversified series of new aircraft testing. These tests are used in the development of components of systems as well as systems within systems. We fly very precise profiles and test points using a carefully planned test program. During a week it is possible to fly 3 to 5 different tests, logging from 15 to 35 hours of flying time. It is also my job to oversee and direct tests in airplanes.

An experimental test pilot certainly must have the appropriate training in test flying as well as just being able to fly an aircraft. You have to have, and maintain, a high degree of concentration at the same time you are gathering and recording test data. Fear can have a very negative effect, but reasonable concern is appropriate.

TEXTILE ARTIST

My career as a textile artist came about by happenstance. I earned my Master's degree in Speech Therapy and practiced in that profession for more than 10 years before changing careers.

As a textile artist, my specialty is painting silk and creating embroideries. My typical activities include stretching and painting silk, delivering the products to shops/people, talking and demonstrating to groups, and being in craft and art shows.

My recommendation for pursuing a career as an artist is being familiar with the medium in order to control it and in order to experiment!

I like my career very much, but wish I had more time to paint. There is personal satisfaction in self-expression as manifested in the finished product and when people admire and buy what I create.

My future plans include opening my own shop and studio.

TEXTILE WORKER

As a weaver in a textile mill which makes woolen, polyester, and cotton cloth, my job is to keep 12 machines going all day. This involves running up and down the aisle tieing knots, taking out mistakes in the cloth, stopping and starting the machines for rethreading or problems, and looking for wrong color or misprints. This kind of work requires keen eyes, good legs, and good hands.

I have somewhat mixed feelings about the work that I do. I would like to have more opportunity for advancement, and for the management to be more fair and to listen to the workers. On the other hand, I like the kind of work I do, and the people I work with.

I do derive satisfaction from making a living, and this job does allow me to do that satisfactorily.

THEATRICAL DIRECTOR/PERFORMER/EDUCATOR

As a theatre director/performer/educator of five years, I perform and participate in a wide variety of theatre and theatre-related productions. There is no such thing as a typical day except for the fact that I start early every day and keep going until late.

My background includes a Bachelor of Arts degree and a Master of Arts degree, with a Master of Fine Arts in progress; previously, I have been employed as a special effects coordinator; a teacher, which I especially enjoyed; a secretary; and a manager of a women's gym. The theatre and all it involves provides me with so much enjoyment that I would not do anything else for a living.

Every project requires a different schedule. There is no typical schedule and there is no such thing as free time; any time that I am not involved actively in a current project, I am spending time reading, researching, or visiting with fellow artists.

The theatre requires a real desire to perform and create, determination, excellent organizational and problem-solving skills, patience, extensive creativity, well-developed interpersonal and communication skills, flexibility, and a stubbornness to hold on to your instinctive senses despite sometimes great adversity. Strong leadership skills, and a never-ending supply of physical energy are helpful.

I personally find project-oriented work very satisfying--it allows me to move from completed project to new project; I enjoy seeing one project to completion and then starting a new one. I really enjoy working with my fellow artists in creating a work of art, especially socially significant art, that the theatre creates to educate.

I would like to see more support in our society for artists, both in societal opinion and monetary compensation. I believe government support, without censorship, would lead to lower ticket prices, making the theatre available to a greater audience and provide more quality employment opportunities with better salaries for artists.

THERAPIST, MEDICAL REHABILITATION

As a teenager, I did volunteer work at a local parks and recreation center with mentally retarded adults and found I enjoyed it. I investigated the various careers in the health field with the aid of my high school counselor and mother. I visited several occupational therapy departments and obtained a fellowship that allowed me to work at a medical center while earning my Bachelor of Science in Occupational Therapy with a minor in humanities.

As the coordinator of occupational therapy rehabilitation, I supervise therapists and treat stroke and head-injured patients so they attain the highest level of functional independence possible in self-care, and mental and physical tasks. In the morning of a typical work day, I prepare the daily schedule for my staff and perform administrative tasks. From 8:40 to 4:15, I'm involved in patient treatment, re-education meetings with interdisciplinary therapists, and family education. From 4:15 on, I document the patient's performance and progress and prepare the schedule for the next day.

You must have a firm belief in being able to take control of a patient's life and change it with therapeutic intervention. Optimism, patience, empathy, intuition, people skills, warmth, and understanding are some of the enabling qualities a good therapist must possess. In addition, your health must be reasonably good because of the physical exertion required. A working knowledge of diseases and basic neurophysiology is also required for occupational therapy.

If I could change anything about my occupation, I would like to raise the status of this field of medicine. Occupational therapy does not have the same level of respect and esteem enjoyed by comparable disciplines in the medical field. Despite this frustrating aspect, I am satisfied with my career. I am able to effect changes in the quality of my patient's lives. Many are able to return home at a good level of independence and require only a small amount of assistance to maintain themselves. Through education, I may help a patient to avoid a similar medical trauma.

THERAPIST/COUNSELOR

I provide counseling for mentally ill and chemically dependent clients on an out-patient basis. Approximately 4 to 5 hours a day is devoted to one-one counseling or group counseling. The remainder of the time is spent doing paperwork--case notes, treatment plans, etc.

In order to perform well at therapy/counseling work, it is important to have a positive attitude and hopeful outlook on life. It is important to be able to detach from others' problems and yet be close enough to empathize with the client.

I started in this job when I graduated from college with a bachelor's degree, but I later went back to school for my Masters in Science in Guidance and Counseling. I plan to go back to school again to earn my Ph.D. in Psychology or Masters in Social Work. I have also considered getting a Masters in Business Administration.

Except for too much paperwork and not liking to give lectures, I like almost every other aspect of my work at the mental health center. I like working and learning with people. It is enjoyable to see others grow and be on a path of recovery from their particular illness.

TICKET ISSUING MACHINE TECH

My degree from college in computer technology made it possible for me to do my present work. I repair ticket issuing machines at racetracks. A typical day consists of performing maintenance on the terminals assigned to me. Then I am on call for the rest of the day.

Although my job pays well, I'd like the salary to be higher. My work is not very physically demanding, and I do enjoy working with my friends. I like my present work as much as I did my previous jobs of construction worker, real estate and retail salesman, and the military. Even though there aren't many ways to progress, my plans are to try to find ways to advance in the company.

The most important skill in my work is problem solving. You have to have a working knowledge of electronic equipment. A positive attitude plus getting along with different types of people has helped me.

TOOL AND DIE MAKER #1

After graduating from high school, I worked as a heavy equipment mechanic and truck driver. Being dissatisfied with those jobs, I enrolled in an apprenticeship program with the company where I am now employed, learning tool and die making.

As a tool and die maker, I do the building and/or repair of tools or fixtures for producing other products. In my particular job, I make the tools and fixtures for the production of office furniture.

In order to work at this trade, it is necessary to have a good mechanical aptitude and then to learn the specific technical skills involved in toolmaking and repair work. It is also important to have the ability to listen to people that you are learning the work from.

I like almost all aspects of my work, including the organization I work for and the people I work with. I get a good feeling out of finishing a job and realizing that I made a part that is used satisfactorily for its intended purpose.

TOOL AND DIE MAKER #2

I've never disliked going to my work as a tool and die maker. I'd make the same choices all over again. The feeling of pride and satisfaction of accomplishment are what gratify me most. It would be an even greater job if new equipment were available to work with.

I spent two years in college, but did not finish. I chose this field after having been introduced to it by a good friend. Previously, I was a TV technician; I've always been mechanically inclined.

You have to be skillful in setting up and running various metal cutting machines, such as lathes, grinders, and milling machines. Patience is also a requirement. The ability to plan by looking ahead to what has to be done is an essential quality.

In my job, guided by blueprints, we form the tools and dies that will produce automobile sheet metal stampings or plastic parts. These tools and dies are manufactured from steel, cast iron, and aluminum. Molds for fenders, hoods, roofs, and dash panels are then made from the dies. We finish these dies and molds by machine or by hand to make parts that are precise in both dimension and appearance.

TOOL DIE & GAUGE MAKER, SUPERVISOR

As a supervisor, I assign all work projects. I pick teams to solve various problems on production machine lines from over 5,000 production employees. Other responsibilities of mine are to conduct personnel interviews for new hires, handle personnel problems and grievances, train and write evaluations for promotions.

Specific skills for this job would include a mechanical aptitude, 1 or 2 years preferably of algebra, 1 year plane geometry, 1 year trigonometry and physics.

I have stayed in this occupation because I find satisfaction working with people, solving problems to cut costs, and designing and making machines and tools that work.

I got into this occupation because my father was a gauge maker and I saw he enjoyed his work.

When I retire as a supervisor, I would like to work part-time as a consultant, setting up machine training programs for Taiwan and Pakistan through an aircraft manufacturer.

TOOL STAMPER

I like my job as tool stamper in a manufacturing plant because of the different machines I get to run and set up, and the variety of jobs I have. It is a good-paying factory job where I am able to see the results of my efforts.

My typical daily assignments include: running the forklift, setting up a variety of machines, running orders, doing quality control checks, and running up to 10,000 parts per day or more if working overtime. The orders I stamp run from 200 parts per order to 15,000 parts per order.

The skills which are important to perform this job well are: good eyesight to see small flaws in characters and to judge if characters are in straight line, and physical strength to move very heavy pans of tools.

I have graduated from high school and have had several other job experiences. I have been a sales clerk, assembler, and freight unloader.

If I could change anything in my occupation, it would be to have the opportunity to select jobs based on the quality of the work performed and loyalty to the job instead of solely on seniority in the plant.

TOWN CLERK AND TAX COLLECTOR

Working in the field of town government for the last year, I perform the duties of Town Clerk, Town Treasurer, and Town Tax Collector. Although there is a general lack of trust among the other local town officials, I like my job(s); I have a very set work schedule and I can depend on only having to work a five-day work week. I supervise an office staff of four persons who process the payroll and expense checks, receive various tax and utility payments, maintain an accurate record of cash transactions and permits issued, and maintain the on-going bank relations.

My background includes a Bachelor of Arts degree in Political Science and a Master's degree in Public Administration, experience in working as a member of the staff for the State Legislature, and experience in working for several political campaigns. The requirements to succeed in town government at my level also include an outgoing and friendly personality, knowledge of local and state government, knowledge of local finances, administrative capabilities, and superior communication skills--both in written and verbal forms.

I enjoy the interaction with my staff, we are a good team; I also enjoy the work itself: it gives me the opportunity to exercise my decision-making capabilities and allows me to work independently. I would like to see a greater sense of mutual trust and understanding among and between all local officials in my organization, but I have been told that this goes with the territory.

I have always been interested in politics and the workings of our government structure; the experience and insight I gained through several, varied volunteering experiences in local government made this position a natural career decision for me.

I would like to someday be appointed to a cabinet position on the state or federal level; then perhaps I would have the opportunity to play golf on the Senior PGA Tour.

TRADE ASSOCIATION EXECUTIVE #1

As Executive Director of a non-profit trade association, my responsibilities include administration, lobbying, program development, financial management, and planning. To accomplish these duties, I work with officers, the board, and committees to plan and execute the various activities of the association. A major portion of my work is done by telephone.

I have now been employed by the association for 14 years, ever since graduating from college with a Bachelor of Arts degree. I was promoted to Executive Director after 4 years with the association. Prior to this job, I was a legislative liaison in the state government.

To perform this kind of work well, it is important to have flexibility, the ability to relate to people, and good writing and organizational skills.

I am very satisfied with this career and plan to continue in it.

I would, however, like to have more staff help to be able to achieve more of our goals. Job satisfaction for me is found in the relationships established with members in the leadership. It is also satisfying because I receive lots of "thank yous," and a fairly good salary.

TRADE ASSOCIATION EXECUTIVE #2

I finished my Masters in Journalism and interviewed at 15-20 ad agencies to get a job as copywriter. All the agencies said they hire only copywriters with experience. I went to work for an association to get needed writing "experience." In two years I was associate publisher and managing editor of their magazine and hooked on association work. I never tried agencies again. Prior to my association work, I was a newspaper writer, reporter, editor, TV news writer and cameraman, and photographer. My educational background also includes a Masters in Business Administration degree.

As a trade association executive I develop services for automotive product manufacturers, supervise market research, represent manufacturers before government agencies and Congress, and do financial management. There is no such thing as a typical day in my job. Each day is different, from: budget planning or review to testifying before Congress and committees, to collecting unpaid invoices, to planning market research, to planning advertising programs, to staff meetings, to visiting the Tokyo office, to meeting with Japanese executives, etc.

To perform my job well, communication abilities are vital (both internal and external). You must have listening skills and the ability to hear and analyze. You should be able to see patterns and trends from individual incidents. It is also important to understand the need of the association's customers, their members.

My work with the association could be more satisfying with more autonomy--less being looked at "over-the-shoulder" and second-guessed. I am, however, basically very satisfied with my kind of work. It offers a variety of work which I have enjoyed these past 23 years. It has given me the opportunity to be deeply involved in many operational and planning areas, handling projects from start to finish. I also derive satisfaction from an occasional public acknowledgement.

TRAINER OF THOROUGHBRED HORSES

I am happy as a trainer of thoroughbred racehorses and intend to stay with this career. To do well as a trainer you must have a love of horses, be open minded to new ideas, and have patience.

I started this career after graduating from college with a bachelor of arts degree and working at several other occupations. I liked my other jobs as an elementary school teacher, a newspaper reporter and a free-lance magazine writer, but my love for horses drew me into this field five years ago. Also, my father used to have a racing stable as a hobby so I was familiar with the career. My job is to supervise the daily training, health, and the nutrition of equine athletes (horses).

A typical day starts at 5:00 a.m. I supervise the exercise of the racehorses from 6:00 a.m. to 10:30 a.m. In the afternoon I take the horses to the races. This is a seven-day-a-week job with no vacations.

I like the people I work with plus I like being self-employed. The things I don't like are the public relations necessary to solicit new clients and the problem with clients who don't pay their bills.

The main satisfaction I get from my work is watching my horses run as well as they can.

TRAVEL AGENT #1

I made a career change from social work to the travel industry because of my personal interest in travel. I have a Bachelor of Arts in Sociology, and Masters in Social Work, and did school social work before making the change.

As a travel agent/branch manager my basic responsibility is to sell travel packages, and sell airline tickets on the computer. My typical daily activities include making reservations over the phone or in person for plane or train packages, scheduling personnel, ordering tickets and brochures for the office, and advertising.

To perform this kind of work well, it is important to have computer expertise, a willingness to work with the public, and attention to detail.

In spite of the low pay, I like my work very much. I like the organization and people I work for, the people I work with, and the kind of work I do. I find job satisfaction from my work because I am continuing to learn, and there is also stimulation from the variety on the job. My future career plans are to continue in my present capacity as travel agent/manager.

TRAVEL AGENT #2

What pleases me most about my job as an independent travel agent is the interaction with people. My fulfillment comes from my clients' satisfaction with my travel services. The feeling of accomplishment is very rewarding.

Being a travel agent is a great occupation. I enjoy dealing with the people, the company, management, and the work itself. There's also opportunities for advancement, a fact I like.

As a travel agent, I work with people to arrange their travel plans: reservations for hotels, airlines, rental cars, and such. I also advise and guide clients about their travel needs. It is work with a lot of variety, but there's not much financial reward and not a lot of benefits.

I got into this work because of my own enjoyment of travel, though that is not a requirement. Mostly, strong people skills are needed in this field. It can be frustrating when people change plans after a great deal of work has been done, but you have to be able to tolerate the whims of the public. Because scheduling and plans are done on the computer, you also need to be adept at its use. Although not required for this work, I have a Bachelor of Science degree.

In spite of my complaints about pay and financial benefits, I like this work because it leads to travel and to knowledge of foreign places, and I find that very rewarding.

TRAVEL MANAGER FOR INTERNATIONAL TOURS

I was working part-time as a tour group host in order to travel. Once in the industry, I wanted to learn more and develop a leisure and commercial travel background. I was quickly promoted in the travel industry and currently hold the position of travel manager for international tours.

As a travel manager, I coordinate staff and operations for all phases of international travel. I have set up my work schedule in the following manner: Mondays are spent on customer service requests (customer service is priority one); Tuesdays through Thursdays are spent on operation fulfillment for all phases of travel; and Fridays are spent on staff briefing on international preparation, documentation, etc.

Effective communications and detail emphasis are critical to operate a travel company and oversee staff. It is important to keep up-to-date with all current affairs world-wide.

The stress level is high due to time deadlines and highly detailed information. You depend on a variety of vendors to perform all aspects of this business. Improved cooperation throughout the industry would help to reduce the negatives.

I enjoy the travel industry and traveling. I have been around the world, including frequent trips to Europe, South America, China, etc. This certainly is a far cry from my earlier job as a fish cutter in my family's store. I have been able to take this experience and enhance the experience of others through educational and recreational tour programs.

TRUCK DRIVER #1

I find satisfaction from my job as a truck driver in giving an honest days work and pleasing my customers. This is very hard physical labor. I work 8 to 10 hour days making local deliveries and pickups. This involves loading and unloading trailers and dealing with customers. The benefit for my hard labor is great pay!

I started in this career after graduating from high school and have now been driving for 8 1/2 years. I like this kind of work, the organization and people I work for, and the people I work with. What I don't like is working in the hot summer climate.

I plan to continue in the transportation field and to possibly move into a management position.

TRUCK DRIVER #2

I have found the occupation I intend to stay with until retirement, although that may be 10 to 15 years "down the road." I am a truck driver, and satisfied that I have this job. I have had many previous jobs including printer, office supervisor, machine operator, factory supervisor, and postal worker, but truck driving seems to suit me best.

I make 2 kinds of deliveries, local and out of state. My local drives are to local retail supermarkets. Out of state deliveries require 22 days and staying in a motel overnight. I pick up the trailer at the warehouse and take the load to different states to unload. I then pick-up loads coming back home. All my unloading is done by hand.

Being alert and aware at all times is critical as a truck driver. You must have patience in dealing with traffic and weather, on road trips especially. Also, to do your job well requires keeping a good reputation with your customers.

Although I like most aspects of my work, I would prefer a little less interstate work and more local so I could be home more often. The positive aspect of my work is the opportunity to be my own boss when out of town. This allows me to make last minute decisions on my own, which is satisfying to me. I take pride in knowing my work commitments have been met with little or no difficulty.

TRUCK DRIVER #3

I had been a mechanic for more than 10 years, during which time I saved enough money to buy my own truck. I was seeking independence in my work and the adventure of seeing the country. Since this is what I have found during my 10 years as a truck driver, I intend to stay with this career.

My basic responsibilities are driving and keeping the books. My typical week includes 50-70 hours of driving. During this time, the most important thing is to stay alert, and to not let frustrating situations bother you. Despite the desire to have freight rates higher, I like most aspects of this occupation. I like the kind of work I do, and the opportunities I have for advancement.

TRUCKING BROKER

My career has just evolved. I was hired by a trucking company after completing college with a Bachelor of Science degree. My career has changed directions with the industry as my knowledge and experience continued to grow. Prior to my current position, I have been a consultant in transportation, a safety director, and director of public relations. I am now a trucking broker and the president of the company licensed by the Interstate Commerce Commission.

As a trucking broker, I sell transportation; customers ship commodities and we arrange transportation at a discount. On a daily and /or weekly basis, my activities include: securing new customers, securing new trucking companies, directing employees in the performance of their individual jobs, instructing and upgrading each individual's knowledge of the computer, and expanding the individual employee's knowledge of our industry.

To succeed in this kind of work, a positive attitude is essential. You should have the desire to learn and expand your knowledge. I would like to see the people in this industry attending seminars to continually expand their knowledge in an ever-increasing area of business. Skills in typing, math and accounting are also important in this occupation.

I like being president of my own company, the people I work with, and the kind of work I do. I find job satisfaction by accomplishment in performance and in seeing employees grow in their individual careers. I plan to continue to expand the business and add an additional office. Ultimately, I plan to sell my business to the employees. Then I will move on to participation in the work of saving our planet!

TURNPIKE TOLL COLLECTOR

I will not suggest that the job of turnpike toll collector is the ultimate occupation, but, frankly, I like this kind of work. I would like it better if I could work a little slower, and if I could work only in good weather conditions. However, I have no complaint with the organization or people I work for.

I like the people I work with and I particularly like meeting the public. What makes my job satisfying is, in fact, the interesting people I meet and work with.

My responsibilities as a toll collector are to collect tolls, assist patrons in an emergency, give directions when needed, provide help in getting medical assistance when necessary, writing accident reports, and balancing transactions at the end of the day.

To perform this kind of work well, it is important to be punctual, accurate, courteous, friendly, and helpful. It is also necessary to have basic math skills.

Prior to this job, I worked as a letter press operator, and a bookbinder. I do feel, however, that if I were given the chance to start again and prepare for another occupation, I would select a career in the medical field.

TUTOR & EDITOR

I did not choose my present occupations. As a matter of fact, I was in the pre-med course at college. What I am doing now is the culmination of that which I have learned thus far about teaching and writing.

All of my occupations have centered on the field of education--teacher (grades 4-12, university level, and learning disabled teacher), senior editor for educational publications, and writer of educational materials.

I am now working as a teacher, tutoring high school learning-disabled students, and as an editor for a leading graduate school of business administration. This allows me to work out my own schedule in order to provide the care for my father that he now needs due to illness. In teaching learning-disabled students, no week is, of course, the same. In editing manuscripts, no manuscript or schedule is the same.

My attitudes are a result of knowing what I can do well and the flexibility of mind required to adapt skills to new experiences--no tunnel vision. The skills I possess are a result of school, learning on the job, the ability to "read people," and the willingness to learn and grow.

I like the teaching I do because of the growth I see, and writing and editing because of the challenges and thinking processes involved. The satisfaction of a job well done is paramount. The knowledge that people have changed and grown because I touched their lives is deeply satisfying. Also, it is good to know I can support myself.

TUTOR & COLLEGE WRITING INSTRUCTOR

I have somewhat of a dual career, although they both involve teaching. I am an instructor of writing at a college, and I own a tutoring business where I teach English as a second language. I chose teaching very early in my life as I was very successful in school. My teachers also inspired me to achieve my goals.

As instructor/tutor, my responsibilities include preparing courses, assigning homework, lecturing, grading, proofreading, typing, giving personal and college counseling, coordinating, supervising, creating, and directing. My schedule varies by semester, but last term's schedule was: 8-9:15 a.m.- prepared lessons; 9:15-11 a.m.- went to office and counseled 2-3 students; 11-1 p.m.- lectured and directed the class in business writing; 1-1:45 p.m.- graded papers and other paperwork; 7-9 p.m.- graded papers. Many afternoons were also spent attending workshops.

To perform this kind of work well, it is important to have the following qualities and skills: giving, kindness, patience, equality consciousness, typing, good knowledge of subject, good self confidence, speaking skills, strong directive personality, open attitude, creativity, flexibility, consistent behavior, logical view, respect for people, intuition, and reliability.

To make my job more satisfying, I would like to see a lower teacher to student ratio. I'd like to see a change of attitude in elementary schools and high schools to take the pain out of learning and allow students to love the subjects. By the time I see them, they are very negative and turned off to the subject. I am also somewhat dissatisfied because I feel there is a lack of compensation for this valuable service of educating our society.

Despite these frustrations, I like my kind of work very much, and the people I work with. I enjoy the opportunity to be creative and the long vacations to help restore my creativity. I like having only short hours of being tied to my office, allowing for a flexible lifestyle and freedom to teach my way. Teaching is satisfying for me because of the visible results I see in my student's lives. It is satisfying helping people - seeing my course creations teach my students what they need to know to succeed. It is a great feeling to see the response to my teaching effort.

UNION CARPENTER, FOREMAN

As a foreman for a union carpenter shop for twenty-eight years, I assign the carpenters their jobs, go over the details of each job, and answer all questions. I work mostly in commercial buildings to make sure the working area is safe and that the carpenters who work for me have safe working tools; I oversee the entire job, checking for quality and efficient use of the worker's time.

To succeed in a position such as mine you should have an Associate's degree in Architectural Engineering; the ability and experience to use the tools of a carpenter, both hand tools and power tools; the ability to work well with others; foresight to see a job through from beginning to end; and the ability to read blueprints.

I enjoy my job for the most part; I especially take great pride in the quality of the finished product. I like the people I work with, the person to whom I report, and this kind of work. My only frustrations arise from the dealings with the union in the course of my work.

As I have good mechanical ability and enjoy working with my hands, this was a natural career choice for me.

I served in the U.S. Navy, then worked as a telephone equipment installer for a non-union house builder. I prefer to work in a non-union shop, but I like the benefits provided with the union.

In the future, I plan to start my own business in this field on a small scale at first.

UNIVERSITY DEAN

I've been in education all my adult life, first as a teacher, then as a school counselor. Currently, I am Dean of Admissions and Registrar at a university where I've been for 15 years. I have a Bachelor of Arts Degree and a Masters in education. My goal is to stay in higher education in a position of growing responsibility.

Job satisfaction for me is maintaining a happy staff and a positive work environment. Helping young professionals learn the profession, planning and organizing an efficient office, and providing service to students, faculty, and administration give me a sense of gratification. My work would be more enjoyable if services in other areas were consolidated to make operations more efficient.

In order to be an effective administrator, you must have strong organizational skills. Good interpersonal and verbal and written communication skills are beneficial as well. It is important to manage projects well, establish performance measurements, and assess personnel based on defined goals and expectations. In supervising personnel, an administrator needs a positive attitude toward subordinates along with a strong belief in that person's ability to do what is best for the organization.

UNIVERSITY FINANCIAL AID ADMINISTRATOR

I have a Bachelor of Science in management and serve as a financial aid administrator for a university. I've been in this work long enough to know that I like it very much.

There is no typical day in my job. The activities vary greatly. Much time is spent with students and families in counseling sessions. I listen, advise them on their financial concerns, and guide them through the application process. Each day applications for aid must be reviewed and addressed; then I evaluate the applications for financial aid. Budgeting and forecasting are also a part of my work. There's a constant flow of paperwork and correspondence which must be processed.

As a financial aid administrator, you must be able to handle a wide variety of information. Abilities to listen, communicate, and evaluate are essential. Policies and regulations relating to financial aid are continually changing. It's vital to understand proposed changes and their impact. Attention to detail is important because of the high volume and fast pace of the work. Finally, you must enjoy working with young people in a counseling setting.

What pleases me most in my work is the feeling that I'm helping others with their own aspirations and dreams. The pleasure of feeling respected because I'm making a difference in people's lives adds to my satisfaction. Dealing with the many complexities of student finances can be frustrating and I often wish I had more control over issues. Often, I can readily identify a problem, but I'm unable to do anything to rectify it.

While attending college, I worked in the financial aid office. I enjoyed the mixture of analytical, creative, and counseling aspects of the work. For now, I'd like to continue to work in academic administration. After further education, I might be able to move toward a more senior level position, such as dean, in the academic world.

URBAN PLANNER #1

In the field of urban planning for twenty-seven years, I specialize in advance planning research. My position as urban planner involves population estimates and forecasts, school enrollment estimates and forecasts, defining census tracts and major retail centers for census enumeration, and housing market analysis. I attend meetings with division colleagues to discuss and plan our work program for the planning department.

My job takes on a more independent nature when I am working on enrollment forecasts for school districts, performing field operations to define and modify census tracts, or preparing reports on housing market activity to be used by housing and commercial planners in the private sector.

A career in urban planning requires: in-depth and current knowledge of economics, the political process, sociology, statistics, and skillful application of these areas of knowledge; an analytical mind; and the ability to communicate with superiors, subordinates, and community groups.

I enjoy seeing the results of my work put to good and productive uses.

Unfortunately, budget cuts, as a result of tax cuts in recent years, resulted in staff and activity reductions that have damaged the quality of urban planning being done; I believe this damage could have been avoided or at least forestalled by rational evaluation of the need for planning. Instead, budget cuts were severe and not well thought out, causing the cuts in fiscal support for urban planning.

It was in my teen years that I chose to pursue a career in urban planning; I attended college and earned a Bachelor of Arts in Political Science degree. While working for the Federal government as a personnel analyst and later for a large oil company as a procedures analyst, I completed a Master's degree program and earned a Master of Public Administration degree.

I am very happy with a career in urban planning; I really like employing the variety of skills that my work requires.

URBAN PLANNER #2

As an Urban Planner, I develop and implement comprehensive land use plans and manage the operation of the planning business.

My background includes a Master of Urban Planning degree; I have always had the desire to build cities. It is essential to enjoy detailed work and dealing with people.

I derive personal and professional satisfaction from getting things done; this is a rewarding job for me. I really like the work I do. I feel that it is very important to build new cities with greater consideration for our sensitive ecological environment.

I believe there is a lot of opportunity for advancement within this field--it is a growing field and I expect to be busy always.

I enjoy the people I meet on my job and the people I work with.

In the future I plan to continue building new structures that will be functional and ecologically safe.

U.S. AIR FORCE COMMAND PILOT

My primary career (and I have had several other jobs) is Command Pilot of Air Force Bombers, and I have had that position for 27 years. During the latter half of that time, I was Squadron Commander and was responsible for flying missions with my crews in experimental reconnaissance aircraft over Siberia. I have also served as Base Commander in connection with the Strategic Air Command.

Do I find this satisfying work? Yes, extremely satisfying. I cannot say as much for some of my other jobs which included running a real-estate office, selling insurance, and property appraisal. Of those, I liked appraising most but disliked selling; it "turned me off." I was also a high school science teacher for one year, and I found that job to be very tough and, for me, unrewarding. One of the reasons I like flying is because I take pride in achieving our objectives, and I was successful at it. In my way of thinking, that was really worthwhile work.

To be an Air Force Officer, you need many skills and attitudes. Those that occur to me are: leadership ability, good vision, health, good depth perception, control of your fears, ability to remain solid under pressure, coordination, and endurance. It was also helpful to be good in science, mainly physics, biology, and chemistry in my case. It is very helpful to have a college degree--a Bachelor of Science or a Bachelor of Arts is sufficient.

As to the future, perhaps I will eventually go into politics. I enjoyed helping in organizing for a political party and, who knows? Maybe I will become a candidate.

U.S. AIR FORCE FLIGHT ENGINEER

I have been a flight engineer for the Air Force for many years. I work on multi-engines aircraft, giving long hours to various duties.

I like everything about my work: my coworkers, my supervisors, the Air Force, and engineering itself. "Getting the job done" is very rewarding to me. After high school, I'd previously worked as a maintenance supervisor at a private club and had owned a small engine shop, but I enjoy the many opportunities for advancement in the Air Force.

My work includes loading air conditioning control engines into aircraft and servicing the air conditioners. I supervise flight crews as well as ground crews. I also keep flight records for our worldwide operations.

A flight engineer needs solid mechanical skills. You should be a good supervisor, a self-starter, and able to cope with many situations. Meticulous attention to details in any mechanical operation is required as well. Of utmost importance is the need to be concerned about safety at all times.

U.S. AIR FORCE MAINTENANCE OFFICER

An Aircraft Maintenance Officer in the U.S. Air Force supervises the maintenance and repair of service aircraft. My duties include managing schedules, plans, and technical information systems. I attend status briefings on aircraft in maintenance and briefings on daily flying schedules. Developing work plans for aircraft repair, releasing aircraft for flight, and long-range work plans for aircraft inspection are also my responsibility. I personally check repairs in progress and perform random checks of equipment and personnel performance.

I have found that the willingness to make the tough calls is necessary in my work. You must be able to allow others to perform their duties with minimum interference. It is necessary to be logical and methodical in making plans, while staying flexible to adapt to changes. A maintenance officer must be self-disciplined, innovative, and dedicated. My Bachelor of Arts Degree is in human resources administration; my Masters Degree is in procurement and acquisitions.

My career plans are to continue to advance in rank and responsibility. At the same time, I want to devote more time to my second career--writing. I'd like to have a book published.

Other jobs I have held are that of a restaurant manager, electrician, and radar technician. I've served 20 years in the Air Force. Job satisfaction is knowing that I contribute to the security of our nation. I am gratified with the successful execution of a mission. I like being a part of historical events others only read about.

U.S. AIR FORCE MAJOR

U.S. Air Force Officers at the rank of Major must have strong leadership skills and the ability to work well with people. One must develop a knowledge of human relations. An Officer needs technical knowledge and experience. Also important are administrative and managerial skills. My degrees are a Bachelor of Science and a Master of Science in Meteorology.

My work is to provide tailored weather briefs for the Armed Services. Forecasting and observing are part of my duties. I provide weather warnings and advisories for resource protection and flying safety. Administratively, I manage 24 people and over 3 million dollars in equipment. My experience has been in some phase of science, weather forecasting, and navigation. I have no additional career plans at this point.

Generally, I find these are difficult times for serving in the military. But, I enjoy helping people and I'm glad when I can provide a good product. We need more people in the unit to provide technical support.

U.S. AIR FORCE OFFICER, RESEARCH PHYSICIST

As a research physicist for the U.S. Air Force, I currently run experiments to study the environment and I also manage several large contracts. I am responsible for our area of work and for the coordination of the work of several scientists.

As an Air Force officer this will change as I am moved to my next assignment in approximately six months.

To perform well at this job it is necessary to have leadership skills, scientific knowledge, organizational skills and motivation.

I am satisfied with my job because of the level of responsibility I have at my young age. I am given the opportunity to accomplish projects which I feel can make a difference. I like the fact that I am allowed to continue my education while working in this setting.

If I were given the opportunity to change anything about my job, I would do away with many of the bureaucratic procedures. I would simplify the regulations which apply to us. I would place more personal responsibility on the members.

I chose the Air Force in eighth grade. I then went to the U.S. Air Force Academy. Before my current occupation I was an aircraft mechanic. I plan on staying in the Air Force for at least 17 more years. At that point I will make a decision to go into private industry or government service. I would plan to go into an area where I thought I could make things better for people.

U.S. AIR FORCE PILOT #1

I can't think of any way I would change my career as an aircraft pilot and a retired officer of the United States Air Force. I have always wanted to fly and the Armed Forces provided me with this opportunity. Years later I still say this would be my career choice.

I now teach students and other members of a flying club how to fly airplanes and gliders. In addition, I race against my own records that I have set earlier in the military.

I think the most important skills to develop for flying are attention to detail and orderly control.

There are definitely times when being a pilot can be stressful and exhausting. However, the thrill and challenge of flying seem to override these negative points. I like the people I work with, and the organization and people I work for. I like the challenge of maintaining my skills. I only hope I know when to quit.

I get job satisfaction now from improving the flying knowledge and skills of younger people.

U.S. AIR FORCE PILOT #2

There is nothing I dislike about my career as a pilot in the Air Force except that we don't get to fly enough. I became a pilot because I have always wanted to fly, and after 20 years of flying, my plans are to continue as a pilot for as long as possible, in the military or for commercial airlines.

In addition to flying and training, I supervise the training and professional development of younger pilots. A typical day would be to prepare for a flight which consists of many things, but, primarily, the mission plan and training objectives. Then, of course, we fly the mission and afterward conduct a thorough critique emphasizing areas of needed improvement.

In order to perform this kind of work well, the following skills and attitudes are important: a positive, self-confident attitude; good hand-eye coordination; the ability to plan for several minutes or events ahead while executing to perfection the current task; the ability to coordinate with others, accept criticism, and help others improve.

My background includes a Bachelor of Science in Math and Philosophy, a Master of Science in Operations Management, and employment as a school teacher. I am definitely glad I made the change to flying. I like every aspect of my work.

I particularly like the camaraderie, the esprit de corps, and the purpose/objectives of this profession. I find job satisfaction in many ways, such as mastering the intricacies of flying modern jet aircraft, working with professionals who have similar goals and aspirations, and being in the military which provides a sense of community, including the families, that is found in very few other occupations.

U.S. AIR FORCE PILOT #3

I was a manager for a country club golf course before joining the Air Force 20 years ago. I've retired now and plan to continue enjoying retirement.

Through an aviation cadet program in the 1950's, I became interested in being a fighter or bomber pilot. I flew high performance airplanes for the Air Force. It is impossible to describe a typical week or day because every flight was different. The variety in each flight was particularly enjoyable to me. I liked the people I worked for and with. In general, flying was very satisfying.

To do this job, you must have excellent health and eye sight. Strong motor skills and a calm personality are important in this profession. You must have a high I.Q., be able to think quickly, and have a sound education, but a college degree is not a requirement.

U.S. ARMY OFFICER

I've spent 30 years as an Army infantry officer and am now at the rank of colonel. Ten years were as an Army aviator. I fought on the front line in World War II and in Korea. Other periods in my career were spent as commander of a rifle company and battalion, serving on general staff at the Pentagon, and commanding a helicopter training base. I also was director of training for a helicopter company in Iran.

A typical day depends on rank and on what work is being done at the time. In the past, I was involved in military planning and operations. My reason for learning to fly was so I could be a part, as commander, of the expanding aviation units for the Vietnam buildup. I've also taught or attended military schools throughout my career.

Career satisfaction for me is doing a job well in peace or in war time. I also enjoy respect from superiors and from subordinates. Being away from my family for long periods of time has been a drawback for me. I'd also like better pay and better living conditions. Otherwise, I've enjoyed my life in the Army, both as an adult and as an "Army brat."

Loving adventure and the unknown is part of the description of an Army officer. You must be a person of integrity and courage. You need to be intelligent, attentive to the welfare of your men, and get along well with people. Planning skills, along with the ability to execute those plans, are also important. You should be able to put leadership and service to your country ahead of material gain. I have a Bachelor of Arts degree which has helped in my promotional climb.

U.S. ARMY RECRUITER

I volunteered for my job as U.S. Army - Soldier/Recruiter after serving two years as a drill instructor to new soldiers. I have now been in recruiting for 7 years and find that I really like this kind of work. I like being in the Army, the people I work with, and the opportunities I have for advancement.

My work as a recruiter is primarily sales work. I telephone people's home to make contacts. I then go out and about talking with and meeting people, in order to find people who I can interest in joining the Army. To accomplish this work, it is important to have administrative skills, know and execute sales techniques, to have a positive attitude, be motivated , and self-disciplined.

I find satisfaction from my work by being able to put someone in the Army who has a strong desire to serve our country. I plan to continue to serve with the U.S. Army for 20 years and to become a sergeant major, the highest ranking non-commissioned officer for the Army.

U.S. GOVERNMENT CONTRACTING OFFICER

I began my career as a Co-operative Education Program participant in college. After earning a Bachelor of Science and Master of Arts degree, I decided to continue my career in federal service work because I find it rewarding. Besides 4 years of military service, this has been my lifetime career for 24 years.

As a Contracting Officer for the U.S. Government Civil Service, I award contracts in support of Federal activities. I provide assistance to small business owners who desire to market and contract with the U.S. Government. Most assistance is provided by telephone with about one-third of the week spent out of the office.

A cooperative willingness to assist those unfamiliar with Federal contracting regulations is essential to perform this kind of work well. Verbal and written communication skills are also necessary.

There really isn't any aspect of my work that I dislike. I only wish there could be an elimination of the aspects of Federal contracting that obviously annoy, frustrate, and discourage business owners when dealing with the U.S. Government. I, therefore, find satisfaction from my work when I help others understand/simplify the sometimes complex rules and regulations that govern Federal Contract expenditures. It is also rewarding to actually see that my efforts benefit small business development.

When my civil service career is completed, I will perhaps open up my own small business.

U.S. GOVERNMENT PUBLIC AFFAIRS OFFICER #1

From childhood, I had special writing abilities and aspirations for a writing career. I started with an after-school job as a cub reporter. In my current position as Public Affairs Officer in a U.S. government environmental department, I write speeches for high officials, and write or supervise other writing projects such as brochures. Some of the regular activities which are involved in my work are: reading reports, newspapers, and other source materials; conferring with speakers; conferring with Deputy Director of Public Affairs; writing speeches; assigning or reviewing work of 4-6 subordinates.

To perform this kind of work well, it is important to have top writing skills in many different subject areas (i.e. history, philosophy, literature); the ability to work under pressure of deadlines; a good knowledge of subject matter; and willingness to accept the anonymity of the ghost writer.

I have found this to be a very satisfying career for me.

I have found personal satisfaction in my accomplishments in that I receive verification of my special skills and talents. I also find satisfaction from the recognition of peers, which makes up for the lack of "public" recognition. The specific writing which I do also allows me to aid in the advancement of worthwhile objectives.

As a retirement job, I am considering doing travel writing, but I guess I don't really need to see my name in print.

U.S. GOVERNMENT PUBLIC AFFAIRS OFFICER #2

Although I am now retired , I can definitely give you some insight into a career as a U.S. Government Public Affairs Officer because I had this position for 30 years. My last 16 years were spent in Berlin, Germany.

I did a variety of things on my way up the ladder that added to my ability and made it possible for me to handle this job. I did not, however, receive a college degree. Prior to becoming a public affairs officer, I was a foreign correspondent, newsreel cameraman, managing editor of a news service, the CEO of a mail order company, and I worked in a department store.

In my capacity as the U.S. public affairs officer in Berlin, I was the liaison with French, British, German and many other government officials. I had the duties of handling relations with the world press for the US government in Berlin, supervising public relation programs, and publishing a newspaper for US personnel in Berlin. I planned and handled congressional visits, presidential, and other foreign visits. I gauged reactions of the Berlin public to programs and events planned for unilateral actions by the US and Allied committees.

If I could change anything about this occupation, it would be to have less emphasis on cultural background and more on practical knowledge for officers in foreign countries.

I particularly like the international ambiance of work and play that this job had. I did not particularly like the visits by some of our government officials. I would certainly, however, choose to do this again if given the chance to start over.

The main satisfaction of my work in Germany came after I retired when The Wall came down and I received mail from officials in the German government and ordinary German friends thanking me for my small part in getting the Wall down and my helping to make reunification a reality.

U.S. IMMIGRATION INSPECTOR

It is my job to inspect applicants at the Maine border for admission into the United States. I primarily work outside checking autos and passengers. I also work inside at the desk where people are sent if there is a need for further inspection.

The mandatory requirement for this job is a knowledge of the United States immigration laws. I find satisfaction from this work because I feel I'm doing my job, I know the laws and apply them correctly.

However, in my opinion, the continual cuts by Congress of our benefits is hurting the morale of government employees. It seems our benefits are usually the first to be cut "for the good of the nation."

I have a Bachelor of Science degree in Education and taught for a number of years. While teaching, I worked as an inspector during my time off in the summer. I eventually decided to make this my full-time job because I could double my teaching salary in two years time.

U.S. MARINE

My career in the U.S. Marines started when I received a college scholarship. As a Marine, I have held the following positions: infantry platoon and company commander, training jobs, personal affairs officer (drugs/education/welfare, etc.) logistics planner, and staff officer.

I am now in logistics planning, and in this capacity I teach senior officers about national security strategy and logistics. My normal work day is from 0700-1700 teaching 2-4 classes per day (1.5 hours each). The rest of my day is spent reading and writing, studying and preparing for class, developing curriculum, and meetings with students/faculty.

To perform this kind of work, it is important to have knowledge of subject matter, self direction, interest in academic subject matter, ability to communicate well with small groups, enthusiasm, writing skills and ability to proof/correct student's work, and the ability to analyze and synthesize diverse material.

If given the chance to change anything in my occupation, I would like to reduce the operational tempo of the military organizations, and reduce the complexity and the "make work" syndrome that is part of the military environment.

Aside from disliking being separated for long periods of time from my family, I like military service.

There is satisfaction from my current position as logistics planner in working with people, the exchange of ideas, and the time to think and study without day-to-day pressure of a normal routine. I find that this job provides me a break from the pressure of normal jobs.

I plan to continue in the U.S. Marines until I can retire at 25-30 years of service.

U.S. MERCHANT MARINE--3RD MATE

With a degree in marine transportation, I became a Third Mate in the US Merchant Marine seven years ago. My duties include handling 2 four-hour watches per day. I'm in charge of the ship's navigation and safety. I direct course changes, avoid collisions, check compasses, and conduct fire and lifeboat drills. From the bridge, I use celestial and terrestrial navigation to direct the ship.

Job satisfaction comes from safely guiding the ship and her crew through foul weather or through areas of congested navigation. I'd like to be home more, or I'd like to be able to have my family with me more often. I dislike some of the people, but I enjoy the solitude, tranquillity, and the beauty I see in my work.

A solid basis in math is required for my work along with understanding of meteorology. You must know the rules of the nautical road, how to handle a ship, and the principles of cargo handling. Knowledge of pollution and maritime law is necessary. You need to think independently and make quick decisions when the situation demands it.

I've loved the ocean from childhood; I wanted to work on or near it. My career aspirations are to continue with my present work in the Merchant Marines.

U.S. NAVAL OFFICER

Before joining the Navy, I was a legislative aide, which I enjoyed, but I volunteered to enlist in the Navy to gain leadership and management experience.

Job satisfaction for me is the pride I have in serving my country. I enjoy the feeling of prestige in being an officer. The sense of accomplishment in a difficult environment is also rewarding to me. The fact that there are opportunities for advancement is important, too.

Days out at sea serving on board a ship are very busy ones. There's not much time for myself or for sleep. Some days are spent doing mundane chores and handling paper work. Mainly at sea, however, an officer must manage his division, stand watch, and be prepared to handle any situation which may arise. As officers, we defend the nation and provide leadership for our sailors.

I've been in the Navy for 7 years; I miss getting enough sleep and miss my family being out at sea so much. One day I'll leave the service and pursue a career as a corporate executive.

An officer must first be a leader. You should have a positive attitude in order to perform well. Good analytical skills are also needed. You must have the necessary training and education; my degree is a Bachelor of Arts in history. Finally, being a good communicator is essential.

U.S. NAVY TECHNICIAN

An electronics technician in the United States Navy needs common sense, logical thinking skills, and patience. Being intelligent and being able to concentrate for long periods are all important for success.

In my work, I maintain and repair radar systems. I test equipment and I also work with transceivers, TVs, and stereo equipment. I get up in the morning at 0600, get to my ship by 0730, and am assigned a piece of equipment to work on. After I test it, I repair it, and go pick up another item.

Gratification comes for me in knowing how much I help my ship's mission and my country. I like most everything about my work except the bad attitudes of some of the people. A high school graduate, I enlisted in the Navy after deciding it was a good alternative to college. My goal is to get my college degree and to become an electronics engineer.

UTILITY WORKER

While in the process of earning a college degree with plans to work for a high tech company or run my own business, I found satisfying employment as a utility worker. The way I got the job was through persistence, going back day after day asking them to hire me. One of my major reasons for choosing this kind of work is that it is outside work.

As a utility worker, I do maintenance on water pipes and install new water service. A typical day could include going out on a service call, talking to people, checking hydrants, and/or installing water services and main lines.

The true skills needed for this kind of work are common sense and patience to be able to work with other people. Aside from that, much of the work is manual labor.

Despite the drawback that there is a lack of opportunity for advancement for me in this job, I like the people I work for and work with, and the kind of work I do. I am learning new things every day and am always meeting new people. Even though this is an interim job for me, I feel there is much that can be gained from this kind of work.

VETERINARIAN #1

I wanted to be a veterinarian since the fifth grade because I wanted to be able to take care of my own horses and dogs. Now that I have earned my degree and practiced for 6 1/2 years, I have found that I like my profession, but I have also been able to see the drawbacks. I like the occupation because I have the ability to solve a problem and help someone's animal. However, I take medical failures personally and find my work to be emotionally draining. I like being busy, but I have found that it is not possible to schedule the work since most of work is dealing with emergencies which, of course, are unpredictable. I find satisfaction in providing a needed service. However, people seem to demand too much sometimes in their non-emergency requests.

As a veterinarian, I vaccinate, treat and do surgeries on companion animals: dogs, cats, horses, and other pets. My work schedule is unpredictable since animals do not get sick only during my scheduled office hours. Aside from dealing with emergencies at any time of the day or night, I try to work by appointments for routine procedures such as vaccinating and neuter surgeries.

To perform this kind of work well, you must be able to communicate well with people, realize this is a service business, and be reasonably available to your clients.

Despite the frustrations I sometimes face with my work as a veterinarian, I do find satisfaction from interacting with nature, helping an animal, solving a problem, and knowing an answer.

My career plans are to keep current in the medical aspects of veterinary life in order to keep up my practice. I would also like to build up my weaving/sheep hobby into a self sufficient or paying proposition.

VETERINARIAN #2

I love my work as a veterinarian mainly because it is a highly respected profession. There is much client appreciation, and I enjoy spending a lot of time with animals. There's always much to learn and each day brings new challenges. Since I was 5, I wanted to be a veterinarian.

My work would be easier if I had more surgical learning experience and if I could be in charge and make decisions. I'd like to be more client and animal friendly so I'd be able to do the best job for the least money. I enjoy the freedom and flexibility of my work.

To be a successful veterinarian one must be a good communicator. The person should have strong people and animal skills, and able to handle difficult situations, such as euthanizing animals, and calming panicked owners and bleeding animals. My degrees are a Bachelor of Science and a Doctorate of Veterinary Medicine.

I usually work a 10-hour day, 4 days a week. Office visits for various procedures--x-rays, fluid therapy, surgery--fill most of the days. I work with a competent staff who can do a great deal of the support work.

My plans are to improve my surgical skills and build a business of my own.

VETERINARY TECHNICIAN

I became a veterinary technician by accident. I graduated from college with a Bachelor of Arts in Art Education. I was unable to find a job teaching art, so I worked in a bookstore. A friend of mine worked for the American Society for the Prevention of Cruelty to Animals and knew I was good with animals. The job paid more, so I took it. I transferred to the ASPCA hospital where they trained me as a technician. I took the licensing tests, passed, and have now liked working in this career for 12 years.

As a veterinary technician, I nurse sick animals--medicate, monitor, treat, clean up after, etc. When I come into work, I am briefed on cases in the "Ill" ward. My typical duties include checking medical, surgical, and isolation wards; cleaning whatever needs cleaning; medically treating, feeding, and cleaning up after cases; helping put in I.V.s; taking radiographs; preparing lab work; keeping records; checking recovery of surgical cases; etc.

The skills and attitudes which I think are important to perform well at this kind of work are organization, ability to work without supervision, a good memory, attention to detail, extremely positive attitude toward cleanliness, fair amount of physical strength, good reflexes (animals bite, scratch, and kick), strong stomach (it can be messy), and good rapport with animals and with people too if you have to handle clients.

I have found satisfaction in this work because animals get well and I helped. If animals die, at least I tried. If euthanasia was necessary, I eased the animals' suffering and they didn't die alone or in pain.

I plan to do this work until I lose interest, which will probably happen no time soon. A friend of mine eventually wants to open a boarding kennel for cats and dogs and has offered me a partnership. I am considering this for the future.

VICE PRESIDENT & DIRECTOR OF IMPORTING COMPANY

My career in business started after earning a Bachelor of Arts degree. Prior to my current position, I was Vice President and General Manager of a health and exercise equipment company and Vice President and General Manager of a computer programming company. Through an executive search company, I found my present position as Executive Vice President and Director of a leather importing company.

It is my responsibility to supervise all USA operations and the New York City sales office and showroom. My typical work schedule includes talking with the parent company in London; checking cash flow, orders received, and inventory; reading balance sheets; administering the general office; scheduling meetings with sales vice presidents and staff; and planning strategy for sales and advertising programs.

To perform this kind of work well, it is important to have a knowledge of the market, the ability to predict trends in fashion and styles and buying habits, the ability to purchase at foreign currency rates favorable to profit margins on sales in USA, and control of inventory according to season trends and buying patterns.

My major frustration with my current position is that I do not have the authority to control the purchases made by the company without permission from the parent Board of Directors in London. I do not feel that foreign companies always keep up on trends in the USA. Therefore, I would like more freedom in selecting lines of merchandise and marketing procedures.

I do, however, like this kind of work very much. I enjoy my ability to predict trends and make a profit for the parent company, and to keep customers happy and satisfied and at the same time ensure that cash flow is satisfactory.

VICE PRESIDENT & NATIONAL SALES MANAGER

As Vice President and National Sales Manager for my company (we sell rugs and towels), I manage and motivate the salespeople, organize the company, set company policy, and develop our marketing strategy. I develop marketing strategy by discussing short- and long-term goals with the President, review sales figures, plan advertising, and enlist the help of the staff of accountants and salespeople to generate more business with new accounts.

The educational requirement for my position is at least a Bachelor's degree in Business Administration. You also need to be experienced and skilled with an overall business sense, get a retail background and sales experience, possess a pleasant personality and positive attitude, have some merchandising ability, and possess the ability to get along with and motivate people to get the work done.

I enjoy dealing with people, receiving recognition from my peers for a job well done, and experiencing the personal sense of achievement and monetary rewards of continued sales growth.

My journey up the retail corporate ladder began after college when I got a job as an assistant buyer in a department store. Shortly thereafter I was promoted to the position of buyer; then I transferred into the sales department as a sales representative. I wanted to learn more about management and importing, so I asked a lot of questions and studied the corporate culture. When the Vice Presidency position opened up, I went for it and got it.

I enjoy my work, I like my job, and I am glad I chose the career steps that led me to my present position.

I plan to be promoted to Executive Vice President, then to Company President; once I achieve that goal I will probably look toward owning and running my own company.

VICE PRESIDENT, CONTROLLER

I chose business when entering college because I felt it was interesting and I had the aptitude. After graduating with a bachelor's degree in business administration, I started with an entry level accounting position. During the course of my career, I have changed companies, but not fields.

Now as Vice President/Controller in a world-wide company, I oversee accounting, budgeting, and financial planning and reporting. My typical activities include: supervising corporate accounting department, and corporate budget and planning department; consulting with other operating and staff department heads to provide financial guidance; participating in CEO staff meetings; traveling to operating locations to oversee financial functions and exposures.

To perform this kind of work well, it is important to have basic accounting knowledge. Imagination and the ability to assess risks and take some risks is a necessary part of this job. Personal integrity is essential to earning respect at all levels.

I have been very satisfied with my career.

I have particularly enjoyed the extensive foreign travel that has been a part of this job. My only complaint is that I feel there is too much emphasis on social status at my high management level. I have found satisfaction in being a part of a successful enterprise and providing well for my family.

My plans for retirement are to do volunteer work.

VICE PRESIDENT, GEOTECHNICAL ENGINEER

I have worked as an engineer in the field of geology for 30 years and like it very much. In my current position I do foundation design. What I do is provide responses, advice, and support to technical questions about the foundation for engineering projects underway.

This is a highly technical field and to prepare for this work I earned a Bachelor of Science degree, a Master's, and a Ph.D. I also have had previous experience as a mining engineer and an engineering geologist before being observed and chosen as vice president.

My advice for those interested in this field is to plan on acquiring years of experience, a solid education, and always to seek new knowledge about this field so you stay current in professional developments.

The main satisfaction I find from this type of work is doing a good job on time.

VICE PRESIDENT, HUMAN RESOURCES

A vice president in human resources, I've worked in this field for 25 years. It is my responsibility to cultivate a work environment which allows people to contribute their maximum ability.

Good listening skills are very important to a human resources manager. Equally critical is the ability to analyze. You need to be able to negotiate well and you should have strong communication skills, both written and verbal.

My time is spent in senior management meetings to discuss policy and strategy. I generate job descriptions as well as interview candidates for employment. Planning the compensation budget for the next fiscal year is my responsibility as well.

While I dislike the need to discipline and fire employees, I do enjoy my work in general. A bookseller for a while, which I also enjoyed doing, I got a Masters of Arts degree and now enjoy helping other people do their jobs. I'd like there to be fewer legal entanglements in my field, but achieving organizational goals is very satisfying to me.

VICE PRESIDENT, INDUSTRIAL RELATIONS

My work in industrial relations has been very satisfying for me. I was led into this occupation because of my father's experience in this field. I earned a Bachelor of Science degree and then immediately started in this kind of work.

My major responsibilities as Vice President of Industrial Relations are handling labor relations, safety, and wage and salary schedules in the corporate headquarters. I supervise about 23 people, perform counseling sessions with managers, deal with labor relations problems, and conduct interviews.

To perform well at industrial relations work, it is important to have credibility, be articulate, and to be comfortable meeting with all types of people.

I like this kind of work, the organization I work for, the opportunity for advancement, and the people I work with. If I were to start my career over, I would still choose industrial relations. I find job satisfaction in doing a job well.

My plan for the future, when I retire, is to completely change my focus and write articles on American history.

VICE PRESIDENT, MANAGEMENT FIRM

A senior vice president for a money management firm, I manage funds for individuals and for businesses. Even though I majored in journalism and got my Bachelor of Arts degree, I've found money management very rewarding and, after 11 years experience in this field, I would choose it again.

I was the editor of, and writer for, a newsletter before becoming a money manager. Working on the newsletter was great, but I really like the people I work with now, my clients, and upper management. That there are opportunities for advancement just adds to my enjoyment.

To be a person who studies the financial world, and decides where other people's money should be invested, you have to be a very thorough person who is detail-oriented. You should have good analytical skills to evaluate information. Finally, being a person of action is a strong asset.

Job satisfaction for me is knowing I'm doing the best I can. Being able to make money for my clients is fantastic. My plans are to continue in this work and retire early.

VICE PRESIDENT, MANUFACTURING #1

I grew into my position by going through the ranks starting at supervisor and advancing with each job change. I have now worked up to the position of vice president. As such, I manage a manufacturing operation for a $30 million company. My responsibilities are in planning, organizing and directing of manufacturing in order to achieve the company and departments goals. This work usually involves constant meetings with people to review status.

I consider the following attitudes to be important for performing this kind of work well: a positive attitude with a will to achieve the goals; an open mind and willingness to work with other people; and the will to continue to learn and help others learn.

I like being in the position that I am, but I would be even more satisfied if I had more control over my and the department's destiny. In fact, my personal career goal is to own my own company to manufacture goods for other companies. In this way I could establish the direction of the organization.

Except for not having as much control as I would like, I like all other aspects of my work.

I find self satisfaction in achieving my goals and helping to teach others how to achieve their goals; and by creating an environment where others can grow and advance.

VICE PRESIDENT, MANUFACTURING #2

I like working with people, plans, and products. I advanced from group leader, through supervisory and management positions with the manufacturing company, to vice president of manufacturing. In this position, I coordinate the efforts of departments toward common goals, plan working schedules, and counsel people. The following activities are typically included in my weekly work schedule: preparing for and attending a weekly staff meeting; discussing general operations; meeting with my staff in smaller meetings to discuss problems or changes in operations; visiting a satellite plant once a week; attending committee meetings; planning operations; solving problems; assisting subordinates in problem solving; and researching alternative manufacturing methods.

In this kind of work, you must know when to solve problems alone or with assistance from your boss or your people. Good listening, math, and science skills are also important for performing this work well. Most important is good hard work and good common sense.

If given the opportunity to make changes in my occupation to make my job more satisfying, I would exercise more authority over the parts of the business I do not run. I would computerize one of the routine planning and scheduling functions, and spend more time and money in research and development. Ultimately, I hope to own my own manufacturing firm and then I will have the opportunity to initiate these changes.

Meanwhile, I find satisfaction from my work when I see my plans become real. It is satisfying to advance someone for doing well, and to work together as a team to accomplish a single goal or set of goals.

VICE PRESIDENT, NURSING HOME

I enjoy working with people as well as helping the elderly make decisions. This is one of the reasons I like my job as Executive Vice President of a nursing home chain. Helping others succeed and working with senior citizens are very rewarding elements of my position.

I have a degree in agriculture economics and worked for some time in farm credit administration, but I enjoy my current position much more. A supervisor of nursing homes must know state and federal rules and regulations. You must have the background to profitably operate a business and must like working with the elderly.

My work day includes dealing with the mail and checking messages on the computer. I talk with co-workers, attend meetings, and travel. I go to the nursing homes, meet with their administrators and employees, and help solve problems. Being responsible for approving capital spending is also my job.

Future plans are to remain in my present position. But my job would be more pleasant if there were fewer state and federal regulations. I'd like, also, more federal and state funding for long-term health care.

VICE PRESIDENT, OPERATIONS FOR INSURANCE AGENCY

Basically my work as a vice president of operations for an insurance agency entails overseeing all the operations of the agency and interviewing applicants for hiring or firing. I must plan the day's events for the agency, place insurance coverages, and plan and execute the agency marketing.

In my position, I feel it is important to have verbal skills. Employees must be aware that you are open for discussion. Above all, you should have a sense of humor!

This work is satisfying for me because I enjoy the interplay with clients and employees. What is dissatisfying at the present time is the public perception of our product. It is at an all-time low.

I like my work at the insurance agency although I did not really choose this as a career. My father had been in the insurance business for many years. When he became ill, I quit my job in order to help him. He died two months later and there I was with an insurance agency. I have now had the agency for 25 years. Prior to this I enjoyed my work as office manager of a consumer finance company.

VICE PRESIDENT, RESEARCH & DEVELOPMENT

I'm interested in getting things done, not just talking about them. Therefore I chose this type of work. As a manager of research and development I am involved in planning, budgeting, reporting, and implementing research and development programs. It is also my job as vice president to handle personnel management and motivation. To accomplish this work I travel 50% of the time. I meet with marketing and manufacturing people to determine the technical work required to support the business. Preparation of lots of reports, presentations, and meetings with customers also are part of my regular schedule.

To perform well in this kind of work it is important to have intelligence, courtesy, assertiveness, honesty, a practical approach, a teamwork attitude, and people sensitivity.

Education has been a major factor in qualifying me for this position. I have earned my Ph.D. degree.

I chose this occupation in science because I had a good aptitude for science and perceived it to have greater job security than the other fields of study, such as English and history, in which I also did well academically. So far I have had security in this career. I also had a diverse background prior to my research and development work, including farming, some laboratory teaching, some "pastoring" for my church, and process development engineering.

I find satisfaction from my work by seeing my people grow and develop, seeing results happen, and being recognized by business people as a key contributor to the success of the business.

VIDEO STORE MANAGER

I was always interested in the movie business which has led me to the video business. As the manager of a video store, I handle the bookkeeping, manage the store employees, help customers, do the scheduling, and decide on the movies to be ordered.

This kind of work requires a person with good communication skills in order to relate well with the customers. Because of the financial responsibilities as a manager, bookkeeping skills are required. Keeping up with all the movies in the theaters is also an important requirement for performing well in this job and one which I particularly enjoy.

I have been working in this field for 5 years and find that I like most aspects of my work. I find job satisfaction from the compliments I receive from customers and my bosses.

My career plans are to continue in the video business, moving my way up in the company to higher management positions.

VOCATIONAL COUNSELOR

I served in the military for 8 years doing clerical and personnel work. I then did graduate work in sociology and decided that I liked the field of vocational rehabilitation. This has now been my career for over 20 years.

As a vocational counselor, I counsel those persons who have mental/physical limitations. I supervise the operation of workshops held by the vocational rehabilitation division of the state.

In order to perform this kind of work well, it is important to have a knowledge of acceptable practices, and the ability to relate to all kinds of people in all types of settings.

I enjoy the kind of work I do, the organization I work for and the people I work with. I would like, however, to be able to have more one on one contact with the disabled. In spite of the limitations under which I work, I still find satisfaction in knowing that my efforts make it easier on those people with limited financial, physical, and mental resources.

VOCATIONAL REHABILITATION COUNSELOR & OWNER

I have always worked with disabled people as a special education teacher and mental health counselor. It was while working for the Social Services Administration that I was approached by some attorneys to assist them in their personal injury cases and that led to the development of my rehabilitation business.

I am the owner of the rehabilitation business and also the vocational rehabilitation counselor. As such, I coordinate the recovery of an injured worker. On a typical day, I review cases for the week, set objectives, list activities to meet objectives and the time frame, and contact support personnel--physicians, attorneys, insurance representatives.

To perform this kind of work well, it is important to have a flexible personality and to have understanding and patience. A college education for foundation of knowledge is also necessary. I have earned a Master of Science in Special Education.

Aside from the frustrations of dealing with too-rigid state insurance regulations, I like all aspects of my job. I would like to see rehabilitation services mandatory for injured workers. A state format should be established for the appropriate application of vocational rehabilitation for injured workers.

I enjoy helping others and the pay is very good as well.

WAREHOUSEMAN

I have been working in the warehousing business for twelve years. My day starts early by filling orders placed by different stores that sell the products in our warehouse; I use a forklift to move the merchandise and prepare the orders to be shipped to or picked up by the stores placing the orders.

To do my job well, I must operate the forklift in tight areas and maneuver through the warehouse traffic. This requires experience in the operation of a forklift so the orders can be filled as quickly as possible. You must be quick, be able to plan the route to be taken, which also means being very familiar with the warehouse layout, and it is essential to keep calm and not be easily flustered. A lot of times there are delays from other warehouse traffic or mechanical problems with the equipment.

I enjoy the companionship of my fellow workers and it is rewarding to know that we reach our production goals by working together as a team. I really like my job, but I would rather be handling lighter items with more room to maneuver. I do not like the heavy lifting.

I previously worked as a forklift operator at a cement roofing tile company and as an aircraft mechanic for the U.S. Air Force. I may use the experience gained in that work by applying it toward a college degree and then move on to the field of computer programming.

WASHER & DRYER MECHANIC

In my work as a washing machine/dryer repairman, I replace or repair broken parts. I am very happy because I enjoy the kind of work I do and the people involved. Since there is also opportunity for advancement, if I could begin again, I'd choose the job I have now.

My main satisfaction is seeing a finished repair job, one I'm almost positive will stay fixed. I try to mind my business, keep my mind on what I am doing, and why I'm doing it as I go from one prearranged location to another. The ability to quickly and accurately diagnose a mechanical problem is valuable along with having good mechanical skills.

I'd like to continue what I'm doing until I reach old age or become ill. Even though I'm old enough to retire, I do not want to quit.

WASTE MANAGEMENT

At age 26, I am a technical coordinator. After earning a Bachelor of Arts degree in communications, I was in landscaping work for a while. Then I found my present job handling hazardous materials.

I am in charge of the storage, treatment, transportation, and disposal of hazardous materials. It is my responsibility to see that all of the above are done in compliance with health and safety regulations. First, I receive and review the paperwork for delivery of these materials. After approving or disapproving the processing of any dangerous matter, I process the paperwork for outgoing shipments of hazardous waste. My job is also to evaluate and prepare the billing information for processed material.

It is satisfying to be able to keep the company in compliance and avoid legal problems. At the same time, it is rewarding to help the business make huge profits. Along with my job, I also enjoy my coworkers. I'd like my work more if there were less pressure and fewer hours required at the office. Eventually, my goal is to be vice president of operations.

My job demands being able to respond well to constant stress with legal time restrictions. You must have solid mathematical skills as well. Good organizational skills with meticulous attention to detail is also needed.

WEATHER RESEARCHER

I am a research associate in the field of atmospheric physics. As such, I do research on the physics of clouds and weather. I design and build scientific instruments, do measurements and computer analyses of data. Basically, I have the freedom to do what I want to do, when I want to. The only thing typical in my work is going there and leaving. Everyday is different, every week and every month as well.

I have been a meteorologist at a national weather service forecasting weather, a snow and avalanche researcher, and a processor in a fish factory. To qualify for my work in meteorology and atmospheric physics, I have earned my Ph.D. degree. I landed my present job by contacting my boss and asking if I could come and work with him.

To perform this kind of work well, it is important to have independent thinking, skill with instruments and tools, knowledge of electronics and physics, and specialization in physics of clouds and precipitation.

I like almost every aspect of my work.

I particularly like having the freedom to do what I want to do. I have an excellent boss and a laboratory full of equipment and junk.

I would like to become a professor of physics or environmental science (atmospheric physics, for example) at a college in the Northeast. There research is considered an integral part of the student's education.

WEAVER

I work as a weaver in a woolen mill operating 12 looms. My primary responsibility is to keep all these machines running and weaving flawless cloth. Most of my time is spent tieing broken threads, threading the machines, and checking for bad threads.

There is no particular schooling for this kind of work. In fact, I have not finished grade school. You just must be willing to work very hard, have a keen eye, be fast, and accurate.

Although there is not much opportunity for advancement in this kind of occupation, I have been fairly satisfied with my job for 21 years. This is basically the best job available for me for the money and the benefits. I enjoy my work and my co-workers in the mill.

WEIGHING INSPECTOR

As a weighing and research coordinator, I inspect freight to ensure that the proper tariffs are applied as they relate to weight and classification. Handling sales problems over the phone, researching local errors, and inspecting shipments are some of my duties. I also coordinate the weighing program. My schedule is very flexible and the tasks vary.

The flexibility of my schedule is what I like most about my work. I like the autonomy I have; my boss is 2,000 miles away. My work would be more rewarding if I had job security and if the people at all levels of my department were held accountable for their work. We need more discipline.

The most important attribute in my work as a coordinator is self-motivation. The willingness to personally follow up on projects each step of the way toward completion is necessary as well. Attention to detail and the ability to motivate others, even if you don't have the authority to hire, fire, or give raises, is valuable. In some ways the qualities of a salesman apply to my work.

I have a Master of Business Administration (M.B.A.) degree and I got into this job because I was one of those people at the right place at the right time. It was just "dumb luck." As for the future, I'd like to remain where I am.

My previous jobs as a market research coordinator, a receiving clerk, and as a teacher were all enjoyable. And, even though I like my present work, I'd like to return some day to teaching.

WELDER

I became a welder because of the money, which used to be better than it is now. After earning my Associates degree, I went through a 4-year apprenticeship program and I've been in welding for 18 1/2 years.

My work requires erecting heavy and light gauge steel and welding high pressure tubes on boilers at 1100-2200 pounds per square inch (PSI). We also do 100% x-ray, which is checking for cracks in the welding so the tubes will not leak with the pressure of the tube's contents. These tubes require welding in all types of positions and in good as well as adverse outside conditions.

To be a good welder, you need good eyes first of all. You also need good hand coordination. Keeping a positive attitude is also important.

I appreciate what I've learned from the trade, but we need better health insurance, more money, better tools and safety conditions. I don't enjoy the extensive travel required, my boss, or the fact that there are few opportunities for advancement.

What I do like is the self-satisfaction of doing a job right when the contractor allows you the time and proper tools. I enjoy my welding work itself and my coworkers. The time off between jobs is great and I'm looking forward to someday being in business for myself.

WRITER

A writer creates written material for the reading enjoyment of others; I entered into the field of writing quite a few years ago, and I have stayed right with it because I enjoy it. I write books and articles for publication in several areas of interest, but mainly I perform research about science philosophy, then write of the knowledge acquired through my research. I generally plan to write several hours each day unless my research prevents it.

I really enjoy writing; there is no limit to one's potential as a writer except those imposed by the mind of the writer.

I am a college graduate, but one also needs typing skills and a never-ending supply of optimism to be a successful writer.

The rewards of a life dedicated to writing are numerous. For me, the rewards come from the frequent letters of appreciation I receive from people who read my books.

The gift of my writing ability was realized at an early age for me; I have spent my life constantly improving my skills and encouraging others to consider a career in writing if they feel so inspired.

Over the years I have been involved in teaching navigation and directing a children's summer camp as sidelines to my work.

I plan to continue writing as long as I possibly can; it is a career that has no mandated retirement age.

WRITER & EDITOR, COMPUTER MAGAZINE

I have used my diverse career and extensive educational background in my present career. Previous occupations include: Air Force officer, college instructor, research scientist, and software engineer. I have earned a bachelor's and three master's degrees. After several years of technical education and experience, I found that my writing skills had atrophied, so I sought a job where writing was an important skill. The job I found is as a computer magazine writer and editor.

My typical duties include: testing computer hardware and software and then writing about the results, maintaining contacts by telephone and through visiting dozens of hardware and software companies, soliciting outside writers and working with them in developing articles, and attending shows and conferences.

The skills and attitudes which I consider important to be able to perform my job well are: flexibility, attention to detail, written and verbal communications skills, technical ability, and the ability to work under constant deadlines.

I like almost every aspect of my work as writer and editor except for the long hours because of the amount of work and the constant deadlines. The things I like this job are: the technical learning opportunities, the writing, people contact, and the variety in the work.

I plan to continue writing, perhaps as an unaffiliated freelancer. To go back to teaching and get a permanent faculty position is another possibility. My other career aspiration is to write books.

WRITER & EDITOR, FREELANCE

I've spent 35 years in my career as a technical writer and editor for several companies. I'd earned a Bachelor of Arts undergraduate degree in English and studied for a career in the ministry, which I decided not to pursue. Since I had many of the basic skills and the interest required for writing, I decided I might try it. The need to eat and pay for a car helped propel me into the field.

Typically, a day begins with my returning to a long technical writing assignment. I write software manuals, data sheets describing products, installation text, and, occasionally, a speech for a company officer. For these projects, I interview knowledgeable parties to prepare my writings properly. The succession of events is: submit projects, re-work them, submit them again, get approval, then perform actual production work with editors.

A good technical writer should be adept with the English language, with knowledge of grammar, and with syntax. I dangle very few participles and split no infinitives. Further, writing style and good form are most important in writing for industry. The ability to gain expertise in a selected specialty field, e.g., electronics, hydraulics--gasoline or diesel--computers, or other area requiring intense training is essential to a technical writer. One should like detail work as well as working, not only with other technical people but also with computers, which have turned typewriters into doorstops.

I've never regretted my work and have made a good living and many friends in my career. I plan to remain in the technical writing profession until eventual retirement. At that time I may take some courses at a local college, and I plan to stay active in my church community. The whole subject of effective communication through the written word intrigues me.

WRITER, ADVERTISING

After earning a Bachelor of Arts in Journalism Communication, I worked in public relations for a computer firm and did some reporting work. I have since changed jobs and am using my writing skills in my work for an advertising communications firm.

My job is to write brochures, videos, slide shows, and technical literature, plus handle public relations for the company. Projects vary in length from 3 hours to 3 months. My days usually consist of writing, placing phone calls to clients for information, meeting with specialists for content of the project, and working with the various artists in the art department.

Excellent writing and oral skills are a necessity. Because of the nature of the advertising industry, one must be open to constructive criticism, harsh deadlines, and unusual client demands.

Although I like my job, I do have a few frustrations with the kind of work I am now doing. I would prefer a little more honesty from client to consumer/public. Advertising tends to encourage people to put aside values/morals and beliefs. I think I would prefer using my writing skills for a charity organization.

Despite this, I like most aspects of my work, and find satisfaction from a job well done within budget.

WRITER, CORPORATE POLICIES

For some years my job has been writing corporate policies and procedures for my company. This work involves writing new or editing existing policies and procedures, as well as the design and implementation of a computer system for on-line viewing of these policies and procedures. I coordinate reviews from departments and input the data into an on-line computer system for viewing by employees, instead of printing and issuing written manuals. I also coordinate corporate personnel programs and the departmental space needs with the architectural department.

In addition to some college classes in journalism to develop good writing skills, you must be creative and possess personal computer skills, a familiarity with programming, the ability to analyze data, the ability to get along with all levels of people, the ability to work on many tasks at one time, and the ability to see different points of view.

I like my work. I enjoy the opportunity to be creative, and I am really proud of the on-line computer system that I designed and implemented.

The only thing I would like to see changed is the time it takes to get all the approvals for changes from the affected departments. It seems to take forever.

I have a varied background; I have held jobs as a file clerk in purchasing, a graphics drafter in engineering, a civil drafter in engineering, an installer of car radios, the section chief of an in-house print shop, an office equipment coordinator, and a staff analyst.

Currently I am working on the completion of a Bachelor of Arts degree in Journalism and Public Relations. Perhaps someday I will work as a political correspondent for a newspaper.

WRITER, SCIENCE AND HEALTH

None of my weeks is typical in my work as a freelance writer of science and health issues. This is one of the reasons I like what I do. A week may include interviewing researchers by phone or in person, I may do research myself, or I may write an article for a publication. For a steady income, I produce newsletters and brochures on the computer and I edit others' writings. For my own satisfaction, I write articles on brain research and topics related to mental health.

My education includes a Bachelor of Arts degree in biology education and graduate work toward a Masters. I got into my work because I wanted to combine my science background and my love of writing. I particularly enjoy the creativity required in my work. I also value the independence and flexibility. Always learning something new, I sometimes am a "cross pollinator" of new ideas. I love the contact with fascinating people. It would be easier if I had a dependable income; with the freedom of freelancing comes unpredictable earnings and little security.

To be an independent writer, you need to ask the right questions and put people at ease during an interview. Intelligence mixed with humility is important. Being a self-disciplined person and someone able to "think on your feet" are necessary as well. I have found excitement in seeking answers these 15 years; I also find joy in the meditative concentration that occurs during writing.

In the past, I worked as a biology teacher and as a program manager for state-wide energy conservation programs. My future plans are to write articles on brain research for nonprofessional science magazines. I'd also like to "ghost write" for professional journals on behalf of clinicians (physicians or psychologists who practice in clinics rather than specializing in research) and other researchers. In addition, it would be interesting to be an author who works with others writing for popular science books.

WRITER, THEATRE & BOOK CRITIC

I am getting paid to do something I love, but I had to strategically plan to get the job. I was a legal secretary in a department for the company I work for. When the time was right, I screamed, kicked, hollered, and threatened to leave the company if I didn't get transferred to the position of writer. I chose it deliberately and waited for the right time and place to move into the position.

As a writer, I go to performing arts events and read books, then write about them. While in the office, I write on a word processor, make telephone calls, and make plans for future editions. My on-the-job time out of the office is spent attending performing arts events and reading voraciously.

In order to perform this kind of work well, it is important to have the following skills and attitudes: writing--clearly, briefly, and specifically; observation--see what others usually miss; dedication to arts and literature; and background in arts and literature.

There is one major drawback to this career, and that is the low pay scale. Our society does not value the arts in terms of pay equity. We need to have someone who will give us financial support or who is independently wealthy or famous.

Aside from this drawback, I like almost every aspect of my occupation.

I love what I do. I find job satisfaction from writing well, feedback from people who read my work, influence of the written word, and getting paid to do something I love.

My plans for the future are to establish a track record in my present job, then go free lance in several years, for the rest of my working life.

YOUTH ADVOCATE

As a high school graduate, I started out as a volunteer in our youth center for homeless kids. Now, I have a job there. It's a drop-in center where kids, ages 12-21, can get the support they need. I've been around the streets before, so I know that what we do means a lot to the young people we serve.

My work at the center is helping serve dinners. We also offer medical services which I help with. I work in the alternative school there too. Helping these kids realize they are worth something is important to me.

To do this work, you need to be a selfless type of person. You must have a desire to achieve goals that many people say are not possible.

We need more money to do our work at the center and more salary for me would help; I have to waitress to make enough to support myself. I also wish that society would not ignore the problems of kids on the streets.

What's kept me going for 5 years is the friendship and love that I receive from the street kids. I like everything about my work: the kids, the center, the supervisors, and my fellow workers. There's a chance to improve myself, too, which I like.

I want to get a Master's degree in Social Work (MAW) and keep on helping juveniles. Crisis intervention and counseling junior high students appeals to me.

YOUTH & YOUNG ADULT ACTIVITIES DIRECTOR

My career life started with work as a customer service representative, executive secretary, office manager, and pension administrator. Then, either through good luck or divine plan, I became a youth and young adult director. A contributing factor was also that I had done volunteer work in youth ministry for 8 years prior to being employed in this job.

As the youth/young adult director, I plan social events, plan and run retreats, counsel teens, and perform family ministry functions. My typical daily and/or weekly activities might include: making arrangements for a hayride for 35 high school students, choir practice for teens, youth committee meetings, meetings with kids and/or families, calling for volunteers to read or serve at church, lunching with youth director from neighbor church.

To perform this kind of work well, you need to have faith in Jesus Christ, a desire to serve, organizational skills, patience, ingenuity, creativity, and understanding.

I like most aspects of my work. I would like more pay, better benefits, and better work space and facilities for activities. Despite these drawbacks, I like the organization and people I work for, the people I work with, and the kind of work I do. I find job satisfaction from helping people, ministering to teens, and bringing God into others' lives.

I plan to continue in youth ministry until I marry and start a family. Even then, I may stay part time or work for diocesan offices as a program director.

YOUTH RELIGIOUS DIRECTOR

My work can be described as organizing and coordinating all the youth activities as a Youth Formation Director of a large denominational parish. I always wanted to work with young people, so when I found out about this job, I went for it.

To do this job well, you must love young people! Being able to work well with anyone and everyone is important as well. It is also necessary to tolerate the politics of church life. Further, you must like the fact that no day is average--that there are new challenges every day.

It's very satisfying to know I have influenced someone's life in a positive way. Although it is often a thankless job, I enjoy the people I work with, the work itself, and the organization. I'm not always happy with the administration for I feel we need physically healthier ordained clergy. Additionally, I'd like my job more if the administration had more vision as to where the diocese is going.

My degree is a Bachelor of Science in education. One day I'd like to have my own private family counseling practice. Coordinating the youth ministry for a whole diocese also appeals to me.

ZOOLOGY PROFESSOR

I am a university professor in biology as a result of an interest in nature, first of all, and subsequently biology--and LOTS of hard work. This has turned out to be an ideal career for me because it incorporates interests which I developed early in life, and those which were tempered by experience as I have progressed through life.

I teach and do research on ecology and related areas, plus, as administrator, I oversee the ecologists in the department. On a typical day, I do research and writing in the A.M. Midmorning and early afternoon are spent sorting through mail and administration duties, lunching with colleagues, or attending seminars. I teach, do administration work and course preparation in the afternoon. In the evening, I work at home handling more administrative work, doing course work and writing.

To perform well as a researcher, you should have skills in logic and creativity. Interpersonal skills and order are important for administration. All of the skills previously mentioned are important for teaching.

I find satisfaction from my work because I have the ability to be my own boss in most facets of my work. I have the ability to do things and make discoveries no one has made before. The ability to help others is also rewarding to me. Also, I feel I have the ability to develop an area of excellence, both personally and in terms of the subdepartment I run.

My future career aspiration is to build the young group I head up into a world-class center of excellence, and to make scientific contributions that will be in this same "ball park."

About the author of the Kuder inventories
... and the compilers of this book...

The evolution of the work that led to production of this book started in 1928 when Frederic Kuder, then 24, entered the graduate school of the University of Michigan under the tutelage of Professor George E. Myers, who was the first president of the National Vocational Guidance Association. At that time there was a remarkable lack of help for young people in finding occupations suitable for their interests. Responding to the influence of Professor Myers, Frederic Kuder began experimenting with ways of helping young people find occupations they would enjoy. Now, at age 92, he is still experimenting; all of the job descriptions in this book were collected in the 1990's.

In developing the *Kuder Preference Record* and its successors, the *Kuder Occupational Interest Survey* and the *Kuder Career Search Schedule*, he introduced a number of practical and theoretical innovations. These included the scoring of vocational interests directly in terms of similarity to occupational groups rather than indirectly in terms of differences between occupational groups and a general reference population. Through this latter insight, Dr. Kuder provided a firm psychometric foundation for a perennial problem in vocational counseling--not matching people to jobs in terms of predicted job performance but, rather, in terms of anticipated job satisfaction. Most recently, Dr. Kuder, using the power of computers, has helped develop a method of matching people to other individuals (rather than occupational groups) in order to measure most accurately one's motivation toward appropriate careers. Dr. Kuder has worked throughout his own long career on ways of helping young people plan their careers and get into jobs they find satisfying. At the same time he has been a highly regarded professor, serving on the faculties of the University of Chicago, Ohio State University, and Duke University. Widely recognized by his colleagues for his achievements in measurement, in 1986 he received from Educational Testing Service its Award for Distinguished Service to Measurement.

Dr. Kuder spent decades of dedicated leadership as founder and editor of *Educational and Psychological Measurement* and as one of the founders and as an editor of *Personnel Psychology*. These are two of the leading journals in the fields of psychology and measurement. With his two collaborators on this volume, he is now working on a new book in the field of interest measurement that will develop further the fundamental conceptual innovations set forth in his 1977 publication, *Activity Interests and Occupational Choice*, and will review the procedures that were used in developing his interest inventories.

******

John A. Hornaday earned the A.B., M.A., and Ph.D. degrees at Duke University. His doctorate was in the field of organizational/industrial psychology, and in pursuing those studies he was much influenced by his mentor, Dr. Frederic Kuder. Since 1948, Drs. Hornaday and Kuder have worked together closely, having collaborated in starting three companies, all of which are still thriving. Although he continued his psychological research throughout, the fundamental principles involved in his own business start-ups intrigued Dr. Hornaday so much that he studied and researched the field of entrepreneurship at Babson College in Wellesley (MA) where he established and taught courses in entrepreneurship during the 1960's through the 1980's. He developed an international reputation as one of the pioneers in the current surge of attention given innovative new businesses. His publications in that field include contributions in the *Encyclopedia of Entrepreneurship, Entrepreneurship Education, The Art and Science of Entrepreneurship,* and the annual editions of *Frontiers of Entrepreneurship Research* from 1982 through 1990. For many years he was editor of *Personnel Psychology.*

During his work with entrepreneurship, Dr. Hornaday did not lose sight of his interest in vocational guidance for young people; in fact, the two fields dove-tailed nicely. During the past five years, Dr. Hornaday and Dr. Kuder, through their Motivation Research Corporation, have completed development of their person-match system that, in turn, led to the publication of this volume.

Although now formally retired from teaching at Daniel Webster College in Nashua (NH), Dr. Hornaday continues his research there in an effort to extend our knowledge of psychological measurement.

******

Lucinda A. Gibson earned her undergraduate degree from Randolph Macon Woman's College and, after a few years' experience in the world of business, she entered Georgia State University to complete the course of study for the Master's degree from the business school in the field of Organizational Behavior. That was followed by a second Master's degree in Human Resource Development, and she is currently completing her Ph.D. at Georgia State University in Human Resource Development; completion is scheduled in 1996.

Ms. Gibson is an owner of The Performance Alliance, Inc. in Atlanta, Georgia. Her company provides a full range of human resource development consulting services, employing organization design and research for improvements in the work life of individuals.

Prior to entering the field of human resource development, she served for many years as an officer in two major southeastern banks, managing funds, human resources, and computer systems.